INTRODUCTION
TO
AUTOMATA
THEORY,
LANGUAGES,
AND
COMPUTATION

INTRODUCTION

TO

AUTOMATA THEORY, LANGUAGES,

AND

COMPUTATION

JOHN E. HOPCROFT
Cornell University

JEFFREY D. ULLMAN
Princeton University

ADDISON-WESLEY PUBLISHING COMPANY

Reading, Massachusetts · Menlo Park, California
London · Amsterdam · Don Mills, Ontario · Sydney

This book is in the
ADDISON–WESLEY SERIES IN COMPUTER SCIENCE

Michael A. Harrison,
Consulting Editor

Library of Congress Cataloging in Publication Data

Hopcroft, John E., 1939-
    Introduction to automata theory, languages, and
computation.

    Bibliography: p.
    Includes index.
    1. Machine theory. 2. Formal languages.
3. Computational complexity. I. Ullman,
Jeffrey D., 1942-   joint author. II. Title.
QA267.H56   629.8'312   78-67950
ISBN 0-201-02988-X

ISBN: 0-201-02988-X

32 DOC 9695

PREFACE

Ten years ago the authors undertook to produce a book covering the known material on formal languages, automata theory, and computational complexity. In retrospect, only a few significant results were overlooked in the 237 pages. In writing a new book on the subject, we find the field has expanded in so many new directions that a uniform comprehensive coverage is impossible. Rather than attempt to be encyclopedic, we have been brutal in our editing of the material, selecting only topics central to the theoretical development of the field or with importance to engineering applications.

Over the past ten years two directions of research have been of paramount importance. First has been the use of language-theory concepts, such as nondeterminism and the complexity hierarchies, to prove lower bounds on the inherent complexity of certain practical problems. Second has been the application of language-theory ideas, such as regular expressions and context-free grammars, in the design of software, such as compilers and text processors. Both of these developments have helped shape the organization of this book.

USE OF THE BOOK

Both authors have used Chapters 1 through 8 for a senior-level course, omitting only the material on inherent ambiguity in Chapter 4 and portions of Chapter 8. Chapters 7, 8, 12, and 13 form the nucleus of a course on computational complexity. An advanced course on language theory could be built around Chapters 2 through 7, 9 through 11, and 14.

EXERCISES

We use the convention that the most difficult problems are doubly starred, and problems of intermediate difficulty are identified by a single star. Exercises marked with an S have solutions at the end of the chapter. We have not attempted to provide a solution manual, but have selected a few exercises whose solutions are particularly instructive.

ACKNOWLEDGMENTS

We would like to thank the following people for their perceptive comments and advice: Al Aho, Nissim Francez, Jon Goldstine, Juris Hartmanis, Dave Maier, Fred Springsteel, and Jacobo Valdes. The manuscript was expertly typed by Marie Olton and April Roberts at Cornell and Gerree Pecht at Princeton.

Ithaca, New York   J. E. H.
Princeton, New Jersey   J. D. U.
March 1979

CONTENTS

PRELIMINARIES

In this chapter we survey the principal mathematical ideas necessary for understanding the material in this book. These concepts include graphs, trees, sets, relations, strings, abstract languages, and mathematical induction. We also provide a brief introduction to, and motivation for, the entire work. The reader with a background in the mathematical subjects mentioned can skip to Section 1.6 for motivational remarks.

1.1 STRINGS, ALPHABETS, AND LANGUAGES

A "symbol" is an abstract entity that we shall not define formally, just as "point" and "line" are not defined in geometry. Letters and digits are examples of frequently used symbols. A *string* (or *word*) is a finite sequence of symbols juxtaposed. For example, a, b, and c are symbols and *abcb* is a string. The *length* of a string w, denoted $|w|$, is the number of symbols composing the string. For example, *abcb* has length 4. The empty string, denoted by ϵ, is the string consisting of zero symbols. Thus $|\epsilon| = 0$.

A *prefix* of a string is any number of leading symbols of that string, and a suffix is any number of trailing symbols. For example, string *abc* has prefixes ϵ, a, *ab*, and *abc*; its suffixes are ϵ, c, *bc*, and *abc*. A prefix or suffix of a string, other than the string itself, is called a *proper* prefix or suffix.

The *concatenation* of two strings is the string formed by writing the first, followed by the second, with no intervening space. For example, the concatenation of *dog* and *house* is *doghouse*. Juxtaposition is used as the concatenation operator. That is, if w and x are strings, then wx is the concatenation of these two strings. The empty string is the identity for the concatenation operator. That is, $\epsilon w = w\epsilon = w$ for each string w.

An *alphabet* is a finite set of symbols. A (*formal*) *language* is a set of strings of symbols from some one alphabet. The empty set, $\emptyset$, and the set consisting of the empty string $\{\epsilon\}$ are languages. Note that they are distinct; the latter has a member while the former does not. The set of *palindromes* (strings that read the same forward and backward) over the alphabet $\{0, 1\}$ is an infinite language. Some members of this language are ϵ, 0, 1, 00, 11, 010, and 1101011. Note that the set of all palindromes over an infinite collection of symbols is technically not a language because its strings are not collectively built from an alphabet.

Another language is the set of all strings over a fixed alphabet Σ. We denote this language by Σ^*. For example, if $\Sigma = \{a\}$, then $\Sigma^* = \{\epsilon, a, aa, aaa, \ldots\}$. If $\Sigma = \{0, 1\}$, then $\Sigma^* = \{\epsilon, 0, 1, 00, 01, 10, 11, 000, \ldots\}$.

1.2 GRAPHS AND TREES

A *graph*, denoted $G = (V, E)$, consists of a finite set of *vertices* (or *nodes*) V and a set of pairs of vertices E called *edges*. An example graph is shown in Fig. 1.1. Here $V = \{1, 2, 3, 4, 5\}$ and $E = \{(n, m) \mid n + m = 4 \text{ or } n + m = 7\}$.

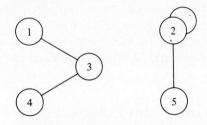

Fig. 1.1 Example of a graph.

A *path* in a graph is a sequence of vertices $v_1, v_2, \ldots, v_k, k \geq 1$, such that there is an edge (v_i, v_{i+1}) for each i, $1 \leq i < k$. The *length* of the path is $k - 1$. For example, 1, 3, 4 is a path in the graph of Fig. 1.1; so is 5 by itself. If $v_1 = v_k$, the path is a *cycle*.

Directed graphs

A *directed graph* (or *digraph*), also denoted $G = (V, E)$, consists of a finite set of vertices V and a set of ordered pairs of vertices E called *arcs*. We denote an arc from v to w by $v \rightarrow w$. An example of a digraph appears in Fig. 1.2.

A *path* in a digraph is a sequence of vertices $v_1, v_2, \ldots, v_k, k \geq 1$, such that $v_i \rightarrow v_{i+1}$ is an arc for each i, $1 \leq i < k$. We say the path is *from* v_1 *to* v_k. Thus $1 \rightarrow 2 \rightarrow 3 \rightarrow 4$ is a path from 1 to 4 in the digraph of Fig. 1.2. If $v \rightarrow w$ is an arc we say v is a *predecessor* of w and w is a *successor* of v.

Fig. 1.2 The digraph $(\{1, 2, 3, 4\}, \{i \rightarrow j \mid i < j\})$.

Trees

A *tree* (strictly speaking, an *ordered, directed tree*) is a digraph with the following properties.

1) There is one vertex, called the *root*, that has no predecessors and from which there is a path to every vertex.

2) Each vertex other than the root has exactly one predecessor.

3) The successors of each vertex are ordered "from the left."

We shall draw trees with the root at the top and all arcs pointing downward. The arrows on the arcs are therefore not needed to indicate direction, and they will not be shown. The successors of each vertex will be drawn in left-to-right order. Figure 1.3 shows an example of a tree which is the "diagram" of the English sentence "The quick brown fox jumped over the lazy dog." The vertices are not named in this example, but are given "labels," which are either words or parts of speech.

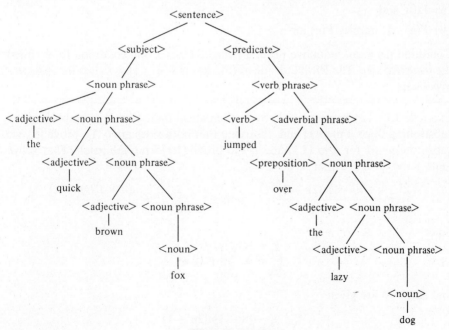

Fig. 1.3 A tree.

There is a special terminology for trees that differs from the general terminology for arbitrary graphs. A successor of a vertex is called a *son*, and the predecessor is called the *father*. If there is a path from vertex v_1 to vertex v_2, then v_1 is said to be an *ancestor* of v_2, and v_2 is said to be a *descendant* of v_1. Note that the case $v_1 = v_2$ is not ruled out; any vertex is an ancestor and a descendant of itself. A vertex with no sons is called a *leaf*, and the other vertices are called *interior* vertices. For example, in Fig. 1.3, the vertex labeled ⟨verb⟩ is a son of the vertex labeled ⟨verb phrase⟩, and the latter is the father of the former. The vertex labeled "dog" is a descendant of itself, the vertex labeled ⟨verb phrase⟩, the vertex labeled ⟨sentence⟩, and six other vertices. The vertices labeled by English words are the leaves, and those labeled by parts of speech enclosed in angle brackets are the interior vertices.

1.3 INDUCTIVE PROOFS

Many theorems in this book are proved by mathematical induction. Suppose we have a statement $P(n)$ about a nonnegative integer n. A commonly chosen example is to take $P(n)$ to be

$$\sum_{i=0}^{n} i^2 = \frac{n(n+1)(2n+1)}{6} \tag{1.1}$$

The principle of mathematical induction is that $P(n)$ follows from

a) $P(0)$, and
b) $P(n-1)$ implies $P(n)$ for $n \geq 1$.

Condition (a) in an inductive proof is called the *basis*, and condition (b) is called the *inductive step*. The left-hand side of (b), that is $P(n-1)$, is called the *inductive hypothesis*.

Example 1.1 Let us prove (1.1) by mathematical induction. We establish (a) by substituting 0 for n in (1.1) and observing that both sides are 0. To prove (b), we substitute $n-1$ for n in (1.1) and try to prove (1.1) from the result. That is, we must show for $n \geq 1$ that

$$\sum_{i=0}^{n-1} i^2 = \frac{(n-1)n(2n-1)}{6} \quad \text{implies} \quad \sum_{i=0}^{n} i^2 = \frac{n(n+1)(2n+1)}{6}.$$

Since

$$\sum_{i=0}^{n} i^2 = \sum_{i=0}^{n-1} i^2 + n^2,$$

and since we are given

$$\sum_{i=0}^{n-1} i^2 = \frac{(n-1)n(2n-1)}{6},$$

we need only show that

$$\frac{(n-1)n(2n-1)}{6} + n^2 = \frac{n(n+1)(2n+1)}{6}.$$

The latter equality follows from simple algebraic manipulation, proving (1.1).

1.4 SET NOTATION

We assume that the reader is familiar with the notion of a *set*, a collection of objects (*members* of the set) without repetition. Finite sets may be specified by listing their members between brackets. For example we used $\{0, 1\}$ to denote the alphabet of symbols 0 and 1. We also specify sets by a *set former*:

$$\{x \mid P(x)\}, \tag{1.2}$$

or

$$\{x \text{ in } A \mid P(x)\}. \tag{1.3}$$

Statement (1.2) is read "the set of objects x such that $P(x)$ is true," where $P(x)$ is some statement about objects x. Statement (1.3) is "the set of x in set A such that $P(x)$ is true," and is equivalent to $\{x \mid P(x) \text{ and } x \text{ is in } A\}$. For example,

$$\{i \mid i \text{ is an integer and there exists integer } j \text{ such that } i = 2j\}$$

is a way of specifying the even integers.

If every member of A is a member of B, then we write $A \subseteq B$ and say A is *contained* in B. $A \supseteq B$ is synonymous with $B \subseteq A$. If $A \subseteq B$ but $A \neq B$, that is, every member of A is in B and there is some member of B that is not in A, then we write $A \subsetneq B$. Sets A and B are *equal* if they have the same members. That is, $A = B$ if and only if $A \subseteq B$ and $B \subseteq A$.

Operations on sets

The usual operations defined on sets are:

1) $A \cup B$, the *union* of A and B, is

$$\{x \mid x \text{ is in } A \text{ or } x \text{ is in } B\}.$$

2) $A \cap B$, the *intersection* of A and B, is

$$\{x \mid x \text{ is in } A \text{ and } x \text{ is in } B\}.$$

3) $A - B$, the *difference* of A and B, is

$$\{x \mid x \text{ is in } A \text{ and } x \text{ is not in } B\}.$$

4) $A \times B$, the *Cartesian product* of A and B, is the set of ordered pairs (a, b) such that a is in A and b is in B.

5) 2^A, the *power set* of A, is the set of all subsets of A.

Example 1.2 Let $A = \{1, 2\}$ and $B = \{2, 3\}$. Then

$$A \cup B = \{1, 2, 3\}, \qquad A \cap B = \{2\}, \qquad A - B = \{1\},$$
$$A \times B = \{(1, 2), (1, 3), (2, 2), (2, 3)\},$$

and

$$2^A = \{\varnothing, \{1\}, \{2\}, \{1, 2\}\}.$$

Note that if A and B have n and m members, respectively, then $A \times B$ has nm members and 2^A has 2^n members.

Infinite sets

Our intuition when extended to infinite sets can be misleading. Two sets S_1 and S_2 have the same *cardinality* (number of members) if there is a one-to-one mapping of the elements of S_1 onto S_2. For finite sets, if S_1 is a proper subset of S_2, then S_1 and S_2 have different cardinality. However, if S_1 and S_2 are infinite, the latter statement may be false. Let S_1 be the set of even integers and let S_2 be the set of all integers. Clearly S_1 is a proper subset of S_2. However, S_1 and S_2 have the same cardinality, since the function f defined by $f(2i) = i$ is a one-to-one mapping of the even integers onto the integers.

Not all infinite sets have the same cardinality. Consider the set of all integers and the set of all reals. Assume that the set of reals can be put in one-to-one-onto correspondence with the integers. Then consider the real number whose ith digit after the decimal is the ith digit of the ith real plus 5 mod 10. This real number cannot be in correspondence with any integer, since it differs from every real that has been mapped to an integer. From this we conclude that the reals cannot be placed in one-to-one correspondence with the integers. Intuitively there are too many real numbers to do so. The above construction is called *diagonalization* and is an important tool in computer science.

Sets that can be placed in one-to-one correspondence with the integers are said to be *countably infinite* or *countable*. The rationals and the set Σ^* of the finite-length strings from an alphabet Σ are countably infinite. The set of all subsets of Σ^* and the set of all functions mapping the integers to $\{0, 1\}$ are of the same cardinality as the reals, and are not countable.

1.5 RELATIONS

A (binary) *relation* is a set of pairs. The first component of each pair is chosen from a set called the *domain*, and the second component of each pair is chosen from a (possibly different) set called the *range*. We shall use primarily relations in which the domain and range are the same set S. In that case we say the relation is *on S*. If R is a relation and (a, b) is a pair in R, then we often write aRb.

Properties of relations

We say a relation R on set S is

1) *reflexive* if aRa for all a in S;
2) *irreflexive* if aRa is false for all a in S;
3) *transitive* if aRb and bRc imply aRc;
4) *symmetric* if aRb implies bRa;
5) *asymmetric* if aRb implies that bRa is false.

Note that any asymmetric relation must be irreflexive.

Example 1.3   The relation $<$ on the set of integers is transitive because $a < b$ and $b < c$ implies $a < c$. It is asymmetric and hence irreflexive because $a < b$ implies $b < a$ is false.

Equivalence relations

A relation R that is reflexive, symmetric, and transitive is said to be an *equivalence* relation. An important property of an equivalence relation R on a set S is that R partitions S into disjoint nonempty equivalence classes (see Exercise 1.8 and its solution). That is, $S = S_1 \cup S_2 \cup \cdots$, where for each i and j, with $i \neq j$:

1) $S_i \cap S_j = \varnothing$;
2) for each a and b in S_i, aRb is true;
3) for each a in S_i and b in S_j, aRb is false.

The S_i's are called *equivalence classes*. Note that the number of classes may be infinite.

Example 1.4   A common example of an equivalence relation is congruence modulo an integer m. We write $i \equiv_m j$ or $i \equiv j$ mod m if i and j are integers such that $i - j$ is divisible by m. The reader may easily prove that $\equiv_m$ is reflexive, transitive, and symmetric. The equivalence classes of $\equiv_m$ are m in number:

$$\{\ldots, -m, 0, m, 2m, \ldots\},$$
$$\{\ldots, -(m-1), 1, m+1, 2m+1, \ldots\},$$
$$\vdots$$
$$\{\ldots, -1, m-1, 2m-1, 3m-1, \ldots\}.$$

Closures of relations

Suppose $\mathscr{P}$ is a set of properties of relations. The $\mathscr{P}$-*closure* of a relation R is the smallest relation R' that includes all the pairs of R and possesses the properties in $\mathscr{P}$. For example, the *transitive closure* of R, denoted R^+, is defined by:

1) If (a, b) is in R, then (a, b) is in R^+.
2) If (a, b) is in R^+ and (b, c) is in R, then (a, c) is in R^+.
3) Nothing is in R^+ unless it so follows from (1) and (2).

It should be evident that any pair placed in R^+ by rules (1) and (2) belongs there, else R^+ would either not include R or not be transitive. Also an easy inductive proof shows that R^+ is in fact transitive. Thus R^+ includes R, is transitive, and contains as few pairs as any relation that includes R and is transitive.

The *reflexive and transitive closure* of R, denoted R^*, is easily seen to be $R^+ \cup \{(a, a)|a$ is in $S\}$.

Example 1.5   Let $R = \{(1, 2), (2, 2), (2, 3)\}$ be a relation on the set $\{1, 2, 3\}$. Then

$$R^+ = \{(1, 2), (2, 2), (2, 3), (1, 3)\},$$

and

$$R^* = \{(1, 1), (1, 2), (1, 3), (2, 2), (2, 3), (3, 3)\}.$$

1.6   SYNOPSIS OF THE BOOK

Computer science is the systematized body of knowledge concerning computation. Its beginnings can be traced back to the design of algorithms by Euclid and the use of asymptotic complexity and reducibility by the Babylonians (Hogben [1955]). Modern interest, however, is shaped by two important events: the advent of modern digital computers capable of many millions of operations per second and the formalization of the concept of an effective procedure, with the consequence that there are provably noncomputable functions.

Computer science has two major components: first, the fundamental ideas and models underlying computing, and second, engineering techniques for the design of computing systems, both hardware and software, especially the application of theory to design. This book is intended as an introduction to the first area, the fundamental ideas underlying computing, although we shall remark briefly on the most important applications.

Theoretical computer science had its beginnings in a number of diverse fields: biologists studying models for neuron nets, electrical engineers developing switching theory as a tool to hardware design, mathematicians working on the foundations of logic, and linguists investigating grammars for natural languages. Out of these studies came models that are central to theoretical computer science.

The notions of finite automata and regular expressions (Chapters 2 and 3) were originally developed with neuron nets and switching circuits in mind. More recently, they have served as useful tools in the design of lexical analyzers, the part of a compiler that groups characters into tokens—indivisible units such as variable names and keywords. A number of compiler-writing systems automatically transform regular expressions into finite automata for use as lexical analyzers. A number of other uses for regular expressions and finite automata have been found in text editors, pattern matching, various text-processing and file-searching programs, and as mathematical concepts with application to other areas, such as logic. At the end of Chapter 2 we shall outline some of the applications of this theory.

The notion of a context-free grammar and the corresponding pushdown automaton (Chapters 4 through 6) has aided immensely the specification of programming languages and in the design of parsers—another key portion of a compiler. Formal specifications of programming languages have replaced extensive and often incomplete or ambiguous descriptions of languages. Understanding the capabilities of the pushdown automaton has greatly simplified parsing. It is interesting to observe that parser design was, for the earliest compilers, a difficult problem, and many of the early parsers were quite inefficient and unnecessarily restrictive. Now, thanks to widespread knowledge of a variety of context-free-grammar-based techniques, parser design is no longer a problem, and parsing occupies only a few percent of the time spent in typical compilation. In Chapter 10 we sketch the principal ways in which efficient parsers that behave as pushdown automata can be built from certain kinds of context-free grammars.

In Chapter 7 we meet Turing machines and confront one of the fundamental problems of computer science; namely, that there are more functions than there are names for functions or than there are algorithms for computing functions. Thus we are faced with the existence of functions that are simply not computable; that is, there is no computer program that can ever be written, which given an argument for the function produces the value of the function for that argument and works for all possible arguments.

Assume that for each computable function there is a computer program or algorithm that computes it, and assume that any computer program or algorithm can be finitely specified. Thus computer programs are no more than finite-length strings of symbols over some finite alphabet. Hence the set of all computer programs is countably infinite. Consider now functions mapping the integers to 0 and 1. Assume that the set of all such functions are countably infinite and that these functions have been placed in correspondence with the integers. Let f_i be the function corresponding to the ith integer. Then the function

$$f(n) = \begin{cases} 0 & \text{if } f_n(n) = 1 \\ 1 & \text{otherwise} \end{cases}$$

cannot correspond to any integer, which is a contradiction. [If $f(n) = f_i(n)$, then we have the contradiction $f(j) = f_j(j)$ and $f(j) \neq f_j(j)$.] This argument is formalized in Chapters 7 and 8, where we shall see that certain easily stated problems cannot be solved on the computer, even though they appear at first glance to be amenable to computation.

However, we can do more than tell whether a problem can be solved by a computer. Just because a problem can be solved doesn't mean there is a practical algorithm to solve it. In Chapter 12 we see that there are abstract problems that are solvable by computer but require inordinate amounts of time and/or space for their solution. Then in Chapter 13 we discover that there are many realistic and important problems that also fall in this category. The nascent theory of "intractable problems" is destined to influence profoundly how we think about problems.

EXERCISES

1.1 In the tree of Fig. 1.4,

a) Which vertices are leaves and which are interior vertices?
b) Which vertices are the sons of 5?
c) Which vertex is the father of 5?
d) What is the length of the path from 1 to 9?
e) Which vertex is the root?

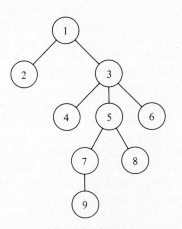

Fig. 1.4 A tree.

1.2 Prove by induction on n that

a) $\displaystyle\sum_{i=0}^{n} i = \frac{n(n+1)}{2}$ b) $\displaystyle\sum_{i=0}^{n} i^3 = \left(\sum_{i=0}^{n} i\right)^2$

*S 1.3   A palindrome can be defined as a string that reads the same forward and backward, or by the following definition.

1) ϵ is a palindrome.
2) If a is any symbol, then the string a is a palindrome.
3) If a is any symbol and x is a palindrome, then axa is a palindrome.
4) Nothing is a palindrome unless it follows from (1) through (3).

Prove by induction that the two definitions are equivalent.

* 1.4   The strings of balanced parentheses can be defined in at least two ways.

1) A string w over alphabet $\{(,)\}$ is balanced if and only if:
   a) w has an equal number of ('s and)'s, and
   b) any prefix of w has at least as many ('s as)'s.
2) a) ϵ is balanced.
   b) If w is a balanced string, then (w) is balanced.
   c) If w and x are balanced strings, then so is wx.
   d) Nothing else is a balanced string.

Prove by induction on the length of a string that definitions (1) and (2) define the same class of strings.

* 1.5   What is wrong with the following inductive "proof" that all elements in any set must be identical? For sets with one element the statement is trivially true. Assume the statement is true for sets with $n - 1$ elements, and consider a set S with n elements. Let a be an element of S. Write $S = S_1 \cup S_2$, where S_1 and S_2 each have $n - 1$ elements, and each contains a. By the inductive hypothesis all elements in S_1 are identical to a and similarly all elements in S_2 are identical to a. Thus all elements in S are identical to a.

1.6   Show that the following are equivalence relations and give their equivalence classes.

a) The relation R_1 on integers defined by $iR_1 j$ if and only if $i = j$.
b) The relation R_2 on people defined by $pR_2 q$ if and only if p and q were born at the same hour of the same day of some year.
c) The same as (b) but "of the same year" instead of "of some year."

1.7   Find the transitive closure, the reflexive and transitive closure, and the symmetric closure of the relation

$$\{(1, 2), (2, 3), (3, 4), (5, 4)\}.$$

*S 1.8   Prove that any equivalence relation R on a set S partitions S into disjoint equivalence classes.

* 1.9   Give an example of a relation that is symmetric and transitive but not reflexive. [*Hint:* Note where reflexivity is needed to show that an equivalence relation defines equivalence classes; see the solution to Exercise 1.8.]

* 1.10   Prove that any subset of a countably infinite set is either finite or countably infinite.

* 1.11   Prove that the set of all ordered pairs of integers is countably infinite.

1.12   Is the union of a countably infinite collection of countably infinite sets countably infinite? is the Cartesian product?

Solutions to Selected Exercises

1.3   Clearly every string satisfying the second definition reads the same forward and backward. Suppose x reads the same forward and backward. We prove by induction on the length of x that x's being a palindrome follows from rules (1) through (3). If $|x| \leq 1$, then x is either ϵ or a single symbol a and rule (1) or (2) applies. If $|x| > 1$, then x begins and ends with some symbol a. Thus $x = awa$, where w reads the same forward and backward and is shorter than x. By the induction hypothesis, rules (1) through (3) imply that w is a palindrome. Thus by rule (3), $x = awa$ is a palindrome.

1.8   Let R be an equivalence relation on S, and suppose a and b are elements of S. Let C_a and C_b be the equivalence classes containing a and b respectively; that is, $C_a = \{c \,|\, aRc\}$ and $C_b = \{c \,|\, bRc\}$. We shall show that either $C_a = C_b$ or $C_a \cap C_b = \varnothing$. Suppose $C_a \cap C_b \neq \varnothing$; let d be in $C_a \cap C_b$. Now let e be an arbitrary member of C_a. Thus aRe. As d is in $C_a \cap C_b$ we have aRd and bRd. By symmetry, dRa. By transitivity (twice), bRa and bRe. Thus e is in C_b and hence $C_a \subseteq C_b$. A similar proof shows that $C_b \subseteq C_a$, so $C_a = C_b$. Thus distinct equivalence classes are disjoint. To show that the classes form a partition, we have only to observe that by reflexivity, each a is in the equivalence class C_a, so the union of the equivalence classes is S.

FINITE AUTOMATA AND REGULAR EXPRESSIONS

2.1 FINITE STATE SYSTEMS

The finite automaton is a mathematical model of a system, with discrete inputs and outputs. The system can be in any one of a finite number of internal configurations or "states." The state of the system summarizes the information concerning past inputs that is needed to determine the behavior of the system on subsequent inputs. The control mechanism of an elevator is a good example of a finite state system. That mechanism does not remember all previous requests for service but only the current floor, the direction of motion (up or down), and the collection of not yet satisfied requests for service.

In computer science we find many examples of finite state systems, and the theory of finite automata is a useful design tool for these systems. A primary example is a switching circuit, such as the control unit of a computer. A switching circuit is composed of a finite number of gates, each of which can be in one of two conditions, usually denoted 0 and 1. These conditions might, in electronic terms, be two different voltage levels at the gate output. The state of a switching network with n gates is thus any one of the 2^n assignments of 0 or 1 to the various gates. Although the voltage on each gate can assume any of an infinite set of values, the electronic circuitry is so designed that only the two voltages corresponding to 0 and 1 are stable, and other voltages will almost instantaneously adjust themselves to one of these voltages. Switching circuits are intentionally designed in this way, so that they can be viewed as finite state systems, thereby separating the logical design of a computer from the electronic implementation.

Certain commonly used programs such as text editors and the lexical analyzers found in most compilers are often designed as finite state systems. For example, a lexical analyzer scans the symbols of a computer program to locate the strings of characters corresponding to identifiers, numerical constants, reserved words, and so on. In this process the lexical analyzer needs to remember only a finite amount of information, such as how long a prefix of a reserved word it has seen since startup. The theory of finite automata is used heavily in the design of efficient string processors of these and other sorts. We mention some of these applications in Section 2.8.

The computer itself can be viewed as a finite state system, although doing so turns out not to be as useful as one would like. Theoretically the state of the central processor, main memory, and auxiliary storage at any time is one of a very large but finite number of states. We are assuming of course that there is some fixed number of disks, drums, tapes, and so on available for use, and that one cannot extend the memory indefinitely. Viewing a computer as a finite state system, however, is not satisfying mathematically or realistically. It places an artificial limit on the memory capacity, thereby failing to capture the real essence of computation. To properly capture the notion of computation we need a potentially infinite memory, even though each computer installation is finite. Infinite models of computers will be discussed in Chapters 7 and 8.

It is also tempting to view the human brain as a finite state system. The number of brain cells or *neurons* is limited, probably 2^{35} at most. It is conceivable, although there is evidence to the contrary, that the state of each neuron can be described by a small number of bits. If so, then finite state theory applies to the brain. However, the number of states is so large that this approach is unlikely to result in useful observations about the human brain, any more than finite state assumptions help us understand large but finite computer systems.

Perhaps the most important reason for the study of finite state systems is the naturalness of the concept as indicated by the fact that it arises in many diverse places. This is an indication that we have captured the notion of a fundamental class of systems, a class that is rich in structure and potential application.

An example

Before formally defining finite state systems let us consider an example. A man with a wolf, goat, and cabbage is on the left bank of a river. There is a boat large enough to carry the man and only one of the other three. The man and his entourage wish to cross to the right bank, and the man can ferry each across, one at a time. However, if the man leaves the wolf and goat unattended on either shore, the wolf will surely eat the goat. Similarly, if the goat and cabbage are left unattended, the goat will eat the cabbage. Is it possible to cross the river without the goat or cabbage being eaten?

The problem is modeled by observing that the pertinent information is the occupants of each bank after a crossing. There are 16 subsets of the man (M), wolf (W), goat (G), and cabbage (C). A state corresponds to the subset that is on the left bank. States are labeled by hyphenated pairs such as *MG-WC*, where the symbols to the left of the hyphen denote the subset on the left bank; symbols to the right of the hyphen denote the subset on the right bank. Some of the 16 states, such as *GC-MW*, are fatal and may never be entered by the system.

The "inputs" to the system are the actions the man takes. He may cross alone (input *m*), with the wolf (input *w*), the goat (input *g*), or cabbage (input *c*). The initial state is *MWGC-$\varnothing$* and the final state is *$\varnothing$-MWGC*. The transition diagram is shown in Fig. 2.1.

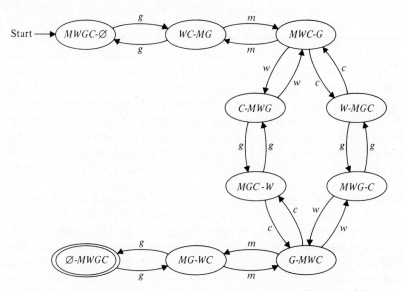

Fig. 2.1 Transition diagram for man, wolf, goat, and cabbage problem.

There are two equally short solutions to the problem, as can be seen by searching for paths from the initial state to the final state (which is doubly circled). There are infinitely many different solutions to the problem, all but two involving useless cycles. The finite state system can be viewed as defining an infinite language, the set of all strings that are labels of paths from the start state to the final state.

Before proceeding, we should note that there are at least two important ways in which the above example is atypical of finite state systems. First, there is only one final state; in general there may be many. Second, it happens that for each transition there is a reverse transition on the same symbol, which need not be the case in general. Also, note that the term "final state," although traditional, does not mean that the computation need halt when it is reached. We may continue making transitions, e.g., to state *MG-WC* in the above example.

2.2 BASIC DEFINITIONS

A *finite automaton* (*FA*) consists of a finite set of states and a set of transitions from state to state that occur on input symbols chosen from an alphabet Σ. For each input symbol there is exactly one transition out of each state (possibly back to the state itself). One state, usually denoted q_0, is the initial state, in which the automaton starts. Some states are designated as final or accepting states.

A directed graph, called a *transition diagram*, is associated with an FA as follows. The vertices of the graph correspond to the states of the FA. If there is a transition from state q to state p on input a, then there is an arc labeled a from state q to state p in the transition diagram. The FA accepts a string x if the sequence of transitions corresponding to the symbols of x leads from the start state to an accepting state.

Example 2.1 The transition diagram of an FA is illustrated in Fig. 2.2. The initial state, q_0, is indicated by the arrow labeled "start." There is one final state, also q_0 in this case, indicated by the double circle. The FA accepts all strings of 0's and 1's in which both the number of 0's and the number of 1's are even. To see this, visualize "control" as traveling from state to state in the diagram. Control starts at q_0 and must finish at q_0 if the input sequence is to be accepted. Each 0-input causes control to cross the horizontal line a–b, while a 1-input does not. Thus control is at a state above the line a–b if and only if the input seen so far contains an even number of 0's. Similarly, control is at a state to the left of the vertical line c–d if and only if the input contains an even number of 1's. Thus control is at q_0 if and only if there are both an even number of 0's and an even number of 1's in the input. Note that the FA uses its state to record only the parity of the number of 0's and the number of 1's, not the actual numbers, which would require an infinite number of states.

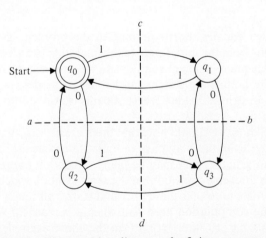

Fig. 2.2 The transition diagram of a finite automaton.

We formally denote a *finite automaton* by a 5-tuple $(Q, \Sigma, \delta, q_0, F)$, where Q is a finite set of *states*, Σ is a finite *input alphabet*, q_0 in Q is the *initial* state, $F \subseteq Q$ is the set of *final* states, and δ is the *transition function* mapping $Q \times \Sigma$ to Q. That is, $\delta(q, a)$ is a state for each state q and input symbol a.

We picture an FA as a *finite control*, which is in some state from Q, reading a sequence of symbols from Σ written on a tape as shown in Fig. 2.3. In one move the FA in state q and scanning symbol a enters state $\delta(q, a)$ and moves its head one symbol to the right. If $\delta(q, a)$ is an accepting state, then the FA is deemed to have accepted the string written on its input tape up to, but not including, the position to which the head has just moved. If the head has moved off the right end of the tape, then it accepts the entire tape. Note that as an FA scans a string it may accept many different prefixes.

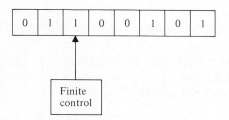

Fig. 2.3 A finite automaton.

To formally describe the behavior of an FA on a string, we must extend the transition function δ to apply to a state and a string rather than a state and a symbol. We define a function $\hat{\delta}$ from $Q \times \Sigma^*$ to Q. The intention is that $\hat{\delta}(q, w)$ is the state the FA will be in after reading w starting in state q. Put another way, $\hat{\delta}(q, w)$ is the unique state p such that there is a path in the transition diagram from q to p, labeled w. Formally we define

1) $\hat{\delta}(q, \epsilon) = q$, and
2) for all strings w and input symbols a,

$$\hat{\delta}(q, wa) = \delta(\hat{\delta}(q, w), a).$$

Thus (1) states that without reading an input symbol the FA cannot change state, and (2) tells us how to find the state after reading a nonempty input string wa. That is, find the state, $p = \hat{\delta}(q, w)$, after reading w. Then compute the state $\delta(p, a)$.

Since $\hat{\delta}(q, a) = \delta(\hat{\delta}(q, \epsilon), a) = \delta(q, a)$ [letting $w = \epsilon$ in rule (2) above], there can be no disagreement between δ and $\hat{\delta}$ on arguments for which both are defined. Thus we shall for convenience use δ instead of $\hat{\delta}$ from here on.

Convention We shall strive to use the same symbols to mean the same thing throughout the material on finite automata. In particular, unless it is stated otherwise, the reader may assume:

1) Q is a set of states. Symbols q and p, with or without subscripts, are states. q_0 is the initial state.
2) Σ is an input alphabet. Symbols a and b, with or without subscripts, and the digits are input symbols.
3) δ is a transition function.
4) F is a set of final states.
5) w, x, y, and z, with or without subscripts, are strings of input symbols.

A string x is said to be *accepted* by a finite automaton $M = (Q, \Sigma, \delta, q_0, F)$ if $\delta(q_0, x) = p$ for some p in F. The *language accepted by M*, designated $L(M)$, is the set $\{x \mid \delta(q_0, x)$ is in $F\}$. A language is a *regular set* (or just *regular*) if it is the set accepted by some finite automaton.† The reader should note that when we talk about a language accepted by a finite automaton M we are referring to the specific set $L(M)$, not just any set of strings all of which happen to be accepted by M.

Example 2.2   Consider the transition diagram of Fig. 2.2 again. In our formal notation this FA is denoted $M = (Q, \Sigma, \delta, q_0, F)$, where $Q = \{q_0, q_1, q_2, q_3\}$, $\Sigma = \{0, 1\}$, $F = \{q_0\}$, and δ is shown in Fig. 2.4.

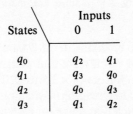

| | Inputs | |
States	0	1
q_0	q_2	q_1
q_1	q_3	q_0
q_2	q_0	q_3
q_3	q_1	q_2

Fig. 2.4 $\delta(q, a)$ for the FA of Fig. 2.2.

Suppose 110101 is input to M. We note that $\delta(q_0, 1) = q_1$ and $\delta(q_1, 1) = q_0$. Thus

$$\delta(q_0, 11) = \delta(\delta(q_0, 1), 1) = \delta(q_1, 1) = q_0.$$

We might remark that thus 11 is in $L(M)$, but we are interested in 110101. We continue by noting $\delta(q_0, 0) = q_2$. Thus

$$\delta(q_0, 110) = \delta(\delta(q_0, 11), 0) = \delta(q_0, 0) = q_2.$$

---

† The term "regular" comes from "regular expressions," a formalism we shall introduce in Section 2.5, and which defines the same class of languages as the FA's.

Continuing in this fashion, we find that

$$\delta(q_0, 1101) = q_3, \qquad \delta(q_0, 11010) = q_1$$

and finally

$$\delta(q_0, 110101) = q_0.$$

The entire sequence of states is

$$q_0 \overset{1}{} q_1 \overset{1}{} q_0 \overset{0}{} q_2 \overset{1}{} q_3 \overset{0}{} q_1 \overset{1}{} q_0.$$

Thus 110101 is in $L(M)$. As we mentioned, $L(M)$ is the set of strings with an even number of 0's and an even number of 1's.

2.3 NONDETERMINISTIC FINITE AUTOMATA

We now introduce the notion of a nondeterministic finite automaton. It will turn out that any set accepted by a nondeterministic finite automaton can also be accepted by a deterministic finite automaton. However, the nondeterministic finite automaton is a useful concept in proving theorems. Also, the concept of non-determinism plays a central role in both the theory of languages and the theory of computation, and it is useful to understand this notion fully in a very simple context initially. Later we shall meet automata whose deterministic and non-deterministic versions are known not to be equivalent, and others for which equivalence is a deep and important open question.

Consider modifying the finite automaton model to allow zero, one, or more transitions from a state on the same input symbol. This new model is called a *nondeterministic finite automaton* (*NFA*). A transition diagram for a nondeterministic finite automaton is shown in Fig. 2.5. Observe that there are two edges labeled 0 out of state q_0, one going back to state q_0 and one going to state q_3.

An input sequence $a_1 a_2 \cdots a_n$ is accepted by a nondeterministic finite automaton if there exists a sequence of transitions, corresponding to the input sequence, that leads from the initial state to some final state. For example, 01001 is accepted by the NFA of Fig. 2.5 because there is a sequence of transitions through the states $q_0, q_0, q_0, q_3, q_4, q_4$, labeled 0, 1, 0, 0, 1. This particular NFA accepts all strings with either two consecutive 0's or two consecutive 1's. Note that the FA of the previous section (*deterministic* FA, or DFA for emphasis) is a special case of the NFA in which for each state there is a unique transition on each symbol. Thus in a DFA, for a given input string w and state q, there will be exactly one path labeled w starting at q. To determine if a string is accepted by a DFA it suffices to check this one path. For an NFA there may be many paths labeled w, and all must be checked to see whether one or more terminate at a final state.

In terms of the picture in Fig. 2.3 with a finite control reading an input tape, we may view the NFA as also reading an input tape. However, the finite control at any time can be in any number of states. When a choice of next state can be

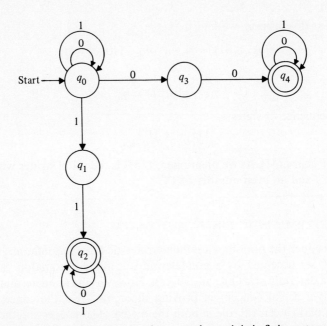

Fig. 2.5   The transition diagram for a nondeterministic finite automaton.

made, as in state q_0 on input 0 in Fig. 2.5, we may imagine that duplicate copies of the automaton are made. For each possible next state there is one copy of the automaton whose finite control is in that state. This proliferation is exhibited in Fig. 2.6 for the NFA of Fig. 2.5 with input 01001.

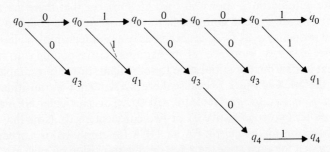

Fig. 2.6   Proliferation of states of an NFA.

Formally we denote a *nondeterministic finite automaton* by a 5-tuple $(Q, \Sigma, \delta, q_0, F)$, where Q, Σ, q_0, and F (states, inputs, start state, and final states) have the same meaning as for a DFA, but δ is a map from $Q \times \Sigma$ to 2^Q. (Recall 2^Q is the power set of Q, the set of all subsets of Q.) The intention is that $\delta(q, a)$ is the set of all states p such that there is a transition labeled a from q to p.

Example 2.3 The function δ for the NFA of Fig. 2.5 is given in Fig. 2.7.

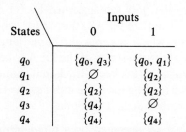

| | Inputs | |
States	0	1
q_0	$\{q_0, q_3\}$	$\{q_0, q_1\}$
q_1	$\varnothing$	$\{q_2\}$
q_2	$\{q_2\}$	$\{q_2\}$
q_3	$\{q_4\}$	$\varnothing$
q_4	$\{q_4\}$	$\{q_4\}$

Fig. 2.7 The mapping δ for the NFA of Fig. 2.5.

The function δ can be extended to a function $\hat{\delta}$ mapping $Q \times \Sigma^*$ to 2^Q and reflecting sequences of inputs as follows:

1) $\hat{\delta}(q, \epsilon) = \{q\}$,
2) $\hat{\delta}(q, wa) = \{p \,|\, \text{for some state } r \text{ in } \hat{\delta}(q, w), p \text{ is in } \delta(r, a)\}$.

Condition (1) disallows a change in state without an input. Condition (2) indicates that starting in state q and reading the string w followed by input symbol a we can be in state p if and only if one possible state we can be in after reading w is r, and from r we may go to p upon reading a.

Note that $\hat{\delta}(q, a) = \delta(q, a)$ for a an input symbol. Thus we may again use δ in place of $\hat{\delta}$. It is also useful to extend δ to arguments in $2^Q \times \Sigma^*$ by

3) $\delta(P, w) = \bigcup_{q \text{ in } P} \delta(q, w)$

for each set of states $P \subseteq Q$. $L(M)$, where M is the NFA $(Q, \Sigma, \delta, q_0, F)$, is $\{w \,|\, \delta(q_0, w) \text{ contains a state in } F\}$.

Example 2.4 Consider again the NFA of Fig. 2.5, whose transition function δ was exhibited in Fig. 2.7. Let the input be 01001.

$$\delta(q_0, 0) = \{q_0, q_3\}.$$

$$\delta(q_0, 01) = \delta(\delta(q_0, 0), 1) = \delta(\{q_0, q_3\}, 1) = \delta(q_0, 1) \cup \delta(q_3, 1) = \{q_0, q_1\}.$$

Similarly, we compute

$$\delta(q_0, 010) = \{q_0, q_3\}, \qquad \delta(q_0, 0100) = \{q_0, q_3, q_4\}$$

and

$$\delta(q_0, 01001) = \{q_0, q_1, q_4\}.$$

The equivalence of DFA's and NFA's

Since every DFA is an NFA, it is clear that the class of languages accepted by NFA's includes the regular sets (the languages accepted by DFA's). However, it turns out that these are the only sets accepted by NFA's. The proof hinges on showing that DFA's can simulate NFA's; that is, for every NFA we can construct an *equivalent* DFA (one which accepts the same language). The way a DFA simulates an NFA is to allow the states of the DFA to correspond to sets of states of the NFA. The constructed DFA keeps track in its finite control of all states that the NFA could be in after reading the same input as the DFA has read. The formal construction is embodied in our first theorem.

Theorem 2.1   Let L be a set accepted by a nondeterministic finite automaton. Then there exists a deterministic finite automaton that accepts L.

Proof   Let $M = (Q, \Sigma, \delta, q_0, F)$ be an NFA accepting L. Define a DFA, $M' = (Q', \Sigma, \delta', q_0', F')$, as follows. The states of M' are all the subsets of the set of states of M. That is, $Q' = 2^Q$. M' will keep track in its state of all the states M could be in at any given time. F' is the set of all states in Q' containing a final state of M. An element of Q' will be denoted by $[q_1, q_2, \ldots, q_i]$, where $q_1, q_2, \ldots, q_i$ are in Q. Observe that $[q_1, q_2, \ldots, q_i]$ is a single state of the DFA corresponding to a set of states of the NFA. Note that $q_0' = [q_0]$.

We define
$$\delta'([q_1, q_2, \ldots, q_i], a) = [p_1, p_2, \ldots, p_j]$$
if and only if
$$\delta(\{q_1, q_2, \ldots, q_i\}, a) = \{p_1, p_2, \ldots, p_j\}.$$

That is, δ' applied to an element $[q_1, q_2, \ldots, q_i]$ of Q' is computed by applying δ to each state of Q represented by $[q_1, q_2, \ldots, q_i]$. On applying δ to each of $q_1, q_2, \ldots, q_i$ and taking the union, we get some new set of states, $p_1, p_2, \ldots, p_j$. This new set of states has a representative, $[p_1, p_2, \ldots, p_j]$ in Q', and that element is the value of $\delta'([q_1, q_2, \ldots, q_i], a)$.

It is easy to show by induction on the length of the input string x that
$$\delta'(q_0', x) = [q_1, q_2, \ldots, q_i]$$
if and only if
$$\delta(q_0, x) = \{q_1, q_2, \ldots, q_i\}.$$

Basis   The result is trivial for $|x| = 0$, since $q_0' = [q_0]$ and x must be ϵ.

Induction   Suppose that the hypothesis is true for inputs of length m or less. Let xa be a string of length $m + 1$ with a in Σ. Then
$$\delta'(q_0', xa) = \delta'(\delta'(q_0', x), a).$$

By the inductive hypothesis,

$$\delta'(q_0', x) = [p_1, p_2, \ldots, p_j]$$

if and only if

$$\delta(q_0, x) = \{p_1, p_2, \ldots, p_j\}.$$

But by definition of δ',

$$\delta'([p_1, p_2, \ldots, p_j], a) = [r_1, r_2, \ldots, r_k]$$

if and only if

$$\delta(\{p_1, p_2, \ldots, p_j\}, a) = \{r_1, r_2, \ldots, r_k\}.$$

Thus,

$$\delta'(q_0', xa) = [r_1, r_2, \ldots, r_k]$$

if and only if

$$\delta(q_0, xa) = \{r_1, r_2, \ldots, r_k\},$$

which establishes the inductive hypothesis.

To complete the proof, we have only to add that $\delta'(q_0', x)$ is in F' exactly when $\delta(q_0, x)$ contains a state of Q that is in F. Thus $L(M) = L(M')$. ☐

Since deterministic and nondeterministic finite automata accept the same sets, we shall not distinguish between them unless it becomes necessary, but shall simply refer to both as finite automata.

Example 2.5 Let $M = (\{q_0, q_1\}, \{0, 1\}, \delta, q_0, \{q_1\})$ be an NFA where

$$\delta(q_0, 0) = \{q_0, q_1\}, \qquad \delta(q_0, 1) = \{q_1\}, \qquad \delta(q_1, 0) = \varnothing, \qquad \delta(q_1, 1) = \{q_0, q_1\}.$$

We can construct a DFA $M' = (Q, \{0, 1\}, \delta', [q_0], F)$, accepting $L(M)$ as follows. Q consists of all subsets of $\{q_0, q_1\}$. We denote the elements of Q by $[q_0]$, $[q_1]$, $[q_0, q_1]$, and $\varnothing$. Since $\delta(q_0, 0) = \{q_0, q_1\}$, we have

$$\delta'([q_0], 0) = [q_0, q_1].$$

Likewise,

$$\delta'([q_0], 1) = [q_1], \qquad \delta'([q_1], 0) = \varnothing, \qquad \text{and} \qquad \delta'([q_1], 1) = [q_0, q_1].$$

Naturally, $\delta'(\varnothing, 0) = \delta'(\varnothing, 1) = \varnothing$. Lastly,

$$\delta'([q_0, q_1], 0) = [q_0, q_1],$$

since

$$\delta(\{q_0, q_1\}, 0) = \delta(q_0, 0) \cup \delta(q_1, 0) = \{q_0, q_1\} \cup \varnothing = \{q_0, q_1\},$$

and

$$\delta'([q_0, q_1], 1) = [q_0, q_1],$$

since

$$\delta(\{q_0, q_1\}, 1) = \delta(q_0, 1) \cup \delta(q_1, 1) = \{q_1\} \cup \{q_0, q_1\} = \{q_0, q_1\}.$$

The set F of final states is $\{[q_1], [q_0, q_1]\}$.

In practice, it often turns out that many states of the NFA are not accessible from the initial state $[q_0]$. It is therefore a good idea to start with state $[q_0]$ and add states to the DFA only if they are the result of a transition from a previously added state.

2.4   FINITE AUTOMATA WITH ϵ-MOVES

We may extend our model of the nondeterministic finite automaton to include transitions on the empty input ϵ. The transition diagram of such an NFA accepting the language consisting of any number (including zero) of 0's followed by any number of 1's followed by any number of 2's is given in Fig. 2.8. As always, we say an NFA accepts a string w if there is some path labeled w from the initial state to a final state. Of course, edges labeled ϵ may be included in the path, although the ϵ's do not appear explicitly in w. For example, the word 002 is accepted by the NFA of Fig. 2.8 by the path $q_0, q_0, q_0, q_1, q_2, q_2$ with arcs labeled 0, 0, ϵ, ϵ, 2.

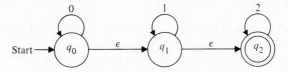

Fig. 2.8   Finite automaton with ϵ-moves.

Formally, define a *nondeterministic finite automaton with ϵ-moves* to be a quintuple $(Q, \Sigma, \delta, q_0, F)$ with all components as before, but δ, the transition function, maps $Q \times (\Sigma \cup \{\epsilon\})$ to 2^Q. The intention is that $\delta(q, a)$ will consist of all states p such that there is a transition labeled a from q to p, where a is either ϵ or a symbol in Σ.

Example 2.6   The transition function for the NFA of Fig. 2.8 is shown in Fig. 2.9.

We shall now extend the transition function δ to a function $\hat{\delta}$ that maps $Q \times \Sigma^*$ to 2^Q. Our expectation is that $\hat{\delta}(q, w)$ will be all states p such that one can

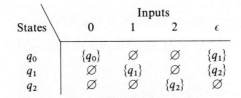

States	Inputs			
	0	1	2	ϵ
q_0	$\{q_0\}$	$\varnothing$	$\varnothing$	$\{q_1\}$
q_1	$\varnothing$	$\{q_1\}$	$\varnothing$	$\{q_2\}$
q_2	$\varnothing$	$\varnothing$	$\{q_2\}$	$\varnothing$

Fig. 2.9 $\delta(q, a)$ for the NFA of Fig. 2.8.

go from q to p along a path labeled w, perhaps including edges labeled ϵ. In constructing $\hat{\delta}$ it will be important to compute the set of states reachable from a given state q using ϵ transitions only. This question is equivalent to the question of what vertices can be reached from a given (*source*) vertex in a directed graph. The source vertex is the vertex for state q in the transition diagram, and the directed graph in question consists of all and only the arcs labeled ϵ. We use ϵ-*CLOSURE*(q) to denote the set of all vertices p such that there is a path from q to p labeled ϵ.

Example 2.7 In Fig. 2.8, ϵ-CLOSURE(q_0) = $\{q_0, q_1, q_2\}$. That is, the path consisting of q_0 alone (there are no arcs on the path), is a path from q_0 to q_0 with all arcs labeled ϵ.† Path q_0, q_1 shows that q_1 is in ϵ-CLOSURE(q_0) and path q_0, q_1, q_2 shows that q_2 is in ϵ-CLOSURE(q_0).

We may naturally let ϵ-CLOSURE(P), where P is a set of states, be $\bigcup_{q \text{ in } P} \epsilon$-CLOSURE($q$). Now we define $\hat{\delta}$ as follows.

1) $\hat{\delta}(q, \epsilon) = \epsilon$-CLOSURE($q$).
2) For w in Σ^* and a in Σ, $\hat{\delta}(q, wa) = \epsilon$-CLOSURE($P$), where $P = \{p \,|\, \text{for some } r$ in $\hat{\delta}(q, w)$, p is in $\delta(r, a)\}$.

It is convenient to extend δ and $\hat{\delta}$ to sets of states by

3) $\delta(R, a) = \bigcup_{q \text{ in } R} \delta(q, a)$, and
4) $\hat{\delta}(R, w) = \bigcup_{q \text{ in } R} \hat{\delta}(q, w)$

for sets of states R. Note that in this case, $\hat{\delta}(q, a)$ is not necessarily equal to $\delta(q, a)$, since $\hat{\delta}(q, a)$ includes all states reachable from q by paths labeled a (including paths with arcs labeled ϵ), while $\delta(q, a)$ includes only those states reachable from q by arcs labeled a. Similarly, $\hat{\delta}(q, \epsilon)$ is not necessarily equal to $\delta(q, \epsilon)$. Therefore it is necessary to distinguish δ from $\hat{\delta}$ when we talk about an NFA with ϵ-transitions.

We define $L(M)$, the *language accepted by* $M = (Q, \Sigma, \delta, q_0, F)$ to be $\{w \,|\, \hat{\delta}(q_0, w)$ contains a state in $F\}$.

---

† Remember that a path of length zero has no arcs, and therefore trivially all its arcs are labeled ϵ.

Example 2.8   Consider again the NFA of Fig. 2.8,

$$\hat{\delta}(q_0, \epsilon) = \epsilon\text{-CLOSURE}(q_0) = \{q_0, q_1, q_2\}.$$

Thus

$$\hat{\delta}(q_0, 0) = \epsilon\text{-CLOSURE}(\delta(\hat{\delta}(q_0, \epsilon), 0))$$
$$= \epsilon\text{-CLOSURE}(\delta(\{q_0, q_1, q_2\}, 0))$$
$$= \epsilon\text{-CLOSURE}(\delta(q_0, 0) \cup \delta(q_1, 0) \cup \delta(q_2, 0))$$
$$= \epsilon\text{-CLOSURE}(\{q_0\} \cup \varnothing \cup \varnothing)$$
$$= \epsilon\text{-CLOSURE}(\{q_0\}) = \{q_0, q_1, q_2\}.$$

Then

$$\hat{\delta}(q_0, 01) = \epsilon\text{-CLOSURE}(\delta(\hat{\delta}(q_0, 0), 1))$$
$$= \epsilon\text{-CLOSURE}(\delta(\{q_0, q_1, q_2\}, 1))$$
$$= \epsilon\text{-CLOSURE}(\{q_1\}) = \{q_1, q_2\}.$$

Equivalence of NFA's with and without ϵ-moves

Like nondeterminism, the ability to make transitions on ϵ does not allow the NFA to accept nonregular sets. We show this by simulating an NFA with ϵ-transitions by an NFA without such transitions.

Theorem 2.2   If L is accepted by an NFA with ϵ-transitions, then L is accepted by an NFA without ϵ-transitions.

Proof   Let $M = (Q, \Sigma, \delta, q_0, F)$ be an NFA with ϵ-transitions. Construct $M' = (Q, \Sigma, \delta', q_0, F')$ where

$$F' = \begin{cases} F \cup \{q_0\} & \text{if } \epsilon\text{-CLOSURE}(q_0) \text{ contains a state of } F, \\ F & \text{otherwise,} \end{cases}$$

and $\delta'(q, a)$ is $\hat{\delta}(q, a)$ for q in Q and a in Σ. Note that M' has no ϵ-transitions. Thus we may use δ' for $\hat{\delta}'$, but we must continue to distinguish between δ and $\hat{\delta}$.

We wish to show by induction on $|x|$ that $\delta'(q_0, x) = \hat{\delta}(q_0, x)$. However, this statement may not be true for $x = \epsilon$, since $\delta'(q_0, \epsilon) = \{q_0\}$, while $\hat{\delta}(q_0, \epsilon) = \epsilon\text{-CLOSURE}(q_0)$. We therefore begin our induction at 1.

Basis $|x| = 1$. Then x is a symbol a, and $\delta'(q_0, a) = \hat{\delta}(q_0, a)$ by definition of δ'.

Induction $|x| > 1$. Let $x = wa$ for symbol a in Σ. Then

$$\delta'(q_0, wa) = \delta'(\delta'(q_0, w), a).$$

By the inductive hypothesis, $\delta'(q_0, w) = \hat{\delta}(q_0, w)$. Let $\hat{\delta}(q_0, w) = P$. We must show that $\delta'(P, a) = \hat{\delta}(q_0, wa)$. But

$$\delta'(P, a) = \bigcup_{q \text{ in } P} \delta'(q, a) = \bigcup_{q \text{ in } P} \hat{\delta}(q, a).$$

Then as $P = \hat{\delta}(q_0, w)$ we have

$$\bigcup_{q \text{ in } P} \hat{\delta}(q, a) = \hat{\delta}(q_0, wa)$$

by rule (2) in the definition of $\hat{\delta}$. Thus

$$\delta'(q_0, wa) = \hat{\delta}(q_0, wa).$$

To complete the proof we shall show that $\delta'(q_0, x)$ contains a state of F' if and only if $\hat{\delta}(q_0, x)$ contains a state of F. If $x = \epsilon$, this statement is immediate from the definition of F'. That is, $\delta'(q_0, \epsilon) = \{q_0\}$, and q_0 is placed in F' whenever $\hat{\delta}(q_0, \epsilon)$, which is ϵ-CLOSURE(q_0), contains a state (possibly q_0) in F. If $x \neq \epsilon$, then $x = wa$ for some symbol a. If $\hat{\delta}(q_0, x)$ contains a state of F, then surely $\delta'(q_0, x)$ contains the same state in F'. Conversely, if $\delta'(q_0, x)$ contains a state in F' other than q_0, then $\hat{\delta}(q_0, x)$ contains a state in F. If $\delta'(q_0, x)$ contains q_0, and q_0 is not in F, then as $\hat{\delta}(q_0, x) = \epsilon$-CLOSURE$(\delta(\hat{\delta}(q_0, w), a))$, the state in ϵ-CLOSURE(q_0) and in F must be in $\hat{\delta}(q_0, x)$. ☐

Example 2.9 Let us apply the construction of Theorem 2.2 to the NFA of Fig. 2.8. In Fig. 2.10 we summarize $\hat{\delta}(q, a)$. We may also regard Fig. 2.10 as the transition function δ' of the NFA without ϵ-transitions constructed by Theorem 2.2. The set of final states F' includes q_2 because that is in F and also includes q_0, because ϵ-CLOSURE(q_0) and F have a state q_2 in common. The transition diagram for M' is shown in Fig. 2.11.

States	Inputs		
	0	1	2
q_0	$\{q_0, q_1, q_2\}$	$\{q_1, q_2\}$	$\{q_2\}$
q_1	$\varnothing$	$\{q_1, q_2\}$	$\{q_2\}$
q_2	$\varnothing$	$\varnothing$	$\{q_2\}$

Fig. 2.10 $\hat{\delta}(q, a)$ for Fig. 2.8.

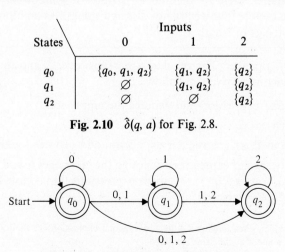

Fig. 2.11 NFA without ϵ-transitions.

2.5   REGULAR EXPRESSIONS

The languages accepted by finite automata are easily described by simple expressions called regular expressions. In this section we introduce the operations of concatenation and closure on sets of strings, define regular expressions, and prove that the class of languages accepted by finite automata is precisely the class of languages describable by regular expressions.

Let Σ be a finite set of symbols and let L, L_1, and L_2 be sets of strings from Σ^*. The *concatenation* of L_1 and L_2, denoted L_1L_2, is the set $\{xy \mid x$ is in L_1 and y is in $L_2\}$. That is, the strings in L_1L_2 are formed by choosing a string L_1 and following it by a string in L_2, in all possible combinations. Define $L^0 = \{\epsilon\}$ and $L^i = LL^{i-1}$ for $i \geq 1$. The *Kleene closure* (or just *closure*) of L, denoted L^*, is the set

$$L^* = \bigcup_{i=0}^{\infty} L^i$$

and the *positive closure* of L, denoted L^+, is the set

$$L^+ = \bigcup_{i=1}^{\infty} L^i.$$

That is, L^* denotes words constructed by concatenating any number of words from L. L^+ is the same, but the case of zero words, whose "concatenation" is defined to be ϵ, is excluded. Note that L^+ contains ϵ if and only if L does.

Example 2.10   Let $L_1 = \{10, 1\}$ and $L_2 = \{011, 11\}$. Then $L_1L_2 = \{10011, 1011, 111\}$. Also,

$$\{10, 11\}^* = \{\epsilon, 10, 11, 1010, 1011, 1110, 1111, \ldots\}.$$

If Σ is an alphabet, then Σ^* denotes all strings of symbols in Σ, as we have previously stated. Note that we are not distinguishing Σ as an alphabet from Σ as a language of strings of length 1.

Let Σ be an alphabet. The regular expressions over Σ and the sets that they denote are defined recursively as follows.

1) $\emptyset$ is a regular expression and denotes the empty set.
2) ϵ is a regular expression and denotes the set $\{\epsilon\}$.
3) For each a in Σ, $\mathbf{a}$† is a regular expression and denotes the set $\{a\}$.
4) If r and s are regular expressions denoting the languages R and S, respectively, then $(r + s)$, (rs), and (r^*) are regular expressions that denote the sets $R \cup S$, RS, and R^*, respectively.

---

† To remind the reader when a symbol is part of a regular expression, we shall write it in boldface. However, we view **a** and a as the same symbol.

In writing regular expressions we can omit many parentheses if we assume that * has higher precedence than concatenation or +, and that concatenation has higher precedence than +. For example, $((0(1^*)) + 0)$ may be written $01^* + 0$. We may also abbreviate the expression rr^* by r^+. When necessary to distinguish between a regular expression r and the language denoted by r, we use $L(r)$ for the latter. When no confusion is possible we use r for both the regular expression and the language denoted by the regular expression.

Example 2.11   **00** is a regular expression representing {00}. The expression $(0 + 1)^*$ denotes all strings of 0's and 1's. Thus, $(0 + 1)^*00(0 + 1)^*$ denotes all strings of 0's and 1's with at least two consecutive 0's. The regular expression $(1 + 10)^*$ denotes all strings of 0's and 1's beginning with 1 and not having two consecutive 0's. In proof, it is an easy induction on i that $(1 + 10)^i$ does not have two consecutive 0's.† Furthermore, given any string beginning with 1 and not having consecutive 0's, one can partition the string into 1's, with a following 0 if there is one. For example, 1101011 is partitioned 1–10–10–1–1. This partition shows that any such string is in $(1 + 10)^i$, where i is the number of 1's. The regular expression $(0 + \epsilon)(1 + 10)^*$ denotes all strings of 0's and 1's whatsoever that do not have two consecutive 0's.

For some additional examples, $(0 + 1)^*011$ denotes all strings of 0's and 1's ending in 011. Also, $0^*1^*2^*$ denotes any number of 0's followed by any number of 1's followed by any number of 2's. This is the language of the NFA of Fig. 2.8. $00^*11^*22^*$ denotes those strings in $0^*1^*2^*$ with at least one of each symbol. We may use the shorthand $0^+1^+2^+$ for $00^*11^*22^*$.

Equivalence of finite automata and regular expressions

We now turn to showing that the languages accepted by finite automata are precisely the languages denoted by regular expressions. This equivalence was the motivation for calling finite automaton languages regular sets. Our plan will be to show by induction on the *size* of (number of operators in) a regular expression that there is an NFA with ϵ-transitions denoting the same language. Finally, we show that for every DFA there is a regular expression denoting its language. These constructions, together with Theorems 2.1 and 2.2, show that all four language defining mechanisms discussed in this chapter define the same class of languages, the regular sets. Figure 2.12 shows the constructions we shall perform or have performed, where an arrow from A to B means that for any descriptor of type A a construction yields an equivalent descriptor of type B.

We proceed to prove that for every regular expression there is an equivalent NFA with ϵ-transitions.

---

† If r is a regular expression, r^i stands for $rr \cdots r$ (i times).

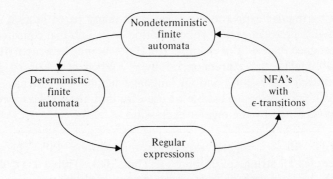

Fig. 2.12   Constructions of this chapter.

Theorem 2.3   Let r be a regular expression. Then there exists an NFA with ϵ-transitions that accepts $L(r)$.

Proof   We show by induction on the number of operators in the regular expression r that there is an NFA M with ϵ-transitions, having one final state and no transitions out of this final state, such that $L(M) = L(r)$.

Basis (Zero operators)   The expression r must be ϵ, $\varnothing$, or $\mathbf{a}$ for some a in Σ. The NFA's in Fig. 2.13(a), (b), and (c) clearly satisfy the conditions.

Fig. 2.13   Finite automata for basis step of Theorem 2.3.

Induction (One or more operators)   Assume that the theorem is true for regular expressions with fewer than i operators, $i \geq 1$. Let r have i operators. There are three cases depending on the form of r.

CASE 1 $r = r_1 + r_2$. Both r_1 and r_2 must have fewer than i operators. Thus there are NFA's $M_1 = (Q_1, \Sigma_1, \delta_1, q_1, \{f_1\})$ and $M_2 = (Q_2, \Sigma_2, \delta_2, q_2, \{f_2\})$ with $L(M_1) = L(r_1)$ and $L(M_2) = L(r_2)$. Since we may rename states of an NFA at will, we may assume Q_1 and Q_2 are disjoint. Let q_0 be a new initial state and f_0 a new final state. Construct

$$M = (Q_1 \cup Q_2 \cup \{q_0, f_0\}, \Sigma_1 \cup \Sigma_2, \delta, q_0, \{f_0\}),$$

where δ is defined by

i) $\delta(q_0, \epsilon) = \{q_1, q_2\}$,

ii) $\delta(q, a) = \delta_1(q, a)$ for q in $Q_1 - \{f_1\}$ and a in $\Sigma_1 \cup \{\epsilon\}$,

iii) $\delta(q, a) = \delta_2(q, a)$ for q in $Q_2 - \{f_2\}$ and a in $\Sigma_2 \cup \{\epsilon\}$,

iv) $\delta(f_1, \epsilon) = \delta_1(f_2, \epsilon) = \{f_0\}$.

Recall by the inductive hypothesis that there are no transitions out of f_1 or f_2 in M_1 or M_2. Thus all the moves of M_1 and M_2 are present in M.

The construction of M is depicted in Fig 2.14(a). Any path in the transition diagram of M from q_0 to f_0 must begin by going to either q_1 or q_2 on ϵ. If the path goes to q_1, it may follow any path in M_1 to f_1 and then go to f_0 on ϵ. Similarly, paths that begin by going to q_2 may follow any path in M_2 to f_2 and then go to f_0 on ϵ. These are the only paths from q_0 to f_0. It follows immediately that there is a path labeled x in M from q_0 to f_0 if and only if there is a path labeled x in M_1 from q_1 to f_1 or a path in M_2 from q_2 to f_2. Hence $L(M) = L(M_1) \cup L(M)_2$ as desired.

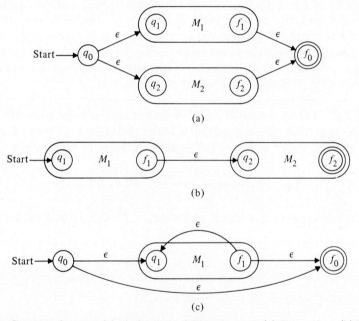

(a)

(b)

(c)

Fig. 2.14 Constructions used in induction of Theorem 2.3. (a) For union. (b) For concatenation. (c) For closure.

CASE 2 $\quad r = r_1 r_2$. Let M_1 and M_2 be as in Case 1 and construct

$$M = (Q_1 \cup Q_2, \Sigma_1 \cup \Sigma_2, \delta, \{q_1\}, \{f_2\}),$$

where δ is given by

i) $\delta(q, a) = \delta_1(q, a)$ for q in $Q_1 - \{f_1\}$ and a in $\Sigma_1 \cup \{\epsilon\}$,

ii) $\delta(f_1, \epsilon) = \{q_2\}$

iii) $\delta(q, a) = \delta_2(q, a)$ for q in Q_2 and a in $\Sigma_2 \cup \{\epsilon\}$.

The construction of M is given in Fig. 2.14(b). Every path in M from q_1 to f_2 is a path labeled by some string x from q_1 to f_1, followed by the edge from f_1 to q_2 labeled ϵ, followed by a path labeled by some string y from q_2 to f_2. Thus $L(M) = \{xy \mid x$ is in $L(M_1)$ and y is in $L(M_2)\}$ and $L(M) = L(M_1)L(M_2)$ as desired.

CASE 3 $r = r_1^*$. Let $M_1 = (Q_1, \Sigma_1, \delta_1, q_1, \{f_1\})$ and $L(M_1) = r_1$. Construct

$$M = (Q_1 \cup \{q_0, f_0\}, \Sigma_1, \delta, q_0, \{f_0\}),$$

where δ is given by

i) $\delta(q_0, \epsilon) = \delta(f_1, \epsilon) = \{q_1, f_0\}$,
ii) $\delta(q, a) = \delta_1(q, a)$ for q in $Q_1 - \{f_1\}$ and a in $\Sigma_1 \cup \{\epsilon\}$.

The construction of M is depicted in Fig. 2.14(c). Any path from q_0 to f_0 consists either of a path from q_0 to f_0 on ϵ or a path from q_0 to q_1 on ϵ, followed by some number (possibly zero) of paths from q_1 to f_1, then back to q_1 on ϵ, each labeled by a string in $L(M_1)$, followed by a path from q_1 to f_1 on a string in $L(M_1)$, then to f_0 on ϵ. Thus there is a path in M from q_0 to f_0 labeled x if and only if we can write $x = x_1 x_2 \cdots x_j$ for some $j \geq 0$ (the case $j = 0$ means $x = \epsilon$) such that each x_i is in $L(M_1)$. Hence $L(M) = L(M_1)^*$ as desired. □

Example 2.12   Let us construct an NFA for the regular expression **01* + 1**. By our precedence rules, this expression is really **(0(1*)) + 1**, so it is of the form $r_1 + r_2$, where $r_1 = $ **01*** and $r_2 = $ **1**. The automaton for r_2 is easy; it is

We may express r_1 as $r_3 r_4$, where $r_3 = $ **0** and $r_4 = $ **1***. The automaton for r_3 is also easy:

In turn, r_4 is r_5^*, where r_5 is **1**. An NFA for r_5 is

Note that the need to keep states of different automata disjoint prohibits us from using the same NFA for r_2 and r_5, although they are the same expression.

To construct an NFA for $r_4 = r_5^*$ use the construction of Fig. 2.14(c). Create states q_7 and q_8 playing the roles of q_0 and f_0, respectively. The resulting NFA for r_4 is shown in Fig. 2.15(a). Then, for $r_1 = r_3 r_4$ use the construction of Fig. 2.14(b). The result is shown in Fig. 2.15(b). Finally, use the construction of Fig. 2.14(a) to find the NFA for $r = r_1 + r_2$. Two states q_9 and q_{10} are created to fill the roles of q_0 and f_0 in that construction, and the result is shown in Fig. 2.15(c).

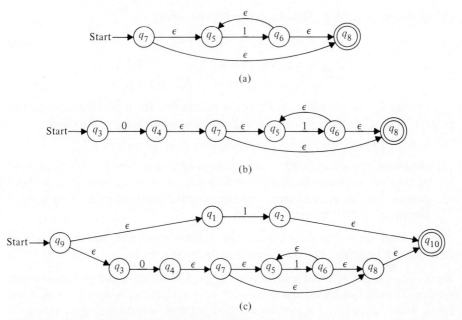

Fig. 2.15 Constructing an NFA from a regular expression. (a) For $r_4 = \mathbf{1}^*$. (b) For $r_1 = \mathbf{01}^*$. (c) For $r = \mathbf{01}^* + \mathbf{1}$.

The proof of Theorem 2.3 is in essence an algorithm for converting a regular expression to a finite automaton. However, the algorithm implicitly assumes that the regular expression is fully parenthesized. For regular expressions without redundant parentheses, we must determine whether the expression is of the form $p + q$, pq, or p^*. This is equivalent to parsing a string in a context-free language, and thus such an algorithm will be delayed until Chapter 5 where it can be done more elegantly.

Now we must show that every set accepted by a finite automaton is denoted by some regular expression. This result will complete the circle shown in Fig. 2.12.

Theorem 2.4 If L is accepted by a DFA, then L is denoted by a regular expression.

Proof Let L be the set accepted by the DFA

$$M = (\{q_1, \ldots, q_n\}, \Sigma, \delta, q_1, F).$$

Let R_{ij}^k denote the set of all strings x such that $\delta(q_i, x) = q_j$, and if $\delta(q_i, y) = q_\ell$, for any y that is a prefix (initial segment) of x, other than x or ϵ, then $\ell \leq k$. That is, R_{ij}^k is the set of all strings that take the finite automaton from state q_i to state q_j without going through any state numbered higher than k. Note that by "going through a state," we mean both entering and then leaving. Thus i or j may be greater than k. Since there is no state numbered greater than n, R_{ij}^n denotes all strings that take q_i to q_j. We can define R_{ij}^k recursively:

$$R_{ij}^k = R_{ik}^{k-1}(R_{kk}^{k-1})^*R_{kj}^{k-1} \cup R_{ij}^{k-1}, \tag{2.1}$$

$$R_{ij}^0 = \begin{cases} \{a \mid \delta(q_i, a) = q_j\} & \text{if } i \neq j, \\ \{a \mid \delta(q_i, a) = q_j\} \cup \{\epsilon\} & \text{if } i = j. \end{cases}$$

Informally, the definition of R_{ij}^k above means that the inputs that cause M to go from q_i to q_j without passing through a state higher than q_k are either

1) in R_{ij}^{k-1} (that is, they never pass through a state as high as q_k); or

2) composed of a string in R_{ik}^{k-1} (which takes M to q_k for the first time) followed by zero or more strings in R_{kk}^{k-1} (which take M from q_k back to q_k without passing through q_k or a higher-numbered state) followed by a string in R_{kj}^{k-1} (which takes M from state q_k to q_j).

We must show that for each i, j, and k, there exists a regular expression r_{ij}^k denoting the language R_{ij}^k. We proceed by induction on k.

Basis $(k = 0)$. R_{ij}^0 is a finite set of strings each of which is either ϵ or a single symbol. Thus r_{ij}^0 can be written as $a_1 + a_2 + \cdots + a_p$ (or $a_1 + a_2 + \cdots + a_p + \epsilon$ if $i = j$), where $\{a_1, a_2, \ldots, a_p\}$ is the set of all symbols a such that $\delta(q_i, a) = q_j$. If there are no such a's, then $\varnothing$ (or ϵ in the case $i = j$) serves as r_{ij}^0.

Induction The recursive formula for R_{ij}^k given in (2.1) clearly involves only the regular expression operators: union, concatenation, and closure. By the induction hypothesis, for each ℓ and m there exists a regular expression $r_{\ell m}^{k-1}$ such that $L(r_{\ell m}^{k-1}) = R_{\ell m}^{k-1}$. Thus for r_{ij}^k we may select the regular expression

$$(r_{ik}^{k-1})(r_{kk}^{k-1})^*(r_{kj}^{k-1}) + r_{ij}^{k-1},$$

which completes the induction.

To finish the proof we have only to observe that

$$L(M) = \bigcup_{q_j \text{ in } F} R_{1j}^n$$

since R_{1j}^n denotes the labels of all paths from q_1 to q_j. Thus $L(M)$ is denoted by the regular expression

$$r_{1j_1}^n + r_{1j_2}^n + \cdots + r_{1j_p}^n,$$

where $F = \{q_{j_1}, q_{j_2}, \ldots, q_{j_p}\}$. $\square$

Example 2.13 Let M be the FA shown in Fig. 2.16. The values of r_{ij}^k for all i and j and for $k = 0$, 1, or 2 are tabulated in Fig. 2.17. Certain equivalences among regular expressions such as $(r + s)t = rt + st$ and $(\epsilon + r)^* = r^*$ have been used to simplify the expressions (see Exercise 2.16). For example, strictly speaking, the expression for r_{22}^1 is given by

$$r_{22}^1 = r_{21}^0(r_{11}^0)^*r_{12}^0 + r_{22}^0 = 0(\epsilon)^*0 + \epsilon.$$

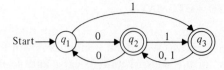

Fig. 2.16   FA for Example 2.13.

	$k = 0$	$k = 1$	$k = 2$
r_{11}^k	ϵ	ϵ	$(00)^*$
r_{12}^k	0	0	$0(00)^*$
r_{13}^k	1	1	0^*1
r_{21}^k	0	0	$0(00)^*$
r_{22}^k	ϵ	$\epsilon + 00$	$(00)^*$
r_{23}^k	1	$1 + 01$	0^*1
r_{31}^k	$\varnothing$	$\varnothing$	$(0 + 1)(00)^*0$
r_{32}^k	$0 + 1$	$0 + 1$	$(0 + 1)(00)^*$
r_{33}^k	ϵ	ϵ	$\epsilon + (0 + 1)0^*1$

Fig. 2.17   Tabulation of r_{ij}^k for FA of Fig. 2.16.

Similarly,

$$r_{13}^2 = r_{12}^1(r_{22}^1)^* r_{23}^1 + r_{13}^1 = 0(\epsilon + 00)^*(1 + 01) + 1.$$

Recognizing that $(\epsilon + 00)^*$ is equivalent to $(00)^*$ and that $1 + 01$ is equivalent to $(\epsilon + 0)1$, we have

$$r_{13}^2 = 0(00)^*(\epsilon + 0)1 + 1.$$

Observe that $(00)^*(\epsilon + 0)$ is equivalent to 0^*. Thus $0(00)^*(\epsilon + 0)1 + 1$ is equivalent to $00^*1 + 1$ and hence to 0^*1.

To complete the construction of the regular expression for M, which is $r_{12}^3 + r_{13}^3$, we write

$$r_{12}^3 = r_{13}^2(r_{33}^2)^* r_{32}^2 + r_{12}^2$$

$$= 0^*1(\epsilon + (0 + 1)0^*1)^*(0 + 1)(00)^* + 0(00)^*$$

$$= 0^*1((0 + 1)0^*1)^*(0 + 1)(00)^* + 0(00)^*$$

and

$$r_{13}^3 = r_{13}^2(r_{33}^2)^* r_{33}^2 + r_{13}^2$$

$$= 0^*1(\epsilon + (0 + 1)0^*1)^*(\epsilon + (0 + 1)0^*1) + 0^*1$$

$$= 0^*1((0 + 1)0^*1)^*.$$

Hence

$$r_{12}^3 + r_{13}^3 = 0^*1((0 + 1)0^*1)^*(\epsilon + (0 + 1)(00)^*) + 0(00)^*.$$

2.6   TWO-WAY FINITE AUTOMATA

We have viewed the finite automaton as a control unit that reads a tape, moving one square right at each move. We added nondeterminism to the model, which allowed many "copies" of the control unit to exist and scan the tape simultaneously. Next we added ϵ-transitions, which allowed change of state without reading the input symbol or moving the tape head. Another interesting extension is to allow the tape head the ability to move left as well as right. Such a finite automaton is called a *two-way finite automaton*. It accepts an input string if it moves the tape head off the right end of the tape, at the same time entering an accepting state. We shall see that even this generalization does not increase the power of the finite automaton; two-way FA accept only regular sets. We give a proof only for a special case of a two-way FA that is deterministic and whose tape head must move left or right (not remain stationary) at each move. A more general model is considered in the exercises.

A *two-way deterministic finite automaton* (2DFA) is a quintuple $M = (Q, \Sigma, \delta, q_0, F)$, where Q, Σ, q_0, and F are as before, and δ is a map from $Q \times \Sigma$ to $Q \times \{L, R\}$. If $\delta(q, a) = (p, L)$, then in state q, scanning input symbol a, the 2DFA enters state p and moves its head left one square. If $\delta(q, a) = (p, R)$, the 2DFA enters state p and moves its head right one square.

In describing the behavior of a one-way FA, we extended δ to $Q \times \Sigma^*$. This corresponds to thinking of the FA as receiving a symbol on an input channel, processing the symbol and requesting the next. This notion is insufficient for the two-way FA, since the 2DFA may move left. Thus the notion of the input being written on the tape is crucial. Instead of trying to extend δ, we introduce the notion of an *instantaneous description* (ID) of a 2DFA, which describes the input string, current state, and current position of the input head. Then we introduce the relation $\vdash_{\overline{M}}$ on ID's such that $I_1 \vdash_{\overline{M}} I_2$ if and only if M can go from the instantaneous description I_1 to I_2 in one move.

An ID of M is a string in $\Sigma^* Q \Sigma^*$. The ID wqx, where w and x are in Σ^* and q is in Q, is intended to represent the facts that

1) wx is the input string,
2) q is the current state, and
3) the input head is scanning the first symbol of x.

If $x = \epsilon$, then the input head has moved off the right end of the input.

We define the relation $\vdash_{\overline{M}}$ or just $\vdash$ if M is understood, by

1) $a_1 a_2 \cdots a_{i-1} q a_i \cdots a_n \vdash a_1 a_2 \cdots a_{i-1} a_i p a_{i+1} \cdots a_n$ whenever $\delta(q, a_i) = (p, R)$, and

2) $a_1 a_2 \cdots a_{i-2} a_{i-1} q a_i \cdots a_n \vdash a_1 a_2 \cdots a_{i-2} p a_{i-1} a_i \cdots a_n$ whenever $\delta(q, a_i) = (p, L)$ and $i > 1$.

The condition $i > 1$ prevents any action in the event that the tape head would move off the left end of the tape. Note that no move is possible if $i = n + 1$ (the tape head has moved off the right end). Let $\overset{*}{\vdash}$ be the reflexive and transitive closure of $\vdash$. That is, $I \overset{*}{\vdash} I$ for all ID's I, and $I_1 \overset{*}{\vdash} I_k$ whenever $I_1 \vdash I_2 \vdash \cdots \vdash I_k$ for some $I_2, \ldots, I_{k-1}$.

We define

$$L(M) = \{w \mid q_0 w \overset{*}{\vdash} wp \quad \text{for some} \quad p \text{ in } F\}.$$

That is, w is accepted by M if, starting in state q_0 with w on the input tape and the head at the left end of w, M eventually enters a final state at the same time it falls off the right end of the input tape.

Example 2.14   Consider a 2DFA M that behaves as follows: Starting in state q_0, M repeats a cycle of moves wherein the tape head moves right until two 1's have been encountered, then left until encountering a 0, at which point state q_0 is reentered and the cycle repeated. More precisely, M has three states, all of which are final; δ is given in Fig. 2.18.

	0	1
q_0	(q_0, R)	(q_1, R)
q_1	(q_1, R)	(q_2, L)
q_2	(q_0, R)	(q_2, L)

Fig. 2.18   The transition function for the 2DFA of Example 2.14.

Consider the input 101001. Since q_0 is the initial state, the first ID is $q_0 101001$. To obtain the second ID, note that the symbol to the immediate right of the state q_0 in the first ID is a 1 and $\delta(q_0, 1)$ is (q_1, R). Thus the second ID is $1q_1 01001$. Continuing in this fashion we get the result shown in Table 2.1. Hence M eventually moves off the right end of the tape in an accepting state. Thus 101001 is in $L(M)$.

Table 2.1

$$
\begin{aligned}
q_0 101001 &\vdash 1q_1 01001 \\
&\vdash 10q_1 1001 \\
&\vdash 1q_2 01001 \\
&\vdash 10q_0 1001 \\
&\vdash 101q_1 001 \\
&\vdash 1010q_1 01 \\
&\vdash 10100q_1 1 \\
&\vdash 1010q_2 01 \\
&\vdash 10100q_0 1 \\
&\vdash 101001q_1
\end{aligned}
$$

Crossing sequences

A useful picture of the behavior of a 2DFA consists of the input, the path followed by the head, and the state each time the boundary between two tape squares is crossed, with the assumption that the control enters its new state prior to moving the head. For example, the behavior of the 2DFA M of Example 2.14 on 101001 is shown in Fig. 2.19.

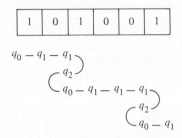

Fig. 2.19 Behavior of the 2DFA of Example 2.14.

The list of states below each boundary between squares is term⌐ ¹ a *crossing sequence*. Note that if a 2DFA accepts its input, no crossing sequence may have a repeated state with the head moving in the same direction, otherwise the 2DFA, being deterministic, would be in a loop and thus could never fall off the right end.

Another important observation about crossing sequences is that the first time a boundary is crossed, the head must be moving right. Subsequent crossings must be in alternate directions. Thus odd-numbered elements of a crossing sequence represent right moves and even-numbered elements represent left moves. If the input is accepted, it follows that all crossing sequences are of odd length.

A crossing sequence $q_1, q_2, \ldots, q_k$ is said to be *valid* if it is of odd length, and no two odd- and no two even-numbered elements are identical. A 2DFA with s states can have valid crossing sequences of length at most $2s$, so the number of valid crossing sequences is finite.

Our strategy for showing that any set accepted by a 2DFA M is regular is to construct an equivalent NFA whose states are the valid crossing sequences of M. To construct the transition function of the NFA we first examine the relationship between adjacent crossing sequences.

Suppose we are given an isolated tape square holding the symbol a and are also given valid crossing sequences $q_1, q_2, \ldots, q_k$ and $p_1, p_2, \ldots, p_\ell$ at the left and right boundaries of the square, respectively. Note that there may be no input strings that could be attached to the left and right of symbol a to actually produce these two crossing sequences. Nevertheless we can test the two sequences for local compatibility as follows. If the tape head moves left from the square holding a in state q_i, restart the automaton on the square holding a in state q_{i+1}. Similarly, whenever the tape head moves right from the square in state p_i, restart the automaton on the square in state p_{i+1}. By this method we can test the two crossing sequences to be sure that they are locally consistent. These ideas are made precise below.

We define *right-matching* and *left-matching* pairs of crossing sequences recursively in (i) through (v) below. The intention is for $q_1, q_2, \ldots, q_k$ to right-match $p_1, p_2, \ldots, p_\ell$ on a if these sequences are consistent, assuming we initially reach a in state q_1 moving right, and for the two crossing sequences to left-match if the sequences are consistent, assuming we initially reach a in state p_1 moving left. In each case, we take $q_1, q_2, \ldots, q_k$ to appear at the left boundary of a and $p_1, p_2, \ldots, p_\ell$ at the right boundary.

i) The null sequence left- and right-matches the null sequence. That is, if we never reach the square holding a, then it is consistent that the boundaries on neither side should be crossed.

ii) If $q_3, \ldots, q_k$ right-matches $p_1, \ldots, p_\ell$ and $\delta(q_1, a) = (q_2, L)$, then $q_1, \ldots, q_k$ right-matches $p_1, \ldots, p_\ell$. That is, if the first crossing of the left boundary is in state q_1 and the head immediately moves left in state q_2, then if we follow these two crossings by any consistent behavior starting from another crossing of the left boundary, we obtain a consistent pair of sequences with first crossing moving right, i.e., a right-matched pair.

iii) If $q_2, \ldots, q_k$ left-matches $p_2, \ldots, p_\ell$ and $\delta(q_1, a) = (p_1, R)$, then $q_1, \ldots, q_k$ right-matches $p_1, \ldots, p_\ell$. That is, if the first crossing of the left boundary is in state q_1 and the head immediately moves right in state p_1, then if we follow these two crossings by any consistent behavior starting from a crossing of the right boundary, we obtain a consistent pair of sequences with the first crossing from the left, i.e., a right-matched pair. Note that this case introduces the need for left-matched sequences, even though we are really only interested in right-matched pairs.

iv) If $q_1, \ldots, q_k$ left-matches $p_3, \ldots, p_\ell$ and $\delta(p_1, a) = (p_2, R)$, then $q_1, \ldots, q_k$ left-matches $p_1, \ldots, p_\ell$. The justification is similar to that for rule (ii).

v) If $q_2, \ldots, q_k$ right-matches $p_2, \ldots, p_\ell$ and $\delta(p_1, a) = (q_1, L)$, then $q_1, \ldots, q_k$ left-matches $p_1, \ldots, p_\ell$. The justification is similar to rule (iii).

Example 2.15 Consider the 2DFA M of Example 2.14 and a tape square containing the symbol 1. The null sequence left-matches the null sequence, and $\delta(q_0, 1) = (q_1, R)$. Thus q_0 right-matches q_1 on 1 by rule (iii). Since $\delta(q_1, 1) = (q_2, L)$, q_1, q_2, q_0 right-matches q_1 on 1 by rule (ii). This must be the case, since there is in fact an accepting computation in which this pair of sequences actually occurs to the left and right of a square holding a 1. Note, however, that a pair of sequences could match, yet there could be no computation in which they appeared adjacent, as it could be impossible to find strings to place to the left and right that would "turn the computation around" in the correct states.

Equivalence of one-way and two-way finite automata

Theorem 2.5   If L is accepted by a 2DFA, then L is a regular set.

Proof   Let $M = (Q, \Sigma, \delta, q_0, F)$ be a 2DFA. The proof consists of constructing an NFA M' which accepts $L(M)$. Define M' to be $(Q', \Sigma, \delta', q_0', F')$, where

1) Q' consists of all valid crossing sequences for M.
2) q_0' is the crossing sequence consisting of q_0 alone.
3) F' is the set of all crossing sequences of length one consisting of a state in F.
4) $\delta'(c, a) = \{d \mid d$ is a valid crossing sequence that is right-matched by c on input $a\}$. Note that as d is valid it must be of odd length.

The intuitive idea is that M' puts together pieces of the computation of M as it scans the input string. This is done by guessing successive crossing sequences. If M' has guessed that c is the crossing sequence at a boundary, and a is the next input symbol, then M' can guess any valid crossing sequence that c right-matches on input a. If the guessed computation results in M moving off the right end of the input in an accepting state, then M' accepts.

We now show that $L(M') = L(M)$. Let w be in $L(M)$. Look at the crossing sequences generated by an accepting computation of M on w. Each crossing sequence right-matches the one at the next boundary, so M' can guess the proper crossing sequences (among other guesses) and accept.

Conversely, if w is in $L(M')$, consider the crossing sequences $c_0, c_1, \ldots, c_n$ of M corresponding to the states of M' as M' scans $w = a_1 a_2 \cdots a_n$. For each i, $0 \le i < n$, c_i right-matches c_{i+1} on a_i. We can construct an accepting computation of M on input w by determining when the head reverses direction. In particular, we prove by induction on i that M' on reading $a_1 a_2 \cdots a_i$ can enter state $c_i = [q_1, \ldots, q_k]$ only if

1) M started in state q_0 on $a_1 a_2 \cdots a_i$ will first move right from position i in state q_1, and
2) for $j = 2, 4, \ldots$, if M is started at position i in state q_j, M will eventually move right from position i in state q_{j+1} (this implies that k must be odd).

Basis $(i = 0)$. As $c_0 = [q_0]$, (1) is satisfied since M begins its computation by "moving right" from position 0 in state q_0. Condition (2) holds vacuously.

Induction   Assume the hypothesis true for $i - 1$. Suppose that M' on reading $a_1 a_2 \cdots a_i$ can enter state $c_i = [p_1, \ldots, p_\ell]$ from state $c_{i-1} = [q_1, \ldots, q_k]$. Since k and ℓ are odd, and c_{i-1} right-matches c_i on a_i, there must exist an odd j such that in state q_j on input a_i, M moves right. Let j_1 be the smallest such j. By definition of "right-matches" it follows that $\delta(q_{j_1}, a_1) = (p_1, R)$. This proves (1). Also by the definition of "right-matches" (rule iii) $[q_{j_1+1}, \ldots, q_k]$ left-matches $[p_2, \ldots, p_\ell]$. Now if $\delta(p_j, a_i) = (p_{j+1}, R)$ for all even j, then (2) follows immediately. In the case that for some smallest even j_2, $\delta(p_{j_2}, a_i) = (q, L)$, then by the definition of "left-matches" (rule v) q must be q_{j_1+1} and $[q_{j_1+2}, \ldots, q_k]$ right-matches $[p_{j_2+1}, \ldots, p_\ell]$. The argument then repeats with the latter sequences in place of c_{i-1} and c_i.

With the induction hypothesis for all i established, the fact that $c_n = [p]$ for some p in F implies that M accepts $a_1 a_2 \cdots a_n$. □

Example 2.16 Consider the construction of an NFA M' equivalent to the 2DFA M of Example 2.14. Since q_2 is only entered on a left move, and q_1 and q_3 are only entered on right moves, all even-numbered components of valid crossing sequences must be q_2. Since a valid crossing sequence must be of odd length, and no two odd-numbered states can be the same, nor can two even-numbered states be the same, there are only four crossing sequences of interest; these are listed in Fig. 2.20 along with their right matches.

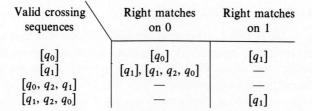

Valid crossing sequences	Right matches on 0	Right matches on 1
$[q_0]$	$[q_0]$	$[q_1]$
$[q_1]$	$[q_1]$, $[q_1, q_2, q_0]$	—
$[q_0, q_2, q_1]$	—	—
$[q_1, q_2, q_0]$	—	$[q_1]$

Fig. 2.20 Valid crossing sequences along with their right matches.

We note immediately that state $[q_0, q_2, q_1]$ may be removed from the constructed NFA M', since it has no right match. The resulting M' is shown in Fig. 2.21. Note that $L(M') = (\epsilon + 1)(0 + 01)^*$, that is, all strings of 0's and 1's without two consecutive 1's.

Consider the input 1001, which is accepted by M' using the sequence of states $[q_0], [q_1], [q_1], [q_1, q_2, q_0], [q_1]$. We can visualize the crossing sequences as in Fig. 2.22. Note that $\delta(q_0, 1) = (q_1, R)$ justifies the first move and that $\delta(q_1, 0) = (q_1, R)$

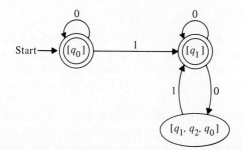

Fig. 2.21 The NFA M' constructed from the 2DFA M.

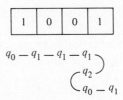

Fig. 2.22   Crossing sequences of 2DFA on input 1001.

justifies the second and third. Since $\delta(q_1, 1) = (q_2, L)$ we see the justification for the fourth move, which reverses the direction of travel. Then $\delta(q_2, 0) = (q_0, R)$ again reverses the direction, and finally $\delta(q_0, 1) = (q_1, R)$ explains the last move.

2.7   FINITE AUTOMATA WITH OUTPUT

One limitation of the finite automaton as we have defined it is that its output is limited to a binary signal: "accept"/"don't accept." Models in which the output is chosen from some other alphabet have been considered. There are two distinct approaches; the output may be associated with the state (called a *Moore machine*) or with the transition (called a *Mealy machine*). We shall define each formally and then show that the two machine types produce the same input-output mappings.

Moore machines

A Moore machine is a six-tuple $(Q, \Sigma, \Delta, \delta, \lambda, q_0)$, where Q, Σ, δ, and q_0 are as in the DFA. Δ is the *output alphabet* and λ is a mapping from Q to Δ giving the output associated with each state. The *output* of M in response to input $a_1 a_2 \cdots a_n, n \geq 0$, is $\lambda(q_0)\lambda(q_1) \cdots \lambda(q_n)$, where $q_0, q_1, \ldots, q_n$ is the sequence of states such that $\delta(q_{i-1}, a_i) = q_i$ for $1 \leq i \leq n$. Note that any Moore machine gives output $\lambda(q_0)$ in response to input ϵ. The DFA may be viewed as a special case of a Moore machine where the output alphabet is $\{0, 1\}$ and state q is "accepting" if and only if $\lambda(q) = 1$.

Example 2.17   Suppose we wish to determine the residue mod 3 for each binary string treated as a binary integer. To begin, observe that if i written in binary is followed by a 0, the resulting string has value $2i$, and if i in binary is followed by a 1, the resulting string has value $2i + 1$. If the remainder of $i/3$ is p, then the remainder of $2i/3$ is $2p \bmod 3$. If $p = 0$, 1, or 2, then $2p \bmod 3$ is 0, 2, or 1, respectively. Similarly, the remainder of $(2i + 1)/3$ is 1, 0, or 2, respectively.

It suffices therefore to design a Moore machine with three states, q_0, q_1, and q_2, where q_j is entered if and only if the input seen so far has residue j. We define

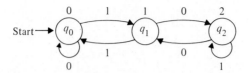

Fig. 2.23   A Moore machine calculating residues.

$\lambda(q_j) = j$ for $j = 0$, 1, and 2. In Fig. 2.23 we show the transition diagram, where outputs label the states. The transition function δ is designed to reflect the rules regarding calculation of residues described above.

On input 1010 the sequence of states entered is q_0, q_1, q_2, q_2, q_1, giving output sequence 01221. That is, ϵ (which has "value" 0) has residue 0, 1 has residue 1, 2 (in decimal) has residue 2, 5 has residue 2, and 10 (in decimal) has residue 1.

Mealy machines

A Mealy machine is also a six-tuple $M = (Q, \Sigma, \Delta, \delta, \lambda, q_0)$, where all is as in the Moore machine, except that λ maps $Q \times \Sigma$ to Δ. That is, $\lambda(q, a)$ gives the output associated with the transition from state q on input a. The *output* of M in response to input $a_1 a_2 \cdots a_n$ is $\lambda(q_0, a_1)\lambda(q_1, a_2) \cdots \lambda(q_{n-1}, a_n)$, where $q_0, q_1, \ldots, q_n$ is the sequence of states such that $\delta(q_{i-1}, a_i) = q_i$ for $1 \le i \le n$. Note that this sequence has length n rather than length $n + 1$ as for the Moore machine, and on input ϵ a Mealy machine gives output ϵ.

Example 2.18   Even if the output alphabet has only two symbols, the Mealy machine model can save states when compared with a finite automaton. Consider the language $(0 + 1)^*(00 + 11)$ of all strings of 0's and 1's whose last two symbols are the same. In the next chapter we shall develop the tools necessary to show that this language is accepted by no DFA with fewer than five states. However, we may define a three-state Mealy machine that uses its state to remember the last symbol read, emits output y whenever the current input matches the previous one, and emits n otherwise. The sequence of y's and n's emitted by the Mealy machine corresponds to the sequence of accepting and nonaccepting states entered by a DFA on the same input; however, the Mealy machine does not make an output prior to any input, while the DFA rejects the string ϵ, as its initial state is nonfinal.

The Mealy machine $M = (\{q_0, p_0, p_1\}, \{0, 1\}, \{y, n\}, \delta, \lambda, q_0)$ is shown in Fig. 2.24. We use the label a/b on an arc from state p to state q to indicate that $\delta(p, a) = q$ and $\lambda(p, a) = b$. The response of M to input 01100 is *nnyny*, with the sequence of states entered being $q_0 p_0 p_1 p_1 p_0 p_0$. Note how p_0 remembers a zero and p_1 remembers a one. State q_0 is initial and "remembers" that no input has yet been received.

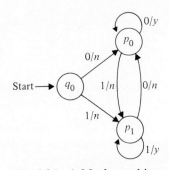

Fig. 2.24 A Mealy machine.

Equivalence of Moore and Mealy machines

Let M be a Mealy or Moore machine. Define $T_M(w)$, for input string w, to be the output produced by M on input w. There can never be exact identity between the functions T_M and $T_{M'}$ if M is a Mealy machine and M' a Moore machine, because $|T_M(w)|$ is one less than $|T_{M'}(w)|$ for each w. However, we may neglect the response of a Moore machine to input ϵ and say that Mealy machine M and Moore machine M' are *equivalent* if for all inputs w, $bT_M(w) = T_{M'}(w)$, where b is the output of M' for its initial state. We may then prove the following theorems, equating the Mealy and Moore models.

Theorem 2.6   If $M_1 = (Q, \Sigma, \Delta, \delta, \lambda, q_0)$ is a Moore machine, then there is a Mealy machine M_2 equivalent to M_1.

Proof   Let $M_2 = (Q, \Sigma, \Delta, \delta, \lambda', q_0)$ and define $\lambda'(q, a)$ to be $\lambda(\delta(q, a))$ for all states q and input symbols a. Then M_1 and M_2 enter the same sequence of states on the same input, and with each transition M_2 emits the output that M_1 associates with the state entered.   □

Theorem 2.7   Let $M_1 = (Q, \Sigma, \Delta, \delta, \lambda, q_0)$ be a Mealy machine. Then there is a Moore machine M_2 equivalent to M_1.

Proof   Let $M_2 = (Q \times \Delta, \Sigma, \Delta, \delta', \lambda', [q_0, b_0])$, where b_0 is an arbitrarily selected member of Δ. That is, the states of M_2 are pairs $[q, b]$ consisting of a state of M_1 and an output symbol. Define $\delta'([q, b], a) = [\delta(q, a), \lambda(q, a)]$ and $\lambda'([q, b]) = b$. The second component of a state $[q, b]$ of M_2 is the output made by M_1 on some transition into state q. Only the first components of M_2's states determine the moves made by M_2. An easy induction on n shows that if M_1 enters states q_0, $q_1, ..., q_n$ on input $a_1a_2 \cdots a_n$, and emits outputs $b_1, b_2, ..., b_n$, then M_2 enters states $[q_0, b_0], [q_1, b_1], ..., [q_n, b_n]$ and emits outputs $b_0, b_1, b_2, ..., b_n$.   □

Example 2.19   Let M_1 be the Mealy machine of Fig. 2.24. The states of M_2 are $[q_0, y]$, $[q_0, n]$, $[p_0, y]$, $[p_0, n]$, $[p_1, y]$, and $[p_1, n]$. Choose $b_0 = n$, making $[q_0, n]$

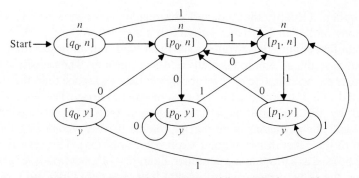

Fig. 2.25 Moore machine constructed from Mealy machine.

M_2's start state. The transitions and outputs of M_2 are shown in Fig. 2.25. Note that state $[q_0, y]$ can never be entered and may be removed.

2.8 APPLICATIONS OF FINITE AUTOMATA

There are a variety of software design problems that are simplified by automatic conversion of regular expression notation to an efficient computer implementation of the corresponding finite automaton. We mention two such applications here; the bibliographic notes contain references to some other applications.

Lexical analyzers

The tokens of a programming language are almost without exception expressible as regular sets. For example, ALGOL identifiers, which are upper- or lower-case letters followed by any sequence of letters and digits, with no limit on length, may be expressed as

$$(\text{letter})(\text{letter} + \text{digit})^*$$

where "letter" stands for $\mathbf{A} + \mathbf{B} + \cdots + \mathbf{Z} + \mathbf{a} + \mathbf{b} + \cdots + \mathbf{z}$, and "digit" stands for $\mathbf{0} + \mathbf{1} + \cdots + \mathbf{9}$. FORTRAN identifiers, with length limit six and letters restricted to upper case and the symbol \$, may be expressed as

$$(\text{letter})(\epsilon + \text{letter} + \text{digit})^5$$

where "letter" now stands for $(\$ + \mathbf{A} + \mathbf{B} + \cdots + \mathbf{Z})$. SNOBOL arithmetic constants (which do not permit the exponential notation present in many other languages) may be expressed as

$$(\epsilon + -)(\text{digit}^+(\cdot \text{digit}^* + \epsilon) + \cdot \text{digit}^+)$$

A number of *lexical-analyzer generators* take as input a sequence of regular expressions describing the tokens and produce a single finite automaton recognizing any token. Usually, they convert the regular expression to an NFA with ϵ-transitions and then construct subsets of states to produce a DFA directly, rather than first eliminating ϵ-transitions. Each final state indicates the particular token found, so the automaton is really a Moore machine. The transition function of the FA is encoded in one of several ways to take less space than the transition table would take if represented as a two-dimensional array. The lexical analyzer produced by the generator is a fixed program that interprets coded tables, together with the particular table that represents the FA recognizing the tokens (specified to the generator in regular expression notation). This lexical analyzer may then be used as a module in a compiler. Examples of lexical analyzer generators that follow the above approach are found in Johnson *et al.* [1968] and Lesk [1975].

Text editors

Certain text editors and similar programs permit the substitution of a string for any string matching a given regular expression. For example, the UNIX text editor allows a command such as

$$s/\text{bbb}*/\text{b}/$$

that substitutes a single blank for the first string of two or more blanks found in a given line. Let "any" denote the expression $a_1 + a_2 + \cdots + a_n$, where the a_i's are all of a computer's characters except the "newline" character. We could convert a regular expression r to a DFA that accepts any$*r$. Note that the presence of any$*$ allows us to recognize a member of $L(r)$ beginning anywhere in the line. However, the conversion of a regular expression to a DFA takes far more time than it takes to scan a single short line using the DFA, and the DFA could have a number of states that is an exponential function of the length of the regular expression.

What actually happens in the UNIX text editor is that the regular expression any$*r$ is converted to an NFA with ϵ-transitions, and the NFA is then simulated directly, as suggested in Fig. 2.6. However, once a column has been constructed listing all the states the NFA can enter on a particular prefix of the input, the previous column is no longer needed and is thrown away to save space. This approach to regular set recognition was first expressed in Thompson [1968].

EXERCISES

*S 2.1   Find a finite automaton whose behavior corresponds to the circuit in Fig. 2.26, in the sense that final states correspond to a 1-output. A circle with a dot represents an *AND-gate*, whose output is 1 only if both inputs have value 1. A circle with a + represents an *OR-gate*, whose output is 1 whenever either input has value 1. A circle with a $\sim$ represents an inverter, whose output is 1 for input 0 and 0 for input 1. Assume there is sufficient time between changes in input values for signals to propagate and for the network to reach a stable configuration.

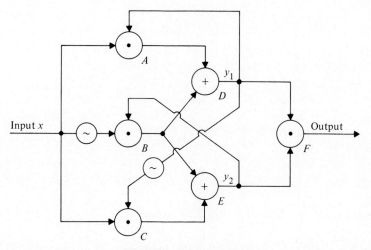

Fig. 2.26 A logic circuit.

2.2 Historically, finite automata were first used to model neuron nets. Find a finite automaton whose behavior is equivalent to the neuron net in Fig. 2.27. Final states of the automaton correspond to a 1-output of the network. Each neuron has excitatory (circles) and inhibitory (dots) synapses. A neuron produces a 1-output if the number of excitatory synapses with 1-inputs exceeds the number of inhibitory synapses with 1-inputs by at least the threshold of the neuron (number inside the triangle). Assume there is sufficient time between changes in input value for signals to propagate and for the network to reach a stable configuration. Further assume that initially the values of y_1, y_2, and y_3 are all 0.

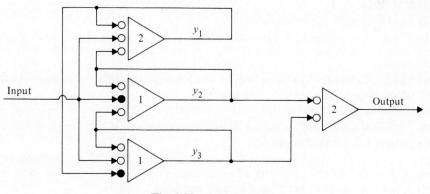

Fig. 2.27 A neuron net.

2.3 Consider the toy shown in Fig. 2.28. A marble is dropped in at A or B. Levers x_1, x_2, and x_3 cause the marble to fall either to the left or right. Whenever a marble encounters a

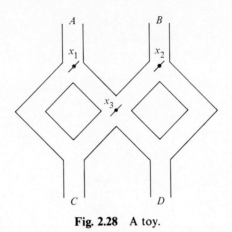

Fig. 2.28   A toy.

lever, it causes the lever to change state, so that the next marble to encounter the lever will take the opposite branch.

a) Model this toy by a finite automaton. Denote a marble in at A by a 0-input and a marble in at B by a 1-input. A sequence of inputs is accepted if the last marble comes out at D.

b) Describe the set accepted by the finite automaton.

c) Model the toy as a Mealy machine whose output is the sequence of C's and D's out of which successive marbles fall.

2.4   Suppose δ is the transition function of a DFA. Prove that for any input strings x and y, $\delta(q, xy) = \delta(\delta(q, x), y)$. [*Hint:* Use induction on $|y|$.]

2.5   Give deterministic finite automata accepting the following languages over the alphabet $\{0, 1\}$.

a) The set of all strings ending in 00.

b) The set of all strings with three consecutive 0's.

c) The set of all strings such that every block of five consecutive symbols contains at least two 0's.

d) The set of all strings beginning with a 1 which, interpreted as the binary representation of an integer, is congruent to zero modulo 5.

e) The set of all strings such that the 10th symbol from the right end is 1.

* **2.6**   Describe in English the sets accepted by the finite automata whose transition diagrams are given in Fig. 2.29(a) through (c).

*S **2.7**   Prove that the FA whose transition diagram is given in Fig. 2.30 accepts the set of all strings over the alphabet $\{0, 1\}$ with an equal number of 0's and 1's, such that each prefix has at most one more 0 than 1's and at most one more 1 than 0's.

2.8   Give nondeterministic finite automata accepting the following languages.

a) The set of strings in $(0 + 1)^*$ such that some two 0's are separated by a string whose length is $4i$, for some $i \geq 0$.

b) The set of all strings over the alphabet $\{a, b, c\}$ that have the same value when evaluated left to right as right to left by multiplying according to the table in Fig. 2.31.

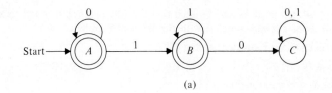

(a)

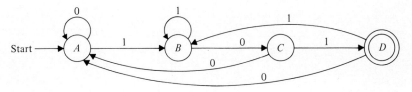

(b)

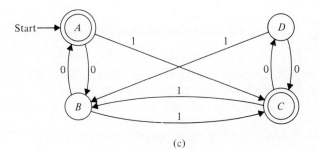

(c)

Fig. 2.29 Transition diagrams for finite automata.

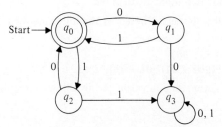

Fig. 2.30 Transition diagram.

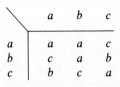

	a	b	c
a	a	a	c
b	c	a	b
c	b	c	a

Fig. 2.31 Nonassociative multiplication table.

c) The set of all strings of 0's and 1's such that the 10th symbol from the right end is a 1. How does your answer compare with the DFA of Problem 2.5(e)?

2.9 Construct DFA's equivalent to the NFA's.

a) $(\{p, q, r, s\}, \{0, 1\}, \delta_1, p, \{s\})$,   b) $(\{p, q, r, s\}, \{0, 1\}, \delta_2, p, \{q, s\})$
where δ_1 and δ_2 are given in Fig. 2.32.

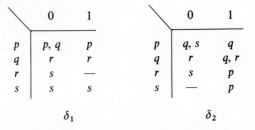

Fig. 2.32   Two transition functions.

2.10 Write regular expressions for each of the following languages over the alphabet $\{0, 1\}$. Provide justification that your regular expression is correct.

* a) The set of all strings with at most one pair of consecutive 0's and at most one pair of consecutive 1's.
 b) The set of all strings in which every pair of adjacent 0's appears before any pair of adjacent 1's.
 c) The set of all strings not containing 101 as a substring.
* d) The set of all strings with an equal number of 0's and 1's such that no prefix has two more 0's than 1's nor two more 1's than 0's.

2.11 Describe in English the sets denoted by the following regular expressions.

a) $(11 + 0)^*(00 + 1)^*$
b) $(1 + 01 + 001)^*(\epsilon + 0 + 00)$
c) $[00 + 11 + (01 + 10)(00 + 11)^*(01 + 10)]^*$

2.12 Construct finite automata equivalent to the following regular expressions.

a) $10 + (0 + 11)0^*1$
b) $01[((10)^* + 111)^* + 0]^*1$
c) $((0 + 1)(0 + 1))^* + ((0 + 1)(0 + 1)(0 + 1))^*$

2.13 Construct regular expressions corresponding to the state diagrams given in Fig. 2.33.

2.14 Use the ideas in the proof of Theorem 2.4 to construct algorithms for the following problems.

a) Find the lowest-cost path between two vertices in a directed graph where each edge is labeled with a nonnegative cost.
b) Determine the number of strings of length n accepted by an FA.

2.15 Construct an NFA equivalent to the 2DFA $(\{q_0, \ldots, q_5\}, \{0, 1\}, \delta, q_0, \{q_2\})$, where δ is given by Fig. 2.34.

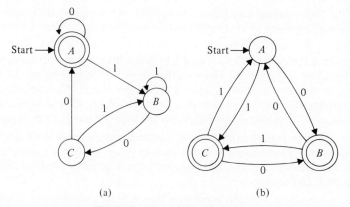

Fig. 2.33 Transition diagrams.

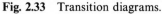

	0	1
q_0	(q_0, R)	(q_1, R)
q_1	(q_1, R)	(q_2, R)
q_2	(q_2, R)	(q_3, L)
q_3	(q_4, L)	(q_3, L)
q_4	(q_0, R)	(q_4, L)

Fig. 2.34 A transition function for a 2DFA.

2.16 Prove the following identities for regular expressions r, s, and t. Here $r = s$ means $L(r) = L(s)$.

a) $r + s = s + r$ b) $(r + s) + t = r + (s + t)$
c) $(rs)t = r(st)$ d) $r(s + t) = rs + rt$
e) $(r + s)t = rt + st$ f) $\emptyset^* = \epsilon$
g) $(r^*)^* = r^*$ h) $(\epsilon + r)^* = r^*$ i) $(r^*s^*)^* = (r + s)^*$

2.17 Prove or disprove the following for regular expressions r, s, and t.
a) $(rs + r)^*r = r(sr + r)^*$ b) $s(rs + s)^*r = rr^*s(rr^*s)^*$
c) $(r + s)^* = r^* + s^*$

2.18 A *two-way nondeterministic finite automaton* (2NFA) is defined in the same manner as the 2DFA, except that the 2NFA has a set of possible moves for each state and input symbol. Prove that the set accepted by any 2NFA is regular. [*Hint:* The observation in the proof of Theorem 2.5 that no state may repeat with the same direction in a valid crossing sequence is no longer true. However, for each accepted input we may consider a shortest computation leading to acceptance.]

2.19 Show that adding the capability of the 2NFA to keep its head stationary (and change state) on a move does not increase the class of languages accepted by 2NFA.

⊦ **2.20** A 2NFA *with endmarkers* is a 2NFA with special symbols ¢ and $ marking the left and right ends of the input. We say that input x, which contains no ¢ or $ symbols, is accepted if the 2NFA started with $\mathcal{c}x\$$ on its tape and with the tape head scanning $\mathcal{c}$ enters an accepting state anywhere on its input. Show that the 2NFA with endmarkers accepts only regular sets.

2.21 Consider a 2DFA $M = (Q, \Sigma, \delta, q_0, F)$. For each string x construct a mapping f from Q to $Q \cup \{\mathcal{c}\}$, where $f(q) = p$ if the 2DFA started on the rightmost symbol of x eventually moves off x to the right, in state p. $f(q) = \mathcal{c}$ means that the 2DFA when started on the rightmost symbol of x either never leaves x or moves off the left end. Construct a DFA which simulates M by storing in its finite control a table f instead of a crossing sequence.

** 2.22 Let r and s be regular expressions. Consider the equation $X = rX + s$, where rX denotes the concatenation of r and X, and $+$ denotes union. Under the assumption that the set denoted by r does not contain ϵ, find the solution for X and prove that it is unique. What is the solution if $L(r)$ contains ϵ?

** 2.23 One can construct a regular expression from a finite automaton by solving a set of linear equations of the form

$$
\begin{pmatrix} x_1 \\ x_2 \\ \vdots \\ x_n \end{pmatrix} = \begin{pmatrix} a_{11} & a_{12} & \cdots & a_{1n} \\ a_{21} & a_{22} & \cdots & a_{2n} \\ \vdots & & & \vdots \\ a_{n1} & a_{n2} & \cdots & a_{nn} \end{pmatrix} \begin{pmatrix} x_1 \\ x_2 \\ \vdots \\ x_n \end{pmatrix} + \begin{pmatrix} c_1 \\ c_2 \\ \vdots \\ c_n \end{pmatrix},
$$

where a_{ij} and c_i are sets of strings denoted by regular expressions, $+$ denotes set union, and multiplication denotes concatenation. Give an algorithm for solving such equations.

2.24 Give Mealy and Moore machines for the following processes:

a) For input from $(0 + 1)^*$, if the input ends in 101, output A; if the input ends in 110, output B; otherwise output C.

b) For input from $(0 + 1 + 2)^*$ print the residue modulo 5 of the input treated as a ternary (base 3, with digits 0, 1, and 2) number.

Solutions to Sample Exercises

2.1 Note that the gate output at y_1 affects the gate output at y_2 and conversely. We shall assume values for y_1 and y_2 and use these assumed values to compute new values. Then we repeat the process with the new values until we reach a stable state of the system. In Fig. 2.35 we have tabulated the stable values of y_1 and y_2 for each possible assumed values for y_1 and y_2 and for input values 0 and 1.

$y_1 y_2$	Input 0	1		0	1
00	00	01	q_0	q_0	q_1
01	11	01	q_1	q_2	q_1
11	11	10	q_2	q_2	q_3
10	00	10	q_3	q_0	q_3
	(a)			(b)	

Fig. 2.35 Transitions of switching circuit.

If y_1 and y_2 are both assumed to have value 0, then gates A and B have output 0 and gate C has output equal to the value of the input x. Since both inputs to gate D are 0, the output of gate D is 0. The output of gate E has the value of the input x. Thus the top row in Fig. 2.35(a) has entries 00 and 01. The remaining entries are computed in a similar manner.

We can model the circuit by assigning a state to each pair of values for $y_1 y_2$. This is done in Fig. 2.35(b). Since $y_1 = y_2 = 1$ produces a 1-output, q_2 is a final state. The circuit can be seen to record the parity of pulses (1-inputs) and produce an output pulse for every odd-numbered input pulse.

2.7   We are asked to prove that a set informally described in English is the set accepted by the FA. Clearly we cannot give a completely formal proof. We must either argue intuitively that some formal description of the set is equivalent to the English description and then proceed formally or else simply give an informal proof. We choose the latter.

The proof consists of deducing the properties of strings, taking the automaton to each of the four states, and then proving by induction on the length of a string that our interpretation is correct.

We say that a string x is *proper* if each prefix of x has at most one more 0 than 1 and at most one more 1 than 0. We argue by induction on the length of a string x that

1) $\delta(q_0, x) = q_0$ if and only if x is proper and contains an equal number of 0's and 1's,

2) $\delta(q_0, x) = q_1$ if and only if x is proper and contains one more 0 than 1's,

3) $\delta(q_0, x) = q_2$ if and only if x is proper and contains one more 1 than 0's,

4) $\delta(q_0, x) = q_3$ if and only if x is not proper.

Observe that the induction hypothesis is stronger than the desired theorem. Conditions (2), (3), and (4) are added to allow the induction to go through.

We prove the "if" portions of (1) through (4) first. The basis of the induction, $|x| = 0$, follows since the empty string has an equal number of 0's and 1's and $\delta(q_0, \epsilon) = q_0$.

Assume the induction hypothesis is true for all x, $|x| < n, n \geq 1$. Consider a string y of length n, such that y is proper and has an equal number of 0's and 1's. First consider the case that y ends in 0. Then $y = x0$, where x is proper and has one more 1 than 0's. Thus $\delta(q_0, x) = q_2$. Hence

$$\delta(q_0, y) = \delta(q_0, x0) = \delta(q_2, 0) = q_0.$$

The case where y ends in a 1 is handled similarly.

Next consider a string y, $|y| = n$ such that y is proper and has one more 0 than 1. If $y = x0$, then x has two more 0's than 1's, contradicting the fact that y is proper. Thus $y = x1$, where x is proper and has an equal number of 0's and 1's. By the induction hypothesis, $\delta(q_0, x) = q_0$; hence $\delta(q_0, y) = q_1$.

The situation where y is proper and has one more 1 than 0, and the situation where y is not proper are treated similarly.

We must now show that strings reaching each state have the interpretations given in (1) through (4). Suppose that $\delta(q_0, y) = q_0$ and $|y| \geq 1$. If $y = x0$, then $\delta(q_0, x) = q_2$, since q_2 is the only state with a 0-transition to state q_0. Thus by the induction hypothesis x is proper and has one more 1 than 0. Thus y is proper and has an equal number of 0's and 1's. The case where y ends in a 1 is similar, as are the cases $\delta(q_0, y) = q_1, q_2,$ or q_3.

BIBLIOGRAPHIC NOTES

The original formal study of finite state systems (neural nets similar to that appearing in Exercise 2.2) is by McCulloch and Pitts [1943]. Kleene [1956] considered regular expressions and modeled the neural nets of McCulloch and Pitts by finite automata, proving the equivalence of the two concepts. Similar models were considered about that time by Huffman [1954], Moore [1956], and Mealy [1955], the latter two being the sources for the terms "Moore machine" and "Mealy machine." Nondeterministic finite automata were introduced by Rabin and Scott [1959], who proved their equivalence to deterministic automata. The notion of a two-way finite automaton and its equivalence to the one-way variety was the independent work of Rabin and Scott [1959] and Shepherdson [1959].

The proof of the equivalence of regular expressions and finite automata as presented here (via NFA's with ϵ-transitions) is patterned after McNaughton and Yamada [1960]. Brzozowski [1962, 1964] developed the theory of regular expressions. The fact that the unique solution to $X = rX + s$ (Exercise 2.22) is r^*s if $L(r)$ does not contain ϵ is known as Arden's [1960] lemma. Floyd [1967] applies the idea of nondeterminism to programs. Salomaa [1966] gives axiomatizations of regular expressions.

Applications of finite automata to switching circuit design can be found in Kohavi [1970] and Friedman [1975]. The use of the theory to design lexical analyzers is treated by Johnson *et al.* [1968] and Lesk [1975]. Other uses of finite automata theory to design text editors and other text processing programs are discussed in Thompson [1968], Bullen and Millen [1972], Aho and Corasick [1975], Knuth, Morris, and Pratt [1977], and Aho and Ullman [1977].

Some additional works treating finite automata are by Arbib [1970], Conway [1971], Minsky [1967], Moore [1964], and Shannon and McCarthy [1956].

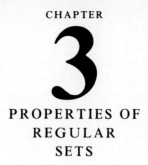

PROPERTIES OF
REGULAR
SETS

There are several questions one can ask concerning regular sets. One important question is: given a language L specified in some manner, is L a regular set? We also might want to know whether the regular sets denoted by different regular expressions are the same, or find the finite automaton with fewest states that denotes the same language as a given FA.

In this chapter we provide tools to deal with questions such as these regarding regular sets. We prove a "pumping lemma" to show that certain languages are nonregular. We provide "closure properties" of regular sets; the fact that languages constructed from regular sets in certain specified ways must also be regular can be used to prove or disprove that certain other languages are regular. The issue of regularity or nonregularity can also be resolved sometimes with the aid of the Myhill-Nerode Theorem of Section 3.4. In addition, we give algorithms to answer a number of other questions about regular expressions and finite automata such as whether a given FA accepts an infinite language.

3.1 THE PUMPING LEMMA FOR REGULAR SETS

In this section we prove a basic result, called the *pumping lemma*, which is a powerful tool for proving certain languages nonregular. It is also useful in the development of algorithms to answer certain questions concerning finite automata, such as whether the language accepted by a given FA is finite or infinite.

If a language is regular, it is accepted by a DFA $M = (Q, \Sigma, \delta, q_0, F)$ with some particular number of states, say n. Consider an input of n or more symbols $a_1 a_2 \cdots a_m$, $m \geq n$, and for $i = 1, 2, \ldots, m$ let $\delta(q_0, a_1 a_2 \cdots a_i) = q_i$. It is not possible for each of the $n + 1$ states $q_0, q_1, \ldots, q_n$ to be distinct, since there are only n different states. Thus there are two integers j and k, $0 \le j < k \le n$, such that $q_j = q_k$. The path labeled $a_1 a_2 \cdots a_m$ in the transition diagram of M is illustrated in Fig. 3.1. Since $j < k$, the string $a_{j+1} \cdots a_k$ is of length at least 1, and since $k \le n$, its length is no more than n.

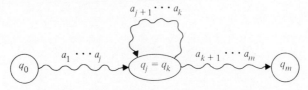

Fig. 3.1 Path in transition diagram of DFA M.

If q_m is in F, that is, $a_1 a_2 \cdots a_m$ is in $L(M)$, then $a_1 a_2 \cdots a_j a_{k+1} a_{k+2} \cdots a_m$ is also in $L(M)$, since there is a path from q_0 to q_m that goes through q_j but not around the loop labeled $a_{j+1} \cdots a_k$. Formally, by Exercise 2.4,

$$\delta(q_0, a_1 \cdots a_j a_{k+1} \cdots a_m) = \delta(\delta(q_0, a_1 \cdots a_j), a_{k+1} \cdots a_m)$$
$$= \delta(q_j, a_{k+1} \cdots a_m)$$
$$= \delta(q_k, a_{k+1} \cdots a_m)$$
$$= q_m.$$

Similarly, we could go around the loop of Fig. 3.1 more than once—in fact, as many times as we like. Thus, $a_1 \cdots a_j(a_{j+1} \cdots a_k)^i a_{k+1} \cdots a_m$ is in $L(M)$ for any $i \ge 0$. What we have proved is that given any sufficiently long string accepted by an FA, we can find a substring near the beginning of the string that may be "pumped," i.e., repeated as many times as we like, and the resulting string will be accepted by the FA. The formal statement of the pumping lemma follows.

Lemma 3.1 Let L be a regular set. Then there is a constant n such that if z is any word in L, and $|z| \ge n$, we may write $z = uvw$ in such a way that $|uv| \le n$, $|v| \ge 1$, and for all $i \ge 0$, $uv^i w$ is in L. Furthermore, n is no greater than the number of states of the smallest FA accepting L.

Proof See the discussion preceding the statement of the lemma. There, z is $a_1 a_2 \cdots a_m$, $u = a_1 a_2 \cdots a_j$, $v = a_{j+1} \cdots a_k$, and $w = a_{k+1} \cdots a_m$. □

Note that the pumping lemma states that if a regular set contains a long string z, then it contains an infinite set of strings of the form $uv^i w$. The lemma does not state that every sufficiently long string in a regular set is of the form $uv^i w$ for some large i. In fact, $(0 + 1)^*$ contains arbitrarily long strings in which no substring appears three times consecutively. (The proof is left as an exercise.)

Applications of the pumping lemma

The pumping lemma is extremely useful in proving that certain sets are not regular. The general methodology in its application is an "adversary argument" of the following form.

1) Select the language L you wish to prove nonregular.

2) The "adversary" picks n, the constant mentioned in the pumping lemma. You must be prepared in what follows for any finite integer n to be picked, but once the adversary has picked n, he may not change it.

3) Select a string z in L. Your choice may depend implicitly on the value of n chosen in (2).

4) The adversary breaks z into u, v, and w, subject to the constraints that $|uv| \le n$ and $|v| \ge 1$.

5) You achieve a contradiction to the pumping lemma by showing, for any u, v, and w determined by the adversary, that there exists an i for which uv^iw is not in L. It may then be concluded that L is not regular. Your selection of i may depend on n, u, v, and w.

It is interesting to note that your choice in the above "game" corresponds to the universal quantifiers ($\forall$, or "for all") and the "adversary's" choices correspond to the existential quantifiers ($\exists$, or "there exists") in the formal statement of the pumping lemma:

$$(\forall L)(\exists n)(\forall z)[z \text{ in } L \text{ and } |z| \ge n \quad \text{implies that}$$

$$(\exists u, v, w)(z = uvw, |uv| \le n, |v| \ge 1 \text{ and } (\forall i)(uv^iw \text{ is in } L))].$$

Example 3.1 The set $L = \{0^{i^2} \,|\, i \text{ is an integer, } i \ge 1\}$, which consists of all strings of 0's whose length is a perfect square, is not regular. Assume L is regular and let n be the integer in the pumping lemma. Let $z = 0^{n^2}$. By the pumping lemma, 0^{n^2} may be written as uvw, where $1 \le |v| \le n$ and uv^iw is in L for all i. In particular, let $i = 2$. However, $n^2 < |uv^2w| \le n^2 + n < (n + 1)^2$. That is, the length of uv^2w lies properly between n^2 and $(n + 1)^2$, and is thus not a perfect square. Thus uv^2w is not in L, a contradiction. We conclude that L is not regular.

Example 3.2 Let L be the set of strings of 0's and 1's, beginning with a 1, whose value treated as a binary number is a prime. We shall make use of the pumping lemma to prove that L is not regular. We need two results from number theory. The first is that the number of primes is infinite and that there are therefore arbitrarily large primes. The second, due to Fermat, is that $2^{p-1} - 1$ is divisible by p for any prime $p > 2$. Stated another way, $2^{p-1} \equiv 1 \bmod p$ (see Hardy and Wright [1938]).

Suppose L were regular, and let n be the integer in the pumping lemma. Let z be the binary representation of a prime p such that $p > 2^n$. Such a prime exists since there are infinitely many primes. By the pumping lemma we may write $z = uvw$, where $|v| \geq 1$ and uv^iw is the binary representation of a prime for all i. Let n_u, n_v, and n_w be the values of u, v, and w treated as binary numbers. If u or w are ϵ, then n_u or n_w, respectively, is 0. Choose $i = p$. Then uv^pw is the binary representation of a prime q. The numerical value of q is

$$n_u 2^{|w| + p|v|} + n_v 2^{|w|}(1 + 2^{|v|} + \cdots + 2^{(p-1)|v|}) + n_w.$$

By Fermat's theorem, $2^{(p-1)} \equiv 1 \bmod p$. If we raise both sides to the power $|v|$, we get $2^{(p-1)|v|} \equiv 1 \bmod p$. Thus

$$2^{p|v|} = 2^{(p-1)|v|}2^{|v|} \equiv 2^{|v|} \bmod p.$$

Let $s = 1 + 2^{|v|} + \cdots + 2^{(p-1)|v|}$. Then

$$(2^{|v|} - 1)s = 2^{p|v|} - 1,$$

which is $2^{|v|} - 1 \bmod p$. Thus $(2^{|v|} - 1)(s - 1)$ is divisible by p. But $1 \leq |v| \leq n$, so $2 \leq 2^{|v|} \leq 2^n < p$. Therefore p cannot divide $2^{|v|} - 1$, so it divides $s - 1$. That is, $s \equiv 1 \bmod p$. But

$$q = n_u 2^{|w| + p|v|} + n_v 2^{|w|}s + n_w,$$

so

$$q \equiv n_u 2^{|w| + |v|} + n_v 2^{|w|} + n_w \bmod p. \tag{3.1}$$

But the right-hand side of (3.1) is the numerical value of p. Thus $q \equiv p \bmod p$, which is to say q is divisible by p. Since $q > p > 1$, q cannot be prime. But by the pumping lemma, the binary representation of q is in L, a contradiction. We conclude that L is not regular.

3.2 CLOSURE PROPERTIES OF REGULAR SETS

There are many operations on languages that preserve regular sets, in the sense that the operations applied to regular sets result in regular sets. For example, the union of two regular sets is a regular set, since if r_1 and r_2 are regular expressions denoting regular sets L_1 and L_2, then $r_1 + r_2$ denotes $L_1 \cup L_2$, so $L_1 \cup L_2$ is also regular. Similarly, the concatenation of regular sets is a regular set and the Kleene closure of a regular set is regular.

If a class of languages is closed under a particular operation, we call that fact a *closure property* of the class of languages. We are particularly interested in *effective closure properties* where, given descriptors for languages in the class, there is an algorithm to construct a representation for the language that results by applying the operation to these languages. For example, we just gave an algorithm to construct a regular expression for the union of two languages denoted by regular expressions, so the class of regular sets is effectively closed under union. Closure properties given in this book are effective unless otherwise stated.

It should be observed that the equivalences shown in Chapter 2 between the various models of finite automata and regular expressions were effective equivalences, in the sense that algorithms were given to translate from one representation to another. Thus in proving effective closure properties we may choose the representation that suits us best, usually regular expressions or deterministic finite automata. We now consider a sequence of closure properties of regular sets; additional closure properties are given in the exercises.

Theorem 3.1   The regular sets are closed under union, concatenation, and Kleene closure.

Proof   Immediate from the definition of regular expressions.   □

Boolean operations

Theorem 3.2   The class of regular sets is closed under complementation. That is, if L is a regular set and $L \subseteq \Sigma^*$, then $\Sigma^* - L$ is a regular set.

Proof   Let L be $L(M)$ for DFA $M = (Q, \Sigma_1, \delta, q_0, F)$ and let $L \subseteq \Sigma^*$. First, we may assume $\Sigma_1 = \Sigma$, for if there are symbols in Σ_1 not in Σ, we may delete all transitions of M on symbols not in Σ. The fact that $L \subseteq \Sigma^*$ assures us that we shall not thereby change the language of M. If there are symbols in Σ not in Σ_1, then none of these symbols appear in words of L. We may therefore introduce a "dead state" d into M with $\delta(d, a) = d$ for all a in Σ and $\delta(q, a) = d$ for all q in Q and a in $\Sigma - \Sigma_1$.

Now, to accept $\Sigma^* - L$, complement the final states of M. That is, let $M' = (Q, \Sigma, \delta, q_0, Q - F)$. Then M' accepts a word w if and only if $\delta(q_0, w)$ is in $Q - F$, that is, w is in $\Sigma^* - L$. Note that it is essential to the proof that M is deterministic and without ϵ moves.   □

Theorem 3.3   The regular sets are closed under intersection.

Proof $L_1 \cap L_2 = \overline{\overline{L_1} \cup \overline{L_2}}$, where the overbar denotes complementation with respect to an alphabet including the alphabets of L_1 and L_2. Closure under intersection then follows from closure under union and complementation.   □

It is worth noting that a direct construction of a DFA for the intersection of two regular sets exists. The construction involves taking the Cartesian product of states, and we sketch the construction as follows.

Let $M_1 = (Q_1, \Sigma, \delta_1, q_1, F_1)$ and $M_2 = (Q_2, \Sigma, \delta_2, q_2, F_2)$ be two deterministic finite automata. Let

$$M = (Q_1 \times Q_2, \Sigma, \delta, [q_1, q_2], F_1 \times F_2),$$

where for all p_1 in Q_1, p_2 in Q_2, and a in Σ,

$$\delta([p_1, p_2], a) = [\delta_1(p_1, a), \delta_2(p_2, a)].$$

It is easily shown that $T(M) = T(M_1) \cap T(M_2)$.

Substitutions and homomorphisms

The class of regular sets has the interesting property that it is closed under substitution in the following sense. For each symbol a in the alphabet of some regular set R, let R_a be a particular regular set. Suppose that we replace each word $a_1 a_2 \cdots a_n$ in R by the set of words of the form $w_1 w_2 \cdots w_n$, where w_i is an arbitrary word in R_{a_i}. Then the result is always a regular set. More formally, a *substitution* f is a mapping of an alphabet Σ onto subsets of Δ^*, for some alphabet Δ. Thus f associates a language with each symbol of Σ. The mapping f is extended to strings as follows:

1) $f(\epsilon) = \epsilon$;
2) $f(xa) = f(x)f(a)$.

The mapping f is extended to languages by defining

$$f(L) = \bigcup_{x \text{ in } L} f(x).$$

Example 3.3   Let $f(0) = \mathbf{a}$ and $f(1) = \mathbf{b}^*$. That is, $f(0)$ is the language $\{a\}$ and $f(1)$ is the language of all strings of b's. Then $f(010)$ is the regular set $\mathbf{ab^*a}$. If L is the language $\mathbf{0^*(0 + 1)1^*}$, then $f(L)$ is $\mathbf{a^*(a + b^*)(b^*)^* = a^*b^*}$.

Theorem 3.4   The class of regular sets is closed under substitution.

Proof   Let $R \subseteq \Sigma^*$ be a regular set and for each a in Σ let $R_a \subseteq \Delta^*$ be a regular set. Let $f: \Sigma \to \Delta^*$ be the substitution defined by $f(a) = R_a$. Select regular expressions denoting R and each R_a. Replace each occurrence of the symbol $\mathbf{a}$ in the regular expression for R by the regular expression for R_a. To prove that the resulting regular expression denotes $f(R)$, observe that the substitution of a union, product, or closure is the union, product, or closure of the substitution. [Thus, for example, $f(L_1 \cup L_2) = f(L_1) \cup f(L_2)$.] A simple induction on the number of operators in the regular expression completes the proof. $\square$

Note that in Example 3.3 we computed $f(L)$ by taking L's regular expression $\mathbf{0^*(1 + 0)1^*}$ and substituting $\mathbf{a}$ for $\mathbf{0}$ and $\mathbf{b}^*$ for $\mathbf{1}$. The fact that the resulting regular expression is equivalent to the simpler regular expression $\mathbf{a^*b^*}$ is a coincidence.

A type of substitution that is of special interest is the homomorphism. A *homomorphism* h is a substitution such that $h(a)$ contains a single string for each a.

We generally take $h(a)$ to be the string itself, rather than the set containing that string. It is useful to define the *inverse homomorphic image* of a language L to be

$$h^{-1}(L) = \{x \mid h(x) \text{ is in } L\}.$$

We also use, for string w;

$$h^{-1}(w) = \{x \mid h(x) = w\}.$$

Example 3.4   Let $h(0) = aa$ and $h(1) = aba$. Then $h(010) = aaabaaa$. If L_1 is $(01)^*$, then $h(L_1)$ is $(\mathbf{aaaba})^*$. Let $L_2 = (\mathbf{ab} + \mathbf{ba})^*\mathbf{a}$. Then $h^{-1}(L_2)$ consists only of the string 1. To see this, observe that a string in L_2 that begins with b cannot be $h(x)$ for any string x of 0's and 1's, since $h(0)$ and $h(1)$ each begin with an a. Thus if $h^{-1}(w)$ is nonempty and w is in L_2, then w begins with a. Now either $w = a$, in which case $h^{-1}(w)$ is surely empty, or w is abw' for some w' in $(\mathbf{ab} + \mathbf{ba})^*\mathbf{a}$. We conclude that every word in $h^{-1}(w)$ begins with a 1, and since $h(1) = aba$, w' must begin with a. If $w' = a$, we have $w = aba$ and $h^{-1}(w) = \{1\}$. However, if $w' \neq a$, then $w' = abw''$ and hence $w = ababw''$. But no string x in $(\mathbf{0} + \mathbf{1})^*$ has $h(x)$ beginning $abab$. Consequently we conclude that $h^{-1}(w)$ is empty in this case. Thus the only string in L_2 which has an inverse image under h is aba, and therefore $h^{-1}(L_2) = \{1\}$.

Observe that $h(h^{-1}(L_2)) = \{aba\} \neq L_2$. On the other hand, it is easily shown that $h(h^{-1}(L)) \subseteq L$ and $h^{-1}(h(L)) \supseteq L$ for any language L.

Theorem 3.5   The class of regular sets is closed under homomorphisms and inverse homomorphisms.

Proof   Closure under homomorphisms follows immediately from closure under substitution, since every homomorphism is a substitution, in which $h(a)$ has one member.

To show closure under inverse homomorphism, let $M = (Q, \Sigma, \delta, q_0, F)$ be a DFA accepting L, and let h be a homomorphism from Δ to Σ^*. We construct a DFA M' that accepts $h^{-1}(L)$ by reading symbol a in Δ and simulating M on $h(a)$. Formally, let $M' = (Q, \Delta, \delta', q_0, F)$ and define $\delta'(q, a)$, for q in Q and a in Δ to be $\delta(q, h(a))$. Note that $h(a)$ may be a long string, or ϵ, but δ is defined on all strings by extension. It is easy to show by induction on $|x|$ that $\delta'(q_0, x) = \delta(q_0, h(x))$. Therefore M' accepts x if and only if M accepts $h(x)$. That is, $L(M') = h^{-1}(L(M))$. $\square$

Example 3.5   The importance of homomorphisms and inverse homomorphisms comes in simplifying proofs. We know for example that $\{0^n1^n \mid n \geq 1\}$ is not regular. Intuitively, $\{a^nba^n \mid n \geq 1\}$ is not regular for the same reasons. That is, if we had an FA M accepting $\{a^nba^n \mid n \geq 1\}$, we could accept $\{0^n1^n \mid n \geq 1\}$ by simulating M on input a for each 0. When the first 1 is seen, simulate M on ba and thereafter simulate M on a for each 1 seen. However, to be rigorous it is necessary to formally prove that $\{a^nba^n \mid n \geq 1\}$ is not regular. This is done by showing that $\{a^nba^n \mid n > 1\}$ can be converted to $\{0^n1^n \mid n \geq 1\}$ by use of operations that preserve regularity. Thus $\{a^nba^n \mid \geq 1\}$ cannot be regular.

Let h_1 and h_2 be the homomorphisms

$$h_1(a) = a, \qquad h_2(a) = 0,$$
$$h_1(b) = ba, \qquad h_2(b) = 1,$$
$$h_1(c) = a, \qquad h_2(c) = 1.$$

Then

$$h_2(h_1^{-1}(\{a^nba^n \mid n \geq 1\}) \cap \mathbf{a^*bc^*}) = \{0^n1^n \mid n \geq 1\}. \tag{3.2}$$

That is, $h_1^{-1}(\{a^nba^n \mid n \geq 1\})$ consists of all strings in $(\mathbf{a + c})\mathbf{^*b(a + c)^*}$ such that the number of symbols preceding the b is one greater than the number of symbols following the b. Thus

$$h_1^{-1}(\{a^nba^n \mid n \geq 1\}) \cap \mathbf{a^*bc^*} = \{a^nbc^{n-1} \mid n \geq 1\}.$$

Line (3.2) then follows immediately by applying homomorphism h_2.

If $\{a^nba^n \mid n \geq 1\}$ were regular, then since homomorphisms, inverse homomorphisms, and intersection with a regular set all preserve the property of being regular, it would follow that $\{0^n1^n \mid n \geq 1\}$ is regular, a contradiction.

Quotients of languages

Now let us turn to the last closure property of regular sets to be proved in this section. A number of additional closure properties are given in the exercises. Define the *quotient* of languages L_1 and L_2, written L_1/L_2, to be

$$\{x \mid \text{there exists } y \text{ in } L_2 \text{ such that } xy \text{ is in } L_1\}.$$

Example 3.6 Let L_1 be $\mathbf{0^*10^*}$ and L_2 be $\mathbf{10^*1}$. Then L_1/L_2 is empty. Since every y in L_2 has two 1's and every string xy which is in L_1 can have only one 1, there is no x such that xy is in L_1 and y is in L_2.

Let L_3 be $\mathbf{0^*1}$. Then L_1/L_3 is $\mathbf{0^*}$, since for any x in $\mathbf{0^*}$ we may choose $y = 1$. Clearly xy is in $L_1 = \mathbf{0^*10^*}$ and y is in $L_3 = \mathbf{0^*1}$. Since words in L_1 and L_3 each have one 1, it is not possible that words not in $\mathbf{0^*}$ are in L_1/L_3. As another example, $L_2/L_3 = \mathbf{10^*}$, since for each x in $\mathbf{10^*}$ we may again choose $y = 1$ from L_3 and xy will be in $L_2 = \mathbf{10^*1}$. If xy is in L_2 and y is in L_3, then evidently, x is in $\mathbf{10^*}$.

Theorem 3.6 The class of regular sets is closed under quotient with arbitrary sets.†

---

† In this theorem the closure is not effective.

Proof Let $M = (Q, \Sigma, \delta, q_0, F)$ be a finite automaton accepting some regular set R, and let L be an arbitrary language. The quotient R/L is accepted by a finite automaton $M' = (Q, \Sigma, \delta, q_0, F')$, which behaves like M except that the final states of M' are all states q of M such that there exists y in L for which $\delta(q, y)$ is in F. Then $\delta(q_0, x)$ is in F' if and only if there exists y such that $\delta(q_0, xy)$ is in F. Thus M' accepts R/L. ☐

One should observe that the construction in Theorem 3.6 is different from all other constructions in this chapter in that it is not effective. Since L is an arbitrary set, there may be no algorithm to determine whether there exists y in L such that $\delta(q, y)$ is in F. Even if we restrict L to some finitely representable class, we still may not have an effective construction unless there is an algorithm to test for the existence of such a y. In effect we are saying that for any L, there is surely some F' such that M with F' as the set of final states accepts R/L. However, we may not be able to tell which subset of Q should be chosen as F'. In the next section we shall see that if L is a regular set, we can determine F', so the regular sets are effectively closed under quotient with a regular set.

3.3 DECISION ALGORITHMS FOR REGULAR SETS

It is important to have algorithms to answer various questions concerning regular sets. The types of questions we are concerned with include: is a given language empty, finite, or infinite? Is one regular set equivalent to another? and so on. Before we can establish the existence of algorithms for answering such questions we must decide on a representation. For our purposes we shall assume regular sets are represented by finite automata. We could just as well have assumed that regular sets were represented by regular expressions or some other notation, since there exist mechanical translations from these notations into finite automata. However, one can imagine representations for which no such translation algorithm exists, and for such representations there may be no algorithm to determine whether or not a particular language is empty.

The reader at this stage may feel that it is obvious that we can determine whether a regular set is empty. We shall see in Chapter 8, however, that for many interesting classes of languages the question cannot be answered.

Emptiness, finiteness, and infiniteness

Algorithms to determine whether a regular set is empty, finite, or infinite may be based on the following theorem. We shall discuss efficient algorithms after presenting the theorem.

Theorem 3.7 The set of sentences accepted by a finite automaton M with n states is:

1) nonempty if and only if the finite automaton accepts a sentence of length less than n.

2) infinite if and only if the automaton accepts some sentence of length ℓ, where $n \leq \ell < 2n$.

Thus there is an algorithm to determine whether a finite automaton accepts zero, a finite number, or an infinite number of sentences.

Proof

1) The "if" portion is obvious. Suppose M accepts a nonempty set. Let w be a word as short as any other word accepted. By the pumping lemma, $|w| < n$, for if w were the shortest and $|w| \geq n$, then $w = uvy$, and uy is a shorter word in the language.

2) If w is in $L(M)$ and $n \leq |w| < 2n$, then by the pumping lemma, $L(M)$ is infinite. That is, $w = w_1 w_2 w_3$, and for all i, $w_1 w_2^i w_3$ is in L. Conversely if $L(M)$ is infinite, then there exists w in $L(M)$, where $|w| \geq n$. If $|w| < 2n$, we are done. If no word is of length between n and $2n - 1$, let w be of length at least $2n$, but as short as any word in $L(M)$ whose length is greater than or equal to $2n$. Again by the pumping lemma, we can write $w = w_1 w_2 w_3$ with $1 \leq |w_2| \leq n$ and $w_1 w_3$ in $L(M)$. Either w was not a shortest word of length $2n$ or more, or $|w_1 w_3|$ is between n and $2n - 1$, a contradiction in either case.

In part (1), the algorithm to decide whether $L(M)$ is empty is: "See if any word of length up to n is in $L(M)$." Clearly there is such a procedure that is guaranteed to halt. In part (2), the algorithm to decide whether $L(M)$ is infinite is: "See if any word of length between n and $2n - 1$ is in $L(M)$." Again, clearly there is such a procedure that is guaranteed to halt. □

It should be appreciated that the algorithms suggested in Theorem 3.7 are highly inefficient. However, one can easily test whether a DFA accepts the empty set by taking its transition diagram and deleting all states that are not reachable on any input from the start state. If one or more final states remain, the language is nonempty. Then without changing the language accepted, we may delete all states that are not final and from which one cannot reach a final state. The DFA accepts an infinite language if and only if the resulting transition diagram has a cycle. The same method works for NFA's, but we must check that there is a cycle labeled by something besides ϵ.

Equivalence

Next we show that there is an algorithm to determine if two finite automata accept the same set.

Theorem 3.8 There is an algorithm to determine if two finite automata are equivalent (i.e., if they accept the same language).

Proof Let M_1 and M_2 be FA accepting L_1 and L_2, respectively. By Theorems 3.1, 3.2, and 3.3, $(L_1 \cap \bar{L}_2) \cup (\bar{L}_1 \cap L_2)$ is accepted by some finite automaton, M_3. It is easy to see that M_3 accepts a word if and only if $L_1 \neq L_2$. Hence, by Theorem 3.7, there is an algorithm to determine if $L_1 = L_2$. □

3.4 THE MYHILL-NERODE THEOREM AND MINIMIZATION OF FINITE AUTOMATA

Recall from Section 1.5 our discussion of equivalence relations and equivalence classes. We may associate with an arbitrary language L a natural equivalence relation R_L; namely, $xR_L y$ if and only if for each z, either both or neither of xz and yz is in L. In the worst case, each string is in an equivalence class by itself, but there may be fewer classes. In particular, the *index* (number of equivalence classes) is always finite if L is a regular set.

There is also a natural equivalence relation on strings associated with a finite automaton. Let $M = (Q, \Sigma, \delta, q_0, F)$ be a DFA. For x and y in Σ^* let $xR_M y$ if and only if $\delta(q_0, x) = \delta(q_0, y)$. The relation R_M is reflexive, symmetric, and transitive, since "$=$" has these properties, and thus R_M is an equivalence relation. R_M divides the set Σ^* into equivalence classes, one for each state that is reachable from q_0. In addition, if $xR_M y$, then $xzR_M yz$ for all z in Σ^*, since by Exercise 2.4,

$$\delta(q_0, xz) = \delta(\delta(q_0, x), z) = \delta(\delta(q_0, y), z) = \delta(q_0, yz).$$

An equivalence relation R such that xRy implies $xzRyz$ is said to be *right invariant (with respect to concatenation)*. We see that every finite automaton induces a right invariant equivalence relation, defined as R_M was defined, on its set of input strings. This result is formalized in the following theorem.

Theorem 3.9 (*The Myhill-Nerode theorem*).   The following three statements are equivalent:

1) The set $L \subseteq \Sigma^*$ is accepted by some finite automaton.
2) L is the union of some of the equivalence classes of a right invariant equivalence relation of finite index.
3) Let equivalence relation R_L be defined by: $xR_L y$ if and only if for all z in Σ^*, xz is in L exactly when yz is in L. Then R_L is of finite index.

Proof

$(1) \rightarrow (2)$ Assume that L is accepted by some DFA $M = (Q, \Sigma, \delta, q_0, F)$. Let R_M be the equivalence relation $xR_M y$ if and only if $\delta(q_0, x) = \delta(q_0, y)$. R_M is right invariant since, for any z, if $\delta(q_0, x) = \delta(q_0, y)$, then $\delta(q_0, xz) = \delta(q_0, yz)$. The index of R_M is finite, since the index is at most the number of states in Q. Furthermore, L is the union of those equivalence classes that include a string x such that $\delta(q_0, x)$ is in F, that is, the equivalence classes corresponding to final states.

$(2) \rightarrow (3)$ We show that any equivalence relation E satisfying (2) is a *refinement* of R_L; that is, every equivalence class of E is entirely contained in some equivalence class of R_L. Thus the index of R_L cannot be greater than the index of E and so is finite. Assume that xEy. Then since E is right invariant, for each z in Σ^*, $xzEyz$, and thus yz is in L if and only if xz is in L. Thus $xR_L y$, and hence the equivalence class of x in E is contained in the equivalence class of x in R_L. We conclude that each equivalence class of E is contained within some equivalence class of R_L.

$(3) \rightarrow (1)$ We must first show that R_L is right invariant. Suppose $xR_L y$, and let w be in Σ^*. We must prove that $xwR_L yw$; that is, for any z, xwz is in L exactly when ywz is in L. But since $xR_L y$, we know by definition of R_L that for any v, xv is in L exactly when yv is in L. Let $v = wz$ to prove that R_L is right invariant.

Now let Q' be the finite set of equivalence classes of R_L and $[x]$ the element of Q' containing x. Define $\delta'([x], a) = [xa]$. The definition is consistent, since R_L is right invariant. Had we chosen y instead of x from the equivalence class $[x]$, we would have obtained $\delta'([x], a) = [ya]$. But $xR_L y$, so xz is in L exactly when yz is in L. In particular, if $z = az'$, xaz' is in L exactly when yaz' is in L, so $xaR_L ya$, and $[xa] = [ya]$. Let $q'_0 = [\epsilon]$ and let $F' = \{[x] \mid x \text{ is in } L\}$. The finite automaton $M' = (Q', \Sigma, \delta', q'_0, F')$ accepts L, since $\delta'(q'_0, x) = [x]$, and thus x is in $L(M')$ if and only if $[x]$ is in F'. $\qquad\square$

Example 3.7 Let L be the language 0^*10^*. L is accepted by the DFA M of Fig. 3.2. Consider the relation R_M defined by M. As all states are reachable from the start state, R_M has six equivalence classes, which are

$$C_a = (00)^*, \qquad C_d = (00)^*01,$$

$$C_b = (00)^*0, \qquad C_e = 0^*100^*,$$

$$C_c = (00)^*1, \qquad C_f = 0^*10^*1(0 + 1)^*$$

L is the union of three of these classes, C_c, C_d, and C_e.

The relation R_L for L has $xR_L y$ if and only if either

i) x and y each have no 1's,

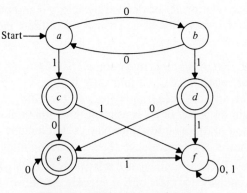

Fig. 3.2 DFA M accepting L.

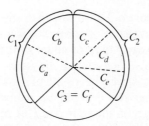

Fig. 3.3 Diagram showing R_M is a refinement of R_L.

ii) x and y each have one 1, or

iii) x and y each have more than one 1.

For example, if $x = 010$ and $y = 1000$, then xz is in L if and only if z is in $\mathbf{0^*}$. But yz is in L under exactly the same conditions. As another example, if $x = 01$ and $y = 00$, then we might choose $z = 0$ to show that $xR_L y$ is false. That is, $xz = 010$ is in L, but $yz = 000$ is not.

We may denote the three equivalence classes of R_L by $C_1 = \mathbf{0^*}$, $C_2 = \mathbf{0^*10^*}$, and $C_3 = \mathbf{0^*10^*1(0 + 1)^*}$. L is the language consisting of only one of these classes, C_2. The relationship of $C_a, \ldots, C_f$ to C_1, C_2, and C_3 is illustrated in Fig. 3.3. For example $C_a \cup C_b = \mathbf{(00)^* + (00)^*0 = 0^*} = C_1$.

From R_L we may construct a DFA as follows. Pick representatives for C_1, C_2, and C_3, say ϵ, 1, and 11. Then let M' be the DFA shown in Fig. 3.4. For example, $\delta'([1], 0) = [1]$, since if w is any string in [1] (note [1] is C_1), say $0^i 10^j$, then $w0$ is $0^i 10^{j+1}$, which is also in $C_1 = \mathbf{0^*10^*}$.

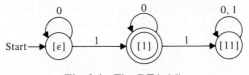

Fig. 3.4 The DFA M'.

Minimizing finite automata

The Myhill-Nerode theorem has, among other consequences, the implication that there is an essentially unique minimum state DFA for every regular set.

Theorem 3.10 The minimum state automaton accepting a set L is unique up to an isomorphism (i.e., a renaming of the states) and is given by M' in the proof of Theorem 3.9.

Proof In the proof of Theorem 3.9 we saw that any DFA $M = (Q, \Sigma, \delta, q_0, F)$ accepting L defines an equivalence relation that is a refinement of R_L. Thus the number of states of M is greater than or equal to the number of states of M' of Theorem 3.9. If equality holds, then each of the states of M can be identified with one of the states of M'. That is, let q be a state of M. There must be some x in Σ^*, such that $\delta(q_0, x) = q$, otherwise q could be removed from Q, and a smaller automaton found. Identify q with the state $\delta'(q_0', x)$, of M'. This identification will be consistent. If $\delta(q_0, x) = \delta(q_0, y) = q$, then, by the proof of Theorem 3.9, x and y are in the same equivalence class of R_L. Thus $\delta'(q_0', x) = \delta'(q_0', y)$. $\square$

A minimization algorithm

There is a simple method for finding the minimum state DFA M' of Theorems 3.9 and 3.10 equivalent to a given DFA $M = (Q, \Sigma, \delta, q_0, F)$. Let $\equiv$ be the equivalence relation on the states of M such that $p \equiv q$ if and only if for each input string x, $\delta(p, x)$ is an accepting state if and only if $\delta(q, x)$ is an accepting state. Observe that there is an isomorphism between those equivalence classes of $\equiv$ that contain a state reachable from q_0 by some input string and the states of the minimum state FA M'. Thus the states of M' may be identified with these classes.

Rather than give a formal algorithm for computing the equivalence classes of $\equiv$ we first work through an example. First some terminology is needed. If $p \equiv q$, we say p is *equivalent* to q. We say that p is *distinguishable* from q if there exists an x such that $\delta(p, x)$ is in F and $\delta(q, x)$ is not, or vice versa.

Example 3.8 Let M be the finite automaton of Fig. 3.5. In Fig. 3.6 we have constructed a table with an entry for each pair of states. An X is placed in the table each time we discover a pair of states that cannot be equivalent. Initially an X is placed in each entry corresponding to one final state and one nonfinal state. In our example, we place an X in the entries (a, c), (b, c), (c, d), (c, e), (c, f), (c, g), and (c, h).

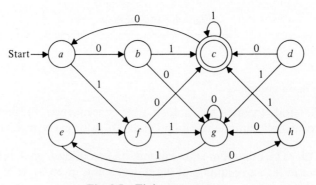

Fig. 3.5 Finite automaton.

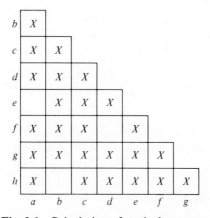

Fig. 3.6 Calculation of equivalent states.

Next for each pair of states p and q that are not already known to be distinguishable we consider the pairs of states $r = \delta(p, a)$ and $s = \delta(q, a)$ for each input symbol a. If states r and s have been shown to be distinguishable by some string x, then p and q are distinguishable by string ax. Thus if the entry (r, s) in the table has an X, an X is also placed at the entry (p, q). If the entry (r, s) does not yet have an X, then the pair (p, q) is placed on a list associated with the (r, s)-entry. At some future time, if the (r, s) entry receives an X, then each pair on the list associated with the (r, s)-entry also receives an X.

Continuing with the example, we place an X in the entry (a, b), since the entry $(\delta(b, 1), \delta(a, 1)) = (c, f)$ already has an X. Similarly, the (a, d)-entry receives an X since the entry $(\delta(a, 0), \delta(d, 0)) = (b, c)$ has an X. Consideration of the (a, e)-entry on input 0 results in the pair (a, e) being placed on the list associated with (b, h). Observe that on input 1, both a and e go to the same state f and hence no string starting with a 1 can distinguish a from e. Because of the 0-input, the pair (a, g) is placed on the list associated with (b, g). When the (b, g)-entry is considered, it receives an X on account of a 1-input, and hence the pair (a, g) receives an X since it was on the list for (b, g). The string 01 distinguishes a from g.

On completion of the table in Fig. 3.6, we conclude that the equivalent states are $a \equiv e$, $b \equiv h$, and $d \equiv f$. The minimum-state finite automaton is given in Fig. 3.7.

The formal algorithm for marking pairs of inequivalent states is shown in Fig. 3.8. Lemma 3.2 proves that the method outlined does indeed mark all pairs of inequivalent states.

Lemma 3.2 Let $M = (Q, \Sigma, \delta, q_0, F)$ be a DFA. Then p is distinguishable from q if and only if the entry corresponding to the pair (p, q) is marked in the above procedure.

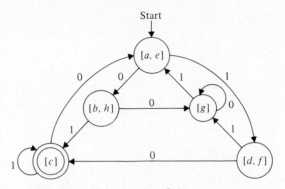

Fig. 3.7   Minimum state finite automaton.

```
        begin
1)      for p in F and q in Q − F do mark (p, q);
2)      for each pair of distinct states (p, q) in F × F or (Q − F) × (Q − F) do
3)          if for some input symbol a, (δ(p, a), δ(q, a)) is marked then
                begin
4)                  mark (p, q);
5)                  recursively mark all unmarked pairs on the list for (p, q) and on the lists
                        of other pairs that are marked at this step.
                end
            else /* no pair (δ(p, a), δ(q, a)) is marked */
6)              for all input symbols a do
7)                  put (p, q) on the list for (δ(p, a), δ(q, a)) unless
                        δ(p, a) = δ(q, a)

        end
```

Fig. 3.8   Algorithm for marking pairs of inequivalent states.

Proof   Assume p is distinguishable from q, and let x be a shortest string distinguishing p from q. We prove by induction on the length of x that the entry corresponding to the pair (p, q) is marked. If $x = \epsilon$ then exactly one of p and q is a final state and hence the entry is marked in line (1). Assume that the hypothesis is true for $|x| < i$, $i \geq 1$, and let $|x| = i$. Write $x = ay$ and let $t = \delta(p, a)$ and $u = \delta(q, a)$. Now y distinguishes t from u and $|y| = i − 1$. Thus by the induction hypothesis the entry corresponding to the pair (t, u) eventually is marked. If this event occurs after the pair (p, q) has been considered, then either the (p, q) entry has already been marked when (t, u) is considered, or the pair (p, q) is on the list associated with (t, u), in which case it is marked at line (5). If (p, q) is considered after (t, u) then (p, q) is marked at the time it is considered. In any event the entry (p, q) is marked. A similar induction on the number of pairs marked shows that if the entry (p, q) is marked then p and q are distinguishable.   □

The algorithm of Fig. 3.8 is more efficient than the obvious marking algorithm, although it is not the most efficient possible. Let Σ have k symbols and Q have n states. Line 1 takes $0(n^2)$ steps.† The loop of lines 2 through 7 is executed $0(n^2)$ times, at most once for each pair of states. The total time spent on lines 2 through 4, 6, and 7 is $0(kn^2)$. The time spent on line 5 is the sum of the length of all lists. But each pair (r, s) is put on at most k lists, at line 7. Thus the time spent on line 5 is $0(kn^2)$, so the total time is also $0(kn^2)$.

Theorem 3.11 The DFA constructed by the algorithm of Fig. 3.8, with inaccessible states removed, is the minimum state DFA for its language.

Proof Let $M = (Q, \Sigma, \delta, q_0, F)$ be the DFA to which the algorithm is applied and $M' = (Q', \Sigma, \delta', [q_0], F')$ be the DFA constructed. That is,

$$Q' = \{[q] \mid q \text{ is accessible from } q_0\},$$

$$F' = \{[q] \mid q \text{ is in } F\}$$

and

$$\delta'([q], a) = [\delta(q, a)].$$

It is easy to show that δ' is consistently defined, since if $q \equiv p$, then $\delta(q, a) \equiv \delta(p, a)$. That is, if $\delta(q, a)$ is distinguished from $\delta(p, a)$ by x, then ax distinguishes q from p. It is also easy to show that $\delta'([q_0], w) = [\delta(q_0, w)]$ by induction on $|w|$. Thus $L(M') = L(M)$.

Now we must show that M' has no more states than R_L has equivalence classes, where $L = L(M)$. Suppose it did; then there are two accessible states q and p in Q such that $[q] \neq [p]$, yet there are x and y such that $\delta(q_0, x) = q$, $\delta(q_0, y) = p$, and $xR_L y$. We claim that $p \equiv q$, for if not, then some w in Σ^* distinguishes p from q. But then $xwR_L yw$ is false, for we may let $z = \epsilon$ and observe that exactly one of xwz and ywz is in L. But since R_L is right invariant, $xwR_L yw$ is true. Hence q and p do not exist, and M' has no more states than the index of R_L. Thus M' is the minimum state DFA for L. $\square$

EXERCISES

3.1   Which of the following languages are regular sets? Prove your answer.

a) $\{0^{2^n} \mid n \geq 1\}$
b) $\{0^m 1^n 0^{m+n} \mid m \geq 1 \text{ and } n \geq 1\}$
c) $\{0^n \mid n \text{ is a prime}\}$
d) the set of all strings that do not have three consecutive 0's.
e) the set of all strings with an equal number of 0's and 1's.
f) $\{x \mid x \text{ in } (0 + 1)^*, \text{ and } x = x^R\}$ x^R is x written backward; for example, $(011)^R = 110$.
g) $\{xwx^R \mid x, w \text{ in } (0 + 1)^+\}$
*h) $\{xx^R w \mid x, w \text{ in } (0 + 1)^+\}$

---

† We say that $g(n)$ is $0(f(n))$ if there exist constants c and n_0 such that $g(n) \leq cf(n)$ for all $n \geq n_0$.

3.2   Prove the following extension of the pumping lemma for regular sets. Let L be a regular set. Then there exists a constant n such that for each z_1, z_2, z_3, with $z_1 z_2 z_3$ in L and $|z_2| = n$, z_2 can be written $z_2 = uvw$ such that $|v| \geq 1$ and for each $i \geq 0$, $z_1 uv^i w z_3$ is in L.

3.3   Use Exercise 3.2 to prove that $\{0^i 1^m 2^m \mid i \geq 1, m \geq 1\}$ is nonregular.

* **3.4**   Let L be a regular set. Which of the following sets are regular? Justify your answers.

   a) $\{a_1 a_3 a_5 \cdots a_{2n-1} \mid a_1 a_2 a_3 a_4 \cdots a_{2n}$ is in $L\}$
S b) $\{a_2 a_1 a_4 a_3 \cdots a_{2n} a_{2n-1} \mid a_1 a_2 \cdots a_{2n}$ is in $L\}$
   c) $\mathrm{CYCLE}(L) = \{x_1 x_2 \mid x_2 x_1$ is in L for strings x_1 and $x_2\}$
   d) $\mathrm{MAX}(L) = \{x$ in $L \mid$ for no y other than ϵ is xy in $L\}$
   e) $\mathrm{MIN}(L) = \{x$ in $L \mid$ no proper prefix of x is in $L\}$
   f) $\mathrm{INIT}(L) = \{x \mid$ for some y, xy is in $L\}$
   g) $L^R = \{x \mid x^R$ is in $L\}$
   h) $\{x \mid xx^R$ is in $L\}$

* **3.5**   Let value(x) be the result when the symbols of x are multiplied from left to right according to the table of Fig. 2.31.

   a) Is $L = \{xy \mid |x| = |y|$ and value(x) = value(y)$\}$ regular?
   b) Is $L = \{xy \mid$ value(x) = value(y)$\}$ regular?

Justify your answers.

* **3.6**   Show that $\{0^i 1^j \mid gcd(i, j) = 1\}$ is not regular.

** **3.7**   Let L be any subset of 0^*. Prove that L^* is regular.

3.8   A set of integers is *linear* if it is of the form $\{c + pi \mid i = 0, 1, 2, \ldots\}$. A set is *semilinear* if it is the finite union of linear sets. Let $R \subseteq 0^*$ be regular. Prove that $\{i \mid 0^i$ is in $R\}$ is semilinear.

3.9   Is the class of regular sets closed under infinite union?

3.10   What is the relationship between the class of regular sets and the least class of languages closed under union, intersection, and complement containing all finite sets?

* **3.11**   Give a finite automaton construction to prove that the class of regular sets is closed under substitution.

** **3.12**   Is the class of regular sets closed under inverse substitution?

3.13   Let h be the homomorphism $h(a) = 01$, $h(b) = 0$.

   a) Find $h^{-1}(L_1)$, where $L_1 = (10 + 1)^*$
   b) Find $h(L_2)$, where $L_2 = (a + b)^*$
   c) Find $h^{-1}(L_3)$, where L_3 is the set of all strings of 0's and 1's with an equal number of 0's and 1's.

3.14   Show that 2DFA with endmarkers (see Exercise 2.20) accept only regular sets by making use of closure properties developed in this chapter.

** **3.15**   The use of $\cap$ with regular expressions does not allow representation of new sets. However it does allow more compact expression. Show that $\cap$ can shorten a regular expression by an exponential amount. [*Hint*: What is the regular expression of shortest length describing the set consisting of the one sentence $(\ldots ((a_0^2 a_1)^2 a_2)^2 \cdots)^2$?]

** **3.16** Let L be a language. Define $\frac{1}{2}(L)$ to be

$$\{x \mid \text{for some } y \text{ such that } |x| = |y|, xy \text{ is in } L\}.$$

That is, $\frac{1}{2}(L)$ is the first halves of strings in L. Prove for each regular L that $\frac{1}{2}(L)$ is regular.

** **3.17** If L is regular, is the set of first thirds of strings in L regular? What about the last third? Middle third? Is the set

$$\{xz \mid \text{for some } y \text{ with } |x| = |y| = |z|, xyz \text{ is in } L\}$$

regular?

** **3.18** Show that if L is regular, so are
  a) $\mathrm{SQRT}(L) = \{x \mid \text{for some } y \text{ with } |y| = |x|^2, xy \text{ is in } L\}$
  b) $\mathrm{LOG}(L) = \{x \mid \text{for some } y \text{ with } |y| = 2^{|x|}, xy \text{ is in } L\}$

* **3.19** A *one-pebble* 2DFA is a 2DFA with the added capability of marking a tape square by placing a pebble on it. The next state function depends on the present state, the tape symbol scanned, and the presence or absence of a pebble on the tape square scanned. A move consists of a change of state, a direction of head motion, and possibly placing or removing the pebble from the scanned tape cell. The automaton "jams" if it attempts to place a second pebble on the input. Prove that one-pebble 2DFA's accept only regular sets. [*Hint:* Add two additional tracks to the input that contain tables indicating for each state p, the state q in which the 2DFA will return if it moves left or right from the tape cell in state p, under the assumption that the pebble is not encountered. Observe that the one-pebble 2DFA operating on the augmented tape need never leave its pebble. Then make use of a homomorphic mapping to remove the additional tracks.]

* **3.20** In converting an NFA to a DFA the number of states may increase substantially. Give upper and lower bounds on the maximum increase in number of states for an n-state NFA. [*Hint:* Consider Exercises 2.5(e) and 2.8(c).]

3.21 Give a decision procedure to determine if the set accepted by a DFA is
  a) the set of all strings over a given alphabet,
  b) *cofinite* (a set whose complement is finite).

** **3.22** Consider a DFA M. Suppose you are told that M has at most n states and you wish to determine the transition diagram of M. Suppose further that the only way you can obtain information concerning M is by supplying an input sequence x and observing the prefixes of x which are accepted.
  a) What assumptions must you make concerning the transition diagram of M in order to be able to determine the transition diagram?
  b) Give an algorithm for determining the transition diagram of M (except for the start state) including the construction of x under your assumptions in part (a).

S **3.23 Give an efficient decision procedure to determine if x is in the language denoted by an *extended regular expression* (a regular expression with operators $\cup$, $\cdot$ (concatenation), *, $\cap$, and $\neg$, that is complement).

3.24 Give an efficient decision procedure for determining if a *semi-extended regular expression* r (a regular expression with $\cup$, $\cdot$, *, $\cap$) denotes a nonempty set. [*Hint:* Space $0(|r|)$ and time $0(2^{|r|})$ are sufficient.]

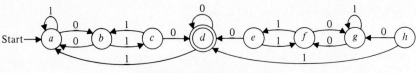

Fig. 3.9   A finite automaton.

3.25   Find the minimum-state finite automaton equivalent to the transition diagram of Fig. 3.9.

3.26

a) What are the equivalence classes of R_L in the Myhill-Nerode theorem (Theorem 3.9) for $L = \{0^n1^n \mid n \geq 1\}$?

b) Use your answer in (a) to show $\{0^n1^n \mid n \geq 1\}$ not regular.

c) Repeat (a) for $\{x \mid x$ has an equal number of 0's and 1's$\}$.

* **3.27** R is a *congruence* relation if xRy implies $wxzRwyz$ for all w and z. Prove that a set is regular if and only if it is the union of some of the congruence classes of a congruence relation of finite index.

* **3.28**   Let M be a finite automaton with n states. Let p and q be distinguishable states of M and let x be a shortest string distinguishing p and q. How long can the string x be as a function of n?

** **3.29**   In a two-tape FA each state is designated as reading tape 1 or tape 2. A pair of strings (x, y) is accepted if the FA, when presented with strings x and y on its respective tapes, reaches a final state with the tape heads immediately to the right of x and y. Let L be the set of pairs accepted by a two-tape FA M. Give algorithms to answer the following questions.

a) Is L empty?   b) Is L finite?

c) Do there exist L_1 and L_2 such that $L = L_1 \times L_2$?

3.30

a) Prove that there exists a constant $c > 0$ such that the algorithm of Fig. 3.8 requires time greater than cn^2 for infinitely many DFA where n is the number of states and the input alphabet has two symbols.

** b) Give an algorithm for minimizing states in a DFA whose execution time is $0(|\Sigma| n \log n)$. Here Σ is the input alphabet. [*Hint:* Instead of asking for each pair of states (p, q) and each input a if $\delta(p, a)$ and $\delta(q, a)$ are distinguishable, partition the states into final and nonfinal states. Then refine the partition by considering all states whose next state under some input symbol is in one particular block of the partition. Each time a block is partitioned, refine the partition further by using the smaller sub-block. Use list processing to make the algorithm as efficient as possible.]

Solutions to Selected Exercises

3.4(b) $L' = \{a_2 a_1 a_4 a_3 \cdots a_{2n} a_{2n-1} \mid a_1 a_2 \cdots a_{2n} \text{ is in } L\}$ is regular. Let $M = (Q, \Sigma, \delta, q_0, F)$ be a DFA accepting L. We construct a DFA M' that accepts L'. M' will process tape symbols in pairs. On seeing the first symbol a in a pair, M' stores a in its finite control. Then on seeing the second symbol b, M' behaves like M on the input ba. More formally

$$M' = (Q \cup Q \times \Sigma, \Sigma, \delta', q_0, F)$$

where

i) $\delta'(q, a) = [q, a]$, and
ii) $\delta'([q, a], b) = \delta(q, ba)$.

To prove that M' accepts L' we show by induction on even i that

$$\delta'(q, a_2 a_1 a_4 a_3 \cdots a_i a_{i-1}) = \delta(q, a_1 a_2 \cdots a_i).$$

Clearly, for $i = 0$, $\delta'(q, \epsilon) = q = \delta(q, \epsilon)$. Assume the hypothesis is true for all even $j < i$. By the induction hypothesis,

$$\delta'(q, a_2 a_1 \cdots a_{i-2} a_{i-3}) = \delta(q, a_1 a_2 \cdots a_{i-2})$$

$$= p \quad \text{for some } p.$$

Thus

$$\delta'(q, a_2 a_1 \cdots a_i a_{i-1}) = \delta'(p, a_i a_{i-1})$$

$$= \delta'([p, a_i], a_{i-1})$$

$$= \delta(p, a_{i-1} a_i)$$

$$= \delta(q, a_1 a_2 \cdots a_i).$$

Therefore $a_2 a_1 a_4 a_3 \cdots a_i a_{i-1}$ is in $L(M')$ if and only if $a_1 a_2 \cdots a_i$ is in $L(M)$, and thus $L(M') = L'$. □

3.23 One can clearly construct a finite automaton equivalent to R by combining finite automata corresponding to subexpressions of R and then simulating the automaton on x. We must examine the combining process to see how it affects the size of the resulting automaton. If we work with DFA's then the number of states for a union or intersection grows as the product. However, concatenation and closure may increase the number of states exponentially, as we need to convert DFA's to NFA's and then perform the subset construction. If we work with NFA's, then the number of states is additive for union, concatenation, and closure and increases as the product for intersection. However, complements require a conversion from an NFA to a DFA and hence an exponential increase in the number of states. Since operators can be nested, the number of states can be exponentiated on the order of n times for an expression with n operators, and thus this technique is not in general feasible.

A more efficient method based on a dynamic programming technique (see Aho, Hopcroft, and Ullman [1974]) yields an algorithm whose execution time is polynomial in the length of the input w and the length of the regular expression s. Let $n = |w| + |s|$. Construct a table which for each subexpression r of s and each substring x_{ij} of w gives the answer to the question: Is x_{ij} in $L(r)$, where x_{ij} is the substring of w of length j beginning at position i? The table is of size at most n^3, since there are at most n subexpressions of s and $n(n + 1)/2$ substrings of w. Fill in the table starting with entries for small subexpressions (those without operators, that is, a, ϵ, or $\varnothing$). Then fill in entries for x and r, where r is of one of the forms $r_1 \cap r_2$, $r_1 + r_2$, $r_1 r_2$, r_1^*, or $\neg r_1$. We handle only the case r_1^*. We proceed in order of the length of x. To determine if x is in r_1^*, given that we already know for each proper substring y of x whether y is in r_1 or in r_1^*, we need only check for each x_1 and x_2 such that $x = x_1 x_2$ and $x_1 \neq \epsilon$, whether x_1 is in r_1 and x_2 is in r_1^*. Thus to calculate the table entry for x and r requires time $O(|x| + |r|)$. Hence the time to fill in the entire table is $O(n^4)$. To determine if w is in s we need only consult the entry for s and w, noting that $w = x_{1k}$, where $k = |w|$.

BIBLIOGRAPHIC NOTES

The pumping lemma for regular sets is based on the formulation of Bar-Hillel, Perles, and Shamir [1961]. Theorem 3.4, closure under substitution, is also from there. Theorem 3.5, closure under inverse homomorphism, is from Ginsburg and Rose [1963b], and Theorem 3.6, on quotients, is from Ginsburg and Spanier [1963]. Theorems 3.7 and 3.8 on decision algorithms are from Moore [1956]. Ginsburg and Rose [1966] give a number of additional closure properties of regular sets.

Theorem 3.9, which we call the Myhill-Nerode Theorem, is actually due to Nerode [1958]. The similar result of Exercise 3.27 on congruence relations is due to Myhill [1957]. The algorithm for minimizing finite automata is due to Huffman [1954] and Moore [1956]. Hopcroft [1971] gives a more efficient algorithm.

Example 3.2, the unrecognizability of the primes in binary, was proved by Minsky and Papert [1966] by another method. Proportional removal operations, such as Exercise 3.16, were first studied in generality by Stearns and Hartmanis [1963]. Generalizations such as Exercise 3.18 were considered by Kosaraju [1974] and Seiferas [1974], and the question of what functions of the string length may be removed from the front to yield regular sets was solved completely by Seiferas and McNaughton [1976]. A solution to Exercise 3.22 was first considered by Hennie [1964]. An algorithm for determining equivalence for deterministic two-tape FA is found in Bird [1973].

CONTEXT-FREE
GRAMMARS

4.1 MOTIVATION AND INTRODUCTION

In this chapter we introduce context-free grammars and the languages they describe—the context-free languages. The context-free languages, like the regular sets, are of great practical importance, notably in defining programming languages, in formalizing the notion of parsing, simplifying translation of programming languages, and in other string-processing applications. As an example, context-free grammars are useful for describing arithmetic expressions, with arbitrary nesting of balanced parentheses, and block structure in programming languages (that is, **begin**'s and **end**'s matched like parentheses). Neither of these aspects of programming languages can be represented by regular expressions.

A *context-free grammar* is a finite set of variables (also called *nonterminals* or *syntactic categories*) each of which represents a language. The languages represented by the variables are described recursively in terms of each other and primitive symbols called *terminals*. The rules relating the variables are called *productions*. A typical production states that the language associated with a given variable contains strings that are formed by concatenating strings from the languages of certain other variables, possibly along with some terminals.

The original motivation for context-free grammars was the description of natural languages. We may write rules such as

$$\langle \text{sentence} \rangle \rightarrow \langle \text{noun phrase} \rangle \langle \text{verb phrase} \rangle$$

$$\langle \text{noun phrase} \rangle \rightarrow \langle \text{adjective} \rangle \langle \text{noun phrase} \rangle$$

$$\langle \text{noun phrase} \rangle \rightarrow \langle \text{noun} \rangle$$

$$\langle \text{noun} \rangle \rightarrow \text{boy}$$

$$\langle \text{adjective} \rangle \rightarrow \text{little} \tag{4.1}$$

where the syntactic categories† are denoted by angle brackets and terminals by unbracketed words like "boy" and "little."

The meaning of

$$\langle \text{sentence} \rangle \rightarrow \langle \text{noun phrase} \rangle \langle \text{verb phrase} \rangle$$

is that one way to form a sentence (a string in the language of the syntactic category $\langle \text{sentence} \rangle$) is to take a noun phrase and follow it by a verb phrase. The meaning of

$$\langle \text{noun} \rangle \rightarrow \text{boy}$$

is that the string consisting of the one-terminal symbol "boy" is in the language of the syntactic category $\langle \text{noun} \rangle$. Note that "boy" is a single terminal symbol, not a string of three symbols.

For a number of reasons, context-free grammars are not in general regarded as adequate for the description of natural languages like English. For example, if we extended the productions of (4.1) to encompass all of English, we would be able to derive "rock" as a noun phrase and "runs" as a verb phrase. Thus "rock runs" would be a sentence, which is nonsense. Clearly some semantic information is necessary to rule out meaningless strings that are syntactically correct. More subtle problems arise when attempts are made to associate the meaning of the sentence with its derivation. Nevertheless context-free grammars play an important role in computer linguistics.

While linguists were studying context-free grammars, computer scientists began to describe programming languages by a notation called *Backus-Naur Form* (*BNF*), which is the context-free grammar notation with minor changes in format and some shorthand. This use of context-free grammars has greatly simplified the definition of programming languages and the construction of compilers. The reason for this success is undoubtedly due in part to the natural way in which most programming language constructs are described by grammars. For example, consider the set of productions

1) $\langle \text{expression} \rangle \rightarrow \langle \text{expression} \rangle + \langle \text{expression} \rangle$

2) $\langle \text{expression} \rangle \rightarrow \langle \text{expression} \rangle * \langle \text{expression} \rangle$

3) $\langle \text{expression} \rangle \rightarrow (\langle \text{expression} \rangle)$

4) $\langle \text{expression} \rangle \rightarrow \textbf{id}$ \hfill (4.2)

which defines the arithmetic expressions with operators $+$ and $*$ and operands represented by the symbol **id**. Here $\langle \text{expression} \rangle$ is the only variable, and the terminals are $+$, $*$, $($, $)$, and **id**. The first two productions say that an expression

---

† Recall that the term "syntactic category" is a synonym for "variable." It is preferred when dealing with natural languages.

can be composed of two expressions connected by an addition or multiplication sign. The third production says that an expression may be another expression surrounded by parentheses. The last says a single operand is an expression.

By applying productions repeatedly we can obtain more and more complicated expressions. For example,

$$\langle \text{expression} \rangle \Rightarrow \langle \text{expression} \rangle * \langle \text{expression} \rangle$$
$$\Rightarrow (\langle \text{expression} \rangle) * \langle \text{expression} \rangle$$
$$\Rightarrow (\langle \text{expression} \rangle) * \mathbf{id}$$
$$\Rightarrow (\langle \text{expression} \rangle + \langle \text{expression} \rangle) * \mathbf{id}$$
$$\Rightarrow (\langle \text{expression} \rangle + \mathbf{id}) * \mathbf{id}$$
$$\Rightarrow (\mathbf{id} + \mathbf{id}) * \mathbf{id} \qquad\qquad (4.3)$$

The symbol $\Rightarrow$ denotes the act of deriving, that is, replacing a variable by the right-hand side of a production for that variable. The first line of (4.3) is obtained from the second production. The second line is obtained by replacing the first $\langle \text{expression} \rangle$ in line 1 by the right-hand side of the third production. The remaining lines are the results of applying productions (4), (1), (4), and (4). The last line, $(\mathbf{id} + \mathbf{id}) * \mathbf{id}$, consists solely of terminal symbols and thus is a word in the language of $\langle \text{expression} \rangle$.

4.2 CONTEXT-FREE GRAMMARS

Now we shall formalize the intuitive notions introduced in the previous section. A *context-free grammar* (*CFG* or just *grammar*) is denoted $G = (V, T, P, S)$, where V and T are finite sets of *variables* and *terminals*, respectively. We assume that V and T are disjoint. P is a finite set of productions; each production is of the form $A \rightarrow \alpha$, where A is a variable and α is a string of symbols from $(V \cup T)^*$. Finally, S is a special variable called the *start symbol*.

Example 4.1 Suppose we use E instead of $\langle \text{expression} \rangle$ for the variable in the grammar (4.2). Then we could formally express this grammar as $(\{E\}, \{+, *, (,), \mathbf{id}\}, P, E)$, where P consists of

$$E \rightarrow E + E$$
$$E \rightarrow E * E$$
$$E \rightarrow (E)$$
$$E \rightarrow \mathbf{id}$$

In this and the next two chapters we use the following conventions regarding grammars.

1) The capital letters A, B, C, D, E, and S denote variables; S is the start symbol unless otherwise stated.

2) The lower-case letters a, b, c, d, e, digits, and boldface strings are terminals.

3) The capital letters X, Y, and Z denote symbols that may be either terminals or variables.

4) The lower-case letters u, v, w, x, y, and z denote strings of terminals.

5) The lower-case Greek letters α, β, and γ denote strings of variables and terminals.

By adhering to the above conventions, we can deduce the variables, terminals, and the start symbol of a grammar solely by examining the productions. Thus we often present a grammar by simply listing its productions. If $A \rightarrow \alpha_1$, $A \rightarrow \alpha_2$, ..., $A \rightarrow \alpha_k$ are the productions for the variable A of some grammar, then we may express them by the notation

$$A \rightarrow \alpha_1 | \alpha_2 | \cdots | \alpha_k,$$

where the vertical line is read "or." The entire grammar of Example 4.1 could be written

$$E \rightarrow E + E | E * E | (E) | \mathbf{id}$$

Derivations and languages

We now formally define the language generated by a grammar $G = (V, T, P, S)$. To do so, we develop notation to represent a derivation. First we define two relations $\underset{G}{\Rightarrow}$ and $\underset{G}{\overset{*}{\Rightarrow}}$ between strings in $(V \cup T)^*$. If $A \rightarrow \beta$ is a production of P and α and γ are any strings in $(V \cup T)^*$, then $\alpha A \gamma \underset{G}{\Rightarrow} \alpha \beta \gamma$. We say that the production $A \rightarrow \beta$ is applied to the string $\alpha A \gamma$ to obtain $\alpha \beta \gamma$ or that $\alpha A \gamma$ *directly derives* $\alpha \beta \gamma$ in grammar G. Two strings are related by $\underset{G}{\Rightarrow}$ exactly when the second is obtained from the first by one application of some production.

Suppose that α_1, α_2, ..., α_m are strings in $(V \cup T)^*$, $m \geq 1$, and

$$\alpha_1 \underset{G}{\Rightarrow} \alpha_2, \ \alpha_2 \underset{G}{\Rightarrow} \alpha_3, \ ..., \ \alpha_{m-1} \underset{G}{\Rightarrow} \alpha_m.$$

Then we say $\alpha_1 \underset{G}{\overset{*}{\Rightarrow}} \alpha_m$ or α_1 *derives* α_m in grammar G. That is, $\underset{G}{\overset{*}{\Rightarrow}}$ is the reflexive and transitive closure of $\underset{G}{\Rightarrow}$ (see Section 1.5 for a discussion of closures of relations). Alternatively, $\alpha \underset{G}{\overset{*}{\Rightarrow}} \beta$ if β follows from α by application of zero or more productions of P. Note that $\alpha \underset{G}{\overset{*}{\Rightarrow}} \alpha$ for each string α. Usually, if it is clear which grammar G is involved, we use $\Rightarrow$ for $\underset{G}{\Rightarrow}$ and $\overset{*}{\Rightarrow}$ for $\underset{G}{\overset{*}{\Rightarrow}}$. If α derives β by exactly i steps, we say $\alpha \overset{i}{\Rightarrow} \beta$.

The *language generated* by G [denoted $L(G)$] is $\{w \,|\, w$ is in T^* and $S \underset{G}{\overset{*}{\Rightarrow}} w\}$. That is, a string is in $L(G)$ if:

1) The string consists solely of terminals.
2) The string can be derived from S.

We call L a *context-free language* (CFL) if it is $L(G)$ for some CFG G. A string of terminals and variables α is called a *sentential form* if $S \overset{*}{\Rightarrow} \alpha$. We define grammars G_1 and G_2 to be *equivalent* if $L(G_1) = L(G_2)$.

Example 4.2 Consider a grammar $G = (V, T, P, S)$, where $V = \{S\}$, $T = \{a, b\}$ and $P = \{S \rightarrow aSb, S \rightarrow ab\}$. Here, S is the only variable; a and b are terminals. There are two productions, $S \rightarrow aSb$ and $S \rightarrow ab$. By applying the first production $n - 1$ times, followed by an application of the second production, we have

$$S \Rightarrow aSb \Rightarrow aaSbb \Rightarrow a^3Sb^3 \Rightarrow \cdots \Rightarrow a^{n-1}Sb^{n-1} \Rightarrow a^nb^n.$$

Furthermore, the only strings in $L(G)$ are a^nb^n for $n \geq 1$. Each time $S \rightarrow aSb$ is used, the number of S's remains the same. After using the production $S \rightarrow ab$ we find that the number of S's in the sentential form decreases by one. Thus, after using $S \rightarrow ab$, no S's remain in the resulting string. Since both productions have an S on the left, the only order in which the productions can be applied is $S \rightarrow aSb$ some number of times followed by one application of $S \rightarrow ab$. Thus, $L(G) = \{a^nb^n \mid n \geq 1\}$.

Example 4.2 was a simple example of a grammar. It was relatively easy to determine which words were derivable and which were not. In general, it may be exceedingly hard to determine what is generated by the grammar. Here is another, more difficult example.

Example 4.3 Consider $G = (V, T, P, S)$, where $V = \{S, A, B\}$, $T = \{a, b\}$, and P consists of the following:

$$S \rightarrow aB \qquad A \rightarrow bAA$$
$$S \rightarrow bA \qquad B \rightarrow b$$
$$A \rightarrow a \qquad B \rightarrow bS$$
$$A \rightarrow aS \qquad B \rightarrow aBB$$

The language $L(G)$ is the set of all words in T^+ consisting of an equal number of a's and b's. We shall prove this statement by induction on the length of a word.

Inductive hypothesis For w in T^+,

1) $S \overset{*}{\Rightarrow} w$ if and only if w consists of an equal number of a's and b's.
2) $A \overset{*}{\Rightarrow} w$ if and only if w has one more a than it has b's.
3) $B \overset{*}{\Rightarrow} w$ if and only if w has one more b than it has a's.

The inductive hypothesis is certainly true if $|w| = 1$, since $A \overset{*}{\Rightarrow} a$, $B \overset{*}{\Rightarrow} b$, and no terminal string of length one is derivable from S. Also, since all productions but $A \to a$ and $B \to b$ increase the length of a string, no strings of length one other than a and b are derivable from A and B, respectively. Also, no strings of length one are derivable from S.

Suppose that the inductive hypothesis is true for all w of length $k - 1$ or less. We shall show that it is true for $|w| = k$. First, if $S \overset{*}{\Rightarrow} w$, then the derivation must begin with either $S \to aB$ or $S \to bA$. In the first case, w is of the form aw_1, where $|w_1| = k - 1$ and $B \overset{*}{\Rightarrow} w_1$. By the inductive hypothesis, the number of b's in w_1 is one more than the number of a's, so w consists of an equal number of a's and b's. A similar argument prevails if the derivation begins with $S \to bA$.

We must now prove the "only if" of part (1), that is, if $|w| = k$ and w consists of an equal number of a's and b's, then $S \overset{*}{\Rightarrow} w$. Either the first symbol of w is a or it is b. Assume that $w = aw_1$. Now $|w_1| = k - 1$, and w_1 has one more b than it has a's. By the inductive hypothesis, $B \overset{*}{\Rightarrow} w_1$. But then $S \Rightarrow aB \overset{*}{\Rightarrow} aw_1 = w$. A similar argument prevails if the first symbol of w is b.

Our task is not done. To complete the proof, we must prove parts (2) and (3) of the inductive hypothesis for w of length k. We do this in a manner similar to our method of proof for part (1); this part is left to the reader.

4.3 DERIVATION TREES

It is useful to display derivations as trees. These pictures, called *derivation* (or *parse*) trees, superimpose a structure on the words of a language that is useful in applications such as the compilation of programming languages. The vertices of a derivation tree are labeled with terminal or variable symbols of the grammar or possibly with ϵ. If an interior vertex n is labeled A, and the sons of n are labeled X_1, $X_2, \ldots, X_k$ from the left, then $A \to X_1 X_2 \cdots X_k$ must be a production. Figure 4.1 shows the parse tree for derivation (4.3). Note that if we read the leaves, in left-to-right order, we get the last line of (4.3), $(\mathbf{id} + \mathbf{id}) * \mathbf{id}$.

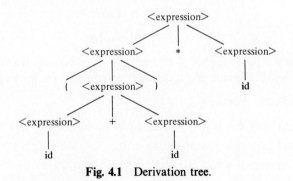

Fig. 4.1 Derivation tree.

More formally, let $G = (V, T, P, S)$ be a CFG. A tree is a *derivation* (or *parse*) *tree* for G if:

1) Every vertex has a *label*, which is a symbol of $V \cup T \cup \{\epsilon\}$.
2) The label of the root is S.
3) If a vertex is interior and has label A, then A must be in V.
4) If n has label A and vertices $n_1, n_2, \ldots, n_k$ are the sons of vertex n, in order from the left, with labels $X_1, X_2, \ldots, X_k$, respectively, then

$$A \rightarrow X_1 X_2 \cdots X_k$$

must be a production in P.

5) If vertex n has label ϵ, then n is a leaf and is the only son of its father.

Example 4.4 Consider the grammar $G = (\{S, A\}, \{a, b\}, P, S)$, where P consists of

$$S \rightarrow aAS \,|\, a$$

$$A \rightarrow SbA \,|\, SS \,|\, ba$$

We draw a tree, just this once, with circles instead of points for the vertices. The vertices will be numbered for reference. The labels will be adjacent to the vertices. See Fig. 4.2.

The interior vertices are 1, 3, 4, 5, and 7. Vertex 1 has label S, and its sons, from the left, have labels a, A, and S. Note that $S \rightarrow aAS$ is a production. Likewise, vertex 3 has label A, and the labels of its sons are S, b, and A from the left. $A \rightarrow SbA$ is also a production. Vertices 4 and 5 each have label S. Their only sons each have label a, and $S \rightarrow a$ is a production. Lastly, vertex 7 has label A and its sons, from the left, have labels b and a. $A \rightarrow ba$ is also a production. Thus, the conditions for Fig. 4.2 to be a derivation tree for G have been met.

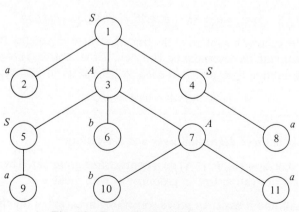

Fig. 4.2 Example of a derivation tree.

We may extend the "from the left" ordering of sons to produce a left-to-right ordering of all the leaves. In fact, for any two vertices, neither of which is an ancestor of the other, one is to the left of the other. Given vertices v_1 and v_2, follow the paths from these vertices toward the root until they meet at some vertex w. Let x_1 and x_2 be the sons of w on the paths from v_1 and v_2, respectively. If v_1 is not an ancestor of v_2, or vice versa, then $x_1 \neq x_2$. Suppose x_1 is to the left of x_2 in the ordering of the sons of w. Then v_1 is to the left of v_2. In the opposite case, v_2 is to the left of v_1. For example, if v_1 and v_2 are 9 and 11 in Fig. 4.2, then w is 3, $x_1 = 5$, and $x_2 = 7$. As 5 is to the left of 7, it follows that 9 is to the left of 11.

We shall see that a derivation tree is a natural description of the derivation of a particular sentential form of the grammar G. If we read the labels of the leaves from left to right, we have a sentential form. We call this string the *yield* of the derivation tree. Later, we shall see that if α is the yield of some derivation tree for grammar $G = (V, T, P, S)$, then $S \overset{*}{\underset{G}{\Rightarrow}} \alpha$, and conversely.

We need one additional concept, that of a *subtree*. A subtree of a derivation tree is a particular vertex of the tree together with all its descendants, the edges connecting them, and their labels. It looks just like a derivation tree, except that the label of the root may not be the start symbol of the grammar. If variable A labels the root, then we call the subtree an *A-tree*. Thus "S-tree" is a synonym for "derivation tree" if S is the start symbol.

Example 4.5   Consider the grammar and derivation tree of Example 4.4. The derivation tree of Fig. 4.2 is reproduced without numbered vertices as Fig. 4.3(a). The yield of the tree in Fig. 4.3(a) is *aabbaa*. Referring to Fig. 4.2 again, we see that the leaves are the vertices numbered 2, 9, 6, 10, 11, and 8, in that order, from the left. These vertices have labels a, a, b, b, a, a, respectively. Note that in this case all leaves had terminals for labels, but there is no reason why this should always be so; some leaves could be labeled by ϵ or by a variable. Note that $S \overset{*}{\underset{G}{\Rightarrow}} aabbaa$ by the derivation

$$S \Rightarrow aAs \Rightarrow aSbAS \Rightarrow aabAS \Rightarrow aabbaS \Rightarrow aabbaa.$$

Figure 4.3(b) shows a subtree of the tree illustrated in part (a). It is vertex 3 of Fig. 4.2, together with its descendants. The yield of the subtree is *abba*. The label of the root of the subtree is A, and $A \overset{*}{\Rightarrow} abba$. A derivation in this case is

$$A \Rightarrow SbA \Rightarrow abA \Rightarrow abba.$$

The relationship between derivation trees and derivations

Theorem 4.1   Let $G = (V, T, P, S)$ be a context-free grammar. Then $S \overset{*}{\Rightarrow} \alpha$ if and only if there is a derivation tree in grammar G with yield α.

Proof   We shall find it easier to prove something in excess of the theorem. What we shall prove is that for any A in V, $A \overset{*}{\Rightarrow} \alpha$ if and only if there is an A-tree with α as the yield.

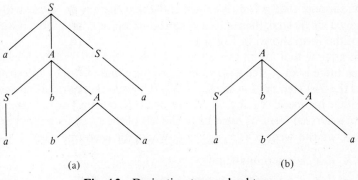

Fig. 4.3   Derivation tree and subtree.

Suppose, first, that α is the yield of an A-tree. We prove, by induction on the number of interior vertices in the tree, that $A \overset{*}{\Rightarrow} \alpha$. If there is only one interior vertex, the tree must look like the one in Fig. 4.4. In that case, $X_1 X_2 \cdots X_n$ must be α, and $A \to \alpha$ must be a production of P, by definition of a derivation tree.

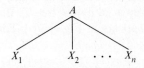

Fig. 4.4   Tree with one interior vertex.

Now, suppose that the result is true for trees with up to $k - 1$ interior vertices. Also, suppose that α is the yield of an A-tree with k interior vertices for some $k > 1$. Consider the sons of the root. These could not all be leaves. Let the labels of the sons be $X_1, X_2, \ldots, X_n$ in order from the left. Then surely, $A \to X_1 X_2 \cdots X_n$ is a production in P. Note that n may be any integer greater than or equal to one in the argument that follows.

If the ith son is not a leaf, it is the root of a subtree, and X_i must be a variable. The subtree must be an X_i-tree and has some yield α_i. If vertex i is a leaf, let $\alpha_i = X_i$. It is easy to see that if $j < i$, vertex j and all of its descendants are to the left of vertex i and all of its descendants. Thus $\alpha = \alpha_1 \alpha_2 \cdots \alpha_n$. A subtree must have fewer interior vertices than its tree does, unless the subtree is the entire tree. By the inductive hypothesis, for each vertex i that is not a leaf, $X_i \overset{*}{\Rightarrow} \alpha_i$, since the subtree with root X_i is not the entire tree. If $X_i = \alpha_i$, then surely $X_i \overset{*}{\Rightarrow} \alpha_i$. We can put all these partial derivations together, to see that

$$A \Rightarrow X_1 X_2 \cdots X_n \overset{*}{\Rightarrow} \alpha_1 X_2 \cdots X_n \overset{*}{\Rightarrow} \alpha_1 \alpha_2 X_3 \cdots X_n \overset{*}{\Rightarrow} \cdots \overset{*}{\Rightarrow} \alpha_1 \alpha_2 \cdots \alpha_n = \alpha.$$

$$(4.4)$$

Thus $A \overset{*}{\Rightarrow} \alpha$. Note that (4.4) is only one of many possible derivations we could produce from the given parse tree.

Now, suppose that $A \overset{*}{\Rightarrow} \alpha$. We must show that there is an A-tree with yield α. If $A \overset{*}{\Rightarrow} \alpha$ by a single step, then $A \to \alpha$ is a production in P, and there is a tree with yield α, of the form shown in Fig. 4.4.

Now, assume that for any variable A if $A \overset{*}{\Rightarrow} \alpha$ by a derivation of fewer than k steps, then there is an A-tree with yield α. Suppose that $A \overset{*}{\Rightarrow} \alpha$ by a derivation of k steps. Let the first step be $A \to X_1 X_2 \cdots X_n$. It should be clear that any symbol in α must either be one of $X_1, X_2, \ldots, X_n$ or be derived from one of these. Also, the portion of α derived from X_i must lie to the left of the symbols derived from X_j, if $i < j$. Thus, we can write α as $\alpha_1 \alpha_2 \cdots \alpha_n$, where for each i between 1 and n,

1) $\alpha_i = X_i$ if X_i is a terminal, and
2) $X_i \overset{*}{\Rightarrow} \alpha_i$ if X_i is a variable.

If X_i is a variable, then the derivation of α_i from X_i must take fewer than k steps, since the entire derivation $A \overset{*}{\Rightarrow} \alpha$ takes k steps, and the first step is surely not part of the derivation $X_i \overset{*}{\Rightarrow} \alpha_i$. Thus, by the inductive hypothesis, for each X_i that is a variable, there is an X_i-tree with yield α_i. Let this tree be T_i.

We begin by constructing an A-tree with n leaves labeled $X_1, X_2, \ldots, X_n$, and no other vertices. This tree is shown in Fig. 4.5(a). Each vertex with label X_i, where X_i is not terminal, is replaced by the tree T_i. If X_i is a terminal, no replacement is made. An example appears in Fig. 4.5(b). The yield of this tree is α. $\square$

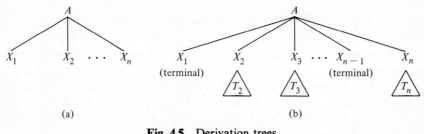

Fig. 4.5 Derivation trees.

Example 4.6 Consider the derivation $S \overset{*}{\Rightarrow} aabbaa$ of Example 4.5. The first step is $S \to aAS$. If we follow the derivation, we see that A eventually is replaced by SbA, then by abA, and finally, by $abba$. Figure 4.3(b) is a parse tree for this derivation. The only symbol derived from S in aAS is a. (This replacement is the last step.) Figure 4.6(a) is a tree for the latter derivation.

Figure 4.6(b) is the derivation tree for $S \to aAS$. If we replace the vertex with label A in Fig. 4.6(b) by the tree of Fig. 4.3(b) and the vertex with label S in Fig. 4.6(b) with the tree of Fig. 4.6(a), we get the tree of Fig. 4.3(a), whose yield is $aabbaa$.

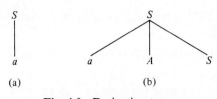

(a)   (b)

Fig. 4.6   Derivation trees.

Leftmost and rightmost derivations; ambiguity

If at each step in a derivation a production is applied to the leftmost variable, then the derivation is said to be *leftmost*. Similarly a derivation in which the rightmost variable is replaced at each step is said to be *rightmost*. If w is in $L(G)$ for CFG G, then w has at least one parse tree, and corresponding to a particular parse tree, w has a unique leftmost and a unique rightmost derivation. In the proof of Theorem 4.1, the derivation of α from A corresponding to the parse tree in question is leftmost, provided the derivations $X_i \overset{*}{\Rightarrow} \alpha_i$ are made leftmost. If instead of derivation (4.4) we (recursively) made the derivation $X_i \overset{*}{\Rightarrow} \alpha_i$ be rightmost and replaced the X_i's by α_i from the right rather than the left, we would obtain the rightmost derivation corresponding to the parse tree.

Of course, w may have several rightmost or leftmost derivations since there may be more than one parse tree for w. However, it is easy to show that from each derivation tree, only one leftmost and one rightmost derivation may be obtained. Also, the construction of Theorem 4.1 produces different derivation trees from different leftmost or different rightmost derivations.

Example 4.7   The leftmost derivation corresponding to the tree of Fig. 4.3(a) is

$$S \Rightarrow aAS \Rightarrow aSbAS \Rightarrow aabAS \Rightarrow aabbaS \Rightarrow aabbaa.$$

The corresponding rightmost derivation is

$$S \Rightarrow aAS \Rightarrow aAa \Rightarrow aSbAa \Rightarrow aSbbaa \Rightarrow aabbaa.$$

A context-free grammar G such that some word has two parse trees is said to be *ambiguous*. From what we have said above, an equivalent definition of ambiguity is that some word has more than one leftmost derivation or more than one rightmost derivation. A CFL for which every CFG is ambiguous is said to be an *inherently ambiguous* CFL. We shall show in Section 4.7 that inherently ambiguous CFL's exist.

4.4   SIMPLIFICATION OF CONTEXT-FREE GRAMMARS

There are several ways in which one can restrict the format of productions without reducing the generative power of context-free grammars. If L is a nonempty context-free language then it can be generated by a context-free grammar G with the following properties.

1) Each variable and each terminal of G appears in the derivation of some word in L.

2) There are no productions of the form $A \to B$ where A and B are variables.

Furthermore, if ϵ is not in L, there need be no productions of the form $A \to \epsilon$. In fact, if ϵ is not in L, we can require that every production of G be of one of the forms $A \to BC$ and $A \to a$, where A, B, and C are arbitrary variables and a is an arbitrary terminal. Alternatively, we could make every production of G be of the form $A \to a\alpha$, where α is a string of variables (perhaps empty). These two special forms are called Chomsky normal form and Greibach normal form, respectively.

Useless symbols

We now undertake the task of eliminating useless symbols from a grammar. Let $G = (V, T, P, S)$ be a grammar. A symbol X is *useful* if there is a derivation $S \overset{*}{\Rightarrow} \alpha X \beta \overset{*}{\Rightarrow} w$ for some α, β, and w, where w is in T^* (recall our convention regarding names of symbols and strings). Otherwise X is *useless*. There are two aspects to usefulness. First some terminal string must be derivable from X and second, X must occur in some string derivable from S. These two conditions are not, however, sufficient to guarantee that X is useful, since X may occur only in sentential forms that contain a variable from which no terminal string can be derived.

Lemma 4.1   Given a CFG $G = (V, T, P, S)$, with $L(G) \neq \varnothing$, we can effectively find an equivalent CFG $G' = (V', T, P', S)$ such that for each A in V' there is some w in T^* for which $A \overset{*}{\Rightarrow} w$.

Proof   Each variable A with production $A \to w$ in P clearly belongs in V'. If $A \to X_1 X_2 \cdots X_n$ is a production, where each X_i is either a terminal or a variable already placed in V', then a terminal string can be derived from A by a derivation beginning $A \Rightarrow X_1 X_2 \cdots X_n$, and thus A belongs in V'. The set V' can be computed by a straightforward iterative algorithm. P' is the set of all productions whose symbols are in $V' \cup T$.

The algorithm of Fig. 4.7 finds all variables A that belong to V'. Surely if A is added to NEWV at line (2) or (5), then A derives a terminal string. To show NEWV is not too small, we must show that if A derives a terminal string w, then A is eventually added to NEWV. We do so by induction on the length of the derivation $A \overset{*}{\Rightarrow} w$.

Basis   If the length is one, then $A \to w$ is a production, and A is added to NEWV in step (2).

Induction   Let $A \Rightarrow X_1 X_2 \cdots X_n \overset{*}{\Rightarrow} w$ by a derivation of k steps. Then we may write $w = w_1 w_2 \cdots w_n$, where $X_i \overset{*}{\Rightarrow} w_i$, for $1 \leq i \leq n$, by a derivation of fewer than

```
        begin
1)          OLDV:= ∅;
2)          NEWV:= {A | A → w for some w in T*};
3)          while OLDV ≠ NEWV do
                begin
4)                  OLDV:= NEWV;
5)                  NEWV:= OLDV ∪ {A | A → α for some α in (T ∪ OLDV)*}
                end;
6)          V':= NEWV
        end
```

Fig. 4.7   Calculation of V'.

k steps. By the inductive hypothesis, those X_i that are variables are eventually added to NEWV. At the while-loop test of line (3), immediately after the last of the X_i's is added to NEWV, we cannot have NEWV = OLDV, for the last of these X_i's is not in OLDV. Thus the while-loop iterates at least once more, and A will be added to NEWV at line (5).

Take V' to be the set computed at line (6) and P' to be all productions whose symbols are in $V' \cup T$. Surely $G' = (V', T, P', S)$ satisfies the property that if A is in V', then $A \xRightarrow{*} w$ for some w. Also, as every derivation in G' is a derivation of G, we know $L(G') \subseteq L(G)$. But if there is some w in $L(G)$ not in $L(G')$, then any derivation of w in G must involve a variable in $V - V'$ or a production in $P - P'$ (which implies there is a variable in $V - V'$ used). But then there is a variable in $V - V'$ that derives a terminal string, a contradiction.   ☐

Lemma 4.2   Given a CFG $G = (V, T, P, S)$ we can effectively find an equivalent CFG $G' = (V', T', P', S)$ such that for each X in $V' \cup T'$ there exist α and β in $(V' \cup T')^*$ for which $S \xRightarrow{*} \alpha X \beta$.

Proof   The set $V' \cup T'$ of symbols appearing in sentential forms of G is constructed by an iterative algorithm. Place S in V'. If A is placed in V' and $A \rightarrow \alpha_1 | \alpha_2 | \cdots | \alpha_n$, then add all variables of $\alpha_1, \alpha_2, \ldots, \alpha_n$ to the set V' and all terminals of $\alpha_1, \alpha_2, \ldots, \alpha_n$ to T'. P' is the set of productions of P containing only symbols of $V' \cup T'$.   ☐

By first applying Lemma 4.1 and then Lemma 4.2, we can convert a grammar to an equivalent one with no useless symbols. It is interesting to note that applying Lemma 4.2 first and Lemma 4.1 second may fail to eliminate all useless symbols.

Theorem 4.2   Every nonempty CFL is generated by a CFG with no useless symbols.

Proof   Let $L = L(G)$ be a nonempty CFL. Let G_1 be the result of applying the construction of Lemma 4.1 to G and let G_2 be the result of applying the construction of Lemma 4.2 to G_1. Suppose G_2 has a useless symbol X. By Lemma 4.2, there is a derivation $S \xRightarrow[G_2]{*} \alpha X \beta$. Since all symbols of G_2 are symbols of G_1, it follows from

Lemma 4.1 that $S \underset{G_1}{\overset{*}{\Rightarrow}} \alpha X \beta \underset{G_1}{\overset{*}{\Rightarrow}} w$ for some terminal string w. Therefore, no symbol in the derivation $\alpha X \beta \underset{G_1}{\overset{*}{\Rightarrow}} w$ is eliminated by Lemma 4.2. Thus, X derives a terminal string in G_2, and hence X is not useless as supposed. □

Example 4.8 Consider the grammar

$$S \rightarrow AB \,|\, a$$

$$A \rightarrow a \qquad\qquad\qquad (4.5)$$

Applying Lemma 4.1, we find that no terminal string is derivable from B. We therefore eliminate B and the production $S \rightarrow AB$. Applying Lemma 4.2 to the grammar

$$S \rightarrow a$$

$$A \rightarrow a \qquad\qquad\qquad (4.6)$$

we find that only S and a appear in sentential forms. Thus $(\{S\}, \{a\}, \{S \rightarrow a\}, S)$ is an equivalent grammar with no useless symbols.

Suppose we first applied Lemma 4.2 to (4.5). We would find that all symbols appeared in sentential forms. Then applying Lemma 4.1 we would be left with (4.6), which has a useless symbol, A.

ϵ-Productions

We now turn our attention to the elimination of productions of the form $A \rightarrow \epsilon$, which we call ϵ-*productions*. Surely if ϵ is in $L(G)$, we cannot eliminate all ϵ-productions from G, but if ϵ is not in $L(G)$, it turns out that we can. The method is to determine for each variable A whether $A \overset{*}{\Rightarrow} \epsilon$. If so, we call A *nullable*. We may replace each production $B \rightarrow X_1 X_2 \cdots X_n$ by all productions formed by striking out some subset of those X_i's that are nullable, but we do not include $B \rightarrow \epsilon$, even if all X_i's are nullable.

Theorem 4.3 If $L = L(G)$ for some CFG $G = (V, T, P, S)$, then $L - \{\epsilon\}$ is $L(G')$ for a CFG G' with no useless symbols or ϵ-productions.

Proof We can determine the nullable symbols of G by the following iterative algorithm. To begin, if $A \rightarrow \epsilon$ is a production, then A is nullable. Then, if $B \rightarrow \alpha$ is a production and all symbols of α have been found nullable, then B is nullable. We repeat this process until no more nullable symbols can be found.

The set of productions P' is constructed as follows. If $A \rightarrow X_1 X_2 \cdots X_n$ is in P, then add all productions $A \rightarrow \alpha_1 \alpha_2 \cdots \alpha_n$ to P' where

1) if X_i is not nullable, then $\alpha_i = X_i$;
2) if X_i is nullable, then α_i is either X_i or ϵ;
3) not all α_i's are ϵ.

Let $G'' = (V, T, P', S)$. We claim that for all A in V and w in T^*, $A \underset{G''}{\Rightarrow} w$ if and only if $w \neq \epsilon$ and $A \underset{G''}{\overset{*}{\Rightarrow}} w$.

If Let $A \underset{G}{\overset{i}{\Rightarrow}} w$ and $w \neq \epsilon$. We prove by induction on i that $A \underset{G''}{\overset{*}{\Rightarrow}} w$. The basis, $i = 1$, is trivial, for $A \to w$ must be a production in P. Since $w \neq \epsilon$, it is also a production of P'. For the inductive step, let $i > 1$. Then $A \underset{G}{\Rightarrow} X_1 X_2 \cdots X_n \underset{G}{\overset{i-1}{\Rightarrow}} w$. Write $w = w_1 w_2 \cdots w_n$ such that for each j, $X_j \overset{*}{\Rightarrow} w_j$ in fewer than i steps. If $w_j \neq \epsilon$ and X_j is a variable, then by the inductive hypothesis we have $X_j \underset{G''}{\overset{*}{\Rightarrow}} w_j$. If $w_j = \epsilon$, then X_j is nullable. Thus, $A \to \beta_1 \beta_2 \cdots \beta_n$ is a production in P', where $\beta_j = X_j$ if $w_j \neq \epsilon$ and $\beta_j = \epsilon$ if $w_j = \epsilon$. Since $w \neq \epsilon$, not all β_j are ϵ. Hence we have a derivation

$$A \Rightarrow \beta_1 \beta_2 \cdots \beta_n \overset{*}{\Rightarrow} w_1 \beta_2 \cdots \beta_n \overset{*}{\Rightarrow} w_1 w_2 \beta_3 \cdots \beta_n \overset{*}{\Rightarrow} \cdots \overset{*}{\Rightarrow} w_1 w_2 \cdots w_n = w$$

in G''.

Only if Suppose $A \underset{G''}{\overset{i}{\Rightarrow}} w$. Surely $w \neq \epsilon$, since G'' has no ϵ-productions. We show by induction on i that $A \underset{G}{\overset{*}{\Rightarrow}} w$. For the basis, $i = 1$, observe that $A \to w$ is a production in P'. There must be a production $A \to \alpha$ in P such that by striking out certain nullable symbols from α we are left with w. Then there is a derivation $A \underset{G}{\Rightarrow} \alpha \overset{*}{\Rightarrow} w$, where the derivation $\alpha \overset{*}{\Rightarrow} w$ involves deriving ϵ from the nullable symbols of α that were struck out in order to get w.

For the induction step, let $i > 1$. Then $A \underset{G''}{\Rightarrow} X_1 X_2 \cdots X_n \underset{G''}{\overset{i-1}{\Rightarrow}} w$. There must be some $A \to \beta$ in P such that $X_1 X_2 \cdots X_n$ is found by striking out some nullable symbols from β. Thus $A \underset{G}{\overset{*}{\Rightarrow}} X_1 X_2 \cdots X_n$. Write $w = w_1 w_2 \cdots w_n$, such that for all j, $X_j \underset{G''}{\overset{*}{\Rightarrow}} w_j$ by fewer than i steps. By the inductive hypothesis, $X_j \underset{G}{\overset{*}{\Rightarrow}} w_j$ if X_j is a variable. Certainly if X_j is a terminal, then $w_j = X_j$, and $X_j \overset{*}{\Rightarrow} w_j$ is trivially true. Thus $A \underset{G}{\overset{*}{\Rightarrow}} w$.

The last step of the proof is to apply Theorem 4.2 to G'' to produce G' with no useless symbols. Since the constructions of Lemmas 4.1 and 4.2 do not introduce any productions, G' has neither nullable symbols nor useless symbols. Furthermore $S \underset{G'}{\overset{*}{\Rightarrow}} w$ if and only if $w \neq \epsilon$ and $S \underset{G}{\overset{*}{\Rightarrow}} w$. That is, $L(G') = L(G) - \{\epsilon\}$.   □

From here on we assume that no grammar has useless symbols. We now turn our attention to productions of the form $A \to B$ whose right-hand side consists of a single variable. We call these *unit* productions. All other productions, including those of the form $A \to a$ and ϵ-productions, are *nonunit* productions.

Theorem 4.4 Every CFL without ϵ is defined by a grammar with no useless symbols, ϵ-productions, or unit productions.

Proof Let L be a CFL without ϵ and $L = L(G)$ for some $G = (V, T, P, S)$. By Theorem 4.3, assume G has no ϵ-productions. Construct a new set of productions P' from P by first including all nonunit productions of P. Then, suppose that $A \underset{G}{\overset{*}{\Rightarrow}} B$, for A and B in V. Add to P' all productions of the form $A \to \alpha$, where $B \to \alpha$ is a nonunit production of P.

Observe that we can easily test whether $A \overset{*}{\underset{G}{\Rightarrow}} B$, since G has no ϵ-productions, and if

$$A \underset{G}{\Rightarrow} B_1 \underset{G}{\Rightarrow} B_2 \underset{G}{\Rightarrow} \cdots \underset{G}{\Rightarrow} B_m \underset{G}{\Rightarrow} B,$$

and some variable appears twice in the sequence, we can find a shorter sequence of unit productions that results in $A \overset{*}{\underset{G}{\Rightarrow}} B$. Thus it is sufficient to consider only those sequences of unit productions that do not repeat any of the variables of G.

We now have a modified grammar, $G' = (V, T, P', S)$. Surely, if $A \to \alpha$ is a production of P', then $A \overset{*}{\underset{G}{\Rightarrow}} \alpha$. Thus, if there is a derivation of w in G', then there is a derivation of w in G.

Suppose that w is in $L(G)$, and consider a leftmost derivation of w in G, say

$$S = \alpha_0 \underset{G}{\Rightarrow} \alpha_1 \underset{G}{\Rightarrow} \cdots \underset{G}{\Rightarrow} \alpha_n = w.$$

If, for $0 \le i < n$, $\alpha_i \underset{G}{\Rightarrow} \alpha_{i+1}$ by a nonunit production, then $\alpha_i \underset{G'}{\Rightarrow} \alpha_{i+1}$. Suppose that $\alpha_i \underset{G}{\Rightarrow} \alpha_{i+1}$ by a unit production, but that $\alpha_{i-1} \Rightarrow \alpha_i$ by a nonunit production, or $i = 0$. Also suppose that $\alpha_{i+1} \underset{G}{\Rightarrow} \alpha_{i+2} \underset{G}{\Rightarrow} \cdots \underset{G}{\Rightarrow} \alpha_j$, all by unit productions, and $\alpha_j \underset{G}{\Rightarrow} \alpha_{j+1}$ by a nonunit production. Then $\alpha_i, \alpha_{i+1}, \ldots, \alpha_j$ are all of the same length, and since the derivation is leftmost, the symbol replaced in each of these must be at the same position. But then $\alpha_i \underset{G'}{\Rightarrow} \alpha_{j+1}$ by one of the productions of $P' - P$. Hence $L(G') = L(G)$. To complete the proof, we observe that G' has no unit productions or ϵ-productions. If we use Lemmas 4.1 and 4.2 to eliminate useless symbols, we do not add any productions, so the result of applying the constructions of these lemmas to G' is a grammar satisfying the theorem. $\quad\square$

4.5   CHOMSKY NORMAL FORM

We now prove the first of two normal-form theorems. These each state that all context-free grammars are equivalent to grammars with restrictions on the forms of productions.

Theorem 4.5 (*Chomsky normal form, or CNF*)   Any context-free language without ϵ is generated by a grammar in which all productions are of the form $A \to BC$ or $A \to a$. Here, A, B, and C, are variables and a is a terminal.

Proof   Let G be a context-free grammar generating a language not containing ϵ. By Theorem 4.4, we can find an equivalent grammar, $G_1 = (V, T, P, S)$, such that P contains no unit productions or ϵ-productions. Thus, if a production has a single symbol on the right, that symbol is a terminal, and the production is already in an acceptable form.

Now consider a production in P, of the form $A \to X_1 X_2 \cdots X_m$, where $m \ge 2$. If X_i is a terminal, a, introduce a new variable C_a and a production $C_a \to a$, which is of an allowable form. Then replace X_i by C_a. Let the new set of variables be V' and the new set of productions be P'. Consider the grammar $G_2 = (V', T, P', S)$.† If

---

† Note that G_2 is not yet in Chomsky normal form.

$\alpha \underset{G_1}{\Rightarrow} \beta$, then $\alpha \underset{G_2}{\overset{*}{\Rightarrow}} \beta$. Thus $L(G_1) \subseteq L(G_2)$. Now we show by induction on the number of steps in a derivation that if $A \underset{G_2}{\overset{*}{\Rightarrow}} w$, for A in V and w in T^*, then $A \underset{G_1}{\overset{*}{\Rightarrow}} w$. The result is trivial for one-step derivations. Suppose that it is true for derivations of up to k steps. Let $A \underset{G_2}{\overset{*}{\Rightarrow}} w$ be a $(k + 1)$-step derivation. The first step must be of the form $A \to B_1 B_2 \cdots B_m$, $m \geq 2$. We can write $w = w_1 w_2 \cdots w_m$, where $B_i \underset{G_2}{\overset{*}{\Rightarrow}} w_i$, $1 \leq i \leq m$.

If B_i is C_{a_i} for some terminal a_i, then w_i must be a_i. By the construction of P', there is a production $A \to X_1 X_2 \cdots X_m$ of P where $X_i = B_i$ if B_i is in V and $X_i = a_i$ if B_i is in $V' - V$. For those B_i in V, we know that the derivation $B_i \underset{G_2}{\overset{*}{\Rightarrow}} w_i$ takes no more than k steps, so by the inductive hypothesis, $X_i \underset{G_1}{\overset{*}{\Rightarrow}} w_i$. Hence $A \underset{G_1}{\overset{*}{\Rightarrow}} w$.

We have now proved the intermediate result that any context-free language can be generated by a grammar for which every production is either of the form $A \to a$ or $A \to B_1 B_2 \cdots B_m$, for $m \geq 2$. Here A and B_1, B_2, ..., B_m are variables, and a is a terminal.

Consider such a grammar $G_2 = (V', T, P', S)$. We modify G_2 by adding some additional symbols to V' and replacing some productions of P'. For each production $A \to B_1 B_2 \cdots B_m$ of P', where $m \geq 3$, we create new variables $D_1, D_2, \ldots, D_{m-2}$ and replace $A \to B_1 B_2 \cdots B_m$ by the set of productions

$$\{A \to B_1 D_1, D_1 \to B_2 D_2, \ldots, D_{m-3} \to B_{m-2} D_{m-2}, D_{m-2} \to B_{m-1} B_m\}.$$

Let V'' be the new nonterminal vocabulary and P'' the new set of productions. Let $G_3 = (V'', T, P'', S)$. G_3 is in CNF. It is clear that if $A \underset{G_2}{\overset{*}{\Rightarrow}} \beta$, then $A \underset{G_3}{\overset{*}{\Rightarrow}} \beta$, so $L(G_2) \subseteq L(G_3)$. But it is also true that $L(G_3) \subseteq L(G_2)$, as can be shown in essentially the same manner as it was shown that $L(G_2) \subseteq L(G_1)$. The proof will be left to the reader. $\square$

Example 4.9 Let us consider the grammar $(\{S, A, B\}, \{a, b\}, P, S)$ that has the productions:

$$S \to bA \mid aB$$

$$A \to bAA \mid aS \mid a$$

$$B \to aBB \mid bS \mid b$$

and find an equivalent grammar in CNF.

First, the only productions already in proper form are $A \to a$ and $B \to b$. There are no unit productions, so we may begin by replacing terminals on the right by variables, except in the case of the productions $A \to a$ and $B \to b$. $S \to bA$ is replaced by $S \to C_b A$ and $C_b \to b$. Similarly, $A \to aS$ is replaced by $A \to C_a S$ and $C_a \to a$; $A \to bAA$ is replaced by $A \to C_b AA$; $S \to aB$ is replaced by $S \to C_a B$; $B \to bS$ is replaced by $B \to C_b S$, and $B \to aBB$ is replaced by $B \to C_a BB$.

In the next stage, the production $A \to C_b AA$ is replaced by $A \to C_b D_1$ and $D_1 \to AA$, and the production $B \to C_a BB$ is replaced by $B \to C_a D_2$ and $D_2 \to BB$.

The productions for the grammar in CNF are shown below.

$$S \rightarrow C_b A \,|\, C_a B \qquad D_1 \rightarrow AA$$
$$A \rightarrow C_a S \,|\, C_b D_1 \,|\, a \qquad D_2 \rightarrow BB$$
$$B \rightarrow C_b S \,|\, C_a D_2 \,|\, b \qquad C_a \rightarrow a$$
$$C_b \rightarrow b$$

4.6 GREIBACH NORMAL FORM

We now develop a normal-form theorem that uses productions whose right-hand sides each start with a terminal symbol perhaps followed by some variables. First we prove two lemmas that say we can modify the productions of a CFG in certain ways without affecting the language generated.

Lemma 4.3   Define an *A-production* to be a production with variable A on the left. Let $G = (V, T, P, S)$ be a CFG. Let $A \rightarrow \alpha_1 B \alpha_2$ be a production in P and $B \rightarrow \beta_1 \,|\, \beta_2 \,|\, \cdots \,|\, \beta_r$ be the set of all B-productions. Let $G_1 = (V, T, P_1, S)$ be obtained from G by deleting the production $A \rightarrow \alpha_1 B \alpha_2$ from P and adding the productions $A \rightarrow \alpha_1 \beta_1 \alpha_2 \,|\, \alpha_1 \beta_2 \alpha_2 \,|\, \cdots \,|\, \alpha_1 \beta_r \alpha_2$. Then $L(G) = L(G_1)$.

Proof   Obviously $L(G_1) \subseteq L(G)$, since if $A \rightarrow \alpha_1 \beta_i \alpha_2$ is used in a derivation of G_1, then $A \underset{G}{\Rightarrow} \alpha_1 B \alpha_2 \underset{G}{\Rightarrow} \alpha_1 \beta_i \alpha_2$ can be used in G. To show that $L(G) \subseteq L(G_1)$, one simply notes that $A \rightarrow \alpha_1 B \alpha_2$ is the only production in G not in G_1. Whenever $A \rightarrow \alpha_1 B \alpha_2$ is used in a derivation by G, the variable B must be rewritten at some later step using a production of the form $B \rightarrow \beta_i$. These two steps can be replaced by the single step $A \underset{G_1}{\Rightarrow} \alpha_1 \beta_i \alpha_2$. $\square$

Lemma 4.4   Let $G = (V, T, P, S)$ be a CFG. Let $A \rightarrow A\alpha_1 \,|\, A\alpha_2 \,|\, \cdots \,|\, A\alpha_r$ be the set of A-productions for which A is the leftmost symbol of the right-hand side. Let $A \rightarrow \beta_1 \,|\, \beta_2 \,|\, \cdots \,|\, \beta_s$ be the remaining A-productions. Let $G_1 = (V \cup \{B\}, T, P_1, S)$ be the CFG formed by adding the variable B to V and replacing all the A-productions by the productions:

1) $\left.\begin{array}{l} A \rightarrow \beta_i \\ A \rightarrow \beta_i B \end{array}\right\} 1 \le i \le s,$ 2) $\left.\begin{array}{l} B \rightarrow \alpha_i \\ B \rightarrow \alpha_i B \end{array}\right\} 1 \le i \le r.$

Then $L(G_1) = L(G)$.

Proof   In a leftmost derivation, a sequence of productions of the form $A \rightarrow A\alpha_i$ must eventually end with a production $A \rightarrow \beta_j$. The sequence of replacements

$$A \Rightarrow A\alpha_{i_1} \Rightarrow A\alpha_{i_2} \alpha_{i_1} \Rightarrow \cdots \Rightarrow A\alpha_{i_p} \alpha_{i_{p-1}} \cdots \alpha_{i_1}$$
$$\Rightarrow \beta_j \alpha_{i_p} \alpha_{i_{p-1}} \cdots \alpha_{i_1}$$

in G can be replaced in G_1 by

$$A \Rightarrow \beta_j B \Rightarrow \beta_j \alpha_{i_p} B \Rightarrow \beta_j \alpha_{i_p} \alpha_{i_{p-1}} B$$
$$\Rightarrow \cdots \Rightarrow \beta_j \alpha_{i_p} \alpha_{i_{p-1}} \cdots \alpha_{i_2} B$$
$$\Rightarrow \beta_j \alpha_{i_p} \alpha_{i_{p-1}} \cdots \alpha_{i_1}.$$

The reverse transformation can also be made. Thus $L(G) = L(G_1)$. Figure 4.8 shows this transformation on derivation trees, where we see that in G, a chain of A's extending to the left is replaced in G_1 by a chain of B's extending to the right. □

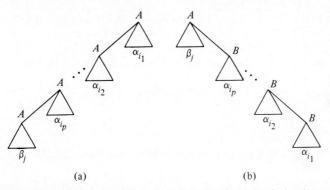

(a)   (b)

Fig. 4.8 Transformation of Lemma 4.4 on portion of a derivation tree.

Theorem 4.6 (*Greibach normal form or GNF*) Every context-free language L without ϵ can be generated by a grammar for which every production is of the form $A \rightarrow a\alpha$, where A is a variable, a is a terminal, and α is a (possibly empty) string of variables.

Proof Let $G = (V, T, P, S)$ be a Chomsky normal form grammar generating the CFL L. Assume that $V = \{A_1, A_2, \ldots, A_m\}$. The first step in the construction is to modify the productions so that if $A_i \rightarrow A_j \gamma$ is a production, then $j > i$. Starting with A_1 and proceeding to A_m, we do this as follows. We assume that the productions have been modified so that for $1 \le i < k$, $A_i \rightarrow A_j \gamma$ is a production only if $j > i$. We now modify the A_k-productions.

If $A_k \rightarrow A_j \gamma$ is a production with $j < k$, we generate a new set of productions by substituting for A_j the right-hand side of each A_j-production according to Lemma 4.3. By repeating the process $k - 1$ times at most, we obtain productions of the form $A_k \rightarrow A_\ell \gamma, \ell \ge k$. The productions with $\ell = k$ are then replaced according to Lemma 4.4, introducing a new variable B_k. The precise algorithm is given in Fig. 4.9.

```
        begin
1)         for k:= 1 to m do
              begin
2)               for j:= 1 to k − 1 do
3)                  for each production of the form A_k → A_j α do
                       begin
4)                        for all productions A_j → β do
5)                            add production A_k → βα;
6)                            remove production A_k → A_j α
                       end;
7)                  for each production of the form A_k → A_k α do
                       begin
8)                        add productions B_k → α and B_k → αB_k;
9)                        remove production A_k → A_k α
                       end;
10)                 for each production A_k → β, where β does not
                       begin with A_k do
11)                       add production A_k → βB_k
              end
        end
```

Fig. 4.9 Step 1 in the Greibach normal-form algorithm.

By repeating the above process for each original variable, we have only productions of the forms:

1) $A_i \to A_j \gamma$, $j > i$,
2) $A_i \to a\gamma$, a in T,
3) $B_i \to \gamma$, γ in $(V \cup \{B_1, B_2, \ldots, B_{i-1}\})^*$.

Note that the leftmost symbol on the right-hand side of any production for A_m must be a terminal, since A_m is the highest-numbered variable. The leftmost symbol on the right-hand side of any production for A_{m-1} must be either A_m or a terminal symbol. When it is A_m, we can generate new productions by replacing A_m by the right-hand side of the productions for A_m according to Lemma 4.3. These productions must have right sides that start with a terminal symbol. We then proceed to the productions for $A_{m-2}, \ldots, A_2, A_1$ until the right side of each production for an A_i starts with a terminal symbol.

As the last step we examine the productions for the new variables, $B_1, B_2, \ldots,$ B_m. Since we began with a grammar in Chomsky normal form, it is easy to prove by induction on the number of applications of Lemmas 4.3 and 4.4 that the right-hand side of every A_i-production, $1 \le i \le n$, begins with a terminal or $A_j A_k$ for some j and k. Thus α in line (7) of Fig. 4.9 can never be empty or begin with some

B_j, so no B_i-production can start with another B_j. Therefore all B_i-productions have right-hand sides beginning with terminals or A_i's, and one more application of Lemma 4.3 for each B_i-production completes the construction.   □

Example 4.10   Let us convert to Greibach normal form the grammar

$$G = (\{A_1, A_2, A_3\}, \{a, b\}, P, A_1),$$

where P consists of the following:

$$A_1 \rightarrow A_2 A_3$$
$$A_2 \rightarrow A_3 A_1 \,|\, b$$
$$A_3 \rightarrow A_1 A_2 \,|\, a$$

Step 1   Since the right-hand side of the productions for A_1 and A_2 start with terminals or higher-numbered variables, we begin with the production $A_3 \rightarrow A_1 A_2$ and substitute the string $A_2 A_3$ for A_1. Note that $A_1 \rightarrow A_2 A_3$ is the only production with A_1 on the left.

The resulting set of productions is:

$$A_1 \rightarrow A_2 A_3$$
$$A_2 \rightarrow A_3 A_1 \,|\, b$$
$$A_3 \rightarrow A_2 A_3 A_2 \,|\, a$$

Since the right side of the production $A_3 \rightarrow A_2 A_3 A_2$ begins with a lower-numbered variable, we substitute for the first occurrence of A_2 both $A_3 A_1$ and b. Thus $A_3 \rightarrow A_2 A_3 A_2$ is replaced by $A_3 \rightarrow A_3 A_1 A_3 A_2$ and $A_3 \rightarrow b A_3 A_2$. The new set is

$$A_1 \rightarrow A_2 A_3$$
$$A_2 \rightarrow A_3 A_1 \,|\, b$$
$$A_3 \rightarrow A_3 A_1 A_3 A_2 \,|\, b A_3 A_2 \,|\, a$$

We now apply Lemma 4.4 to the productions

$$A_3 \rightarrow A_3 A_1 A_3 A_2 \,|\, b A_3 A_2 \,|\, a.$$

Symbol B_3 is introduced, and the production $A_3 \rightarrow A_3 A_1 A_3 A_2$ is replaced by $A_3 \rightarrow b A_3 A_2 B_3$, $A_3 \rightarrow a B_3$, $B_3 \rightarrow A_1 A_3 A_2$, and $B_3 \rightarrow A_1 A_3 A_2 B_3$. The resulting set is

$$A_1 \rightarrow A_2 A_3$$
$$A_2 \rightarrow A_3 A_1 \,|\, b$$
$$A_3 \rightarrow b A_3 A_2 B_3 \,|\, a B_3 \,|\, b A_3 A_2 \,|\, a$$
$$B_3 \rightarrow A_1 A_3 A_2 \,|\, A_1 A_3 A_2 B_3$$

Step 2   Now all the productions with A_3 on the left have right-hand sides that start with terminals. These are used to replace A_3 in the production $A_2 \to A_3 A_1$ and then the productions with A_2 on the left are used to replace A_2 in the production $A_1 \to A_2 A_3$. The result is the following.

$$A_3 \to b A_3 A_2 B_3 \qquad\qquad A_3 \to b A_3 A_2$$
$$A_3 \to a B_3 \qquad\qquad\qquad A_3 \to a$$
$$A_2 \to b A_3 A_2 B_3 A_1 \qquad\quad A_2 \to b A_3 A_2 A_1$$
$$A_2 \to a B_3 A_1 \qquad\qquad\quad A_2 \to a A_1$$
$$A_2 \to b$$
$$A_1 \to b A_3 A_2 B_3 A_1 A_3 \qquad A_1 \to b A_3 A_2 A_1 A_3$$
$$A_1 \to a B_3 A_1 A_3 \qquad\qquad A_1 \to a A_1 A_3$$
$$A_1 \to b A_3$$
$$B_3 \to A_1 A_3 A_2 \qquad\qquad B_3 \to A_1 A_3 A_2 B_3$$

Step 3   The two B_3-productions are converted to proper form, resulting in 10 more productions. That is, the productions

$$B_3 \to A_1 A_3 A_2 \qquad \text{and} \qquad B_3 \to A_1 A_3 A_2 B_3$$

are altered by substituting the right side of each of the five productions with A_1 on the left for the first occurrences of A_1. Thus $B_3 \to A_1 A_3 A_2$ becomes

$$B_3 \to b A_3 A_2 B_3 A_1 A_3 A_3 A_2, \qquad B_3 \to a B_3 A_1 A_3 A_3 A_2.$$
$$B_3 \to b A_3 A_3 A_2, \qquad B_3 \to b A_3 A_2 A_1 A_3 A_3 A_2, \qquad B_3 \to a A_1 A_3 A_3 A_2.$$

The other production for B_3 is replaced similarly. The final set of productions is

$$A_3 \to b A_3 A_2 B_3 \qquad\qquad A_3 \to b A_3 A_2$$
$$A_3 \to a B_3 \qquad\qquad\qquad A_3 \to a$$
$$A_2 \to b A_3 A_2 B_3 A_1 \qquad\quad A_2 \to b A_3 A_2 A_1$$
$$A_2 \to a B_3 A_1 \qquad\qquad\quad A_2 \to a A_1$$
$$A_2 \to b$$
$$A_1 \to b A_3 A_2 B_3 A_1 A_3 \qquad A_1 \to b A_3 A_2 A_1 A_3$$
$$A_1 \to a B_3 A_1 A_3 \qquad\qquad A_1 \to a A_1 A_3$$
$$A_1 \to b A_3$$
$$B_3 \to b A_3 A_2 B_3 A_1 A_3 A_3 A_2 B_3 \qquad B_3 \to b A_3 A_2 B_3 A_1 A_3 A_3 A_2$$

$$B_3 \rightarrow aB_3 A_1 A_3 A_3 A_2 B_3 \qquad\qquad B_3 \rightarrow aB_3 A_1 A_3 A_3 A_2$$

$$B_3 \rightarrow bA_3 A_3 A_2 B_3 \qquad\qquad B_3 \rightarrow bA_3 A_3 A_2$$

$$B_3 \rightarrow bA_3 A_2 A_1 A_3 A_3 A_2 B_3 \qquad\qquad B_3 \rightarrow bA_3 A_2 A_1 A_3 A_3 A_2$$

$$B_3 \rightarrow aA_1 A_3 A_3 A_2 B_3 \qquad\qquad B_3 \rightarrow aA_1 A_3 A_3 A_2$$

4.7   THE EXISTENCE OF INHERENTLY AMBIGUOUS CONTEXT-FREE LANGUAGES

It is easy to exhibit ambiguous context-free grammars. For example, consider the grammar with productions $S \rightarrow A$, $S \rightarrow B$, $A \rightarrow a$, and $B \rightarrow a$. What is not so easy to do is to exhibit a context-free language for which every CFG is ambiguous. In this section we show that there are indeed inherently ambiguous CFL's. The proof is somewhat tedious, and the student may skip this section without loss of continuity. The existence of such a language is made use of only in Theorem 8.16.

We shall show that the language

$$L = \{a^n b^n c^m d^m \,|\, n \geq 1, m \geq 1\} \cup \{a^n b^m c^m d^n \,|\, n \geq 1, m \geq 1\}$$

is inherently ambiguous by showing that infinitely many strings of the form $a^n b^n c^n d^n$, $n \geq 1$, must have two distinct leftmost derivations. We proceed by first establishing two technical lemmas.

Lemma 4.5   Let (N_i, M_i), $1 \leq i \leq r$, be pairs of sets of integers. (The sets may be finite or infinite.) Let

$$S_i = \{(n, m) \,|\, n \text{ in } N_i, m \text{ in } M_i\}$$

and let

$$S = S_1 \cup S_2 \cup \cdots \cup S_r.$$

If each pair of integers (n, m) is in S for all n and m, where $n \neq m$, then (n, n) is in S for all but some finite set of n.

Proof   Assume that for all n and m, where $n \neq m$, each (n, m) is in S, and that there are infinitely many n such that (n, n) is not in S. Let J be the set of all n such that (n, n) is not in S. We construct a sequence of sets $J_r, J_{r-1}, \ldots, J_1$ such that

$$J \supseteq J_r \supseteq J_{r-1} \supseteq \cdots \supseteq J_1.$$

Each J_i will be infinite, and for each n and m in J_i, (n, m) is not in

$$S_i \cup S_{i+1} \cup \cdots \cup S_r.$$

For n in J, either n is not in N_r or n is not in M_r; otherwise (n, n) would be in S_r and hence in S. Thus there is an infinite subset of J, call it J_r, such that either for all n in J_r, n is not in N_r, or for all n in J_r, n is not in M_r. Now for n and m in J_r, (n, m) is not in S_r.

Assume that $J_r, J_{r-1}, \ldots, J_{i+1}$ have been constructed, where $i \leq r - 1$. Then J_i is constructed as follows. For each n in J_{i+1}, either n is not in N_i or not in M_i; otherwise (n, n) would be in S_i and hence in S, a contradiction since $J_{i+1} \subseteq J$. Thus, either an infinite subset of J_{i+1} is not in N_i or an infinite subset of J_{i+1} is not in M_i. In either case, let the infinite subset be J_i. Now for all n and m in J_i, (n, m) is not in S_i and hence not in $S_i \cup S_{i+1} \cup \cdots \cup S_r$.

Since J_1 contains an infinite number of elements, there exist n and m in J_1, $n \neq m$. Now (n, m) is not in $S_1 \cup S_2 \cup \cdots \cup S_r = S$, contradicting the assumption that all (n, m), where $n \neq m$, are in S. Thus (n, n) is in S for all but some finite set of n. $\square$

Lemma 4.6 Let G be an unambiguous CFG. Then we can effectively construct an unambiguous CFG G' equivalent to G, such that G' has no useless symbols or productions, and for every variable A other than possibly the start symbol of G', we have the derivation $A \underset{G'}{\overset{*}{\Rightarrow}} x_1 A x_2$, where x_1 and x_2 are not both ϵ.

Proof The construction of Lemmas 4.1 and 4.2, removing useless symbols and productions, cannot convert an unambiguous grammar into an ambiguous one, since the set of derivation trees for words does not change. The construction of Theorem 4.4, removing unit productions, cannot introduce ambiguities. This is because if we introduce production $A \to \alpha$, there must be a unique B such that $A \overset{*}{\Rightarrow} B$ and $B \to \alpha$ is a production, else the original grammar was not unambiguous. Similarly, the construction of Theorem 4.3, removing ϵ-productions, does not introduce ambiguity.

Let us therefore assume that G has no useless symbols or productions, no ϵ-productions, and no unit productions. Suppose that for no x_1 and x_2 not both ϵ does $A \overset{*}{\Rightarrow} x_1 A x_2$. Then replace each occurrence of A on the right side of any production by all the right sides of A-productions. As there are no unit productions, ϵ-productions or useless symbols, there cannot be a production $A \to \alpha_1 A \alpha_2$, else there is a derivation $A \overset{*}{\Rightarrow} x_1 A x_2$, with x_1 and x_2 not both ϵ. The above change does not modify the generated language, by Lemma 4.3. Each new production comes from a unique sequence of old productions, else G was ambiguous. Thus the resulting grammar is unambiguous. We see that A is now useless and may be eliminated. After removing variables violating the condition of the lemma in this manner, the new grammar is equivalent to the old, is still unambiguous, and satisfies the lemma. $\square$

Theorem 4.7 The CFL,

$$L = \{a^n b^n c^m d^m \mid n \geq 1, m \geq 1\} \cup \{a^n b^m c^m d^n \mid n \geq 1, m \geq 1\},$$

is inherently ambiguous.

Proof Assume that there is an unambiguous grammar generating L. By Lemma 4.6 we can construct an unambiguous grammar $G = (V, T, P, S)$ generating L with no useless symbols, and for each A in $V - \{S\}$, $A \overset{*}{\Rightarrow} x_1 A x_2$ for some x_1 and x_2 in T^*, not both ϵ.

We note that the grammar G has the following properties:

1) If $A \overset{*}{\Rightarrow} x_1 A x_2$, then x_1 and x_2 each consist of only one type of symbol (a, b, c, or d); otherwise

$$S \overset{*}{\Rightarrow} w_1 A w_3 \overset{*}{\Rightarrow} w_1 x_1 x_1 A x_2 x_2 w_3 \overset{*}{\Rightarrow} w_1 x_1 x_1 w_2 x_2 x_2 w_3,$$

for some w_1, w_2, and w_3. This last terminal string is not in L.

2) If $A \overset{*}{\Rightarrow} x_1 A x_2$, then x_1 and x_2 consist of different symbols. Otherwise, in a derivation involving A, we could increase the number of one type of symbol in a sentence of L without increasing the number of any other type of symbols, thereby generating a sentence not in L.

3) If $A \overset{*}{\Rightarrow} x_1 A x_2$, then $|x_1| = |x_2|$. Otherwise we could find words in L having more of one symbol than any other.

4) If $A \overset{*}{\Rightarrow} x_1 A x_2$ and $A \overset{*}{\Rightarrow} x_3 A x_4$, then x_1 and x_3 consist of the same type of symbol. Likewise x_2 and x_4. Otherwise Property 1 above would be violated.

5) If $A \overset{*}{\Rightarrow} x_1 A x_2$, then either

a) x_1 consists solely of a's and x_2 solely of b's or of d's,
b) x_1 consists solely of b's and x_2 solely of c's, or
c) x_1 consists solely of c's and x_2 solely of d's.

In any of the other cases it is easy to derive a string not in L. Thus the variables other than S can be divided into four classes, C_{ab}, C_{ad}, C_{bc}, and C_{cd}. C_{ab} is the set of all A in V such that $A \overset{*}{\Rightarrow} x_1 A x_2$, with x_1 in $\mathbf{a}^*$ and x_2 in $\mathbf{b}^*$; C_{ad}, C_{bc}, and C_{cd} are defined analogously.

6) A derivation containing a symbol in C_{ab} or C_{cd} cannot contain a symbol in C_{ad} or C_{bc} or vice versa. Otherwise, we could increase the number of three types of symbols of a sentence in L without increasing the number of the fourth type of symbol. In that case, there would be a sentence in L for which the number of occurrences of one type of symbol is smaller than that of any other.

We now note that if a derivation contains a variable in C_{ab} or C_{cd}, then the terminal string generated must be in $\{a^n b^n c^m d^m \mid n \geq 1, m \geq 1\}$. For assume that A in C_{ab} appears in a derivation of a sentence x not in $\{a^n b^n c^m d^m \mid n \geq 1, m \geq 1\}$. Then x must be of the form $a^n b^m c^m d^n$, $m \neq n$. Since A is in C_{ab}, a sentence $a^{n+p} b^{m+p} c^m d^n$, $m \neq n$, for some $p > 0$, could be generated. Such a sentence is not in L. A similar argument holds for A in C_{cd}. Similar reasoning implies that if a derivation contains a variable in C_{ad} or C_{bc}, then the sentence generated must be in $\{a^n b^m c^m d^n \mid n \geq 1, m \geq 1\}$.

We divide G into two grammars,

$$G_1 = (\{S\} \cup C_{ab} \cup C_{cd}, T, P_1, S)$$

and

$$G_2 = (\{S\} \cup C_{ad} \cup C_{bc}, T, P_2, S),$$

where P_1 contains all productions of P with a variable form C_{ab} or C_{cd} on either the right or left, and P_2 contains all productions of P with a variable from C_{ad} or C_{bc} on either the right or left. In addition, P_1 contains all productions from P of the form $S \rightarrow a^n b^n c^m d^m$, $n \neq m$, and P_2 contains all productions from P of the form $S \rightarrow a^n b^m c^m d^n$, $n \neq m$. Productions of P of the form $S \rightarrow a^n b^n c^n d^n$ are not in either P_1 or P_2.

Since G generates

$$\{a^n b^n c^m d^m \mid n \geq 1, m \geq 1\} \cup \{a^n b^m c^m d^n \mid n \geq 1, m \geq 1\},$$

G_1 must generate all sentences in

$$\{a^n b^n c^m d^m \mid n \geq 1, m \geq 1, n \neq m\}$$

plus possibly some sentences in $\{a^n b^n c^n d^n \mid n \geq 1\}$, and G_2 must generate all sentences in

$$\{a^n b^m c^m d^n \mid n \geq 1, m \geq 1, n \neq m\}$$

plus possibly some sentences in $\{a^n b^n c^n d^n \mid n \geq 1\}$. We now show that this cannot be the case unless G_1 and G_2 both generate all but a finite number of sentences in $\{a^n b^n c^n d^n \mid n \geq 1\}$. Thus all but a finite number of sentences in $\{a^n b^n c^n d^n \mid n \geq 1\}$ are generated by both G_1 and G_2 and hence by two distinct derivations in G. This contradicts the assumption that G was unambiguous.

To see that G_1 and G_2 generate all but a finite number of sentences in $\{a^n b^n c^n d^n \mid n \geq 0\}$, number the productions in P_1 of the form $S \rightarrow \alpha$ from 1 to r. For $1 \leq i \leq r$, if $S \rightarrow \alpha$ is the ith production, let N_i be the set of all n such that

$$S \underset{G_1}{\Rightarrow} \alpha \underset{G_1}{\overset{*}{\Rightarrow}} a^n b^n c^m d^m$$

for some m, and let M_i be the set of all m such that

$$S \underset{G_1}{\Rightarrow} \alpha \underset{G_1}{\overset{*}{\Rightarrow}} a^n b^n c^m d^m$$

for some n. We leave it to the reader to show that for any n in N_i and any m in M_i,

$$S \underset{G_1}{\Rightarrow} \alpha \underset{G_1}{\overset{*}{\Rightarrow}} a^n b^n c^m d^m.$$

[*Hint:* Recall that the variables of α are in C_{ab} or C_{cd}.] It follows immediately from Lemma 4.5 that G_1 must generate all but a finite number of sentences in $\{a^n b^n c^n d^n \mid n \geq 1\}$.

A similar argument applies to G_2. The reader can easily show that G_2 cannot have a right side with two or more variables. We number certain productions and pairs of productions in a single ordering. Productions of the form $S \rightarrow \alpha_1 B \alpha_2$, where B is in C_{bc}, will receive a number, and if this number is i, let N_i be the set of all n such that for some m,

$$S \Rightarrow \alpha_1 B \alpha_2 \overset{*}{\Rightarrow} a^n b^m c^m d^n.$$

Also let M_i be the set of m such that for some n,

$$S \Rightarrow \alpha_1 B \alpha_2 \overset{*}{\Rightarrow} a^n b^m c^m d^n.$$

The pair of productions $S \to \alpha$ and $A \to \alpha_1 B \alpha_2$ will receive a number if α contains a variable in C_{ad}, A is in C_{ad}, and B is in C_{bc}. If this pair is assigned the number i, then define N_i to be the set of n such that for some m,

$$S \Rightarrow \alpha \overset{*}{\Rightarrow} x_1 A x_2 \Rightarrow x_1 \alpha_1 B \alpha_2 x_2 \overset{*}{\Rightarrow} a^n b^m c^m d^n.$$

Also define M_i to be the set of m such that for some n,

$$S \Rightarrow \alpha \overset{*}{\Rightarrow} x_1 A x_2 \Rightarrow x_1 \alpha_1 B \alpha_2 x_2 \overset{*}{\Rightarrow} a^n b^m c^m d^n.$$

Once again, for any n in N_i and m in M_i,

$$S \overset{*}{\underset{G_2}{\Rightarrow}} a^n b^m c^m d^n,$$

and thus it follows from Lemma 4.5 that G_2 generates all but a finite number of sentences in $\{a^n b^n c^n d^n \mid n \geq 1\}$. We conclude that for some n, $a^n b^n c^n d^n$ is in both $L(G_1)$ and $L(G_2)$. This sentence has two leftmost derivations in G. $\square$

EXERCISES

4.1   Give context-free grammars generating the following sets.

S a) The set of palindromes (strings that read the same forward as backward) over alphabet $\{a, b\}$.

  b) The set of all strings of balanced parentheses, i.e., each left parenthesis has a matching right parenthesis and pairs of matching parentheses are properly nested.

  * c) The set of all strings over alphabet $\{a, b\}$ with exactly twice as many a's as b's.

  d) The set of all strings over alphabet $\{a, b, \cdot, +, *, (,), \epsilon, \varnothing\}$ that are well-formed regular expressions over alphabet $\{a, b\}$. Note that we must distinguish between ϵ as the empty string and as a symbol in a regular expression. We use ϵ in the latter case.

  * e) The set of all strings over alphabet $\{a, b\}$ not of the form ww for some string w.

  f) $\{a^i b^j c^k \mid i \neq j \text{ or } j \neq k\}$.

* 4.2   Let G be the grammar

$$S \to aS \mid aSbS \mid \epsilon.$$

Prove that

$$L(G) = \{x \mid \text{each prefix of } x \text{ has at least as many } a\text{'s as } b\text{'s}\}.$$

* 4.3   For $i \geq 1$, let b_i denote the string in $1(0 + 1)^*$ that is the binary representation of i. Construct a CFG generating

$$\{0, 1, \#\}^+ - \{b_1 \# b_2 \# \cdots \# b_n \mid n \geq 1\}.$$

* 4.4   Construct a CFG generating the set

$$\{w \# w^R \# \mid w \text{ in } (0 + 1)^+\}^*.$$

* 4.5   The grammar

$$E \to E + E \mid E * E \mid (E) \mid \mathbf{id}$$

generates the set of arithmetic expressions with $+$, $*$, parentheses and $\mathbf{id}$. The grammar is ambiguous since $\mathbf{id} + \mathbf{id} * \mathbf{id}$ can be generated by two distinct leftmost derivations.

  a) Construct an equivalent unambiguous grammar.

b) Construct an unambiguous grammar for all arithmetic expressions with no redundant parentheses. A set of parentheses is redundant if its removal does not change the expression, e.g., the parentheses are redundant in $id + (id * id)$ but not in $(id + id) * id$.

* **4.6**   Suppose G is a CFG with m variables and no right side of a production longer than ℓ. Show that if $A \overset{*}{\underset{G}{\Rightarrow}} \epsilon$, then there is a derivation of no more than $\dfrac{\ell^m - 1}{\ell - 1}$ steps by which A derives ϵ. How close to this bound can you actually come?

* **4.7**   Show that for each CFG G there is a constant c such that if w is in $L(G)$, and $w \neq \epsilon$, then w has a derivation of no more than $c|w|$ steps.

4.8   Let G be the grammar

$$S \rightarrow aB \,|\, bA$$

$$A \rightarrow a \,|\, aS \,|\, bAA$$

$$B \rightarrow b \,|\, bS \,|\, aBB$$

For the string $aaabbabbba$ find a

a) leftmost derivation,   b) rightmost derivation,   c) parse tree.

* **4.9**   Is the grammar in Exercise 4.8 unambiguous?

4.10   Find a CFG with no useless symbols equivalent to

$$S \rightarrow AB \,|\, CA \qquad B \rightarrow BC \,|\, AB$$

$$A \rightarrow a \qquad\qquad C \rightarrow aB \,|\, b$$

4.11   Suppose G is a CFG and w, of length ℓ, is in $L(G)$. How long is a derivation of w in G if

a) G is in CNF   b) G is in GNF.

4.12   Let G be the CFG generating well-formed formulas of propositional calculus with predicates p and q:

$$S \rightarrow \sim S \,|\, [S \supset S] \,|\, p \,|\, q.$$

The terminals are p, q, $\sim$, $[$, $]$, and $\supset$. Find a Chomsky normal-form grammar generating $L(G)$.

4.13   Show that conversion to Chomsky normal form can square the number of productions in a grammar. [*Hint:* Consider the removal of unit productions.]

4.14   Find a Greibach normal-form grammar equivalent to the following CFG:

$$S \rightarrow AA \,|\, 0$$

$$A \rightarrow SS \,|\, 1$$

4.15   Show that every CFL without ϵ can be generated by a CFG all of whose productions are of the form $A \rightarrow a$, or $A \rightarrow BC$, where $B \neq C$ and if $A \rightarrow \alpha_1 B \alpha_2$ and $A \rightarrow \gamma_1 B \gamma_2$ are productions, then $\alpha_1 = \gamma_1 = \epsilon$ or $\alpha_2 = \gamma_2 = \epsilon$.

*S **4.16**   Show that every CFL without ϵ is generated by a CFG all of whose productions are of the form $A \rightarrow a$, $A \rightarrow aB$, and $A \rightarrow aBC$.

4.17   Show that every CFL without ϵ is generated by a CFG all of whose productions are of the form $A \to a$ and $A \to a\alpha b$.

4.18   Can every CFL without ϵ be generated by a CFG all of whose productions are of the forms $A \to BCD$ and $A \to a$?

* **4.19**   Show that if all productions of a CFG are of the form $A \to wB$ or $A \to w$, then $L(G)$ is a regular set.

** **4.20**   A CFG is said to be *linear* if no right side of a production has more than one instance of a variable. Which of the languages of Exercise 4.1 have linear grammars?

S **4.21   An *operator grammar* is a CFG with no ϵ-productions such that no consecutive symbols on the right sides of productions are variables. Show that every CFL without ϵ has an operator grammar.

** **4.22**   The algorithm given in Fig. 4.7 to determine which variables derive terminal strings is not the most efficient possible. Give a computer program to perform the task in $O(n)$ steps if n is the sum of the length of all the productions.

** **4.23**   Is $\{a^i b^j c^k \,|\, i \neq j$ and $j \neq k$ and $k \neq i\}$ a CFL? [*Hint*: Develop a normal form similar to that in Theorem 4.7. (A pumping lemma is developed in Section 6.1 that makes exercises of this type much easier. The reader may wish to compare his solution to that in Example 6.3).]

Solutions to Selected Exercises

4.1   a) The definition of "palindrome," a string reading the same forward as backward is of no help in finding a CFG. What we must do in this and many other cases is rework the definition into a recursive form. We may define palindromes over $\{0, 1\}$ recursively, as follows:

1) ϵ, 0, and 1 are palindromes;
2) if w is a palindrome, so are $0w0$ and $1w1$;
3) nothing else is a palindrome.

We proved in Exercise 1.3 that this is a valid definition of palindromes. A CFG for palindromes now follows immediately from (1) and (2). It is:

$$S \to 0\,|\,1\,|\,\epsilon \qquad \text{(from 1)};$$

$$S \to 0S0\,|\,1S1 \qquad \text{(from 2)}.$$

4.16   Let $G = (V, T, P, S)$ be a GNF grammar generating L. Suppose k is the length of the longest right side of a production of G. Let $V' = \{[\alpha]\,|\,\alpha$ is in V^+ and $|\alpha| < k\}$. For each production $A \to a\alpha$ in P and each variable $[A\beta]$ in V' place $[A\beta] \to a[\alpha][\beta]$ in P'. In the case where α or β is ϵ, $[\epsilon]$ is deleted from the right side of the production.

4.21   Let $G = (V, T, P, S)$ be a GNF grammar generating L. By Exercise 4.16 we may assume all productions are of the form $A \to a$, $A \to aB$ and $A \to aBC$. First replace each production $A \to aBC$ by $A \to a[BC]$, where $[BC]$ is a new variable. After having replaced all productions of the form $A \to aBC$, then for each newly introduced variable $[BC]$, B-production $B \to \alpha$, and C-production $C \to \beta$, add production $[BC] \to \alpha\beta$. Note that α and β are either single terminals or of the form bE, where E may be either a new or old variable. The resulting grammar is an operator grammar equivalent to the original.

BIBLIOGRAPHIC NOTES

The origin of the context-free grammar formalism is found in Chomsky [1956]; important later writings by Chomsky on the subject appear in Chomsky [1959, 1963]. The related Backus-Naur form notation was used for the description of ALGOL in Backus [1959] and Naur [1960]. The relationship between CFG's and BNF was perceived in Ginsburg and Rice [1962].

Chomsky normal form is based on Chomsky [1959]. Actually, Chomsky proved the stronger result stated in Exercise 4.15. Greibach normal form was proved by Greibach [1965]. The method of proof used here is due to M. C. Paull. The reader should also consider the algorithm of Rosenkrantz [1967], which has the property that it never more than squares the number of variables, while the algorithm of Theorem 4.6 may exponentiate the number. Solutions to Exercises 4.16, 4.17, and 4.21 can be found there as well.

Ambiguity in CFG's was first studied formally by Floyd [1962a], Cantor [1962], Chomsky and Schutzenberger [1963], and Greibach [1963]. Inherent ambiguity was studied by Gross [1964], and Ginsburg and Ullian [1966a, b].

Important applications of context-free grammar theory have been made to compiler design. See Aho and Ullman [1972, 1973, 1977], Lewis, Rosenkrantz, and Stearns [1976], and the bibliographic notes to Chapter 10 for a description of some of the work in this area. Additional material on context-free languages can be found in Ginsburg [1966] and Salomaa [1973].

CHAPTER

PUSHDOWN
AUTOMATA

5.1 INFORMAL DESCRIPTION

Just as the regular expressions have an equivalent automaton—the finite automaton, the context-free grammars have their machine counterpart—the pushdown automaton. Here the equivalence is somewhat less satisfactory, since the pushdown automaton is a nondeterministic device, and the deterministic version accepts only a subset of all CFL's. Fortunately, this subset includes the syntax of most programming languages. (See Chapter 10 for a detailed study of deterministic pushdown automaton languages.)

The pushdown automaton is essentially a finite automaton with control of both an input tape and a stack, or "first in–last out" list. That is, symbols may be entered or removed only at the top of the list. When a symbol is entered at the top, the symbol previously at the top becomes second from the top, the symbol previously second from the top becomes third, and so on. Similarly, when a symbol is removed from the top of the list, the symbol previously second from the top becomes the top symbol, the symbol previously third from the top becomes second, and so on.

A familiar example of a stack is the stack of plates on a spring that one sees in cafeterias. There is a spring below the plates with just enough strength so that exactly one plate appears above the level of the counter. When that top plate is removed, the load on the spring is lightened, and the plate directly below appears above the level of the counter. If a plate is then put on top of the stack, the pile is pushed down, and only the new plate appears above the counter. For our purposes, we make the assumption that the spring is arbitrarily long, so we may add as many plates as we desire.

107

Such a stack of plates, coupled with a finite control, can be used to recognize a nonregular set. The set $L = \{wcw^R \,|\, w$ in $(0 + 1)^*\}$ is a context-free language, generated by the grammar $S \to 0S0 \,|\, 1S1 \,|\, c$. It is not hard to show that L cannot be accepted by any finite automaton. To accept L, we shall make use of a finite control with two states, q_1 and q_2, and a stack on which we place blue, green, and red plates. The device will operate by the following rules.

1) The machine starts with one red plate on the stack and with the finite control in state q_1.

2) If the input to the device is 0 and the device is in state q_1, a blue plate is placed on the stack. If the input to the device is 1 and the device is in state q_1, a green plate is placed on the stack. In both cases the finite control remains in state q_1.

3) If the input is c and the device is in state q_1, it changes state to q_2 while no plates are added or removed.

4) If the input is 0 and the device is in state q_2 with a blue plate, which represents 0, on top of the stack, the plate is removed. If the input is 1 and the device is in state q_2 with a green plate, which represents 1, on top of the stack, the plate is removed. In both cases the finite control remains in state q_2.

5) If the device is in state q_2 and a red plate is on top of the stack, the plate is removed without waiting for the next input.

6) For all cases other than those described above, the device can make no move.

The preceding rules are summarized in Fig. 5.1.

We say that the device described above accepts an input string if, on processing the last symbol of the string, the stack of plates becomes completely empty. Note that, once the stack is empty, no further moves are possible.

Essentially, the device operates in the following way. In state q_1, the device makes an image of its input by placing a blue plate on top of the stack of plates each time a 0 appears in the input, and a green plate each time a 1 appears in the input. When c is the input, the device enters state q_2. Next, the remaining input is compared with the stack by removing a blue plate from the top of the stack each time the input symbol is a 0, and a green plate each time the input symbol is a 1. Should the top plate be of the wrong color, the device halts and no further processing of the input is possible. If all plates match the inputs, eventually the red plate at the bottom of the stack is exposed. The red plate is immediately removed and the device is said to accept the input string. All plates can be removed only when the string that enters the device after the c is the reverse of what entered before the c.

5.2 DEFINITIONS

We shall now formalize the concept of a pushdown automaton (PDA). The PDA will have an *input tape*, a *finite control*, and a *stack*. The stack is a string of symbols from some alphabet. The leftmost symbol of the stack is considered to be at the

Top plate	State	Input 0	1	c
Blue	q_1	Add blue plate; stay in state q_1.	Add green plate; stay in state q_1.	Go to state q_2.
	q_2	Remove top plate; stay in state q_2.	—	—
Green	q_1	Add blue plate; stay in state q_1.	Add green plate; stay in state q_1.	Go to state q_2.
	q_2	—	Remove top plate; stay in state q_2.	—
Red	q_1	Add blue plate; stay in state q_1.	Add green plate; stay in state q_1.	Go to state q_2.
	q_2	Without waiting for next input, remove top plate.		

Fig. 5.1 Finite control for pushdown automaton accepting $\{wcw^R \mid w$ in $(0 + 1)^*\}$.

"top" of the stack. The device will be nondeterministic, having some finite number of choices of moves in each situation. The moves will be of two types. In the first type of move, an input symbol is used. Depending on the input symbol, the top symbol on the stack, and the state of the finite control, a number of choices are possible. Each choice consists of a next state for the finite control and a (possibly empty) string of symbols to replace the top stack symbol. After selecting a choice, the input head is advanced one symbol.

The second type of move (called an ϵ-move) is similar to the first, except that the input symbol is not used, and the input head is not advanced after the move. This type of move allows the PDA to manipulate the stack without reading input symbols.

Finally, we must define the language accepted by a pushdown automaton. There are two natural ways to do this. The first, which we have already seen, is to define the language accepted to be the set of all inputs for which some sequence of moves causes the pushdown automaton to empty its stack. This language is referred to as the language accepted by empty stack.

The second way of defining the language accepted is similar to the way a finite automaton accepts inputs. That is, we designate some states as final states and define the accepted language as the set of all inputs for which some choice of moves causes the pushdown automaton to enter a final state.

As we shall see, the two definitions of acceptance are equivalent in the sense that if a set can be accepted by empty stack by some PDA, it can be accepted by final state by some other PDA, and vice versa.

Acceptance by final state is the more common notion, but it is easier to prove the basic theorem of pushdown automata by using acceptance by empty stack. This theorem is that a language is accepted by a pushdown automaton if and only if it is a context-free language.

A *pushdown automaton M* is a system $(Q, \Sigma, \Gamma, \delta, q_0, Z_0, F)$, where

1) Q is a finite set of *states*;
2) Σ is an alphabet called the *input alphabet*;
3) Γ is an alphabet, called the *stack alphabet*;
4) q_0 in Q is the *initial state*;
5) Z_0 in Γ is a particular stack symbol called the *start symbol*;
6) $F \subseteq Q$ is the set of *final states*;
7) δ is a mapping from $Q \times (\Sigma \cup \{\epsilon\}) \times \Gamma$ to finite subsets of $Q \times \Gamma^*$.

Unless stated otherwise, we use lower-case letters near the front of the alphabet to denote input symbols and lower-case letters near the end of the alphabet to denote strings of input symbols. Capital letters denote stack symbols and Greek letters indicate strings of stack symbols.

Moves

The interpretation of

$$\delta(q, a, Z) = \{(p_1, \gamma_1), (p_2, \gamma_2), \ldots, (p_m, \gamma_m)\}$$

where q and p_i, $1 \le i \le m$, are states, a is in Σ, Z is a stack symbol, and γ_i is in Γ^*, $1 \le i \le m$, is that the PDA in state q, with input symbol a and Z the top symbol on the stack can, for any i, enter state p_i, replace symbol Z by string γ_i, and advance the input head one symbol. We adopt the convention that the leftmost symbol of γ_i will be placed highest on the stack and the rightmost symbol lowest on the stack. Note that it is not permissible to choose state p_i and string γ_j for some $j \ne i$ in one move.

The interpretation of

$$\delta(q, \epsilon, Z) = \{(p_1, \gamma_1), (p_2, \gamma_2), \ldots, (p_m, \gamma_m)\}$$

is that the PDA in state q, independent of the input symbol being scanned and with Z the top symbol on the stack, can enter state p_i and replace Z by γ_i for any i, $1 \le i \le m$. In this case, the input head is not advanced.

Example 5.1 Figure 5.2 gives a formal pushdown automaton that accepts $\{wcw^R \,|\, w$ in $(0 + 1)^*\}$ by empty stack. Note that for a move in which the PDA writes a symbol on the top of the stack, δ has a value (q, γ) where $|\gamma| = 2$. For example, $\delta(q_1, 0, R) = \{(q_1, BR)\}$. If γ were of length one, the PDA would simply replace the top symbol by a new symbol and not increase the length of the stack. This allows us to let γ equal ϵ when we wish to pop the stack.

Note that the rule $\delta(q_2, \epsilon, R) = \{(q_2, \epsilon)\}$ means that the PDA, in state q_2 with R the top stack symbol, can erase the R independently of the input symbol. In this case, the input head is not advanced, and in fact, there need not be any remaining input.

$$M = (\{q_1, q_2\}, \{0, 1, c\}, \{R, B, G\}, \delta, q_1, R, \varnothing)$$

$\delta(q_1, 0, R) = \{(q_1, BR)\}$	$\delta(q_1, 1, R) = \{(q_1, GR)\}$
$\delta(q_1, 0, B) = \{(q_1, BB)\}$	$\delta(q_1, 1, B) = \{(q_1, GB)\}$
$\delta(q_1, 0, G) = \{(q_1, BG)\}$	$\delta(q_1, 1, G) = \{(q_1, GG)\}$
$\delta(q_1, c, R) = \{(q_2, R)\}$	
$\delta(q_1, c, B) = \{(q_2, B)\}$	
$\delta(q_1, c, G) = \{(q_2, G)\}$	
$\delta(q_2, 0, B) = \{(q_2, \epsilon)\}$	$\delta(q_2, 1, G) = \{(q_2, \epsilon)\}$
$\delta(q_2, \epsilon, R) = \{(q_2, \epsilon)\}$	

Fig. 5.2 Formal pushdown automaton accepting $\{wcw^R \,|\, w$ in $(0 + 1)^*\}$ by empty stack.

Instantaneous descriptions

To formally describe the configuration of a PDA at a given instant we define an *instantaneous description* (*ID*). The ID must, of course, record the state and stack contents. However, we find it useful to include the "unexpended input" as well. Thus we define an ID to be a triple (q, w, γ), where q is a state, w a string of input symbols, and γ a string of stack symbols. If $M = (Q, \Sigma, \Gamma, \delta, q_0, Z_0, F)$ is a PDA, we say $(q, aw, Z\alpha) \underset{M}{\vdash} (p, w, \beta\alpha)$ if $\delta(q, a, Z)$ contains (p, β). Note that a may be ϵ or an input symbol. For example, in the PDA of Fig. 5.2, the fact that (q_1, BG) is in $\delta(q_1, 0, G)$ tells us that $(q_1, 011, GGR) \vdash (q_1, 11, BGGR)$.

We use $\underset{M}{\overset{*}{\vdash}}$ for the reflexive and transitive closure of $\underset{M}{\vdash}$. That is, $I \overset{*}{\vdash} I$ for each ID I, and $I \underset{M}{\vdash} J$ and $J \underset{M}{\overset{*}{\vdash}} K$ imply $I \underset{M}{\overset{*}{\vdash}} K$. We write $I \overset{i}{\vdash} K$ if ID I can become K after exactly i moves. The subscript is dropped from $\underset{M}{\vdash}, \underset{M}{\overset{i}{\vdash}}$, and $\underset{M}{\overset{*}{\vdash}}$ whenever the particular PDA M is understood.

Accepted languages

For PDA $M = (Q, \Sigma, \Gamma, \delta, q_0, Z_0, F)$ we define $L(M)$, the *language accepted by final state*, to be

$$\{w \,|\, (q_0, w, Z_0) \overset{*}{\vdash} (p, \epsilon, \gamma) \text{ for some } p \text{ in } F \text{ and } \gamma \text{ in } \Gamma^*\}.$$

We define $N(M)$, the *language accepted by empty stack* (or *null stack*) to be

$$\{w \,|\, (q_0, w, Z_0) \overset{*}{\vdash} (p, \epsilon, \epsilon) \text{ for some } p \text{ in } Q\}.$$

When acceptance is by empty stack, the set of final states is irrelevant, and, in this case, we usually let the set of final states be the empty set.

Example 5.2 Figure 5.3 gives a PDA that accepts $\{ww^R \,|\, w \text{ in } (0 + 1)^*\}$. Rules (1) through (6) allow M to store the input on the stack. In rules (3) and (6), M has a choice of two moves. M may decide that the middle of the input string has been reached and make the second choice: M goes to state q_2 and tries to match the remaining input symbols with the contents of the stack. If M guessed right, and if the input is of the form ww^R, then the inputs will match, M will empty its stack and thus accept the input string.

$$M = (\{q_1, q_2\}, \{0, 1\}, \{R, B, G\}, \delta, q_1, R, \varnothing)$$

1) $\delta(q_1, 0, R) = \{(q_1, BR)\}$	6) $\delta(q_1, 1, G) = \{(q_1, GG), (q_2, \epsilon)\}$
2) $\delta(q_1, 1, R) = \{(q_1, GR)\}$	7) $\delta(q_2, 0, B) = \{(q_2, \epsilon)\}$
3) $\delta(q_1, 0, B) = \{(q_1, BB), (q_2, \epsilon)\}$	8) $\delta(q_2, 1, G) = \{(q_2, \epsilon)\}$
4) $\delta(q_1, 0, G) = \{(q_1, BG)\}$	9) $\delta(q_1, \epsilon, R) = \{(q_2, \epsilon)\}$
5) $\delta(q_1, 1, B) = \{(q_1, GB)\}$	10) $\delta(q_2, \epsilon, R) = \{(q_2, \epsilon)\}$

Fig. 5.3 A nondeterministic PDA that accepts $\{ww^R \,|\, w \text{ in } (0 + 1)^*\}$ by empty stack.

Like the nondeterministic finite automaton, a nondeterministic PDA M accepts an input if any sequence of choices causes M to empty its stack. Thus M always "guesses right," because wrong guesses, in themselves, do not cause an input to be rejected. An input is rejected only if there is no "right guess." Figure 5.4 shows the accessible ID's of M when M processes the string 001100.

Deterministic PDA's

The PDA of Example 5.1 is deterministic in the sense that at most one move is possible from any ID. Formally, we say that a PDA $M = (Q, \Sigma, \Gamma, \delta, q_0, Z_0, F)$, is

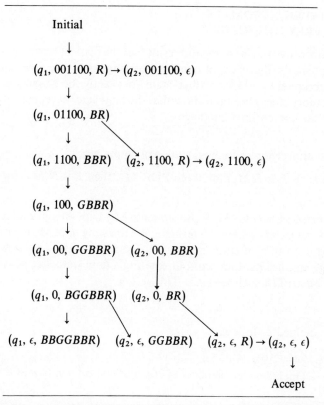

Initial

↓

$(q_1, 001100, R) \rightarrow (q_2, 001100, \epsilon)$

↓

$(q_1, 01100, BR)$

↓

$(q_1, 1100, BBR)$ $(q_2, 1100, R) \rightarrow (q_2, 1100, \epsilon)$

↓

$(q_1, 100, GBBR)$

↓

$(q_1, 00, GGBBR)$ $(q_2, 00, BBR)$

↓

$(q_1, 0, BGGBBR)$ $(q_2, 0, BR)$

↓

$(q_1, \epsilon, BBGGBBR)$ $(q_2, \epsilon, GGBBR)$ $(q_2, \epsilon, R) \rightarrow (q_2, \epsilon, \epsilon)$

↓

Accept

Fig. 5.4 Accessible ID's for the PDA of Fig. 5.3 with input 001100.

deterministic if:

1) for each q in Q and Z in Γ, whenever $\delta(q, \epsilon, Z)$ is nonempty, then $\delta(q, a, Z)$ is empty for all a in Σ;

2) for no q in Q, Z in Γ, and a in $\Sigma \cup \{\epsilon\}$ does $\delta(q, a, Z)$ contain more than one element.

Condition 1 prevents the possibility of a choice between a move independent of the input symbol (ϵ-move) and a move involving an input symbol. Condition 2 prevents a choice of move for any (q, a, Z) or (q, ϵ, Z). Note that unlike the finite automaton, a PDA is assumed to be nondeterministic unless we state otherwise.

For finite automata, the deterministic and nondeterministic models were equivalent with respect to the languages accepted. The same is not true for PDA. In fact ww^R is accepted by a nondeterministic PDA, but not by any deterministic PDA.

5.3   PUSHDOWN AUTOMATA AND CONTEXT-FREE LANGUAGES

We shall now prove the fundamental result that the class of languages accepted by PDA's is precisely the class of context-free languages. We first show that the languages accepted by PDA's by final state are exactly the languages accepted by PDA's by empty stack. We then show that the languages accepted by empty stack are exactly the context-free languages.

Equivalence of acceptance by final state and empty stack

Theorem 5.1   If L is $L(M_2)$ for some PDA M_2, then L is $N(M_1)$ for some PDA, M_1.

Proof   In brief, we would like M_1 to simulate M_2, with the option for M_1 to erase its stack whenever M_2 enters a final state. We use state q_e of M_1 to erase the stack, and we use a bottom of stack marker X_0 for M_1, so M_1 does not accidentally accept if M_2 empties its stack without entering a final state. Let $M_2 = (Q, \Sigma, \Gamma, \delta, q_0, Z_0, F)$ be a PDA such that $L = L(M_2)$. Let

$$M_1 = (Q \cup \{q_e, q_0'\}, \Sigma, \Gamma \cup \{X_0\}, \delta', q_0', X_0, \varnothing),$$

where δ' is defined as follows.

1) $\delta'(q_0', \epsilon, X_0) = \{(q_0, Z_0 X_0)\}$.
2) $\delta'(q, a, Z)$ includes the elements of $\delta(q, a, Z)$ for all q in Q, a in Σ or $a = \epsilon$, and Z in Γ.
3) For all q in F, and Z in $\Gamma \cup \{X_0\}$, $\delta'(q, \epsilon, Z)$ contains (q_e, ϵ).
4) For all Z in $\Gamma \cup \{X_0\}$, $\delta'(q_e, \epsilon, Z)$ contains (q_e, ϵ).

Rule (1) causes M_1 to enter the initial ID of M_2, except that M_1 will have its own bottom of the stack marker X_0, which is below the symbols of M_2's stack. Rule (2) allows M_1 to simulate M_2. Should M_2 ever enter a final state, rules (3) and (4) allow M_1 the choice of entering state q_e and erasing its stack, thereby accepting the input, or continuing to simulate M_2. One should note that M_2 may possibly erase its entire stack for some input x not in $L(M_2)$. This is the reason that M_1 has its own special bottom-of-stack marker. Otherwise M_1, in simulating M_2, would also erase its entire stack, thereby accepting x when it should not.

Let x be in $L(M_2)$. Then $(q_0, x, Z_0) \vdash^*_{M_2} (q, \epsilon, \gamma)$ for some q in F. Now consider M_1 with input x. By rule (1),

$$(q_0', x, X_0) \vdash^*_{M_1} (q_0, x, Z_0 X_0),$$

By rule (2), every move of M_2 is a legal move for M_1, thus

$$(q_0, x, Z_0) \vdash^*_{M_1} (q, \epsilon, \gamma).$$

If a PDA can make a sequence of moves from a given ID, it can make the same sequence of moves from any ID obtained from the first by inserting a fixed string of stack symbols below the original stack contents. Thus

$$(q_0', x, X_0) \vdash_{\overline{M_1}} (q_0, x, Z_0 X_0) \vdash_{\overline{M_1}}^{*} (q, \epsilon, \gamma X_0).$$

By rules (3) and (4),

$$(q, \epsilon, \gamma X_0) \vdash_{\overline{M_1}}^{*} (q_e, \epsilon, \epsilon).$$

Therefore,

$$(q_0', x, X_0) \vdash_{\overline{M_1}}^{*} (q_e, \epsilon, \epsilon),$$

and M_1 accepts x by empty stack.

Conversely, if M_1 accepts x by empty stack, it is easy to show that the sequence of moves must be one move by rule (1), then a sequence of moves by rule (2) in which M_1 simulates acceptance of x by M_2, followed by the erasure of M_1's stack using rules (3) and (4). Thus x must be in $L(M_2)$. ☐

Theorem 5.2 If L is $N(M_1)$ for some PDA M_1, then L is $L(M_2)$ for some PDA M_2.

Proof Our plan now is to have M_2 simulate M_1 and detect when M_1 empties its stack. M_2 enters a final state when and only when this occurs. Let $M_1 = (Q, \Sigma, \Gamma, \delta, q_0, Z_0, \varnothing)$ be a PDA such that $L = N(M_1)$. Let

$$M_2 = (Q \cup \{q_0', q_f\}, \Sigma, \Gamma \cup \{X_0\}, \delta', q_0', X_0, \{q_f\}),$$

where δ' is defined as follows:

1) $\delta'(q_0', \epsilon, X_0) = \{(q_0, Z_0 X_0)\}$.
2) For all q in Q, a in $\Sigma \cup \{\epsilon\}$, and Z in Γ,

$$\delta'(q, a, Z) = \delta(q, a, Z).$$

3) For all q in Q, $\delta'(q, \epsilon, X_0)$ contains (q_f, ϵ).

Rule (1) causes M_2 to enter the initial ID of M_1, except that M_2 will have its own bottom-of-stack marker X_0, which is below the symbols of M_1's stack. Rule (2) allows M_2 to simulate M_1. Should M_1 ever erase its entire stack, then M_2, when simulating M_1, will erase its entire stack except the symbol X_0 at the bottom. Rule (3) causes M_2, when the X_0 appears, to enter a final state, thereby accepting the input x. The proof that $L(M_2) = N(M_1)$ is similar to the proof of Theorem 5.1 and is left as an exercise. ☐

Equivalence of PDA's and CFL's

Theorem 5.3 If L is a context-free language, then there exists a PDA M such that $L = N(M)$.

Proof We assume that ϵ is not in $L(G)$. The reader may modify the construction for the case where ϵ is in $L(G)$. Let $G = (V, T, P, S)$ be a context-free grammar in Greibach normal form generating L. Let

$$M = (\{q\}, T, V, \delta, q, S, \varnothing),$$

where $\delta(q, a, A)$ contains (q, γ) whenever $A \to a\gamma$ is in P.

The PDA M simulates leftmost derivations of G. Since G is in Greibach normal form, each sentential form in a leftmost derivation consists of a string of terminals x followed by a string of variables α. M stores the suffix α of the left sentential form on its stack after processing the prefix x. Formally we show that

$$S \overset{*}{\Rightarrow} x\alpha \text{ by a leftmost derivation if and only if } (q, x, S) \overset{*}{\underset{M}{\vdash}} (q, \epsilon, \alpha). \quad (5.1)$$

First we suppose that $(q, x, S) \overset{i}{\vdash} (q, \epsilon, \alpha)$ and show by induction on i that $S \overset{*}{\Rightarrow} x\alpha$. The basis, $i = 0$, is trivial since $x = \epsilon$ and $\alpha = S$. For the induction, suppose $i \geq 1$, and let $x = ya$. Consider the next-to-last step,

$$(q, ya, S) \overset{i-1}{\vdash} (q, a, \beta) \vdash (q, \epsilon, \alpha). \quad (5.2)$$

If we remove a from the end of the input string in the first i ID's of the sequence (5.2), we discover that $(q, y, S) \overset{i-1}{\vdash} (q, \epsilon, \beta)$, since a can have no effect on the moves of M until it is actually consumed from the input. By the inductive hypothesis $S \overset{*}{\Rightarrow} y\beta$. The move $(q, a, \beta) \vdash (q, \epsilon, \alpha)$ implies that $\beta = A\gamma$ for some A in V, $A \to a\eta$ is a production of G and $\alpha = \eta\gamma$. Hence

$$S \overset{*}{\Rightarrow} y\beta \Rightarrow ya\eta\gamma = x\alpha,$$

and we conclude the "if" portion of (5.1).

Now suppose that $S \overset{i}{\Rightarrow} x\alpha$ by a leftmost derivation. We show by induction on i that $(q, x, S) \overset{*}{\vdash} (q, \epsilon, \alpha)$. The basis, $i = 0$, is again trivial. Let $i \geq 1$ and suppose

$$S \overset{i-1}{\Rightarrow} yA\gamma \Rightarrow ya\eta\gamma,$$

where $x = ya$ and $\alpha = \eta\gamma$. By the inductive hypothesis, $(q, y, S) \overset{*}{\vdash} (q, \epsilon, A\gamma)$ and thus $(q, ya, S) \overset{*}{\vdash} (q, a, A\gamma)$. Since $A \to a\eta$ is a production, it follows that $\delta(q, a, A)$ contains (q, η). Thus

$$(q, x, S) \overset{*}{\vdash} (q, a, A\gamma) \vdash (q, \epsilon, \alpha),$$

and the "only if" portion of (5.1) follows.

To conclude the proof, we have only to note that (5.1) with $\alpha = \epsilon$ says $S \overset{*}{\Rightarrow} x$ if and only if $(q, x, S) \overset{*}{\vdash} (q, \epsilon, \epsilon)$. That is, x is in $L(G)$ if and only if x is in $N(M)$. $\square$

Theorem 5.4 If L is $N(M)$ for some PDA M, then L is a context-free language.

Proof Let M be the PDA $(Q, \Sigma, \Gamma, \delta, q_0, Z_0, \varnothing)$. Let $G = (V, \Sigma, P, S)$ be a context-free grammar where V is the set of objects of the form $[q, A, p]$, q and p in

Q, and A in Γ, plus the new symbol S. P is the set of productions

1) $S \rightarrow [q_0, Z_0, q]$ for each q in Q;

2) $[q, A, q_{m+1}] \rightarrow a[q_1, B_1, q_2][q_2, B_2, q_3] \cdots [q_m, B_m, q_{m+1}]$ for each $q, q_1, q_2, \ldots,$ q_{m+1} in Q, each a in $\Sigma \cup \{\epsilon\}$, and $A, B_1, B_2, \ldots, B_m$ in Γ, such that $\delta(q, a, A)$ contains $(q_1, B_1 B_2 \cdots B_m)$. (If $m = 0$, then the production is $[q, A, q_1] \rightarrow a$.)

To understand the proof it helps to know that the variables and productions of G have been defined in such a way that a leftmost derivation in G of a sentence x is a simulation of the PDA M when fed the input x. In particular, the variables that appear in any step of a leftmost derivation in G correspond to the symbols on the stack of M at a time when M has seen as much of the input as the grammar has already generated. Put another way, the intention is that $[q, A, p]$ derive x if and only if x causes M to erase an A from its stack by some sequence of moves beginning in state q and ending in state p.

To show that $L(G) = N(M)$, we prove by induction on the number of steps in a derivation of G or number of moves of M that

$$[q, A, p] \overset{*}{\underset{G}{\Rightarrow}} x \qquad \text{if and only if} \qquad (q, x, A) \overset{*}{\underset{M}{\vdash}} (p, \epsilon, \epsilon). \qquad (5.3)$$

First we show by induction on i that if $(q, x, A) \overset{i}{\vdash} (p, \epsilon, \epsilon)$, then $[q, A, p] \overset{*}{\Rightarrow} x$. If $i = 1$, then $\delta(q, x, A)$ must contain (p, ϵ). (Here x is ϵ or a single input symbol.) Thus $[q, A, p] \rightarrow x$ is a production of G.

Now suppose $i > 1$. Let $x = ay$ and

$$(q, ay, A) \vdash (q_1, y, B_1 B_2 \cdots B_n) \overset{i-1}{\vdash} (p, \epsilon, \epsilon).$$

The string y can be written $y = y_1 y_2 \cdots y_n$, where y_j has the effect of popping B_j from the stack, possibly after a long sequence of moves. That is, let y_1 be the prefix of y at the end of which the stack first becomes as short as $n - 1$ symbols. Let y_2 be the symbols of y following y_1 such that at the end of y_2 the stack first becomes as short as $n - 2$ symbols, and so on. The arrangement is shown in Fig. 5.5. Note that B_1 need not be the nth stack symbol from the bottom during the entire time y_1 is being read by M, since B_1 may be changed if it is at the top of stack and is replaced by one or more symbols. However, none of $B_2 B_3 \cdots B_n$ are ever at the top while y_1 is being read and so cannot be changed or influence the computation. In general, B_j remains on the stack unchanged while $y_1 y_2 \cdots y_{j-1}$ is read.

There exist states $q_2, q_3, \ldots, q_{n+1}$, where $q_{n+1} = p$, such that

$$(q_j, y_j, B_j) \overset{*}{\vdash} (q_{j+1}, \epsilon, \epsilon)$$

by fewer than i moves (q_j is the state entered when the stack first becomes as short as $n - j + 1$). Thus the inductive hypothesis applies and

$$[q_j, B_j, q_{j+1}] \overset{*}{\Rightarrow} y_j \qquad \text{for} \quad 1 \le j \le n.$$

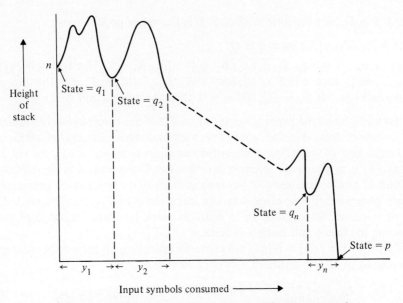

Fig. 5.5   Height of stack as a function of input consumed.

Recalling the original move $(q, ay, A) \vdash (q_1, y, B_1 B_2 \cdots B_n)$, we know that

$$[q, A, p] \Rightarrow a[q_1, B, q_2][q_2, B_2, q_3] \cdots [q_n, B_n, q_{n+1}],$$

so $[q, A, p] \overset{*}{\Rightarrow} ay_1 y_2 \cdots y_n = x$.

Now suppose $[q, A, p] \overset{i}{\Rightarrow} x$. We show by induction on i that $(q, x, A) \overset{*}{\vdash} (p, \epsilon, \epsilon)$. The basis, $i = 1$, is immediate, since $[q, A, p] \to x$ must be a production of G and therefore $\delta(q, x, A)$ must contain (p, ϵ). Note x is ϵ or in Σ here.

For the induction, suppose

$$[q, A, p] \Rightarrow a[q_1, B_1, q_2] \cdots [q_n, B_n, q_{n+1}] \overset{i-1}{\Rightarrow} x,$$

where $q_{n+1} = p$. Then we may write $x = ax_1 x_2 \cdots x_n$, where $[q_j, B_j, q_{j+1}] \overset{*}{\Rightarrow} x_j$ for $1 \leq j \leq n$, with each derivation taking fewer than i steps. By the inductive hypothesis, $(q_j, x_j, B_j) \overset{*}{\vdash} (q_{j+1}, \epsilon, \epsilon)$ for $1 \leq j \leq n$. If we insert $B_{j+1} \cdots B_n$ at the bottom of each stack in the above sequence of ID's we see that

$$(q_j, x_j, B_j B_{j+1} \cdots B_n) \overset{*}{\vdash} (q_{j+1}, \epsilon, B_{j+1} \cdots B_n). \tag{5.4}$$

From the first step in the derivation of x from $[q, A, p]$ we know that

$$(q, x, A) \vdash (q_1, x_1 x_2 \cdots x_n, B_1 B_2 \cdots B_n)$$

is a legal move of M, so from this move and (5.4) for $j = 1, 2, \ldots, n$, $(q, x, A) \overset{*}{\vdash} (p, \epsilon, \epsilon)$ follows.

The proof concludes with the observation that (5.3) with $q = q_0$ and $A = Z_0$ says

$$[q_0, Z_0, p] \overset{*}{\Rightarrow} x \qquad \text{if and only if} \qquad (q_0, x, Z_0) \overset{*}{\vdash} (p, \epsilon, \epsilon).$$

This observation, together with rule (1) of the construction of G, says that

$$S \overset{*}{\Rightarrow} x \qquad \text{if and only if} \qquad (q_0, x, Z_0) \overset{*}{\vdash} (p, \epsilon, \epsilon) \quad \text{for some state } p.$$

That is, x is in $L(G)$ if and only if x is in $N(M)$. $\qquad\qquad\qquad\qquad\square$

Example 5.3 Let

$$M = (\{q_0, q_1\}, \{0, 1\}, \{X, Z_0\}, \delta, q_0, Z_0, \varnothing),$$

where δ is given by

$$\delta(q_0, 0, Z_0) = \{(q_0, XZ_0)\}, \qquad \delta(q_1, 1, X) = \{(q_1, \epsilon)\},$$
$$\delta(q_0, 0, X) = \{(q_0, XX)\}, \qquad \delta(q_1, \epsilon, X) = \{(q_1, \epsilon)\},$$
$$\delta(q_0, 1, X) = \{(q_1, \epsilon)\}, \qquad \delta(q_1, \epsilon, Z_0) = \{(q_1, \epsilon)\}.$$

To construct a CFG $G = (V, T, P, S)$ generating $N(M)$ let

$$V = \{S, [q_0, X, q_0], [q_0, X, q_1], [q_1, X, q_0], [q_1, X, q_1],$$
$$[q_0, Z_0, q_0], [q_0, Z_0, q_1], [q_1, Z_0, q_0], [q_1, Z_0, q_1]\}$$

and $T = \{0, 1\}$. To construct the set of productions easily, we must realize that some variables may not appear in any derivation starting from the symbol S. Thus, we can save some effort if we start with the productions for S, then add productions only for those variables that appear on the right of some production already in the set. The productions for S are

$$S \to [q_0, Z_0, q_0]$$
$$S \to [q_0, Z_0, q_1]$$

Next we add productions for the variable $[q_0, Z_0, q_0]$. These are

$$[q_0, Z_0, q_0] \to 0[q_0, X, q_0][q_0, Z_0, q_0]$$
$$[q_0, Z_0, q_0] \to 0[q_0, X, q_1][q_1, Z_0, q_0]$$

These productions are required by $\delta(q_0, 0, Z_0) = \{(q_0, XZ_0)\}$. Next, the productions for $[q_0, Z_0, q_1]$ are

$$[q_0, Z_0, q_1] \to 0[q_0, X, q_0][q_0, Z_0, q_1]$$
$$[q_0, Z_0, q_1] \to 0[q_0, X, q_1][q_1, Z_0, q_1]$$

These are also required by $\delta(q_0, 0, Z_0) = \{(q_0, XZ_0)\}$. The productions for the remaining variables and the relevant moves of the PDA are:

1) $[q_0, X, q_0] \rightarrow 0[q_0, X, q_0][q_0, X, q_0]$
$[q_0, X, q_0] \rightarrow 0[q_0, X, q_1][q_1, X, q_0]$
$[q_0, X, q_1] \rightarrow 0[q_0, X, q_0][q_0, X, q_1]$
$[q_0, X, q_1] \rightarrow 0[q_0, X, q_1][q_1, X, q_1]$

       since $\delta(q_0, 0, X) = \{(q_0, XX)\}$.

2) $[q_0, X, q_1] \rightarrow 1$ since $\delta(q_0, 1, X) = \{(q_1, \epsilon)\}$.

3) $[q_1, Z_0, q_1] \rightarrow \epsilon$ since $\delta(q_1, \epsilon, Z_0) = \{(q_1, \epsilon)\}$.

4) $[q_1, X, q_1] \rightarrow \epsilon$ since $\delta(q_1, \epsilon, X) = \{(q_1, \epsilon)\}$.

5) $[q_1, X, q_1] \rightarrow 1$ since $\delta(q_1, 1, X) = \{(q_1, \epsilon)\}$.

It should be noted that there are no productions for the variables $[q_1, X, q_0]$ and $[q_1, Z_0, q_0]$. As all productions for $[q_0, X, q_0]$ and $[q_0, Z_0, q_0]$ have $[q_1, X, q_0]$ or $[q_1, Z_0, q_0]$ on the right, no terminal string can be derived from $[q_0, X, q_0]$ or $[q_0, Z_0, q_0]$ either. Deleting all productions involving one of these four variables on either the right or left, we end up with the following productions.

$$S \rightarrow [q_0, Z_0, q_1], \qquad\qquad [q_1, Z_0, q_1] \rightarrow \epsilon,$$
$$[q_0, Z_0, q_1] \rightarrow 0[q_0, X, q_1][q_1, Z_0, q_1], \qquad [q_1, X, q_1] \rightarrow \epsilon,$$
$$[q_1, X, q_1] \rightarrow 0[q_0, X, q_1][q_1, X, q_1], \qquad [q_1, X, q_1] \rightarrow 1.$$
$$[q_0, X, q_1] \rightarrow 1,$$

We summarize Theorems 5.1 through 5.4 as follows. The three statements below are equivalent:

1) L is a context-free language.
2) $L = N(M_1)$ for some PDA M_1.
3) $L = L(M_2)$ for some PDA M_2.

EXERCISES

5.1 Construct pushdown automata for each of the languages in Exercise 4.1.

5.2 Construct a PDA equivalent to the following grammar.

$$S \rightarrow aAA, \qquad A \rightarrow aS \,|\, bS \,|\, a.$$

5.3 Complete the proof of Theorem 5.3 by showing that every CFL L is the set accepted by some PDA even if ϵ is in L. [*Hint:* Add a second state to the PDA for $L - \{\epsilon\}$.]

5.4 Show that if L is a CFL, then there is a PDA M accepting L by final state such that M has at most two states and makes no ϵ-moves.

* **5.5**

a) Show that if L is a CFL, then L is $L(M)$ for some PDA M such that if $\delta(q, a, X)$ contains (p, γ), then $|\gamma| \le 2$.

b) Show that M of part (a) can be further restricted so that if $\delta(q, a, X)$ contains (p, γ), then γ is either ϵ (a pop move), X (no change to the stack), or YX for some stack symbol Y (a push move).

c) Can we put a bound on the number of states of M in part (a) and still have a PDA for any CFL?

d) Can we put a bound on the number of states in part (b)?

5.6   Give a grammar for the language $N(M)$ where

$$M = (\{q_0, q_1\}, \{0, 1\}, \{Z_0, X\}, \delta, q_0, Z_0, \varnothing)$$

and δ is given by

$$\delta(q_0, 1, Z_0) = \{(q_0, XZ_0)\}, \qquad \delta(q_0, \epsilon, Z_0) = \{(q_0, \epsilon)\},$$

$$\delta(q_0, 1, X) = \{(q_0, XX)\}, \qquad \delta(q_1, 1, X) = \{(q_1, \epsilon)\},$$

$$\delta(q_0, 0, X) = \{(q_1, X)\}, \qquad \delta(q_1, 0, Z_0) = \{(q_0, Z_0)\}.$$

5.7   The deterministic PDA (DPDA) is not equivalent to the nondeterministic PDA. For example, the language

$$L = \{0^n 1^n \mid n \ge 1\} \cup \{0^n 1^{2n} \mid n \ge 1\}$$

is a CFL that is not accepted by any DPDA.

a) Show that L is a CFL.

** b) Prove that L is not accepted by a DPDA.

5.8   A language L is said to have the *prefix property* if no word in L is a proper prefix of another word in L. Show that if L is $N(M)$ for DPDA M, then L has the prefix property. Is the foregoing necessarily true if L is $N(M)$ for a nondeterministic PDA M?

* **5.9**   Show that L is $N(M)$ for some DPDA M if and only if L is $L(M')$ for some DPDA M', and L has the prefix property.

5.10   A *two-way PDA* (2PDA) is a PDA that is permitted to move either way on its input. Like the two-way FA, it accepts by moving off the right end of its input in a final state. Show that $L = \{0^n 1^n 2^n \mid n \ge 1\}$ is accepted by a 2PDA. We shall show in the next chapter that L is not a CFL, by the way, so 2PDA's are not equivalent to PDA's.

*S **5.11**   Write a program to translate a regular expression to a finite automaton.

* **5.12**   The grammar

$$E \to E + E \mid E * E \mid (E) \mid \mathbf{id} \qquad (5.5)$$

generates the set of arithmetic expressions with $+$, $*$, parentheses and id in *infix* notation (operator between the operands). The grammar

$$P \to +PP \mid *PP \mid \mathbf{id}$$

generates the set of arithmetic expressions in *prefix* notation (operator precedes the operands). Construct a program to translate arithmetic expressions from infix to prefix notation using the following technique. Design a deterministic PDA that parses an infix expression according to the grammar in (5.5). For each vertex in the parse tree determine the necessary action to produce the desired prefix expression. [*Hint:* See the solution to Exercise 5.11.]

5.13 Construct a compiler for infix arithmetic expressions that produces an assembly language program to evaluate the expression. Assume the assembly language has the single address instructions: LOAD x (copy x to accumulator), ADD x (add x to accumulator), MULT x (multiply contents of the accumulator by x) and STO x (store the contents of the accumulator in x).

Solutions to Selected Exercises

5.11 Writing a program to translate a regular expression to a finite automaton can be thought of as constructing a rudimentary compiler. We have already seen (Theorem 2.3) that finite automata accepting $\varnothing$, ϵ, 0, and 1 can be combined to obtain an automaton equivalent to a given regular expression. The only problem is parsing the regular expression to determine the order in which to combine the automata.

Our first step is to construct a CFG for the set of regular expressions. The next step is to write a parser and finally the automaton-generating routines.

A grammar for regular expressions that groups subexpressions according to the conventional precedence of operations is given below. Note that ϵ is used for the symbol ϵ.

$$E \to P + E \,|\, P$$
$$P \to T \cdot P \,|\, T$$
$$T \to 0 \,|\, 1 \,|\, \epsilon \,|\, \varnothing \,|\, T* \,|\, (E)$$

The parsing routine is constructed directly from the grammar by writing a procedure for each variable. A global variable STRING initially contains the following regular expression.

```
procedure FIND_EXPRESSION;
begin
     FIND_PRODUCT;
     while first symbol of STRING is + do
     begin
          delete first symbol of STRING;
          FIND_PRODUCT
     end;
end FIND_EXPRESSION;
procedure FIND_PRODUCT;
begin
     FIND_TERM;
     while first symbol of STRING is · do
          begin
               delete first symbol of STRING;
               FIND_TERM
          end
end FIND_PRODUCT;
```

procedure FIND_TERM;
begin
    if first symbol of STRING is 0, 1, ϵ, or $\emptyset$ **then**
        delete first symbol of STRING;
    else if first symbol of STRING is (**then**
        begin
            delete first symbol of STRING;
            FIND_EXPRESSION;
            if first symbol of STRING is) **then**
                delete first symbol of STRING
            else error
        end
    while first symbol of STRING is * **do**
        delete first symbol of STRING
end FIND_TERM

The actual parsing program consists of a single procedure call:

FIND_EXPRESSION;

Note that the recursive procedures FIND_EXPRESSION, FIND_PRODUCT, and FIND_TERM have no local variables. Thus they may be implemented by a stack that pushes E, P, or T, respectively, when a procedure is called, and pops the symbol when the procedure returns. (Although FIND_EXPRESSION has two calls to FIND_PRODUCT, both calls return to the same point in FIND_EXPRESSION. Thus the return location need not be stored. Similar comments apply to FIND_PRODUCT). Thus, a deterministic PDA suffices to execute the program we have defined.

Having developed a procedure to parse a regular expression, we now add statements to output a finite automaton. Each procedure is modified to return a finite automaton. In procedure FIND_TERM, if the input symbol is 0, 1, ϵ, or $\emptyset$, a finite automaton accepting 0, 1, ϵ, or $\emptyset$ is created and FIND_TERM returns this automaton. If the input symbol is (, then the finite automaton returned by FIND_EXPRESSION is the value of FIND_TERM. In either case, if the while loop for * is executed, the automaton is modified to accept the closure.

In procedure FIND_PRODUCT, the value of FIND_PRODUCT is assigned the value of the first call of FIND_TERM. Each time the "while" statement is executed, the value of FIND_PRODUCT is set to an automaton accepting the concatenation of the sets accepted by the current value of FIND_PRODUCT and the automaton returned by the call to FIND_TERM in the "while" loop. Similar statements are added to the procedure FIND_EXPRESSION.

BIBLIOGRAPHIC NOTES

The pushdown automaton appears as a formal construction in Oettinger [1961] and Schutzenberger [1963]. Its equivalence to context-free grammars was perceived by Chomsky [1962] and Evey [1963].

A variety of similar devices have been studied. *Counter machines* have only one pushdown symbol, with the exception of a bottom-of-stack marker. They are discussed in

Fischer [1966], and Fischer, Meyer, and Rosenberg [1968]; see also the bibliographic notes to Chapter 7. *Pushdown transducers* are PDA's that may print symbols at each move. They have been studied by Evey [1963], Fischer [1963], Ginsburg and Rose [1966], Ginsburg and Greibach [1966b], and Lewis and Stearns [1968].

The two-way PDA mentioned in Exercise 5.10 has been studied by Hartmanis, Lewis, and Stearns [1965]. Its closure properties were considered by Gray, Harrison, and Ibarra [1967], and characterizations of the class of languages accepted by the deterministic (2DPDA) and nondeterministic (2NPDA) varieties have been given by Aho, Hopcroft, and Ullman [1968], and Cook [1971c]. The latter contains the remarkable result that any language accepted by a 2DPDA is recognizable in linear time on a computer. Thus, the existence of a CFL requiring more than linear time to recognize on a computer, would imply that there are CFL's not accepted by 2DPDA's. However, no one to date has proved that such a language exists. Incidentally, the language $\{0^n 1^n 2^n \mid n \geq 1\}$ is an example of a non-CFL accepted by a 2DPDA.

CHAPTER

6

PROPERTIES OF
CONTEXT-FREE
LANGUAGES

To a large extent this chapter parallels Chapter 3. We shall first give a pumping lemma for context-free languages and use it to show that certain languages are not context free. We then consider closure properties of CFL's and finally we give algorithms to answer certain questions about CFL's.

6.1 THE PUMPING LEMMA FOR CFL's

The pumping lemma for regular sets states that every sufficiently long string in a regular set contains a short substring that can be pumped. That is, inserting as many copies of the substring as we like always yields a string in the regular set. The pumping lemma for CFL's states that there are always two short substrings close together that can be repeated, both the same number of times, as often as we like. The formal statement of the pumping lemma is as follows.

Lemma 6.1 (The pumping lemma for context-free languages). Let L be any CFL. Then there is a constant n, depending only on L, such that if z is in L and $|z| \geq n$, then we may write $z = uvwxy$ such that

1) $|vx| \geq 1$,
2) $|vwx| \leq n$, and
3) for all $i \geq 0$ uv^iwx^iy is in L.

Proof Let G be a Chomsky normal-form grammar generating $L - \{\epsilon\}$. Observe that if z is in $L(G)$ and z is long, then any parse tree for z must contain a long path. More precisely, we show by induction on i that if the parse tree of a word

125

generated by a Chomsky normal-form grammar has no path of length greater than i, then the word is of length no greater than 2^{i-1}. The basis, $i = 1$, is trivial, since the tree must be of the form shown in Fig. 6.1(a). For the induction step, let $i > 1$. Let the root and its sons be as shown in Fig. 6.1(b). If there are no paths of length greater than $i - 1$ in trees T_1 and T_2, then the trees generate words of 2^{i-2} or fewer symbols. Thus the entire tree generates a word no longer than 2^{i-1}

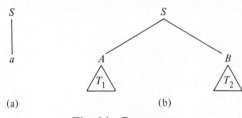

(a)   (b)

Fig. 6.1   Parse trees.

Let G have k variables and let $n = 2^k$. If z is in $L(G)$ and $|z| \geq n$, then since $|z| > 2^{k-1}$, any parse tree for z must have a path of length at least $k + 1$. But such a path has at least $k + 2$ vertices, all but the last of which are labeled by variables. Thus there must be some variable that appears twice on the path.

We can in fact say more. Some variable must appear twice near the bottom of the path. In particular, let P be a path that is as long or longer than any path in the tree. Then there must be two vertices v_1 and v_2 on the path satisfying the following conditions.

1) The vertices v_1 and v_2 both have the same label, say A.

2) Vertex v_1 is closer to the root than vertex v_2.

3) The portion of the path from v_1 to the leaf is of length at most $k + 1$.

To see that v_1 and v_2 can always be found, just proceed up path P from the leaf, keeping track of the labels encountered. Of the first $k + 2$ vertices, only the leaf has a terminal label. The remaining $k + 1$ vertices cannot have distinct variable labels.

Now the subtree T_1 with root v_1 represents the derivation of a subword of length at most 2^k. This is true because there can be no path in T_1 of length greater than $k + 1$, since P was a path of longest length in the entire tree. Let z_1 be the yield of the subtree T_1. If T_2 is the subtree generated by vertex v_2, and z_2 is the yield of the subtree T_2, then we can write z_1 as $z_3 z_2 z_4$. Furthermore, z_3 and z_4 cannot both be ϵ, since the first production used in the derivation of z_1 must be of the form $A \rightarrow BC$ for some variables B and C. The subtree T_2 must be completely within either the subtree generated by B or the subtree generated by C. The above is illustrated in Fig. 6.2.

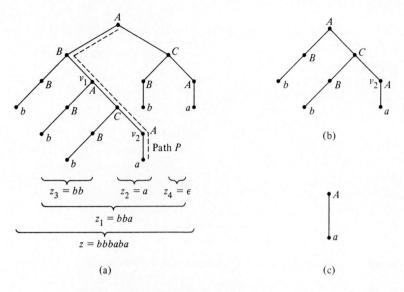

$z_1 = z_3 z_2 z_4$, where $z_3 = bb$ and $z_4 = \epsilon$

$G = (\{A, B, C\}, \{a, b\}, \{A \rightarrow BC, B \rightarrow BA, C \rightarrow BA, A \rightarrow a, B \rightarrow b\}, A)$

Fig. 6.2 Illustration of subtrees T_1 and T_2 of Lemma 6.1. (a) Tree. (b) Subtree T_1. (c) Subtree T_2.

We now know that

$$A \underset{G}{\overset{*}{\Rightarrow}} z_3 A z_4 \quad \text{and} \quad A \overset{*}{\Rightarrow} z_2, \quad \text{where} \quad |z_3 z_2 z_4| \leq 2^k = n.$$

But it follows that $A \underset{G}{\overset{*}{\Rightarrow}} z_3^i z_2 z_4^i$ for each $i \geq 0$. (See Fig. 6.3.) The string z can clearly be written as $u z_3 z_2 z_4 y$, for some u and y. We let $z_3 = v$, $z_2 = w$, and $z_4 = x$, to complete the proof. $\quad\square$

Applications of the pumping lemma

The pumping lemma can be used to prove a variety of languages not to be context free, using the same "adversary" argument as for the regular set pumping lemma.

Example 6.1 Consider the language $L_1 = \{a^i b^i c^i \mid i \geq 1\}$. Suppose L were context free and let n be the constant of Lemma 6.1. Consider $z = a^n b^n c^n$. Write $z = uvwxy$ so as to satisfy the conditions of the pumping lemma. We must ask ourselves where v and x, the strings that get pumped, could lie in $a^n b^n c^n$. Since $|vwx| \leq n$, it is not possible for vx to contain instances of a's and c's, because the rightmost a is $n + 1$ positions away from the leftmost c. If v and x consist of a's only, then uwy (the string $uv^i wx^i y$ with $i = 0$) has n b's and n c's but fewer than n a's, since $|vx| \geq 1$.

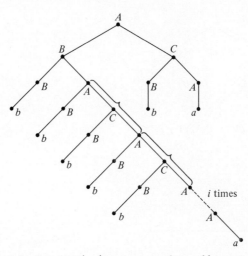

Fig. 6.3   The derivation of uv^iwx^iy, where $u = b$, $v = bb$, $w = a$, $x = \epsilon$, $y = ba$.

Thus, uwy is not of the form $a^jb^jc^j$. But by the pumping lemma vwy is in L_1, a contradiction.

The cases where v and x consist only of b's or only of c's are disposed of similarly. If vx has a's and b's, then uwy has more c's than a's or b's, and again it is not in L_1. If vx contains b's and c's, a similar contradiction results. We conclude that L_1 is not a context-free language.

The pumping lemma can also be used to show that certain languages similar to L_1 are not context free. Some examples are

$$\{a^ib^ic^j \mid j \geq i\} \quad \text{and} \quad \{a^ib^jc^k \mid i \leq j \leq k\}.$$

Another type of relationship that CFG's cannot enforce is illustrated in the next example.

Example 6.2   Let $L_2 = \{a^ib^jc^id^j \mid i \geq 1 \text{ and } j \geq 1\}$. Suppose L_2 is a CFL, and let n be the constant in Lemma 6.1. Consider the string $z = a^nb^nc^nd^n$. Let $z = uvwxy$ satisfy the conditions of the pumping lemma. Then as $|vwx| \leq n$, vx can contain at most two different symbols. Furthermore, if vx contains two different symbols, they must be consecutive, for example, a and b. If vx has only a's, then uwy has fewer a's than c's and is not in L_2, a contradiction. We proceed similarly if vx consists of only b's, only c's, or only d's. Now suppose vx has a's and b's. Then vwy still has fewer a's than c's. A similar contradiction occurs if vx consists of b's and c's or c's and d's. Since these are the only possibilities, we conclude that L_2 is not context free.

Ogden's lemma

There are certain non-CFL's for which the pumping lemma is of no help. For example,

$$L_3 = \{a^i b^j c^k d^\ell | \text{either } i = 0 \text{ or } j = k = \ell\}$$

is not context free. However, if we choose $z = b^j c^k d^\ell$, and write $z = uvwxy$, then it is always possible to choose u, v, w, x, and y so that $uv^m wx^m y$ is in L_3 for all m. For example, choose vwx to have only b's. If we choose $z = a^i b^j c^j d^j$, then v and x might consist only of a's, in which case $uv^m wx^m y$ is again in L_3 for all m.

What we need is a stronger version of the pumping lemma that allows us to focus on some small number of positions in the string and pump them. Such an extension is easy for regular sets, as any sequence of $n + 1$ states of an n-state FA must contain some state twice, and the intervening string can be pumped. The result for CFL's is much harder to obtain but can be shown. Here we state and prove a weak version of what is known as Ogden's lemma.

Lemma 6.2 (Ogden's lemma). Let L be a CFL. Then there is a constant n (which may in fact be the same as for the pumping lemma) such that if z is any word in L, and we mark any n or more positions of z "distinguished," then we can write $z = uvwxy$, such that:

1) v and x together have at least one distinguished position,
2) vwx has at most n distinguished positions, and
3) for all $i \geq 0$, $uv^i wx^i y$ is in L.

Proof Let G be a Chomsky normal-form grammar generating $L - \{\epsilon\}$. Let G have k variables and choose $n = 2^k + 1$. We must construct a path P in the tree analogous to path P in the proof of the pumping lemma. However, since we worry only about distinguished positions here, we cannot concern ourselves with every vertex along P, but only with *branch points*, which are vertices both of whose sons have distinguished descendants.

Construct P as follows. Begin by putting the root on path P. Suppose r is the last vertex placed on P. If r is a leaf, we end. If r has only one son with distinguished descendants, add that son to P and repeat the process there. If both sons of r have distinguished descendants, call r a branch point and add the son with the larger number of distinguished descendants to P (break a tie arbitrarily). This process is illustrated in Fig. 6.4.

It follows that each branch point on P has at least half as many distinguished descendants as the previous branch point. Since there are at least n distinguished positions in z, and all of these are descendants of the root, it follows that there are at least $k + 1$ branch points on P. Thus among the last $k + 1$ branch points are two with the same label. We may select v_1 and v_2 to be two of these branch points with the same label and with v_1 closer to the root than v_2. The proof then proceeds exactly as for the pumping lemma. □

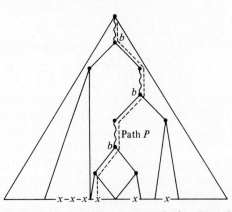

Fig. 6.4   The path P. Distinguished positions are marked x. Branch points are marked b.

Example 6.3   Let $L_4 = \{a^i b^j c^k \,|\, i \neq j, j \neq k \text{ and } i \neq k\}$. Suppose L_4 were a context-free language. Let n be the constant in Ogden's lemma and consider the string $z = a^n b^{n+n!} c^{n+2n!}$. Let the positions of the a's be distinguished and let $z = uvwxy$ satisfy the conditions of Ogden's lemma. If either v or x contains two distinct symbols, then uv^2wx^2y is not in L_4. (For example, if v is in $a^+ b^+$, then uv^2wx^2y has a b preceding an a.) Now at least one of v and x must contain a's since only a's are in distinguished positions. Thus, if x is in b^* or c^*, v must be in a^+. If x is in a^+, then v must be in a^*, otherwise a b or c would precede an a. We consider in detail the situation where x is in b^*. The other cases are handled similarly. Suppose x is in b^* and v in a^+. Let $p = |v|$. Then $1 \leq p \leq n$, so p divides $n!$ Let q be the integer such that $pq = n!$ Then

$$z' = uv^{2q+1}wx^{2q+1}y$$

is in L_4. But $v^{2q+1} = a^{2pq+p} = a^{2n!+p}$. Since uwy contains exactly $(n-p)$ a's, z' has $(2n!+n)$ a's. However, since v and x have no c's, z' also has $(2n!+n)$ c's and hence is not in L_4, a contradiction. A similar contradiction occurs if x is in a^+ or c^*. Thus L_4 is not a context-free language.

Note that Lemma 6.1 is a special case of Ogden's lemma in which all positions are distinguished.

6.2   CLOSURE PROPERTIES OF CFL's

We now consider some operations that preserve context-free languages. The operations are useful not only in constructing or proving that certain languages are context free, but also in proving certain languages not to be context free. A given language L can be shown not to be context free by constructing from L a language that is not context free using only operations preserving CFL's.

Theorem 6.1 Context-free languages are closed under union, concatenation and Kleene closure.

Proof Let L_1 and L_2 be CFL's generated by the CFG's

$$G_1 = (V_1, T_1, P_1, S_1) \quad \text{and} \quad G_2 = (V_2, T_2, P_2, S_2),$$

respectively. Since we may rename variables at will without changing the language generated, we assume that V_1 and V_2 are disjoint. Assume also that S_3, S_4, and S_5 are not in V_1 or V_2.

For $L_1 \cup L_2$ construct grammar $G_3 = (V_1 \cup V_2 \cup \{S_3\}, T_1 \cup T_2, P_3, S_3)$, where P_3 is $P_1 \cup P_2$ plus the productions $S_3 \to S_1 | S_2$. If w is in L_1, then the derivation $S_3 \underset{G_3}{\Rightarrow} S_1 \underset{G_1}{\overset{*}{\Rightarrow}} w$ is a derivation in G_3, as every production of G_1 is a production of G_3. Similarly, every word in L_2 has a derivation in G_3 beginning with $S_3 \Rightarrow S_2$. Thus $L_1 \cup L_2 \subseteq L(G_3)$. For the converse, let w be in $L(G_3)$. Then the derivation $S_3 \underset{G_3}{\overset{*}{\Rightarrow}} w$ begins with either $S_3 \underset{G_3}{\Rightarrow} S_1 \underset{G_3}{\overset{*}{\Rightarrow}} w$ or $S_3 \underset{G_3}{\Rightarrow} S_2 \underset{G_3}{\overset{*}{\Rightarrow}} w$. In the former case, as V_1 and V_2 are disjoint, only symbols of G_1 may appear in the derivation $S_1 \underset{G_3}{\overset{*}{\Rightarrow}} w$. As the only productions of P_3 that involve only symbols of G_1 are those from P_1, we conclude that only productions of P_1 are used in the derivation $S_1 \underset{G_3}{\overset{*}{\Rightarrow}} w$. Thus $S_1 \underset{G_1}{\overset{*}{\Rightarrow}} w$, and w is in L_1. Analogously, if the derivation starts $S_3 \underset{G_3}{\Rightarrow} S_2$, we may conclude w is in L_2. Hence $L(G_3) \subseteq L_1 \cup L_2$, so $L(G_3) = L_1 \cup L_2$, as desired.

For concatenation, let $G_4 = (V_1 \cup V_2 \cup \{S_4\}, T_1 \cup T_2, P_4, S_4)$, where P_4 is $P_1 \cup P_2$ plus the production $S_4 \to S_1 S_2$. A proof that $L(G_4) = L(G_1)L(G_2)$ is similar to the proof for union and is omitted.

For closure, let $G_5 = (V_1 \cup \{S_5\}, T_1, P_5, S_5)$, where P_5 is P_1 plus the productions $S_5 \to S_1 S_5 | \epsilon$. We again leave the proof that $L(G_5) = L(G_1)^*$ to the reader.

$\square$

Substitution and homomorphisms

Theorem 6.2 The context-free languages are closed under substitution.

Proof Let L be a CFL, $L \subseteq \Sigma^*$, and for each a in Σ let L_a be a CFL. Let L be $L(G)$ and for each a in Σ let L_a be $L(G_a)$. Without loss of generality assume that the variables of G and the G_a's are disjoint. Construct a grammar G' as follows. The variables of G' are all the variables of G and the G_a's; the terminals of G' are the terminals of the G_a's. The start symbol of G' is the start symbol of G. The productions of G' are all the productions of the G_a's together with those productions formed by taking a production $A \to \alpha$ of G and substituting S_a, the start symbol of G_a, for each instance of an a in Σ appearing in α. $\square$

Example 6.4 Let L be the set of words with an equal number of a's and b's, $L_a = \{0^n 1^n \mid n \geq 1\}$ and $L_b = \{ww^R \mid w \text{ is in } (0 + 2)^*\}$. For G we may choose

$$S \to aSbS \mid bSaS \mid \epsilon$$

For G_a take

$$S_a \to 0S_a 1 \,|\, 01$$

For G_b take

$$S_b \to 0S_b 0 \,|\, 2S_b 2 \,|\, \epsilon$$

If f is the substitution $f(a) = L_a$ and $f(b) = L_b$, then $f(L)$ is generated by the grammar

$$S \to S_a SS_b S \,|\, S_b SS_a S \,|\, \epsilon$$

$$S_a \to 0S_a 1 \,|\, 01$$

$$S_b \to 0S_b 0 \,|\, 2S_b 2 \,|\, \epsilon$$

One should observe that since $\{a, b\}$, $\{ab\}$, and $\mathbf{a}^*$ are CFL's, the closure of CFL's under substitution implies closure under union, concatenation, and $*$. The union of L_a and L_b is simply the substitution of L_a and L_b into $\{a, b\}$ and similarly $L_a L_b$ and L_a^* are the substitutions into $\{ab\}$ and $\mathbf{a}^*$, respectively. Thus Theorem 6.1 could be presented as a corollary of Theorem 6.2.

Since a homomorphism is a special type of substitution we state the following corollary.

Corollary   The CFL's are closed under homomorphism.

Theorem 6.3   The context-free languages are closed under inverse homomorphism.

Proof   As with regular sets, a machine-based proof for closure under inverse homomorphism is easiest to understand. Let $h: \Sigma \to \Delta$ be a homomorphism and L be a CFL. Let $L = L(M)$, where M is the PDA $(Q, \Delta, \Gamma, \delta, q_0, Z_0, F)$. In analogy with the finite-automaton construction of Theorem 3.5, we construct PDA M' accepting $h^{-1}(L)$ as follows. On input a, M' generates the string $h(a)$ and simulates M on $h(a)$. If M' were a finite automaton, all it could do on a string $h(a)$ would be to change state, so M' could simulate such a composite move in one of its moves. However, in the PDA case, M could pop many symbols on a string, or, since it is nondeterministic, make moves that push an arbitrary number of symbols on the stack. Thus M' cannot necessarily simulate M's moves on $h(a)$ with one (or any finite number of) moves of its own.

What we do is give M' a buffer, in which it may store $h(a)$. Then M' may simulate any ϵ-moves of M it likes and consume the symbols of $h(a)$ one at a time, as if they were M's input. As the buffer is part of M''s finite control, it cannot be allowed to grow arbitrarily long. We ensure that it does not, by permitting M' to read an input symbol only when the buffer is empty. Thus the buffer holds a suffix of $h(a)$ for some a at all times. M' accepts its input w if the buffer is empty and M is in a final state. That is, M has accepted $h(w)$. Thus $L(M') = \{w \,|\, h(w) \text{ is in } L\}$, that is

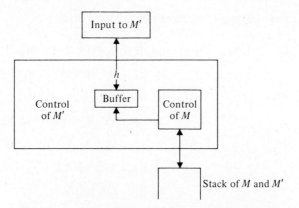

Fig. 6.5 Construction of a PDA accepting $h^{-1}(L)$.

$L(M') = h^{-1}(L(M))$. The arrangement is depicted in Fig. 6.5; the formal construction follows.

Let $M' = (Q', \Sigma, \Gamma, \delta', [q_0, \epsilon], Z_0, F \times \{\epsilon\})$, where Q' consists of pairs $[q, x]$ such that q is in Q and x is a (not necessarily proper) suffix of some $h(a)$ for a in Σ. δ' is defined as follows:

1) $\delta'([q, x], \epsilon, Y)$ contains all $([p, x], \gamma)$ such that $\delta(q, \epsilon, Y)$ contains (p, γ). Simulate ϵ-moves of M independent of the buffer contents.

2) $\delta'([q, ax], \epsilon, Y)$ contains all $([p, x], \gamma)$ such that $\delta(q, a, Y)$ contains (p, γ). Simulate moves of M on input a in Δ, removing a from the front of the buffer.

3) $\delta'([q, \epsilon], a, Y)$ contains $([q, h(a)], Y)$ for all a in Σ and Y in Γ. Load the buffer with $h(a)$, reading a from M''s input; the state and stack of M remain unchanged.

To show that $L(M') = h^{-1}(L(M))$ first observe that by one application of rule (3), followed by applications of rules (1) and (2), if $(q, h(a), \alpha) \vdash_M^* (p, \epsilon, \beta)$, then

$$([q, \epsilon], a, \alpha) \vdash_{M'} ([q, h(a)], \epsilon, \alpha) \vdash_{M'}^* ([p, \epsilon], \epsilon, \beta).$$

Thus if M accepts $h(w)$, that is,

$$(q_0, h(w), Z_0) \vdash_M^* (p, \epsilon, \beta)$$

for some p in F and β in Γ^*, it follows that

$$([q_0, \epsilon], w, Z_0) \vdash_{M'}^* ([p, \epsilon], \epsilon, \beta),$$

so M' accepts w. Thus $L(M') \supseteq h^{-1}(L(M))$.

Conversely, suppose M' accepts $w = a_1 a_2 \cdots a_n$. Then since rule (3) can be applied only with the buffer (second component of M''s state) empty, the sequence of the moves of M' leading to acceptance can be written

$$([q_0, \epsilon], a_1 a_2 \cdots a_n, Z_0) \overset{*}{\underset{M'}{\vdash}} ([p_1, \epsilon], a_1 a_2 \cdots a_n, \alpha_1),$$
$$\underset{M'}{\vdash} ([p_1, h(a_1)], a_2 a_3 \cdots a_n, \alpha_1),$$
$$\overset{*}{\underset{M'}{\vdash}} ([p_2, \epsilon], a_2 a_3 \cdots a_n, \alpha_2),$$
$$\underset{M'}{\vdash} ([p_2, h(a_2)], a_3 a_4 \cdots a_n, \alpha_2),$$
$$\vdots$$
$$\overset{*}{\underset{M'}{\vdash}} ([p_{n-1}, \epsilon], a_n, \alpha_n),$$
$$\underset{M'}{\vdash} ([p_{n-1}, h(a_n)], \epsilon, \alpha_n),$$
$$\overset{*}{\underset{M'}{\vdash}} ([p_n, \epsilon], \epsilon, \alpha_{n+1}),$$

where p_n is in F. The transitions from state $[p_i, \epsilon]$ to $[p_i, h(a_i)]$ are by rule (3), the other transitions are by rules (1) and (2). Thus, $(q_0, \epsilon, Z_0) \overset{*}{\underset{M}{\vdash}} (p_1 \epsilon, \alpha_1)$, and for all i,

$$(p_i, h(a_i), \alpha_i) \overset{*}{\underset{M}{\vdash}} (p_{i+1}, \epsilon, \alpha_{i+1}).$$

Putting these moves together, we have

$$(q_0, h(a_1 a_2 \cdots a_n), Z_0) \overset{*}{\underset{M}{\vdash}} (p_n, \epsilon, \alpha_{n+1}),$$

so $h(a_1 a_2 \cdots a_n)$ is in $L(M)$. Hence $L(M') \subseteq h^{-1}(L(M))$, whereupon we conclude $L(M') = h^{-1}(L(M))$. $\square$

Boolean operations

There are several closure properties of regular sets that are not possessed by the context-free languages. Notable among these are closure under intersection and complementation.

Theorem 6.4   The CFL's are not closed under intersection.

Proof   In Example 6.1 we showed the language $L_1 = \{a^i b^i c^i \mid i \geq 1\}$ was not a CFL. We claim that $L_2 = \{a^i b^i c^j \mid i \geq 1 \text{ and } j \geq 1\}$ and $L_3 = \{a^i b^j c^j \mid i \geq 1 \text{ and } j \geq 1\}$ are both CFL's. For example, a PDA to recognize L_2 stores the a's on its stack and cancels them against b's, then accepts its input after seeing one or more c's. Alternatively L_2 is generated by the grammar

$$S \to AB$$
$$A \to aAb \mid ab$$
$$B \to cB \mid c$$

where A generates $a^i b^i$ and B generates c^j. A similar grammar

$$S \to CD$$
$$C \to aC \,|\, a$$
$$D \to bDc \,|\, bc$$

generates L_3.

However, $L_2 \cap L_3 = L_1$. If the CFL's were closed under intersection, L_1 would thus be a CFL, contradicting Example 6.1. $\square$

Corollary The CFL's are not closed under complementation.

Proof We know the CFL's are closed under union. If they were closed under complementation, they would, by DeMorgan's law, $L_1 \cap L_2 = \overline{\overline{L_1} \cup \overline{L_2}}$ be closed under intersection, contradicting Theorem 6.4. $\square$

Although the class of CFL's is not closed under intersection it is closed under intersection with a regular set.

Theorem 6.5 If L is a CFL and R is a regular set, then $L \cap R$ is a CFL.

Proof Let L be $L(M)$ for PDA $M = (Q_M, \Sigma, \Gamma, \delta_M, q_0, Z_0, F_M)$, and let R be $L(A)$ for DFA $A = (Q_A, \Sigma, \delta_A, p_0, F_A)$. We construct a PDA M' for $L \cap R$ by "running M and A in parallel," as shown in Fig. 6.6. M' simulates moves of M on input ϵ without changing the state of A. When M' makes a move on input symbol a, M simulates that move and also simulates A's change of state on input a. M' accepts if and only if both A and M accept. Formally, let

$$M' = (Q_A \times Q_M, \Sigma, \Gamma, \delta, [p_0, q_0], Z_0, F_A \times F_M),$$

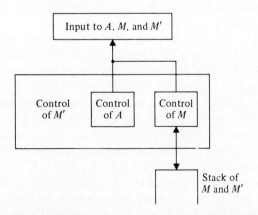

Fig. 6.6 Running an FA and a PDA in parallel.

where δ is defined by $\delta([p, q], a, X)$, contains $([p', q'], \gamma)$ if and only if $\delta_A(p, a) = p'$, and $\delta_M(q, a, X)$ contains (q', γ). Note that a may be ϵ, in which case $p' = p$.

An easy induction on i shows that

$$([p_0, q_0], w, Z_0) \mathrel{\vert\frac{i}{M'}} ([p, q], \epsilon, \gamma)$$

if and only if

$$(q_0, w, Z_0) \mathrel{\vert\frac{i}{M}} (q, \epsilon, \gamma) \qquad \text{and} \qquad \delta(p_0, w) = p.$$

The basis, $i = 0$, is trivial, since $p = p_0$, $q = q_0$, $\gamma = Z_0$, and $w = \epsilon$. For the induction, assume the statement for $i - 1$, and let

$$([p_0, q_0], xa, Z_0) \mathrel{\vert\frac{i-1}{M'}} ([p', q'], a, \beta) \mathrel{\overline{M'}} ([p, q], \epsilon, \gamma),$$

where $w = xa$, and a is ϵ or a symbol of Σ. By the inductive hypothesis,

$$\delta_A(p_0, x) = p' \qquad \text{and} \qquad (q_0, x, Z_0) \mathrel{\vert\frac{i-1}{M}} (q', \epsilon, \beta).$$

By the definition of δ, the fact that $([p', q'], a, \beta) \mathrel{\vert_{\overline{M'}}} ([p, q], \epsilon, \gamma)$ tells us that $\delta_A(p', a) = p$ and $(q', a, \beta) \mathrel{\vert_{\overline{M}}} (q, \epsilon, \gamma)$. Thus $\delta_A(p_0, w) = p$ and

$$(q_0, w, Z_0) \mathrel{\vert\frac{i}{M}} (q, \epsilon, \gamma).$$

The converse, showing that $(q_0, w, Z_0) \mathrel{\vert\frac{i}{M}} (q, \epsilon, \gamma)$ and $\delta_A(p_0, w) = p$ imply

$$([p_0, q_0], w, Z_0) \mathrel{\vert\frac{i}{M'}} ([p, q], \epsilon, \gamma),$$

is similar and left as an exercise. $\qquad\qquad\qquad\qquad\qquad\qquad\qquad\qquad\qquad\square$

Use of closure properties

We conclude this section with an example illustrating the use of closure properties of context-free languages to prove that certain languages are not context free.

Example 6.5 Let $L = \{ww \mid w \text{ is in } (\mathbf{a} + \mathbf{b})^*\}$. That is, L consists of all words whose first and last halves are the same. Suppose L were context free. Then by Theorem 6.5, $L_1 = L \cap \mathbf{a}^+\mathbf{b}^+\mathbf{a}^+\mathbf{b}^+$ would also be a CFL. But $L_1 = \{a^i b^j a^i b^j \mid i \ge 1, j \ge 1\}$. L_1 is almost the same as the language proved not to be context free in Example 6.2, using the pumping lemma. The same argument shows that L_1 is not a CFL. We thus contradict the assumption that L is a CFL.

If we did not want to use the pumping lemma on L_1, we could reduce it to $L_2 = \{a^i b^j c^i d^j \mid i \ge 1 \text{ and } j \ge 1\}$, the exact language discussed in Example 6.2. Let h be the homomorphism $h(a) = h(c) = a$ and $h(b) = h(d) = b$. Then $h^{-1}(L_1)$ consists of all words of the form $x_1 x_2 x_3 x_4$, where x_1 and x_3 are of the same length and in $(\mathbf{a} + \mathbf{c})^+$, and x_2 and x_4 are of equal length and in $(\mathbf{b} + \mathbf{d})^+$. Then $h^{-1}(L_1) \cap \mathbf{a}^*\mathbf{b}^*\mathbf{c}^*\mathbf{d}^* = L_2$. By Theorems 6.3 and 6.5, if L_1 were a CFL, so would be L_2. Since L_2 is known not to be a CFL, we conclude that L_1 is not a CFL.

6.3 DECISION ALGORITHMS FOR CFL's

There are a number of questions about CFL's we can answer. These include whether a given CFL is empty, finite, or infinite and whether a given word is in a given CFL. There are, however, certain questions about CFL's that no algorithm can answer. These include whether two CFG's are equivalent, whether a CFL is cofinite, whether the complement of a given CFL is also a CFL, and whether a given CFG is ambiguous. In the next two chapters we shall develop tools for showing that no algorithm to do a particular job exists. In Chapter 8 we shall actually prove that the above questions and others have no algorithms. In this chapter we shall content ourselves with giving algorithms for some of the questions that have algorithms.

As with regular sets, we have several representations for CFL's, namely context-free grammars and pushdown automata accepting by empty stack or by final state. As the constructions of Chapter 5 are all effective, an algorithm that uses one representation can be made to work for any of the others. We shall use the CFG representation in this section.

Theorem 6.6   There are algorithms to determine if a CFL is (a) empty, (b) finite, or (c) infinite.

Proof   The theorem can be proved by the same technique (Theorem 3.7) as the analogous result for regular sets, by making use of the pumping lemma. However, the resulting algorithms are highly inefficient. Actually, we have already given a better algorithm to test whether a CFL is empty. For a CFG $G = (V, T, P, S)$, the test of Lemma 4.1 determines if a variable generates any string of terminals. Clearly, $L(G)$ is nonempty if and only if the start symbol S generates some string of terminals.

To test whether $L(G)$ is finite, use the algorithm of Theorem 4.5 to find a CFG $G' = (V', T, P', S)$ in CNF and with no useless symbols, generating $L(G) - \{\epsilon\}$. $L(G')$ is finite if and only if $L(G)$ is finite. A simple test for finiteness of a CNF grammar with no useless symbols is to draw a directed graph with a vertex for each variable and an edge from A to B if there is a production of the form $A \to BC$ or $A \to CB$ for any C. Then the language generated is finite if and only if this graph has no cycles.

If there is a cycle, say $A_0, A_1, \ldots, A_n, A_0$, then

$$A_0 \Rightarrow \alpha_1 A_1 \beta_1 \Rightarrow \alpha_2 A_2 \beta_2 \cdots \Rightarrow \alpha_n A_n \beta_n \Rightarrow \alpha_{n+1} A_0 \beta_{n+1},$$

where the α's and β's are strings of variables, with $|\alpha_i \beta_i| = i$. Since there are no useless symbols, $\alpha_{n+1} \xRightarrow{*} w$ and $\beta_{n+1} \xRightarrow{*} x$ for some terminal strings w and x of total length at least $n + 1$. Since $n \geq 0$, w and x cannot both be ϵ. Next, as there are no useless symbols, we can find terminal strings y and z such that $S \xRightarrow{*} yA_0 z$, and a terminal string v such that $A_0 \xRightarrow{*} v$. Then for all i,

$$S \xRightarrow{*} yA_0 z \xRightarrow{*} ywA_0 xz \xRightarrow{*} yw^2 A_0 x^2 z \xRightarrow{*} \cdots \xRightarrow{*} yw^i A_0 x^i z \xRightarrow{*} yw^i v x^i z.$$

As $|wx| > 0$, $yw^i vx^i z$ cannot equal $yw^j vx^j z$ if $i \neq j$. Thus the grammar generates an infinite number of strings.

Conversely, suppose the graph has no cycles. Define the *rank* of a variable A to be the length of the longest path in the graph beginning at A. The absence of cycles implies that the rank of A is finite. We also observe that if $A \rightarrow BC$ is a production, then the rank of B and C must be strictly less than the rank of A, because for every path from B or C, there is a path of length one greater from A. We show by induction on r that if A has rank r, then no terminal string derived from A has length greater than 2^r.

Basis $r = 0$. If A has rank 0, then its vertex has no edges out. Therefore all A-productions have terminals on the right, and A derives only strings of length 1.

Induction $r > 0$. If we use a production of the form $A \rightarrow a$, we may derive only a string of length 1. If we begin with $A \rightarrow BC$, then as B and C are of rank $r - 1$ or less, by the inductive hypothesis, they derive only strings of length 2^{r-1} or less. Thus BC cannot derive a string of length greater than 2^r.

Since S is of finite rank r_0, and in fact, is of rank no greater than the number of variables, S derives strings of length no greater than 2^{r_0}. Thus the language is finite. $\qquad\qquad\square$

Example 6.6 Consider the grammar

$$S \rightarrow AB$$
$$A \rightarrow BC \,|\, a$$
$$B \rightarrow CC \,|\, b$$
$$C \rightarrow a$$

whose graph is shown in Fig. 6.7(a). This graph has no cycles. The ranks of S, A, B, and C are 3, 2, 1, and 0, respectively. For example, the longest path from S is S, A, B, C. Thus this grammar derives no string of length greater than $2^3 = 8$ and therefore generates a finite language. In fact, a longest string generated from S is

$$S \Rightarrow AB \Rightarrow BCB \Rightarrow CCCB \Rightarrow CCCCC \overset{*}{\Rightarrow} aaaaa.$$

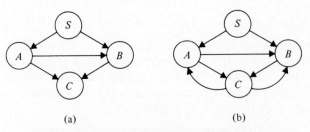

(a)   (b)

Fig. 6.7 Graphs corresponding to CNF grammars.

If we add production $C \rightarrow AB$, we get the graph of Fig. 6.7(b). This new graph has several cycles, such as A, B, C, A. Thus we can find a derivation $A \overset{*}{\Rightarrow} \alpha_3 A \beta_3$, in particular $A \Rightarrow BC \Rightarrow CCC \Rightarrow CABC$, where $\alpha_3 = C$ and $\beta_3 = BC$. Since $C \overset{*}{\Rightarrow} a$ and $BC \overset{*}{\Rightarrow} ba$, we have $A \overset{*}{\Rightarrow} aAba$. Then as $S \overset{*}{\Rightarrow} Ab$ and $A \overset{*}{\Rightarrow} a$, we now have $S \overset{*}{\Rightarrow} a^i a(ba)^i b$ for every i. Thus the language is infinite.

Membership

Another question we may answer is: Given a CFG $G = (V, T, P, S)$ and string x in T^*, is x in $L(G)$? A simple but inefficient algorithm to do so is to convert G to $G' = (V', T, P', S)$, a grammar in Greibach normal form generating $L(G) - \{\epsilon\}$. Since the algorithm of Theorem 4.3 tests whether $S \overset{*}{\Rightarrow} \epsilon$, we need not concern ourselves with the case $x = \epsilon$. Thus assume $x \neq \epsilon$, so x is in $L(G')$ if and only if x is in $L(G)$. Now, as every production of a GNF grammar adds exactly one terminal to the string being generated, we know that if x has a derivation in G', it has one with exactly $|x|$ steps. If no variable of G' has more than k productions, then there are at most $k^{|x|}$ leftmost derivations of strings of length $|x|$. We may try them all systematically.

However, the above algorithm can take time which is exponential in $|x|$. There are several algorithms known that take time proportional to the cube of $|x|$ or even a little less. The bibliographic notes discuss some of these. We shall here present a simple cubic time algorithm known as the Cocke-Younger-Kasami or *CYK* algorithm. It is based on the dynamic programming technique discussed in the solution to Exercise 3.23. Given x of length $n \geq 1$, and a grammar G, which we may assume is in Chomsky normal form, determine for each i and j and for each variable A, whether $A \overset{*}{\Rightarrow} x_{ij}$, where x_{ij} is the substring of x of length j beginning at position i.

We proceed by induction on j. For $j = 1$, $A \overset{*}{\Rightarrow} x_{ij}$ if and only if $A \rightarrow x_{ij}$ is a production, since x_{ij} is a string of length 1. Proceeding to higher values of j, if $j > 1$, then $A \overset{*}{\Rightarrow} x_{ij}$ if and only if there is some production $A \rightarrow BC$ and some k, $1 \leq k < j$, such that B derives the first k symbols of x_{ij} and C derives the last $j - k$ symbols of x_{ij}. That is, $B \overset{*}{\Rightarrow} x_{ik}$ and $C \overset{*}{\Rightarrow} x_{i+k, j-k}$. Since k and $j - k$ are both less than j, we already know whether each of the last two derivations exists. We may thus determine whether $A \overset{*}{\Rightarrow} x_{ij}$. Finally, when we reach $j = n$, we may determine whether $S \overset{*}{\Rightarrow} x_{1n}$. But $x_{1n} = x$, so x is in $L(G)$ if and only if $S \overset{*}{\Rightarrow} x_{1n}$.

To state the CYK algorithm precisely, let V_{ij} be the set of variables A such that $A \overset{*}{\Rightarrow} x_{ij}$. Note that we may assume $1 \leq i \leq n - j + 1$, for there is no string of length greater than $n - i + 1$ beginning at position i. Then Fig. 6.8 gives the CYK algorithm formally.

Steps (1) and (2) handle the case $j = 1$. As the grammar G is fixed, step (2) takes a constant amount of time. Thus steps (1) and (2) take $0(n)$ time. The nested for-loops of lines (3) and (4) cause steps (5) through (7) to be executed at most n^2 times, since i and j range in their respective for-loops between limits that are at

begin
1)   **for** $i:= 1$ **to** n **do**
2) $V_{i1} := \{A \mid A \to a$ is a production and the ith symbol of x is $a\}$;
3)   **for** $j:= 2$ **to** n **do**
4)   **for** $i:= 1$ **to** $n - j + 1$ **do**
            begin
5) $V_{ij} := \varnothing$;
6)   **for** $k:= 1$ **to** $j - 1$ **do**
7) $V_{ij} := V_{ij} \cup \{A \mid A \to BC$ is a production, B is in V_{ik} and C
                    is in $V_{i+k, j-k}\}$

        end

    end

Fig. 6.8.   The CYK algorithm.

most n apart. Step (5) takes constant time at each execution, so the aggregate time spent at step (5) is $0(n^2)$. The for-loop of line (6) causes step (7) to be executed n or fewer times. Since step (7) takes constant time, steps (6) and (7) together take $0(n)$ time. As they are executed $0(n^2)$ times, the total time spent in step (7) is $0(n^3)$. Thus the entire algorithm is $0(n^3)$.

Example 6.7   Consider the CFG

$$S \to AB \mid BC$$

$$A \to BA \mid a$$

$$B \to CC \mid b$$

$$C \to AB \mid a$$

and the input string *baaba*. The table of V_{ij}'s is shown in Fig. 6.9. The top row is filled in by steps (1) and (2) of the algorithm in Fig. 6.8. That is, for positions 1 and 4, which are b, we set $V_{11} = V_{41} = \{B\}$, since B is the only variable which derives b.

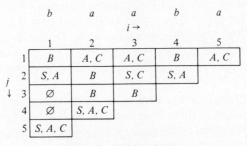

Fig. 6.9   Table of V_{ij}'s.

Similarly, $V_{21} = V_{31} = V_{51} = \{A, C\}$, since only A and C have productions with a on the right.

To compute V_{ij} for $j > 1$, we must execute the for-loop of steps (6) and (7). We must match V_{ik} against $V_{i+k,j-k}$ for $k = 1, 2, \ldots, j - 1$, seeking variable D in V_{ik} and E in $V_{i+k,j-k}$ such that DE is the right side of one or more productions. The left sides of these productions are adjoined to V_{ij}. The pattern in the table which corresponds to visiting V_{ik} and $V_{i+k,j-k}$ for $k = 1, 2, \ldots, j - 1$ in turn is to simultaneously move down column i and up the diagonal extending from V_{ij} to the right, as shown in Fig. 6.10.

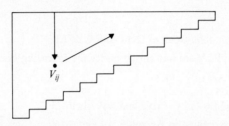

Fig. 6.10   Traversal pattern for computation of V_{ij}.

For example, let us compute V_{24}, assuming that the top three rows of Fig. 6.9 are filled in. We begin by looking at $V_{21} = \{A, C\}$ and $V_{33} = \{B\}$. The possible right-hand sides in $V_{21}V_{33}$ are AB and CB. Only the first of these is actually a right side, and it is a right side of two productions $S \to AB$ and $C \to AB$. Hence we add S and C to V_{24}. Next we consider $V_{22}V_{42} = \{B\}\{S, A\} = \{BS, BA\}$. Only BA is a right side, so we add the corresponding left side A to V_{24}. Finally, we consider $V_{23}V_{51} = \{B\}\{A, C\} = \{BA, BC\}$. BA and BC are each right sides, with left sides A and S, respectively. These are already in V_{24}, so we have $V_{24} = \{S, A, C\}$. Since S is a member of V_{15}, the string $baaba$ is in the language generated by the grammar.

EXERCISES

6.1   Show that the following are not context-free languages.

a) $\{a^i b^j c^k \mid i < j < k\}$
b) $\{a^i b^j \mid j = i^2\}$
c) $\{a^i \mid i$ is a prime$\}$
d) the set of strings of a's, b's, and c's with an equal number of each
e) $\{a^n b^n c^m \mid n \leq m \leq 2n\}$

* 6.2   Which of the following are CFL's?

a) $\{a^i b^j \mid i \neq j$ and $i \neq 2j\}$
b) $(\mathbf{a} + \mathbf{b})^* - \{(a^n b^n)^n \mid n \geq 1\}$
c) $\{ww^R w \mid w$ is in $(\mathbf{a} + \mathbf{b})^*\}$
d) $\{b_i \# b_{i+1} \mid b_i$ is i in binary, $i \geq 1\}$

e) $\{wxw \mid w \text{ and } x \text{ are in } (\mathbf{a} + \mathbf{b})^*\}$

f) $(\mathbf{a} + \mathbf{b})^* - \{(a^n b)^n \mid n \geq 1\}$

6.3 Prove that the following are not CFL's.

a) $\{a^i b^j a^k \mid j = \max \{i, k\}\}$

b) $\{a^n b^n c^i \mid i \neq n\}$

[*Hint:* Use Ogden's lemma on a string of the form $a^n b^n c^{n!}$.]

6.4 Show that the CFL's are closed under the following operations:

* a) Quotient with a regular set, that is, if L is a CFL and R a regular set, then L/R is a CFL.

b) INIT

S** c) CYCLE

d) reversal

See Exercise 3.4 for the definitions of INIT and CYCLE.

* **6.5** Show that the CFL's are not closed under the following operations.

S a) MIN   b) MAX   c) $\frac{1}{2}$

d) Inverse substitution

e) INV, where $\text{INV}(L) = \{x \mid x = wyz \text{ and } wy^R z \text{ is in } L\}$

MIN, MAX, and $\frac{1}{2}$ are defined in Exercises 3.4 and 3.16.

* **6.6** Let Σ be an alphabet. Define homomorphisms h, h_1, and h_2 by $h(a) = h(\bar{a}) = a$, $h_1(a) = a$, $h_1(\bar{a}) = \epsilon$, $h_2(a) = \epsilon$, and $h_2(\bar{a}) = a$ for each a in Σ^*. For $L_1 \subseteq \Sigma^*$ and $L_2 \subseteq \Sigma^*$, define

$$\text{Shuffle } (L_1, L_2) = \{x \mid \text{for some } y \text{ in } h^{-1}(x), h_1(y) \text{ is in } L_1 \text{ and } h_2(y) \text{ is in } L_2\}.$$

That is, the Shuffle of L_1 and L_2 is the set of words formed by "shuffling" a word of L_1 with a word of L_2. Symbols from the two words need not alternate as in a "perfect shuffle."

a) Show that the Shuffle of two regular sets is regular.

b) Prove that the Shuffle of two CFL's is not necessarily a CFL.

c) Prove that the Shuffle of a CFL and a regular set is a CFL.

* **6.7** A *Dyck Language* is a language with k types of balanced parentheses. Formally, each Dyck language is, for some k, $L(G_k)$, where G_k is the grammar

$$S \to SS \mid [_1 S]_1 \mid [_2 S]_2 \mid \cdots \mid [_k S]_k \mid \epsilon.$$

For example, $[_1[_2[_1]_1[_2]_2]_2]_1$ is in the Dyck language with two kinds of parentheses. Prove that every CFL L is $h(L_D \cap R)$, where h is a homomorphism, R a regular set, and L_D a Dyck language. [*Hint:* Let L be accepted by empty stack by a PDA in the normal form of Exercise 5.5(b) where the moves only push or pop single symbols. Let the parentheses be $[_{abX}$ and $]_{abX}$, where $[_{abX}$ "means" on input a, stack symbol X is pushed, and matching parenthesis $]_{abX}$ "means" on input b, X may be popped (a or b may be ϵ). Then the Dyck language enforces the condition that the stack be handled consistently, i.e., if X is pushed, then it will still be X when it is popped. Let the regular set R enforce the condition that there be a sequence of states for which the push and pop moves are legal for inputs a and b, respectively. Let $h([_{abX}) = a$ and $h(]_{abX}) = b$.]

* **6.8** Show that if L is a CFL over a one-symbol alphabet, then L is regular. [*Hint:* Let n be the pumping lemma constant for L and let $L \subseteq 0^*$. Show that for every word of length n or more, say 0^m, there are p and q no greater than n such that 0^{p+iq} is in L for all $i \geq 0$. Then show that L consists of perhaps some words of length less than n plus a finite number of linear sets, i.e., sets of the form $\{0^{p+iq} \,|\, i \geq 0\}$ for fixed p and q, $q \leq n$.]

** **6.9**   Prove that the set of primes in binary is not a CFL.

6.10   Show that the linear languages (see Exercise 4.20 for a definition) are closed under

a) union   b) homomorphism   c) intersection with a regular set

6.11   Prove the following pumping lemma for linear languages. If L is a linear language, then there is a constant L such that if z in L is of length n or greater, then we may write $z = uvwxy$, such that $|uvxy| \leq n$, $|vx| \geq 1$, and for all $i \geq 0$, uv^iwx^iy is in L.

6.12   Show that $\{a^ib^ic^jd^j \,|\, i \geq 1 \text{ and } j \geq 1\}$ is not a linear language.

* **6.13**   A PDA is said to make a *turn* if it enters a sequence of ID's

$$(q_1, w_1, \gamma_1) \vdash (q_2, w_2, \gamma_2) \vdash (q_3, w_3, \gamma_3)$$

and $|\gamma_2|$ is strictly greater than $|\gamma_1|$ and $|\gamma_3|$. That is, a turn occurs when the length of the stack "peaks." A PDA M is said to be a *k-turn* PDA if for every word w in $L(M)$, w is accepted by a sequence of ID's making no more than k turns. If a PDA is k-turn for some finite k, it is said to be *finite-turn*. If L is accepted by a finite-turn PDA, L is *metalinear*.

a) Show that a language is linear if and only if it is accepted by a one-turn PDA.
b) Show that the linear languages are closed under inverse homomorphism.
c) Show that the metalinear languages are closed under union, concatenation, homomorphism, inverse homomorphism, and intersection with a regular set.

** **6.14**   Show that the set of strings with an equal number of a's and b's is a CFL that is not a metalinear language.

6.15   Show that

a) the linear languages   ** b) the metalinear languages

are not closed under $*$.

6.16   Give an algorithm to decide for two sentential forms α and β of a CFG G, whether $\alpha \overset{*}{\underset{G}{\Rightarrow}} \beta$.

6.17   Use the CYK algorithm to determine whether

a) *aaaaa*   b) *aaaaaa*

are in the grammar of Example 6.7.

6.18   Let G be a context-free grammar in CNF.

a) Give an algorithm to determine the number of distinct derivations of a string x.
b) Associate a cost with each production of G. Give an algorithm to produce a minimum-cost parse of a string x. The cost of a parse is the sum of the costs of the productions used.

[*Hint*: Modify the CYK algorithm of Section 6.3.]

Solutions to Selected Exercises

6.4   c) Let $G = (V, T, P, S)$ be a CFG in CNF. To construct $\hat{G}$ such that $L(\hat{G}) = \text{CYCLE}(L(G))$ consider a derivation tree of a string $x_1 x_2$ in grammar G. Follow the path from S to the leftmost symbol of x_2. We wish to generate the path in reverse order (bottom to top) and output symbols on opposite sides of the path from which they originally appeared. To do this construct

$$\hat{G} = (V \cup \{\hat{A} \,|\, A \text{ is in } V\} \cup \{S_0\}, T, \hat{P}, S_0),$$

where $\hat{P}$ contains

1) all productions of P,
2) $\hat{C} \to \hat{A}B$ and $\hat{B} \to C\hat{A}$ if P contains $A \to BC$,
3) $\hat{S} \to \epsilon$,
4) $S_0 \to a\hat{A}$ if P contains $A \to a$,
5) $S_0 \to S$.

To see that $L(\hat{G}) = \text{CYCLE}(L(G))$ show by induction on the length of a derivation that $A \overset{*}{\Rightarrow} A_1 A_2 \cdots A_n$ if and only if for each i

$$\hat{A}_i \overset{*}{\Rightarrow} A_{i+1} \cdots A_n \hat{A} A_1 \cdots A_{i-1}.$$

Then

$$S \overset{*}{\Rightarrow} A_1 \cdots A_n \Rightarrow A_1 \cdots A_{i-1} a A_{i+1} \cdots A_n$$

iff

$$S_0 \Rightarrow a\hat{A}_i \overset{*}{\Rightarrow} aA_{i+1} \cdots A_n \hat{S} A_1 \cdots A_{i-1}$$

$$\Rightarrow aA_{i+1} \cdots A_n A_1 \cdots A_{i-1}.$$

A derivation tree of G is shown in Fig. 6.11(a) with a corresponding tree for $\hat{G}$ in Fig. 6.11(b).

6.5 a) Let L be the CFL $\{0^i 1^j 2^k \,|\, i \leq k \text{ or } j \leq k\}$. L is generated by the CFG

$$S \to AB \,|\, C, \qquad A \to 0A \,|\, \epsilon, \qquad B \to 1B2 \,|\, B2 \,|\, \epsilon, \qquad C \to 0C2 \,|\, C2 \,|\, D, \qquad D \to 1D \,|\, \epsilon$$

$\text{MIN}(L) = \{0^i 1^j 2^k \,|\, k = \min(i, j)\}$. We claim $\text{MIN}(L)$ is not a CFL. Suppose it were, and let n be the pumping lemma constant. Consider $z = 0^n 1^n 2^n = uvwxy$. If vx contains no 2's, then uwy is not in $\text{MIN}(L)$. If vx has a 2, it cannot have a 0, since $|vwx| \leq n$. Thus $uv^2 wx^2 y$ has at least $n + 1$ 2's, at least n 1's and exactly n 0's; it is thus not in $\text{MIN}(L)$.

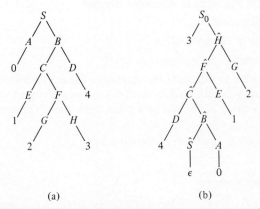

(a)   (b)

Fig. 6.11 Tree transformation used for Exercise 6.4(c).

BIBLIOGRAPHIC NOTES

The pumping lemma for context-free languages is from Bar-Hillel, Perles, and Shamir [1961]; Ogden's lemma, in its stronger version, is found in Ogden [1968]. Wise [1976] gives a necessary and sufficient condition for a language to be context free. Parikh [1966] gives necessary conditions in terms of the distribution of symbols in words of the language. Pumping lemmas for other classes of languages are given in Boasson [1973] and Ogden [1969].

Theorem 6.2, closure under substitution, and Theorem 6.5, closure under intersection with a regular set, are from Bar-Hillel, Perles, and Shamir [1961]. Theorem 6.3 is from Ginsburg and Rose [1963b]. Theorem 6.4 and its corollary, nonclosure under intersection or complementation, are from Scheinberg [1960]. Theorem 6.6, the existence of an algorithm to tell whether a CFL is finite, is also from Bar-Hillel, Perles, and Shamir [1961]. Floyd [1962b] shows how to apply closure properties to prove language constructs not to be context free.

The CYK algorithm was originally discovered by J. Cocke, but its first publication was due independently to Kasami [1965] and Younger [1967]. The most practical, general, context-free recognition and parsing algorithm is by Earley [1970]. This algorithm is $O(n^3)$ in general, but takes only $O(n^2)$ on any unambiguous CFG and is actually linear on a wide variety of useful grammars. The algorithm of Valiant [1975a] is asymptotically the most efficient, taking $O(n^{2.8})$ steps, while the algorithm of Graham, Harrison, and Ruzzo [1976] takes $O(n^3/\log n)$ steps. A related result, that membership for unambiguous CFG's can be tested in $O(n^2)$ time, is due to Kasami and Torii [1969] and Earley [1970].

Exercise 6.4(a), closure of CFL's under quotient with a regular set, was shown by Ginsburg and Spanier [1963]. Additional closure properties of CFL's can be found in Ginsburg and Rose [1963b, 1966]. Exercise 6.7, the characterization of CFL's by Dyck languages, is from Chomsky [1962]. Stanley [1965] showed the stronger result that the Dyck language used need depend only on the size of the terminal alphabet. The proof that the primes in binary are not a CFL (Exercise 6.9) is from Hartmanis and Shank [1968]. Finite-turn PDA's, mentioned in Exercise 6.13, were studied by Ginsburg and Spanier [1966]. Exercise 6.8, that CFL's over a one-symbol alphabet are regular, was shown by Ginsburg and Rice [1962].

7

TURING MACHINES

In this chapter we introduce the Turing machine, a simple mathematical model of a computer. Despite its simplicity, the Turing machine models the computing capability of a general-purpose computer. The Turing machine is studied both for the class of languages it defines (called the recursively enumerable sets) and the class of integer functions it computes (called the partial recursive functions). A variety of other models of computation are introduced and shown to be equivalent to the Turing machine in computing power.

7.1 INTRODUCTION

The intuitive notion of an algorithm or effective procedure has arisen several times. In Chapter 3 we exhibited an effective procedure to determine if the set accepted by a finite automation was empty, finite, or infinite. One might naively assume that for any class of languages with finite descriptions, there exists an effective procedure for answering such questions. However, this is not the case. For example, there is no algorithm to tell whether the complement of a CFL is empty (although we can tell whether the CFL itself is empty). Note that we are not asking for a procedure that answers the question for a specific context-free language, but rather a single procedure that will correctly answer the question for all CFL's. It is clear that if we need only determine whether one specific CFL has an empty complement, then an algorithm to answer the question exists. That is, there is one algorithm that says "yes" and another that says "no," independent of their inputs. One of these must be correct. Of course, which of the two algorithms answers the question correctly may not be obvious.

At the turn of the century, the mathematician David Hilbert set out on a program to find an algorithm for determining the truth or falsity of any mathematical proposition. In particular, he was looking for a procedure to determine if an arbitrary formula in the first-order predicate calculus, applied to integers, was true. Since the first-order predicate calculus is powerful enough to express the statement that the language generated by a context-free grammar is Σ^*, had Hilbert been successful, our problem of deciding whether the complement of a CFL is empty would be solved. However, in 1931, Kurt Gödel published his famous incompleteness theorem, which proved that no such effective procedure could exist. He constructed a formula in the predicate calculus applied to integers, whose very definition stated that it could neither be proved nor disproved within this logical system. The formalization of this argument and the subsequent clarification and formalization of our intuitive notion of an effective procedure is one of the great intellectual achievements of this century.

Once the notion of an effective procedure was formalized, it was shown that there was no effective procedure for computing many specific functions. Actually the existence of such functions is easily seen from a counting argument. Consider the class of functions mapping the nonnegative integers onto $\{0, 1\}$. These functions can be put into one-to-one correspondence with the reals. However, if we assume that effective procedures have finite descriptions, then the class of all effective procedures can be put into one-to-one correspondence with the integers. Since there is no one-to-one correspondence between the integers and the reals, there must exist functions with no corresponding effective procedures to compute them. There are simply too many functions, a noncountable number, and only a countable number of procedures. Thus the existence of noncomputable functions is not surprising. What is surprising is that some problems and functions with genuine significance in mathematics, computer science, and other disciplines are noncomputable.

Today the Turing machine has become the accepted formalization of an effective procedure. Clearly one cannot prove that the Turing machine model is equivalent to our intuitive notion of a computer, but there are compelling arguments for this equivalence, which has become known as Church's hypothesis. In particular, the Turing machine is equivalent in computing power to the digital computer as we know it today and also to all the most general mathematical notions of computation.

7.2 THE TURING MACHINE MODEL

A formal model for an effective procedure should possess certain properties. First, each procedure should be finitely describable. Second, the procedure should consist of discrete steps, each of which can be carried out mechanically. Such a model was introduced by Alan Turing in 1936. We present a variant of it here.

The basic model, illustrated in Fig. 7.1, has a finite control, an input tape that is divided into cells, and a tape head that scans one cell of the tape at a time. The tape has a leftmost cell but is infinite to the right. Each cell of the tape may hold exactly one of a finite number of tape symbols. Initially, the n leftmost cells, for some finite $n \geq 0$, hold the input, which is a string of symbols chosen from a subset of the tape symbols called the input symbols. The remaining infinity of cells each hold the blank, which is a special tape symbol that is not an input symbol.

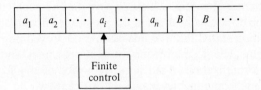

Finite
control

Fig. 7.1   Basic Turing machine.

In one move the Turing machine, depending upon the symbol scanned by the tape head and the state of the finite control,

1) changes state,
2) prints a symbol on the tape cell scanned, replacing what was written there, and
3) moves its head left or right one cell.

Note that the difference between a Turing machine and a two-way finite automaton lies in the former's ability to change symbols on its tape.

Formally, a Turing machine (TM) is denoted

$$M = (Q, \Sigma, \Gamma, \delta, q_0, B, F),$$

where

Q is the finite set of *states*,
Γ is the finite set of allowable *tape symbols*,
B, a symbol of Γ, is the *blank*,
Σ, a subset of Γ not including B, is the set of *input symbols*,
δ is the *next move function*, a mapping from $Q \times \Gamma$ to $Q \times \Gamma \times \{L, R\}$ (δ may, however, be undefined for some arguments),
q_0 in Q is the *start state*,
$F \subseteq Q$ is the set of *final states*.

We denote an *instantaneous description* (ID) of the Turing machine M by $\alpha_1 q \alpha_2$. Here q, the current state of M, is in Q; $\alpha_1 \alpha_2$ is the string in Γ^* that is the contents of the tape up to the rightmost nonblank symbol or the symbol to the left of the head, whichever is rightmost. (Observe that the blank B may occur in $\alpha_1 \alpha_2$.)

We assume that Q and Γ are disjoint to avoid confusion. Finally, the tape head is assumed to be scanning the leftmost symbol of α_2, or if $\alpha_2 = \epsilon$, the head is scanning a blank.

We define a *move* of M as follows. Let $X_1 X_2 \cdots X_{i-1} q X_i \cdots X_n$ be an ID. Suppose $\delta(q, X_i) = (p, Y, L)$, where if $i - 1 = n$, then X_i is taken to be B. If $i = 1$, then there is no next ID, as the tape head is not allowed to fall off the left end of the tape. If $i > 1$, then we write

$$X_1 X_2 \cdots X_{i-1} q X_i \cdots X_n \underset{M}{\vdash} X_1 X_2 \cdots X_{i-2} p X_{i-1} Y X_{i+1} \cdots X_n. \quad (7.1)$$

However, if any suffix of $X_{i-1} Y X_{i+1} \cdots X_n$ is completely blank, that suffix is deleted in (7.1).

Alternatively, suppose $\delta(q, X_i) = (p, Y, R)$. Then we write:

$$X_1 X_2 \cdots X_{i-1} q X_i X_{i+1} \cdots X_n \underset{M}{\vdash} X_1 X_2 \cdots X_{i-1} Y p X_{i+1} \cdots X_n. \quad (7.2)$$

Note that in the case $i - 1 = n$, the string $X_i \cdots X_n$ is empty, and the right side of (7.2) is longer than the left side.

If two ID's are related by $\underset{M}{\vdash}$, we say that the second results from the first by one move. If one ID results from another by some finite number of moves, including zero moves, they are related by the symbol $\overset{*}{\underset{M}{\vdash}}$. We drop the subscript M from $\underset{M}{\vdash}$ or $\overset{*}{\underset{M}{\vdash}}$ when no confusion results.

The *language accepted by* M, denoted $L(M)$, is the set of those words in Σ^* that cause M to enter a final state when placed, justified at the left, on the tape of M, with M in state q_0, and the tape head of M at the leftmost cell. Formally, the language accepted by $M = (Q, \Sigma, \Gamma, \delta, q_0, B, F)$ is

$$\{w \mid w \text{ in } \Sigma^* \text{ and } q_0 w \overset{*}{\vdash} \alpha_1 p \alpha_2 \text{ for some } p \text{ in } F, \text{ and } \alpha_1 \text{ and } \alpha_2 \text{ in } \Gamma^*\}.$$

Given a TM recognizing a language L, we assume without loss of generality that the TM halts, i.e., has no next move, whenever the input is accepted. However, for words not accepted, it is possible that the TM will never halt.

Example 7.1 The design of a TM M to accept the language $L = \{0^n 1^n \mid n \geq 1\}$ is given below. Initially, the type of M contains $0^n 1^n$ followed by an infinity of blanks. Repeatedly, M replaces the leftmost 0 by X, moves right to the leftmost 1, replacing it by Y, moves left to find the rightmost X, then moves one cell right to the leftmost 0 and repeats the cycle. If, however, when searching for a 1, M finds a blank instead, then M halts without accepting. If, after changing a 1 to a Y, M finds no more 0's, then M checks that no more 1's remain, accepting if there are none.

Let $Q = \{q_0, q_1, q_2, q_3, q_4\}$, $\Sigma = \{0, 1\}$, $\Gamma = \{0, 1, X, Y, B\}$, and $F = \{q_4\}$. Informally, each state represents a statement or a group of statements in a program. State q_0 is entered initially and also immediately prior to each replacement of a leftmost 0 by an X. State q_1 is used to search right, skipping over 0's and Y's until it finds the leftmost 1. If M finds a 1 it changes it to Y, entering state q_2.

State q_2 searches left for an X and enters state q_0 upon finding it, moving right, to the leftmost 0, as it changes state. As M searches right in state q_1, if a B or X is encountered before a 1, then the input is rejected; either there are too many 0's or the input is not in $0*1*$.

State q_0 has another role. If, after state q_2 finds the rightmost X, there is a Y immediately to its right, then the 0's are exhausted. From q_0, scanning Y, state q_3 is entered to scan over Y's and check that no 1's remain. If the Y's are followed by a B, state q_4 is entered and acceptance occurs; otherwise the string is rejected. The function δ is shown in Fig. 7.2. Figure 7.3 shows the computation of M on input 0011. For example, the first move is explained by the fact that $\delta(q_0, 0) = (q_1, X, R)$; the last move is explained by the fact that $\delta(q_3, B) = (q_4, B, R)$. The reader should simulate M on some rejected inputs such as 001101, 001, and 011.

	Symbol				
State	0	1	X	Y	B
q_0	(q_1, X, R)	—	—	(q_3, Y, R)	—
q_1	$(q_1, 0, R)$	(q_2, Y, L)	—	(q_1, Y, R)	—
q_2	$(q_2, 0, L)$	—	(q_0, X, R)	(q_2, Y, L)	—
q_3	—	—	—	(q_3, Y, R)	(q_4, B, R)
q_4	—	—	—	—	—

Fig. 7.2   The function δ.

$$q_00011 \vdash Xq_1011 \quad \vdash X0q_111 \quad \vdash Xq_20Y1 \quad \vdash$$
$$q_2X0Y1 \vdash Xq_00Y1 \quad \vdash XXq_1Y1 \quad \vdash XXYq_11 \vdash$$
$$XXq_2YY \vdash Xq_2XYY \quad \vdash XXq_0YY \vdash XXYq_3Y \vdash$$
$$XXYYq_3 \vdash XXYYBq_4$$

Fig. 7.3   A computation of M.

7.3 COMPUTABLE LANGUAGES AND FUNCTIONS

A language that is accepted by a Turing machine is said to be *recursively enumerable* (r.e.). The term "enumerable" derives from the fact that it is precisely these languages whose strings can be enumerated (listed) by a Turing machine. "Recursively" is a mathematical term predating the computer, and its meaning is similar to what the computer scientist would call "recursion." The class of r.e. languages is very broad and properly includes the CFL's.

The class of r.e. languages includes some languages for which we cannot mechanically determine membership. If $L(M)$ is such a language, then any Turing machine recognizing $L(M)$ must fail to halt on some input not in $L(M)$. If w is in $L(M)$, M eventually halts on input w. However, as long as M is still running on some input, we can never tell whether M will eventually accept if we let it run long enough, or whether M will run forever.

It is convenient to single out a subclass of the r.e. sets, called the *recursive sets*, which are those languages accepted by at least one Turing machine that halts on all inputs (note that halting may or may not be preceded by acceptance). We shall see in Chapter 8 that the recursive sets are a proper subclass of the r.e. sets. Note also that by the algorithm of Fig. 6.8, every CFL is a recursive set.

The Turing machine as a computer of integer functions

In addition to being a language acceptor, the Turing machine may be viewed as a computer of functions from integers to integers. The traditional approach is to represent integers in *unary*; the integer $i \geq 0$ is represented by the string 0^i. If a function has k arguments, $i_1, i_2, \ldots, i_k$, then these integers are initially placed on the tape separated by 1's, as $0^{i_1}10^{i_2}1 \cdots 10^{i_k}$.

If the TM halts (whether or not in an accepting state) with a tape consisting of 0^m for some m, then we say that $f(i_1, i_2, \ldots, i_k) = m$, where f is the function of k arguments computed by this Turing machine. Note that one TM may compute a function of one argument, a different function of two arguments, and so on. Also note that if TM M computes function f of k arguments, then f need not have a value for all different k-tuples of integers $i_1, \ldots, i_k$.

If $f(i_1, \ldots, i_k)$ is defined for all $i_1, \ldots, i_k$, then we say f is a *total recursive function*. A function $f(i_1, \ldots, i_k)$ computed by a Turing machine is called a *partial recursive function*. In a sense, the partial recursive functions are analogous to the r.e. languages, since they are computed by Turing machines that may or may not halt on a given input. The total recursive functions correspond to the recursive languages, since they are computed by TM's that always halt. All common arithmetic functions on integers, such as multiplication, $n!$, $\lceil \log_2 n \rceil$ and 2^{2^n} are total recursive functions.

Example 7.2 *Proper subtraction* $m \dot{-} n$ is defined to be $m - n$ for $m \geq n$, and zero for $m < n$. The TM

$$M = (\{q_0, q_1, \ldots, q_6\}, \{0, 1\}, \{0, 1, B\}, \delta, q_0, B, \varnothing)$$

defined below, started with 0^m10^n on its tape, halts with $0^{m \dot{-} n}$ on its tape. M repeatedly replaces its leading 0 by blank, then searches right for a 1 followed by a 0 and changes the 0 to 1. Next, M moves left until it encounters a blank and then repeats the cycle. The repetition ends if

i) Searching right for a 0, M encounters a blank. Then, the n 0's in 0^m10^n have all been changed to 1's, and $n + 1$ of the m 0's have been changed to B. M replaces the $n + 1$ 1's by a 0 and n B's, leaving $m - n$ 0's on its tape.

ii) Beginning the cycle, M cannot find a 0 to change to a blank, because the first m 0's already have been changed. Then $n \geq m$, so $m \dot{-} n = 0$. M replaces all remaining 1's and 0's by B.

The function δ is described below.

1) $\delta(q_0, 0) = (q_1, B, R)$
Begin the cycle. Replace the leading 0 by B.

2) $\delta(q_1, 0) = (q_1, 0, R)$
$\delta(q_1, 1) = (q_2, 1, R)$
Search right, looking for the first 1.

3) $\delta(q_2, 1) = (q_2, 1, R)$
$\delta(q_2, 0) = (q_3, 1, L)$
Search right past 1's until encountering a 0. Change that 0 to 1.

4) $\delta(q_3, 0) = (q_3, 0, L)$
$\delta(q_3, 1) = (q_3, 1, L)$
$\delta(q_3, B) = (q_0, B, R)$
Move left to a blank. Enter state q_0 to repeat the cycle.

5) $\delta(q_2, B) = (q_4, B, L)$
$\delta(q_4, 1) = (q_4, B, L)$
$\delta(q_4, 0) = (q_4, 0, L)$
$\delta(q_4, B) = (q_6, 0, R)$
If in state q_2 a B is encountered before a 0, we have situation (i) described above. Enter state q_4 and move left, changing all 1's to B's until encountering a B. This B is changed back to a 0, state q_6 is entered, and M halts.

6) $\delta(q_0, 1) = (q_5, B, R)$
$\delta(q_5, 0) = (q_5, B, R)$
$\delta(q_5, 1) = (q_5, B, R)$
$\delta(q_5, B) = (q_6, B, R)$
If in state q_0 a 1 is encountered instead of a 0, the first block of 0's has been exhausted, as in situation (ii) above. M enters state q_5 to erase the rest of the tape, then enters q_6 and halts.

A sample computation of M on input 0010 is:

$$q_0 0010 \vdash Bq_1 010 \vdash B0q_1 10 \vdash B01q_2 0 \vdash$$
$$B0q_3 11 \vdash Bq_3 011 \vdash q_3 B011 \vdash Bq_0 011 \vdash$$
$$BBq_1 11 \vdash BB1q_2 1 \vdash BB11q_2 \vdash BB1q_4 1 \vdash$$
$$BBq_4 1 \vdash Bq_4 \quad \vdash B0q_6$$

On input 0100, M behaves as follows:

$$q_0 0100 \vdash Bq_1 100 \vdash B1q_2 00 \vdash Bq_3 110 \vdash$$
$$q_3 B110 \vdash Bq_0 110 \vdash BBq_5 10 \vdash BBBq_5 0 \vdash$$
$$BBBBq_5 \vdash BBBBBq_6$$

7.4 TECHNIQUES FOR TURING MACHINE CONSTRUCTION

Designing Turing machines by writing out a complete set of states and a next-move function is a noticeably unrewarding task. In order to describe complicated Turing machine constructions we need some "higher-level" conceptual tools. In this section we shall discuss the principal ones.

Storage in the finite control

The finite control can be used to hold a finite amount of information. To do so, the state is written as a pair of elements, one exercising control and the other storing a symbol. It should be emphasized that this arrangement is for conceptual purposes only. No modification in the definition of the Turing machine has been made.

Example 7.3 Consider a Turing machine M that looks at the first input symbol, records it in its finite control, and checks that the symbol does not appear elsewhere on its input. Note that M accepts a regular set, but M will serve for demonstration purposes:

$$M = (Q, \{0, 1\}, \{0, 1, B\}, \delta, [q_0, B], B, F),$$

where Q is $\{q_0, q_1\} \times \{0, 1, B\}$. That is, Q consists of the pairs $[q_0, 0]$, $[q_0, 1]$, $[q_0, B]$, $[q_1, 0]$, $[q_1, 1]$, and $[q_1, B]$. The set F is $\{[q_1, B]\}$. The intention is that the first component of the state controls the action, while the second component "remembers" a symbol.

We define δ as follows.

1) a) $\delta([q_0, B], 0) = ([q_1, 0], 0, R)$,   b) $\delta([q_0, B], 1) = ([q_1, 1], 1, R)$.

   Initially, q_0 is the control component of the state, and M moves right. The first component of M's state becomes q_1, and the first symbol seen is stored in the second component.

2) a) $\delta([q_1, 0], 1) = ([q_1, 0], 1, R)$,   b) $\delta([q_1, 1], 0) = ([q_1, 1], 0, R)$.

   If M has a 0 stored and sees a 1 or vice versa, then M continues to move to the right.

3) a) $\delta([q_1, 0], B) = ([q_1, B], 0, L)$,   b) $\delta([q_1, 1], B) = ([q_1, B], 0, L)$.
M enters the final state $[q_1, B]$ if it reaches a blank symbol without having first encountered a second copy of the leftmost symbol.

If M reaches a blank in state $[q_1, 0]$, or $[q_1, 1]$, it accepts. For state $[q_1, 0]$ and symbol 0 or for state $[q_1, 1]$ and symbol 1, δ is not defined. Thus if M encounters the tape symbol stored in its state, M halts without accepting.

In general, we can allow the finite control to have k components, all but one of which store information.

Multiple tracks

We can imagine that the tape of the Turing machine is divided into k tracks, for any finite k. This arrangement is shown in Fig. 7.4, with $k = 3$. The symbols on the tape are considered k-tuples, one component for each track.

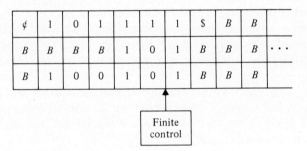

Fig. 7.4   A three-track Turing machine.

Example 7.4   The tape in Fig. 7.4 belongs to a Turing machine that takes a binary input greater than 2, written on the first track, and determines whether it is a prime. The input is surrounded by ¢ and $ on the first track. Thus, the allowable input symbols are $[¢, B, B]$, $[0, B, B]$, $[1, B, B]$, and $[\$, B, B]$. These symbols can be identified with ¢, 0, 1, and $, respectively, when viewed as input symbols. The blank symbol can be identified with $[B, B, B]$.

To test if its input is a prime, the TM first writes the number two in binary on the second track and copies the first track onto the third. Then the second track is subtracted, as many times as possible, from the third track, effectively dividing the third track by the second and leaving the remainder.

If the remainder is zero, the number on the first track is not a prime. If the remainder is nonzero, the number on the second track is increased by one. If the second track equals the first, the number on the first track is a prime, because it cannot be divided by any number lying properly between one and itself. If the second is less than the first, the whole operation is repeated for the new number on the second track.

In Fig. 7.4, the TM is testing to determine if 47 is a prime. The TM is dividing by 5; already 5 has been subtracted twice, so 37 appears on the third track.

Checking off symbols

Checking off symbols is a useful trick for visualizing how a TM recognizes languages defined by repeated strings, such as

$$\{ww \mid w \text{ in } \Sigma^*\}, \qquad \{wcy \mid w \text{ and } y \text{ in } \Sigma^*, w \neq y\} \qquad \text{or} \qquad \{ww^R \mid w \text{ in } \Sigma^*\}.$$

It is also useful when lengths of substrings must be compared, such as in the languages

$$\{a^i b^i \mid i \geq 1\} \qquad \text{or} \qquad \{a^i b^j c^k \mid i \neq j \text{ or } j \neq k\}.$$

We introduce an extra track on the tape that holds a blank or $\sqrt{}$. The $\sqrt{}$ appears when the symbol below it has been considered by the TM in one of its comparisons.

Example 7.5 Consider a Turing machine $M = (Q, \Sigma, \Gamma, \delta, q_0, B, F)$, which recognizes the language $\{wcw \mid w \text{ in } (\mathbf{a} + \mathbf{b})^+\}$. Let

$$Q = \{[q, d] \mid q = q_1, q_2, \ldots, q_9 \text{ and } d = a, b, \text{ or } B\}.$$

The second component of the state is used to store an input symbol,

$$\Sigma = \{[B, d] \mid d = a, b, \text{ or } c\}.$$

The input symbol $[B, d]$ is identified with d. Remember that the two "tracks" are just conceptual tools; that is, $[B, d]$ is just another "name" for d:

$$\Gamma = \{[X, d] \mid X = B \text{ or } \sqrt{} \quad \text{and} \quad d = a, b, c, \text{ or } B\},$$

$$q_0 = [q_1, B], \quad \text{and} \quad F = \{[q_9, B]\};$$

$[B, B]$ is identified with B, the blank symbol. For $d = a$ or b and $e = a$ or b we define δ as follows.

1) $\delta([q_1, B], [B, d]) = ([q_2, d], [\sqrt{}, d], R)$.

   M checks the symbol scanned on the tape, stores the symbol in the finite control, and moves right.

2) $\delta([q_2, d], [B, e]) = ([q_2, d], [B, e], R)$.

   M continues to move right, over unchecked symbols, looking for c.

3) $\delta([q_2, d], [B, c]) = ([q_3, d], [B, c], R)$.

   On finding c, M enters a state with first component q_3.

4) $\delta([q_3, d], [\sqrt{}, e]) = ([q_3, d], [\sqrt{}, e], R)$.

   M moves right over checked symbols.

5) $\delta([q_3, d], [B, d]) = ([q_4, B], [\sqrt{}, d], L)$.

   M encounters an unchecked symbol. If the unchecked symbol matches the symbol stored in the finite control, M checks it and begins moving left. If the symbols disagree, M has no next move and so halts without accepting. M also halts if in state q_3 it reaches $[B, B]$ before finding an unchecked symbol.

6) $\delta([q_4, B], [\sqrt{}, d]) = ([q_4, B], [\sqrt{}, d], L)$.

   M moves left over checked symbols.

7) $\delta([q_4, B], [B, c]) = ([q_5, B], [B, c], L)$.

   M encounters the symbol c.

8) $\delta([q_5, B], [B, d]) = ([q_6, B], [B, d], L)$.

   If the symbol immediately to the left of c is unchecked, M proceeds left to find the rightmost checked symbol.

9) $\delta([q_6, B], [B, d]) = ([q_6, B], [B, d], L)$.

   M proceeds left.

10) $\delta([q_6, B], [\sqrt{}, d]) = ([q_1, B], [\sqrt{}, d], R)$.

   M encounters a checked symbol and moves right to pick up another symbol for comparison. The first component of state becomes q_1 again.

11) $\delta([q_5, B], [\sqrt{}, d]) = ([q_7, B], [\sqrt{}, d], R)$.

   M will be in state $[q_5, B]$ immediately after crossing c moving left. (See rule 7.) If a checked symbol appears immediately to the left of c, all symbols to the left of c have been checked. M must test whether all symbols to the right have been checked. If so, they must have compared properly with the symbols to the left of c, so M will accept.

12) $\delta([q_7, B], [B, c]) = ([q_8, B], [B, c], R)$.

   M moves right over c.

13) $\delta([q_8, B], [\sqrt{}, d]) = ([q_8, B], [\sqrt{}, d], R)$.

   M moves to the right over checked symbols.

14) $\delta([q_8, B], [B, B]) = ([q_9, B], [\sqrt{}, B], L)$.

   If M finds $[B, B]$, the blank, it halts and accepts. If M finds an unchecked symbol when its first component of state is q_8, it halts without accepting.

Shifting over

A Turing machine can make space on its tape by shifting all nonblank symbols a finite number of cells to the right. To do so, the tape head makes an excursion to the right, repeatedly storing the symbols read in its finite control and replacing them with symbols read from cells to the left. The TM can then return to the vacated cells and print symbols of its choosing. If space is available, it can push blocks of symbols left in a similar manner.

Example 7.6 We construct part of a Turing machine, $M = (Q, \Sigma, \Gamma, \delta, q_0, B, F)$, which may occasionally have a need to shift nonblank symbols two cells to the right. We suppose that M's tape does not contain blanks between nonblanks, so when it reaches a blank it knows to stop the shifting process. Let Q contain states of the form $[q, A_1, A_2]$ for $q = q_1$ or q_2, and A_1 and A_2 in Γ. Let X be a special symbol not used by M except in the shifting process. M starts the shifting process in state $[q_1, B, B]$. The relevant portions of the function δ are as follows.

1) $\delta([q_1, B, B], A_1) = ([q_1, B, A_1], X, R)$ for A_1 in $\Gamma - \{B, X\}$.

   M stores the first symbol read in the third component of its state. X is printed on the cell scanned, and M moves to the right.

2) $\delta([q_1, B, A_1], A_2) = ([q_1, A_1, A_2], X, R)$ for A_1 and A_2 in $\Gamma - \{B, X\}$.

   M shifts the symbol in the third component to the second component, stores the symbol being read in the third component, prints an X, and moves right.

3) $\delta([q_1, A_1, A_2], A_3) = ([q_1, A_2, A_3], A_1, R)$ for A_1, A_2,   and A_3 in $\Gamma - \{B, X\}$.

   M now repeatedly reads a symbol A_3, stores it in the third component of state, shifts the symbol previously in the third component, A_2, to the second component, deposits the previous second component, A_1, on the cell scanned, and moves right. Thus a symbol will be deposited two cells to the right of its original position.

4) $\delta([q_1, A_1, A_2], B) = ([q_1, A_2, B], A_1, R)$ for A_1 and A_2 in $\Gamma - \{B, X\}$.

   When a blank is seen on the tape, the stored symbols are deposited on the tape.

5) $\delta([q_1, A_1, B], B) = ([q_2, B, B], A_1, L)$.

   After all symbols have been deposited, M sets the first component of state to q_2 and moves left to find an X, which marks the rightmost vacated cell.

6) $\delta([q_2, B, B], A) = ([q_2, B, B], A, L)$ for A in $\Gamma - \{B, X\}$.

   M moves left until an X is found. When X is found, M transfers to a state that we have assumed exists in Q and resumes its other functions.

Subroutines

As with programs, a "modular" or "top-down" design is facilitated if we use subroutines to define elementary processes. A Turing machine can simulate any type of subroutine found in programming languages, including recursive procedures and any of the known parameter-passing mechanisms. We shall here describe only the use of parameterless, nonrecursive subroutines, but even these are quite powerful tools.

The general idea is to write part of a TM program to serve as a subroutine; it will have a designated initial state and a designated return state which temporarily has no move and which will be used to effect a return to the calling routine. To design a TM that "calls" the subroutine, a new set of states for the subroutine is made, and a move from the return state is specified. The call is effected by entering the initial state for the subroutine, and the return is effected by the move from the return state.

Example 7.7 The design of a TM M to implement the total recursive function "multiplication" is given below. M starts with 0^m10^n on its tape and ends with 0^{mn} surrounded by blanks. The general idea is to place a 1 after 0^m10^n and then copy the block of n 0's onto the right end m times, each time erasing one of the m 0's. The result is 10^n10^{mn}. Finally the prefix 10^n1 is erased, leaving 0^{mn}. The heart of the algorithm is a subroutine COPY, which begins in an ID $0^m1q_10^n10^i$ and eventually enters an ID $0^m1q_50^n10^{i+n}$. COPY is defined in Fig. 7.5. In state q_1, on seeing a 0, M changes it to a 2 and enters state q_2. In state q_2, M moves right, to the next blank, deposits the 0, and starts left in state q_3. In state q_3, M moves left to a 2. On reaching a 2, state q_1 is entered and the process repeats until the 1 is encountered, signaling that the copying process is complete. State q_4 is used to convert the 2's back to 0's, and the subroutine halts in q_5.

	0	1	2	B
q_1	$(q_2, 2, R)$	$(q_4, 1, L)$		
q_2	$(q_2, 0, R)$	$(q_2, 1, R)$		$(q_3, 0, L)$
q_3	$(q_3, 0, L)$	$(q_3, 1, L)$	$(q_1, 2, R)$	
q_4		$(q_5, 1, R)$	$(q_4, 0, L)$	

Fig. 7.5 δ for subroutine COPY.

To complete the program for multiplication, we add states to convert initial ID $q_00^m10^n$ to $B0^{m-1}1q_10^n1$. That is, we need the rules

$$\delta(q_0, 0) = (q_6, B, R),$$
$$\delta(q_6, 0) = (q_6, 0, R),$$
$$\delta(q_6, 1) = (q_1, 1, R).$$

Additional states are needed to convert an ID $B^i0^{m-i}1q_50^n10^{ni}$ to $B^{i+1}0^{m-i-1}1q_10^n10^{ni}$, which restarts COPY, and to check whether $i = m$, that is, all m 0's have been erased. In the case that $i = m$, the leading 10^n1 is erased and the computation halts in state q_{12}. These moves are shown in Fig. 7.6.

	0	1	2	B
q_5	$(q_7, 0, L)$			
q_7		$(q_8, 1, L)$		
q_8	$(q_9, 0, L)$			(q_{10}, B, R)
q_9	$(q_9, 0, L)$			(q_0, B, R)
q_{10}		(q_{11}, B, R)		
q_{11}	(q_{11}, B, R)	(q_{12}, B, R)		

Fig. 7.6 Additional moves for TM performing multiplication.

Note that we could make more than one call to a subroutine if we rewrote the subroutine using a new set of states for each call.

7.5 MODIFICATIONS OF TURING MACHINES

One reason for the acceptance of the Turing machine as a general model of a computation is that the model with which we have been dealing is equivalent to many modified versions that would seem off-hand to have increased computing power. In this section we give informal proofs of some of these equivalence theorems.

Two-way infinite tape

A Turing machine with a two-way infinite tape is denoted by $M = (Q, \Sigma, \Gamma, \delta, q_0, B, F)$, as in the original model. As its name implies, the tape is infinite to the left as well as to the right. We denote an ID of such a device as for the one-way infinite TM. We imagine, however, that there is an infinity of blank cells both to the left and right of the current nonblank portion of the tape.

The relation $\vdash_M$, which relates two ID's if the ID on the right is obtained from the one on the left by a single move, is defined as for the original model with the exception that if $\delta(q, X) = (p, Y, L)$, then $qX\alpha \vdash_M pBY\alpha$ (in the original model, no move could be made), and if $\delta(q, X) = (p, B, R)$, then $qX\alpha \vdash p\alpha$ (in the original, the B would appear to the left of p).

The initial ID is $q_0 w$. While there was a left end to the tape in the original model, there is no left end of the tape for the Turing machine to "fall off," so it can proceed left as far as it wishes. The relation $\vdash_M^*$, as usual, relates two ID's if the one on the right can be obtained from the one on the left by some number of moves.

Theorem 7.1 L is recognized by a Turing machine with a two-way infinite tape if and only if it is recognized by a TM with a one-way infinite tape.

Proof The proof that a TM with a two-way infinite tape can simulate a TM with a one-way infinite tape is easy. The former marks the cell to the left of its initial head position and then simulates the latter. If during the simulation the marked cell is reached, the simulation terminates without acceptance.

Conversely, let $M_2 = (Q_2, \Sigma_2, \Gamma_2, \delta_2, q_2, B, F_2)$ be a TM with a two-way infinite tape. We construct M_1, a Turing machine simulating M_2 and having a tape that is infinite to the right only. M_1 will have two tracks, one to represent the cells of M_2's tape to the right of, and including, the tape cell initially scanned, the other to represent, in reverse order, the cells to the left of the initial cell. The relationship between the tapes of M_2 and M_1 is shown in Fig. 7.7, with the initial cell of M_2 numbered 0, the cells to the right 1, 2, ..., and the cells to the left $-1, -2, \ldots$.

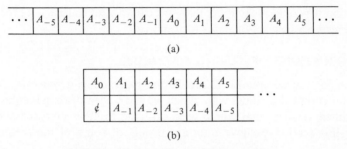

(a)

(b)

Fig. 7.7   (a) Tape of M_2. (b) Tape of M_1.

The first cell of M_1's tape holds the symbol $\rlap{/}{c}$ in the lower track, indicating that it is the leftmost cell. The finite control of M_1 tells whether M_2 would be scanning a symbol appearing on the upper or on the lower track of M_1.

It should be fairly evident that M_1 can be constructed to simulate M_2, in the sense that while M_2 is to the right of the initial position of its input head, M_1 works on the upper track. While M_2 is to the left of its initial tape head position, M_1 works on its lower track, moving in the direction opposite to the direction in which M_2 moves. The input symbols of M_1 are symbols with a blank on the lower track and an input symbol of M_2 on the upper track. Such a symbol can be identified with the corresponding input symbol of M_2. B is identified with $[B, B]$.

We now give a formal construction of $M_1 = (Q_1, \Sigma_1, \Gamma_1, \delta_1, q_1, B, F_1)$. The states, Q_1, of M_1 are all objects of the form $[q, U]$ or $[q, D]$, where q is in Q_2, plus the symbol q_1. Note that the second component will indicate whether M_1 is working on the upper (U for up) or lower (D for down) track. The tape symbols in Γ_1 are all objects of the form $[X, Y]$, where X and Y are in Γ_2. In addition, Y may be $\rlap{/}{c}$, a symbol not in Γ_2. Σ_1 consists of all symbols $[a, B]$, where a is in Σ_2. F_1 is $\{[q, U], [q, D] \mid q$ is in $F_2\}$. We define δ_1 as follows.

1) For each a in $\Sigma_2 \cup \{B\}$,

$$\delta_1(q_1, [a, B]) = ([q, U], [X, \rlap{/}{c}], R) \quad \text{if} \quad \delta_2(q_2, a) = (q, X, R).$$

If M_2 moves right on its first move, M_1 prints $\rlap{/}{c}$ in the lower track to mark the end of tape, sets its second component of state to U, and moves right. The first component of M_1's state holds the state of M_2. On the upper track, M_1 prints the symbol X that is printed by M_2.

2) For each a in $\Sigma_2 \cup \{B\}$,

$$\delta_1(q_1, [a, B]) = ([q, D], [X, \mathcal{c}], R) \quad \text{if} \quad \delta_2(q_2, a) = (q, X, L).$$

If M_2 moves left on its first move, M_1 records the next state of M_2 and the symbol printed by M_2 as in (1) but sets the second component of its state to D and moves right. Again, $\mathcal{c}$ is printed in the lower track to mark the left end of the tape.

3) For each $[X, Y]$ in Γ_1, with $Y \neq \mathcal{c}$, and $A = L$ or R,

$$\delta_1([q, U], [X, Y]) = ([p, U], [Z, Y], A) \quad \text{if} \quad \delta_2(q, X) = (p, Z, A).$$

M_1 simulates M_2 on the upper track.

4) For each $[X, Y]$ in Γ_1, with $Y \neq \mathcal{c}$,

$$\delta_1([q, D], [X, Y]) = ([p, D], [X, Z], A) \quad \text{if} \quad \delta_2(q, Y) = (p, Z, \bar{A}).$$

Here A is L if $\bar{A}$ is R, and A is R if $\bar{A}$ is L. M_1 simulates M_2 on the lower track of M_1. The direction of head motion of M_1 is opposite to that of M_2.

5) $$\delta_1([q, U], [X, \mathcal{c}]) = \delta_1([q, D], [X, \mathcal{c}])$$
$$= ([p, C], [Y, \mathcal{c}], R) \quad \text{if} \quad \delta_2(q, X) = (p, Y, A).$$

Here $C = U$ if $A = R$, and $C = D$ if $A = L$. M_1 simulates a move of M_2 on the cell initially scanned by M_2. M_1 next works on the upper or lower track, depending on the direction in which M_2 moves. M_1 will always move right in this situation. □

Multitape Turing machines

A multitape Turing machine is shown in Fig. 7.8. It consists of a finite control with k tape heads and k tapes; each tape is infinite in both directions. On a single move, depending on the state of the finite control and the symbol scanned by each of the tape heads, the machine can:

1) change state;
2) print a new symbol on each of the cells scanned by its tape heads;
3) move each of its tape heads, independently, one cell to the left or right, or keep it stationary.

Initially, the input appears on the first tape, and the other tapes are blank. We shall not define the device more formally, as the formalism is cumbersome and a straightforward generalization of the notation for single-tape TM's.

Theorem 7.2 If a language L is accepted by a multitape Turing machine, it is accepted by a single-tape Turing machine.

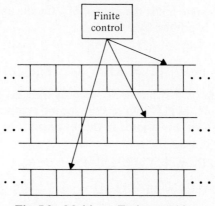

Fig. 7.8   Multitape Turing machine.

Proof   Let L be accepted by M_1, a TM with k tapes. We can construct M_2, a one-tape TM with $2k$ tracks, two tracks for each of M_1's tapes. One track records the contents of the corresponding tape of M_1 and the other is blank, except for a marker in the cell that holds the symbol scanned by the corresponding head of M_1. The arrangement is illustrated in Fig. 7.9. The finite control of M_2 stores the state of M_1, along with a count of the number of head markers to the right of M_2's tape head.

Head 1		X				
Tape 1	A_1	A_2	...		...	A_m
Head 2				X		
Tape 2	B_1	B_2	...		...	B_m
Head 3	X					
Tape 3	C_1	C_2	...		...	C_m

Fig. 7.9   Simulation of three tapes by one.

Each move of M_1 is simulated by a sweep from left to right and then from right to left by the tape head of M_2. Initially, M_2's head is at the leftmost cell containing a head marker. To simulate a move of M_1, M_2 sweeps right, visiting each of the cells with head markers and recording the symbol scanned by each head of M_1. When M_2 crosses a head marker, it must update the count of head markers to its right. When no more head markers are to the right, M_2 has seen the symbols scanned by each of M_1's heads, so M_2 has enough information to determine the move of M_1. Now M_2 makes a pass left, until it reaches the leftmost head marker. The count of markers to the right enables M_2 to tell when it has gone far enough. As M_2 passes each head marker on the leftward pass, it updates the tape symbol of M_1 "scanned" by that head marker, and it moves the head marker one symbol left or right to simulate the move of M_1. Finally, M_2 changes the state of M_1 recorded in M_2's control to complete the simulation of one move of M_1. If the new state of M_1 is accepting, then M_2 accepts.   □

Note that in the first simulation of this section—that of a two-way infinite tape TM by a one-way infinite tape TM, the simulation was move for move. In the present simulation, however, many moves of M_2 are needed to simulate one move of M_1. In fact, since after k moves, the heads of M_1 can be $2k$ cells apart, it takes about $\sum_{i=1}^{k} 2i \approx 2k^2$ moves of M_2 to simulate k moves of M_1. (Actually, $2k$ more moves may be needed to simulate heads moving to the right.) This quadratic slowdown that occurs when we go from a multitape TM to a single tape TM is inherently necessary for certain languages. While we defer a proof to Chapter 12, we shall here give an example of the efficiency of multitape TM's.

Example 7.8 The language $L = \{ww^R \mid w \text{ in } (0 + 1)^*\}$ can be recognized on a single-tape TM by moving the tape head back and forth on the input, checking symbols from both ends, and comparing them. The process is similar to that of Example 7.5.

To recognize L with a two-tape TM, the input is copied onto the second tape. The input on one tape is compared with the reversal on the other tape by moving the heads in opposite directions, and the length of the input checked to make sure it is even.

Note that the number of moves used to recognize L by the one-tape machine is approximately the square of the input length, while with a two-tape machine, time proportional to the input length is sufficient.

Nondeterministic Turing machines

A nondeterministic Turing machine is a device with a finite control and a single, one-way infinite tape. For a given state and tape symbol scanned by the tape head, the machine has a finite number of choices for the next move. Each choice consists of a new state, a tape symbol to print, and a direction of head motion. Note that the nondeterministic TM is not permitted to make a move in which the next state is selected from one choice, and the symbol printed and/or direction of head motion are selected from other choices. The nondeterministic TM accepts its input if any sequence of choices of moves leads to an accepting state.

As with the finite automaton, the addition of nondeterminism to the Turing machine does not allow the device to accept new languages. In fact, the combination of nondeterminism with any of the extensions presented or to be presented, such as two-way infinite or multitape TM's, does not add additional power. We leave these results as exercises, and prove only the basic result regarding the simulation of a nondeterministic TM by a deterministic one.

Theorem 7.3   If L is accepted by a nondeterministic Turing machine, M_1, then L is accepted by some deterministic Turing machine, M_2.

Proof   For any state and tape symbol of M_1, there is a finite number of choices for the next move. These can be numbered 1, 2, ... Let r be the maximum number of choices for any state-tape symbol pair. Then any finite sequence of choices can be represented by a sequence of the digits 1 through r. Not all such sequences may represent choices of moves, since there may be fewer than r choices in some situations.

M_2 will have three tapes. The first will hold the input. On the second, M_2 will generate sequences of the digits 1 through r in a systematic manner. Specifically, the sequences will be generated with the shortest appearing first. Sequences of equal length are generated in numerical order.

For each sequence generated on tape 2, M_2 copies the input onto tape 3 and then simulates M_1 on tape 3, using the sequence on tape 2 to dictate the moves of M_1. If M_1 enters an accepting state, M_2 also accepts. If there is a sequence of choices leading to acceptance, it will eventually be generated on tape 2. When simulated, M_2 will accept. But if no sequence of choices of moves of M_1 leads to acceptance, M_2 will not accept.   □

Multidimensional Turing machines

Let us consider another modification of the Turing machine that adds no additional power—the multidimensional Turing machine. The device has the usual finite control, but the tape consists of a k-dimensional array of cells infinite in all $2k$ directions, for some fixed k. Depending on the state and symbol scanned, the device changes state, prints a new symbol, and moves its tape head in one of $2k$ directions, either positively or negatively, along one of the k axes. Initially, the input is along one axis, and the head is at the left end of the input.

At any time, only a finite number of rows in any dimension contain nonblank symbols, and these rows each have only a finite number of nonblank symbols. For example, consider the tape configuration of the two-dimensional TM shown in Fig. 7.10(a). Draw a rectangle about the nonblank symbols, as also shown in Fig. 7.10(a). The rectangle can be represented row by row on a single tape, as shown in Fig. 7.10(b). The *'s separate the rows. A second track may be used to indicate the position of the two-dimensional TM's tape head.

We shall prove that a one-dimensional TM can simulate a two-dimensional TM, leaving the generalization to more than two dimensions as an exercise.

Theorem 7.4   If L is accepted by a two-dimensional TM M_2, then L is accepted by a one-dimensional TM M_1.

B	B	B	a_1	B	B	B
B	B	a_2	a_3	a_4	a_5	B
a_6	a_7	a_8	a_9	B	a_{10}	B
B	a_{11}	a_{12}	a_{13}	B	a_{14}	a_{15}
B	B	a_{16}	a_{17}	B	B	B

$**BBBa_1 BBB*BBa_2 a_3 a_4 a_5 B*a_6 a_7 a_8 a_9 Ba_{10} B*Ba_{11} a_{12} a_{13} Ba_{14} a_{15} *BBa_{16} a_{17} BBB**$

Fig. 7.10 Simulation of two dimensions by one. (a) Two-dimensional tape. (b) One-dimensional simulation.

Proof M_1 represents the tape of M_2 as in Fig. 7.10(b). M_1 will also have a second tape used for purposes we shall describe, and the tapes are two-way infinite. Suppose that M_2 makes a move in which the head does not leave the rectangle already represented by M_1's tape. If the move is horizontal, M_1 simply moves its head marker one cell left or right after printing a new symbol and changing the state of M_2 recorded in M_1's control. If the move is vertical, T_1 uses its second tape to count the number of cells between the tape head position and the $*$ to its left. Then M_1 moves to the $*$ to the right, if the move is down, or the $*$ to the left if the move is up, and puts the tape head marker at the corresponding position in the new *block* (region between $*$'s) by using the count on the second tape.

Now consider the situation when M_2's head moves off the rectangle represented by M_1. If the move is vertical, add a new block of blanks to the left or right, using the second tape to count the current length of blocks. If the move is horizontal, M_1 uses the "shifting over" technique to add a blank at the left or right end of each block, as appropriate. Note that double $*$'s mark the ends of the region used to hold blocks, so M_1 can tell when it has augmented all blocks. After creating room to make the move, M_1 simulates the move of M_2 as described above. $\square$

Multihead Turing machines

A k-head Turing machine has some fixed number, k, of heads. The heads are numbered 1 through k, and a move of the TM depends on the state and on the symbol scanned by each head. In one move, the heads may each move independently left, right, or remain stationary.

Theorem 7.5 If L is accepted by some k-head TM M_1, it is accepted by a one-head TM M_2.

Proof The proof is similar to that of Theorem 7.2 for multitape TM's. M_2 has $k + 1$ tracks on its tape; the last holds the tape of M_1 and the ith holds a marker indicating the position of the ith tape head for $1 \leq i \leq k$. The details are left for an exercise. □

Off-line Turing machines

An *off-line* Turing machine is a multitape TM whose input tape is read-only. Usually we surround the input by endmarkers, ¢ on the left and \$ on the right. The Turing machine is not allowed to move the input tape head off the region between ¢ and \$. It should be obvious that the off-line TM is just a special case of the multitape TM, and therefore is no more powerful than any of the models we have considered. Conversely, an off-line TM can simulate any TM M by using one more tape than M. The first thing the off-line TM does is copy its own input onto the extra tape, and it then simulates M as if the extra tape were M's input. The need for off-line TM's will become apparent in Chapter 12, when we consider limiting the amount of storage space to less than the input length.

7.6 CHURCH'S HYPOTHESIS

The assumption that the intuitive notion of "computable function" can be identified with the class of partial recursive functions is known as *Church's hypothesis* or the *Church-Turing thesis*. While we cannot hope to "prove" Church's hypothesis as long as the informal notion of "computable" remains an informal notion, we can give evidence for its reasonableness. As long as our intuitive notion of "computable" places no bound on the number of steps or the amount of storage, it would seem that the partial recursive functions are intuitively computable, although some would argue that a function is not "computable" unless we can bound the computation in advance or at least establish whether or not the computation eventually terminates.

What is less clear is whether the class of partial recursive functions includes all "computable" functions. Logicians have presented many other formalisms such as the λ-calculus, Post systems, and general recursive functions. All have been shown to define the same class of functions, i.e., the partial recursive functions. In addition, abstract computer models, such as the *random access machine* (RAM), also give rise to the partial recursive functions.

The RAM consists of an infinite number of memory words, numbered 0, 1, ..., each of which can hold any integer, and a finite number of arithmetic registers capable of holding any integer. Integers may be decoded into the usual sorts of computer instructions. We shall not define the RAM model more formally, but it should be clear that if we choose a suitable set of instructions, the RAM may simulate any existing computer. The proof that the Turing machine formalism is as powerful as the RAM formalism is given below. Some other formalisms are discussed in the exercises.

Simulation of random access machines by Turing machines

Theorem 7.6   A Turing machine can simulate a RAM, provided that the elementary RAM instructions can themselves be simulated by a TM.

Proof   We use a multitape TM M to perform the simulation. One tape of M holds the words of the RAM that have been given values. The tape looks like

$$\#0*v_0 \# 1*v_1 \# 10*v_2 \# \cdots \# i*v_i \# \cdots,$$

where v_i is the contents, in binary, of the ith word. At all times, there will be some finite number of words of the RAM that have been used, and M needs only to keep a record of values up to the largest numbered word that has been used so far.

The RAM has some finite number of arithmetic registers. M uses one tape to hold each register's contents, one tape to hold the *location counter*, which contains the number of the word from which the next instruction is to be taken, and one tape as a *memory address register* on which the number of a memory word may be placed.

Suppose that the first 10 bits of an instruction denote one of the standard computer operations, such as LOAD, STORE, ADD, and so on, and that the remaining bits denote the address of an operand. While we shall not discuss the details of implementation for all standard computer instructions, an example should make the techniques clear. Suppose the location counter tape of M holds number i in binary. M searches its first tape from the left, looking for $\# i*$. If a blank is encountered before finding $\# i*$, there is no instruction in word i, so the RAM and M halt. If $\# i*$ is found, the bits following $*$ up to the next $\#$ are examined. Suppose the first 10 bits are the code for "ADD to register 2," and the remaining bits are some number j in binary. M adds 1 to i on the location counter tape and copies j onto the memory address tape. Then M searches for $\# j*$ on the first tape, again starting from the left (note that $\#0*$ marks the left end). If $\# j*$ is not found, we assume word j holds 0 and go on to the next instruction of the RAM. If $\# j*v_j \#$ is found, v_j is added to the contents of register 2, which is stored on its own tape. We then repeat the cycle with the next instruction.

Observe that although the RAM simulation used a multitape Turing machine, by Theorem 7.2 a single tape TM would suffice, although the simulation would be more complicated.   □

7.7   TURING MACHINES AS ENUMERATORS

We have viewed Turing machines as recognizers of languages and as computers of functions on the nonnegative integers. There is a third useful view of Turing machines, as generating devices. Consider a multitape TM M that uses one tape as an *output tape*, on which a symbol, once written, can never be changed, and whose tape head never moves left. Suppose also that on the output tape, M writes strings over some alphabet Σ, separated by a marker symbol $\#$. We can define $G(M)$, the *language generated by* M, to be the set of w in Σ^* such that w is eventually printed between a pair of $\#$'s on the output tape.

Note that unless M runs forever, $G(M)$ is finite. Also, we do not require that words be generated in any particular order, or that any particular word be generated only once. If L is $G(M)$ for some TM M, then L is an r.e. set, and conversely. The recursive sets also have a characterization in terms of generators; they are exactly the languages whose words can be generated in order of increasing size. These equivalences will be proved in turn.

Characterization of r.e. sets by generators

Lemma 7.1   If L is $G(M_1)$ for some TM M_1, then L is an r.e. set.

Proof   Construct TM M_2 with one more tape than M_1. M_2 simulates M_1 using all but M_2's input tape. Whenever M_1 prints $\#$ on its output tape, M_2 compares its input with the word just generated. If they are the same, M_2 accepts; otherwise M_2 continues to simulate M_1. Clearly M_2 accepts an input x if and only if x is in $G(M_1)$. Thus $L(M_2) = G(M_1)$.   □

The converse of Lemma 7.1 is somewhat more difficult. Suppose M_1 is a recognizer for some r.e. set $L \subseteq \Sigma^*$. Our first (and unsuccessful) attempt at designing a generator for L might be to generate the words in Σ^* in some order w_1, $w_2, \ldots$, run M_1 on w_1, and if M_1 accepts, generate w_1. Then run M_1 on w_2, generating w_2 if M_1 accepts, and so on. This method works if M_1 is guaranteed to halt on all inputs. However, as we shall see in Chapter 8, there are languages L that are r.e. but not recursive. If such is the case, we must contend with the possibility that M_1 never halts on some w_i. Then M_2 never considers w_{i+1}, $w_{i+2}, \ldots$, and so cannot generate any of these words, even if M_1 accepts them.

We must therefore avoid simulating M_1 indefinitely on any one word. To do this we fix an order for enumerating words in Σ^*. Next we develop a method of generating all pairs (i, j) of positive integers. The simulation proceeds by generating a pair (i, j) and then simulating M_1 on the ith word, for j steps.

We fix a *canonical order* for Σ^* as follows. List words in order of size, with words of the same size in "numerical order." That is, let $\Sigma = \{a_0, a_1, \ldots, a_{k-1}\}$, and imagine that a_i is the "digit" i in base k. Then the words of length n are the numbers 0 through $k^n - 1$ written in base k. The design of a TM to generate words in canonical order is not hard, and we leave it as an exercise.

Example 7.9   If $\Sigma = \{0, 1\}$, the canonical order is ϵ, 0, 1, 00, 01, 10, 11, 000, 001, $\ldots$

Note that the seemingly simpler order in which we generate the shortest representation of $0, 1, 2, \ldots$ in base k will not work as we never generate words like $a_0 a_0 a_1$, which have "leading 0's."

Next consider generating pairs (i, j) such that each pair is generated after some finite amount of time. This task is not so easy as it seems. The naive approach, $(1, 1), (1, 2), (1, 3), \ldots$ never generates any pairs with $i > 1$. Instead, we shall generate pairs in order of the sum $i + j$, and among pairs of equal sum, in order of increasing i. That is, we generate $(1, 1), (1, 2), (2, 1), (1, 3), (2, 2), (3, 1), (1, 4), \ldots$ The pair (i, j) is the $\{[(i + j - 1)(i + j - 2)]/2 + i\}$th pair generated. Thus this ordering has the desired property that there is a finite time at which any particular pair (i, j) is generated.

A TM generating pairs (i, j) in this order in binary is easy to design, and we leave its construction to the reader. We shall refer to such a TM as the *pair generator* in the future. Incidentally, the ordering used by the pair generator demonstrates that pairs of integers can be put into one-to-one correspondence with the integers themselves, a seemingly paradoxical result that was discovered by Georg Kantor when he showed that the rationals (which are really the ratios of two integers) are equinumerous with the integers.

Theorem 7.7 A language is r.e. if and only if it is $G(M_2)$ for some TM M_2.

Proof With Lemma 7.1 we have only to show how an r.e. set $L = L(M_1)$ can be generated by a TM M_2. M_2 simulates the pair generator. When (i, j) is generated, M_2 produces the ith word w_i in canonical order and simulates M_1 on w_i for j steps. If M_1 accepts on the jth step (counting the initial ID as step 1), then M_2 generates w_i.

Surely M_2 generates no word not in L. If w is in L, let w be the ith word in canonical order for the alphabet of L, and let M_1 accept w after exactly j moves. As it takes only a finite amount of time for M_2 to generate any particular word in canonical order or to simulate M_1 for any particular number of steps, we know that M_2 will eventually produce the pair (i, j). At that stage, w will be generated by M_2. Thus $G(M_2) = L$. □

Corollary If L is an r.e. set, then there is a generator for L that enumerates each word in L exactly once.

Proof M_2 described above has that property, since it generates w_i only when considering the pair (i, j), where j is exactly the number of steps taken by M_1 to accept w_i. □

Characterization of recursive sets by generators

We shall now show that the recursive sets are precisely those sets whose words can be generated in canonical order.

Lemma 7.2   If L is recursive, then there is a generator for L that prints the words of L in canonical order and prints no other words.

Proof   Let $L = L(M_1) \subseteq \Sigma^*$, where M_1 halts on every input. Construct M_2 to generate L as follows. M_2 generates (on a scratch tape) the words in Σ^*, one at a time, in canonical order. After generating some word w, M_2 simulates M_1 on w. If M_1 accepts w, M_2 generates w. Since M_1 is guaranteed to halt, we know that M_2 will finish processing each word after a finite time and will therefore eventually consider each particular word in Σ^*. Clearly M_2 generates L in canonical order. $\square$

The converse of Lemma 7.2, that if L can be generated in canonical order then L is recursive, is also true. However, there is a subtlety of which we should be aware. In Lemma 7.2 we could actually construct M_2 from M_1. However, given a TM M generating L in canonical order, we know a halting TM recognizing L exists, but there is no algorithm to exhibit that TM.

Suppose M_1 generates L in canonical order. The natural thing to do is to construct a TM M_2 that on input w simulates M_1 until M_1 either generates w or a word beyond w in canonical order. In the former case, M_2 accepts w, and in the latter case, M_2 halts without accepting w. However, if L is finite, M_1 may never halt after generating the last word in L, so M_1 may generate neither w nor any word beyond. In this situation M_2 would not halt. This problem arises only when L is finite, even though we know every finite set is accepted by a Turing machine that halts on all inputs. Unfortunately, we cannot determine whether a TM generates a finite set or, if finite, which finite set it is. Thus we know that a halting Turing machine accepting L, the language generated by M_1, always exists, but there is no algorithm to exhibit the Turing machine.

Theorem 7.8 L is recursive if and only if L is generated in canonical order.

Proof   The "only if" part was established by Lemma 7.2. For the "if" part, when L is infinite, M_2 described above is a halting Turing machine for L. Clearly, when L is finite, there is a finite automaton accepting L, and thus L can be accepted by a TM that halts on all inputs. Note that in general we cannot exhibit a particular halting TM that accepts L, but the theorem merely states that one such TM exists. $\square$

7.8   RESTRICTED TURING MACHINES EQUIVALENT TO THE BASIC MODEL

In Section 7.5 we considered generalizations of the basic TM model. As we have seen, these generalizations have no more computational power than the basic model. We conclude this chapter by considering some models that at first appear less powerful than the TM but indeed are just as powerful. For the most part, these models will be variations of the pushdown automaton defined in Chapter 5.

In passing, we note that a pushdown automaton is equivalent to a nondeterministic TM with a read-only input on which the input head cannot move left, plus a storage tape with a rather peculiar restriction on the tape head. Whenever the storage tape head moves left, it must print a blank. Thus the storage tape to the right of the head is always completely blank, and the storage tape is effectively a stack, with the top at the right, rather than the left as in Chapter 5.

Multistack machines

A deterministic two-stack machine is a deterministic Turing machine with a read-only input and two storage tapes. If a head moves left on either tape, a blank is printed on that tape.

Lemma 7.3 An arbitrary single-tape Turing machine can be simulated by a deterministic two-stack machine.

Proof The symbols to the left of the head of the TM being simulated can be stored on one stack, while the symbols on the right of the head can be placed on the other stack. On each stack, symbols closer to the TM's head are placed closer to the top of the stack than symbols farther from the TM's head. □

Counter machines

We can prove a result stronger than Lemma 7.3. It concerns *counter machines*, which are off-line Turing machines whose storage tapes are semi-infinite, and whose tape alphabets contain only two symbols, Z and B (blank). Furthermore, the symbol Z, which serves as a bottom of stack marker, appears initially on the cell scanned by the tape head and may never appear on any other cell. An integer i can be stored by moving the tape head i cells to the right of Z. A stored number can be incremented or decremented by moving the tape head right or left. We can test whether a number is zero by checking whether Z is scanned by the head, but we cannot directly test whether two numbers are equal.

An example of a counter machine is shown in Fig. 7.11; ¢ and \$ are customarily used for end markers on the input. Here Z is the nonblank symbol on each tape. An instantaneous description of a counter machine can be described by the state, the input tape contents, the position of the input head, and the distance of the storage heads from the symbol Z (shown here as d_1 and d_2). We call these distances the *counts* on the tapes. The counter machine, then, can really only store a count on each tape and tell if that count is zero.

Lemma 7.4 A four-counter machine can simulate an arbitrary Turing machine.

Proof From Lemma 7.3, it suffices to show that two counter tapes can simulate one stack. Let a stack have $k - 1$ tape symbols, $Z_1, Z_2, \ldots, Z_{k-1}$. Then we can

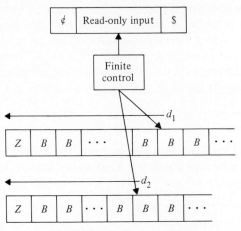

Fig. 7.11 Counter machine.

represent the stack $Z_{i_1} Z_{i_2} \cdots Z_{i_m}$ uniquely by the count in base k

$$j = i_m + k i_{m-1} + k^2 i_{m-2} + \cdots + k^{m-1} i_1. \tag{7.3}$$

Note that not every integer represents a stack; in particular, those whose base-k representation contains the digit 0 do not.

Suppose that the symbol Z_r is pushed onto the top (right end) of the stack $Z_{i_1} Z_{i_2} \cdots Z_{i_m}$. The count associated with $Z_{i_1} Z_{i_2} \cdots Z_{i_m} Z_r$ is $jk + r$. To get this new count, the counter machine repeatedly moves the head of the first counter one cell to the left and the head of the second, k cells to the right. When the head of the first counter reaches the nonblank symbol, the second counter will hold the count jk. It is a simple matter to add r to the count.

If, instead, the top symbol Z_{i_m} of the stack were popped, j should be replaced by $\lfloor j/k \rfloor$, the integer part of j/k. We repeatedly decrement the count on the first counter by k and then add one to the second count. When the first count is zero, the second count will be $\lfloor j/k \rfloor$.

To complete the description of the simulation, we must show how the four-counter machine can tell what symbol is at the top of each stack. If the count j is stored on one counter, the four-counter machine can copy j to another counter, computing $j \bmod k$ in its finite control. Note that $j \bmod k$ is i_m if j is given by (7.3). □

Theorem 7.9 A two-counter machine can simulate an arbitrary Turing machine.

Proof By Lemma 7.4, it is sufficient to show how to simulate four counters with two. Let four counters have counts $i, j, k,$ and ℓ. One counter can represent these four by the number $n = 2^i 3^j 5^k 7^\ell$. Since 2, 3, 5, and 7 are primes, $i, j, k,$ and ℓ can be uniquely recovered from n.

To increment $i, j, k,$ or ℓ by 1, we multiply n by 2, 3, 5, or 7, respectively. To do so, if we have another counter set to zero, we can move the head of this counter 2, 3, 5, or 7 cells to the right each time we move the head of the first counter one cell to the left. When the first counter holds zero, the second will hold $2n, 3n, 5n,$ or $7n$, respectively. To decrement $i, j, k,$ or ℓ by 1, n is, by a similar process, divided by 2, 3, 5, or 7, respectively.

We must also show how the two-counter machine can determine the next move of the four-counter machine. The two-counter machine always scans the same cell of the input tape as the four-counter machine does. The state of the four-counter machine is stored in the finite control of the two-counter machine. Thus, to determine the move of the four-counter machine, the two-counter machine has only to determine which, if any, of $i, j, k,$ and ℓ are 0. By passing n from one counter to the other, the finite control of the two-counter machine can determine if n is divisible by 2, 3, 5, 7, or any product of these. ☐

Limits on the number of states and symbols

Another way to restrict a TM is to limit the size of the tape alphabet or the number of states. If the tape alphabet, number of tapes, and number of states are all limited, then there is only a finite number of different Turing machines, so the restricted model is less powerful than the original.† If we do not restrict the tape alphabet, then three states and one tape are sufficient to recognize any r.e. set; this result is left as an exercise. We shall, however, prove a result about limited tape alphabets.

Theorem 7.10 If $L \subseteq (0 + 1)^*$ and L is r.e., then L is accepted by a one-tape TM with tape alphabet $\{0, 1, B\}$.

Proof Let $L = L(M_1)$, where $M_1 = (Q, \{0, 1\}, \Gamma, \delta, q_0, B, F)$. Suppose Γ has between $2^{k-1} + 1$ and 2^k symbols, so k bits are sufficient to encode any tape symbol of M_1. We may design M_2, with tape alphabet $\{0, 1, B\}$ to simulate M_1. The tape of M_2 will consist of a sequence of codes for symbols of M_1. The finite control of M_2 remembers the state of M_1 and also remembers the position of M_2's tape head, modulo k, so M_2 can know when it is at the beginning of a coded tape symbol of M_1.

At the beginning of the simulation of a move of M_1, the head of M_2 is at the left end of a binary-coded symbol of M_1. M_2 scans the next $k - 1$ symbols to its right, to determine the move of M_1. Then M_1 replaces the symbols scanned to reflect the move of M_1, positions its tape head at the left end of the code for the next symbol scanned by M_1, and changes the state of M_1. If that state is accepting,

---

† However, there are such restricted Turing machines that are "universal" (see Section 8.3) in the sense that given as input an encoding of a transition function for some TM M and an input w to M, the universal machine accepts if and only if M accepts w. For example, it is known that there is a universal TM with one tape, 5 states, and 7 tape symbols.

M_2 accepts; otherwise, M_2 is ready to simulate the next move of M_1. A special case occurs if M_2 finds its head positioned at a blank when it should be reading a code for a tape symbol of M_1. In this case, M_1 has just moved to a position it has never before reached. M_2 must write the binary code for M_1's blank on the cell scanned and the $k - 1$ cells to its right, after which it may simulate a move of M_1 as before.

One important detail is left to be explained. M_2's input is a binary string w in $(0 + 1)^*$ representing w itself, rather than a string of coded 0's and 1's representing w. Therefore, before simulating M_1, M_2 must replace w by its code. To do so, M_2 uses the "shifting over" trick, using B for the symbol X described in Section 7.4, where "shifting over" was introduced. For each input symbol, starting with the leftmost, the string to the right of the symbol is shifted $k - 1$ places right, and then the symbol and the $k - 1$ B's introduced are replaced by the k-bit binary code for the symbol. $\square$

We can apply the same binary coding technique even if the input alphabet is not $\{0, 1\}$. We therefore state the following corollary and leave its proof as an exercise.

Corollary If L is an r.e. set over any alphabet whatsoever, then L is accepted by an off-line TM that has only one tape besides the input, and whose alphabet for that tape is $\{0, 1, B\}$.

Theorem 7.11 Every Turing machine can be simulated by an off-line Turing machine having one storage tape with two symbols, 0 (blank) and 1. The Turing machine can print a 0 or 1 over a 0, but cannot print a 0 over a 1.

Proof We leave this to the reader. The "trick" is to create successive ID's of the original Turing machine on the tape of the new one. Tape symbols are, of course, encoded in binary. Each ID is copied over, making the changes necessary to simulate a move of the old machine.

In addition to the binary encoding of the original symbol, the TM doing the simulating needs cells to indicate the position of the head in the ID being copied, and cells to indicate that the binary representation of a symbol has already been copied. $\square$

EXERCISES

7.1 Design Turing machines to recognize the following languages.

a) $\{0^n 1^n 0^n \mid n \geq 1\}$.

b) $\{ww^R \mid w \text{ is in } (0 + 1)^*\}$.

c) The set of strings with an equal number of 0's and 1's.

7.2 Design Turing machines to compute the following functions.

a) $\lceil \log_2 n \rceil$ b) $n!$ c) n^2

7.3   Show that if L is accepted by a k-tape, ℓ-dimensional, nondeterministic TM with m heads per tape, then L is accepted by a deterministic TM with one semi-infinite tape and one tape head.

7.4   A *recursive function* is a function defined by a finite set of rules that for various arguments specify the function in terms of variables, nonnegative integer constants, the *successor* (add one) function, the function itself, or an expression built from these by composition of functions. For example, *Ackermann's function* is defined by the rules:

1) $A(0, y) = 1$
2) $A(1, 0) = 2$
3) $A(x, 0) = x + 2$ for $x \geq 2$
4) $A(x + 1, y + 1) = A(A(x, y + 1), y)$
   a) Evaluate $A(2, 1)$.
 * b) What function of one variable is $A(x, 2)$?
 * c) Evaluate $A(4, 3)$.

 * **7.5**   Give recursive definitions for

   a) $n + m$ b) $n \dot{-} m$ c) nm d) $n!$

** **7.6**   Show that the class of recursive functions is identical to the class of partial recursive functions.

7.7   A function is *primitive recursive* if it is a finite number of applications of composition and *primitive recursion*† applied to constant 0, the successor function, or a projection function $P_i(x_1, \ldots, x_n) = x_i$.

   a) Show that every primitive recursive function is a total recursive function.
** b) Show that Ackermann's function is not primitive recursive.
** c) Show that adding the minimization operator, min $(f(x))$ defined as the least x such that $f(x) = 0$, yields all partial recursive functions.

7.8   Design a Turing machine to enumerate $\{0^n 1^n \mid n \geq 1\}$.

** **7.9**   Show that every r.e. set is accepted by a TM with only two nonaccepting states and one accepting state.

 * **7.10**   Complete the proof of Theorem 7.11, that tapes symbols 0 (blank) and 1, with no 1 overprinted by 0, are sufficient for an off-line TM to accept any r.e. language.

7.11   Consider an off-line TM model that cannot write on any tape but has three pebbles that can be placed on the auxiliary tape. Show that the model can accept any r.e. language.

---

† A primitive recursion is a definition of $f(x_1, \ldots, x_n)$ by

$$f(x_1, \ldots, x_n) = \text{if } x_n = 0 \text{ then}$$

$$g(x_1, \ldots, x_{n-1})$$

else

$$h(x_1, \ldots, x_n, f(x_1, \ldots, x_{n-1}, x_n - 1))$$

where g and h are primitive recursive functions.

BIBLIOGRAPHIC NOTES

The Turing machine is the invention of Turing [1936]. Alternative formulations can be found in Kleene [1936], Church [1936], or Post [1936]. For a discussion of Church's hypothesis, see Kleene [1952], Davis [1958], or Rogers [1967]. Other formalisms equivalent to the partial recursive functions include the λ-calculus (Church [1941]), recursive functions (Kleene [1952]), and Post systems (Post [1943]).

Off-line TM's are discussed by Hartmanis, Lewis, and Stearns [1965]. An important result about multihead TM's—that they can be simulated without loss of time with one head per tape—is found in Hartmanis and Stearns [1965]. The one case not covered by the latter paper, when the multihead machine runs in *real* time (a number of moves proportional to the input length), was handled by Fischer, Meyer, and Rosenberg [1972], and Leong and Seiferas [1977] contains the latest on reducing the complexity of that construction. RAM's were formally considered by Cook and Reckhow [1973].

Theorem 7.9, that two counters can simulate a TM, was proved by Minsky [1961]; the proof given here is taken from Fischer [1966]. Theorem 7.11, on TM's that can only print 1's over 0's, is from Wang [1957]. Exercise 7.9, limiting the number of states, is from Shannon [1956]. In fact, as the latter paper assumes acceptance by halting rather than by final state, it shows that only two states are needed.

A number of texts provide an introduction to the theory of Turing machines and recursive functions. These include Davis [1958, 1965], Rogers [1967], Yasuhara [1971], Jones [1973], Brainerd and Landweber [1974], Hennie [1977], and Machtey and Young [1978].

CHAPTER

8

UNDECIDABILITY

We now consider the classes of recursive and recursively enumerable languages. The most interesting aspect of this study concerns languages whose strings are interpreted as codings of instances of problems. Consider the problem of determining if an arbitrary Turing machine accepts the empty string. This problem may be formulated as a language problem by encoding TM's as strings of 0's and 1's. The set of all strings encoding TM's that accept the empty string is a language that is recursively enumerable but not recursive. From this we conclude that there can be no algorithm to decide which TM's accept the empty string and which do not.

In this chapter we shall show that many questions about TM's, as well as some questions about context-free languages and other formalisms, have no algorithms for their solution. In addition we introduce some fundamental concepts from the theory of recursive functions, including the hierarchy of problems induced by the consideration of Turing machines with "oracles."

8.1 PROBLEMS

Informally we use the word *problem* to refer to a question such as: "Is a given CFG ambiguous?" In the case of the *ambiguity problem*, above, an instance of the problem is a particular CFG. In general, an *instance* of a problem is a list of arguments, one argument for each parameter of the problem. By restricting our attention to problems with yes-no answers and encoding instances of the problem by strings over some finite alphabet, we can transform the question of whether there exists an algorithm for solving a problem to whether or not a particular language is recursive. While it may seem that we are throwing out a lot of impor-

177

tant problems by looking only at yes-no problems, in fact such is not the case. Many general problems have yes-no versions that are provably just as difficult as the general problem.

Consider the ambiguity problem for CFG's. Call the yes-no version AMB. A more general version of the problem, called FIND, requires producing a word with two or more parses if one exists and answering "no" otherwise. An algorithm for FIND can be used to solve AMB. If FIND produces a word w, then answer "yes"; if FIND answers "no," then answer "no." Conversely, given an algorithm for AMB we can produce an algorithm for FIND. The algorithm first applies AMB to the grammar G. If AMB answers "no" our algorithm answers "no." If AMB answers "yes," the algorithm systematically begins to generate all words over the terminal alphabet of G. As soon as a word w is generated, it is tested to see if it has two or more parse trees. Note that the algorithm does not begin generating words unless G is ambiguous, so some w eventually will be found and printed. Thus we indeed have an algorithm. The portion of the algorithm that tests w for two or more parses is left as an exercise.

The process whereby we construct an algorithm for one problem (such as FIND), using a supposed algorithm for another (AMB), is called a *reduction* (of FIND to AMB). In general, when we reduce problem A to problem B we are showing that B is at least as hard as A. Thus in this case, as in many others, the yes-no problem AMB is no easier than the more general version of the problem. Later we shall show that there is no algorithm for AMB. By the reduction of AMB to FIND we conclude there is no algorithm for FIND either, since the existence of an algorithm for FIND implies the existence of an algorithm for AMB, a contradiction.

One further instructive point concerns the coding of the grammar G. As all Turing machines have a fixed alphabet, we cannot treat the 4-tuple notation $G = (V, T, P, S)$ as the encoding of G without modification. We can encode 4-tuples as binary strings as follows. Let the metasymbols in 4-tuples, that is, the left and right parentheses, brackets, comma and $\rightarrow$, be encoded by $1, 10, 100, \ldots,$ 10^5, respectively. Let the ith grammar symbol (in any chosen order) be encoded by 10^{i+5}. In this encoding, we cannot tell the exact symbols used for either terminals or nonterminals. Of course renaming nonterminals does not affect the language generated, so their symbols are not important. Although we ordinarily view the identities of the terminals as important, for this problem the actual symbols used for the terminals is irrelevant, since renaming the terminals does not affect the ambiguity or unambiguity of a grammar.

Decidable and undecidable problems

A problem whose language is recursive is said to be *decidable*. Otherwise, the problem is *undecidable*. That is, a problem is undecidable if there is no algorithm that takes as input an instance of the problem and determines whether the answer to that instance is "yes" or "no."

An unintuitive consequence of the definition of "undecidable" is that problems with only a single instance are trivially decidable. Consider the following problem based on Fermat's conjecture. Is there no solution in positive integers to the equation $x^i + y^i = z^i$ if $i \geq 3$? Note that x, y, z, and i are not parameters but bound variables in the statement of the problem. There is one Turing machine that accepts any input and one that rejects any input. One of these answers Fermat's conjecture correctly, even though we do not know which one. In fact there may not even be a resolution to the conjecture using the axioms of arithmetic. That is, Fermat's conjecture may be true, yet there may be no arithmetic proof of that fact. The possibility (though not the certainty) that this is the case follows from Godel's incompleteness theorem, which states that any consistent formal system powerful enough to encompass number theory must have statements that are true but not provable within the system.

It should not disturb the reader that a conundrum like Fermat's conjecture is "decidable." The theory of undecidability is concerned with the existence or non-existence of algorithms for solving problems with an infinity of instances.

8.2 PROPERTIES OF RECURSIVE AND RECURSIVELY ENUMERABLE LANGUAGES

A number of theorems in this chapter are proved by reducing one problem to another. These reductions involve combining several Turing machines to form a composite machine. The state of the composite TM has a component for each individual component machine. Similarly the composite machine has separate tapes for each individual machine. The details of the composite machine are usually tedious and provide no insight. Thus we choose to informally describe the constructions.

Given an algorithm (TM that always halts), we can allow the composite TM to perform one action if the algorithm accepts and another if it does not accept. We could not do this if we were given an arbitrary TM rather than an algorithm, since if the TM did not accept, it might run forever, and the composite machine would never initiate the next task. In pictures, an arrow into a box labeled "start" indicates a start signal. Boxes with no "start" signal are assumed to begin operating when the composite machine does. Algorithms have two outputs, "yes" and "no," which can be used as start signals or as a response by the composite machine. Arbitrary TM's have only a "yes" output, which can be used for the same purposes.

We now turn to some basic closure properties of the classes of recursive and r.e. sets.

Theorem 8.1 The complement of a recursive language is recursive.

Proof Let L be a recursive language and M a Turing machine that halts on all inputs and accepts L. Construct M' from M so that if M enters a final state on input w, then M' halts without accepting. If M halts without accepting, M' enters a

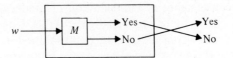

Fig. 8.1 Construction showing that recursive languages are closed under complementation.

final state. Since one of these two events occurs, M' is an algorithm. Clearly $L(M')$ is the complement of L and thus the complement of L is a recursive language. Figure 8.1 pictures the construction of M' from M. □

Theorem 8.2 The union of two recursive languages is recursive. The union of two recursively enumerable languages is recursively enumerable.

Proof Let L_1 and L_2 be recursive languages accepted by algorithms M_1 and M_2. We construct M, which first simulates M_1. If M_1 accepts, then M accepts. If M_1 rejects, then M simulates M_2 and accepts if and only if M_2 accepts. Since both M_1 and M_2 are algorithms, M is guaranteed to halt. Clearly M accepts $L_1 \cup L_2$.

For recursively enumerable languages the above construction does not work, since M_1 may not halt. Instead M can simultaneously simulate M_1 and M_2 on separate tapes. If either accepts, then M accepts. Figure 8.2 shows the two constructions of this theorem. □

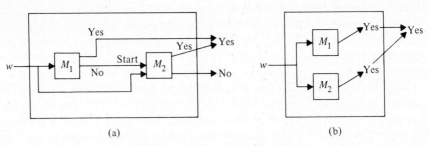

(a)   (b)

Fig. 8.2 Construction for union.

Theorem 8.3 If a language L and its complement $\bar{L}$ are both recursively enumerable, then L (and hence $\bar{L}$) is recursive.

Proof Let M_1 and M_2 accept L and $\bar{L}$ respectively. Construct M as in Fig. 8.3 to simulate simultaneously M_1 and M_2. M accepts w if M_1 accepts w and rejects w if M_2 accepts w. Since w is in either L or $\bar{L}$, we know that exactly one of M_1 or M_2 will accept. Thus M will always say either "yes" or "no," but will never say both. Note that there is no *a priori* limit on how long it may take before M_1 or M_2 accepts, but it is certain that one or the other will do so. Since M is an algorithm that accepts L, it follows that L is recursive. □

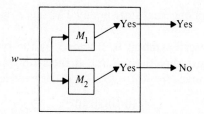

Fig. 8.3 Construction for Theorem 8.3.

Theorems 8.1 and 8.3 have an important consequence. Let L and $\bar{L}$ be a pair of complementary languages. Then either

1) both L and $\bar{L}$ are recursive,
2) neither L nor $\bar{L}$ is r.e., or
3) one of L and $\bar{L}$ is r.e. but not recursive; the other is not r.e.

An important technique for showing a problem undecidable is to show by diagonalization that the complement of the language for that problem is not r.e. Thus case (2) or (3) above must apply. This technique is essential in proving our first problem undecidable. After that, various forms of reductions may be employed to show other problems undecidable.

8.3 UNIVERSAL TURING MACHINES AND AN UNDECIDABLE PROBLEM

We shall now use diagonalization to show a particular problem to be undecidable. The problem is: "Does Turing machine M accept input w?" Here, both M and w are parameters of the problem. In formalizing the problem as a language we shall restrict w to be over alphabet $\{0, 1\}$ and M to have tape alphabet $\{0, 1, B\}$. As the restricted problem is undecidable, the more general problem is surely undecidable as well. We choose to work with the more restricted version to simplify the encoding of problem instances as strings.

Turing machine codes

To begin, we encode Turing machines with restricted alphabets as strings over $\{0, 1\}$. Let

$$M = (Q, \{0, 1\}, \{0, 1, B\}, \delta, q_1, B, \{q_2\})$$

be a Turing machine with input alphabet $\{0, 1\}$ and the blank as the only additional tape symbol. We further assume that $Q = \{q_1, q_2, \ldots, q_n\}$ is the set of states, and that q_2 is the only final state. Theorem 7.10 assures us that if $L \subseteq (0 + 1)^*$ is accepted by any TM, then it is accepted by one with alphabet $\{0, 1, B\}$. Also, there is no need for more than one final state in any TM, since once it accepts it may as well halt.

It is convenient to call symbols 0, 1, and B by the synonyms X_1, X_2, X_3, respectively. We also give directions L and R the synonyms D_1 and D_2, respectively. Then a generic move $\delta(q_i, X_j) = (q_k, X_\ell, D_m)$ is encoded by the binary string

$$0^i 1 0^j 1 0^k 1 0^\ell 1 0^m. \tag{8.1}$$

A binary code for Turing machine M is

$$111 \text{ code}_1 11 \text{ code}_2 11 \cdots 11 \text{ code}_r 111, \tag{8.2}$$

where each code$_i$ is a string of the form (8.1), and each move of M is encoded by one of the code$_i$'s. The moves need not be in any particular order, so each TM actually has many codes. Any such code for M will be denoted $\langle M \rangle$.

Every binary string can be interpreted as the code for at most one TM; many binary strings are not the code of any TM. To see that decoding is unique, note that no string of the form (8.1) has two 1's in a row, so the code$_i$'s can be found directly. If a string fails to begin and end with exactly three 1's, has three 1's other than at the end, or has two pair of 1's with other than five blocks of 0's in between, then the string represents no TM.

The pair M and w is represented by a string of the form (8.2) followed by w. Any such string will be denoted $\langle M, w \rangle$.

Example 8.1 Let $M = (\{q_1, q_2, q_3\}, \{0, 1\}, \{0, 1, B\}, \delta, q_1, B, \{q_2\})$ have moves:

$$\delta(q_1, 1) = (q_3, 0, R),$$
$$\delta(q_3, 0) = (q_1, 1, R),$$
$$\delta(q_3, 1) = (q_2, 0, R),$$
$$\delta(q_3, B) = (q_3, 1, L).$$

Thus one string denoted by $\langle M, 1011 \rangle$ is

$$1110100100010100110001010100010011$$

$$0001001001010011000100010001001011111011$$

Note that many different strings are also codes for the pair $\langle M, 1011 \rangle$, and any of these may be referred to by the notation $\langle M, 1011 \rangle$.

A non-r.e. language

Suppose we have a list of $(0 + 1)^*$ in canonical order (see Section 7.7), where w_i is the ith word, and M_j is the TM whose code, as in (8.2) is the integer j written in

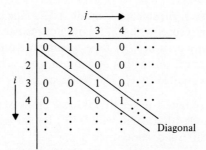

Fig. 8.4 Hypothetical table indicating acceptance of words by TM's.

binary. Imagine an infinite table that tells for all i and j whether w_i is in $L(M_j)$. Figure 8.4 suggests such a table;† 0 means w_i is not in $L(M_j)$ and 1 means it is.

We construct a language L_d by using the diagonal entries of the table to determine membership in L_d. To guarantee that no TM accepts L_d, we insist that w_i is in L_d if and only if the (i, i) entry is 0, that is, if M_i does not accept w_i. Suppose that some TM M_j accepted L_d. Then we are faced with the following contradiction. If w_j is in L_d, then the (j, j) entry is 0, implying that w_j is not in $L(M_j)$ and contradicting $L_d = L(M_j)$. On the other hand, if w_j is not in L_d, then the (j, j) entry is 1, implying that w_j is in $L(M_j)$, which again contradicts $L_d = L(M_j)$. As w_j is either in or not in L_d, we conclude that our assumption, $L_d = L(M_j)$, is false. Thus, no TM in the list accepts L_d, and by Theorem 7.10, no TM whatsoever accepts L_d.

We have thus proved

Lemma 8.1 L_d is not r.e.

The universal language

Define L_u, the "universal language," to be $\{\langle M, w \rangle \mid M \text{ accepts } w\}$. We call L_u "universal" since the question of whether any particular string w in $(0 + 1)^*$ is accepted by any particular Turing machine M is equivalent to the question of whether $\langle M', w \rangle$ is in L_u, where M' is the TM with tape alphabet $\{0, 1, B\}$ equivalent to M constructed as in Theorem 7.10.

Theorem 8.4 L_u is recursively enumerable.

Proof   We shall exhibit a three-tape TM M_1 accepting L_u. The first tape of M_1 is the input tape, and the input head on that tape is used to look up moves of the TM M when given code $\langle M, w \rangle$ as input. Note that the moves of M are found between the first two blocks of three 1's. The second tape of M_1 will simulate the tape of M.

---

† Actually as all low-numbered Turing machines accept the empty set, the correct portion of the table shown has all 0's.

The alphabet of M is $\{0, 1, B\}$, so each symbol of M's tape can be held in one tape cell of M_1's second tape. Observe that if we did not restrict the alphabet of M, we would have to use many cells of M_1's tape to simulate one of M's cells, but the simulation could be carried out with a little more work. The third tape holds the state of M, with q_i represented by 0^i. The behavior of M_1 is as follows:

1) Check the format of tape 1 to see that it has a prefix of the form (8.2) and that there are no two codes that begin with $0^i 10^j 1$ for the same i and j. Also check that if $0^i 10^j 10^k 10^\ell 10^m$ is a code, then $1 \leq j \leq 3$, $1 \leq \ell \leq 3$, and $1 \leq m \leq 2$. Tape 3 can be used as a scratch tape to facilitate the comparison of codes.

2) Initialize tape 2 to contain w, the portion of the input beyond the second block of three 1's. Initialize tape 3 to hold a single 0, representing q_1. All three tape heads are positioned on the leftmost symbols. These symbols may be marked so the heads can find their way back.

3) If tape 3 holds 00, the code for the final state, halt and accept.

4) Let X_j be the symbol currently scanned by tape head 2 and let 0^i be the current contents of tape 3. Scan tape 1 from the left end to the second 111, looking for a substring beginning $110^i 10^j 1$. If no such string is found, halt and reject; M has no next move and has not accepted. If such a code is found, let it be $0^i 10^j 10^k 10^\ell 10^m$. Then put 0^k on tape 3, print X_ℓ on the tape cell scanned by head 2 and move that head in direction D_m. Note that we have checked in (1) that $1 \leq \ell \leq 3$ and $1 \leq m \leq 2$. Go to step (3).

It is straightforward to check that M_1 accepts $\langle M, w \rangle$ if and only if M accepts w. It is also true that if M runs forever on w, M_1 will run forever on $\langle M, w \rangle$, and if M halts on w without accepting, M_1 does the same on $\langle M, w \rangle$. $\square$

The existence of M_1 is sufficient to prove Theorem 8.4. However, by Theorems 7.2 and 7.10, we can find a TM with one semi-infinite tape and alphabet $\{0, 1, B\}$ accepting L_u. We call this particular TM M_u, the *universal Turing machine*, since it does the work of any TM with input alphabet $\{0, 1\}$.

By Lemma 8.1, the diagonal language L_d is not r.e., and hence not recursive. Thus by Theorem 8.1, $\bar{L}_d$ is not recursive. Note that $\bar{L}_d = \{w_i \mid M_i \text{ accepts } w_i\}$. We can prove the universal language $L_u = \{\langle M, w \rangle \mid M \text{ accepts } w\}$ not to be recursive by reducing $\bar{L}_d$ to L_u. Thus L_u is an example of a language that is r.e. but not recursive. In fact, $\bar{L}_d$ is another example of such a language.

Theorem 8.5 L_u is not recursive.

Proof   Suppose A were an algorithm recognizing L_u. Then we could recognize $\bar{L}_d$ as follows. Given string w in $(0 + 1)^*$, determine by an easy calculation the value of i such that $w = w_i$. Integer i in binary is the code for some TM M_i. Feed $\langle M_i, w_i \rangle$ to algorithm A and accept w if and only if M_i accepts w_i. The construction is shown in Fig. 8.5. It is easy to check that the constructed algorithm accepts w if

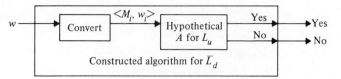

Fig. 8.5 Reduction of $\bar{L}_d$ to L_u.

and only if $w = w_i$ and w_i is in $L(M_i)$. Thus we have an algorithm for $\bar{L}_d$ Since no such algorithm exists, we know our assumption, that algorithm A for L_u exists, is false. Hence L_u is r.e. but not recursive. □

8.4 RICE'S THEOREM AND SOME MORE UNDECIDABLE PROBLEMS

We now have an example of an r.e. language that is not recursive. The associated problem "Does M accept w?" is undecidable, and we can use this fact to show that other problems are undecidable. In this section we shall give several examples of undecidable problems concerning r.e. sets. In the next three sections we shall discuss some undecidable problems taken from outside the realm of TM's.

Example 8.2 Consider the problem: "Is $L(M) \neq \varnothing$?" Let $\langle M \rangle$ denote a code for M as in (8.2). Then define

$$L_{ne} = \{\langle M \rangle \,|\, L(M) \neq \varnothing\} \qquad \text{and} \qquad L_e = \{\langle M \rangle \,|\, L(M) = \varnothing\}.$$

Note that L_e and L_{ne} are complements of one another, since every binary string denotes some TM; those with a bad format denote the TM with no moves. All these strings are in L_e. We claim that L_{ne} is r.e. but not recursive and that L_e is not r.e.

We show that L_{ne} is r.e. by constructing a TM M to recognize codes of TM's that accept nonempty sets. Given input $\langle M_i \rangle$, M nondeterministically guesses a string x accepted by M_i and verifies that M_i does indeed accept x by simulating M_i on input x. This step can also be carried out deterministically if we use the pair generator described in Section 7.7. For pair (j, k) simulate M_i on the jth binary string (in canonical order) for k steps. If M_i accepts, then M accepts $\langle M_i \rangle$.

Now we must show that L_e is not recursive. Suppose it were. Then we could construct an algorithm for L_u, violating Theorem 8.5. Let A be a hypothetical algorithm accepting L_e. There is an algorithm B that, given $\langle M, w \rangle$, constructs a TM M' that accepts $\varnothing$ if M does not accept w and accepts $(0 + 1)^*$ if M accepts w. The plan of M' is shown in Fig. 8.6. M' ignores its input x and instead simulates M on input w, accepting if M accepts.

Note that M' is not B. Rather, B is like a compiler that takes $\langle M, w \rangle$ as "source program" and produces M' as "object program." We have described what B must do, but not how it does it. The construction of B is simple. It takes $\langle M, w \rangle$

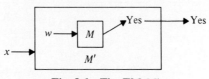

Fig. 8.6 The TM M'.

and isolates w. Say $w = a_1 a_2 \cdots a_n$ is of length n. B creates $n + 3$ states $q_1, q_2, \ldots,$ q_{n+3} with moves

$$\delta(q_1, X) = (q_2, \$, R) \text{ for any } X \text{ (print marker)},$$

$$\delta(q_i, X) = (q_{i+1}, a_{i-1}, R) \text{ for any } X \text{ and } 2 \le i \le n + 1 \text{ (print } w\text{)},$$

$$\delta(q_{n+2}, X) = (q_{n+2}, B, R) \text{ for } X \ne B \text{ (erase tape)},$$

$$\delta(q_{n+2}, B) = (q_{n+3}, B, L),$$

$$\delta(q_{n+3}, X) = (q_{n+3}, X, L) \text{ for } X \ne \$ \text{ (find marker)}.$$

Having produced the code for these moves, B then adds $n + 3$ to the indices of the states of M and includes the move

$$\delta(q_{n+3}, \$) = (q_{n+4}, \$, R) \text{ /* start up } M \text{ */}$$

and all the moves of M in its generated TM. The resulting TM has an extra tape symbol \$, but by Theorem 7.10 we may construct M' with tape alphabet $\{0, 1, B\}$, and we may surely make q_2 the accepting state. This step completes the algorithm B, and its output is the desired M' of Fig. 8.6.

Now suppose algorithm A accepting L_e exists. Then we construct an algorithm C for L_u as in Fig. 8.7. If M accepts w, then $L(M') \ne \emptyset$; so A says "no" and C says "yes." If M does not accept w, then $L(M') = \emptyset$, A says "yes," and C says "no." As C does not exist by Theorem 8.5, A cannot exist. Thus, L_e is not recursive. If L_{ne} were recursive, L_e would be also by Theorem 8.1. Thus L_{ne} is r.e. but not recursive. If L_e were r.e., then L_e and L_{ne} would be recursive by Theorem 8.3. Thus L_e is not r.e.

Example 8.3 Consider the language

$$L_r = \{\langle M \rangle \mid L(M) \text{ is recursive}\}$$

and

$$L_{nr} = \{\langle M \rangle \mid L(M) \text{ is not recursive}\}.$$

Note that L_r is not $\{\langle M \rangle \mid M \text{ halts on all inputs}\}$, although it includes the latter language. A TM M could accept a recursive language even though M itself might loop forever on some words not in $L(M)$; some other TM equivalent to M must always halt, however. We claim neither L_r nor L_{nr} is r.e.

Suppose L_r were r.e. Then we could construct a TM for $\bar{L}_u$ which we know

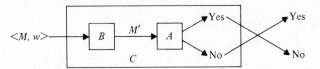

Fig. 8.7 Algorithm constructed for L_u assuming that algorithm A for L_e exists.

does not exist. Let M_r be a TM accepting L_r. We may construct an algorithm A that takes $\langle M, w \rangle$ as input and produces as output a TM M' such that

$$L(M') = \begin{cases} \varnothing & \text{if } M \text{ does not accept } w, \\ L_u & \text{if } M \text{ accepts } w. \end{cases}$$

Note that L_u is not recursive, so M' accepts a recursive language if and only if M does not accept w. The plan of M' is shown in Fig. 8.8. As in the previous example, we have described the output of A. We leave the construction of A to the reader.

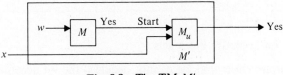

Fig. 8.8 The TM M'.

Given A and M_r, we could construct a TM accepting $\bar{L}_u$, shown in Fig. 8.9, which behaves as follows. On input $\langle M, w \rangle$ the TM uses A to produce M', uses M_r to determine if the set accepted by M' is recursive, and accepts if and only if $L(M')$ is recursive. But $L(M')$ is recursive if and only if $L(M') = \varnothing$, which means M does not accept w. Thus the TM of Fig. 8.9 accepts $\langle M, w \rangle$ if and only if $\langle M, w \rangle$ is in $\bar{L}_u$.

Now let us turn to L_{nr}. Suppose we have a TM M_{nr} accepting L_{nr}. Then we may use M_{nr} and an algorithm B, to be constructed by the reader, to accept $\bar{L}_u$. B takes $\langle M, w \rangle$ as input and produces as output a TM M' such that

$$L(M') = \begin{cases} \Sigma^* & \text{if } M \text{ accepts } w, \\ L_u & \text{if } M \text{ does not accept } w. \end{cases}$$

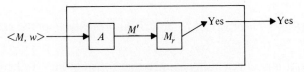

Fig. 8.9 Hypothetical TM for $\bar{L}_u$.

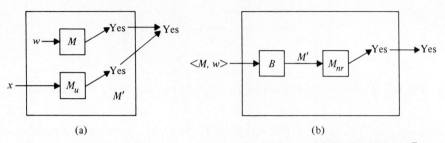

Fig. 8.10 Constructions used in proof that L_{nr} is not r.e. (a) M'. (b) TM for $\bar{L}_u$.

Thus M' accepts a recursive language if and only if M accepts w. M', which B must produce, is shown in Fig. 8.10(a), and a TM to accept $\bar{L}_u$ given B and M_{nr}, is shown in Fig. 8.10(b). The TM of Fig. 8.10(b) accepts $\langle M, w \rangle$ if and only if $L(M')$ is not recursive, or equivalently, if and only if M does not accept w. That is, the TM accepts $\langle M, w \rangle$ if and only if $\langle M, w \rangle$ is in $\bar{L}_u$. Since we have already shown that no such TM exists, the assumption that M_{nr} exists is false. We conclude that L_{nr} is not r.e.

Rice's Theorem for recursive index sets

The above examples show that we cannot decide if the set accepted by a Turing machine is empty or recursive. The technique of proof can also be used to show that we cannot decide if the set accepted is finite, infinite, regular, context free, has an even number of strings, or satisfies many other predicates. What then can we decide about the set accepted by a TM? Only the trivial predicates, such as "Does the TM accept an r.e. set?," which are either true for all TM's or false for all TM's.

In what follows we shall discuss languages that represent properties of r.e. languages. That is, the languages are sets of TM codes such that membership of $\langle M \rangle$ in the language depends only on $L(M)$, not on M itself. Later we shall consider languages of TM codes that depend on the TM itself, such as "M has 27 states," which may be satisfied for some but not all of the TM's accepting a given language.

Let $\mathscr{S}$ be a set of r.e. languages, each a subset of $(0 + 1)^*$. $\mathscr{S}$ is said to be a *property of the r.e. languages*. A set L has property $\mathscr{S}$ if L is an element of $\mathscr{S}$. For example, the property of being infinite is $\{L \mid L \text{ is infinite}\}$. $\mathscr{S}$ is a *trivial* property if $\mathscr{S}$ is empty or $\mathscr{S}$ consists of all r.e. languages. Let $L_{\mathscr{S}}$ be the set $\{\langle M \rangle \mid L(M) \text{ is in } \mathscr{S}\}$.

Theorem 8.6 (*Rice's Theorem*)   Any nontrivial property $\mathscr{S}$ of the r.e. languages is undecidable.

Proof   Without loss of generality assume that $\emptyset$ is not in $\mathscr{S}$ (otherwise consider $\bar{\mathscr{S}}$). Since $\mathscr{S}$ is nontrivial, there exists L with property $\mathscr{S}$. Let M_L be a TM accepting L. Suppose $\mathscr{S}$ were decidable. Then there exists an algorithm $M_{\mathscr{S}}$ accepting $L_{\mathscr{S}}$. We use M_L and $M_{\mathscr{S}}$ to construct an algorithm for L_u as follows. First construct an algorithm A that takes $\langle M, w \rangle$ as input and produces $\langle M' \rangle$ as output, where $L(M')$ is in $\mathscr{S}$ if and only if M accepts w ($\langle M, w \rangle$ is in L_u).

The design of M' is shown in Fig. 8.11. First M' ignores its input and simulates M on w. If M does not accept w, then M' does not accept x. If M accepts w, then M' simulates M_L on x, accepting x if and only if M_L accepts x. Thus M' either accepts $\varnothing$ or L depending on whether M accepts w.

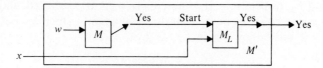

Fig. 8.11 M' used in Rice's theorem.

We may use the hypothetical $M_{\mathscr{S}}$ to determine if $L(M')$ is in $\mathscr{S}$. Since $L(M')$ is in $\mathscr{S}$ if and only if $\langle M, w \rangle$ is in L_u, we have an algorithm for recognizing L_u, a contradiction. Thus $\mathscr{S}$ must be undecidable. Note how this proof generalizes Example 8.2. □

Theorem 8.6 has a great variety of consequences, some of which are summarized in the following corollary.

Corollary The following properties of r.e. sets are not decidable:

a) emptiness,

b) finiteness,

c) regularity,

d) context-freedom.

Rice's Theorem for recursively enumerable index sets

The condition under which a set $L_{\mathscr{S}}$ is r.e. is far more complicated. We shall show that $L_{\mathscr{S}}$ is r.e. if and only if $\mathscr{S}$ satisfies the following three conditions.

1) If L is in $\mathscr{S}$ and $L \subseteq L'$, for some r.e. L', then L' is in $\mathscr{S}$ (the *containment property*).

2) If L is an infinite language in $\mathscr{S}$, then there is a finite subset of L in $\mathscr{S}$.

3) The set of finite languages in $\mathscr{S}$ is *enumerable*, in the sense that there is a Turing machine that generates the (possibly) infinite string $\text{code}_1 \# \text{code}_2 \# \ldots$, where code_i is a code for the ith finite language in $\mathscr{S}$ (in

any order). The code for the finite language $\{w_1, w_2, \ldots, w_n\}$ is just w_1, $w_2, \ldots, w_n$.

We prove this characterization with a series of lemmas.

Lemma 8.2 If $\mathscr{S}$ does not have the containment property, then $L_{\mathscr{S}}$ is not r.e.

Proof We generalize the proof that L_{nr} is not r.e. Let L_1 be in $\mathscr{S}$, $L_1 \subseteq L_2$, and let L_2 not be in $\mathscr{S}$. [For the case where $\mathscr{S}$ was the nonrecursive sets, we chose $L_1 = L_u$ and $L_2 = (0 + 1)^*$.] Construct algorithm A that takes as input $\langle M, w \rangle$ and produces as output TM M' with the behavior shown in Fig. 8.12, where M_1 and M_2 accept L_1 and L_2, respectively. If M accepts w, then M_2 is started, and M' accepts x whenever x is in either L_1 or L_2. If M does not accept w, then M_2 never starts, so M' accepts x if and only if x is in L_1. As $L_1 \subseteq L_2$,

$$L(M') = \begin{cases} L_2 & \text{if } M \text{ accepts } w, \\ L_1 & \text{if } M \text{ does not accept } w. \end{cases}$$

Thus $L(M')$ is in $\mathscr{S}$ if and only if M does not accept w.

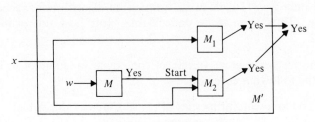

Fig. 8.12 The TM M'.

We again leave it to the reader to design the "compiler" A that takes $\langle M, w \rangle$ as input and connects them with the fixed Turing machines M_1 and M_2 to construct the M' shown in Fig. 8.12. Having constructed A, we can use a TM $M_{\mathscr{S}}$ for $L_{\mathscr{S}}$ to accept $\bar{L}_u$, as shown in Fig. 8.13. This TM accepts $\langle M, w \rangle$ if and only if M' accepts a language in $\mathscr{S}$, or equivalently, if and only if M does not accept w. As such a TM does not exist, we know $M_{\mathscr{S}}$ cannot exist, so $L_{\mathscr{S}}$ is not r.e. $\quad\square$

We now turn to the second property of recursively enumerable index sets.

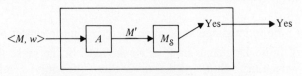

Fig. 8.13 Hypothetical TM to accept $\bar{L}_u$.

Lemma 8.3 If $\mathscr{S}$ has an infinite language L such that no finite subset of L is in $\mathscr{S}$, then $L_{\mathscr{S}}$ is not r.e.

Proof Suppose $L_{\mathscr{S}}$ were r.e. We shall show that $\bar{L}_u$ would be r.e. as follows. Let M_1 be a TM accepting L. Construct algorithm A to take a pair $\langle M, w \rangle$ as input and produce as output a TM M' that accepts L if w is not in $L(M)$ and accepts some finite subset of L otherwise. As shown in Fig. 8.14, M' simulates M_1 on its input x. If M_1 accepts x, then M' simulates M on w for $|x|$ moves. If M fails to accept w after $|x|$ moves, then M' accepts x. We leave the design of algorithm A as an exercise.

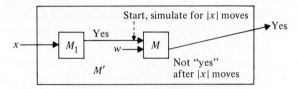

Fig. 8.14 Construction of M'.

If w is in $L(M)$, then M accepts w after some number of moves, say j. Then $L(M') = \{x \mid x$ is in L and $|x| < j\}$, which is a finite subset of L. If w is not in $L(M)$, then $L(M') = L$. Hence, if M does not accept w, $L(M')$ is in $\mathscr{S}$, and if M accepts w, $L(M')$, being a finite subset of L, is not in $\mathscr{S}$ by the hypothesis of the lemma. An argument that is by now standard proves that if $L_{\mathscr{S}}$ is r.e., so is L_u. Since the latter is not r.e., we conclude the former is not either. □

Finally, consider the third property of r.e. index sets.

Lemma 8.4 If $L_{\mathscr{S}}$ is r.e., then the list of binary codes for the finite sets in $\mathscr{S}$ is enumerable.

Proof We use the pair generator described in Section 7.7. When (i, j) is generated, we treat i as the binary code of a finite set, assuming 0 is the code for comma, 10 the code for zero, and 11 the code for one. We may in a straightforward manner construct a TM $M^{(i)}$ (essentially a finite automaton) that accepts exactly the words in the finite language represented by i. We then simulate the enumerator for $L_{\mathscr{S}}$ for j steps. If it has printed $M^{(i)}$, we print the code for the finite set represented by i, that is, the binary representation of i itself, followed by a delimiter symbol $\#$. In any event, after the simulation we return control to the pair generator, which generates the pair following (i, j). □

Theorem 8.7 $L_{\mathscr{S}}$ is r.e. if and only if

1) If L is in $\mathscr{S}$ and $L \subseteq L'$, for some r.e. L', then L' is in $\mathscr{S}$.
2) If L is an infinite set in $\mathscr{S}$, then there is some finite subset L' of L that is in $\mathscr{S}$.
3) The set of finite languages in $\mathscr{S}$ is enumerable.

Proof The "only if" part is Lemmas 8.2, 8.3, and 8.4. For the "if" part, suppose (1), (2), and (3) hold. We construct a TM M_1 that recognizes $\langle M \rangle$ if and only if $L(M)$ is in $\mathscr{S}$ as follows. M_1 generates pairs (i, j) using the pair generator. In response to (i, j), M_1 simulates M_2, which is an enumerator of the finite sets in $\mathscr{S}$, for i steps. We know M_2 exists by condition (3). Let L_1 be the last set completely printed out by M_2. [If there is no set completely printed, generate the next (i, j) pair.] Then simulate M for j steps on each word in L_1. If M accepts all words in L_1, then M_1 accepts $\langle M \rangle$. If not, M_1 generates the next (i, j)-pair.

We use conditions (1) and (2) to show that $L(M_1) = L_{\mathscr{S}}$. Suppose L is in $L_{\mathscr{S}}$, and let M be any TM with $L(M) = L$. By condition (2), there is a finite $L' \subseteq L$ in $\mathscr{S}$ (take $L' = L$ if L is finite). Let L' be generated after i steps of M_2, and let j be the maximum number of steps taken by M to accept a word in L' (if $L' = \varnothing$, let $j = 1$). Then when M_1 generates (i, j), if not sooner, M_1 will accept $\langle M \rangle$.

Conversely, suppose M_1 accepts $\langle M \rangle$. Then there is some (i, j) such that within j steps M accepts every word in some finite language L' such that M_2 generates L' within its first i steps. Then L' is in $\mathscr{S}$, and $L' \subseteq L(M)$. By condition (1), $L(M)$ is in $\mathscr{S}$, so $\langle M \rangle$ is in $L_{\mathscr{S}}$. We conclude that $L(M_1) = L_{\mathscr{S}}$. $\square$

Theorem 8.7 has a great variety of consequences. We summarize some of them as corollaries and leave others as exercises.

Corollary 1 The following properties of r.e. sets are not r.e.

a) $L = \varnothing$.

b) $L = \Sigma^*$.

c) L is recursive.

d) L is not recursive.

e) L is a *singleton* (has exactly one member).

f) L is a regular set.

g) $L - L_u \neq \varnothing$.

Proof In each case condition (1) is violated, except for (b), where (2) is violated, and (g), where (3) is violated. $\square$

Corollary 2 The following properties of r.e. sets are r.e.

a) $L \neq \varnothing$.

b) L contains at least 10 members.

c) w is in L for some fixed word w.

d) $L \cap L_u \neq \varnothing$.

Problems about Turing machines

Does Theorem 8.6 say that everything about Turing machines is undecidable? The answer is no. That theorem has to do only with properties of the language accepted, not properties of the Turing machine itself. For example, the question "Does a given Turing machine have an even number of states?" is clearly decidable. When dealing with properties of Turing machines themselves, we must use our ingenuity. We give two examples.

Example 8.4   It is undecidable if a Turing machine with alphabet $\{0, 1, B\}$ ever prints three consecutive 1's on its tape. For each Turing machine M_i we construct $\hat{M}_i$, which on blank tape simulates M_i on blank tape. However, $\hat{M}_i$ uses 01 to encode a 0 and 10 to encode a 1. If M_i's tape has a 0 in cell j, $\hat{M}_i$ has 01 in cells $2j - 1$ and $2j$. If M_i changes a symbol, $\hat{M}_i$ changes the corresponding 1 to 0, then the paired 0 to 1. One can easily design $\hat{M}_i$ so that $\hat{M}_i$ never has three consecutive 1's on its tape. Now further modify $\hat{M}_i$ so that if M_i accepts, $\hat{M}_i$ prints three consecutive 1's and halts. Thus $\hat{M}_i$ prints three consecutive 1's if and only if M_i accepts ϵ. By Theorem 8.6, it is undecidable whether a TM accepts ϵ, since the predicate "ϵ is in L" is not trivial. Thus the question of whether an arbitrary Turing machine ever prints three consecutive 1's is undecidable.

Example 8.5   It is decidable whether a single-tape Turing machine started on blank tape scans any cell four or more times. If the Turing machine never scans any cell four or more times, than every *crossing sequence* (sequence of states in which the boundary between cells is crossed, assuming states change before the head moves) is of length at most three. But there is a finite number of distinct crossing sequences of length three or less. Thus either the Turing machine stays within a fixed bounded number of tape cells, in which case finite automaton techniques answer the question, or some crossing sequence repeats. But if some crossing sequence repeats, then the TM moves right with some easily detectable pattern, and the question is again decidable.

8.5 UNDECIDABILITY OF POST'S CORRESPONDENCE PROBLEM

Undecidable problems arise in a variety of areas. In the next three sections we explore some of the more interesting problems in language theory and develop techniques for proving particular problems undecidable. We begin with Post's Correspondence Problem, it being a valuable tool in establishing other problems to be undecidable.

An instance of *Post's Correspondence Problem* (*PCP*) consists of two lists, $A = w_1, \ldots, w_k$ and $B = x_1, \ldots, x_k$, of strings over some alphabet Σ. This instance of PCP *has a solution* if there is any sequence of integers $i_1, i_2, \ldots, i_m$, with $m \geq 1$, such that

$$w_{i_1}, w_{i_2}, \ldots, w_{i_m} = x_{i_1}, x_{i_2}, \ldots, x_{i_m}.$$

The sequence $i_1, \ldots, i_m$ is a solution to this instance of PCP.

Example 8.6 Let $\Sigma = \{0, 1\}$. Let A and B be lists of three strings each, as defined in Fig. 8.15. In this case PCP has a solution. Let $m = 4$, $i_1 = 2$, $i_2 = 1$, $i_3 = 1$, and $i_4 = 3$. Then

$$w_2 w_1 w_1 w_3 = x_2 x_1 x_1 x_3 = 101111110.$$

	List A	List B
i	w_i	x_i
1	1	111
2	10111	10
3	10	0

Fig. 8.15 An instance of PCP.

Example 8.7 Let $\Sigma = \{0, 1\}$. Let A and B be lists of three strings as shown in Fig. 8.16.

	List A	List B
i	w_i	x_i
1	10	101
2	011	11
3	101	011

Fig. 8.16 Another PCP instance.

Suppose that this instance of PCP has a solution $i_1, i_2, \ldots, i_m$. Clearly, $i_1 = 1$, since no string beginning with $w_2 = 011$ can equal a string beginning with $x_2 = 11$; no string beginning with $w_3 = 101$ can equal a string beginning with $x_3 = 011$.

We write the string from list A above the corresponding string from B. So far we have

10

101

The next selection from A must begin with a 1. Thus $i_2 = 1$ or $i_2 = 3$. But $i_2 = 1$ will not do, since no string beginning with $w_1 w_1 = 1010$ can equal a string beginning with $x_1 x_1 = 101101$. With $i_2 = 3$, we have

$$10101$$

$$101011$$

Since the string from list B again exceeds the string from list A by the single symbol 1, a similar argument shows that $i_3 = i_4 = \cdots = 3$. Thus there is only one sequence of choices that generates compatible strings, and for this sequence string B is always one character longer. Thus this instance of PCP has no solution.

A modified version of PCP

We show that PCP is undecidable by showing that if it were decidable, we would have an algorithm for L_u. First, we show that, if PCP were decidable, a modified version of PCP would also be decidable.

The *Modified Post's Correspondence Problem* (MPCP) is the following: Given lists A and B, of k strings each from Σ^*, say

$$A = w_1, w_2, \ldots, w_k \qquad \text{and} \qquad B = x_1, x_2, \ldots, x_k,$$

does there exist a sequence of integers, $i_1, i_2, \ldots, i_r$, such that

$$w_1 w_{i_1} w_{i_2} \cdots w_{i_r} = x_1 x_{i_1} x_{i_2} \cdots x_{i_r}?$$

The difference between the MPCP and PCP is that in the MPCP, a solution is required to start with the first string on each list.

Lemma 8.5 If PCP were decidable, then MPCP would be decidable. That is, MPCP reduces to PCP.

Proof Let

$$A = w_1, w_2, \ldots, w_k \qquad \text{and} \qquad B = x_1, x_2, \ldots, x_k$$

be an instance of the MPCP. We convert this instance of MPCP to an instance of PCP that has a solution if and only if our MPCP instance has a solution. If PCP were decidable, we would then be able to solve the MPCP, proving the lemma.

Let Σ be the smallest alphabet containing all the symbols in lists A and B, and let ϕ and \$ not be in Σ. Let y_i be obtained from w_i by inserting the symbol ϕ after each character of w_i and let z_i be obtained from x_i by inserting the symbol ϕ ahead of each character of x_i. Create new words

$$y_0 = \phi y_1, \qquad z_0 = z_1,$$

$$y_{k+1} = \$, \qquad z_{k+1} = \phi\$.$$

Let $C = y_0, y_1, \ldots, y_{k+1}$ and $D = z_0, z_1, \ldots, z_{k+1}$. For example, the lists C and D constructed from the lists A and B of Example 8.6 are shown in Fig. 8.17.

		List A	List B		List C	List D	
	i	w_i	x_i	i	y_i	z_i	
	1	1	111	0	¢1¢	¢1¢1¢1	PCP
MPCP	2	10111	10	1	1¢	¢1¢1¢	
	3	10	0	2	1¢0¢1¢1¢1¢	¢1¢0	
				3	1¢0¢	¢0	
				4	$	¢$	

Fig. 8.17   Corresponding instances of MPCP and PCP.

In general, the lists C and D represent an instance of PCP. We claim that this instance of PCP has a solution if and only if the instance of MPCP represented by lists A and B has a solution. To see this, note that if $1, i_1, i_2, \ldots, i_r$ is a solution to MPCP with lists A and B, then

$$0, i_1, i_2, \ldots, i_r, k+1$$

is a solution to PCP with lists C and D. Likewise, if $i_1, i_2, \ldots, i_r$ is a solution to PCP with lists C and D, then $i_1 = 0$ and $i_r = k+1$, since y_0 and z_0 are the only words with the same index that begin with the same symbol, and y_{k+1} and z_{k+1} are the only words with the same index that end with the same symbol. Let j be the smallest integer such that $i_j = k+1$. Then $i_1, i_2, \ldots, i_j$ is also a solution, since the symbol $ occurs only as the last symbol of y_{k+1} and z_{k+1}, and, for no ℓ, where $1 \leq \ell < j$, is $i_\ell = k+1$. Clearly $1, i_2, i_3, \ldots, i_{j-1}$ is a solution to MPCP for lists A and B.

If there is an algorithm to decide PCP, we can construct an algorithm to decide MPCP by converting any instance of MPCP to PCP as above.   ☐

Undecidability of PCP

Theorem 8.8   PCP is undecidable.

Proof   With Lemma 8.5, it is sufficient to show that if MPCP were decidable, then it would be decidable whether a TM accepts a given word. That is, we reduce L_u to MPCP, which by Lemma 8.5 reduces to PCP. For each M and w we construct an instance of MPCP that has a solution if and only if M accepts w. We do this by constructing an instance of MPCP that, if it has a solution, has one that starts with $\#q_0 w \# \alpha_1 q_1 \beta_1 \# \cdots \# \alpha_k q_k \beta_k \#$, where strings between successive #'s are successive ID's in a computation of M with input w, and q_k is a final state.

Formally, the pairs of strings forming lists A and B of the instance of MPCP are given below. Since, except for the first pair, which must be used first, the order of the pairs is irrelevant to the existence of a solution, the pairs will be given without indexing numbers. We assume there are no moves from a final state.

The first pair is:

List A	List B
#	$\#q_0 w\#$

The remaining pairs are grouped as follows:
Group I

List A	List B	
X	X	for each X in Γ.
#	#	

Group II. For each q in $Q - F$, p in Q, and X, Y, and Z in Γ:

List A	List B	
qX	Yp	if $\delta(q, X) = (p, Y, R)$
ZqX	pZY	if $\delta(q, X) = (p, Y, L)$
$q\#$	$Yp\#$	if $\delta(q, B) = (p, Y, R)$
$Zq\#$	$pZY\#$	if $\delta(q, B) = (p, Y, L)$

Group III. For each q in F, and X and Y in Γ:

List A	List B
XqY	q
Xq	q
qY	q

Group IV

List A	List B	
$q\#\#$	#	for each q in F.

Let us say that (x, y) is a *partial solution* to MPCP with lists A and B if x is a prefix of y, and x and y are the concatenation of corresponding strings of lists A and B respectively. If $xz = y$, then call z the *remainder* of (x, y).

Suppose that from ID $q_0 w$ there is a valid sequence of k more ID's. We claim that there is a partial solution

$$(x, y) = (\#q_0 w\#\alpha_1 q_1 \beta_1\# \cdots \#\alpha_{k-1} q_{k-1}\beta_{k-1}\#,$$

$$\#q_0 w\#\alpha_1 q_1 \beta_1\# \cdots \#\alpha_k q_k \beta_k\#).$$

Moreover, this is the only partial solution whose larger string is as long as $|y|$.

The above statement is easy to prove by induction k. It is trivial for $k = 0$, since the pair $(\#, \#q_0 w\#)$ must be chosen first.

Suppose that the statement is true for some k and that q_k is not in F. We can easily show that it is true for $k + 1$. The remainder of the pair (x, y) is $z = \alpha_k q_k \beta_k \#$. The next pairs must be chosen so that their strings from list A form z. No matter what symbols appear to the right and left of q_k, there is at most one pair in Group II that will enable the partial solution to be continued past q_k. This pair represents, in a natural way, the move of M from ID $\alpha_k q_k \beta_k$. The other symbols of z force choices from Group I. No other choices will enable z to be composed of elements in list A.

We can thus obtain a new partial solution, $(y, y\alpha_{k+1} q_{k+1} \beta_{k+1}\#)$. It is straightforward to see that $\alpha_{k+1} q_{k+1} \beta_{k+1}$ is the one ID that M can reach on one move from $\alpha_k q_k \beta_k$. Also, there is no other partial solution whose length of the second string equals $|y\alpha_{k+1} q_{k+1} \beta_{k+1}\#|$.

In addition, if q_k is in F, it is easy to find pairs from Groups I and III which, when preceded by the partial solution (x, y) and followed by the pair in Group IV, provide a solution to MPCP with lists A and B.

Thus if M, started in ID $q_0 w$, reaches an accepting state, the instance of MPCP with lists A and B has a solution. If M does not reach an accepting state, no pairs from groups III or IV may be used. Therefore, there may be partial solutions, but the string from B must exceed the string from A in length, so no solution is possible.

We conclude that the instance of MPCP has a solution if and only if M with input w halts in an accepting state. Since the above construction can be carried out for arbitrary M and w, it follows that if there were an algorithm to solve MPCP, then there would be an algorithm to recognize L_u, contradicting Theorem 8.5. ☐

Example 8.8 Let

$$M = (\{q_1, q_2, q_3\}, \{0, 1, B\}, \{0, 1\}, \delta, q_1, B, \{q_3\}),$$

and let δ be defined by:

q_i	$\delta(q_i, 0)$	$\delta(q_i, 1)$	$\delta(q_i, B)$
q_1	$(q_2, 1, R)$	$(q_2, 0, L)$	$(q_2, 1, L)$
q_2	$(q_3, 0, L)$	$(q_1, 0, R)$	$(q_2, 0, R)$
q_3	—	—	—

Let $w = 01$. We construct an instance of MPCP with lists A and B. The first pair is $\#$ for list A and $\#q_1 01\#$ for list B. The remaining pairs are:
Group I

List A	List B
0	0
1	1
$\#$	$\#$

Group II

List A	List B	
$q_1 0$	$1q_2$	from $\delta(q_1, 0) = (q_2, 1, R)$
$0q_1 1$	$q_2 00$ ⎫	
$1q_1 1$	$q_2 10$ ⎭	from $\delta(q_1, 1) = (q_2, 0, L)$
$0q_1 \#$	$q_2 01\#$ ⎫	
$1q_1 \#$	$q_2 11\#$ ⎭	from $\delta(q_1, B) = (q_2, 1, L)$†
$0q_2 0$	$q_3 00$ ⎫	
$1q_2 0$	$q_3 10$ ⎭	from $\delta(q_2, 0) = (q_3, 0, L)$
$q_2 1$	$0q_1$	from $\delta(q_2, 1) = (q_1, 0, R)$
$q_2 \#$	$0q_2 \#$	from $\delta(q_2, B) = (q_2, 0, R)$

Group III

List A	List B
$0q_3 0$	q_3
$0q_3 1$	q_3
$1q_3 0$	q_3
$1q_3 1$	q_3
$0q_3$	q_3
$1q_3$	q_3
$q_3 0$	q_3
$q_3 1$	q_3

Group IV

List A	List B
$q_3 \#\#$	$\#$

Note that M accepts input $w = 01$ by the sequence of ID's:

$$q_1 01, \ 1q_2 1, \ 10q_1, \ 1q_2 01, \ q_3 101.$$

Let us see if there is a solution to the MPCP we have constructed. The first pair gives a partial solution $(\#, \#q_1 01\#)$. Inspection of the pairs indicates that the only way to get a longer partial solution is to use the pair $(q_1 0, 1q_2)$ next. The resulting partial solution is $(\#q_1 0, \#q_1 01\#1q_2)$. The remainder is now $1\#1q_2$. The next three pairs chosen must be $(1, 1)$, $(\#, \#)$, and $(1, 1)$. The partial solution becomes $(\#q_1 01\#1, \#q_1 01\#1q_2 1\#1)$. The remainder is now $q_2 1\#1$. Continuing the argument, we see that the only partial solution, the length of whose second string is 14, is $(x, x0q_1 \#1)$, where $x = \#q_1 01\#1q_2 1\#1$.

Here, we seemingly have a choice, because the next pair used could be $(0, 0)$ or $(0q_1 \#, q_2 01\#)$. In the former case we have $(x0, x0q_1 \#10)$ as a partial solution. But this partial solution is a "dead end." No pair can be added to it to make another partial solution, so, surely, it cannot lead to a solution.

---

† Since B is never printed, we can omit pairs where B is to the right of the state. Group III pairs also omit those with B on one or both sides of the state.

In a similar manner, we continue to be forced by our desire to reach a solution to choose one particular pair to continue each partial solution. Finally, we reach the partial solution $(y, y1\#q_310)$, where

$$y = \#q_101\#1q_21\#10q_1\#1q_20.$$

Since q_3 is a final state, we can now use pairs in Groups I, III, and IV to find a solution to the instance of MPCP. The choice of pairs is

$$(1, 1), (\#, \#), (q_31, q_3), (0, 0), (1, 1), (\#, \#), (q_30, q_3),$$
$$(1, 1), (\#, \#), (q_31, q_3), (\#, \#), (q_3\#\#, \#).$$

Thus, the shortest word that can be composed of corresponding strings from lists A and B, starting with pair 1 is

$$\#q_101\#1q_21\#10q_1\#1q_201\#q_3101\#q_301\#q_31\#q_3\#\#.$$

An application of PCP

Post's correspondence problem can be used to show that a wide variety of problems are undecidable. We give only one application here: the undecidability of ambiguity for context-free grammars. The reader should consult the exercises at the end of the chapter for additional applications.

Theorem 8.9 It is undecidable whether an arbitrary CFG is ambiguous.

Proof Let

$$A = w_1, w_2, \ldots, w_n \qquad \text{and} \qquad B = x_1, x_2, \ldots, x_n$$

be two lists of words over a finite alphabet Σ. Let $a_1, a_2, \ldots, a_n$ be new symbols. Let

$$L_A = \{w_{i_1} w_{i_2} \cdots w_{i_m} a_{i_m} a_{i_{m-1}} \cdots a_{i_1} \,|\, m \geq 1\}$$

and

$$L_B = \{x_{i_1} x_{i_2} \cdots x_{i_m} a_{i_m} a_{i_{m-1}} \cdots a_{i_1} \,|\, m \geq 1\}.$$

Let G be the CFG

$$(\{S, S_1, S_2\}, \Sigma \cup \{a_1, \ldots, a_n\}, P, S),$$

where P contains the productions $S \to S_A$, $S \to S_B$ and for $1 \leq i \leq n$, $S_A \to w_i S_A a_i$, $S_A \to w_i a_i$, $S_B \to x_i S_B a_i$, and $S_B \to x_i a_i$. The grammar G generates the language $L_A \cup L_B$.

If the instance (A, B) of PCP has a solution, say $i_1, i_2, \ldots, i_m$, then there is a word $x_{i_1} x_{i_2} \cdots x_{i_m} a_{i_m} a_{i_{m-1}} \cdots a_{i_1}$ in L_A that equals the word $w_{i_1} w_{i_2} \cdots w_{i_m} a_{i_m} a_{i_{m-1}} \cdots a_{i_1}$ in L_B. This word has a leftmost derivation beginning $S \to S_A$, and another beginning $S \to S_B$. Hence in this case G is ambiguous.

Conversely, suppose G is ambiguous. Since the a's dictate the productions used, it is easy to show that any word derived from S_A has only one leftmost derivation from S_A. Similarly, no word derived from S_B has more than one leftmost derivation from S_B. Thus it must be that some word has leftmost deviations from both S_A and S_B. If this word is $ya_{i_m} a_{i_{m-1}} \cdots a_{i_1}$, where y is in Σ^*, then i_1, $i_2, \ldots, i_m$ is a solution to PCP.

Thus G is ambiguous if and only if the instance (A, B) of PCP has a solution. We have thus reduced PCP to the ambiguity problem for CFG's. That is, if there were an algorithm for the latter problem, we could construct an algorithm for PCP, which by Theorem 8.8 does not exist. Thus the ambiguity problem for CFG's is undecidable.   □

8.6 VALID AND INVALID COMPUTATIONS OF TM'S: A TOOL FOR PROVING CFL PROBLEMS UNDECIDABLE

While PCP can be reduced easily to most of the known undecidable problems about CFL's, there is a more direct method that is instructive. We shall in this section show direct reductions of the membership problem for TM's to various problems about CFL's. To do so we need to introduce the notions of valid and invalid Turing machine computations.

A *valid computation* of a Turing machine $M = (Q, \Sigma, \Gamma, \delta, q_0, B, F)$, for the purposes of this section, is a string $w_1 \# w_2^R \# w_3 \# w_4^R \# \cdots$ such that:

1) each w_i is an ID of M, a string in $\Gamma^* Q \Gamma^*$ not ending with B,

2) w_1 is an initial ID, one of the form $q_0 x$ for x in Σ^*,

3) w_n is a final ID, that is, one in $\Gamma^* F \Gamma^*$, and

4) $w_i \vdash_{\overline{M}} w_{i+1}$ for $1 \le i < n$.

We assume without loss of generality that Q and Γ are disjoint, and $\#$ is in neither Q nor Γ.

The *set of invalid computations* of a Turing machine is the complement of the set of valid computations with respect to the alphabet $\Gamma \cup Q \cup \{\#\}$.

The notions of valid and invalid computations are useful in proving many properties of CFL's to be undecidable. The reason is that the set of invalid computations is a CFL, and the set of valid computations is the intersection of two CFL's.

Lemma 8.6 The set of valid computations of a Turing machine M is the intersection of two CFL's, L_1 and L_2, and grammars for these CFL's can be effectively constructed from M.

Proof Let $M = (Q, \Sigma, \Gamma, \delta, q_0, B, F)$ be a TM. Both CFL's L_1 and L_2 will consist of strings of the form $x_1 \# x_2 \# \cdots \# x_m \#$. We use L_1 to enforce the condition that $x_i \vdash (x_{i+1})^R$ for odd i and L_2 to enforce the condition $x_i^R \vdash x_{i+1}$ for even i. L_2 also enforces the condition that x_1 is an initial ID. That x_m is a final ID or its reverse is enforced by L_1 or L_2 depending on whether m is odd or even, respectively. Then $L_1 \cap L_2$ is the set of valid computations of M.

To begin, let L_3 be $\{y\#z^R \mid y \vdash_{\overline{M}} z\}$. It is easy to construct a PDA P to accept L_3. P reads y, the input up to the $\#$, checking in its finite control that y is of the form $\Gamma^*Q\Gamma^*$. In the process, P places on its stack the ID z such that $y \vdash_{\overline{M}} z$, where y is the input before the $\#$. That is, when the input to P is a symbol of Γ, P pushes that symbol onto the stack. If the input is a state q in Q, P stores q in the finite control and reads the next input symbol, say X (if the next symbol is $\#$, take X to be B). If $\delta(q, X) = (p, Y, R)$, then P pushes Yp onto the stack. If $\delta(q, X) = (p, Y, L)$, let Z be on top of the stack. Then P replaces Z by pZY (but if the input last read was $\#$, and $Y = B$, just replace Z by pZ, or by p if Z is also B). After reading the $\#$, P compares each input symbol with the top stack symbol. If they differ, P has no next move and so dies. If they are equal, P pops the top stack symbol. When the stack is emptied, P accepts.

Now, let $L_1 = (L_3\#)^*(\{\epsilon\} \cup \Gamma^*F\Gamma^*\#)$. By Theorems 5.4 and 6.1, there is an algorithm to construct a CFG for L_1. In a similar way, we can construct a PDA for $L_4 = \{y^R\#z \mid y \vdash_{\overline{M}} z\}$. The construction of G_2 for

$$L_2 = q_0\Sigma^*\#(L_4\#)^*(\{\epsilon\} \cup \Gamma^*F\Gamma^*\#)$$

is then easy, and by Theorem 6.1 there is an algorithm to construct a CFG G_2 for L_2. Now $L_1 \cap L_2$ is the set of valid computations of M. That is, if $x_1\#x_2\# \cdots \#x_m\#$ is in $L_1 \cap L_2$, then L_1 requires that $x_i \vdash_{\overline{M}} (x_{i+1})^R$ for odd i; L_2 requires that x_1 is initial, and $x_i^R \vdash_{\overline{M}} x_{i+1}$ for even i. That the last ID has an accepting state is enforced by L_1 for m odd and by L_2 for m even. $\square$

Theorem 8.10 It is undecidable for arbitrary CFG's G_1 and G_2 whether $L(G_1) \cap L(G_2)$ is empty.

Proof By Lemma 8.6 we can construct from M grammars G_1 and G_2 such that $L(G_1) \cap L(G_2)$ is the set of valid computations of M. If there is an algorithm A to tell whether the intersection of the languages of two CFG's is empty, we can construct an algorithm B to tell whether $L(M) = \emptyset$ for arbitrary TM M. Simply design B to construct G_1 and G_2 from M as in Lemma 8.6, then apply Algorithm A to tell whether $L(G_1) \cap L(G_2)$ is empty. If the intersection is empty, then there are no valid computations of M, so $L(M) = \emptyset$. If the intersection is not empty, $L(M) \neq \emptyset$. That is, the problem of emptiness for r.e. sets reduces to the problem of intersection for CFG's.

Algorithm B cannot exist, however, since $L(M) = \emptyset$ is undecidable by Theorem 8.6. Therefore A does not exist, so it is undecidable whether the intersection of two CFL's is empty. $\square$

Although two context-free languages are required to represent the valid computations of a Turing machine, the set of invalid computations is itself a CFL. The reason is that we no longer need to guarantee simultaneously for each i that

$w_i \vdash w_{i+1}$. We need only guess where an error occurs. That is, we must verify for one i that $w_i \vdash w_{i+1}$ is false.

Lemma 8.7 The set of invalid computations of a Turing machine $M = (Q, \Sigma, \Gamma, \delta, q_0, B, F)$ is a CFL.

Proof If a string w is an invalid computation, then one of the following conditions holds.

1) w is not of the form $x_1 \# x_2 \# \cdots \# x_m \#$, where each x_i is an ID of M.
2) x_1 is not initial; that is, x_1 is not in $q_0 \Sigma^*$.
3) x_m is not final; that is, x_m is not in $\Gamma^* F \Gamma^*$.
4) $x_i \vdash_{\overline{M}} (x_{i+1})^R$ is false for some odd i.
5) $x_i^R \vdash_{\overline{M}} x_{i+1}$ is false for some even i.

The set of strings satisfying (1), (2), and (3) is regular, and an FA accepting it is easily constructed. The sets of strings satisfying (4) and (5) are each CFL's. We prove this contention for (4); a similar argument prevails for (5). A PDA P for (4) nondeterministically selects some x_i that is preceded by an even number of #'s and while reading x_i stores on its stack the ID z such that $x_i \vdash z$, with the right end of z at the top of the stack. After finding # on the input, P compares z with the following x_{i+1}. If $z \neq x_{i+1}$, then P scans its remaining input and accepts.

The set of invalid computations is the union of two CFL's and a regular set. By Theorem 6.1 it is a CFL, and a grammar for this language can be constructed effectively. $\square$

Theorem 8.11 It is undecidable for any arbitrary CFG G whether $L(G) = \Sigma^*$.

Proof Given an arbitrary TM M, we can effectively construct a CFG G with terminal alphabet Σ, such that $L(G) = \Sigma^*$ if and only if $L(M) = \emptyset$. That is, by Lemma 8.7 we may construct a CFG G that generates the invalid computations of M. Thus if for arbitrary G, $L(G) = \Sigma^*$ were decidable, then we could decide for arbitrary M whether $L(M) = \emptyset$, a contradiction. $\square$

Other consequences of characterization of computations by CFL's

Many other results follow from Theorem 8.11.

Theorem 8.12 Let G_1 and G_2 be arbitrary CFG's and R an arbitrary regular set. The following problems are undecidable.

1) $L(G_1) = L(G_2)$.   2) $L(G_2) \subseteq L(G_1)$.
3) $L(G_1) = R$.   4) $R \subseteq L(G_1)$.

Proof Fix G_2 to be a grammar generating Σ^*, where Σ is the terminal alphabet of G_1. Then (1) and (2) are equivalent to $L(G_1) = \Sigma^*$. Fix $R = \Sigma^*$, and (3) and (4) are equivalent to $L(G_1) = \Sigma^*$. Thus the undecidable problem of whether a CFL is Σ^* reduces to (1) through (4), and each of these problems is undecidable as well.

$\square$

Note that by Theorems 5.3 and 5.4, one can convert effectively between PDA's and CFG's, so Theorems 8.10, 8.11, and 8.12 remain true if CFL's are represented by PDA's instead of CFG's. Also, the regular set R in Theorem 8.12 can be represented by a DFA, NFA, or regular expression as we choose.

One should observe also that the question $L(G) \subseteq R$ is decidable. The reason is that $L(G) \subseteq R$ if and only if $L(G) \cap \bar{R} = \varnothing$. But $L(G) \cap \bar{R}$ is a CFL, and hence its emptiness is decidable.

There are some additional properties of context-free languages that we can show to be undecidable by observing that if a TM has valid computations on an infinite set of inputs, its set of valid computations is not, in general, a CFL. However, we first modify each Turing machine M in a trivial way by adding two extra states whose sole purpose is to ensure that M makes at least two moves in every computation. This can be done without otherwise modifying the computation performed by M. The purpose of the modification is to force each valid computation to contain at least three ID's and thus ensure that the set of valid computations is a CFL if and only if M accepts a finite set.

Lemma 8.8 Let M be a Turing machine that makes at least three moves on every input. The set of valid computations of M is a CFL if and only if the set accepted by M is a finite set.

Proof If the set accepted by M is finite, the set of valid computations of M is finite and hence a CFL. Assume the set accepted by M is infinite and the set L of valid computations is a CFL. Since M accepts an infinite set, there exists a valid computation

$$w_1 \# w_2^R \# w_3 \# \cdots$$

where the w_i's are ID's, and $|w_2|$ is greater than the constant n in Ogden's lemma. Mark the symbols of w_2 as distinguished. Then we can "pump" w_2 without pumping both w_1 and w_3, thus getting an invalid computation that must be in L. We conclude that the valid computations do not form a CFL. $\square$

Theorem 8.13 It is undecidable for arbitrary CFG's G_1 and G_2 whether

1) $\overline{L(G_1)}$ is a CFL;   2) $L(G_1) \cap L(G_2)$ is a CFL.

Proof
1) Given an arbitrary Turing machine M, modify M without changing the set accepted, so that M makes at least two moves on every input. Construct CFG G generating the invalid computations. $\overline{L(G)}$ is a CFL if and only if M accepts a finite set.
2) Proceed as in (1), but construct CFG's G_1 and G_2 such that $L(G_1) \cap L(G_2)$ is the set of valid computations of M. $\square$

8.7 GREIBACH'S THEOREM

There is a striking similarity among the proofs of undecidability in language theory. This suggests that there is an analog of Rice's theorem for classes of languages such as the CFL's, and indeed there is.

Let us focus our attention on a class of languages $\mathscr{C}$, such as the CFL's, and on a particular system (such as CFG's or PDA's) for interpreting finite-length strings as names of languages. Consider a class $\mathscr{C}$ of languages with the property that, given names (e.g., grammars) of languages L_1 and L_2 in $\mathscr{C}$ and a name (e.g., a finite automaton) for a regular set R, we can effectively construct names for RL_1, $L_1 R$, and $L_1 \cup L_2$. Then we say that the class $\mathscr{C}$ is *effectively closed* under concatenation with regular sets and union. Assume furthermore that $L = \Sigma^*$ is undecidable for the class $\mathscr{C}$, as is the case for the CFL's. The next theorem shows that a wide variety of problems are undecidable for the class $\mathscr{C}$.

Theorem 8.14 (*Greibach's Theorem*) Let $\mathscr{C}$ be a class of languages that is effectively closed under concatenation with regular sets and union, and for which "$= \Sigma^*$" is undecidable for any sufficiently large fixed Σ. Let P be any nontrivial property† that is true for all regular sets and that is preserved under $/a$, where a is a single symbol. (That is, if L has the property P, so does $L/a = \{w \mid wa \text{ is in } L\}$.) Then P is undecidable for $\mathscr{C}$.

Proof Let $L_0 \subseteq \Sigma^*$ be a member of $\mathscr{C}$ for which $P(L_0)$ is false where Σ^* is sufficiently large so that "$= \Sigma^*$" is undecidable. For any $L \subseteq \Sigma^*$ in $\mathscr{C}$ construct $L_1 = L_0 \# \Sigma^* \cup \Sigma^* \# L$. L_1 is in $\mathscr{C}$, since $\mathscr{C}$ is effectively closed under concatenation with regular sets and under union. Now if $L = \Sigma^*$, then $L_1 = \Sigma^* \# \Sigma^*$, which is a regular set, and hence $P(L_1)$ is true. If $L \neq \Sigma^*$, then there exists w not in L. Hence $L_1 / \# w = L_0$. Since P is preserved under quotient with a single symbol, it is preserved under quotient with the string $\# w$, by induction on $|w|$. Thus $P(L_1)$ must be false, or else $P(L_0)$ would be true, contrary to our assumption. Therefore $P(L_1)$ is true if and only if $L = \Sigma^*$. Thus "$= \Sigma^*$" for $\mathscr{C}$ reduces to property P for $\mathscr{C}$, and hence P is undecidable for $\mathscr{C}$. ☐

Applications of Greibach's theorem

Theorem 8.14 can be used to show, for example, that it is undecidable if the language generated by a CFG is regular. Note that this question is different from asking if the language generated is equal to some particular regular set R, as was asked in Theorem 8.12.

Theorem 8.15 Let G be an arbitrary CFG. It is undecidable whether $L(G)$ is regular.

Proof The CFL's are effectively closed under concatenation with regular sets and under union. Let P be the property that L is regular. P is nontrivial for the CFL's,

---

† Technically, a property is just a subset of $\mathscr{C}$. We say "L has property P" or "$P(L)$" to mean L is a member of P.

is true for all the regular sets, and is preserved under quotient with a single symbol by Theorem 3.6. Note that the regular sets are effectively closed under quotient with another regular set, although Theorem 3.6 does not claim this (see the discussion following that theorem). Thus by Theorem 8.14, P is undecidable for CFL's. $\quad\square$

Theorem 8.15 allows us to show that a property is undecidable by showing that the property is preserved under quotient with a single symbol. This latter task is often relatively easy as, for example, in proving that inherent ambiguity is undecidable.

Lemma 8.9 Let P be the property that a CFL is not inherently ambiguous. Then P is preserved under quotient with a single symbol.

Proof Let $G = (V, T, P, S)$ be an unambiguous CFG. Let

$$G_a = (V \cup \{[A/a] \,|\, A \text{ is in } V\}, T, P_a, [S/a]),$$

where P_a contains

1) all productions of P,
2) $[A/a] \to \alpha$ if $A \to \alpha a$ is in P,
3) $[A/a] \to \alpha[B/a]$ if $A \to \alpha B\beta$ is in P, and $\beta \overset{*}{\Rightarrow} \epsilon$.

We claim that $L(G_a) = L(G)/a$ and that G_a is unambiguous. To see this, first show by an easy induction that

1) $[S/a] \overset{*}{\Rightarrow} \alpha$ if and only if $S \overset{*}{\Rightarrow} \alpha a$, and
2) $[S/a] \overset{*}{\Rightarrow} \alpha[A/a]$ if and only if $S \overset{*}{\Rightarrow} \alpha A$.

That $L(G_a) = L(G)/a$ follows immediately. Assume G_a is ambiguous. Then there must be two leftmost derivations

1) $[S/a] \overset{*}{\Rightarrow} \beta \overset{*}{\Rightarrow} \alpha \overset{*}{\Rightarrow} x$ and
2) $[S/a] \overset{*}{\Rightarrow} \gamma \overset{*}{\Rightarrow} \alpha \overset{*}{\Rightarrow} x$ where $\beta \neq \gamma$.

But then in G we have two leftmost derivations of the string xa, a contradiction. Thus G_a must be unambiguous. We conclude that unambiguity is preserved under quotient with a single symbol. $\quad\square$

Theorem 8.16 Inherent ambiguity for CFL's is undecidable.

Proof By Theorem 4.7, P is nontrivial. By Lemma 8.9 it is preserved under quotient with a single symbol. It is easy to show that P is true for all regular sets. That is, every regular set has an unambiguous CFG. (The reader may look ahead to Theorem 9.2 for a construction of an unambiguous CFG from an arbitrary DFA.) Thus by Theorem 8.14, inherent ambiguity for CFL's is undecidable. $\quad\square$

8.8 INTRODUCTION TO RECURSIVE FUNCTION THEORY

We mentioned in Section 7.3 that each Turing machine can be thought of as computing a function from integers to integers, as well as being a language recognizer. For every Turing machine M and every k, there is a function $f_M^{(k)}(i_1, i_2, \ldots, i_k)$ that takes k integers as arguments and produces an integer answer or is undefined for those arguments. If M started with $0^{i_1}10^{i_2}1 \cdots 0^{i_k}$ on its tape halts with 0^j on its tape, then we say $f_M^{(k)}(i_1, \ldots, i_k) = j$. If M does not halt with a tape consisting of a block of 0's with all other cells blank, then $f_M^{(k)}(i_1, \ldots, i_k)$ is undefined. Note that the same Turing machine can be thought of as a language recognizer, a computer of a function with one argument, a computer of a different function of two arguments, and so on.

If i is an integer code for a TM M, as described in Section 8.3, and k is understood, then we shall often write f_i in place of $f_M^{(k)}$.

Recall that a function computed by a Turing machine is called a (partial) recursive function. If it happens to be defined for all values of its arguments, then it is also called a total recursive function.

The constructions on Turing machines given earlier in this chapter and the previous one can be expressed as total recursive functions of a single variable. That is, an algorithm A that takes as input the binary code for a TM M and produces as output the binary code for another TM M' can be viewed as a function g of one variable. In particular, let i be the integer representing M and j be the integer representing M'. Then $g(i) = j$. Technically, the TM B that computes g is not A, but rather one that converts its unary input to binary, simulates A and then converts its output to unary.

The S_{mn}-theorem

Our first theorem, called the S_{mn}-*theorem*, says that given a partial recursive function $g(x, y)$ of two variables, there is an algorithm one can use to construct from a TM for g and a value for x, another TM which with input y computes $g(x, y)$.

Theorem 8.17 Let $g(x, y)$ be a partial recursive function. Then there is a total recursive function σ of one variable, such that $f_{\sigma(x)}(y) = g(x, y)$ for all x and y. That is, if $\sigma(x)$ is treated as the integer representing some TM M_x, then $f_{M_x}^{(1)}(y) = g(x, y)$.

Proof Let M compute g. Let A be a TM that given input x, written in unary, constructs a TM M_x that when given input y, shifts it right and writes 0^x1 to its left; M_x then returns its head to the left end and simulates M. The output of A is the unary representation of an integer $\langle M_x \rangle$ that represents M_x. Then A computes a total recursive function σ, and $f_{\sigma(x)}(y) = g(x, y)$. In proof, note that for each x, $\sigma(x)$ is an integer representing M_x above, and for each x, M_x is designed to produce $g(x, y)$ when given input y. Since $f_{\sigma(x)}$ is the function computed by M_x, the equality $f_{\sigma(x)}(y) = g(x, y)$ follows. $\qquad \square$

The recursion theorem

The second theorem, called the *recursion theorem*, states that every total recursive function σ mapping *indices* (integers denoting Turing machines) of partial recursive functions into indices of partial recursive functions has a fixed point x_0 such that $f_{x_0}(y) = f_{\sigma(x_0)}(y)$ for all y. In other words, if we modify all Turing machines in some manner, there is always some Turing machine M_{x_0} for which the modified Turing machine $M_{\sigma(x_0)}$ computes the same function as the unmodified Turing machine. At first this sounds impossible, since we can modify each Turing machine to add 1 to the originally computed function. One is tempted to say that $f(y) + 1 \neq f(y)$. But note that if $f(y)$ is everywhere undefined, then $f(y) + 1$ does equal $f(y)$ for all y.

Theorem 8.18   For any total recursive function σ there exists an x_0 such that $f_{x_0}(x) = f_{\sigma(x_0)}(x)$ for all x.

Proof   For each integer i construct a TM that on input x computes $f_i(i)$ and then simulates, by means of a universal TM, the $f_i(i)$th TM on x. Let $g(i)$ be index of the TM so constructed. Thus for all i and x,

$$f_{g(i)}(x) = f_{f_i(i)}(x). \tag{8.3}$$

Observe that $g(i)$ is a total function even if $f_i(i)$ is not defined. Let j be an index of the function σg. That is, j is an integer code for a TM that, given input i, computes $g(i)$ and then applies σ to $g(i)$. Then for $x_0 = g(j)$ we have

$$\begin{aligned}
f_{x_0}(x) &= f_{g(j)}(x) \\
&= f_{f_j(j)}(x) &&\text{by (8.3)} \\
&= f_{\sigma(g(j))}(x) &&\text{since } f_j \text{ is the function } \sigma g \\
&= f_{\sigma(x_0)}(x).
\end{aligned}$$

Thus x_0 is a fixed point of the mapping σ. That is, TM x_0 and TM $\sigma(x_0)$ compute the same function.   □

Applications of the recursion and S_{mn} theorems

Example 8.9   Let $M_1, M_2, \ldots$ be any enumeration of all Turing machines. We do not require that this enumeration be the "standard" one introduced in Section 8.3, but only that whatever representation is used for a TM, we can by an algorithm convert from that representation to the 7-tuple notation introduced in Section 7.2, and vice versa. Then we can use the recursion theorem to show that for some i, M_i and M_{i+1} both compute the same function.

Let $\sigma(i)$ be the total recursive function defined as follows. Enumerate TM's $M_1, M_2, \ldots$ until one with integer code i as in (8.2) is found. Note that the states of the TM must be considered in all possible orders to see if i is a code for this TM, since in the notation introduced in Section 8.3, the order in which the moves for the various states is written affects the code. Having found that M_j has code i, enumerate one more TM, M_{j+1}, and let $\sigma(i)$ be the code for M_{j+1}. Then the recursion theorem applied to this σ says there is some x_0 for which M_{x_0} and M_{x_0+1} define the same function of one variable.

Example 8.10 Given a formal system F, such as set theory, we can exhibit a Turing machine M such that there is no proof in F that M started on any particular input halts, and no proof that it does not halt. Construct M, a TM computing a two-input function $g(i, j)$, such that

$$g(i, j) = \begin{cases} 1 & \text{if there is a proof in } F \text{ that } f_i(j) \text{ is} \\ & \text{not defined; that is, there is a proof} \\ & \text{that the } i\text{th TM does not halt when given input } j; \\ \text{undefined} & \text{otherwise.} \end{cases}$$

M enumerates proofs in F in some order, printing 1 if a proof that the ith TM does not halt on input j is found. Further, we may construct M so that if $g(i, j) = 1$, then M halts, and M does not halt otherwise. By the S_{mn}-theorem there exists σ such that

$$f_{\sigma(i)}(j) = g(i, j).$$

By the recursion theorem, we may effectively construct an integer i_0 such that

$$f_{i_0}(j) = f_{\sigma(i_0)}(j) = g(i_0, j).$$

But $g(i_0, j) = 1$, and is therefore defined, if and only if there is a proof in F that $f_{i_0}(j)$ is undefined. Thus if F is consistent (i.e., there cannot be proofs of a statement and its negation), there can be no proof in F that the i_0th TM either halts or does not halt on any particular input j.

8.9 ORACLE COMPUTATIONS

One is tempted to ask what would happen if the emptiness problem, or some other undecidable problem, were decidable? Could we then compute everything? To answer the question we must be careful. If we start out by assuming that the emptiness problem is decidable, we have a contradictory set of assumptions and may conclude anything. We avoid this problem by defining a Turing machine with oracle.

Let A be a language, $A \subseteq \Sigma^*$. A *Turing machine with oracle* A is a single-tape Turing machine with three special states $q_?$, q_y, and q_n. The state $q_?$ is used to ask whether a string is in the set A. When the Turing machine enters state $q_?$ it requests an answer to the question: "Is the string of nonblank symbols to the right of the tape head in A?" The answer is supplied by having the state of the Turing machine change on the next move to one of the two states q_y or q_n, depending on whether the answer is yes or no.† The computation continues normally until the next time $q_?$ is entered, when the "oracle" answers another question.

Observe that if A is a recursive set, then the oracle can be simulated by another Turing machine, and the set accepted by the TM with oracle A is recursively enumerable. On the other hand, if A is not a recursive set and an oracle is available to supply the correct answer, then the TM with oracle A may accept a set that is not recursively enumerable. We denote the Turing machine M with oracle A by M^A. A set L is *recursively enumerable with respect to A* if $L = L(M^A)$ for some TM M. A set L is *recursive with respect to A* if $L = L(M^A)$ for some TM M^A that always halts. Two oracle sets are *equivalent* if each is recursive in the other.

A hierarchy of undecidable problems

We can now rephrase the question at the beginning of the section as "What sets can be recognized given an oracle for the emptiness problem?" Clearly not all sets can be r.e. with respect to the emptiness problem, since there is an uncountable number of sets and only a countable number of TM's. Consider the oracle set $S_1 = \{\langle M \rangle \mid L(M) = \varnothing\}$, which is not an r.e. set (recall that $\langle M \rangle$ is the binary code for TM M). Now consider TM's with oracle S_1. These machines have a halting problem that is not recursive in S_1. By defining an oracle for the emptiness problems for TM's with oracle S_1, and so on, we can develop an infinite hierarchy of undecidable problems. More specifically, define

$$S_{i+1} = \{\langle M \rangle \mid L^{S_i}(M) = \varnothing\}.$$

S_{i+1} is an oracle for solving the emptiness problem for computations with respect to S_i. We can now classify some undecidable problems (but not all such problems) by showing their equivalence to a set S_i for some particular i.

Theorem 8.19 The membership problem for TM's without oracles is equivalent to S_1.

Proof Construct M^{S_1} that, given $\langle M, w \rangle$ on its input, constructs the code for a TM M' that accepts $\varnothing$ if w is not in $L(M)$ and accepts $(0 + 1)^*$ otherwise. The construction of M' was given in Example 8.2. M^{S_1} then enters state $q_?$ with the code for M' to the right of its head and accepts if and only if q_n is entered. Thus the membership problem for TM's without oracle is recursive in S_1.

Conversely, we can show there is a Turing machine with the membership problem as oracle, that recognizes S_1. (Strictly speaking, the oracle is L_u.) To show S_1 is recursive in L_u, construct a TM M_2 that, given $\langle M \rangle$, constructs a new TM M' operating as follows: M' ignores its input; instead, M' uses the pair generator to generate all pairs (i, j). When (i, j) is generated, M' simulates M for i steps on the

---

† Note that the TM can remember its prior state by writing that state on its tape just before entering $q_?$.

*j*th input word to M, words being numbered in the usual ordering. If M accepts, M' accepts its own input. If $L(M) = \varnothing$, then $L(M') = \varnothing$. If $L(M) \neq \varnothing$, then M' accepts all its own inputs, ϵ in particular. Thus $M_2^{L_u}$ may query its oracle whether M' accepts ϵ, that is, whether $\langle M', \epsilon \rangle$ is in L_u. If so, M_2 rejects M. Otherwise M_2 accepts M. Thus S_1 is recursive in L_u.   □

Next consider the problem whether $L(M) = \Sigma^*$, where Σ is the input alphabet for TM M. In a sense, this problem is "harder" than membership or emptiness, because, as we shall see, the "$=\Sigma^*$" problem is equivalent to S_2, while emptiness and membership are equivalent to S_1. While this difference means nothing in practical terms since all these problems are undecidable, the results on comparative degree of difficulty suggest that when we consider restricted versions of the problems, the "$=\Sigma^*$" problem really is harder than membership or emptiness. For context-free grammars, the emptiness and membership problems are decidable, while by Theorem 8.11 the problem whether $L(G) = \Sigma^*$ is undecidable. For another example, consider regular expressions. The emptiness and membership problems are each decidable efficiently, in time polynomial in the length of the expression, while the problem whether a given regular expression r is equivalent to Σ^* has been proved almost certainly to require time exponential in the length of r.†

Theorem 8.20   The problem whether $L(M) = \Sigma^*$ is equivalent to S_2.

Proof   We construct a TM $M_3^{S_2}$ that takes an arbitrary TM M and constructs from it $\hat{M}^{S_1}$, a TM with oracle S_1 that behaves as follows. $\hat{M}^{S_1}$ enumerates words x, and for each x uses oracle S_1 to tell whether M accepts x. The technique whereby S_1 can be used to answer the membership question was covered in Theorem 8.19. $\hat{M}^{S_1}$ accepts its own input if any x is not accepted by M. Thus

$$ L(\hat{M}^{S_1}) = \begin{cases} \varnothing & \text{if } L(M) = \Sigma^*, \\ \Sigma^* & \text{otherwise.} \end{cases} $$

$M_3^{S_2}$ with input M constructs $\hat{M}^{S_1}$,‡ then asks its own oracle, S_2, whether $L(\hat{M}^{S_1}) = \varnothing$. If so, $M_3^{S_2}$ accepts M, and $M_3^{S_2}$ rejects otherwise. Thus $M_3^{S_2}$ accepts $\{\langle M \rangle \mid L(M) = \Sigma^*\}$.

Now we must show that S_2 is recursive in the "$=\Sigma^*$" problem. That is, let L_* be the set of codes for ordinary Turing machines that accept all strings over their input alphabet. Then there is a TM $M_4^{L_*}$ that accepts S_2.

Before constructing $M_4^{L_*}$, we first define a *valid* computation of a TM M^{S_1} using oracle S_1. A valid computation is a sequence of ID's, just as for ordinary Turing machines. However, if one ID has state $q_?$, and the next ID has state q_n, then M^{S_1} has queried the oracle whether some TM N accepts $\varnothing$ and received the

---

† Technically, the problem is "complete in polynomial space"; see Chapter 13.

‡ Note that S_1 is not part of $\hat{M}$. Actually $M_3^{S_2}$ constructs the state transitions of oracle machine $\hat{M}$, which will work correctly given S_1 as oracle.

answer "no." To demonstrate that this answer is correct, we insert a valid computation of ordinary TM N, showing that N accepts some particular input. If the next state is q_y, however, we insert no computation of N.

Now, let us describe how $M_4^{L}*$ behaves on input M^{S_1}. $M_4^{L}*$ creates an ordinary TM M' that accepts all the invalid computations of M^{S_1}. To check that a string is not a valid computation, M' checks if the format is invalid (as in Lemma 8.7), or if one ID of M^{S_1} does not follow on one move from the previous ID of M^{S_1} in the sequence, or if a computation of an ordinary TM N inserted between ID's of M^{S_1} with states $q_?$ and q_n is not valid.

The only difficult part to check is when one ID of M^{S_1} has state $q_?$, and the next ID has state q_y. Then M' must determine if "yes" is not the correct answer, so these two ID's do not follow in sequence. Let N be the TM about which the query is made. M' uses the pair generator and, when (i, j) is generated, simulates N for i steps on the jth input. If N accepts, M' determines that $L(N) \neq \varnothing$, so "yes" is the wrong answer. Thus the computation is not a valid one, and M' accepts this computation.

Now M' accepts all strings over its input alphabet if and only if $L(M^{S_1}) = \varnothing$, that is, M^{S_1} has no valid computations. $M_4^{L}*$ may query its oracle whether M' accepts Σ^*. The code for M^{S_1} is in S_2 if and only if $L(M') = \Sigma^*$. Thus S_2 is recursive in L_*.   □

Turing reducibility

We have, throughout this chapter, dealt with a notion called "reducibility," in which we reduced language L_1 to L_2 by finding an algorithm that mapped strings in L_1 to strings in L_2 and strings not in L_1 to strings not in L_2. This notion of reducibility is often called *many-one reducibility*, and while it was all we needed, it is not the most general notion. A more general technique is called *Turing reducibility*, and consists simply of showing that L_1 is recursive in L_2.

If L_1 is many-one reducible to L_2, then surely L_1 is Turing-reducible to L_2. In proof, suppose f is a function computable by a TM that always halts, such that $f(x)$ is in L_2 if and only if x is in L_1. Then consider the oracle TM M^{L_2} that, given input x, computes $f(x)$ and then enters state $q_?$ with $f(x)$ to the right of its head. M^{L_2} accepts if and only if it then enters q_y. Surely $L(M^{L_2}) = L_1$, so L_1 Turing-reduces to L_2. The converse is false, and a proof is suggested in the exercises.

If L_1 Turing-reduces to L_2, and L_1 is undecidable, then so is L_2. For if L_2 were recursive, then the oracle TM M^{L_2} such that $L(M^{L_2}) = L_1$ can be simulated by an ordinary TM that always halts. Thus one could use a Turing reduction to show that L_2 is undecidable, given that L_1 was undecidable, even in circumstances where a many-one reduction of L_1 to L_2 did not exist, or was hard to find.

The notion of many-one reducibility has its virtues, however. If L_1 is many-one reducible to L_2, and L_1 is not r.e., we can conclude L_2 is not r.e. Yet this conclusion cannot be drawn for Turing reducibility. For example, $\bar{L}_u$ is a non-r.e. language that Turing-reduces to the r.e. language L_u. We can recognize $\bar{L}_u$ given L_u as an oracle, by asking whether $\langle M, w \rangle$ is in L_u and accepting if and only if the answer is no.

We see that the more difficult form of reducibility (many-one) enables us to draw conclusions we cannot draw with the easier form of reducibility (Turing). In Chapter 13, where we study bounded reducibility, we shall see additional examples of how more difficult forms of reductions yield conclusions not achievable by easier forms.

EXERCISES

8.1   Suppose the tape alphabets of all Turing machines are selected from some infinite set of symbols $a_1, a_2, \ldots$ Show how each TM may be encoded as a binary string.

8.2   Which of the following properties of r.e. sets are themselves r.e.?

a) L contains at least two strings.
b) L is infinite.
c) L is a context-free language.
d) $L = L^R$.

8.3   Show that it is undecidable whether a TM halts on all inputs.

8.4   A *Post Tag System* is a finite set P of pairs (α, β) chosen from some finite alphabet, and a *start string* γ. We say that $\alpha\delta \Rightarrow \delta\beta$ if (α, β) is a pair. Define $\overset{*}{\Rightarrow}$ to be the reflexive, transitive closure of $\Rightarrow$, as for grammars. Show that for given tag system (P, γ) and string δ it is undecidable whether $\gamma \overset{*}{\Rightarrow} \delta$. [*Hint:* For each TM M let γ be the initial ID of M with blank tape, followed by a marker #, and select the pairs so that any ID must become the next ID after a sequence of applications of the rules, unless that ID has an accepting state, in which case the ID can eventually become ϵ. Then ask if $\gamma \overset{*}{\Rightarrow} \epsilon$.]

8.5   Show that there is no algorithm which given a TM M defining a partial recursive function f of one variable, produces a TM M' that defines a different function of one variable.

*8.6   For ordinary Turing machines M, show that

a) the problem of determining whether $L(M)$ is finite is equivalent to S_2;
b) the problem of determining whether $L(M)$ is a regular set is equivalent to S_3.

8.7   Show that the following problems about programs in a real programming language are undecidable.

a) Whether a given program can loop forever on some input.
b) Whether a given program ever produces an output.
c) Whether two programs produce the same output on all inputs.

8.8   Use Theorem 8.14 to show that the following properties of CFL's are undecidable.

a) L is a linear language.
b) $\bar{L}$ is a CFL.

S 8.9   Show that Theorem 8.14 applies to the linear languages. [*Hint:* Consult Theorem 9.2 for a proof that every regular set has a linear grammar. The hard part is showing that "$= \Sigma^*$," is undecidable for linear languages.

*8.10   Show that the following properties of linear languages are undecidable. You may use the fact that every regular set is a linear language.

a) L is a regular set.
b) $\bar{L}$ is a linear language.
c) $\bar{L}$ is a CFL.
d) L has no unambiguous linear CFG.

*8.11   Show that for CFL L, it is undecidable whether $L = L^R$.

*8.12

a) Show that if L_1 many-one reduces to L_2, and L_2 is (i) recursive in L_3 or (ii) r.e. in L_3, then L_1 is recursive or r.e. in L_3, respectively.
b) Show that $\bar{L}_u$ Turing-reduces to S_1.
c) Show that $\bar{L}_u$ does not many-one reduce to S_1. [*Hint:* Use part (a).]

8.13   We say that L_1 "*truth-table*" *reduces* to L_2 if:

1) There are k algorithms mapping any string x over the alphabet of L_1 to strings over the alphabet L_2. Let $g_i(x)$ be the result of applying the ith algorithm to x.
2) There is a Boolean function $f(y_1, \ldots, y_k)$ such that if y_i is true when $g_i(x)$ is in L_2, and y_i is false otherwise, then $f(y_1, \ldots, y_k)$ is true if and only if x is in L_1.

For example, let L_1 be the set of strings with equal numbers of 0's and 1's, and let L_2 be the set of strings with no fewer 0's than 1's. Let $g_1(x) = x$ and $g_2(x)$ be formed from x by replacing 0's by 1's and vice versa. Let $f(y_1, y_2) = y_1 \wedge y_2$. Then $f(y_1, y_2)$ is true if and only if $g_1(x)$ and $g_2(x)$ both have no fewer 0's than 1's; that is, x has an equal number of 0's and 1's. Thus L_1 truth-table reduces to L_2.

a) Show that if L_1 truth-table reduces to L_2, then L_1 Turing-reduces to L_2.
b) Show that if L_1 many-one reduces to L_2, then L_1 truth-table reduces to L_2.
c) Show that $\bar{L}_u$ truth-table reduces to S_1.

8.14   Consider a multitape TM with oracle which, when it queries its oracle, refers to the entire contents of a designated tape, say the last. Show that this model is equivalent to the oracle TM as defined in Section 8.9.

8.15   Show that PCP is decidable for words over a one-symbol alphabet.

8.16   Show that PCP is equivalent to S_1.

*8.17   Show that PCP is undecidable if strings are restricted to have length one or two. What if strings are restricted to have length exactly two?

*8.18   Let σ be a total recursive function mapping indices of partial recursive functions to indices of partial recursive functions. Give an algorithm to enumerate an infinite set of fixed points of σ; that is, infinitely many i's such that $f_i(y) = f_{\sigma(i)}(y)$ for all y.

*8.19   Does there exist an effective enumeration of Turing machines $M_1, M_2, \ldots$ such that no three consecutive TM's compute the same function?

Solutions to Selected Exercises

8.3 Let $M = (Q, \Sigma, \Gamma, \delta, q_0, B, F)$ be a TM. We construct another TM M', such that M' halts on x if and only if M accepts x. We shall thus have shown that the question whether a TM halts on all inputs reduces to the question whether a TM accepts all inputs, which we know is undecidable. Incidentally, we shall also show by this construction that a question such as "Does a TM halt on a given input?" or "Does a TM halt on some input?" is also undecidable.

M' is designed to behave as follows. First, it shifts its input one position right, placing a left end marker \$ on the leftmost cell. M' then simulates M. If $\delta(q, X)$ is undefined, and either (i) q is nonaccepting and X is any symbol in $\Gamma \cup \{\$\}$ [note that $\delta(q, \$)$ is surely undefined], or (ii) q is accepting and X is \$, then M' scanning X in state q moves right and enters state p_1. In state p_1, scanning any symbol, M' moves left and enters state p_2; in that state, M' moves right and enters p_1 again. Thus M' loops forever if M either halts in a nonaccepting state or falls off the left end of the tape in any state. If M enters an accepting state, not scanning \$, then M' halts. Thus M' halts if and only if M accepts its input, as desired.

8.9 We must first show that the linear languages are closed under union and concatenation with regular sets. We look ahead to Theorem 9.2 for a proof that every regular set is generated by CFG all of whose productions are of the forms $A \to Bw$ and $A \to w$ for nonterminals A and B and string of terminals w. Any such grammar is surely linear. The proof that linear languages are closed under union is just like Theorem 6.1. For concatenation with a regular set, let $G_1 = (V_1, T_1, P_1, S_1)$ be a linear grammar and $G_2 = (V_2, T_2, P_2, S_2)$ be a grammar with all productions of the forms $A \to Bw$ and $A \to w$. Assume V_1 and V_2 are disjoint. Let

$$G = (V_1 \cup V_2, T_1 \cup T_2, P, S_2),$$

where P consists of

i) all productions $A \to Bw$ of P_2,
ii) production $A \to S_1 w$ whenever $A \to w$ is a production of P_2, and
iii) all productions of P_1.

Then $L(G)$ is easily seen to be $L(G_1)L(G_2)$, since all derivations in G are of the form $S_2 \overset{*}{\underset{G}{\Rightarrow}} S_1 x \overset{*}{\underset{G}{\Rightarrow}} yx$, where $S_2 \overset{*}{\underset{G_2}{\Rightarrow}} x$ and $S_1 \overset{*}{\underset{G_1}{\Rightarrow}} y$. Since regular sets and linear languages are closed under reversal, concatenation on the left by a regular set follows similarly.

Now we must show that "$= \Sigma^*$" is undecidable for linear languages. The proof closely parallels Lemma 8.7 and Theorem 8.11, the analogous results for general CFG's. The important difference is that we must redefine the form of valid computations so the set of invalid computations is a linear CFG. Let us define a valid computation of TM M to be a string

$$w_1 \# w_2 \# \cdots \# w_{n-1} \# w_n \# \# w_n^R \# w_{n-1}^R \# \cdots \# w_2^R \# w_1^R, \tag{8.4}$$

where each w_i is an ID, $w_i \underset{M}{\mid\!\!-} w_{i+1}$ for $1 \le i < n$, w_1 is an initial ID and w_n is a final ID. Then it is not hard to construct a linear grammar for strings not of the form (8.4), paralleling the ideas of Lemma 8.7. Then the analog of Theorem 8.11 shows that "$= \Sigma^*$" is undecidable for linear grammars.

BIBLIOGRAPHIC NOTES

The undecidability of L_u is the basic result of Turing [1936]. Theorems 8.6 and 8.7, characterizing recursive and r.e. index sets, are from Rice [1953, 1956]. Post's correspondence problem was shown undecidable in Post [1946], and the proof of undecidability used here is patterned after Floyd [1964]. Lemmas 8.6 and 8.7, relating Turing machine computations to CFG's, are from Hartmanis [1967].

The fundamental papers on undecidable properties of CFL's are Bar Hillel, Perles, and Shamir [1961] and Ginsburg and Rose [1963a]. However, Theorem 8.9, on ambiguity, was proved independently by Cantor [1962], Floyd [1962a], and Chomsky and Schutzenberger [1963]. Theorem 8.16, undecidability of inherent ambiguity, is taken from Ginsburg and Ullian [1966]. Linear grammars and their decision properties have been studied by Greibach [1963, 1966] and Gross [1964]. The approach used in the solution to Exercise 8.9 is from Baker and Book [1974].

Greibach's theorem is from Greibach [1968]. A generalization appears in Hunt and Rosenkrantz [1974], which includes a solution to Exercise 8.11. Hopcroft and Ullman [1968a] shows that for certain classes of languages defined by automata, the decidability of membership and emptiness are related. The S_{mn}- and recursion theorems are from Kleene [1952]. Example 8.10, on the nonexistence of proofs of halting or nonhalting for all TM's, is from Hartmanis and Hopcroft [1976].

Hartmanis and Hopcroft [1968] are the authors of the basic paper relating problems about CFL's to the hierarchy of undecidable problems. Theorems 8.19 and 8.20, as well as Exercise 8.6, are from there. Additional results of this nature have been obtained by Cudia and Singletary [1968], Cudia [1970], Hartmanis [1969], and Reedy and Savitch [1975]. Exercise 8.4, on tag systems, is from Minsky [1961].

THE CHOMSKY HIERARCHY

Of the three major classes of languages we have studied—the regular sets, the context-free languages, and the recursively enumerable languages—we have grammatically characterized only the CFL's. In this chapter we shall give grammatical definitions of the regular sets and the r.e. languages. We shall also introduce a new class of languages, lying between the CFL's and the r.e. languages, giving both machine and grammatical characterizations for this new class. The four classes of languages are often called the *Chomsky hierarchy*, after Noam Chomsky, who defined these classes as potential models of natural languages.

9.1 REGULAR GRAMMARS

If all productions of a CFG are of the form $A \to wB$ or $A \to w$, where A and B are variables and w is a (possibly empty) string of terminals, then we say the grammar is *right-linear*. If all productions are of the form $A \to Bw$ or $A \to w$, we call it *left-linear*. A right- or left-linear grammar is called a *regular grammar*.

Example 9.1 The language **0(10)*** is generated by the right-linear grammar

$$S \to 0A$$
$$A \to 10A \,|\, \epsilon$$

(9.1)

and by the left-linear grammar

$$S \to S10 \,|\, 0$$

(9.2)

217

Equivalence of regular grammars and finite automata

The regular grammars characterize the regular sets, in the sense that a language is regular if and only if it has a left-linear grammar and if and only if it has a right-linear grammar. These results are proved in the next two theorems.

Theorem 9.1   If L has a regular grammar, then L is a regular set.

Proof   First, suppose $L = L(G)$ for some right-linear grammar $G = (V, T, P, S)$. We construct an NFA with ϵ-moves, $M = (Q, T, \delta, [S], \{[\epsilon]\})$ that simulates derivations in G.

Q consists of the symbols $[\alpha]$ such that α is S or a (not necessarily proper) suffix of some right-hand side of a production in P.

We define δ by:

1) If A is a variable, then $\delta([A], \epsilon) = \{[\alpha] \mid A \to \alpha \text{ is a production}\}$.
2) If a is in T and α in $T^* \cup T^*V$, then $\delta([a\alpha], a) = \{[\alpha]\}$.

Then an easy induction on the length of a derivation or move sequence shows that $\delta([S], w)$ contains $[\alpha]$ if and only if $S \overset{*}{\Rightarrow} xA \Rightarrow xy\alpha$, where $A \to y\alpha$ is a production and $xy = w$, or if $\alpha = S$ and $w = \epsilon$. As $[\epsilon]$ is the unique final state, M accepts w if and only if $S \overset{*}{\Rightarrow} xA \Rightarrow w$. But since every derivation of a terminal string has at least one step, we see that M accepts w if and only if G generates w. Hence every right-linear grammar generates a regular set.

Now let $G = (V, T, P, S)$ be a left-linear grammar. Let $G' = (V, T, P', S)$, where P' consists of the productions of G with right sides reversed, that is,

$$P' = \{A \to \alpha \mid A \to \alpha^R \text{ is in } P\}.$$

If we reverse the productions of a left-linear grammar we get a right-linear grammar, and vice versa. Thus G' is a right-linear grammar, and it is easy to show that $L(G') = L(G)^R$. By the preceding paragraph, $L(G')$ is a regular set. But the regular sets are closed under reversal (Exercise 3.4g), so $L(G')^R = L(G)$ is also a regular set. Thus every right- or left-linear grammar defines a regular set.   □

Example 9.2   The NFA constructed by Theorem 9.1 from grammar (9.1) is shown in Fig. 9.1.

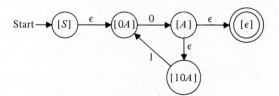

Fig. 9.1   NFA accepting 0(10)*.

Now consider grammar (9.2). If we reverse its productions we get

$$S \rightarrow 01S \,|\, 0$$

The construction of Theorem 9.1 for this grammar yields the NFA of Fig. 9.2(a). If we reverse the edges of that NFA and exchange initial and final states, we get another NFA for $0(10)^*$.

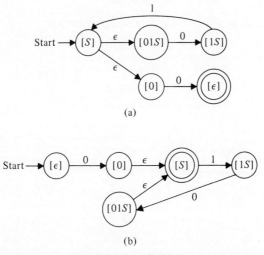

(a)

(b)

Fig. 9.2 Construction of an NFA for $0(10)^*$ from a left-linear grammar.

Theorem 9.2 If L is a regular set, then L is generated by some left-linear grammar and by some right-linear grammar.

Proof Let $L = L(M)$ for DFA $M = (Q, \Sigma, \delta, q_0, F)$. First suppose that q_0 is not a final state. Then $L = L(G)$ for right-linear grammar $G = (Q, \Sigma, P, q_0)$, where P consists of production $p \rightarrow aq$ whenever $\delta(p, a) = q$ and also $p \rightarrow a$ whenever $\delta(p, a)$ is a final state. Then clearly $\delta(p, w) = q$ if and only if $p \overset{*}{\Rightarrow} wq$. If wa is accepted by M, let $\delta(q_0, w) = p$, implying $q_0 \overset{*}{\Rightarrow} wp$. Also, $\delta(p, a)$ is final, so $p \rightarrow a$ is a production. Thus $q_0 \overset{*}{\Rightarrow} wa$. Conversely, let $q_0 \overset{*}{\Rightarrow} x$. Then $x = wa$, and $q_0 \overset{*}{\Rightarrow} wp \Rightarrow wa$ for some state (variable) p. Then $\delta(q_0, w) = p$, and $\delta(p, a)$ is final. Thus x is in $L(M)$. Hence $L(M) = L(G) = L$.

Now let q_0 be in F, so ϵ is in L. We note that the grammar G defined above generates $L - \{\epsilon\}$. We may modify G by adding a new start symbol S with productions $S \rightarrow q_0 \,|\, \epsilon$. The resulting grammar is still right-linear and generates L.

To produce a left-linear grammar for L, start with an NFA for L^R and then reverse the right sides of all productions of the resulting right-linear grammar. $\square$

Example 9.3   In Fig. 9.3 we see a DFA for **0(10)***.
The right-linear grammar from this DFA is

$$A \rightarrow 0B\,|\,1D\,|\,0$$
$$B \rightarrow 0D\,|\,1C$$
$$C \rightarrow 0B\,|\,1D\,|\,0$$
$$D \rightarrow 0D\,|\,1D$$

As D is useless we may eliminate it, obtaining grammar

$$A \rightarrow 0B\,|\,0$$
$$B \rightarrow 1C$$
$$C \rightarrow 0B\,|\,0$$

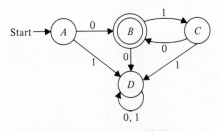

Fig. 9.3   DFA for **0(10)***.

9.2   UNRESTRICTED GRAMMARS

The largest family of grammars in the Chomsky hierarchy permits productions of the form $\alpha \rightarrow \beta$, where α and β are arbitrary strings of grammar symbols, with $\alpha \neq \epsilon$. These grammars are known as *semi-Thue, type 0, phrase structure* or *unrestricted grammars*. We shall continue to use the 4-tuple notation $G = (V, T, P, S)$ for unrestricted grammars. We say $\gamma\alpha\delta \Rightarrow \gamma\beta\delta$ whenever $\alpha \rightarrow \beta$ is a production. As before, $\overset{*}{\Rightarrow}$ stands for the reflexive and transitive closure of the relation $\Rightarrow$:

$$L(G) = \{w\,|\,w \text{ is in } T^* \text{ and } S \overset{*}{\Rightarrow} w\},$$

exactly as for context-free grammars.

Example 9.4   A grammar generating $\{a^i\,|\,i$ is a positive power of $2\}$ is given below.

1) $S \rightarrow ACaB$	5) $aD \rightarrow Da$
2) $Ca \rightarrow aaC$	6) $AD \rightarrow AC$
3) $CB \rightarrow DB$	7) $aE \rightarrow Ea$
4) $CB \rightarrow E$	8) $AE \rightarrow \epsilon$

A and *B* serve as left and right endmarkers for sentential forms; *C* is a marker that moves through the string of *a*'s between *A* and *B*, doubling their number by production (2). When *C* hits the right endmarker *B*, it becomes a *D* or *E* by production (3) or (4). If a *D* is chosen, that *D* migrates left by production (5) until the left endmarker *A* is reached. At that point the *D* becomes a *C* again by production (6), and the process starts over. If an *E* is chosen, the right endmarker is consumed. The *E* migrates left by production (7) and consumes the left endmarker, leaving a string of 2^i *a*'s for some $i > 0$. We can prove by induction on the number of steps in the derivation that if production (4) is never used, then any sentential form is either

i) *S*,

ii) of the form Aa^iCa^jB, where $i + 2j$ is a positive power of 2, or

iii) of the form Aa^iDa^jB, where $i + j$ is a positive power of 2.

When we use production (4) we are left with a sentential form Aa^iE, where *i* is a positive power of 2. Then the only possible steps in a derivation are *i* applications of (7) to yield AEa^i followed by one application of (8), producing sentence a^i, where *i* is a positive power of 2.

Equivalence of type 0 grammars and Turing machines

We shall prove in the next two theorems that unrestricted grammars characterize the r.e. languages. The first theorem states that every type-0 language generates an r.e. set. An easy proof would be to give an algorithm for enumerating all strings generated by a type-0 grammar. Instead we construct a Turing machine recognizer for sentences generated by a type-0 grammar, since this construction will be useful later for a similar proof about context-sensitive grammars (the remaining class in the Chomsky hierarchy).

Theorem 9.3 If *L* is *L*(*G*) for unrestricted grammar $G = (V, T, P, S)$, then *L* is an r.e. language.

Proof Let us construct a nondeterministic two-tape Turing machine *M* to recognize *L*. *M*'s first tape is the input, on which a string *w* will be placed. The second tape is used to hold a sentential form α of *G*. *M* initializes α to *S*. Then *M* repeatedly does the following:

1) Nondeterministically select a position *i* in α, so that any *i* between 1 and $|\alpha|$ can be chosen. That is, start at the left, and repeatedly choose to move right or select the present position.

2) Nondeterministically select a production $\beta \to \gamma$ of *G*.

3) If β appears beginning in position *i* of α, replace β by γ there, using the "shifting-over" technique of Section 7.4, perhaps shifting left if $|\gamma| < |\beta|$.

4) Compare the resulting sentential form with w on tape 1. If they match, accept; w is a sentence of G. If not, go back to Step (1).

It is easy to show that all and only the sentential forms of G appear on tape 2 when Step (4) is executed after some sequence of choices. Thus $L(M) = L(G) = L$, so L is r.e. $\square$

Theorem 9.4 If L is an r.e. language, then $L = L(G)$ for some unrestricted grammar G.

Proof Let L be accepted by Turing machine $M = (Q, \Sigma, \Gamma, \delta, q_0, B, F)$. Construct a grammar G that "nondeterministically" generates two copies of a representation of some word in Σ^* and then simulates the action of M on one copy. If M accepts the word, then G converts the second copy to a terminal string. If M does not accept, the derivation never results in a terminal string.

Formally, let

$$G = (V, \Sigma, P, A_1), \quad \text{where } V = ((\Sigma \cup \{\epsilon\}) \times \Gamma) \cup \{A_1, A_2, A_3\}$$

and the productions in P are:

1) $A_1 \to q_0 A_2$
2) $A_2 \to [a, a]A_2$ for each a in Σ.
3) $A_2 \to A_3$
4) $A_3 \to [\epsilon, B]A_3$
5) $A_3 \to \epsilon$
6) $q[a, X] \to [a, Y]p$ for each a in $\Sigma \cup \{\epsilon\}$ and each q in Q and X and Y in Γ, such that $\delta(q, X) = (p, Y, R)$.
7) $[b, Z]q[a, X] \to p[b, Z][a, Y]$ for each X, Y, and Z in Γ, a and b in $\Sigma \cup \{\epsilon\}$, and q in Q, such that $\delta(q, X) = (p, Y, L)$.
8) $[a, X]q \to qaq$, $q[a, X] \to qaq$, and $q \to \epsilon$ for each a in $\Sigma \cup \{\epsilon\}$, X in Γ, and q in F.

Using rules 1 and 2, we have

$$A_1 \overset{*}{\Rightarrow} q_0[a_1, a_1][a_2, a_2] \cdots [a_n, a_n]A_2,$$

where a_i is in Σ for each i. Suppose that M accepts the string $a_1 a_2 \cdots a_n$. Then for some m, M uses no more than m cells to the right of its input. Using rule 3, then rule 4 m times, and finally rule 5, we have

$$A_1 \overset{*}{\Rightarrow} q_0[a_1, a_1][a_2, a_2] \cdots [a_n, a_n][\epsilon, B]^m.$$

From this point on, only rules 6 and 7 can be used until an accepting state is generated. Note that the first components of variables in $(\Sigma \cup \{\epsilon\}) \times \Gamma$ are never changed. We can show by induction on the number of moves made by M that if

$$q_0 a_1 a_2 \cdots a_n \overset{*}{\underset{M}{\vdash}} X_1 X_2 \cdots X_{r-1} q X_r \cdots X_s, \tag{9.3}$$

then

$$q_0[a_1, a_1][a_2, a_2] \cdots [a_n, a_n][\epsilon, B]^m \underset{G}{\overset{*}{\Rightarrow}}$$

$$[a_1, X_1][a_2, X_2] \cdots [a_{r-1}, X_{r-1}]q[a_r, X_r] \cdots [a_{n+m}, X_{n+m}], \qquad (9.4)$$

where $a_1, a_2, \ldots, a_n$ are in Σ, $a_{n+1} = a_{n+2} = \cdots = a_{n+m} = \epsilon$, $X_1, X_2, \ldots, X_{n+m}$ are in Γ, and $X_{s+1} = X_{s+2} = \cdots = X_{n+m} = B$.

The inductive hypothesis is trivially true for zero moves, since $r = 1$ and $s = n$. Suppose it is true for $k - 1$ moves and let

$$q_0 a_1 a_2 \cdots a_n \underset{M}{\overset{k-1}{\vdash}} X_1 X_2 \cdots X_{r-1}qX_r \cdots X_s \underset{M}{\overline{}} Y_1 Y_2 \cdots Y_{t-1}pY_t \cdots Y_u.$$

By the inductive hypothesis,

$$q_0[a_1, a_1] \cdots [a_n, a_n][\epsilon, B]^m \underset{G}{\overset{*}{\Rightarrow}} [a_1, X_1] \cdots [a_{r-1}, X_{r-1}]q[a_r, X_r] \cdots [a_{n+m}, X_{n+m}],$$

where the a's and X's satisfy the conditions of (9.4).

If $t = r + 1$, then the kth move of M is to the right, so $\delta(q, X_r) = (p, Y_r, R)$. By rule (6), $q[a_r, X_r] \to [a_r, Y_r]p$ is a production of G. Thus

$$q_0[a_1, a_1] \cdots [a_n, a_n][\epsilon, B]^m \underset{G}{\overset{*}{\Rightarrow}}$$

$$[a_1, Y_1] \cdots [a_{t-1}, Y_{t-1}]p[a_t, Y_t] \cdots [a_{n+m}, Y_{n+m}], \qquad (9.5)$$

where $Y_i = B$ for $i > u$.

If $t = r - 1$, then the kth move of M is to the left, and we prove (9.5) using rule (7) and the observations that $r > 1$ and $\delta(q, X_r) = (p, Y_r, L)$.

By rule (8), if p is in F then

$$[a_1, Y_1] \cdots [a_{t-1}, Y_{t-1}]p[a_t, Y_t] \cdots [a_{n+m}, Y_{n+m}] \overset{*}{\Rightarrow} a_1 a_2 \cdots a_n.$$

We have thus shown that if w is in $L(M)$, then $A_1 \overset{*}{\Rightarrow} w$, so w is in $L(G)$.

For the converse, that w in $L(G)$ implies w in $L(M)$, an induction similar to the above shows that (9.4) implies (9.3). We leave this part as an exercise. Then we note that there is no way to remove the state of M from sentential forms of G without using rule (8). Thus G cannot derive a terminal string without simulating an accepting computation of M. By rule (8), the string derived must be the first components of the variables in $(\Sigma \cup \{\epsilon\}) \times \Gamma$, which are never changed as moves of M are simulated. $\qquad \square$

9.3 CONTEXT-SENSITIVE LANGUAGES

Suppose we place the restriction on productions $\alpha \to \beta$ of a phrase structure grammar that β be at least as long as α. Then we call the resulting grammar *context-sensitive* and its language a *context-sensitive language* (CSG and CSL respectively). The term "context-sensitive" comes from a normal form for these grammars, where each production is of the form $\alpha_1 A \alpha_2 \to \alpha_1 \beta \alpha_2$, with $\beta \neq \epsilon$. Productions of the latter form look almost like context-free productions, but they permit replacement of variable A by string β only in the "context" $\alpha_1 - \alpha_2$. We leave this normal form as an exercise.

Almost any language one can think of is context-sensitive; the only known proofs that certain languages are not CSL's are ultimately based on diagonalization. These include L_u of Chapter 8 and the languages to which we may reduce L_u, for example, the languages proved undecidable in Chapter 8. We shall prove in Section 9.4 that there are recursive languages that are non-CSL's, and in Chapter 12 we shall refine this statement somewhat. In both cases the proofs proceed by diagonalization.

Example 9.5 Consider again the grammar of Example 9.4. There are two productions that violate the definition of a context-sensitive grammar. These are $CB \to E$ and $AE \to \epsilon$. We can create a CSG for the language $\{a^{2^i} \mid i \geq 1\}$ by realizing that A, B, C, D, and E are nothing but markers, which eventually disappear. Instead of using separate symbols for the markers, we can incorporate these markers into the a's by creating "composite" variables like $[CaB]$, which is a single symbol appearing in place of the string CaB.

The complete set of composite symbols we need to mimic the grammar of Example 9.4 is $[ACaB]$, $[Aa]$, $[ACa]$, $[ADa]$, $[AEa]$, $[Ca]$, $[Da]$, $[Ea]$, $[aCB]$, $[CaB]$, $[aDB]$, $[aE]$, $[DaB]$, and $[aB]$. The productions of our context-sensitive grammars, which we group according to the production from Example 9.4 that they mimic, are:

1) $S \to [ACaB]$

2) $[Ca]a \to aa[Ca]$
$[Ca][aB] \to aa[CaB]$
$[ACa]a \to [Aa]a[Ca]$
$[ACa][aB] \to [Aa]a[CaB]$
$[ACaB] \to [Aa][aCB]$
$[CaB] \to a[aCB]$

3) $[aCB] \to [aDB]$

4) $[aCB] \to [aE]$

5) $a[Da] \to [Da]a$
$[aDB] \to [DaB]$
$[Aa][Da] \to [ADa]a$
$a[DaB] \to [Da][aB]$
$[Aa][DaB] \to [ADa][aB]$

6) $[ADa] \to [ACa]$

7) $a[Ea] \to [Ea]a$
$[aE] \to [Ea]$
$[Aa][Ea] \to [AEa]a$

8) $[AEa] \to a$

It is straightforward to show that $S \overset{*}{\Rightarrow} \alpha$ in the grammar of Example 9.4 if and only if $S \overset{*}{\Rightarrow} \alpha'$ in the present CSG, where α' is formed from α by grouping with an a all markers (A through E) appearing between it and the a to its left and also grouping with the first a any markers to its left and with the last a any markers to its right. For example, if $\alpha = AaaCaB$, then α' is $[Aa]a[CaB]$.

Linear bounded automata

Now we introduce a machine characterization of the CSL's. A *linear bounded automaton* (LBA) is a nondeterministic Turing machine satisfying the following two conditions.

1) Its input alphabet includes two special symbols ¢ and $, the *left* and *right endmarkers*, respectively.

2) The LBA has no moves left from ¢ or right from $, nor may it print another symbol over ¢ or $.

The linear bounded automaton is simply a Turing machine which, instead of having potentially infinite tape on which to compute, is restricted to the portion of the tape containing the input x plus the two tape squares holding the endmarkers. We shall see in Chapter 12 that restricting the Turing machine to an amount of tape that, on each input, is bounded by some linear function of the length of the input would result in the identical computational ability as restricting the Turing machine to the portion of the tape containing the input—hence the name "linear bounded automaton."

An LBA will be denoted $M = (Q, \Sigma, \Gamma, \delta, q_0, ¢, \$, F)$, where $Q, \Sigma, \Gamma, \delta, q_0$ and F are as for a nondeterministic TM; ¢ and $ are symbols in Σ, the left and right endmarkers. $L(M)$, the *language* accepted by M, is

$$\{w \,|\, w \text{ is in } (\Sigma - \{¢, \$\})^* \text{ and } q_0 ¢ w \$ \vdash_M^* \alpha q \beta \text{ for some } q \text{ in } F\}.$$

Note that the endmarkers are on the input tape initially but are not considered part of the word to be accepted or rejected. Since an LBA cannot move off the input, there is no need to suppose that there is blank tape to the right of the $.

Equivalence of LBA's and CSG's

We now show that except for the fact that an LBA can accept ϵ while a CSG cannot generate ϵ, the LBA's accept exactly the CSL's.

Theorem 9.5 If L is a CSL, then L is accepted by some LBA.

Proof The proof is almost the same as that for Theorem 9.3. The only difference is that while the TM of Theorem 9.3 generated sentential forms of an unrestricted grammar on a second tape, the LBA uses a second track of its input tape. Presented with ¢$w$$ on its tape, the LBA starts by writing the symbol S on a second track below the leftmost symbol of w. If $w = \epsilon$, the LBA instead halts without accepting. Next the LBA repeatedly guesses a production and a position in the sentential form written on the second track. It applies the production, shifting the portion of the sentential form to the right whenever the sentential form expands. If, however, the new sentential form is longer than w, the LBA halts without acceptance. Thus the LBA will accept w if there is a derivation $S \overset{*}{\Rightarrow} w$ such that no intermediate sentential form is longer than w. But since the right side of any production in a CSG is as long or longer than the left side, there could not be a derivation $S \overset{*}{\Rightarrow} \alpha \overset{*}{\Rightarrow} w$, where α is longer than w. Thus the LBA accepts all and only the words generated by the CSG.   □

Theorem 9.6 If $L = L(M)$ for LBA $M = (Q, \Sigma, \Gamma, \delta, q_0, \mathcal{c}, \$, F)$, then $L - \{\epsilon\}$ is a CSL.

Proof The proof parallels the construction of an unrestricted grammar from a TM in Theorem 9.4. The differences are that the endmarkers on the LBA tape must be incorporated into adjacent tape symbols, and the state must likewise be incorporated into the symbol scanned by the tape head. The reason for this is that if the CSG simulated the LBA using separate symbols for the endmarkers, or state, it could not erase these symbols afterward, since that would necessitate shortening a sentential form, and the right side of every CSG production is at least as long as the left side. The generation of a sequence of pairs, the first component of which forms the terminal string $a_1 a_2 \cdots a_n$ and the second of which forms the LBA tape is accomplished by the productions

$$A_1 \to [a, q_0 \mathcal{c} a] A_2, \qquad A_1 \to [a, q_0 \mathcal{c} a \$],$$
$$A_2 \to [a, a] A_2, \qquad A_2 \to [a, a \$],$$

for all a in $\Sigma - \{\mathcal{c}, \$\}$.

The LBA-simulating rules are similar to rules 6 and 7 in Theorem 9.4 and are left as an exercise.

If q is final, then we have production

$$[a, \alpha q \beta] \to a$$

for all a in $\Sigma - \{\mathcal{c}, \$\}$ and all possible α and β (that is, α and/or β could include $\mathcal{c}$, $\$$, and one tape symbol). Note that the number of productions defined is finite. We also allow deletion of the second component of a variable if it is adjacent to a terminal, by

$$[a, \alpha] b \to ab,$$
$$b [a, \alpha] \to ba$$

for any a and b in $\Sigma - \{\mathcal{c}, \$\}$ and all possible α's.

The productions shown explicitly are clearly context-sensitive. The LBA-simulating productions can easily be made length preserving, so the resulting grammar is a CSG. A proof that any word w but ϵ is accepted by M if and only if it is generated by the grammar parallels Theorem 9.4, and we omit it. Note that there is no way for the grammar to set up the LBA input $\mathcal{c}\$$ or simulate M on that input. Thus ϵ is not generated by the grammar whether or not it is in $L(M)$.   □

9.4 RELATIONS BETWEEN CLASSES OF LANGUAGES

The four classes of languages—r.e. sets, CSL's, CFL's, and regular sets—are often referred to as languages of types 0, 1, 2, and 3, respectively. We can show that except for the matter of the empty string, the type-i languages properly include the type-$(i + 1)$ languages for $i = 0$, 1, and 2. We first need to show that every CSL is recursive, and in fact, there are recursive languages that are not CSL's.

CSL's and recursive sets

Theorem 9.7 Every CSL is recursive.

Proof Given a CSG $G = (V, T, P, S)$ and a word w in Σ^* of length n, we can test whether w is in $L(G)$ as follows. Construct a graph whose vertices are the strings in $(V \cup T)^*$ of length n or less. Put an arc from α to β if $\alpha \Rightarrow \beta$. Then paths in the graph correspond to derivations in G, and w is in $L(G)$ if and only if there is a path from the vertex for S to the vertex for w. Use any of a number of path-finding algorithms (see Aho, Hopcroft, and Ullman [1974]) to decide whether such a path exists. □

Example 9.6 Consider the CSG of Example 9.5 and input $w = aa$. One way to test for paths in the graph is to start with string S, and at the ith step find the strings of length n or less having a path from S of length i or less. If we have the set for $i - 1$, say $\mathscr{S}$, then the set for i is $\mathscr{S} \cup \{\beta \mid \alpha \Rightarrow \beta \text{ for some } \alpha \text{ in } \mathscr{S} \text{ and } |\beta| \leq n\}$. In our example we get the following sets:

$$i = 0: \quad \{S\}$$

$$i = 1: \quad \{S, [ACaB]\}$$

$$i = 2: \quad \{S, [ACaB], [Aa][aCB]\}$$

$$i = 3: \quad \{S, [ACaB], [Aa][aCB], [Aa][aDB], [Aa][aE]\}$$

$$\vdots$$

$$i = 6: \quad \{S, [ACaB], [Aa][aCB], [Aa][aDB], [Aa][aE],$$
$$[Aa][DaB], [Aa][Ea], [ADa][aB], [AEa]a,$$
$$[ACa][aB], aa\}$$

Since for $i = 6$ we discover that aa is reachable from S we need go no further. In general, since the number of sentential forms of length n or less is finite for any fixed grammar and fixed n, we know we shall eventually come to a point where no new sentential forms are added. Since the set for i depends only on the set for $i - 1$, we shall never add any new strings, so if we have not yet produced w, we never will. In that case w is not in the language.

To prove that the CSL's are a proper subset of the recursive languages we prove something more general. In particular, we show that any class of languages that can be effectively enumerated, by listing one or more Turing machines that halt on all inputs, for each member of the class, is a proper subclass of the recursive languages.

Lemma 9.1   Let $M_1, M_2, \ldots$ be an enumeration of some set of Turing machines that halt on all inputs. Then there is some recursive language that is not $L(M_i)$ for any i.

Proof   Let L be the subset of $(0 + 1)^*$ such that w is in L if and only if M_i does not accept w, where i is the integer whose binary representation is w. L is recursive, since given w we can generate M_i and test whether or not w is in $L(M_i)$. But no TM on the list accepts L. Suppose L were $L(M_j)$, and let x be the binary representation of j. If x is in L, then x is not in $L(M_j)$, and if x is not in L, then x is in $L(M_j)$. Thus $L \neq L(M_j)$ as supposed. Hence L is a recursive language that is not $L(M_j)$ for any j.   □

Theorem 9.8   There is a recursive language that is not context-sensitive.

Proof   By Lemma 9.1 we need only show that we can enumerate halting TM's for the CSL's over alphabet $\{0, 1\}$. Let the 4-tuple representation for CSG's with terminal alphabet $\{0, 1\}$ be given some binary coding. For example, we could let 0, 1, comma, $\rightarrow$, $\{$, $\}$, (, and) be denoted by 10, 100, ..., 10^8, respectively, and let the ith variable be denoted by 10^{i+8}. Let M_j be the Turing machine implementing the algorithm of Theorem 9.7 that recognizes the language of the CSG with binary code j. Clearly M_j always halts whether its input is accepted or not. The theorem then follows immediately from Lemma 9.1.   □

The hierarchy theorem

Theorem 9.9   (a) The regular sets are properly contained in the context-free languages. (b) The CFL's not containing the empty string are properly contained in the context-sensitive languages. (c) The CSL's are properly contained in the r.e. sets.

Proof   Part (a) follows from the fact that every regular grammar is a CFG, and $\{0^n1^n \mid n \geq 1\}$ is an example of a CFL that is not regular. Part (b) is proved by noting that every CFG in Chomsky normal form is a CSG. $\{a^{2^i} \mid i \geq 1\}$ is a CSL that is easily shown not to be a CFL by the pumping lemma. For part (c) every CSG is surely an unrestricted grammar. Proper containment follows from Theorem 9.8.   □

EXERCISES

9.1   Construct left-linear and right-linear grammars for the languages

a) $(0 + 1)^*00(0 + 1)^*$
b) $0^*(1(0 + 1))^*$
c) $(((01 + 10)^*11)^*00)^*$

9.2   Show the following normal form for right-linear grammars and the analogous result for left-linear grammars: If L is a regular set, then $L - \{\epsilon\}$ is generated by a grammar in which all productions are of the form $A \to aB$ or $A \to a$ for terminal a and variables A and B.

9.3   A context-free grammar is said to be *simple* if it is in Greibach normal form, and for every variable A and terminal a, there is at most one string α such that $A \to a\alpha$ is a production. A language is *simple* if it has a simple grammar. For example, $L = \{0^n1^n \mid n \geq 1\}$ has the simple grammar:

$$S \to 0A$$
$$A \to 0AB \mid 1$$
$$B \to 1$$

Note that the more natural GNF grammar for L,

$$S \to 0SB \mid 0B$$
$$B \to 1$$

is not simple because there are two S-productions whose right sides begin with 0. Prove that every regular set not containing ϵ is a simple language. [*Hint*: Use a DFA representation for the regular set.]

*9.4   A CFG is said to be *self-embedding* if there is some useful variable A such that $A \overset{*}{\Rightarrow} wAx$, and neither w nor x is ϵ. Prove that a CFL is regular if and only if it has a CFG that is not self-embedding. [*Hint*: It is easy to show that no regular grammar is self-embedding. For the "if" portion, show that a non-self-embedding grammar may be put in Greibach normal form without making it self-embedding. Then show that for every non-self-embedding GNF grammar, there is a constant k such that no left-sentential form has more than k variables. Finally, show from the above that the non-self-embedding GNF grammar can be converted to a regular grammar.]

*9.5   Give unrestricted grammars for

a) $\{ww \mid w$ is in $(0 + 1)^*\}$ b) $\{0^{i^2} \mid i \geq 1\}$
c) $\{0^i \mid i$ is not a prime$\}$ d) $\{0^i1^i2^i \mid i \geq 1\}$

9.6   Give context-sensitive grammars for the languages of Exercise 9.5, excluding ϵ in (a).

9.7   A CSL is said to be *deterministic* if it is accepted by some deterministic LBA. Show that the complement of a deterministic CSL is also a deterministic CSL. [*Hint*: Show that for every deterministic LBA there is an equivalent LBA that halts on every input.] It is, incidentally, open whether every CSL is a deterministic CSL, and whether the CSL's are closed under complementation. Obviously a positive answer to the former question would imply a positive answer to the latter.

*9.8

a) Show that every context-free language is accepted by a deterministic LBA.

b) Show that the Boolean closure of the CFL's is contained within the class of sets accepted by deterministic LBA's.

c) Show that the containment in (b) is proper. [*Hint:* Consider languages over a one-symbol alphabet.]

*9.9   Show that every CSL is generated by a grammar in which all productions are of the form $\alpha A\beta \rightarrow \alpha\gamma\beta$, where A is a variable, α, β, and γ are strings of grammar symbols, and $\gamma \neq \epsilon$.

*S9.10   Show that the CSL's are closed under the following operations:

a) union	b) concatenation
c) intersection	d) substitution
e) inverse homomorphism	f) positive closure (recall $L^+ = \bigcup_{i=1} L^i$)

*9.11   Show that the r.e. sets are closed under the following operations:

a) through e) same as Exercise 9.10.

f) Kleene closure.

9.12

a) Show that all the undecidable properties of CFL's mentioned in Sections 8.5, 8.6, and 8.7 are undecidable for CSL's, with the exception that "$= \Sigma^*$" is trivially decidable because no CSL contains ϵ.

b) Show that "$= \Sigma^+$" is undecidable for CSL's.

S9.13   Show that it is undecidable whether a given CSL is empty.

*S9.14   Show that every r.e. set is $h(L)$, where h is a homomorphism and L a CSL.

Solutions to Selected Exercises

9.10   The proofs are similar to the proofs of Theorems 6.1, 6.2, and 6.3 for CFL's. However, there is one problem with which we have to deal. Consider the concatenation construction. Suppose

$$G_1 = (V_1, T_1, P_1, S_1) \qquad \text{and} \qquad G_2 = (V_2, T_2, P_2, S_2)$$

are CSG's generating L_1 and L_2, respectively. In Theorem 6.1 for CFG's, we constructed grammar

$$G_4 = (V_1 \cup V_2 \cup \{S_4\}, T_1 \cup T_2, P_1 \cup P_2 \cup \{S_4 \rightarrow S_1 S_2\}, S_4)$$

to generate $L_1 L_2$. This construction is correct for CFG's, provided V_1 and V_2 are disjoint. For CSG's, however, we could have a production $\alpha \rightarrow \beta$ in P_1 or P_2 that was applicable in a sentential form of G_4, say $\gamma\delta$, where $S_1 \underset{G_1}{\overset{*}{\Rightarrow}} \gamma$ and $S_2 \underset{G_2}{\overset{*}{\Rightarrow}} \delta$, in such a position that α straddles the boundary between γ and δ. We might thus derive a string not in $L_1 L_2$.

Assuming $V_1 \cap V_2 = \varnothing$ doesn't help, since α could consist of terminals only, and of course we cannot assume that $T_1 \cap T_2 = \varnothing$. What we need is a normal form for CSG's that allows only variables on the left sides of productions. Such a lemma is easy to prove. Let $G = (V, T, P, S)$ be a CSG. Construct $G' = (V', T, P', S)$, where V' consists of V plus the variables A_a for each a in T. P' consists of productions $A_a \to a$ for each a, and production $\alpha' \to \beta'$ for each $\alpha \to \beta$ in P, where α' is α with each occurrence of a terminal a replaced by A_a, and β' is similarly related to β.

Now, if we assume that G_1 and G_2 have disjoint sets of variables and are in the above normal form, the constructions of Theorem 6.1 for union and concatenation carry over to CSL's.

Positive closure presents another problem. If, in analogy with Theorem 6.1, we construct

$$G_5 = (V_1 \cup \{S_5\}, T_1, P_1 \cup \{S_5 \to S_1 S_5 | S_1\}, S_5),$$

we have not avoided the problem of the potential for applying a production $\alpha \to \beta$ in such a way that it straddles the strings derived from two or more instances of S_1. What we can do is create grammar G_1', which is G_1 with each variable A replaced by a new symbol A'. Then we construct the grammar $G_5 = (V_5, T_1, P_5', S_5)$, where V_5 consists of the variables of G_1 and G_1', plus the symbols S_5 and S_5'; P_5' consists of the productions of G_1 and G_1', plus

$$S_5 \to S_1 S_5' | S_1$$

$$S_5' \to S_1' S_5 | S_1'$$

As no CSL contains ϵ, we can never have symbols derived from two instances of S_1 or two instances of S_1' adjacent, and we may be sure that each production of G_5 is applied to a string derived from one instance of S_1 or S_1'.

Inverse homomorphism, intersection, and substitution are best handled by machine-based proofs. Let L be a CSL accepted by LBA M and h a homomorphism. Suppose that $|h(a)| \le k$ for any a. Then we may construct LBA M' for $h^{-1}(L)$ as follows. M' takes its input x and computes $h(x)$, storing k symbols per cell. There is sufficient space, since $|h(x)| \le k|x|$. Then M' simulates M on $h(x)$, accepting if M accepts.

For intersection, let L_1 and L_2 be CSL's accepted by LBA's M_1 and M_2. Construct LBA M_3 that treats its input as if it were written on two tracks. That is, we identify input symbol a with $[a, a]$. On the first track, M_3 simulates M_1. If some sequence of choices of move by M_1 causes it to accept, M_3 begins to simulate M_2 on the second track, accepting if M_2 accepts. Thus M_3 accepts $L_1 \cap L_2$.

For substitution into CSL $L \subseteq \Sigma$ of CSL's L_a for symbols a in Σ, construct an LBA that works as follows. Given input $a_1 a_2 \cdots a_n$, nondeterministically guess which positions end strings in some L_a, and mark them. If we guess that $a_i a_{i+1} \cdots a_j$ is in some particular L_a, simulate the LBA for L_a on that substring. If $a_i a_{i+1} \cdots a_j$ is in L_a, replace it by a. If all our guesses are correct, take the resulting string in Σ^* and simulate an LBA for L on it, accepting $a_1 a_2 \cdots a_n$ if that LBA accepts.

9.13 It is easy to design an LBA to accept the valid computations of a given Turing machine. Thus the emptiness problem for Turing machines is reducible to the question whether a given CSL is empty.

9.14 Let L_1 be an r.e. set and c a symbol not in the alphabet of L_1. Let M_1 be a TM accepting L_1 and define

$$L_2 = \{wc^i \,|\, M_1 \text{ accepts } w \text{ by a sequence of moves in which the head never}$$

$$\text{moves more than } i \text{ positions to the right of } w\}.$$

Then L_2 is accepted by an LBA that simulates M_1, treating c as the blank and halting if it ever goes beyond the sequence of c's on its input. We have only to show that $L_1 = h(L_2)$ for some homomorphism h. Let $h(a) = a$ for all symbols in the alphabet of L, and $h(c) = \epsilon$.

Combining Exercise 9.14 with Theorem 9.9, we observe that the CSL's are not closed under homomorphism. This may seem paradoxical, since Exercise 9.10 claimed the CSL's were closed under substitution. However, homomorphism is not a special case of substitution by a CSL, as a CSL may not contain ϵ. In particular, for h defined above, $h(c) = \epsilon$ is not a CSL. The CSL's are, however, closed under homomorphisms that do not map any symbol to ϵ.

BIBLIOGRAPHIC NOTES

The Chomsky hierarchy was defined in Chomsky [1956, 1959]. Chomsky and Miller [1958] showed the equivalence of regular grammars and regular sets. Kuroda [1964] showed the equivalence of LBA's and CSG's. Previously, Myhill [1960] had defined deterministic LBA's, and Landweber [1963] showed that the deterministic LBA languages are contained in the CSL's. Chomsky [1959] showed that the r.e. sets are equivalent to the languages generated by type-0 grammars. Fischer [1969] gives some interesting characterizations of the CSL's. Hibbard [1974] discusses a restriction on CSG's that yields the context-free languages. Additional closure properties of CSL's are studied in Ginsburg and Griebach [1966b] and Wegbreit [1969]. Basic decision properties of CSL's are given in Landweber [1964].

10

DETERMINISTIC CONTEXT-FREE LANGUAGES

We now have machine models that define each class of languages in the Chomsky hierarchy. At the extreme ends of the hierarchy, the machines—finite automata and Turing machines—exhibit no difference in accepting ability between their deterministic and nondeterministic models. For the linear-bounded automaton, it is unknown whether the deterministic and nondeterministic varieties accept the same class of languages. However, for pushdown automata, we do know that the deterministic PDA's accept a family of languages, the *deterministic context-free languages* (DCFL's), lying properly between the regular sets and the context-free languages.

It turns out that the syntax of many programming languages can be described by means of DCFL's. Moreover, modern compiler writing systems usually require that the syntax of the language for which they are to produce a compiler be described by a context-free grammar of restricted form. These restricted forms almost invariably generate only DCFL's. We shall meet what is probably the most important of these restricted forms—the *LR*-grammars. The *LR*-grammars have the property that they generate exactly the DCFL's.

If a compiler writing system is to be used, it is generally necessary that the language designer choose a syntax for his language that makes it a DCFL. Thus it is useful to be able to determine whether a proposed language is in fact a DCFL. If it is, one can often prove it so by producing a DPDA or *LR*-grammar defining the language. But if the language L is not a DCFL, how are we to prove it? If L is not a CFL at all, we could use the pumping lemma, perhaps. However, L will often be a CFL but not a DCFL. There is no known pumping lemma specifically for DCFL's, so we must fall back on closure properties. Fortunately, the DCFL's are closed under a number of operations, such as complementation, that do not preserve CFL's in general. Thus, if L is a CFL but its complement is not, then L is not a DCFL.

Sections 10.1 through 10.4 develop various closure properties of DCFL's. Section 10.5 briefly covers decision properties. Sections 10.6 and 10.7 treat *LR*-grammars.

10.1 NORMAL FORMS FOR DPDA's

Recall that PDA $M = (Q, \Sigma, \Gamma, \delta, q_0, Z_0, F)$ is deterministic if:

1) whenever $\delta(q, a, X)$ is nonempty for some a in Σ, then $\delta(q, \epsilon, X)$ is empty, and
2) for each q in Q, a in $\Sigma \cup \{\epsilon\}$ and X in Γ, $\delta(q, a, X)$ contains at most one element.

Rule (1) prevents a choice between using the next input or making an ϵ-move. Rule (2) prevents a choice on the same input. For deterministic PDA's we shall hereafter write $\delta(q, a, X) = (p, \gamma)$ rather than $\delta(q, a, X) = \{(p, \gamma)\}$.

Like PDA's in general, we can put DPDA's in a *normal form* where the only stack operations are to erase the top symbol or to push one symbol. This form will be proved in the next two lemmas. The first lemma shows that the DPDA need never push more than one symbol per move, since it can push a string of symbols one at a time, using ϵ-moves. The second lemma shows that DPDA's need never change the top stack symbol. Changes are avoided by storing the top stack symbol in the finite control and recording changes to it there. The reader who grasps these ideas should skip to the start of the next section.

Lemma 10.1 Every DCFL is $L(M)$ for a DPDA $M = (Q, \Sigma, \Gamma, \delta, q_0, Z_0, F)$ such that if $\delta(q, a, X) = (p, \gamma)$, then $|\gamma| \leq 2$.

Proof If $\delta(q, a, X) = (r, \gamma)$ and $|\gamma| > 2$, let $\gamma = Y_1 Y_2 \cdots Y_n$, where $n \geq 3$. Create new nonaccepting states $p_1, p_2, \ldots, p_{n-2}$, and redefine

$$\delta(q, a, X) = (p_1, Y_{n-1} Y_n).$$

Then define

$$\delta(p_i, \epsilon, Y_{n-i}) = (p_{i+1}, Y_{n-i-1} Y_{n-i})$$

for $1 \leq i \leq n - 3$ and $\delta(p_{n-2}, \epsilon, Y_2) = (r, Y_1 Y_2)$. Thus, in state q, on input a, with X on top of the stack, the revised DPDA still replaces X with $Y_1 Y_2 \cdots Y_n = \gamma$ and enters state r, but it now takes $n - 1$ moves to do so. $\square$

Lemma 10.2 Every DCFL is $L(M)$ for a DPDA $M = (Q, \Sigma, \Gamma, \delta, q_0, Z_0, F)$ such that if $\delta(q, a, X) = (p, \gamma)$, then γ is either ϵ (a pop), X (no stack move), or of the form YX (a push) for some stack symbol Y.

Proof Assume $L = L(M')$, where $M' = (Q', \Sigma, \Gamma', \delta', q'_0, X_0, F')$ satisfies Lemma 10.1. We construct M to simulate M' while keeping the top stack symbol of M' in

M's control. Formally, let

$$Q = Q' \times \Gamma', \; q_0 = [q_0', X_0], \qquad F = F' \times \Gamma' \quad \text{and} \quad \Gamma = \Gamma' \cup \{Z_0\},$$

where Z_0 is a new symbol not in Γ'. Define δ by:

i) If $\delta'(q, a, X) = (p, \epsilon)$, then for all Y, $\delta([q, X], a, Y) = ([p, Y], \epsilon)$. If M' pops its stack, M pops its stack, picking up the symbol popped for its control.

ii) If $\delta'(q, a, X) = (p, Y)$, then for all Z, $\delta([q, X], a, Z) = ([p, Y], Z)$. If M' changes its top stack symbol, M records the change in its own control but does not alter its stack.

iii) If $\delta'(q, a, X) = (p, YZ)$, then for all W, $\delta([q, X], a, W) = ([p, Y], ZW)$. If the stack of M' grows, M pushes a symbol onto its stack.

It is easy to show by induction on the number of moves made that

$$(q_0', w, X_0) \models_{M'}^* (q, \epsilon, X_1 X_2 \cdots X_n)$$

if and only if

$$([q_0', X_0], w, Z_0) \models_M^* ([q, X_1], \epsilon, X_2 X_3 \cdots X_n Z_0).$$

Thus $L(M) = L(M')$. $\qquad\qquad\qquad\qquad\qquad\qquad\qquad\qquad\qquad\qquad\qquad\qquad$ □

10.2 CLOSURE OF DCFL's UNDER COMPLEMENTATION

To show that the complement of a DCFL is also a DCFL we would like to use the approach employed in Theorem 3.2 to show closure of the regular sets under complementation. That is, given a DPDA M we would like to interchange final and nonfinal states and then be able to claim that the resulting DPDA accepts the complement of $L(M)$.

There are two difficulties that complicate the above approach. The first difficulty is that the original DPDA might never move beyond some point on an input string, because on reading input w either it reaches an ID in which no move is possible or it makes an infinity of moves on ϵ-input and never uses another input symbol. In either case, the DPDA does not accept any input with w as a prefix, and thus a DPDA accepting the complement should accept every string with prefix w. However, if we simply changed final and nonfinal states, the resulting DPDA still would not move beyond w and therefore would not accept strings with prefix w.

The second difficulty is due to the fact that after seeing a sentence x, the DPDA may make several moves on ϵ-input. The DPDA may be in final states after some of these moves and in nonfinal states after others. In this case, interchanging the final and nonfinal states results in the DPDA still accepting x.

Forcing DPDA's to scan their input

To remove the first difficulty, we prove a lemma stating that, given a DPDA M, we can always find an equivalent DPDA M' that will never enter an ID from which it will not eventually use another input symbol.

Lemma 10.3 Let M be a DPDA. There exists an equivalent DPDA M' such that on every input, M' scans the entire input.

Proof We can assume without loss of generality that for every accessible ID and input symbol, M has a next move. Otherwise, one can add an endmarker on the stack to prevent M from erasing the stack entirely and thereby halting, without scanning, the entire input. In addition, one can add a "dead state," d so that for any combination of state, input symbol, and stack symbol for which M has no next move, either using the input symbol or an ϵ-input, a transfer to state d occurs. On any input symbol, the only transition from state d is to state d, and no change of the stack occurs. Of course, d is not an accepting state.

Now, if for every ID and input symbol, M has a next move, then the only way in which M might never reach the end of its input is if in some ID, M makes an infinity of moves on ϵ input. If in state q with Z on top of the stack, M makes an infinity of ϵ-moves without erasing the symbol Z, then let M instead enter the dead state d. This change cannot affect the language accepted unless M entered an accepting state at some time during the infinite sequence of ϵ-moves. However, in this case, we introduce a new final state f, letting $\delta(q, \epsilon, Z) = (f, Z)$ and $\delta(f, \epsilon, Z) = (d, Z)$.

Formally, we propose the following construction. Let $M = (Q, \Sigma, \Gamma, \delta, q_0, Z_0, F)$. Define

$$M' = (Q \cup \{q_0', d, f\}, \Sigma, \Gamma \cup \{X_0\}, \delta', q_0', X_0, F \cup \{f\}),$$

where:

1) $\delta'(q_0', \epsilon, X_0) = (q_0, Z_0 X_0)$. X_0 marks the bottom of the stack.

2) If for some q in Q, a in Σ and Z in Γ, $\delta(q, a, Z)$ and $\delta(q, \epsilon, Z)$ are both empty, then

$$\delta'(q, a, Z) = (d, Z).$$

Also for all q in Q and a in Σ,

$$\delta'(q, a, X_0) = (d, X_0).$$

Enter the dead state if no move is possible.

3) $\delta'(d, a, Z) = (d, Z)$ for all a in Σ and Z in $\Gamma \cup \{X_0\}$.

4) If for q and Z and all i there exist q_i and γ_i for which $(q, \epsilon, Z) \overset{i}{\vdash} (q_i, \epsilon, \gamma_i)$, then $\delta'(q, \epsilon, Z) = (d, Z)$ provided no q_i is final and $\delta'(q, \epsilon, Z) = (f, Z)$ whenever one or more of the q_i's is final. (Note we have not claimed that we can determine whether $\delta'(q, \epsilon, Z)$ should be (d, Z) or (f, Z). However, there are

only a finite number of such decisions to be made. For each possible set of choices there exists a DPDA. One of these DPDA's will be the desired one. We shall subsequently show that the construction is effective.)

5) $\delta'(f, \epsilon, Z) = (d, Z)$ for all Z in $\Gamma \cup \{X_0\}$.

6) For any q in Q, a in $\Sigma \cup \{\epsilon\}$, and Z in Γ, if $\delta'(q, a, Z)$ has not been defined by rule (2) or (4), then $\delta'(q, a, Z) = \delta(q, a, Z)$.

The argument preceding the formal construction should convince us that $L(M') = L(M)$. To prove that M' uses all its input, suppose that for some proper prefix x of xy,

$$(q'_0, xy, X_0) \vdash^*_M (q, y, Z_1 Z_2 \cdots Z_k X_0),$$

and from ID $(q, y, Z_1 Z_2 \cdots Z_k X_0)$, no symbol of y is ever consumed. By rule (2) it is not possible that M' halts. By rule (4), it is not possible that M' makes an infinite sequence of ϵ-moves without erasing Z_1. Therefore M_1 must eventually erase Z_1. Similarly M_1 must erase $Z_2, \ldots, Z_k$ and eventually enter an ID (q', y, X_0). By rule (2) $(q', y, X_0) \vdash_{M'} (d, y', X_0)$, where $y = ay'$ and a is in Σ. Thus M' did not fail to read past x as supposed, and M' satisfies the conditions of the lemma.   □

Let us now observe that the construction in rule (4) of Lemma 10.3 can be made effective. Assume without loss of generality that M is in normal form. We shall compute more information than is actually needed. In particular, we determine for each q and p in Q and Z in Γ, whether

1) $(q, \epsilon, Z) \vdash^*_M (p, \epsilon, Z)$,
2) $(q, \epsilon, Z) \vdash^*_M (p, \epsilon, \epsilon)$,
3) $(q, \epsilon, Z) \vdash^*_M (p, \epsilon, \gamma)$ for some γ in Γ^*.

For each q and Z we can determine from (3) whether M ever enters a state that consumes the next symbol of y without erasing Z.† If not, then from (2) we can determine if M erases Z. If neither event occurs, then either M' must enter the dead state by rule (2), or rule (4) applies and again (3) tells us whether $\delta'(q, \epsilon, Z)$ is (d, Z) or (f, Z).

Construct Boolean-valued tables T_1, T_2, and T_3 such that for $i = 1, 2$, and 3, $T_i(q, Z, p)$ is **true** if and only if statement (i) is **true** for q, Z, and p. The tables are initially all false and are filled inductively. The basis is to set $T_3(q, Z, p) =$ **true** if $\delta(q, \epsilon, Z) = (p, YZ)$, to set $T_1(q, Z, p) = T_3(q, Z, p) =$ **true** if $\delta(q, \epsilon, Z) = (p, Z)$, and to set $T_2(q, Z, p) =$ **true** if $\delta(q, \epsilon, Z) = (p, \epsilon)$. The inductive inferences are:

1) Whenever $\delta(q, \epsilon, Z) = (r, YZ)$, then
   a) if $T_2(r, Y, s)$ and $T_2(s, Z, p)$ are **true**, set $T_2(q, Z, p) =$ **true**;
   b) if $T_2(r, Y, s)$ and $T_1(s, Z, p)$ are **true**, set $T_1(q, Z, p) =$ **true**;

---

† Note that by the construction of Lemma 10.2, the state p alone determines whether a non-ϵ input move is to be made.

c) if $T_2(r, Y, s)$ and $T_3(s, Z, p)$ are **true**, or $T_1(r, Y, s)$ and $T_3(s, Y, p)$ are **true**, set $T_3(q, Z, p) = $ **true**;

d) if $T_3(r, Y, p)$ is **true**, set $T_3(q, Z, p) = $ **true**.

2) Whenever $\delta(q, \epsilon, Z) = (r, Z)$ then

a) if $T_1(r, Z, p)$ is **true**, set $T_1(q, Z, p) = $ **true**;

b) if $T_2(r, Z, p)$ is **true**, set $T_2(q, Z, p) = $ **true**;

c) if $T_3(r, Z, p)$ is **true**, set $T_3(q, Z, p) = $ **true**.

We leave as an exercise an efficient algorithm for filling in the true entries in the tables and proving that the only true entries are the ones that follow from the basis and rules (1) and (2) above.

Closure under complementation

We are now ready to prove that the DCFL's are closed under complementation. To do so we must deal with the second problem mentioned at the beginning of this section; the possibility that after reading input w, the DPDA makes a sequence of ϵ-moves, entering both final and nonfinal states. The solution is to modify the DPDA by adding a second component to the state. The second component records whether a final state of the original DPDA has been entered since the last time a *true* (non-ϵ)-input was used in a move. If not, the DPDA accepting the complement enters a final state of its own, just before it is ready to use the next true input symbol.

Theorem 10.1   The complement of a DCFL is a DCFL.

Proof   Let $M = (Q, \Sigma, \Gamma, \delta, q_0, Z_0, F)$ be a DPDA satisfying Lemma 10.3. Let $M' = (Q', \Sigma, \Gamma, \delta', q_0', Z_0, F')$ be a DPDA simulating M, where

$$Q' = \{[q, k] \mid q \text{ is in } Q \text{ and } k = 1, 2, \text{ or } 3\}.$$

Let $F' = \{[q, 3] \mid q \text{ in } Q\}$, and let

$$q_0' = \begin{cases} [q_0, 1] & \text{if } q_0 \text{ is in } F; \\ [q_0, 2] & \text{if } q_0 \text{ is not in } F. \end{cases}$$

The purpose of k in $[q, k]$ is to record, between true inputs, whether or not M has entered an accepting state. If M has entered an accepting state since the last true input, then $k = 1$. If M has not entered an accepting state since the last true input, then $k = 2$. If $k = 1$ when M reads a true input symbol, then M' simulates the move of M and changes k to 1 or 2, depending on whether the new state of M is or is not in F. If $k = 2$, M' first changes k to 3 and then simulates the move of M, changing k to 1 or 2, depending on whether the new state of M is or is not in F.

Thus, δ' is defined as follows, for q and p in Q, and a in Σ.

1) If $\delta(q, \epsilon, Z) = (p, \gamma)$, then for $k = 1$ or 2,

$$\delta'([q, k], \epsilon, Z) = ([p, k'], \gamma),$$

where $k' = 1$ if $k = 1$ or p is in F; otherwise $k' = 2$.

2) If $\delta(q, a, Z) = (p, \gamma)$, for a in Σ, then

$$\delta'([q, 2], \epsilon, Z) = ([q, 3], Z)$$

and

$$\delta'([q, 1], a, Z) = \delta'([q, 3], a, Z) = ([p, k], \gamma)$$

where $k = 1$ or 2 for p in F or not in F, respectively.

We claim that $L(M')$ is the complement of $L(M)$. Suppose that $a_1 a_2 \cdots a_n$ is in $L(M)$. Then M enters an accepting state after using a_n as an input. In that case, the second component of the state of M' will be 1 before it is possible for M' to use a true input after a_n. Therefore, M' does not accept (enter a state whose second component is 3) while a_n was the last true input used.

If $a_1 a_2 \cdots a_n$ is not in $L(M)$, by Lemma 10.3 M' will some time after reading a_n have no ϵ-moves to make and will have to use a true input symbol. But, at this time, the second component of M''s state is 2, since $a_1 a_2 \cdots a_n$ is not in $L(M)$. By rule (2), M' will accept before attempting to use a true input symbol. □

Before concluding this section we state the following corollary.

Corollary Every deterministic CFL is accepted by some DPDA that, in an accepting state, may make no move on ϵ-input.

Proof The statement is implicit in the proof of Theorem 10.1. Note that in a final state (one in which $k = 3$) no ϵ-move is possible. □

It is possible to use Theorem 10.1 to show certain languages not to be DCFL's.

Example 10.1 The language $L = \{0^i 1^j 2^k \mid i = j \text{ or } j = k\}$ is a CFL generated by the grammar

$$S \rightarrow AB \mid CD \qquad A \rightarrow 0A1 \mid \epsilon$$

$$B \rightarrow 2B \mid \epsilon \qquad C \rightarrow 0C \mid \epsilon \qquad D \rightarrow 1D2 \mid \epsilon$$

However, L is not a DCFL. If it were, then $\bar{L}$ would be a DCFL and hence a CFL. By Theorem 6.5, $L_1 = \bar{L} \cap 0^*1^*2^*$ would be a CFL. But $L_1 = \{0^i 1^j 2^k \mid i \neq j \text{ and } j \neq k\}$. A proof using Odgen's lemma similar to that of Example 6.3 shows that L_1 is not a CFL, so L is not a DCFL.

10.3 PREDICTING MACHINES

For a number of other closure properties of DCFL's we need a construction in which the stack symbols of DPDA M are modified to contain information about a certain finite automaton A. The information associated with the top stack symbol tells, for each state q of M and p of A, whether there is some input string that causes M to accept when started in state q with its current stack and simultaneously causes A to accept if started in state p.

Formally, let $M = (Q_M, \Sigma, \Gamma, \delta_M, q_0, Z_0, F_M)$ be a normal form DPDA and $A = (Q_A, \Sigma, \delta_A, p_0, F_A)$. Then $\pi(M, A)$, the *predicting machine* for M and A, is defined by $(Q_M, \Sigma, \Gamma \times \Delta, \delta, q_0, X_0, F_M)$, where Δ is the set of subsets of $Q_M \times Q_A$. The intention is that if $\pi(M, A)$ is in ID $(r, x, [Z, \mu]\gamma)$, then μ consists of exactly those pairs (q, p) such that there is a w in Σ^* for which $\delta_A(p, w)$ is in F_A, and $(q, w, Z\beta) \models^*_M (s, \epsilon, \alpha)$ for some s in F_M and α and β in Γ^*, where β is the string of first components of γ.

To define δ and X_0 we need additional notation. Let $M_{q,Z}$ be M with q and Z made the start state and start symbol respectively. Let A_p be A with p made the start state. Then by our usual notation,

$$L(M_{q,Z}) = \{w \,|\, (q, w, Z) \models^*_M (s, \epsilon, \gamma) \text{ for some } s \text{ in } F_M \text{ and } \gamma \text{ in } \Gamma^*\}$$

and

$$L(A_p) = \{w \,|\, \delta_A(p, w) \text{ is in } F_A\}.$$

Let $N_r(M_{q,Z})$ be the set of strings that cause $M_{q,Z}$ to erase its stack and enter state r, that is,

$$N_r(M_{q,Z}) = \{w \,|\, (q, w, Z) \models^*_M (r, \epsilon, \epsilon)\}.$$

Surely $L(M_{q,Z})$ is a DCFL and $L(A_p)$ is a regular set. It is also true that $N_r(M_{q,Z})$ is a DCFL. In proof, modify M to place a marker Y_0 at the bottom of stack and then simulate M in state q with stack ZY_0. If Y_0 becomes the top stack symbol, then accept if the state is r and reject if not. Finally, let $L_s(A_p) = \{w \,|\, \delta(p, w) = s\}$. Clearly $L_s(A_p)$ is regular.

Now we may define $\delta(r, a, [Z, \mu])$, for r in Q_M, a in $\Sigma \cup \{\epsilon\}$, Z in Γ, and μ in Δ as follows.

1) If $\delta_M(r, a, Z) = (s, \epsilon)$, then $\delta(r, a, [Z, \mu]) = (s, \epsilon)$. Note that μ does not influence the action of $\pi(M, A)$, except in rule (3) below, where it influences the second component of the stack symbol pushed.

2) If $\delta_M(r, a, Z) = (s, Z)$, then $\delta(r, a, [Z, \mu]) = (s, [Z, \mu])$.

3) If $\delta_M(r, a, Z) = (s, YZ)$, then $\delta(r, a, [Z, \mu]) = (s, [Y, v][Z, \mu])$, where v consists of those pairs (q, p) such that either
   a) $L(M_{q,Y}) \cap L(A_p)$ is nonempty, or

b) there is some t in Q_M and u in Q_A such that

$$N_t(M_{q,Y}) \cap L_u(A_p)$$

is nonempty and (t, u) is in μ.

Note that $L(M_{q,Y})$ and $N_t(M_{q,Y})$ are CFL's, and $L(A_p)$ and $L_u(A_p)$ are regular, so by Theorems 6.5 and 6.6, we may determine whether the languages mentioned in (a) and (b) are empty.

Finally, let $X_0 = [Z_0, \mu_0]$, where

$$\mu_0 = \{(q, p) \mid L(M_{q,Z_0}) \cap L(A_p) \neq \varnothing\}.$$

Lemma 10.4 $\pi(M, A)$ as defined above has the property that

$$(q_0, x, [Z_0, \mu_0]) \xvdash{*}{\pi(M,A)} (r, y, [Z_1, \mu_1][Z_2, \mu_2] \cdots [Z_n, \mu_n])$$

if and only if

a) $(q_0, x, Z_0) \xvdash{*}{M} (r, y, Z_1 Z_2 \cdots Z_n)$, and

b) for $1 \leq i \leq n$,

$$\mu_i = \{(q, p) \mid \text{for some } w, (q, w, Z_i Z_{i+1} \cdots Z_n) \xvdash{*}{M} (s, \epsilon, \gamma) \text{ for some}$$

$$s \text{ in } F_M \text{ and } \gamma \text{ in } \Gamma^*, \text{ and } \delta_A(p, w) \text{ is in } F_A\}.$$

Proof (a) is obvious, since $\pi(M, A)$ simulates M, carrying along the second component of stack symbols but not allowing them to influence anything but other second components of stack symbols.

We prove (b) by induction on i, starting at $i = n$ and working down. The basis, $i = n$ is easy. Z_n must be Z_0, since M is in normal form. The definition of X_0 plus rule (2) in the definition of δ gives us the basis.

For the induction, suppose the result is true for $i + 1$. Then μ_i was constructed from μ_{i+1} as v is constructed from μ in rule (3). Suppose there is some w such that

$$(q, w, Z_i Z_{i+1} \cdots Z_n) \xvdash{*}{} (s, \epsilon, \gamma)$$

for s in F_M, and $\delta_A(p, w)$ is in F_A. Then there are two cases depending on whether Z_i is ever erased. If it is not, then w is in $L(M_{q,Z_i})$ and also in $L(A_p)$, so by rule (3a), (q, p) is in μ_i. If Z_i is erased, let $w = w_1 w_2$, where

$$(q, w_1, Z_i) \xvdash{*}{M} (t, \epsilon, \epsilon) \quad \text{and} \quad (t, w_2, Z_{i+1} Z_{i+2} \cdots Z_n) \xvdash{*}{M} (s, \epsilon, \gamma)$$

for some s in F_M. Also let $\delta_A(p, w_1) = u$, so $\delta_A(u, w_2)$ is in F_A. Then w_1 is in $N_t(M_{q,Z_i})$ and also in $L_u(A_p)$. By the inductive hypothesis, (t, u) is in μ_{i+1}. Thus by rule (3b), (q, p) is in μ_i.

Conversely, if (q, p) is in μ_i by rule (3a), then there is a w such that $\delta_A(p, w)$ is in F_A and $(q, w, Z_i Z_{i+1} \cdots Z_n) \xvdash{*}{M} (s, \epsilon, \gamma)$ for s in F_M, by a sequence of moves in which Z_i is never erased. If (q, p) is in μ_i by rule (3b), then there exists w_1 in Σ^*, t in

Q_M and u in Q_A such that $(q, w_1, Z_i) \overset{*}{\vdash_M} (t, \epsilon, \epsilon)$, $\delta_A(p, w_1) = u$, and (t, u) is in μ_{i+1}. By the inductive hypothesis, there exists w_2 in Σ^* such that $(t, w_2, Z_{i+1} Z_{i+2} \cdots Z_n) \overset{*}{\vdash_M} (s, \epsilon, \gamma)$ for some s in F_M, and $\delta_A(u, w_2)$ is in F_A. Thus $(q, w_1 w_2, Z_i Z_{i+1} \cdots Z_n) \overset{*}{\vdash_M} (s, \epsilon, \gamma)$, and $\delta_A(p, w_1 w_2)$ is in F_A, so (q, p) belongs in μ_i. This completes the induction and the proof of the lemma. ☐

Example 10.2 Let

$$M = (\{q_0, q_1, q_2, q_3\}, \{0, 1\}, \{X, Z_0\}, \delta_M, q_0, Z_0, \{q_3\}),$$

where

$$\delta_M(q_0, 0, Z_0) = (q_0, XZ_0), \qquad \delta_M(q_1, 0, X) = (q_2, \epsilon),$$
$$\delta_M(q_0, 0, X) = (q_0, XX), \qquad \delta_M(q_2, 0, X) = (q_2, \epsilon),$$
$$\delta_M(q_0, 1, X) = (q_1, XX), \qquad \delta_M(q_2, \epsilon, Z_0) = (q_3, \epsilon).$$
$$\delta_M(q_1, 1, X) = (q_1, XX),$$

Also let $A = (\{p_0, p_1\}, \{0, 1\}, \delta_A, p_0, \{p_0\})$, where

$$\delta_A(p_0, 0) = p_1, \qquad \delta_A(p_0, 1) = p_0,$$
$$\delta_A(p_1, 0) = p_0, \qquad \delta_A(p_1, 1) = p_1.$$

Observe that

$$L(M) = L(M_{q_0, Z_0}) = \{0^i 1^j 0^k \,|\, i + j = k, i > 0 \text{ and } j > 0\}.$$

Also $L(M_{q_1, Z_0}) = \varnothing$ and $L(M_{q_2, Z_0}) = L(M_{q_3, Z_0}) = \{\epsilon\}$.

$$L(A) = L(A_{p_0}) = (1 + 01^*0)^*;$$

that is, strings with an even number of 0's, and $L(A_{p_1}) = 1^*0(1 + 01^*0)^*$ that is, strings with an odd number of 0's. Thus $L(M_{q_0, Z_0}) \cap L(A_{p_0})$ contains strings such as 00110000, and $L(M_{q_0, Z_0}) \cap L(A_{p_1})$ contains strings such as 01110000. $L(M_{q_2, Z_0}) \cap L(A_{p_0})$ and $L(M_{q_3, Z_0}) \cap L(A_{p_0})$ each contain ϵ, but the other four intersections of the form $L(M_{q_i, Z_0}) \cap L(A_{p_j})$ are empty. Thus the start symbol of $\pi(M, A)$ is $[Z_0, \mu_0]$, where

$$\mu_0 = \{(q_0, p_0), (q_0, p_1), (q_2, p_0), (q_3, p_0)\}.$$

Now let us compute

$$\delta(q_0, 0, [Z_0, \mu_0]) = (q_0, [X, v][Z_0, \mu_0]).$$

To do so we need to deduce that $L(M_{q_i, X}) = \varnothing$ for $i = 0, 1$, or 2, since we cannot accept without a Z_0 on the stack and cannot write Z_0 if it wasn't there originally. Thus there is no contribution to v from rule (3a). However, $L(M_{q_3, X}) \cap L(A_{p_0}) = \{\epsilon\}$, so we add (q_3, p_0) to v.

Consider rule (3b).

$$N_{q_2}(M_{q_0,x}) = \{0^i 1^j 0^k \,|\, i + j = k - 1 \text{ and } j > 0\},$$

$$N_{q_2}(M_{q_1,x}) = \{1^j 0^k \,|\, j = k - 1\},$$

and

$$N_{q_2}(M_{q_2,x}) = \{0\}.$$

The other sets of the form $N_{q_i}(M_{q_j,x})$ are empty. Also, $L_{p_i}(A_{p_j})$ is all strings with an even number of 0's if $i = j$ and all strings with an odd number of 0's if $i \neq j$.

Since $N_{q_i}(M_{q_j,x})$ is nonempty only if $i = 2$ and $j = 0, 1,$ or 2, we can only apply rule (3b) successfully if the pair (q_2, p_0) is chosen from μ_0. We see $N_{q_2}(M_{q_0,x}) \cap L_{p_0}(A_{p_0})$ and $N_{q_2}(M_{q_0,x}) \cap L_{p_0}(A_{p_1})$ are both nonempty, yielding (q_0, p_0) and (q_0, p_1) for v. Similarly $N_{q_2}(M_{q_1,x}) \cap L_{p_0}(A_{p_0})$ and $N_{q_2}(M_{q_1,x}) \cap L_{p_0}(A_{p_1})$ are nonempty, yielding (q_1, p_0) and (q_1, p_1) for v. Also, $N_{q_2}(M_{q_2,x}) \cap L_{p_0}(A_{p_1})$ is nonempty, yielding (q_2, p_1) for v, but

$$N_{q_2}(M_{q_2,x}) \cap L_{p_0}(A_{p_0}) = \varnothing.$$

Thus,

$$v = \{(q_0, p_0), (q_0, p_1), (q_1, p_0), (q_1, p_1), (q_2, p_1), (q_3, p_0)\}.$$

10.4 ADDITIONAL CLOSURE PROPERTIES OF DCFL's

Using the idea developed in the previous section we can prove a few closure properties of deterministic context-free languages. Before proceeding, we present one more technical lemma. The lemma asserts that we can define acceptance for a DPDA by a combination of state and the top stack symbol; the language so defined is still a deterministic language.

Lemma 10.5 Let $M = (Q, \Sigma, \Gamma, \delta, q_0, Z_0, F)$ be a DPDA. Let B be any subset of $Q \times \Gamma$, that is, pairs of state and stack symbol. Define

$$L = \{w \,|\, (q_0, w, Z_0) \underset{M}{\overset{*}{\vdash}} (q, \epsilon, Z\gamma) \text{ for some } (q, Z) \text{ in } B\}.$$

Then L is a DCFL.

Proof We define a DPDA M', accepting L, as follows.

$$M' = (Q', \Sigma, \Gamma, \delta', q_0, Z_0, F'),$$

where

$$Q' = \{q, q', q'' \,|\, q \text{ in } Q\} \qquad \text{and} \qquad F' = \{q'' \,|\, q \text{ in } Q\}.$$

M' makes the same moves as M, except that M' moves from an unprimed state to a singly primed state and then, on ϵ-input, moves back to the corresponding unprimed state, either directly or through a doubly primed version. The latter case applies only if the pair of state and top symbol of the stack is in B.

Formally,

1) if $\delta(q, a, Z) = (p, \gamma)$, then $\delta'(q, a, Z) = (p', \gamma)$;
2) $\delta'(q', \epsilon, Z) = (q, Z)$ provided (q, Z) is not in B;
3) $\delta'(q', \epsilon, Z) = (q'', Z)$ and $\delta'(q'', \epsilon, Z) = (q, Z)$ if (q, Z) is in B. $\qquad\square$

Quotient with a regular set

Recall that the quotient of L_1 with respect to L_2, denoted L_1/L_2, is

$$\{x \mid \text{there exists } w \text{ in } L_2 \text{ such that } xw \text{ is in } L_1\}.$$

In Exercise 6.4 we claimed that the CFL's were closed under quotient with a regular set. (See Theorem 11.3 for a proof.) We shall now prove a similar result for DCFL's.

Theorem 10.2   Let L be a DCFL and R a regular set. Then L/R is a DCFL.

Proof   Let $L = L(M)$ for M a DPDA that always scans its entire input.

Let $R = L(A)$ for finite automaton A. Suppose $M = (Q_M, \Sigma, \Gamma, \delta_M, q_0, Z_0, F_M)$ and $A = (Q_A, \Sigma, \delta_A, p_0, F_A)$. Then let

$$M' = (Q_M, \Sigma, \Gamma \times \Delta, \delta, q_0, [Z_0, \mu_0], F_M)$$

be $\pi(M, A)$, the predicting machine for M and A. Let B be the subset of $Q_M \times (\Gamma \times \Delta)$ containing all $(q, [Z, \mu])$ such that (q, p_0) is in μ.

Then by Lemma 10.5,

$$L_1 = \{x \mid (q_0, x, [Z_0, \mu_0]) \underset{M'}{\overset{*}{\vdash}} (q, \epsilon, [Z, \mu]\gamma) \text{ and } (q, p_0) \text{ is in } \mu\}$$

is a DCFL. By Lemma 10.4,

$$L_1 = \{x \mid \text{for some } w \text{ in } \Sigma^*, (q_0, x, Z_0) \underset{M}{\overset{*}{\vdash}} (q, \epsilon, Z\gamma')$$

$$\text{and } (q, w, Z\gamma') \underset{M}{\overset{*}{\vdash}} (s, \epsilon, \beta),$$

where s is in F_M, γ' is the first components of γ, and $\delta_A(p_0, w)$ is in $F_A\}$.

Equivalently,

$$L_1 = \{x \mid \text{for some } w \text{ in } \Sigma^*, xw \text{ is in } L(M) \text{ and } w \text{ is in } L(A)\}.$$

That is, $L_1 = L/R$. Thus L/R is a DCFL. $\qquad\square$

MIN and MAX

We now show two operations that preserve DCFL's but not arbitrary CFL's.

Recall that for each language L:

$$\text{MIN}(L) = \{x \mid x \text{ is in } L \text{ and no } w \text{ in } L \text{ is a proper prefix of } x\},$$

and

$$\text{MAX}(L) = \{x \mid x \text{ is in } L \text{ and } x \text{ is not a proper prefix of any word in } L\}.$$

Example 10.3 Let
$$L = \{0^i 1^j 0^k \,|\, i, j, k > 0, i + j \geq k\}.$$
Then $\mathrm{MIN}(L) = \mathbf{00^*110}$, and $\mathrm{MAX}(L) = \{0^i 1^j 0^{i+j} \,|\, i, j > 0\}$.

Theorem 10.3 If L is a DCFL, then $\mathrm{MIN}(L)$ and $\mathrm{MAX}(L)$ are DCFL's.

Proof Let $M = (Q_M, \Sigma, \Gamma, \delta_M, q_0, Z_0, F_M)$ be a DPDA that accepts L and always scans its entire input. Modify M to make no move in a final state. Then the resulting DPDA M_1 accepts $\mathrm{MIN}(L)$. In proof, if w is in $\mathrm{MIN}(L)$, then let

$$(q_0, w, Z_0) = I_0 \vdash_{\overline{M}} I_1 \vdash_{\overline{M}} \cdots \vdash_{\overline{M}} I_m \tag{10.1}$$

be the sequence of ID's entered by M, where $I_m = (q, \epsilon, \gamma)$ for some γ, and q is in F_M. Furthermore, since w is in $\mathrm{MIN}(L)$, none of $I_0, I_1, \ldots, I_{m-1}$ has an accepting state. Thus (10.1) is also a computation of M_1, so w is in $L(M)$.

Conversely, if $(q_0, w, Z_0) = I_0 \vdash_{\overline{M_1}} I_1 \vdash_{\overline{M_1}} \cdots \vdash_{\overline{M_1}} I_m$ is an accepting computation of M_1, then none of $I_0, I_1, \ldots, I_{m-1}$ has an accepting state. Thus w is in $\mathrm{MIN}(L)$.

For MAX we must use the predicting machine. Let $A = (Q_A, \Sigma, \delta_A, p_0, F_A)$ be the simple *FA* of Fig. 10.1 accepting Σ^+. Let $M = (Q_M, \Sigma, \Gamma \times \Delta, \delta, q_0, [Z_0, \mu_0], F_M)$ be $\pi(M, A)$. Let $B = \{(q, [Z, \mu]) \,|\, q$ is in F_M and (q, p_0) is not in $\mu\}$. Then by Lemma 10.5,

$$L_1 = \{x \,|\, (q_0, x, Z_0) \vdash_{\overline{M}}^{*} (q, \epsilon, \gamma)$$

$$\text{for some } q \text{ in } F_M, \text{ and for no } w \neq \epsilon$$

$$\text{does } (q, w, \gamma) \vdash^{*} (s, \epsilon, \beta) \text{ for } s \text{ in } F_M\}$$

is a DCFL. But $L_1 = \mathrm{MAX}(L)$, so $\mathrm{MAX}(L)$ is a DCFL. ☐

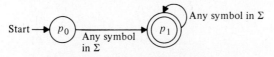

Fig. 10.1 The automaton A.

Example 10.4 Let us use Theorem 10.3 to show a CFL not to be a DCFL. Let $L_1 = \{0^i 1^j 2^k \,|\, k \leq i \text{ or } k \leq j\}$. Then L_1 is a CFL generated by the grammar

$$S \rightarrow AB \,|\, C$$

$$A \rightarrow 0A \,|\, \epsilon$$

$$B \rightarrow 1B2 \,|\, 1B \,|\, \epsilon$$

$$C \rightarrow 0C2 \,|\, 0C \,|\, D$$

$$D \rightarrow 1D \,|\, \epsilon$$

Suppose L_1 were a DCFL. Then $L_2 = \text{MAX}(L_1)$ would be a DCFL and hence a CFL. But $L_2 = \{0^i1^j2^k \mid k = \max(i, j)\}$. Suppose L_2 were a CFL. Let n be the pumping lemma constant and consider $z = uvwxy = 0^n1^n2^n$. If neither v nor x has a 2, then $z' = uv^2wx^2y$ has n 2's and at least $(n + 1)$ 0's or at least $(n + 1)$ 1's. Thus z' would not be in L_2 as supposed.

Now consider the case where vx has a 2. If either v or x has more than one symbol, then $z' = uv^2wx^2y$ is not of the form $0^i1^j2^k$ and would not be L_2. Thus either 0 or 1 is not present in vx. Hence uwy has fewer than n 2's but has n 0's or n 1's and is not in L_2. We conclude L_2 is not a CFL, so L_1 is not a DCFL.

Other closure properties

As a general rule, only those closure properties of CFL's mentioned in Section 6.2 that were given proofs using the PDA characterization carry over to DCFL's. In particular, we can state the following.

Theorem 10.4 The DCFL's are closed under (a) inverse homomorphism, and (b) intersection with a regular set.

Proof The arguments used in Theorems 6.3 and 6.5 work for DPDA's. □

Theorem 10.5 The DCFL's are not closed under (a) homomorphism, (b) union, (c) concatenation, or (d) Kleene closure.

Proof See Exercise 10.4 and its solution. □

10.5 DECISION PROPERTIES OF DCFL's

A number of problems that are undecidable for CFL's are decidable for DCFL's.

Theorem 10.6 Let L be a DCFL and R a regular set. The following problems are decidable.

1) Is $L = R$?
2) Is $R \subseteq L$?
3) Is $\bar{L} = \varnothing$?
4) Is $\bar{L}$ a CFL?
5) Is L regular?

Proof

1) $L = R$ if and only if $L_1 = (L \cap \bar{R}) \cup (\bar{L} \cap R)$ is empty. Since the DCFL's are effectively closed under complementation and intersection with a regular set, and since the CFL's are effectively closed under union, L_1 is a CFL, and emptiness for CFL's is decidable.
2) $R \subseteq L$ if and only if $\bar{L} \cap R = \varnothing$. Since $\bar{L} \cap R$ is a CFL, $\bar{L} \cap R = \varnothing$ is decidable.

3) Since the DCFL's are effectively closed under complementation, $\bar{L}$ is a DCFL and hence $\bar{L} = \emptyset$ is decidable.

4) The property $\bar{L}$ is a CFL is trivial for DCFL's and hence is decidable.

5) Regularity for DCFL's is decidable. The proof is lengthy and the reader is referred to Stearns [1967] or Valiant [1975b]. □

Undecidable properties of DCFL's

Certain other properties undecidable for CFL's remain so even when restricted to the DCFL's. Many of these problems can be proved undecidable by observing that the languages L_1 and L_2 of Section 8.6, whose intersection is the valid computations of a Turing machine M, are DCFL's.

Theorem 10.7 Let L and L' be arbitrary DCFL's. Then the following problems are undecidable.

1) Is $L \cap L' = \emptyset$?
2) Is $L \subseteq L'$?
3) Is $L \cap L'$ a DCFL?
4) Is $L \cap L'$ a CFL?
5) Is $L \cup L'$ a DCFL?

Proof   Given an arbitrary TM M we showed in Lemma 8.6 how to construct languages L_1 and L_2 such that $L_1 \cap L_2 = \emptyset$ if and only if $L(M) = \emptyset$. It is easy to show that L_1 and L_2 are DCFL's by exhibiting DPDA's that accept them. Thus (1) follows immediately from the fact that it is undecidable whether $L(M) = \emptyset$. Since DCFL's are closed under complement, and $L \subseteq \bar{L}'$ if and only if $L \cap L' = \emptyset$, (2) follows from (1).

To prove (3), (4), and (5), modify each TM M to make at least two moves before accepting, as in Lemma 8.8. Then $L_1 \cap L_2$ is either a finite set (in which case it is surely a CFL and a DCFL) or is not a CFL depending on whether $L(M)$ is finite. Thus decidability of (3) or (4) would imply decidability of finiteness for $L(M)$, a known undecidable property. Since DCFL's are closed under complementation, deciding whether $L \cup L'$ is a DCFL is equivalent to deciding if $L \cap L'$ is a DCFL. Thus (5) follows from (3). □

Theorem 10.8   Let L be an arbitrary CFL. It is undecidable whether L is a DCFL.

Proof   Let L be the CFL of invalid computations of an arbitrary TM M that makes at least two moves on every input. L is regular and, hence, a DCFL if and only if M accepts a finite set. □

Finally we observe that the question of whether two DCFL's are equivalent is an important unresolved problem of language theory.

10.6 *LR*(0) GRAMMARS

Recall that one motivation for studying DCFL's is their ability to describe the syntax of programming languages. Various compiler writing systems require syntactic specification in the form of restricted CFG's, which allow only the representation of DCFL's. Moreover, the parser produced by such compiler writing systems is essentially a DPDA. In this section we introduce a restricted type of CFG called an *LR*(0) grammar. This class of grammars is the first in a family collectively called *LR*-grammars. Incidentally, *LR*(0) stands for "left-to-right scan of the input producing a rightmost derivation and using 0 symbols of lookahead on the input."

The *LR*(0) grammars define exactly the DCFL's having the prefix property. (*L* is said to have the *prefix property* if, whenever *w* is in *L*, no proper prefix of *w* is in *L*.) Note that the prefix property is not a severe restriction, since the introduction of an endmarker converts any DCFL to a DCFL with the prefix property. Thus $L\$ = \{w\$ | w$ is in $L\}$ is a DCFL with the prefix property whenever L is a DCFL.

While the *LR*(0) restriction is too severe to provide convenient and natural grammars for many programming languages, the *LR*(0) condition captures the flavor of its more useful generalizations, which we discuss in Section 10.8, and which have been successfully used in several parser-generating systems.

LR-items

To introduce the *LR*(0) grammars we need some preliminary definitions. First, an *item* for a given CFG is a production with a dot anywhere in the right side, including the beginning or end. In the case of an ϵ-production, $B \rightarrow \epsilon$, $B \rightarrow \cdot$ is an item.

Example 10.5 We now introduce a grammar that we shall use in a series of examples.

$$S' \rightarrow Sc \qquad S \rightarrow SA \,|\, A \qquad A \rightarrow aSb \,|\, ab \qquad (10.2)$$

This grammar, with start symbol S', generates strings of "balanced parentheses," treating a and b as left and right parentheses, respectively, and c as an endmarker.

The items for grammar (10.2) are

$$
\begin{array}{lll}
S' \rightarrow \cdot Sc & S \rightarrow \cdot SA & A \rightarrow \cdot aSb \\
S' \rightarrow S \cdot c & S \rightarrow S \cdot A & A \rightarrow a \cdot Sb \\
S' \rightarrow Sc \cdot & S \rightarrow SA \cdot & A \rightarrow aS \cdot b \\
 & S \rightarrow \cdot A & A \rightarrow aSb \cdot \\
 & S \rightarrow A \cdot & A \rightarrow \cdot ab \\
 & & A \rightarrow a \cdot b \\
 & & A \rightarrow ab \cdot
\end{array}
$$

In what follows, we use the symbols $\underset{rm}{\overset{*}{\Rightarrow}}$ and $\underset{rm}{\Rightarrow}$ to denote rightmost derivations and single steps in a rightmost derivation, respectively. A *right-sentential* form is a sentential form that can be derived by a rightmost derivation. A *handle* of a right-sentential form γ for CFG G is a substring β, such that

$$S \underset{rm}{\overset{*}{\Rightarrow}} \delta Aw \underset{rm}{\Rightarrow} \delta\beta w,$$

and $\delta\beta w = \gamma$. That is, a handle of γ is a substring that could be introduced at the last step in a rightmost derivation of γ. Note that in this context, the position of β within γ is important.

A *viable prefix* of a right-sentential form γ is any prefix of γ ending no farther right than the right end of a handle of γ.

Example 10.6   In grammar (10.2) there is a rightmost derivation

$$S' \Rightarrow Sc \Rightarrow SAc \Rightarrow SaSbc.$$

Thus $SaSbc$ is a right-sentential form, and its handle is aSb. Note that in any unambiguous grammar with no useless symbols, such as grammar (10.2), the rightmost derivation of a given right-sentential form is unique, so its handle is unique. Thus we may speak of "the handle" rather than "a handle." The viable prefixes of $SaSbc$ are ϵ, S, Sa, SaS, and $SaSb$.

We say an item $A \to \alpha \cdot \beta$ is *valid* for a viable prefix γ if there is a rightmost derivation

$$S \underset{rm}{\overset{*}{\Rightarrow}} \delta Aw \underset{rm}{\Rightarrow} \delta\alpha\beta w$$

and $\delta\alpha = \gamma$. Knowing which items are valid for a given viable prefix helps us find a rightmost derivation in reverse, as follows. An item is said to be *complete* if the dot is the rightmost symbol in the item. If $A \to \alpha \cdot$ is a complete item valid for γ, then it appears that $A \to \alpha$ could have been used at the last step and that the previous right-sentential form in the derivation of γw was δAw.

Of course, we cannot more than suspect this since $A \to \alpha \cdot$ may be valid for γ because of a rightmost derivation $S \overset{*}{\Rightarrow} \delta Aw' \Rightarrow \gamma w'$. Clearly, there could be two or more complete items valid for γ, or there could be a handle of γw that includes symbols of w. Intuitively, a grammar is defined to be *LR*(0) if in each such situation δAw is indeed the previous right-sentential form for γw. In that case, we can start with a string of terminals x that is in $L(G)$ and hence is a right-sentential form of G, and work backward to previous right-sentential forms until we get to S. We then have a rightmost derivation of x.

Example 10.7   Consider grammar (10.2) and the right-sentential form abc. Since

$$S' \underset{rm}{\overset{*}{\Rightarrow}} Ac \Rightarrow abc,$$

we see that $A \to ab \cdot$ is valid for viable prefix ab. We also see that $A \to a \cdot b$ is valid for viable prefix a, and $A \to \cdot ab$ is valid for viable prefix ϵ. As $A \to ab \cdot$ is a complete item, we might be able to deduce that Ac was the previous right-sentential form for abc.

Computing sets of valid items

The definition of $LR(0)$ grammars and the method of accepting $L(G)$ for $LR(0)$ grammar G by a DPDA each depend on knowing the set of valid items for each viable prefix γ. It turns out that for every CFG G whatsoever, the set of viable prefixes is a regular set, and this regular set is accepted by an NFA whose states are the items for G. Applying the subset construction to this NFA yields a DFA whose state in response to the viable prefix γ is the set of valid items for γ.

The NFA M recognizing the viable prefixes for CFG $G = (V, T, P, S)$ is defined as follows. Let $M = (Q, V \cup T, \delta, q_0, Q)$, where Q is the set of items for G plus the state q_0, which is not an item. Define

1) $\delta(q_0, \epsilon) = \{S \rightarrow \cdot\, \alpha \,|\, S \rightarrow \alpha \text{ is a production}\}$,
2) $\delta(A \rightarrow \alpha \cdot B\beta, \epsilon) = \{B \rightarrow \cdot\, \gamma \,|\, B \rightarrow \gamma \text{ is a production}\}$,
3) $\delta(A \rightarrow \alpha \cdot X\beta, X) = \{A \rightarrow \alpha X \cdot \beta\}$.

Rule (2) allows expansion of a variable B appearing immediately to the right of the dot. Rule (3) permits moving the dot over any grammar symbol X if X is the next input symbol.

Example 10.8   The NFA for grammar (10.2) is shown in Fig. 10.2.

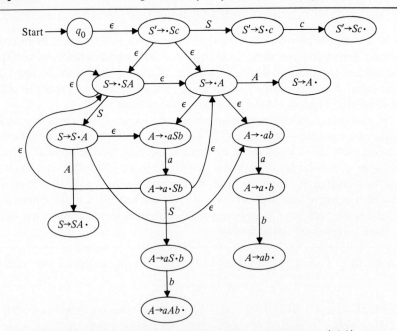

Fig. 10.2   NFA recognizing viable prefixes for Grammar (10.2).

Theorem 10.9 The NFA M defined above has the property that $\delta(q_0, \gamma)$ contains $A \to \alpha \cdot \beta$ if and only if $A \to \alpha \cdot \beta$ is valid for γ.

Proof

Only if: We must show that each item $A \to \alpha \cdot \beta$ contained in $\delta(q_0, \gamma)$ is valid for γ. We proceed by induction on the length of the shortest path labeled γ from q_0 to $A \to \alpha \cdot \beta$ in the transition diagram for M. The basis (length 1) is straightforward. The only paths of length one from q_0 are labeled ϵ and go to items of the form $S \to \cdot \alpha$. Each of these items is valid for ϵ because of the rightmost derivation $S \underset{rm}{\Rightarrow} \alpha$.

For the induction, suppose that the result is true for paths shorter than k, and let there be a path of length k labeled γ from q_0 to $A \to \alpha \cdot \beta$. There are two cases depending on whether the last edge is labeled ϵ or not.

CASE 1 The last edge is labeled X, for X in $V \cup T$. The edge must come from a state $A \to \alpha' \cdot X\beta$, where $\alpha = \alpha'X$. Then by the inductive hypothesis, $A \to \alpha' \cdot X\beta$ is valid for γ', where $\gamma = \gamma'X$. Thus there is a rightmost derivation

$$S \underset{rm}{\overset{*}{\Rightarrow}} \delta Aw \underset{rm}{\Rightarrow} \delta \alpha' X\beta w,$$

where $\delta \alpha' = \gamma'$. This same derivation shows that $A \to \alpha'X \cdot \beta$ (which is $A \to \alpha \cdot \beta$) is valid for γ.

CASE 2 The last edge is labeled ϵ. In this case α must be ϵ, and $A \to \alpha \cdot \beta$ is really $A \to \cdot \beta$. The item in the previous state is of the form $B \to \alpha_1 \cdot A\beta_1$, and is also valid for γ. Thus there is a derivation

$$S \overset{*}{\Rightarrow} \delta Bw \Rightarrow \delta \alpha_1 A\beta_1 w,$$

where $\gamma = \delta \alpha_1$. Let $\beta_1 \overset{*}{\Rightarrow} x$ for some terminal string x. Then the derivation

$$S \underset{rm}{\overset{*}{\Rightarrow}} \delta Bw \underset{rm}{\Rightarrow} \delta \alpha_1 A\beta_1 w \underset{rm}{\overset{*}{\Rightarrow}} \delta \alpha_1 Axw \underset{rm}{\Rightarrow} \delta \alpha_1 \beta xw$$

can be written

$$S \underset{rm}{\overset{*}{\Rightarrow}} \delta \alpha_1 Axw \underset{rm}{\Rightarrow} \delta \alpha_1 \beta xw.$$

Thus $A \to \cdot \beta$ is valid for γ, as $\gamma = \delta \alpha_1$.

If: Suppose $A \to \alpha \cdot \beta$ is valid for γ. Then

$$S \overset{*}{\Rightarrow} \gamma_1 Aw \underset{rm}{\Rightarrow} \gamma_1 \alpha\beta w, \tag{10.3}$$

where $\gamma_1 \alpha = \gamma$. If we can show that $\delta(q_0, \gamma_1)$ contains $A \to \cdot \alpha\beta$, then by rule (3) we know that $\delta(q_0, \gamma)$ contains $A \to \alpha \cdot \beta$. We therefore prove by induction on the length of derivation (10.3) that $\delta(q_0, \gamma_1)$ contains $A \to \cdot \alpha\beta$.

The basis, one step, follows from rule (1). For the induction, consider the step in $S \underset{rm}{\overset{*}{\Rightarrow}} \gamma_1 Aw$ in which the explicitly shown A was introduced. That is, write $S \underset{rm}{\overset{*}{\Rightarrow}} \gamma_1 Aw$ as

$$S \underset{rm}{\overset{*}{\Rightarrow}} \gamma_2 Bx \underset{rm}{\Rightarrow} \gamma_2 \gamma_3 A\gamma_4 x \underset{rm}{\overset{*}{\Rightarrow}} \gamma_2 \gamma_3 Ayx,$$

where $\gamma_2 \gamma_3 = \gamma_1$ and $yx = w$. Then by the inductive hypothesis applied to the derivation

$$S \overset{*}{\underset{rm}{\Rightarrow}} \gamma_2 Bx \underset{rm}{\Rightarrow} \gamma_2 \gamma_3 A\gamma_4 x,$$

we know that $B \rightarrow \cdot \gamma_3 A\gamma_4$ is in $\delta(q_0, \gamma_2)$. By rule (3), $B \rightarrow \gamma_3 \cdot A\gamma_4$ is in $\delta(q_0, \gamma_2 \gamma_3)$, and by rule (2), $A \rightarrow \cdot \alpha\beta$ is in $\delta(q_0, \gamma_2 \gamma_3)$. Since $\gamma_2 \gamma_3 = \gamma_1$, we have proved the inductive hypothesis. ☐

Definition of $LR(0)$ grammar

We are now prepared to define an $LR(0)$ grammar. We say that G is an $LR(0)$ *grammar* if

1) its start symbol does not appear on the right side of any production, and
2) for every viable prefix γ of G, whenever $A \rightarrow \alpha \cdot$ is a complete item valid for γ, then no other complete item nor any item with a terminal to the right of the dot is valid for γ.†

There is no prohibition against several incomplete items being valid for γ, as long as no complete item is valid.

Theorem 10.9 gives a method for computing the sets of valid items for any viable prefix. Just convert the NFA whose states are items to a DFA. In the DFA, the path from the start state labeled γ leads to the state that is the set of valid items for γ. Thus construct the DFA and inspect each state to see if a violation of the $LR(0)$ condition occurs.

Example 10.9 The DFA constructed from the NFA of Fig. 10.2, with the dead state (empty set of items) and transitions to the dead state removed, is shown in Fig. 10.3. Of these states, all but I_0, I_1, I_3, and I_6 consist of a single complete item. The states with more than one item have no complete items, and surely S', the start symbol, does not appear on the right side of any production. Hence grammar (10.2) is $LR(0)$.

10.7 $LR(0)$ GRAMMARS AND DPDA's

We now show that every $LR(0)$ grammar generates a DCFL, and every DCFL with the prefix property has an $LR(0)$ grammar. Since every language with an $LR(0)$ grammar will be shown to have the prefix property, we have an exact characterization of the DCFL's; namely L is a DCFL if and only if $L\$$ has an $LR(0)$ grammar.

---

† The only items that could be valid simultaneously with $A \rightarrow \alpha \cdot$ are productions with a nonterminal to the right of the dot, and this can occur only if $\alpha = \epsilon$; otherwise another violation of the $LR(0)$ conditions can be shown to occur.

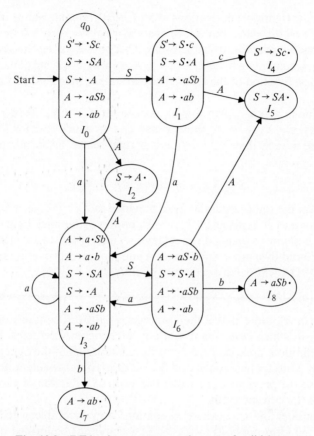

Fig. 10.3   DFA whose states are the sets of valid items.

DPDA's from *LR*(0) grammars

The way in which we construct a DPDA from an *LR*(0) grammar differs from the
way in which we constructed a (nondeterministic) PDA from an arbitrary CFL in
Theorem 5.3. In the latter theorem we traced out a leftmost derivation of the word
on the PDA's input, using the stack to hold the suffix of a left-sentential form
beginning at the leftmost variable. Now we shall trace out a rightmost derivation,
in reverse, using the stack to hold a viable prefix of a right-sentential form,
including all variables of that right-sentential form, allowing the remainder of the
form to appear on the input.

In order to clearly describe this process, it is useful to develop a new notation
for ID's of a PDA. We picture the stack with its top at the right end, rather than
the left. To distinguish the new notation from the old we use brackets rather than
parentheses: $[q, \alpha, w]$ is our synonym for (q, w, α^R).

To simulate rightmost derivations in an $LR(0)$ grammar not only do we keep a viable prefix on the stack, but above every symbol we keep a state of the DFA recognizing viable prefixes. If viable prefix $X_1 X_2 \cdots X_k$ is on the stack, then the complete stack contents will be $s_0 X_1 s_1 \cdots X_k s_k$, where s_i is $\delta(q_0, X_1 \cdots X_i)$ and δ is the transition function of the DFA. The top state s_k provides the valid items for $X_1 X_2 \cdots X_k$.

If s_k contains $A \to \alpha \cdot$, then $A \to \alpha \cdot$ is valid for $X_1 \cdots X_k$. Thus α is a suffix of $X_1 \cdots X_k$, say $\alpha = X_{i+1} \cdots X_k$ (note α may be ϵ, in which case $i = k$). Moreover, there is some w such that $X_1 \cdots X_k w$ is a right-sentential form, and there is a derivation

$$S \underset{rm}{\overset{*}{\Rightarrow}} X_1 \cdots X_i A w \underset{rm}{\Rightarrow} X_1 \cdots X_k w.$$

Thus to obtain the right-sentential form previous to $X_1 \cdots X_k w$ in a right derivation we *reduce* α to A, replacing $X_{i+1} \cdots X_k$ on top of the stack by A. That is, by a sequence of pop moves (using distinct states so the DPDA can remember what it is doing) followed by a move that pushes A and the correct covering state onto the stack, our DPDA will enter a sequence of ID's

$$[q, s_0 X_1 \cdots s_{k-1} X_k s_k, w] \overset{*}{\vdash} [q, s_0 X_1 \cdots s_{i-1} X_i s_i A s, w], \qquad (10.4)$$

where $s = \delta(s_i, A)$. Note that if the grammar is $LR(0)$, s_k contains only $A \to \alpha \cdot$, unless $\alpha = \epsilon$, in which case s_k may contain some incomplete items. However, by the $LR(0)$ definition, none of these items have a terminal to the right of the dot, or are complete. Thus for any y such that $X_1 \cdots X_k y$ is a right-sentential form, $X_1 \cdots X_i A y$ must be the previous right-sentential form, so reduction of α to A is correct regardless of the current input.

Now consider the case where s_k contains only incomplete items. Then the right-sentential form previous to $X_1 \cdots X_k w$ could not be formed by reducing a suffix of $X_1 \cdots X_k$ to some variable, else there would be a complete item valid for $X_1 \cdots X_k$. There must be a handle ending to the right of X_k in $X_1 \cdots X_k w$, as $X_1 \cdots X_k$ is a viable prefix. Thus the only appropriate action for the DPDA is to shift the next input symbol onto the stack. That is,

$$[q, s_0 X_1 \cdots s_{k-1} X_k s_k, ay] \vdash [q, s_0 X_1 \cdots s_{k-1} X_k s_k at, y], \qquad (10.5)$$

where $t = \delta(s_k, a)$. If t is not the empty set of items, $X_1 \cdots X_k a$ is a viable prefix. If t is empty, we shall prove there is no possible previous right-sentential form for $X_1 \cdots X_k ay$, so the original input is not in the grammar's language, and the DPDA "dies" instead of making the move (10.5). We summarize the above observations in the next theorem.

Theorem 10.10   If L is $L(G)$ for an $LR(0)$ grammar G, then L is $N(M)$ for a DPDA M.

Proof   Construct from G the DFA D, with transition function δ, that recognizes G's viable prefixes. Let the stack symbols of M be the grammar symbols of G and the states of *D*. *M* has state *q*, which is its start state, along with the additional states used to perform reductions by sequences of moves such as (10.4) above. We assume the reader can specify the set of states for each reduction and the ϵ-transitions needed to effect a reduction. We also leave to the reader the specification of the transition function of *M* needed to implement the moves indicated by (10.4) and (10.5).

We have previously indicated why, if *G* is *LR*(0), reductions are the only possible way to get the previous right-sentential form when the state of the DFA on the top of *M*'s stack contains a complete item. We claim that when *M* starts with *w* in *L*(*G*) on its input and only s_0 on its stack, it will construct a rightmost derivation for *w* in reverse order. The only point still requiring proof is that when a shift is called for, as in (10.5), because the top DFA state on *M*'s stack has only incomplete items, then there could not be a handle among the grammar symbols $X_1 \cdots X_k$ found on the stack at that time. If there were such a handle, then some DFA state on the stack, below the top, would have a complete item.

Suppose there were such a state containing $A \rightarrow \alpha \cdot$. Note that each state, when it is first put on the stack either by (10.4) or (10.5), is on top of the stack. Therefore it will immediately call for reduction of α to *A*. If $\alpha \neq \epsilon$, then $\{A \rightarrow \alpha \cdot\}$ is removed from the stack and cannot be buried. If $\alpha = \epsilon$, then reduction of ϵ to *A* occurs by (10.4), causing *A* to be put on the stack above $X_1 \cdots X_k$. In this case, there will always be a variable above X_k on the stack as long as $X_1 \cdots X_k$ occupies the bottom positions on the stack. But $A \rightarrow \epsilon$ at position *k* could not be the handle of any right-sentential form $X_1 \cdots X_k \beta$, where β contains a variable.

One last point concerns acceptance by *G*. If the top state on the stack is $\{S \rightarrow \alpha \cdot\}$, where *S* is *G*'s start symbol, then *G* pops its stack, accepting. In this case we have completed the reverse of a rightmost derivation of the original input. Note that as *S* does not appear on the right of any production, it is impossible that there is an item of the form $A \rightarrow S \cdot \alpha$ valid for viable prefix *S*. Thus there is never a need to shift additional input symbols when *S* alone appears on the stack. Put another way, *L*(*G*) always has the prefix property if *G* is *LR*(0).

We have thus proved that if *w* is in *L*(*G*), *M* finds a rightmost derivation of *w*, reduces *w* to *S*, and accepts. Conversely, if *M* accepts *w*, the sequence of right-sentential forms represented by the ID's of *M* provides a derivation of *w* from *S*. Thus $N(M) = L(G)$. $\square$

Corollary Every *LR*(0) grammar is unambiguous.

Proof The above argument shows that the rightmost derivation of *w* is unique. $\square$

Example 10.10 Consider the DFA of Fig. 10.3. Let 0, 1, ..., 8 be the names of the states corresponding to the sets of items $I_0, I_1, \ldots, I_8$, respectively. Let the input be *aababbc*. The DPDA *M* constructed as in Theorem 10.10 makes the sequence of moves listed in Fig. 10.4.

	Stack	Remaining input	Comments
1)	0	*aababbc*	Initial ID
2)	0*a*3	*ababbc*	Shift
3)	0*a*3*a*3	*babbc*	Shift
4)	0*a*3*a*3*b*7	*abbc*	Shift
5)	0*a*3*A*2	*abbc*	Reduce by $A \rightarrow ab$
6)	0*a*3*S*6	*abbc*	Reduce by $S \rightarrow A$
7)	0*a*3*S*6*a*3	*bbc*	Shift
8)	0*a*3*S*6*a*3*b*7	*bc*	Shift
9)	0*a*3*S*6*A*5	*bc*	Reduce by $A \rightarrow ab$
10)	0*a*3*S*6	*bc*	Reduce by $S \rightarrow SA$
11)	0*a*3*S*6*b*8	*c*	Shift
12)	0*A*2	*c*	Reduce by $A \rightarrow aSb$
13)	0*S*1	*c*	Reduce by $S \rightarrow A$
14)	0*S*1*c*4	—	Shift
15)	—	—	Accept

Fig. 10.4   Sequence of moves of DPDA M.

For example, in line (1), state 0 is on top of the stack. There is no complete item in set I_0, so we shift. The first input symbol is a, and there is a transition from I_0 to I_3 labeled a. Thus in line (2) the stack is $0a3$. In line (9), 5 is the top state. I_5 consists of complete item $S \rightarrow SA$. We pop SA off the stack, leaving $0a3$. We then push S onto the stack. There is a transition from I_3 to I_6 labeled S, so we cover S by 6, yielding the stack $0a3S6$ in line (10).

$LR(0)$ grammars from DPDA's

We now begin our study of the converse result—if L is $N(M)$ for a DPDA M, then L has an $LR(0)$ grammar. In fact, the grammar of Theorem 5.4 is $LR(0)$ whenever M is deterministic, but it is easier to prove that a modification of that grammar is $LR(0)$. The change we make is to put at the beginning of the right side of each production a symbol telling which PDA move gave rise to that production.

Formally, let $M = (Q, \Sigma, \Gamma, \delta, q_0, Z_0, \varnothing)$ be a DPDA. We define grammar $G_M = (V, \Sigma, P, S)$ such that $L(G_M) = N(M)$. V consists of the symbol S, the symbols $[qXp]$ for q and p in Q and X in Γ, and the symbols A_{qaY} for q in Q, a in $\Sigma \cup \{\epsilon\}$ and Y in Γ. S and the $[qXp]$'s play the same role as in Theorem 5.3. Symbol A_{qaY} indicates that the production is obtained from the move of M in $\delta(q, a, Y)$. The productions of G_M are as follows (with useless symbols and productions removed).

1) $S \rightarrow [q_0 Z_0 p]$ for all p in Q.
2) If $\delta(q, a, Y) = (p, \epsilon)$, then there is a production $[qYp] \rightarrow A_{qaY}$.

3) If $\delta(q, a, Y) = (p_1, X_1 X_2 \cdots X_k)$ for $k \geq 1$, then for each sequence of states p_2, $p_3, \ldots, p_{k+1}$ there is a production

$$[qYp_{k+1}] \to A_{qaY}[p_1 X_1 p_2] \cdots [p_k X_k p_{k+1}].$$

4) For all q, a, and Y, $A_{qaY} \to a$.

Consider a rightmost derivation in G_M. It starts with $S \Rightarrow [q_0 Z_0 p]$ for some state p. Suppose for the sake of argument that $\delta(q_0, a, Z_0) = (r, XYZ)$. Then the only productions for $[q_0 Z_0 p]$ that derive strings beginning with a (a may be ϵ) have right sides $A_{q_0aZ_0}[rXs][sYt][tZp]$ for some states s and t. Suppose that the rightmost derivation eventually derives some string w from $[tZp]$. Then, if $\delta(s, b, Y) = (u, VW)$, we might continue the rightmost derivation as

$$S \overset{*}{\underset{rm}{\Rightarrow}} A_{q_0aZ_0}[rXs][sYt]w \underset{rm}{\Rightarrow} A_{q_0aZ_0}[rXs]A_{sbY}[uVv][vWt]w. \tag{10.6}$$

Now consider the moves made by M before reading input w. The input corresponding to derivation (10.6) is of the form $ax_1 bx_2 x_3 w$, where $[rXs] \overset{*}{\Rightarrow} x_1$, $[uVv] \overset{*}{\Rightarrow} x_2$, and $[vWt] \overset{*}{\Rightarrow} x_3$. The corresponding sequence of moves is of the form†

$$(q_0, ax_1 bx_2 x_3 w, Z_0) \vdash (r, x_1 bx_2 x_3 w, XYZ)$$

$$\vdash^* (s, bx_2 x_3 w, YZ)$$

$$\vdash (u, x_2 x_3 w, VWZ)$$

$$\vdash (v, x_3 w, WZ)$$

$$\vdash (t, w, Z). \tag{10.7}$$

If we compare (10.6) and (10.7) we note that stack symbols (Z in particular) which remain on the stack at the end of (10.7) are the symbols that do not appear (with two states attached in a bracketed variable) in the longest viable prefix of (10.6). The stack symbols popped from the stack in (10.7), namely X, V, and W, are the symbols that appear in the viable prefix of (10.6). This situation makes sense, since the symbols at the left end of a sentential form derive a prefix of a sentence, and that prefix is read first by the PDA.

In general, given any viable prefix α of G_M, we can find a corresponding ID I of M in which the stack contains all and only the stack symbols that were introduced in a rightmost derivation of some αw and later replaced by a string of terminals. Moreover, I is obtained by having M read any string derived from α. In the case that M is deterministic, we can argue that the derivations of right-sentential forms with prefix α have a specific form and translate these limitations on derivations into restrictions on the set of items for α.

Lemma 10.6 If M is a DPDA and G_M is the grammar constructed from M as above, then whenever $[qXp] \overset{*}{\Rightarrow} w$, there is a unique computation $(q, w, X) \vdash^* (p, \epsilon,$

---

† Note that we have reverted to our original notation for ID's.

ϵ). Moreover, the sequence of moves made by M corresponds to the reverse of the sequence in which subscripted A_{say}'s are replaced by a, where A_{say} is deemed to "correspond" to a move in which the state is s, Y is on top of the stack, and input a is used.

Proof The existence of such a computation was proved in Theorem 5.3. Its uniqueness follows from the fact that M is deterministic. To show the correspondence between the moves of M and the reverse of the sequence of expansions of subscripted A's, we perform an easy induction on the length of a derivation. The key portion of the inductive step is when the first expansion is by rule (3):

$$[qXp] \Rightarrow A_{qax}[p_1 X_1 p_2][p_2 X_2 p_3] \cdots [p_k X_k p].$$

Then the explicitly shown A_{qaX} will be expanded after all subscripted A's derived from the other variables are expanded.

As the first move of M,

$$(q, w, X) \vdash (p_1, w', X_1 X_2 \cdots X_k),$$

where $w = aw'$, corresponds to A_{qaX}, we have part of the induction proved. The remainder of the induction follows from observing that in the moves of M, X_1, X_2, ..., X_k are removed from the stack in order, by using inputs $w_1, w_2, \ldots, w_k$, where $w_1 w_2 \cdots w_k = w'$, while in the rightmost derivation of w from $[qXp]$, the derivation of w_1 from $[p_1 X_1 p_2]$ follows the derivation of w_2 from $[p_2 X_2 p_3]$, and so on. Since all these derivations are shorter than $[qXp] \overset{*}{\underset{rm}{\Rightarrow}} w$, we may use the inductive hypothesis to complete the proof. $\square$

Now, for each variable $[qXp]$ of G_M, let us fix on a particular string w_{qXp} derived from $[qXp]$.† Let h be the homomorphism from the variables of G_M to Σ^* defined by

$$h(A_{qay}) = a, \qquad h([qXp]) = w_{qXp}.$$

Let $N(A_{qay}) = 1$ and $N([qXp])$ be the number of moves in the computation corresponding to $[qXp] \overset{*}{\underset{rm}{\Rightarrow}} w_{qXp}$. Extend N to V^* by $N(B_1 B_2 \cdots B_k) = \sum_{i=1}^{k} N(B_i)$. Finally, let us represent a move $\delta(q, a, Y)$ of M by the triple (qaY). Let m be the homomorphism from V^* to moves defined by

1) $m(A_{qaY}) = (qaY)$;
2) $m([qXp])$ is the reverse of the sequence of subscripts of the A's expanded in the derivation of w_{qXp} from $[qXp]$. By Lemma 10.6, $m([qXp])$ is also the sequence of moves $(q, w_{qXp}, X) \vdash^* (p, \epsilon, \epsilon)$.

We can now complete our characterization of $LR(0)$ grammars.

Lemma 10.7 Let γ be a viable prefix of G_M. (Note that by the construction of G_M, γ is in V^*). Then $(q_0, h(\gamma), Z_0) \vdash^{N(\gamma)} (p, \epsilon, \beta)$ for some p and β, by the sequence of moves $m(\gamma)$.

---

† We assume G_M has no useless symbols, so w_{qXp} exists.

Proof As γ is a viable prefix, there is some y in Σ^* such that γy is a right-sentential form. Then for some state r, $[q_0 Z_0 r] \overset{*}{\underset{rm}{\Rightarrow}} h(\gamma)y$. By Lemma 10.6, the last $N(\gamma)$ expansions of A's in that derivation take place after the right-sentential form γy is reached. Also by Lemma 10.6, there is a unique sequence of moves $(q_0, h(\gamma)y, Z_0) \overset{*}{\vdash} (r, \epsilon, \epsilon)$, and the first $N(\gamma)$ of these must be $m(\gamma)$. $\square$

We are now ready to show that G_M is $LR(0)$. Since the start symbol obviously does not appear in any right side, it suffices to show that each set of items with a complete item $B \to \beta \cdot$ contains no other complete item and no item of the form $A_{qaY} \to \cdot a$ for a in Σ. We prove these facts in two lemmas.

Lemma 10.8 If I is a set of items of G_M, and $B \to \beta \cdot$ is in I, then there is no item $A_{qaY} \to \cdot a$ in I.

Proof Let I be the set of items for viable prefix γ.

CASE 1 If $B \to \beta$ is a production from rule (1), then $\gamma = \beta$, and γ is a single variable $[q_0 Z_0 p]$, since S appears on no right side. If $A_{qaY} \to \cdot a$ is valid for γ, then there is a derivation $S \overset{*}{\Rightarrow} \gamma A_{qaY} y \underset{rm}{\Rightarrow} \gamma ay$. However, no right-sentential form begins with a variable $[q_0 Z_0 p]$ unless it is the first step of a derivation; all subsequent right-sentential forms begin with a subscripted A, until the last, which begins with a terminal. Thus γ could not be followed by A_{qaY} in a right-sentential form.

CASE 2 If $B \to \beta$ is introduced by rules (2) or (3), then we can again argue that $\gamma' \beta A_{qaY}$ is a viable prefix, where $\gamma = \gamma' \beta$. However, in any rightmost derivation, when $B \to \beta$ is applied, the last symbol of β is immediately expanded by rules (2), (3), or (4), so β could not appear intact in a right-sentential form followed by A_{qaY}.

CASE 3 If $B \to \beta$ is $A_{pbZ} \to b$ introduced by rule (4), and $A_{qaY} \to \cdot a$ is valid for γ, then b must be ϵ, else γA_{qaY}, which is a viable prefix, has a terminal in it. As $A_{p\epsilon Z} \to \cdot$ is valid for γ, it follows that $\gamma A_{p\epsilon Z}$ is a viable prefix. Thus, by Lemma 10.7 applied to γA_{qaY} and $\gamma A_{p\epsilon Z}$, the first $N(\gamma) + 1$ moves made by M when given input $h(\gamma)a$ are both $m(\gamma)(p\epsilon Z)$ and $m(\gamma)(qaY)$, contradicting the determinism of M. (Note that in the first of these sequences, a is not consumed.) $\square$

Lemma 10.9 If I is a set of items of G_M, and $B \to \beta \cdot$ is in I, then there is no other item $C \to \alpha \cdot$ in I.

Proof Again let γ be a viable prefix with set of valid items I.

CASE 1 Neither $B \to \beta$ nor $C \to \alpha$ is a production introduced by rule (4). Then the form of productions of types (2) and (3), and the fact that productions of type (1) are applied only at the first step tell us that as α and β are both suffixes of γ, we must have $\beta = \alpha$. If these productions are of type (1), $B = C = S$, so the two items are really the same. If the productions are of type (2) or (3), it is easy to check that $B = C$. For example, if $\alpha = \beta = A_{qaY}$, then the productions are of type (2), and B and C are each $[qYp]$ for some p. But rule (2) requires that $\delta(q, a, Y) = (p, \epsilon)$, so the determinism of M assures that p is unique.

CASE 2 $B \rightarrow \beta$ and $C \rightarrow \alpha$ are type (4) productions. Then γB and γC are viable prefixes, and Lemma 10.7 provides a contradiction to the determinism of M. That is, if $\beta = \alpha = \epsilon$, then the first $N(\gamma) + 1$ moves of M on input $h(\gamma)$ must be $m(\gamma B)$ and must also be $m(\gamma C)$. If $\beta = a \neq \epsilon$ and $\alpha = b \neq \epsilon$, then $a = b$, and the first $N(\gamma) + 1$ moves of M on input $h(\gamma)a$ must be $m(\gamma B)$ and $m(\gamma C)$. If $\beta = a \neq \epsilon$ and $\alpha = \epsilon$, then the first $N(\gamma) + 1$ moves of M on input $h(\gamma)a$ provides a similar contradiction.

CASE 3 $B \rightarrow \beta$ is from rule (1), (2), or (3) and $C \rightarrow \alpha$ is from rule (4), or vice versa. Then γC is a right-sentential form, and γ ends in β. We can rule out this possibility as in cases (1) and (2) of Lemma 10.8.   □

Theorem 10.11   If M is a DPDA, then G_M is an $LR(0)$ grammar.

Proof   Immediate from Lemmas 10.8 and 10.9.   □

We can now complete our characterization of $LR(0)$ grammars.

Theorem 10.12   A language L has an $LR(0)$ grammar if and only if L is a DCFL with the prefix property.

Proof

If: Suppose L is a DCFL with the prefix property. Then L is $L(M')$ for a DPDA M'. We can make M' accept L by empty stack by putting a bottom-of-stack marker on M' and causing M' to enter a new state that erases the stack whenever it enters a final state. As L has the prefix property, we do not change the language accepted, and L is accepted by empty stack by the new DPDA, M. Thus $L = L(G_M)$, and the desired conclusion follows from Theorem 10.11.

Only if: Theorem 10.10 says that L is $N(M)$ for a DPDA, M. We may use the construction of Theorem 5.2 to show that L is $L(M')$ for a DPDA M'. The fact that L has the prefix property follows from the fact that a DPDA "dies" when it empties its stack.   □

Corollary $L\$$ has $LR(0)$ grammar if and only if L is a DCFL, where \$ is not a symbol of L's alphabet.

Proof $L\$$ surely has the prefix property. If $L\$$ is a DCFL, then $L = L\$/\$$ is a DCFL by Theorem 10.2. Conversely, if L is a DCFL, it is easy to construct a DPDA for $L\$$.   □

10.8 $LR(k)$ GRAMMARS

It is interesting to note that if we add one symbol of "lookahead," by determining the set of following terminals on which reduction by $A \rightarrow \alpha$ could possibly be performed, then we can use DPDA's to recognize the languages of a wider class of grammars. These grammars are called $LR(1)$ grammars, for the one symbol of lookahead. It is known that all and only the deterministic CFL's have $LR(1)$

grammars. This class of grammars has great importance for compiler design, since they are broad enough to include the syntax of almost all programming languages, yet restrictive enough to have efficient parsers that are essentially DPDA's.

It turns out that adding more than one symbol of lookahead to guide the choice of reductions does not add to the class of languages definable, although for any k, there are grammars, called $LR(k)$, that may be parsed with k symbols of lookahead but not with $k - 1$ symbols of lookahead.

Let us briefly give the definition and an example of $LR(1)$ grammars, without proving any of the above contentions. The key extension of $LR(0)$ grammars is that an $LR(1)$ *item* consists of an $LR(0)$ item followed by a *lookahead set* consisting of terminals and/or the special symbol \$, which serves to denote the right end of a string. The generic form of an $LR(1)$ item is thus

$$A \rightarrow \alpha \cdot \beta, \{a_1, a_2, \ldots, a_n\}.$$

We say $LR(1)$ item $A \rightarrow \alpha \cdot \beta, \{a\}$ is *valid* for viable prefix γ if there is a rightmost derivation $S \overset{*}{\underset{rm}{\Rightarrow}} \delta Ay \underset{rm}{\Rightarrow} \delta \alpha \beta y$, where $\delta \alpha = \gamma$, and either

i) a is the first symbol of y, or

ii) $y = \epsilon$ and a is \$.

Also, $A \rightarrow \alpha \cdot \beta, \{a_1, a_2, \ldots, a_n\}$ is valid for γ if for each i, $A \rightarrow \alpha \cdot \beta, \{a_i\}$ is valid for γ.

Like the $LR(0)$ items, the set of $LR(1)$ items forms the states of a viable prefix recognizing NFA, and we can compute the set of valid items for each viable prefix by converting this NFA to a DFA. The transitions of this NFA are defined as follows.

1) There is a transition on X from $A \rightarrow \alpha \cdot X\beta, \{a_1, a_2, \ldots, a_n\}$ to $A \rightarrow \alpha X \cdot \beta$, $\{a_1, a_2, \ldots, a_n\}$.

2) There is a transition on ϵ from $A \rightarrow \alpha \cdot B\beta, \{a_1, a_2, \ldots, a_n\}$ to $B \rightarrow \cdot \gamma, T$, if $B \rightarrow \gamma$ is a production and T is the set of terminals and/or \$ such that b is in T if and only if either

   i) β derives a terminal string beginning with b, or

   ii) $\beta \overset{*}{\Rightarrow} \epsilon$, and b is a_i for some $1 \le i \le n$.

3) There is an initial state q_0 with transitions on ϵ to $S \rightarrow \cdot \alpha, \{\$\}$ for each production $S \rightarrow \alpha$.

Example 10.11   Consider the grammar

$$S \rightarrow A \qquad A \rightarrow BA \mid \epsilon \qquad B \rightarrow aB \mid b \qquad (10.8)$$

which happens to generate a regular set, $(\mathbf{a^*b})^*$. The NFA for grammar (10.8) is shown in Fig. 10.5, and the corresponding DFA is shown in Fig. 10.6. The NFA of Fig. 10.5 is unusual in that no two items differ only in the lookahead sets. In general, we may see two items with the same dotted production.

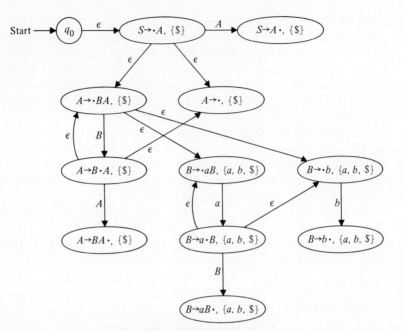

Fig. 10.5 NFA for *LR*(1) items.

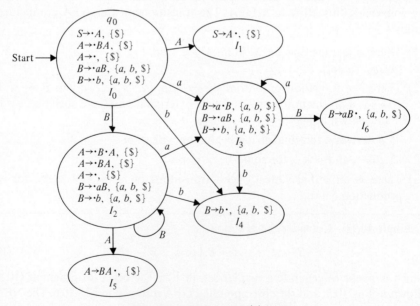

Fig. 10.6 DFA for *LR*(1) items.

To see how Fig. 10.5 is constructed, consider item $S \to \cdot A$, {$}. It has ϵ-transitions to items of the form $A \to \cdot AB$, T, and $A \to \cdot$, T, but what should T be? In rule (2) above, β is ϵ, so (2i) yields no symbols for T. Rule (2ii) tells us that $ is in T, so $T = \{\$\}$. Now consider item $A \to \cdot BA$, {$}. There are ϵ-transitions to $B \to \cdot aB$, U and $B \to \cdot b$, U for some U. Here, $\beta = A$. It is easy to check that A derives strings beginning with a and b, so a and b are in U. A also derives ϵ, so $ is in U because it is the lookahead set of $A \to \cdot BA$, {$}. Thus $U = \{a, b, \$\}$.

A grammar is said to be *LR(1)* if

1) the start symbol appears on no right side, and

2) whenever the set of items I valid for some viable prefix includes some complete item $A \to \alpha \cdot$, $\{a_1, a_2, \ldots, a_n\}$, then

   i) no a_i appears immediately to the right of the dot in any item of I, and
   ii) if $B \to \beta \cdot$, $\{b_1, b_2, \ldots, b_k\}$ is another complete item in I, then $a_i \neq b_j$ for any $1 \leq i \leq n$ and $1 \leq j \leq k$.

Example 10.12 Consider Fig. 10.6. Sets of items I_1, I_4, I_5, and I_6 consist of only one item and so satisfy (2). Set I_0 has one complete item, $A \to \cdot$, {$}. But $ does not appear to the right of a dot in any item of I_0. A similar remark applies to I_2, and I_3 has no complete items. Thus grammar (10.8) is $LR(1)$. Note that this grammar is not $LR(0)$; its language does not have the prefix property.

The automaton that accepts an $LR(1)$ language is like a DPDA, except that it is allowed to use the next input symbol in making its decisions even if it makes a move that does not consume its input. We can simulate such an automaton by an ordinary DPDA if we append $ to the end of the input. Then the DPDA can keep the next symbol or $ in its state to indicate the symbol scanned. The stack of our automaton is like the stack of the $LR(0)$ grammar recognizing DPDA: it has alternating grammar symbols and sets of items. The rules whereby it decides to reduce or shift an input symbol onto the stack are:

1) If the top set of items has complete item $A \to \alpha \cdot$, $\{a_1, a_2, \ldots, a_n\}$, where $A \neq S$, reduce by $A \to \alpha$ if the current input symbol is in $\{a_1, a_2, \ldots, a_n\}$.

2) If the top set of items has an item $S \to \alpha \cdot$, {$}, then reduce by $S \to \alpha$ and accept if the current symbol is $, that is, the end of the input is reached.

3) If the top set of items has an item $A \to \alpha \cdot aB$, T, and a is the current input symbol, then shift.

Note that the definition of an $LR(1)$ grammar guarantees that at most one of the above will apply for any particular input symbol or $. We customarily summarize these decisions by a table whose rows correspond to the sets of items and whose columns are the terminals and $.

Example 10.13   The table for grammar (10.8), built from Fig. 10.6, is shown in Fig. 10.7. Empty entries indicate an error; the input is not in the language. The sequence of actions taken by the parser on input *aabb* is shown in Fig. 10.8. The number *i* on the stack represents set of items I_i from Fig. 10.6. The proper set of items with which to cover a given grammar symbol is determined from the DFA transitions (Fig. 10.6) exactly as for an $LR(0)$ grammar.

	a	b	$
I_0	Shift	Shift	Reduce by $A \to \epsilon$
I_1			Accept
I_2	Shift	Shift	Reduce by $A \to \epsilon$
I_3	Shift	Shift	
I_4	Reduce by $B \to b$	Reduce by $B \to b$	Reduce by $B \to b$
I_5			Reduce by $A \to BA$
I_6	Reduce by $B \to aB$	Reduce by $B \to aB$	Reduce by $B \to aB$

Fig. 10.7   Decision table for grammar (10.8).

Stack	Remaining input	Comments
0	aabb$	Initial
0a3	abb$	Shift
0a3a3	bb$	Shift
0a3a3b4	b$	Shift
0a3a3B6	b$	Reduce by $B \to b$
0a3B6	b$	Reduce by $B \to aB$
0B2	b$	Reduce by $B \to aB$
0B2b4	$	Shift
0B2B2	$	Reduce by $B \to b$
0B2B2A5	$	Reduce by $A \to \epsilon$
0B2A5	$	Reduce by $A \to BA$
0A1	$	Reduce by $A \to BA$
—	$	Reduce by $S \to A$ and accept

Fig. 10.8   Action of $LR(1)$ parser on input *aabb*.

EXERCISES

10.1   Show that the normal form of Lemma 10.2 holds for nondeterministic PDA's.

10.2

a) Show that every DCFL is accepted by a DPDA whose only ϵ moves are pop moves.

b) Show that the DPDA of part (a) can be made to satisfy the normal form of Lemma 10.2.

*10.3   Give an efficient algorithm to implement rule (4) of Lemma 10.3.

*S10.4   Show that the DCFL's are not closed under union, concatenation, Kleene closure, or homomorphism.

**10.5   Show that the following are not DCFL's.

$$\text{Sa) } \{ww^R \,|\, w \text{ is in } (0 + 1)^*\} \qquad \text{b) } \{0^n1^n \,|\, n \geq 1\} \cup \{0^n1^{2n} \,|\, n \geq 1\}$$

**10.6   Prove that

$$\{0^i1^ja2^i \,|\, i, j \geq 1\} \cup \{0^i1^jb2^j \,|\, i, j \geq 1\}$$

is a DCFL, but is not accepted by any DPDA without ϵ-moves.

10.7   Show that if L is a DCFL, then L is accepted by a DPDA which, if it accepts $a_1 a_2 \cdots a_n$, does so immediately upon consuming a_n (without subsequent ϵ-moves). [*Hint:* Use the predicting machine.]

10.8   Does Greibach's Theorem (Theorem 8.14) apply to the DCFL's?

10.9   Construct the nonempty sets of items for the following grammars. Which are $LR(0)$?

a) $S' \to S$
   $S \to aSa \,|\, bSb \,|\, c$

b) $S' \to S$
   $S \to aSa \,|\, bSb \,|\, \epsilon$

Sc) $S \to E_1$
   $E_1 \to T_3 E_1 \,|\, T_1$
   $E_2 \to T_3 E_2 \,|\, T_2$
   $T_1 \to a\$ \,|\, (E_2\$$
   $T_2 \to a) \,|\, (E_2)$
   $T_3 \to a + \,|\, (E_2 +$

10.10   Show the sequence of stacks used by the DPDA constructed from grammar 10.9(c) when the input is $a + (a + a)\$$.

10.11   Construct the nonempty sets of $LR(1)$ items for the following grammars. Which are $LR(1)$?

a) $S \to A$
   $A \to AB \,|\, \epsilon$
   $B \to aB \,|\, b$

b) $S \to E$
   $E \to E + T \,|\, T$
   $T \to a \,|\, (E)$

10.12   Repeat Exercise 10.10 for grammar 10.11(b).

10.13   Let G be an $LR(0)$ grammar with $A \to \alpha \cdot$, $\alpha \neq \epsilon$, valid for some viable prefix γ. Prove that no other production can be valid for γ.

Solutions to selected exercises

10.4   Let $L_1 = \{0^i1^i2^j \,|\, i, j \geq 0\}$ and $L_2 = \{0^i1^j2^j \,|\, i, j \geq 0\}$. It is easy to show that L_1 and L_2 are DCFL's. However, $L_1 \cup L_2$ is the CFL shown not to be a DCFL in Example 10.1. Thus the DCFL's are not closed under union.

For concatenation, let $L_3 = aL_1 \cup L_2$. Then L_3 is a DCFL, because the presence or absence of symbol a tells us whether to look for a word in L_1 or a word in L_2. Surely $\mathbf{a}^*$ is a DCFL. However $\mathbf{a}^*L_3$ is not a DCFL. If it were, then $L_4 = \mathbf{a}^*L_3 \cap \mathbf{a0}^*\mathbf{1}^*\mathbf{2}^*$ would be a DCFL by Theorem 10.4. But $L_4 = aL_1 \cup aL_2$. If L_4 is a DCFL, accepted by DPDA M, then we could recognize $L_1 \cup L_2$ by simulating M on (imaginary) input a and then on the real input. As $L_1 \cup L_2$ is not a DCFL, neither is L_4, and therefore the DCFL's are not closed under concatenation.

The proof for closure is similar, if we let $L_5 = \{a\} \cup L_3$. L_5 is a DCFL, but L_5^* is not, by a proof similar to the above.

For homomorphism, let $L_6 = aL_1 \cup bL_2$, which is a DCFL. Let L be the homomorphism that maps b to a and maps other symbols to themselves. Then $h(L_6) = L_4$, so the DCFL's are not closed under homomorphism.

10.5(a) Suppose $L_1 = \{ww^R \mid w \text{ is in } (0 + 1)^+\}$ were a DCFL. Then by Theorem 10.4, so would be

$$L_2 = L_1 \cap (01)^*(10)^*(01)^*(10)^*.$$

Now

$$L_2 = \{(01)^i(10)^j(01)^j(10)^i \mid i, j \geq 0, i \text{ and } j \text{ not both } 0\}.$$

By Theorem 10.3, $L_3 = \text{MIN}(L_2)$ is a DCFL. But

$$L_3 = \{(01)^i(10)^j(01)^j(10)^i \mid 0 \leq j < i\},$$

since if $j \geq i$, a prefix is in L_2. Let L be the homomorphism $h(a) = 01$ and $h(b) = 10$. Then

$$L_4 = h^{-1}(L_3) = \{a^ib^ja^jb^i \mid 0 \leq j < i\}$$

is a DCFL by Theorem 10.4. However, the pumping lemma with $z = a^{n+1}b^na^nb^{n+1}$ shows that L_4 is not even a CFL.

10.9(c) Before tackling this project, let us describe the language of the grammar. We first describe "expression" and "term" recursively, as follows.

1) A term is a single symbol a which stands for any "argument" of an arithmetic expression or a parenthesized expression.
2) An expression is one or more terms connected by plus signs.

Then the language of this grammar is the set of all expressions followed by an endmarker, $. E_1 and T_1 generate expressions and terms followed by a $. E_2 and T_2 generate expressions and terms followed by a right parenthesis, and T_3 generates a term followed by a plus sign.

It turns out that $LR(0)$ grammars to define arithmetic expressions, of which our grammar is a simple example, are quite contorted, in comparison with an $LR(1)$ grammar for the same language [see Exercise 10.11(b)]. For this reason, practical compiler-writing systems never require that the syntax of a language be described by an $LR(0)$ grammar; $LR(1)$ grammars, or a subset of these, are preferred. Nevertheless, the present grammar will serve as a useful exercise. The DFA accepting viable prefixes has 20 states, not counting the dead state. We tabulate these sets of items in Fig. 10.9. Figure 10.10 gives the transition table for the DFA; blanks indicate transitions to the dead state.

Inspection of the sets of items tells us that certain sets, namely 1, 3, 6, 7, 8, 11, 14, 15, 16, 17, and 19, consist of a single complete item, while the remainder have no complete items. Thus the grammar is $LR(0)$.

I_0	I_5	I_{10}	I_{14}

I_0

$S \rightarrow \cdot E_1$
$E_1 \rightarrow \cdot T_3 E_1$
$E_1 \rightarrow \cdot T_1$
$T_3 \rightarrow \cdot a +$
$T_3 \rightarrow \cdot (E_2 +$
$T_1 \rightarrow \cdot a\$$
$T_1 \rightarrow \cdot (E_2 \$$

I_5

$T_3 \rightarrow (\cdot E_2 +$
$T_1 \rightarrow (\cdot E_2 \$$
$E_2 \rightarrow \cdot T_3 E_2$
$E_2 \rightarrow \cdot T_2$
$T_3 \rightarrow \cdot a +$
$T_3 \rightarrow \cdot (E_2 +$
$T_2 \rightarrow \cdot a)$
$T_2 \rightarrow \cdot (E_2)$

I_{10}

$E_2 \rightarrow T_3 \cdot E_2$
$E_2 \rightarrow \cdot T_3 E_2$
$E_2 \rightarrow \cdot T_2$
$T_3 \rightarrow \cdot a +$
$T_3 \rightarrow \cdot (E_2 +$
$T_2 \rightarrow \cdot a)$
$T_2 \rightarrow \cdot (E_2)$

I_{14}

$T_3 \rightarrow (E_2 + \cdot$

I_{15}

$T_1 \rightarrow (E_2 \$ \cdot$

I_{16}

$E_2 \rightarrow T_3 E_2 \cdot$

I_1

$S \rightarrow E_1 \cdot$

I_6

$E_1 \rightarrow T_3 E_1 \cdot$

I_{11}

$E_2 \rightarrow T_2 \cdot$

I_{17}

$T_2 \rightarrow a) \cdot$

I_2

$E_1 \rightarrow T_3 \cdot E_1$
$E_1 \rightarrow \cdot T_3 E_1$
$E_1 \rightarrow \cdot T_1$
$T_3 \rightarrow \cdot a +$
$T_3 \rightarrow \cdot (E_2 +$
$T_1 \rightarrow \cdot a\$$
$T_1 \rightarrow \cdot (E_2 \$$

I_7

$T_3 \rightarrow a + \cdot$

I_{12}

$T_3 \rightarrow a \cdot +$
$T_2 \rightarrow a \cdot)$

I_{18}

$T_3 \rightarrow (E_2 \cdot +$
$T_2 \rightarrow (E_2 \cdot)$

I_3

$E_1 \rightarrow T_1 \cdot$

I_8

$T_1 \rightarrow a\$ \cdot$

I_{13}

$T_3 \rightarrow (\cdot E_2 +$
$T_2 \rightarrow (\cdot E_2)$
$E_2 \rightarrow \cdot T_3 E_2$
$E_2 \rightarrow \cdot T_2$
$T_3 \rightarrow \cdot a +$
$T_3 \rightarrow \cdot (E_2 + \cdot$
$T_2 \rightarrow \cdot a)$
$T_2 \rightarrow \cdot (E_2)$

I_{19}

$T_2 \rightarrow (E_2) \cdot$

I_4

$T_3 \rightarrow a \cdot +$
$T_1 \rightarrow a \cdot \$$

I_9

$T_3 \rightarrow (E_2 \cdot +$
$T_1 \rightarrow (E_2 \cdot \$$

Fig. 10.9 Sets of items for Exercise 10.9(c).

BIBLIOGRAPHIC NOTES

Deterministic pushdown automata were first studied by Fischer [1963], Schutzenberger [1963], Haines [1965], and Ginsburg and Greibach [1966a]. Lemma 10.3, the fact that DPDA's can be made to consume all their input, is from Schutzenberger [1963]; Theorem 10.1, closure under complementation, was observed independently by various people. Most of the closure and decision properties, Theorems 10.2 through 10.8, were first proved by Ginsburg and Greibach [1966a]. An exception is the fact that it is decidable whether a DCFL is regular, which was proved by Stearns [1967]. The predicting-machine construction is from Hopcroft and Ullman [1969b].

	a	$+$	$($	$)$	$\$$	E_1	E_2	T_1	T_2	T_3
0	4		5			1		3		2
1										
2	4		5			6		3		2
3										
4		7			8					
5	12		13				9		11	10
6										
7										
8										
9		14			15					
10	12		13				16		11	10
11										
12		7		17						
13	12		13				18		11	10
14										
15										
16										
17										
18		14		19						
19										

Fig. 10.10   Transition table of viable prefix recognizing DFA.

$LR(k)$ grammars and the equivalence of DPDA's to $LR(1)$ grammars is from Knuth [1965]. The latter work generalized a sequence of papers dealing with subclasses of the CFG's having efficient parsing algorithms. The history of this development is described in Aho and Ullman [1972, 1973]. Graham [1970] shows that a number of other classes of grammars define exactly the CFL's.

Subsequent to Knuth [1965], a series of papers examined the class of $LR(1)$ grammars for a useful subclass for which parsers of reasonable size could be built. Korenjak's [1969] was the first such method, although two subclasses of $LR(1)$ grammars, called $SLR(1)$ (for "simple" LR) and $LALR(1)$ (for "lookahead LR"), due to DeRemer [1969, 1971] are the methods used most commonly today. By way of comparison, a typical programming language, such as ALGOL, has an $LR(1)$ parser (viable prefix recognizing DFA) with several thousand states, and even more are needed for an $LR(0)$ parser. As the transition table must be part of the parser for a language, it is not feasible to store such a large parser in the main memory of the computer, even if the table is compacted. However, the same languages have $SLR(1)$ or $LALR(1)$ parsers of a few hundred states, which fit easily with compaction. See Aho and Johnson [1974] or Aho and Ullman [1977] for a description of how LR-based parsers are designed and used.

A good deal of research has been focused on the open question of whether equivalence is decidable for DPDA's. Korenjak and Hopcroft [1966] showed that equivalence is decidable for a subclass of the DCFL's called "simple" languages.† These are defined by gram-

---

† These are not related to "simple" LR grammars in any substantial way.

mars in Greibach normal form such that no two productions $A \to a\alpha$ and $A \to a\beta$ exist. The decidability of equivalence was extended to the $LL(k)$ grammars of Lewis and Stearns [1968], which are a proper subset of the $LR(k)$ grammars, by Rosenkrantz and Stearns [1970]. Valiant [1973] showed that equivalence was decidable for finite-turn DPDA's (see Exercise 6.13 for a definition), among other classes; see also Valiant [1974], Beeri [1976], and Taniguchi and Kasami [1976]. Friedman [1977] showed that equivalence for DPDA's is decidable if and only if it is decidable for "monadic recursion schemes," which in terms of automata can be viewed as one-state DPDA's that can base their next move on the current input symbol, without consuming that symbol.

Additionally, work was done on extending the undecidability of containment for DCFL's to small subsets of the DCFL's. The work culminated in Friedman [1976], which proved that containment is undecidable even for the simple languages of Korenjak and Hopcroft [1966].

A solution to Exercise 10.5(b) is found in Ginsburg and Greibach [1966a], and Exercise 10.6 is based on Cole [1969].

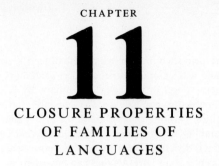

CHAPTER

11

CLOSURE PROPERTIES
OF FAMILIES OF
LANGUAGES

There are striking similarities among the closure properties of the regular sets, the context-free languages, the r.e. sets, and other classes. Not only are the closure properties similar, but so are the proof techniques used to establish these properties. In this chapter we take a general approach and study all families of languages having certain closure properties. This will provide new insight into the underlying structure of closure properties and will simplify the study of new classes of languages.

11.1 TRIOS AND FULL TRIOS

Recall that a language is a set of finite-length strings over some finite alphabet. A *family of languages* is a collection of languages containing at least one nonempty language. A *trio* is a family of languages closed under intersection with a regular set, inverse homomorphism, and ϵ-free (forward) homomorphism. [We say a homomorphism h is *ϵ-free* if $h(a) \neq \epsilon$ for any symbol a.] If the family of languages is closed under all homomorphisms, as well as inverse homomorphism and intersection with a regular set, then it is said to be a *full trio*.

Example 11.1 The regular sets, the context-free languages, and the r.e. sets are full trios. The context-sensitive languages and the recursive sets are trios but not full trios, since they are not closed under arbitrary homomorphisms. In fact, closing the CSL's or the recursive sets under arbitrary homomorphisms yields the r.e. sets (see Exercise 9.14 and its solution).

Theorem 3.3 showed that regular sets are closed under intersection; hence they are closed under "intersection with a regular set." Theorem 3.5 showed closure of the regular sets under homomorphisms and inverse homomorphism, completing the proof that the regular sets form a full trio. The corollary to Theorems 6.2, 6.3, and 6.5 show that the CFL's are a full trio. Exercise 9.10 and its solution provide a proof that the CSL's are closed under inverse homomorphism, intersection (hence intersection with a regular set), and substitution (hence ϵ-free homomorphism, but not all homomorphisms, since ϵ is not permitted in a CSL). Thus the CSL's are a trio but not a full trio.

We shall prove that the recursive sets are a trio, leaving the proof that the r.e. sets are a full trio as an exercise. Let h be a homomorphism and L a recursive language recognized by algorithm A. Then $h^{-1}(L)$ is recognized by algorithm B, which simply applies A to $h(w)$, where w is B's input. Let g be an ϵ-free homomorphism. Then $g(L)$ is recognized by algorithm C which, given input w of length n, enumerates all the words x of length up to n over the domain alphabet of g. For each x such that $g(x) = w$, algorithm A is applied to x, and if x is in L, algorithm C accepts w. Note that since g is ϵ-free, w cannot be $g(x)$ if $|x| > |w|$. Finally, if R is a regular set accepted by DFA M, we may construct algorithm D that accepts input w if and only if A accepts w and M accepts w.

We conclude this section by observing that every full trio contains all regular sets. Thus the regular sets are the smallest full trio. Also, the ϵ-free regular sets are the smallest trio. (A language is ϵ-*free* if ϵ is not a member of the language.)

Lemma 11.1 Every full trio contains all regular sets; every trio contains all ϵ-free regular sets.

Proof Let $\mathscr{C}$ be a trio, Σ an alphabet, and $R \subseteq \Sigma^*$ an ϵ-free regular set. Since $\mathscr{C}$ contains at least one nonempty language, let L be in $\mathscr{C}$ and w be in L. Define $\Sigma' = \{a' \mid a \text{ is in } \Sigma\}$ and let h be the homomorphism that maps each a in Σ to ϵ and each a' in Σ' to w. Then $L_1 = h^{-1}(L)$ is in $\mathscr{C}$ because $\mathscr{C}$ is a trio. As w is in L, L_1 contains all strings in $\Sigma'\Sigma^*$, and others as well. Let g be the homomorphism $g(a') = g(a) = a$ for all a in Σ. Then g being ϵ-free, we know that $L_2 = g(L_1)$ is in $\mathscr{C}$ and is either Σ^* or Σ^+, depending on whether or not L_1 contains ϵ. Thus $L_2 \cap R = R$ is in $\mathscr{C}$, proving our contention that every trio contains all ϵ-free regular sets.

If $\mathscr{C}$ is a full trio, we may modify the above proof by letting $g'(a') = \epsilon$ and $g'(a) = a$ for all a in Σ. Then $L_2 = g'(L_1) = \Sigma^*$. If R is any regular set whatsoever, $L_2 \cap R = R$ is in $\mathscr{C}$. □

We leave it as an exercise to show that the ϵ-free regular sets are a trio and hence the smallest trio. Note that they do not form a full trio, because they are not closed under all homomorphisms.

11.2   GENERALIZED SEQUENTIAL MACHINE MAPPINGS

In studying closure properties, one quickly observes that certain properties follow automatically from others. Thus to establish a set of closure properties for a class of languages one need only establish a set of properties from which the others follow. In this section we shall establish a number of closure properties that follow from the basic properties of trios and full trios.

The first operation we consider is a generalization of a homomorphism. Consider a Mealy machine that is permitted to emit any string, including ϵ, in a move. This device is called a generalized sequential machine, and the mapping it defines is called a generalized sequential machine mapping.

More formally a *generalized sequential machine* (GSM) is a 6-tuple $M = (Q, \Sigma, \Delta, \delta, q_0, F)$, where Q, Σ, and Δ are the *states*, *input alphabet*, and *output alphabet*, respectively, δ is a mapping from $Q \times \Sigma$ to finite subsets of $Q \times \Delta^*$, q_0 is the *initial state*, and F is the set of *final states*. The interpretation of (p, w) in $\delta(q, a)$ is that M in state q with input symbol a may, as one possible choice of move, enter state p and emit the string w.

We extend the domain of δ to $Q \times \Sigma^*$ as follows.

1) $\delta(q, \epsilon) = \{(q, \epsilon)\}$.
2) For x in Σ^* and a in Σ,

$$\delta(q, xa) = \{(p, w) \,|\, w = w_1 w_2 \text{ and for some } p',$$
$$(p', w_1) \text{ is in } \delta(q, x) \text{ and } (p, w_2) \text{ is in } \delta(p', a)\}.$$

A GSM is *ϵ-free* if δ maps $Q \times \Sigma$ to finite subsets of $Q \times \Delta^+$. Let $M(x)$, where M is a GSM as defined above, denote the set

$$\{y \,|\, (p, y) \text{ is in } \delta(q_0, x) \text{ for some } p \text{ in } F\}.$$

If L is a language over Σ, let $M(L)$ denote

$$\{y \,|\, y \text{ is in } M(x) \text{ for some } x \text{ in } L\}.$$

We say that $M(L)$ is a *GSM mapping*. If M is ϵ-free, then $M(L)$ is an *ϵ-free GSM mapping*. Note that L is a parameter of the mapping, not a given language.

Also let

$$M^{-1}(x) = \{y \,|\, M(y) \text{ contains } x\},$$

and

$$M^{-1}(L) = \{y \,|\, x \text{ is in } M(y) \text{ for some } x \text{ in } L\}.$$

We say that M^{-1} is an *inverse GSM mapping*. It is not necessarily true that $M^{-1}(M(L)) = M(M^{-1}(L)) = L$, so M^{-1} is not a true inverse.

Example 11.2   Let

$$M = (\{q_0, q_1\}, \{0, 1\}, \{a, b\}, \delta, q_0, \{q_1\}).$$

We define δ by

$$\delta(q_0, 0) = \{(q_0, aa), (q_1, b)\},$$
$$\delta(q_0, 1) = \{(q_0, a)\},$$
$$\delta(q_1, 0) = \varnothing,$$
$$\delta(q_1, 1) = \{(q_1, \epsilon)\}.$$

We may draw a GSM as a finite automaton, with an edge labeled a/w from state q to state p if $\delta(q, a)$ contains (p, w). The diagram for M above is shown in Fig. 11.1. Intuitively, as 0's are input to M, M has the choice of either emitting two a's or one b. If M emits the b, it goes to state q_1. If 1 is input to M, and M is in state q_0, M can only output an a. In state q_1, M dies on a 0-input, but can remain in state q_1 with no output on a 1-input.

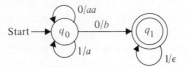

Fig. 11.1 A GSM.

Let $L = \{0^n1^n \,|\, n \geq 1\}$. Then

$$M(L) = \{a^{2n}b \,|\, n \geq 0\}.$$

For as 0's are read by M, it emits two a's per 0, until at some time it guesses that it should emit the symbol b and go to state q_1. If 1's do not follow immediately on the input, M dies. Or if M chooses to stay in q_0 when the first 1 is read, it can never reach q_1 if the input is of the form 0^n1^n. Thus the only output made by M when given input 0^n1^n is $a^{2n-2}b$.

If $L_1 = \{a^{2n}b \,|\, n \geq 0\}$, then

$$M^{-1}(L_1) = \{w01^i \,|\, i \geq 0 \text{ and } w \text{ has an even number of 1's}\}.$$

Note that $M^{-1}(M(L)) \supsetneq L$.

The GSM mapping is a useful tool for expressing one language in terms of a second language having essentially the same structure but different external trappings. For example, $L_1 = \{a^nb^n \,|\, n \geq 1\}$ and $L_2 = \{a^nba^n \,|\, n \geq 1\}$ in some sense have the same structure, but differ slightly. L_1 and L_2 are easily expressible in terms of each other by GSM mappings. Figure 11.2(a) shows a GSM mapping L_1 to L_2, and Fig. 11.2(b) shows a GSM mapping L_2 to L_1.

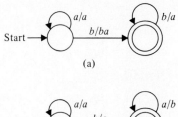

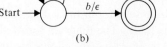

Fig. 11.2   Two GSM's.

Closure under GSM mappings

A key fact about GSM mappings is that they can be expressed in terms of homomorphisms, inverse homomorphisms, and intersection with regular sets. Thus any class of languages closed under the latter operations is closed under GSM mappings.

Theorem 11.1   Every full trio is closed under GSM mappings. Every trio is closed under ϵ-free GSM mappings.

Proof   Let $\mathscr{C}$ be a full trio, L a member of $\mathscr{C}$, and $M = (Q, \Sigma, \Delta, \delta, q_0, F)$ a GSM. We must prove that $M(L)$ is in $\mathscr{C}$. Let

$$\Delta_1 = \{[q, a, x, p] \mid \delta(q, a) \text{ contains } (p, x)\}$$

and let h_1 and h_2 be the homomorphisms from Δ_1^* to Σ^* and Δ_1^* to Δ^* defined by $h_1([q, a, x, p]) = a$ and $h_2([q, a, x, p]) = x$. Let R be the regular set of all strings in Δ_1^* such that

1) the first component of the first symbol is q_0, the start state of M;
2) the last component of the last symbol is a final state of M;
3) the last component of each symbol is the same as the first component of the succeeding symbol.

It is easy to check that R is a regular set. A DFA can verify condition (3) by remembering the previous symbol in its state and comparing it with the current symbol.

   If ϵ is not in L, then $M(L) = h_2(h_1^{-1}(L) \cap R)$. That is, h_1^{-1} maps M's input to a string that has encoded in it, for each symbol of the input string, a possible state transition of M on the input symbol and a corresponding output string. The regular set forces the sequence of states to be a possible sequence of state transitions of M. Finally, h_2 erases the input and state transitions, leaving only the output string. Formally,

$$h_1^{-1}(L) = \{[p_1, a_1, x_1, q_1][p_2, a_2, x_2, q_2] \cdots [p_k, a_k, x_k, q_k] \,|\, a_1 a_2 \cdots a_k$$

is in L, the p_i's are arbitrary, and (q_i, x_i) is in $\delta(p_i, a_i)\}$.

Intersecting $h_1^{-1}(L)$ with R yields

$$L' = \{[q_0, a_1, x_1, q_1][q_1, a_2, x_2, q_2] \cdots [q_{k-1}, a_k, x_k, q_k] \,|\, a_1 a_2 \cdots a_k$$

is in L, q_k is in F, and $\delta(q_{i-1}, a_i)$ contains (q_i, x_i) for all $i\}$.

Hence $h_2(L')$ is $M(L)$ by definition.

If ϵ is in L and q_0 is not a final state, then $h_2(L')$ is still $M(L)$. But if ϵ is in L and q_0 is a final state, then $M(\epsilon) = \epsilon$, so we must modify the construction above to make sure ϵ is in the resulting language. Let $L'' = h_1^{-1}(L) \cap (R + \epsilon)$. Then $L'' = L' \cup \{\epsilon\}$, since ϵ is in $h^{-1}(L)$. Hence $h_2(L'') = M(L)$. Since every full trio is closed under intersection with a regular set, homomorphism, and inverse homomorphism, $M(L)$ is in $\mathscr{C}$.

The proof for trios and ϵ-free GSM mappings proceeds in a similar fashion. Since the GSM never emits ϵ, the x in $[q, a, x, p]$ is never ϵ, and consequently h_2 is an ϵ-free homomorphism. $\qquad\square$

Limited erasing and inverse GSM mappings

Trios are not necessarily closed under homomorphisms that result in arbitrary erasing. However, trios are closed under certain homomorphisms that allow erasing, provided the erasing is limited. A class of languages is said to be closed under *k-limited erasing* if for any language L of the class and any homomorphism h such that h never maps more than k consecutive symbols of any sentence x in L to ϵ, $h(L)$ is in the class. The class is closed under *limited erasing* if it is closed under k-limited erasing for all k. Note that if $h(a)$ is ϵ for some a, then whether h is a limited erasing on L depends on L.

Lemma 11.2 Every trio is closed under limited erasing.

Proof Let $\mathscr{C}$ be a trio, $L \subseteq \Sigma_1^*$ be a member of $\mathscr{C}$, and h a homomorphism that is k-limited on L. Let

$$\Sigma_2 = \{[x] \,|\, x \text{ is in } \Sigma_1^*, |x| \le k + 1, \text{ and } h(x) \ne \epsilon\}.$$

Let h_1 and h_2 be homomorphisms defined by

$$h_1([a_1 a_2 \cdots a_m]) = a_1 a_2 \cdots a_m \text{ and } h_2([a_1 a_2 \cdots a_m]) = h(a_1 a_2 \cdots a_m).$$

Since $[a_1 a_2 \cdots a_m]$ is only in Σ_2 if $h(a_1 a_2 \cdots a_m) \ne \epsilon$, h_2 is ϵ-free. Then $h_2(h_1^{-1}(L))$ is in $\mathscr{C}$ since $\mathscr{C}$ is closed under ϵ-free homomorphisms and all inverse homomorphisms. It is easy to check that $h_2(h_1^{-1}(L)) = h(L)$. $\qquad\square$

Theorem 11.2 Every trio is closed under inverse GSM mappings.

Proof Let $\mathscr{C}$ be a trio, L a member of $\mathscr{C}$, and let $M = (Q, \Sigma, \Delta, \delta, q_0, F)$ be a GSM. Without loss of generality assume that the sets Σ and Δ are disjoint. If not, replace symbols in Δ by new symbols and restore them at the end of the construction by an ϵ-free homomorphism mapping each new symbol to the corresponding old symbol. Let h_1 be the homomorphism mapping $(\Sigma \cup \Delta)^*$ to Δ^* defined by

$$h_1(a) = \begin{cases} a & \text{for } a \text{ in } \Delta, \\ \epsilon & \text{for } a \text{ in } \Sigma. \end{cases}$$

Let $L_1 = h_1^{-1}(L)$. Then L_1 is the set of strings in $\Sigma^* b_1 \Sigma^* b_2 \cdots \Sigma^* b_n \Sigma^*$, such that $b_1 b_2 \cdots b_n$ is in L.

Let R be the regular set consisting of all words of the form $a_1 x_1 a_2 x_2 \cdots a_m x_m$ such that

1) the a's are in Σ,
2) the x's are in Δ^*,
3) there exist states $q_0, q_1, \ldots, q_m$ such that q_m is in F and for $1 \le i \le m$, $\delta(q_{i-1}, a_i)$ contains (q_i, x_i).

Note that x_i may be ϵ. The reader may easily show R to be a regular set by constructing a nondeterministic finite automaton accepting R. This NFA guesses the sequence of states $q_1, q_2, \ldots, q_m$.

Now $L_1 \cap R$ is the set of all words in R of the form $a_1 x_1 a_2 x_2 \cdots a_m x_m$, $m \ge 0$, where the a's are in Σ, the x's are in Δ^*, $x_1 x_2 \cdots x_m$ is in L, and $\delta(q_0, a_1 a_2 \cdots a_m)$ contains $(p, x_1 x_2 \cdots x_m)$, for some p in F. None of the x_i's is of length greater than k, where k is the length of the longest x such that (p, x) is in $\delta(q, a)$ for some p and q in Q and a in Σ.

Finally, let h_2 be the homomorphism that maps a to a for each a in Σ, and b to ϵ for each b in Δ. Then

$$M^{-1}(L) = h_2(L_1 \cap R)$$

is in $\mathscr{C}$ by Lemma 11.2, since h_2 never causes more than k consecutive symbols to be mapped to ϵ. $\square$

11.3 OTHER CLOSURE PROPERTIES OF TRIOS

Trios and full trios are closed under many other operations. In this section we present several of these closure properties.

Theorem 11.3 Every full trio is closed under quotient with a regular set.

Proof Let $\mathscr{C}$ be a full trio, $L \subseteq \Sigma_1^*$ a member of $\mathscr{C}$, and $R \subseteq \Sigma_1^*$ a regular set. For each a in Σ_1 let a' be a new symbol, and let Σ_1' be the set of all such symbols. Let h_1

and h_2 be the homomorphisms from $(\Sigma_1 \cup \Sigma_1')^*$ to Σ_1^* defined by $h_1(a) = h_1(a') = a$, $h_2(a) = \epsilon$ and $h_2(a') = a$. Then $L/R = h_2(h_1^{-1}(L) \cap (\Sigma_1')^*R)$, and hence L/R is in $\mathscr{C}$. That is, $h_1^{-1}(L)$ is the words in L with each symbol primed or unprimed independently. Thus $h_1^{-1}(L) \cap (\Sigma_1')^*R$ is those words xy such that x consists only of primed symbols, y consists only of unprimed symbols, y is in R, and if z is x with the primes removed, then zy is in L. It follows that

$$h_2(h_1^{-1}(L) \cap (\Sigma_1')^*R)$$

is all strings z as described above, that is, L/R. □

Theorem 11.4 Trios are closed under substitution by ϵ-free regular sets, and full trios are closed under substitution by regular sets.

Proof Let $\mathscr{C}$ be a trio, $L \subseteq \Sigma_1^*$ a member of $\mathscr{C}$ and $s: \Sigma_1^* \to \Sigma_2^*$ a substitution such that for each a in Σ_1, $s(a)$ is regular. For the time being assume Σ_1 and Σ_2 are disjoint, and $s(a)$ does not contain ϵ.

Let x be a string in L. By an inverse homomorphism we can insert arbitrary strings from Σ_2^* among symbols of x. By intersecting with a regular set we can assure that the string inserted after the symbol a is in $s(a)$. Then by limited erasing we can erase the symbols of x, leaving a string from $s(x)$.

More precisely let $h_1: (\Sigma_1 \cup \Sigma_2)^* \to \Sigma_1^*$ be the homomorphism defined by $h_1(a) = a$ for a in Σ_1 and $h_1(a) = \epsilon$ for a in Σ_2 and let $h_2: (\Sigma_1 \cup \Sigma_2)^* \to \Sigma_2^*$ be the homomorphism defined by $h_2(a) = \epsilon$ for a in Σ_1 and $h_2(a) = a$ for a in Σ_2. Then

$$s(L) = h_2\left(h_1^{-1}(L) \cap \left(\bigcup_{a \text{ in } \Sigma_1} as(a)\right)^*\right)$$

Now

$$\left(\bigcup_{a \text{ in } \Sigma_1} as(a)\right)^*$$

is a regular set, since each $s(a)$ is. Since $s(a)$ is ϵ-free, h_2 erases at most every other symbol, so $s(L)$ is in $\mathscr{C}$ by Lemma 11.2. The proof that full trios are closed under substitution by regular sets is identical except for the fact that s may not be ϵ-free. If Σ_1 and Σ_2 are not disjoint, replace each symbol of Σ_2 by a new symbol, and follow the above operations by an ϵ-free homomorphism to restore the old symbols. □

11.4 ABSTRACT FAMILIES OF LANGUAGES

Many of the families of languages we have studied have closure properties that are not implied by the trio or full trio operations. Predominant among these are union, concatenation, and Kleene closure. For this reason, two other sets of closure properties have had their consequences heavily studied, and in fact were studied long before the trio and full trio. Define a class of languages to be an *abstract family of languages* (*AFL*) if it is a trio and also closed under union, concatenation, and positive closure (recall that L^+, the positive closure of L, is $\bigcup_{i=1}^{\infty} L^i$). Call a class of languages a *full AFL* if it is a full trio and closed under union, concatenation, and Kleene closure.

For example, we proved in Chapters 3 and 6 that the regular sets and context-free languages are full AFL's. The r.e. sets are also a full AFL, and we leave the proof as an exercise. The CSL's are an AFL, but not a full AFL, since they are not closed under general homomorphism (see Exercises 9.10 and 9.14).

We saw that the regular sets are the smallest full trio. They are also a full AFL and therefore the smallest full AFL. The ϵ-free regular sets are the smallest AFL, as well as the smallest trio.

The next theorem states that AFL's are closed under substitution into regular sets. That is, for each symbol of an alphabet, we associate a language from an AFL $\mathscr{C}$. Then replacing each symbol in each string in some regular set by the associated language yields a language in $\mathscr{C}$.

Theorem 11.5   Let $\mathscr{C}$ be an AFL that contains some language containing ϵ, and let $R \subseteq \Sigma^*$ be a regular set. Let s be a substitution defined by $s(a) = L_a$ for each a in Σ, where L_a is a member of $\mathscr{C}$. Then $s(R)$ is in $\mathscr{C}$.

Proof   The proof is by induction on the number of operators in a regular expression denoting R. If there are zero operators, then the regular expression must be one of $\varnothing$, ϵ, or a, for a in Σ. If it is a, then the result of the substitution is L_a, which is in $\mathscr{C}$. If the regular expression is $\varnothing$, the result of substitution is $\varnothing$, which is in $\mathscr{C}$ by Lemma 11.1. If the regular expression is ϵ, the result of the substitution is $\{\epsilon\}$. We claim $\{\epsilon\}$ is in $\mathscr{C}$, because some L containing ϵ is in $\mathscr{C}$, and $L \cap \{\epsilon\} = \{\epsilon\}$ is in $\mathscr{C}$ by closure under intersection with a regular set.

The induction step is easy. AFL's are closed under union and concatenation, and we can show closure under * easily, given L in $\mathscr{C}$ containing ϵ. That is, we already showed $\{\epsilon\}$ is in $\mathscr{C}$. If L_1 is any language in $\mathscr{C}$, then L_1^+ is in $\mathscr{C}$, so $L_1^* = L_1^+ \cup \{\epsilon\}$ is in $\mathscr{C}$. Therefore, the AFL $\mathscr{C}$ is closed under $\cup$, $\cdot$ and *, from which the inductive step follows. Thus $\mathscr{C}$ is closed under substitution into a regular set. $\square$

In general, AFL's are not closed under substitution of languages in the family into other languages in the family, although most of the common AFL's such as the CFL's, the recursive sets, and the r.e. sets are. However, any AFL closed under $\cap$ is closed under substitution. The proof is similar to that of Theorem 11.5 and is left as an exercise. We also leave as an exercise the fact that all AFL's, even those with no language containing ϵ, are closed under substitution into ϵ-free regular sets.

11.5 INDEPENDENCE OF THE AFL OPERATIONS

The definition of an AFL requires six closure properties. However, to show that a family of languages is an AFL, one need not show all six properties, since they are not independent. For example, any family of languages closed under $\cup$, $^+$, ϵ-free h, h^{-1} and $\cap R$ is necessarily closed under $\cdot$.† Similarly, $\cup$ follows from the other five operations and the same holds for $\cap R$. We shall only prove the dependence of $\cdot$.

Theorem 11.6 Any family of languages closed under $\cup$, $^+$, ϵ-free h, h^{-1}, and $\cap R$ is closed under $\cdot$.

Proof Let $\mathscr{C}$ be such a family of languages, and let $L_1 \subseteq \Sigma^*$ and $L_2 \subseteq \Sigma^*$ be in $\mathscr{C}$. We may assume without loss of generality that ϵ is not in L_1 or L_2. This assumption is justified by the fact that

$$L_1 L_2 = (L_1 - \{\epsilon\})(L_2 - \{\epsilon\}) \cup L_1' \cup L_2',$$

where L_1' is L_1 if ϵ is in L_2 and $\varnothing$ otherwise; L_2' is L_2 if ϵ is in L_1 and $\varnothing$ otherwise. As $\mathscr{C}$ is closed under union, if we can show that $(L_1 - \{\epsilon\})(L_2 - \{\epsilon\})$ is in $\mathscr{C}$, we shall have shown that $L_1 L_2$ is in $\mathscr{C}$.

Let a and b be symbols not in Σ. As $\mathscr{C}$ is a trio, Theorem 11.1 tells us $\mathscr{C}$ is closed under ϵ-free GSM mappings. Let M_1 be the GSM that prints a, followed by its first input symbol, then copies its input, and let M_2 be another GSM that prints b with its first input symbol, then copies its input. Then as ϵ is not in L_1 or L_2, $M_1(L_1) = aL_1$ and $M_2(L_2) = bL_2$, and both are in $\mathscr{C}$. By closure under $\cup$, $^+$, and $\cap R$,

$$(aL_1 \cup bL_2)^+ \cap a\Sigma^* b\Sigma^* = aL_1 bL_2$$

is in $\mathscr{C}$. Define g to be the homomorphism $g(a) = g(b) = \epsilon$, and $g(c) = c$ for all c in Σ. Then g is a 2-limited erasing, since L_1 and L_2 are assumed ϵ-free. By Lemma 11.2, $g(aL_1 bL_2) = L_1 L_2$ is in $\mathscr{C}$. $\square$

11.6 SUMMARY

We list in Fig. 11.3 some operations under which trios, full trios, AFL's and full AFL's are closed. The properties have all been proved in this chapter or are exercises. Recall that the regular sets, CFL's, and r.e. sets are full AFL's; the CSL's and recursive sets are AFL's. The DCFL's are not even trios, however.

Some other operations do not fit into the theory of trios and AFL's. In Fig. 11.4 we summarize the closure properties of six classes of languages under these operations. The question of whether the CSL's are closed under complementation is a long-standing open problem, and is equivalent to their closure under MIN.

---

† We use $\cap R$ for "intersection with a regular set," h for "homomorphism," and h^{-1} for "inverse homomorphism." The dot stands for concatenation.

	Trio	Full trio	AFL	Full AFL
$\cup$			✓	✓
·			✓	✓
+			✓	✓
*				✓
h^{-1}	✓	✓	✓	✓
ϵ-free h	✓	✓	✓	✓
h		✓		✓
$\cap R$	✓	✓	✓	✓
ϵ-free GSM mappings	✓	✓	✓	✓
GSM mappings		✓		✓
Inverse GSM mappings	✓	✓	✓	✓
Limited erasing	✓	✓	✓	✓
Quotient with regular set		✓		✓
INIT		✓		✓
Substitution into regular sets			✓	✓
Substitution by ϵ-free regular sets	✓	✓	✓	✓
Substitution by regular sets		✓		✓

Fig. 11.3 Summary of closure properties.

While this chapter has concerned itself with closure properties and not decision properties, we have reached a good point to summarize these properties as well, for the six classes of languages mentioned in Fig. 11.4. We show in Fig. 11.5 whether each of 10 important properties is decidable for the six classes. D means decidable, U means undecidable, T means trivially decidable (because the answer is always "yes"), and ? means the answer is not known. The results in Fig. 11.5 are proved in various chapters, chiefly Chapters 3, 6, 8, and 10.

	Regular sets	CFL's	DCFL's	CSL's	Recursive sets	r.e. sets
Complementation	✓		✓	?	✓	
Intersection	✓			✓	✓	✓
Substitution	✓	✓		✓		✓
MIN	✓		✓	?	✓	✓
MAX	✓		✓			
CYCLE	✓	✓		✓	✓	✓
Reversal	✓	✓		✓	✓	✓

Fig. 11.4 Some other closure properties.

Question	Regular sets	DCFL's	CFL's	CSL's	Recursive sets	r.e. sets
Is w in L?	D	D	D	D	D	U
Is $L = \varnothing$?	D	D	D	U	U	U
Is $L = \Sigma^*$?	D	D	U	U	U	U
Is $L_1 = L_2$?	D	?	U	U	U	U
Is $L_1 \subseteq L_2$?	D	U	U	U	U	U
Is $L_1 \cap L_2 = \varnothing$?	D	U	U	U	U	U
Is $L = R$, where R is a given regular set?	D	D	U	U	U	U
Is L regular?	T	D	U	U	U	U
Is the intersection of two languages a language of the same type?	T	U	U	T	T	T
Is the complement of a language also a language of the same type?	T	U	U	?	T	U

Fig. 11.5 Some decision properties.

EXERCISES

*S11.1   Show that the linear languages are a full trio but not an AFL.

11.2   Show that the ϵ-free regular sets are an AFL.

11.3   Show that a full trio is closed under INIT, SUB, and FIN, where

$$SUB(L) = \{x \mid wxy \text{ is in } L \text{ for some } w \text{ and } y\},$$

and

$$FIN(L) = \{x \mid wx \text{ is in } L \text{ for some } w\}.$$

11.4   Show that not every AFL is closed under *, h, INIT, SUB, FIN, quotient with a regular set or substitution by regular sets.

*11.5   Show that not every full trio is closed under $\cup$, $\cdot$, *, $^+$, or substitution into regular sets. [*Hint:* The linear languages suffice for all but union. (To prove that certain languages are not linear, use Exercise 6.11). To show nonclosure under union, find two full trios $\mathscr{C}_1$ and $\mathscr{C}_2$ containing languages L_1 and L_2, respectively, such that $L_1 \cup L_2$ is in neither $\mathscr{C}_1$ nor $\mathscr{C}_2$. Show that $\mathscr{C}_1 \cup \mathscr{C}_2$ is also a full trio.]

11.6   Prove each of the closure and nonclosure properties in Fig. 11.4 (some have been asked for in previous exercises or proved in previous theorems).

*11.7   The *interleaving* of two languages L_1 and L_2, denoted $IL(L_1, L_2)$, is

$$\{w_1 x_1 w_2 x_2 \cdots w_k x_k \mid k \text{ is arbitrary, } w_1 w_2 \cdots w_k \text{ is in } L_1 \text{ and } x_1 x_2 \cdots x_k \text{ is in } L_2\}.\dagger$$

Show that if $\mathscr{C}$ is any trio, L is in $\mathscr{C}$, and R is a regular set, then $IL(L, R)$ is in $\mathscr{C}$.

11.8   Are the following closed under IL?
a) regular sets   b) CFL's   c) CSL's   d) recursive sets   e) r.e. sets

11.9   An *A-transducer* is a GSM that may move (make output and change state) on ϵ-input. Show that every full trio is closed under A-transductions.

11.10   Find a GSM that maps a^i to the set $\{a^j b^k \mid i \le j + k \le 2i\}$ for all i.

*11.11   Show that any class of languages closed under $\cdot$, h, h^{-1}, and $\cap R$ is closed under union.

*11.12   Show that any class of languages closed under h, h^{-1}, $\cdot$, and $\cup$ is closed under $\cap R$.

**11.13   Give examples of classes of languages closed under
a) $\cup$, $\cdot$, ϵ-free h, h^{-1}, and $\cap R$, but not $^+$;
b) $\cup$, $\cdot$, $^+$, ϵ-free h, and $\cap R$, but not h^{-1};
c) $\cup$, $\cdot$, $^+$, h^{-1}, and $\cap R$, but not ϵ-free h.

*11.14   Show that an AFL is closed under complementation if and only if it is closed under MIN.

*11.15   A *scattered-context grammar*, $G = (V, T, P, S)$, has productions of the form $(A_1, \ldots, A_n) \to (\alpha_1, \ldots, \alpha_n)$, where each α_i is in $(V \cup T)^+$. If $(A_1, \ldots, A_n) \to (\alpha_1, \ldots, \alpha_n)$ is in P, then we write

$$\beta_1 A_1 \beta_2 A_2 \cdots \beta_n A_n \beta_{n+1} \Rightarrow \beta_1 \alpha_1 \beta_2 \alpha_2 \cdots \beta_n \alpha_n \beta_{n+1}.$$

† Note some w's and x's may be ϵ.

Let $\overset{*}{\Rightarrow}$ be the reflexive, transitive closure of $\Rightarrow$. The language generated by G is $\{x \mid x$ is in T^+ and $S \overset{*}{\Rightarrow} x\}$.

a) Prove that the scattered-context languages form an AFL.

b) What class of languages is generated by the scattered-context grammars if we allow productions with the α_i's possibly ϵ?

**11.16 An AFL $\mathscr{C}$ is said to be *principal* if there is a language L such that $\mathscr{C}$ is the least AFL containing L.

a) Do the CFL's form a principal AFL?

b) Prove that the least AFL containing $\{a^n b^n \mid n \geq 0\}$ is properly contained in the CFL's.

c) Let $\mathscr{C}_0, \mathscr{C}_1, \mathscr{C}_2, \ldots$ be an infinite sequence of AFL's such that $\mathscr{C}_{i-1} \subsetneqq \mathscr{C}_i$ for all $i > 0$. Prove that the union of the $\mathscr{C}_i$'s forms an AFL that is not principal.

d) Give an example of a nonprincipal AFL.

*11.17 Show that if an AFL is closed under intersection, then it is closed under substitution.

Solutions to Selected Exercises

11.1 To prove that the linear languages are closed under homomorphism, let G be a linear grammar and h a homomorphism. If each production $A \rightarrow wBx$ or $A \rightarrow y$ is replaced by $A \rightarrow h(w)Bh(x)$ or $A \rightarrow h(y)$, respectively, then the resulting grammar generates $h(L(G))$. To show closure under h^{-1} and $\cap R$, we could use machine-based proofs analogous to the proofs for CFL's, since by Exercise 6.13(a), the linear languages are characterized by one-turn PDA's. We shall instead give grammar-based proofs.

Let $G = (V, T, P, S)$ be a linear CFG, and $M = (Q, T, \delta, q_0, F)$ a DFA. Construct linear grammar $G' = (V', T, P', S')$ generating $L(G) \cap L(M)$. Let $V' = \{[qAp] \mid q$ and p are in Q and A in $V\} \cup \{S'\}$. Then define P' to have productions

1) $S' \rightarrow [q_0 Sp]$ for all p in F,

2) $[qAp] \rightarrow w[rBs]x$ whenever $A \rightarrow wBx$ is in P, $\delta(q, w) = r$ and $\delta(s, x) = p$, and

3) $[qAp] \rightarrow y$ whenever $A \rightarrow y$ is in P and $\delta(q, y) = p$.

An easy induction on derivation length shows that $[qAp] \overset{*}{\underset{G'}{\Rightarrow}} w$ if and only if $A \overset{*}{\underset{G}{\Rightarrow}} w$ and $\delta(q, w) = p$. Thus $S' \overset{*}{\underset{G'}{\Rightarrow}} w$ if and only if $S \overset{*}{\underset{G}{\Rightarrow}} w$ and $\delta(q_0, w)$ is a final state. Hence $L(G') = L(G) \cap L(M)$.

Now, let $G = (V, T, P, S)$ be a linear grammar and $h: \Sigma^* \rightarrow T^*$ a homomorphism. Suppose k is such that for all a in Σ, $|h(a)| \leq k$, and if $A \rightarrow wBx$ or $A \rightarrow w$ is in P, then $|w| \leq k$ and $|x| \leq k$. Let $G'' = (V'', \Sigma, P'', [S])$, where V'' consists of all symbols $[wAx]$ such that A is in V, and w and x in T^* are each of length at most $2k - 1$. Also in V'' are symbols $[y]$, where $|y| \leq 3k - 1$. Intuitively G'' simulates a derivation of G in its variable until the string of terminals either to the right or to the left of the variable of G is of length at least k. Then G'' produces a terminal a on the right or left and deletes $h(a)$ from what is stored in the variable.

The productions of P'' are:

1) If $A \rightarrow w_1 B x_1$ is in P, then for all w_2 and x_2 of length at most $k - 1$, $[w_2 A x_2] \rightarrow [w_2 w_1 B x_1 x_2]$ is in P''. If $A \rightarrow y$ is in P, then $[w_2 A x_2] \rightarrow [w_2 y x_2]$ is in P''.

2) For a in Σ,

$$[h(a)w_1 A x_1] \rightarrow a[w_1 A x_1], \qquad [w_1 A x_1 h(a)] \rightarrow [w_1 A x_1]a, \qquad \text{and} \qquad [h(a)y] \rightarrow a[y].$$

3) $[\epsilon] \rightarrow \epsilon$.

It follows by induction on derivation length that

$$[S] \overset{*}{\underset{G''}{\Rightarrow}} w_1[w_2 A x_2]x_1$$

if and only if

$$S \overset{*}{\underset{G}{\Rightarrow}} h(w_1)w_2 A x_2 h(x_1).$$

Thus $[S] \overset{*}{\underset{G''}{\Rightarrow}} v$ if and only if $S \overset{*}{\underset{G}{\Rightarrow}} h(v)$, and hence $L(G'') = h^{-1}(L(G))$.

To show that the linear languages are not an AFL, we show they are not closed under concatenation. Surely $\{a^i b^i \mid i \geq 1\}$ and $\{c^j d^j \mid j \geq 1\}$ are linear languages, but their concatenation is not, by Exercise 6.12.

BIBLIOGRAPHIC NOTES

The study of abstract families of languages was initiated by Ginsburg and Greibach [1969], who proved Theorems 11.1 through 11.5 and Lemma 11.1. The central importance of the trio in this theory is pointed out by Ginsburg [1975]. Theorem 11.6 on independence of the operators appears in Greibach and Hopcroft [1969]; a solution to Exercise 11.13 can also be found there. The notion of limited erasing is also due to Greibach and Hopcroft [1969]. That AFL's closed under intersection are closed under substitution was first proved by Ginsburg and Hopcroft [1970]. An enormous amount of literature concerns itself with abstract families of languages; we mention only Ginsburg and Greibach [1970], dealing with principal AFL's (Exercise 11.16), and Greibach [1970], who attempts to work substitution into the theory. A summary and additional references can be found in Ginsburg [1975].

The theory of families of languages has, from its inception, been connected with the theory of automata. Ginsburg and Greibach [1969] show that a family of languages is a full AFL if and only if it is defined by a family of nondeterministic automata with a one-way input. Of course, the notion of a "family of automata" must be suitably defined, but, roughly, each such family is characterized by a set of rules whereby it may access or update its storage. The "if" part was proved independently in Hopcroft and Ullman [1967b]. Chandler [1969] characterized families of deterministic automata with a one-way input, in terms of closure properties, and Aho and Ullman [1970] did the same for deterministic automata with a two-way input. Curiously, no characterization for two-way nondeterministic automata is known.

There have also been attempts to codify a theory of grammars, chiefly subfamilies of the CFG's. Gabriellian and Ginsburg [1974] and Cremers and Ginsburg [1975] wrote the basic papers in this area.

The GSM was defined by Ginsburg [1962], and the study of GSM mappings and their properties commenced with Ginsburg and Rose [1963b]. An important unresolved issue concerns testing for equivalence of two sequential transducers. That equivalence is decidable for Moore machines (and hence for Mealy machines, which GSM's generalize) was known since Moore [1956]. Griffiths [1968] showed that the equivalence problem for ϵ-free GSM's was undecidable, while Bird [1973] gave a decision algorithm for the equivalence of two-tape automata, which are more general than deterministic GSM's.

Scattered-context grammars (Exercise 11.15) are discussed in Greibach and Hopcroft [1969].

12

COMPUTATIONAL
COMPLEXITY
THEORY

Language theory classifies sets by their structural complexity. Thus regular sets are regarded as "simpler" than CFL's, because the finite automaton has less complex structure than a PDA. Another classification, called computational complexity, is based on the amount of time, space, or other resource needed to recognize a language on some universal computing device, such as a Turing machine.

Although computational complexity is primarily concerned with time and space, there are many other possible measures, such as the number of reversals in the direction of travel of the tape head on a single-tape TM. In fact one can define a complexity measure abstractly and prove many of the results in a more general setting. We choose to present the results for the specific examples of time and space, since this approach renders the proofs more intuitive. In Section 12.7 we briefly outline the more abstract approach.

12.1 DEFINITIONS

Space complexity

Consider the off-line Turing machine M of Fig. 12.1. M has a read-only input tape with endmarkers and k semi-infinite storage tapes. If for every input word of length n, M scans at most $S(n)$ cells on any storage tape, then M is said to be an $S(n)$ *space-bounded Turing machine*, or *of space complexity* $S(n)$. The language recognized by M is also said to be of space complexity $S(n)$.

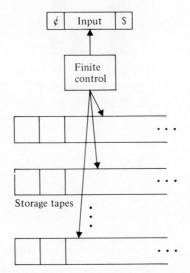

Fig. 12.1   Multitape Turing machine with read-only input.

Note that the Turing machine cannot rewrite on the input and that only the length of the storage tapes used counts in computing the tape bound. This restriction enables us to consider tape bounds of less than linear growth. If the TM could rewrite on the input tape, then the length of the input would have to be included in calculating the space bound. Thus no space bound could be less than linear.

Time complexity

Consider the multitape TM M of Fig. 12.2. The TM has k two-way infinite tapes, one of which contains the input. All tapes, including the input tape, may be written

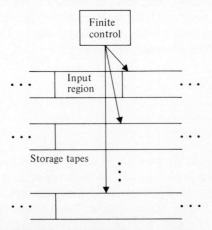

Fig. 12.2   Multitape Turing machine.

upon. If for every input word of length n, M makes at most $T(n)$ moves before halting, then M is said to be a $T(n)$ *time-bounded Turing machine*, or *of time complexity* $T(n)$. The language recognized by M is said to be of time complexity $T(n)$.

The two different models for time and space complexity were selected with an eye toward making certain proofs simple, and some variation in the models is feasible. For example, if $S(n) \geq n$, then we can use the single tape TM as our model without changing the class of languages accepted in space $S(n)$. We cannot, however, when discussing time complexity, use the single tape TM, or TM's with any fixed number of tapes, without possibly losing some languages from the class of languages accepted in time $T(n)$.

Example 12.1 Consider the language

$$L = \{wcw^R \,|\, w \text{ in } (0 + 1)^*\}.$$

Language L is of time complexity $n + 1$, since there is a Turing machine M_1, with two tapes, that copies the input to the left of the c onto the second tape. Then, when a c is found, M_1 moves its second tape head to the left, through the string it has just copied, and simultaneously continues to move its input tape head to the right. The symbols under the two heads are compared as the heads move. If all pairs of symbols match and if, in addition, the number of symbols to the right and left of the lone c are equal, then M_1 accepts. It is easy to see that M_1 makes at most $n + 1$ moves if the input is of length n.

There is another Turing machine, M_2, of space complexity $\log_2 n$ accepting L. M_2 uses two storage tapes for binary counters. First, the input is checked to see that only one c appears, and that there are equal numbers of symbols to the right and left of the c. Next the words on the right and left are compared symbol by symbol, using the counters to find corresponding symbols. If they disagree, M_2 halts without accepting. If all symbols match, M_2 accepts.

Special assumptions about time and space complexity functions

It should be obvious that every TM uses at least one cell on all inputs, so if $S(n)$ is a space complexity measure, we may assume $S(n) \geq 1$ for all n. We make the useful assumption that when we talk of "space complexity $S(n)$," we really mean max $(1, \lceil S(n) \rceil)$. For example, in Example 12.1, we said that TM M_2 was of "space complexity $\log_2 n$." This makes no sense for $n = 0$ or 1, unless one accepts that "$\log_2 n$" is shorthand for max $(1, \lceil \log_2 n \rceil)$.

Similarly, it is reasonable to assume that any time complexity function $T(n)$ is at least $n + 1$, for this is the time needed just to read the input and verify that the end has been reached by reading the first blank.† We thus make the convention

---

† Note, however, that there are TM's that accept or reject without reading all their input. We choose to eliminate them from consideration.

that "time complexity $T(n)$" means max $(n + 1, \lceil T(n) \rceil)$. For example, the value of time complexity $n \log_2 n$ at $n = 1$ is 2, not 0, and at $n = 2$, its value is 3.

Nondeterministic time and space complexity

The concepts of time- and space-bounded Turing machines apply equally well to nondeterministic machines. A nondeterministic TM is of time complexity $T(n)$ if no sequence of choices of move causes the machine to make more than $T(n)$ moves. It is of space complexity $S(n)$ if no sequence of choices enables it to scan more than $S(n)$ cells on any storage tape.

Complexity classes

The family of languages of space complexity $S(n)$ is denoted by DSPACE($S(n)$); the languages of nondeterministic space complexity $S(n)$ are collectively called NSPACE($S(n)$). The family of languages of time complexity $T(n)$ is denoted DTIME($T(n)$) and that of nondeterministic time complexity $T(n)$ is denoted NTIME($T(n)$). All these families of languages are called *complexity classes*. For example, language L of Example 12.1 is in DTIME(n)† and in DSPACE($\log_2 n$). L is therefore also in NTIME(n) and NSPACE($\log_2 n$) as well as larger classes such as DTIME(n^2) or NSPACE($\sqrt{n}$).

12.2   LINEAR SPEED-UP, TAPE COMPRESSION, AND REDUCTIONS IN THE NUMBER OF TAPES

Since the number of states and the tape alphabet size of a Turing machine can be arbitrarily large, the amount of space needed to recognize a set can always be compressed by a constant factor. This is achieved by encoding several tape symbols into one. Similarly one can speed up a computation by a constant factor. Thus in complexity results it is the functional rate of growth (e.g., linear, quadratic, exponential) that is important, and constant factors may be ignored. For example, we shall talk about complexity $\log n$ without specifying the base of logarithms, since $\log_b n$ and $\log_c n$ differ by a constant factor, namely $\log_b c$. In this section we establish the basic facts concerning linear speed up and compression as well as considering the effect of the number of tapes on complexity.

Tape compression

Theorem 12.1   If L is accepted by an $S(n)$ space-bounded Turing machine with k storage tapes, then for any $c > 0$, L is accepted by a $cS(n)$ space-bounded TM.‡

---

† Recall that n really means max $(n + 1, n) = n + 1$ for time complexity.
‡ Note that by our convention, $cS(n)$ is regarded as max $(1, \lceil cS(n) \rceil)$.

Proof Let M_1 be an $S(n)$ tape-bounded off-line Turing machine accepting L. The proof turns on constructing a new Turing machine M_2 that simulates M_1, where for some constant r, each storage tape cell of M_2 holds a symbol representing the contents of r adjacent cells of the corresponding tape of M_1. The finite control of M_2 can keep track of which of the cells of M_1, among those represented, is actually scanned by M_1.

Detailed construction of the rules of M_2 from the rules of M_1 are left to the reader. Let r be such that $rc \geq 2$. M_2 can simulate M_1 using no more than $\lceil S(n)/r \rceil$ cells on any tape. If $S(n) \geq r$, this number is no more than $cS(n)$. If $S(n) < r$, then M_2 can store in one cell the contents of any tape. Thus, M_2 uses only one cell in the latter case. $\qquad\square$

Corollary If L is in NSPACE($S(n)$), then L is in NSPACE($cS(n)$), where c is any constant greater than zero.

Proof If M_1 above is nondeterministic, let M_2 be nondeterministic in the above construction. $\qquad\square$

Reduction in the number of tapes for space complexity classes

Theorem 12.2 If a language L is accepted by an $S(n)$ space-bounded TM with k storage tapes, it is accepted by an $S(n)$ space-bounded TM with a single storage tape.

Proof Let M_1 be an $S(n)$ space-bounded TM with k storage tapes, accepting L. We may construct a new TM M_2 with one storage tape, which simulates the storage tapes of M_1 on k tracks. The technique was used in Theorem 7.2. M_2 uses no more than $S(n)$ cells. $\qquad\square$

From now on we assume that any $S(n)$ space-bounded TM has but one storage tape, and if $S(n) \geq n$, then it is a single-tape TM, rather than an off-line TM with one storage tape and one input tape.

Linear speed up

Before considering time bounds, let us introduce the following notation. Let $f(n)$ be a function of n. The expression $\sup_{n \to \infty} f(n)$ is taken to be the limit as $n \to \infty$ of the least upper bound of $f(n), f(n+1), f(n+2), \ldots$ Likewise, $\inf_{n \to \infty} f(n)$ is the limit as $n \to \infty$ of the greatest lower bound of $f(n), f(n+1), f(n+2), \ldots$ If $f(n)$ converges to a limit as $n \to \infty$, then that limit is both $\inf_{n \to \infty} f(n)$ and $\sup_{n \to \infty} f(n)$.

Example 12.2 Let $f(n) = 1/n$ for n even, and $f(n) = n$ for n odd. The least upper bound of $f(n), f(n+1), \ldots$ is clearly ∞ for any n, because of the terms for odd n. Hence $\sup_{n \to \infty} f(n) = \infty$. However, because of the terms with n even, it is also true that $\inf_{n \to \infty} f(n) = 0$.

For another example, suppose $f(n) = n/(n + 1)$. Then the least upper bound of $n/(n + 1)$, $(n + 1)/(n + 2)$, ... is 1 for any n. Thus

$$\sup_{n \to \infty} \frac{n}{n + 1} = 1.$$

The greatest lower bound of $n/(n + 1)$, $(n + 1)/(n + 2)$, ... is $n/(n + 1)$ and $\lim_{n \to \infty} n/(n + 1) = 1$, so $\inf_{n \to \infty} n/(n + 1) = 1$ as well.

Theorem 12.3 If L is accepted by a k-tape $T(n)$ time-bounded Turing machine M_1, then L is accepted by a k-tape $cT(n)$ time-bounded TM M_2 for any $c > 0$, provided that $k > 1$ and $\inf_{n \to \infty} T(n)/n = \infty$.

Proof A TM M_2 can be constructed to simulate M_1 in the following manner. First M_2 copies the input onto a storage tape, encoding m symbols into one. (The value of m will be determined later.) From this point on, M_2 uses this storage tape as the input tape and uses the old input tape as a storage tape. M_2 will encode the contents of M_1's storage tapes by combining m symbols into one. During the course of the simulation, M_2 simulates a large number of moves of M_1 in one *basic step* consisting of eight moves of M_2. Call the cells currently scanned by each of M_2's heads the *home cells*. The finite control of M_2 records, for each tape, which of the m symbols of M_1 represented by each home cell is scanned by the corresponding head of M_2.

To begin a basic step, M_2 moves each head to the left once, to the right twice, and to the left once, recording the symbols to the left and right of the home cells in its finite control. Four moves of M_2 are required, after which M_2 has returned to its home cells.

Next, M_2 determines the contents of all of M_1's tape cells represented by the home cells and their left and right neighbors at the time when some tape head of M_1 first leaves the region represented by the home cell and its left and right neighbors. (Note that this calculation by M_2 takes no time. It is built into the transition rules of M_2.) If M_1 accepts before some tape head leaves the represented region, M_2 accepts. If M_1 halts, M_2 halts. Otherwise M_2 then visits, on each tape, the two neighbors of the home cell, changing these symbols and that of the home cell if necessary. M_2 positions each of its heads at the cell that represents the symbol that M_1's corresponding head is scanning at the end of the moves simulated. At most four moves of M_2 are needed.

It takes at least m moves for M_1 to move a head out of the region represented by a home cell and its neighbors. Thus, in eight moves, M_2 has simulated at least m moves of M_1. Choose m such that $cm \geq 16$.

If M_1 makes $T(n)$ moves, then M_2 simulates these in at most $8\lceil T(n)/m \rceil$ moves. Also, M_2 must copy and encode its input (m cells to one), then return the head of the simulated input tape to the left end. This takes $n + \lceil n/m \rceil$ moves, for a total of

$$n + \lceil n/m \rceil + 8\lceil T(n)/m \rceil \tag{12.1}$$

moves. As $\lceil x \rceil < x + 1$ for any x, (12.1) is upper bounded by

$$n + n/m + 8T(n)/m + 2. \tag{12.2}$$

Now we have assumed that $\inf_{n \to \infty} T(n)/n = \infty$, so for any constant d there is an n_d such that for all $n \geq n_d$, $T(n)/n \geq d$, or put another way, $n \leq T(n)/d$. Thus whenever $n \geq 2$ (so $n + 2 \leq 2n$) and $n \geq n_d$, (12.2) is bounded above by

$$T(n) \left[\frac{8}{m} + \frac{2}{d} + \frac{1}{md} \right]. \tag{12.3}$$

We have not yet specified d. Remembering that m was chosen so that $cm \geq 16$, choose $d = m/4 + \frac{1}{8}$, and substitute $16/c$ for m in (12.3). Then for all $n \geq \max(2, n_d)$ the number of moves made by M_2 does not exceed $cT(n)$.

To recognize the finite number of words of length less than the maximum of 2 and n_d, M_2 uses its finite control only, taking $n + 1$ moves to read its input and reach the blank marking the end of the input. Thus the time complexity of M_2 is $cT(n)$. Recall that for time complexity, $cT(n)$ stands for $\max(n + 1, \lceil cT(n) \rceil)$. □

Corollary If $\inf_{n \to \infty} T(n)/n = \infty$ and $c > 0$, then

$$\text{DTIME}(T(n)) = \text{DTIME}(cT(n)).$$

Proof Theorem 12.3 is a direct proof for any language L accepted by a DTM with 2 or more tapes in time $T(n)$. Clearly if L is accepted by a 1-tape TM, it is accepted by a 2-tape TM of the same time complexity. □

Theorem 12.3 does not apply if $T(n)$ is a constant multiple of n, as then $\inf_{n \to \infty} T(n)/n$ is a constant, not infinity. However, the construction of Theorem 12.3, with a more careful analysis of the time bound of M_2 shows the following.

Theorem 12.4 If L is accepted by a k-tape cn time-bounded TM, for $k > 1$ and for some constant c, then for every $\epsilon > 0$, L is accepted by a k-tape $(1 + \epsilon)n$ time-bounded TM.

Proof Pick $m = 1/16\epsilon$ in the proof of Theorem 12.3. □

Corollary If $T(n) = cn$ for some $c > 1$, then $\text{DTIME}(T(n)) = \text{DTIME}((1 + \epsilon)n)$ for any $\epsilon > 0$.

Corollary (of Theorems 12.3 and 12.4)

a) If $\inf_{n \to \infty} T(n)/n = \infty$, then $\text{NTIME}(T(n)) = \text{NTIME}(cT(n))$ for any $c > 0$.

b) If $T(n) = cn$ for some constant c, then $\text{NTIME}(T(n)) = \text{NTIME}((1 + \epsilon)n)$, for any $\epsilon > 0$.

Proof The proofs are analogous to Theorems 12.3 and 12.4. □

Reduction in the number of tapes for time complexity classes

Now let us see what happens to time complexity when we restrict ourselves to one tape. A language like $L = \{wcw^R \mid w \text{ is in } (\mathbf{a} + \mathbf{b})^*\}$ can be recognized in linear time on a two-tape machine, as we saw in Example 12.1. However, on a one-tape machine, L requires time cn^2 for some $c > 0$. (The exercises give hints how this may be proved.) Thus permitting only one tape can square the time necessary to recognize a language. That this is the worst that can happen is expressed in the next theorem.

Theorem 12.5 If L is in DTIME($T(n)$), then L is accepted in time $T^2(n)$ by a one-tape TM.

Proof In the construction of Theorem 7.2, going from a multitape TM to a one-tape TM, M_2 uses at most $6T^2(n)$ steps to simulate $T(n)$ steps of M_1. By Theorem 12.3, we may speed up M_1 to run in time $T(n)/\sqrt{6}$. Then M_2 is a one-tape TM accepting L in $T^2(n)$ steps. □

Corollary If L is in NTIME($T(n)$), then L is accepted by a one-tape NTM of nondeterministic time complexity $T^2(n)$.

Proof Analogous to the proof of the theorem. □

If we restrict ourselves to two tapes, the time loss is considerably less than if we restrict ourselves to one tape, as the next theorem shows.

Theorem 12.6 If L is accepted by a k-tape $T(n)$ time-bounded Turing machine M_1, then L is accepted by a two-storage tape TM M_2 in time $T(n) \log T(n)$.

Proof The first storage tape of M_2 will have two tracks for each storage tape of M_1. For convenience, we focus on two tracks corresponding to a particular tape of M_1. The other tapes of M_1 are simulated in exactly the same way. The second tape of M_2 is used only for scratch, to transport blocks of data on tape 1.

One particular cell of tape 1, known as B_0, will hold the storage symbols scanned by each of the heads of M_1. Rather than moving head markers, M_2 will transport data across B_0 in the direction opposite to that of the motion of the head of M_1 being simulated. Thus M_2 can simulate each move of M_1 by looking only at B_0. To the right of cell B_0 will be blocks $B_1, B_2, \ldots$ of exponentially increasing length; that is, B_i is of length 2^{i-1}. Likewise, to the left of B_0 are blocks B_{-1}, $B_{-2}, \ldots$, with B_{-i} having length 2^{i-1}. The markers between blocks are assumed to exist, although they will not actually appear until the block is used.

Let a_0 denote the contents of the cell initially scanned by this tape head of M_1. The contents of the cells to the right of this cell are $a_1, a_2, \ldots$, and those to the left, $a_{-1}, a_{-2}, \ldots$ The values of the a_i's may change when they enter B_0; it is not their values, but their positions on the tracks of tape 1 of M_2, that is important. Initially the upper track of M_2 for the tape of M_1 in question is assumed to be empty, while the lower track is assumed to hold $\ldots, a_{-2}, a_{-1}, a_0, a_1, a_2, \ldots$ These are placed in blocks $\ldots, B_{-2}, B_{-1}, B_0, B_1, B_2, \ldots$, as shown in Fig. 12.3.

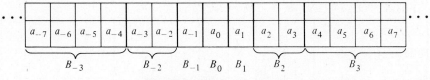

Fig. 12.3 Blocks on tape 1.

As mentioned previously, data will be shifted across B_0 and perhaps changed as it passes through. After the simulation of each move of M_1, the following will hold.

1) For any $i > 0$, either B_i is full (both tracks) and B_{-i} is empty, or B_i is empty and B_{-i} is full, or the bottom tracks of both B_i and B_{-i} are full, while the upper tracks are empty.

2) The contents of any B_i or B_{-i} represent consecutive cells on the tape of M_1 represented. For $i > 0$, the upper track represents cells to the left of those of the lower track; for $i < 0$, the upper track represents cells to the right of those of the lower track.

3) For $i < j$, B_i represents cells to the left of those of B_j.

4) B_0 always has only its lower track filled, and its upper track is specially marked.

To see how data is transferred, imagine that the tape head of M_1 in question moves to the left. Then M_2 must shift the corresponding data right. To do so, M_2 moves the head of tape 1 from B_0, where it rests, and goes to the right until it finds the first block, say B_i, that does not have both tracks full. Then M_2 copies all the data of $B_0, B_1, \ldots, B_{i-1}$ onto tape 2 and stores it in the lower track of $B_1, B_2, \ldots,$ B_{i-1} plus the lower track of B_i, assuming that the lower track of B_i is not already filled. If the lower track of B_i is already filled, the upper track of B_i is used instead. In either case, there is just enough room to distribute the data. Also note the data can be picked up and stored in its new location in time proportional to the length of B_i.

Next, in time proportional to the length of B_i, T_1 can find B_{-i} (using tape 2 to measure the distance from B_i to B_0 makes this easy). If B_{-i} is completely full, T_1 picks up the upper track of B_{-i} and stores it on tape 2. If B_{-i} is half full, the lower track is put on tape 2. In either case, what has been copied to tape 2 is next copied to the lower tracks of $B_{-(i-1)}, B_{-(i-2)}, \ldots, B_0$. (By Rule 1, these tracks have to be empty, since $B_1, B_2, \ldots, B_{i-1}$ were full.) Again, note that there is just enough room to store the data, and all the above operations can be carried out in time proportional to the length of B_i. Also note that the data can be distributed in a manner that satisfies rules (1), (2), and (3), above.

We call all that we have described above a B_i-*operation*. The case in which the head of M_1 moves to the right is analogous. The successive contents of the blocks as M_1 moves its tape head in question five cells to the left are shown in Fig. 12.4.

	B_{-3}			B_{-2}		B_{-1}	B_0	B_1	B_2		B_3				
a_{-7}	a_{-6}	a_{-5}	a_{-4}	a_{-3}	a_{-2}	a_{-1}	a_0	a_1	a_2	a_3	a_4	a_5	a_6	a_7	
							a_0								
a_{-7}	a_{-6}	a_{-5}	a_{-4}	a_{-3}	a_{-2}		a_{-1}	a_1	a_2	a_3	a_4	a_5	a_6	a_7	
							a_0	a_1							
a_{-7}	a_{-6}	a_{-5}	a_{-4}			a_{-3}	a_{-2}	a_{-1}	a_2	a_3	a_4	a_5	a_6	a_7	
						a_{-2}	a_0	a_1							
a_{-7}	a_{-6}	a_{-5}	a_{-4}			a_{-3}	a_{-1}	a_2	a_3		a_4	a_5	a_6	a_7	
											a_0	a_1	a_2	a_3	
				a_{-7}	a_{-6}	a_{-5}	a_{-4}	a_{-3}	a_{-2}	a_{-1}	a_4	a_5	a_6	a_7	
						a_{-4}					a_0	a_1	a_2	a_3	
				a_{-7}	a_{-6}		a_{-5}	a_{-3}	a_{-2}	a_{-1}	a_4	a_5	a_6	a_7	

Fig. 12.4   Contents of blocks of M_1.

We note that for each tape of M_1, M_2 must perform a B_i-operation at most once per 2^{i-1} moves of M_1, since it takes this long for $B_1, B_2, \ldots, B_{i-1}$, which are half empty after a B_i-operation, to fill. Also, a B_i-operation cannot be performed for the first time until the 2^{i-1}th move of M_1. Hence, if M_1 operates in time $T(n)$, M_2 will perform only B_i-operations, for those i such that $i \leq \log_2 T(n) + 1$.

We have seen that there is a constant m, such that M_2 uses at most $m2^i$ moves to perform a B_i-operation. If M_1 makes $T(n)$ moves, M_2 makes at most

$$T_1(n) = \sum_{i=1}^{\log_2 T(n)+1} m2^i \, \frac{T(n)}{2^{i-1}} \tag{12.4}$$

moves when simulating one tape of M_1.

From (12.4), we obtain

$$T_1(n) = 2mT(n)\lceil \log_2 T(n) + 1 \rceil, \tag{12.5}$$

and from (12.5),

$$T_1(n) < 4mT(n) \log_2 T(n).$$

The reader should be able to see that M_2 operates in time proportional to $T_1(n)$ even when M_1 makes moves using different storage tapes rather than only the one upon which we have concentrated. By Theorem 12.3, we can modify M_2 to run in no more than $T(n) \log_2 T(n)$ steps. □

Corollary If L is accepted by a k-tape NTM of time complexity $T(n)$, then L is accepted by a two-tape NTM of time complexity $T(n) \log T(n)$.

Proof Analogous to the proof of the theorem. □

12.3 HIERARCHY THEOREMS

Intuitively, given more time or space, we should be able to recognize more languages or compute more functions. However, the linear speed-up and compression theorems tell us that we have to increase the available space or time by more than a constant factor. But what if we multiply the space or time by a slowly growing function such as log log n? Is it possible that we cannot then recognize any new languages? Is there a time or space bound $f(n)$ such that every recursive language is in DTIME($f(n)$), or perhaps in DSPACE($f(n)$)?

The answer to the last question is "no," as we shall prove in the next theorem. However, the answer to the first question depends on whether or not we start with a "well-behaved" function. In this section we shall give suitable definitions of "well behaved" and show that for well-behaved functions, small amounts of extra time and space do add to our ability to compute.

In Section 12.6 we shall consider arbitrary total recursive functions and the complexity classes they define. There we shall see that strange behavior is exhibited. There are "gaps" in any complexity hierarchy, that is, there exists a function $T(n)$ for which DTIME($T^2(n)$) = DTIME($T(n)$), and in general, for any total recursive function f there is a time complexity $T_f(n)$ for which DTIME($T_f(n)$) = DTIME($f(T_f(n))$). Similar statements hold for space, and indeed for any reasonable measure of computational complexity. We shall also see that there are languages L for which no "best" recognizer exists; rather there is an infinite sequence of TM's recognizing L, each of which runs much faster than the previous one.

Theorem 12.7 Given any total recursive time-bound (space-bound) $T(n)$, there is a recursive language L not in DTIME($T(n)$) or DSPACE($T(n)$), respectively.

Proof We shall show the result for time; the argument for space is analogous. The argument is basically a diagonalization. Since $T(n)$ is total recursive, there is a halting TM M that computes it. We construct $\hat{M}$ to accept a language $L \subseteq (0 + 1)^*$ that is recursive but not in DTIME($T(n)$). Let x_i be the ith string in the canonical ordering of $(0 + 1)^*$. In Chapter 8, we ordered single-tape TM's with tape alphabet $\{0, 1, B\}$. We can similarly order multitape TM's with arbitrary tape alphabets by replacing their transition functions by binary strings. The only substantial point is that the names of the tape symbols, like those of states, don't matter, so we may assume that all TM's whose input alphabet is $\{0, 1\}$ have tape alphabet $0, 1, B, X_4, X_5, \ldots$ up to some finite X_m, then encode 0, 1, and B by 0, 00, and 000 and encode X_i by 0^i, $i \geq 4$. We also permit an arbitrary number of 1's in front of the code for M to represent M as well, so M has arbitrarily long encodings.

We are thus free to talk about M_i, the ith multitape TM. Now define $L = \{x_i \mid M_i \text{ does not accept } x_i \text{ within } T(|x_i|) \text{ moves}\}$. We claim L is recursive. To recognize L, execute the following algorithm, which can surely be implemented on a Turing machine. Given input w of length n, simulate M on n to compute $T(n)$. Then determine i such that $w = x_i$. The integer i written in binary is the transition function of some multitape TM M_i (if i in binary is of improper form for a transition function, then M_i has no moves). Simulate M_i on w for $T(n)$ moves, accepting if M_i either halts without accepting or runs for more than $T(n)$ moves and does not accept.

To see that L is not in DTIME($T(n)$), suppose $L = L(M_i)$, and M_i is $T(n)$ time bounded. Is x_i in L? If so, M_i accepts x_i within $T(n)$ steps, where $n = |x_i|$. Thus by definition of L, x_i is not in L, a contradiction. If x_i is not in L, then M_i does not accept x_i, so by definition of L, x_i is in L, again a contradiction. Both assumptions lead to contradictions, so the supposition that M_i is $T(n)$ time bounded must be false. ☐

If $T'(n) \geq T(n)$ for all n, it follows immediately from the definition of a time complexity class that DTIME($T(n)$) $\subseteq$ DTIME($T'(n)$). If $T(n)$ is a total recursive function, Theorem 12.7 implies there exists a recursive set L not in DTIME($T(n)$). Let $\hat{T}(n)$ be the running time of some Turing machine accepting L and let $T'(n) = \max\{T(n), \hat{T}(n)\}$. Then DTIME($T(n)$) $\subsetneqq$ DTIME($T'(n)$), since L is in the latter but not the former. Thus we know that there is an infinite hierarchy of deterministic time complexity classes. A similar result holds for deterministic space complexity classes, and for nondeterministic time and space classes.

Theorem 12.7 demonstrates that for any recursive time or space complexity $f(n)$, there is an $f'(n)$ such that some language is in the complexity class defined by $f'(n)$ but not $f(n)$. We now show that for a well-behaved function $f(n)$ only a slight increase in the growth rate of $f(n)$ is required to yield a new complexity class. Theorems 12.8 and 12.9 are concerned with the increase needed in order to obtain a new deterministic complexity class. These theorems are used later to establish lower bounds on the complexity of various problems. Similar results for nondeterministic classes are very much more difficult; we shall touch on a dense hierarchy for nondeterministic space in Section 12.5.

A space hierarchy

We now introduce our notion of a "well-behaved" space complexity function. A function $S(n)$ is said to be *space constructible* if there is some Turing machine M that is $S(n)$ space bounded, and for each n, there is some input of length n on which M actually uses $S(n)$ tape cells. The set of space-constructible functions includes log n, n^k, 2^n, and $n!$. If $S_1(n)$ and $S_2(n)$ are space constructible, then so are $S_1(n)S_2(n)$, $2^{S_1(n)}$, and $S_1(n)^{S_2(n)}$. Thus the set of space-constructible functions is very rich.

Note that M above need not use $S(n)$ space on all inputs of length n, just on some one input of that length. If for all n, M in fact uses exactly $S(n)$ cells on any input of length n, then we say $S(n)$ is *fully space constructible*. Any space-constructible $S(n) \geq n$ is fully space constructible (exercise).

In order to simplify the next result we prove the following lemma.

Lemma 12.1 If L is accepted by an $S(n) \geq \log_2 n$ space-bounded TM, then L is accepted by an $S(n)$ space-bounded TM that halts on all inputs.

Proof Let M be an $S(n)$ space-bounded off-line Turing machine with s states and t tape symbols accepting L. If M accepts, it does so by a sequence of at most $(n + 2)sS(n)t^{S(n)}$ moves, since otherwise some ID repeats. That is, there are $n + 2$ input head positions, s states, $S(n)$ tape head positions, and $t^{S(n)}$ storage tape contents. If an additional track is added as a move counter, M can shut itself off after $(4st)^{S(n)} \geq (n + 2)sS(n)t^{S(n)}$ moves. Actually, M sets up a counter of length log n, and counts in base $4st$. Whenever M scans a new cell beyond the cells containing the counter, M increases the counter length. Thus if M loops having used only i tape cells, then the counter will detect this when the count reaches $(4st)^{\max(i, \log_2 n)}$, which is at least $(n + 2)sS(n)t^{S(n)}$. $\qquad\square$

Theorem 12.8 If $S_2(n)$ is a fully space-constructible function,

$$\inf_{n \to \infty} \frac{S_1(n)}{S_2(n)} = 0,$$

and $S_1(n)$ and $S_2(n)$ are each at least $\log_2 n$, then there is a language in DSPACE($S_2(n)$) not in DSPACE($S_1(n)$).

Proof The theorem is proved by diagonalization. Consider an enumeration of off-line Turing machines with input alphabet $\{0, 1\}$ and one storage tape, based on the binary encoding of Section 8.3, but with a prefix of 1's permitted, so each TM has arbitrarily long encodings. We construct a TM M that uses $S_2(n)$ space and disagrees on at least one input with any $S_1(n)$ space-bounded TM.

On input w, M begins by marking $S_2(n)$ cells on a tape, where n is the length of w. Since $S_2(n)$ is fully space constructible, this can be done by simulating a TM that uses exactly $S_2(n)$ cells on each input of length n. In what follows, if M attempts to leave the marked cells, M halts and rejects w. This guarantees that M is $S_2(n)$ space bounded.

Next M begins a simulation on input w of TM M_w, the TM encoded by binary string w. If M_w is $S_1(n)$ space bounded and has t tape symbols, then the simulation requires space $\lceil \log_2 t \rceil S_1(n)$. M accepts w only if M can complete the simulation in $S_2(n)$ space and M_w halts without accepting x.

Since M is $S_2(n)$ space bounded, $L(M)$ is in DSPACE$(S_2(n))$. $L(M)$ is not in DSPACE$(S_1(n))$. For suppose there were an $S_1(n)$ space-bounded TM $\hat{M}$ with t tape symbols accepting $L(M)$. By Lemma 12.1 we may assume that $\hat{M}$ halts on all inputs. Since $\hat{M}$ appears infinitely often in the enumeration, and

$$\inf_{n \to \infty} \frac{S_1(n)}{S_2(n)} = 0,$$

there exists a sufficiently long w, $|w| = n$, such that $\lceil \log_2 t \rceil S_1(n) < S_2(n)$ and M_w is $\hat{M}$. On input w, M has sufficient space to simulate M_w and accept if and only if M_w rejects. Thus $L(M_w) \neq L(M)$, a contradiction. Thus $L(M)$ is in DSPACE$(S_2(n))$ but not in DSPACE$(S_1(n))$. □

While most common functions are fully space constructible, we need only space constructibility to make Theorem 12.8 go through. We therefore state the following.

Corollary Theorem 12.8 holds even if $S_2(n)$ is space constructible but not fully space constructible.

Proof Let M_1 be a TM that constructs $S_2(n)$ on some input. Let Σ be the input alphabet of M_1. We design M to accept a language over alphabet $\Sigma \times \{0, 1\}$. That is, the input to M is treated as if it had two tracks: the first is used as input to M_1, the second as the code of a TM with input alphabet $\Sigma \times \{0, 1\}$. The only modification to the design of M is that M must lay off blocks on tapes 1 and 2 by simulating M_1 on M's first track. We may show that M disagrees with any $S_1(n)$ space-bounded TM $\hat{M}$ on an input whose length, n, is sufficiently large, whose first track is a string in Σ^n that causes M_1 to use $S_2(n)$ cells, and whose second track is an encoding of $\hat{M}$. □

We leave as an exercise a proof that the condition $S_2(n) \geq \log_2 n$ in Theorem 12.8 and its corollary are not really needed. The proof is not a diagonalization, but hinges on showing that

$$\{wc^i w \mid w \text{ is in } (\mathbf{a} + \mathbf{b})^*, \quad |w| = S_2(n) \quad \text{and} \quad i = n - 2S_2(n)\}$$

is accepted in $S_2(n)$ space but not in $S_1(n)$ space if

$$\inf_{n \to \infty} \frac{S_1(n)}{S_2(n)} = 0,$$

and $S_2(n) < \log_2 n$.

Note that if $\inf_{n \to \infty} [S_1(n)/S_2(n)] = 0$ and $S_1(n) \leq S_2(n)$ for all n, then

$$\text{DSPACE}(S_1(n)) \subsetneq \text{DSPACE}(S_2(n)).$$

However, if we do not have $S_1(n) \leq S_2(n)$, then it is possible that DSPACE($S_1(n)$) and DSPACE($S_2(n)$) each have languages not in the other.

A time hierarchy

The deterministic time hierarchy is not as tight as the space hierarchy. The reason is that a TM which diagonalizes over all multitape TM's has some fixed number of tapes. To simulate a TM with a larger number of tapes we make use of the two-tape simulation of a multitape TM, thereby introducing a logarithmic slow-down. Before giving the construction we introduce the notion of time constructibility.

A function $T(n)$ is said to be *time constructible* if there exists a $T(n)$ time-bounded multitape Turing machine M such that for each n there exists some input on which M actually makes $T(n)$ moves. Just as for space-constructible functions there is a rich hierarchy of time-constructible functions. We say that $T(n)$ is *fully time-constructible* if there is a TM that uses $T(n)$ time on all inputs of length n. Again, most common functions are fully time-constructible.

Theorem 12.9 If $T_2(n)$ is a fully time-constructible function and

$$\inf_{n \to \infty} \frac{T_1(n) \log T_1(n)}{T_2(n)} = 0,$$

then there is a language in DTIME($T_2(n)$) but not DTIME($T_1(n)$).

Proof The proof is similar to that of Theorem 12.8, and only a brief sketch of the necessary construction is given. A $T_2(n)$ time-bounded TM M is constructed to operate as follows. M treats the input w as an encoding of a Turing machine $\hat{M}$ and simulates $\hat{M}$ on w. A difficulty arises because M has some fixed number of tapes, so for some w's $\hat{M}$ will have more tapes than M. Fortunately, by Theorem 12.6, only two tapes are needed to simulate any $\hat{M}$, although the simulation costs a factor of $\log T_1(n)$. Also, since $\hat{M}$ may have many tape symbols, which must be encoded into some fixed number of symbols, the simulation of $T_1(n)$ moves of $\hat{M}$ by M requires time $cT_1(n) \log T_1(n)$, where c is a constant depending on $\hat{M}$.

In order to assure that the simulation of $\hat{M}$ is $T_2(n)$ time bounded, M simultaneously executes steps of a TM (using additional tapes) that uses exactly $T_2(n)$ time on all inputs of length n. This is the reason that $T_2(n)$ must be fully time constructible. After $T_2(n)$ steps, M halts. M accepts w only if the simulation of $\hat{M}$ is completed and $\hat{M}$ rejects w. The encoding of $\hat{M}$ is designed as in the previous theorem, so each $\hat{M}$ has arbitrarily long encodings. Thus, if $\hat{M}$ is a $T_1(n)$ time-bounded Turing machine, there will be a sufficiently large w encoding $\hat{M}$ so that

$$cT_1(|w|) \log T_1(|w|) \leq T_2(|w|),$$

and the simulation will carry to completion. In this case, w is in $L(M)$ if and only if w is not in $L(\hat{M})$. Thus $L(M) \neq L(\hat{M})$ for any $\hat{M}$ that is $T_1(n)$ time bounded. Therefore $L(M)$ is in DTIME($T_2(n)$) − DTIME($T_1(n)$). $\square$

Example 12.3   Let $T_1(n) = 2^n$ and $T_2(n) = n^2 2^n$. Then

$$\inf_{n \to \infty} \frac{T_1(n) \log_2 T_1(n)}{T_2(n)} = \inf_{n \to \infty} \frac{1}{n} = 0.$$

Thus Theorem 12.9 applies, and DTIME$(2^n) \neq$ DTIME$(n^2 2^n)$. Since $T_1(n) \leq T_2(n)$ for all n, we may conclude that DTIME$(2^n) \subsetneqq$ DTIME$(n^2 2^n)$.

12.4   RELATIONS AMONG COMPLEXITY MEASURES

There are several straightforward relationships and one not-so-obvious relationship among the complexities of a given language L according to the four complexity measures we have defined. The straightforward relationships are stated in one theorem.

Theorem 12.10

a) If L is in DTIME$(f(n))$, then L is in DSPACE$(f(n))$.

b) If L is in DSPACE$(f(n))$ and $f(n) \geq \log_2 n$, then there is some constant c, depending on L, such that L is in DTIME$(c^{f(n)})$.

c) If L is in NTIME$(f(n))$, then there is some constant c, depending on L, such that L is in DTIME$(c^{f(n)})$.

Proof

a) If TM M makes no more than $f(n)$ moves, it cannot scan more than $f(n) + 1$ cells on any tape. By modifying M to hold two symbols per cell we can lower the storage requirements to $\lceil [f(n) + 1]/2 \rceil$, which is at most $f(n)$.

b) Observe that if TM M_1 has s states and t tape symbols, and uses at most $f(n)$ space, then the number of different ID's of M_1 with input of length n is at most $s(n + 2)f(n)t^{f(n)}$. Since $f(n) \geq \log_2 n$, there is some constant c such that for all $n \geq 1$, $c^{f(n)} \geq s(n + 2)f(n)t^{f(n)}$.

   Construct from M_1 a multitape TM M_2 that uses one tape to count to $c^{f(n)}$, and two others to simulate M_2. If M_1 has not accepted when the count reaches $c^{f(n)}$, M_2 halts without accepting. After this number of moves, M_1 must have repeated an ID and so is never going to accept. Clearly M_2 is $c^{f(n)}$ time bounded.

c) Let M_1 be an $f(n)$ time-bounded nondeterministic TM with s states, t tape symbols, and k tapes. The number of possible ID's of M_1 given input of length n is at most $s(f(n) + 1)^k t^{kf(n)}$, the product of the number of states, head positions, and tape contents. Thus $d = s(t + 1)^{3k}$ satisfies

$$d^{f(n)} \geq s(f(n) + 1)^k t^{kf(n)} \qquad \text{for all} \quad n \geq 1.$$

   A deterministic multitape TM can determine if M_1 accepts input w of length n by constructing a list of all the ID's of M_1 that are accessible from the initial ID. This process can be carried out in time bounded by the square of the length of the list. Since the list of accessible ID's has length no greater than $d^{f(n)}$ times the length of an ID, which can be encoded in $1 + k(f(n) + 1)$ symbols, the time is bounded by $c^{f(n)}$ for some constant c. $\qquad\square$

Theorem 12.11 (*Savitch's theorem*) If L is in NSPACE($S(n)$), then L is in DSPACE($S^2(n)$) provided $S(n)$ is fully space constructible and $S(n) \geq \log_2 n$.

Proof Let $L = L(M_1)$, where M_1 is an $S(n)$ space-bounded nondeterministic TM. For some constant c, there are at most $c^{S(n)}$ ID's for an input of length n. Thus, if M_1 accepts its input, it does so by some sequence of at most $c^{S(n)}$ moves, since no ID is repeated in the shortest computation of M_1 leading to acceptance.

Let $I_1 \overset{(i)}{\vdash} I_2$ denote that the ID I_2 can be reached from I_1 by a sequence of at most 2^i moves. For $i \geq 1$, we can determine if $I_1 \overset{(i)}{\vdash} I_2$ by testing each I' to see if $I_1 \overset{(i-1)}{\vdash} I'$ and $I' \overset{(i-1)}{\vdash} I_2$. Thus the space needed to determine if we can get from one ID to another in 2^i moves is equal to the space needed to record the ID I' currently being tested plus the space needed to determine if we can get from one ID to another in 2^{i-1} moves. Observe that the space used to test whether one ID is reachable from another in 2^{i-1} moves can be reused for each such test.

The details for testing if w is in $L(M_1)$ are given in Fig. 12.5. The algorithm of Fig. 12.5 may be implemented on a Turing machine M_2 that uses a tape as a stack of activation records† for the calls to TEST. Each call has an activation record in which the values of parameters I_1, I_2, and i are placed, as well as the value of local variable I'. As I_1, I_2 and I' are ID's with no more than $S(n)$ cells, we can represent each of them in $S(n)$ space. The input head position in binary uses $\log n \leq S(n)$ cells. Note that the input tape in all ID's is fixed and is the same as the input to

---

```
begin
        let |w| = n and m = ⌈log₂ c⌉;
        let I₀ be the initial ID of M₁ with input w;
        for each final ID I_f of length at most S(n) do
            if TEST (I₀, I_f, mS(n)) then accept;
end;


procedure TEST (I₁, I₂, i);
        if i = 0 and (I₁ = I₂ or I₁ ⊢ I₂) then return true;
        if i ≥ 1 then
            for each ID I' of length at most S(n) do
                if TEST (I₁, I', i − 1) and TEST (I', I₂, i − 1) then
                    return true;
        return false
    end TEST
```

Fig. 12.5 Algorithm to simulate M_1.

---

† An "activation record" is the area used for the data belonging to one call of one procedure.

M_2, so we need not copy the input in each ID. The parameter i can be coded in binary using at most $mS(n)$ cells. Thus each activation record takes space $O(S(n))$.

As the third parameter decreases by one each time TEST is called, the initial call has $i = mS(n)$, and no call is made when i reaches zero, the maximum number of activation records on the stack is $O(S(n))$. Thus the total space used is $O(S^2(n))$, and by Theorem 12.1, we may redesign M_2 to make the space be exactly $S^2(n)$.

□

Example 12.4

$$\text{NSPACE}(\log n) \subseteq \text{DSPACE}(\log^2 n)$$

$$\text{NSPACE}(n^2) \subseteq \text{DSPACE}(n^4) \quad \text{and} \quad \text{NSPACE}(2^n) \subseteq \text{DSPACE}(4^n).$$

Note that for $S(n) \geq n$, Savitch's theorem holds even if $S(n)$ is space constructible rather than fully space constructible. M_2 begins by simulating a TM M that constructs $S(n)$, on each input of length n, taking the largest amount of space used as $S(n)$ and using this length to lay out the space for the activation records. Observe, however, that if we have no way of computing $S(n)$ in even $S^2(n)$ space, then we cannot cycle through all possible values of I_f or I' without getting some that take too much space.

12.5 TRANSLATIONAL LEMMAS AND NONDETERMINISTIC HIERARCHIES

In Theorems 12.8 and 12.9 we saw that the deterministic space and time hierarchies were very dense. It would appear that corresponding hierarchies for nondeterministic machines would require an increase of a square for space and an exponential for time, to simulate a nondeterministic machine for diagonalization purposes. However, a translational argument can be used to give a much denser hierarchy for nondeterministic machines. We illustrate the technique for space.

A translation lemma

The first step is to show that containment translates upward. For example, suppose it happened to be true (which it is not) that $\text{NSPACE}(n^3) \subseteq \text{NSPACE}(n^2)$. This relation could be translated upward by replacing n by n^2, yielding

$$\text{NSPACE}(n^6) \subseteq \text{NSPACE}(n^4).$$

Lemma 12.2   Let $S_1(n)$, $S_2(n)$, and $f(n)$ be fully space constructible, with $S_2(n) \geq n$ and $f(n) \geq n$. Then

$$\text{NSPACE}(S_1(n)) \subseteq \text{NSPACE}(S_2(n))$$

implies

$$\text{NSPACE}(S_1(f(n))) \subseteq \text{NSPACE}(S_2(f(n))).$$

Proof Let L_1 be accepted by M_1, a nondeterministic $S_1(f(n))$ space-bounded TM. Let

$$L_2 = \{x\$^i \mid M_1 \text{ accepts } x \text{ in space } S_1(|x| + i)\},$$

where $\$$ is a new symbol not in the alphabet of L_1. Then L_2 is accepted by a TM M_2 as follows. On input $x\$^i$, M_2 marks off $S_1(|x| + i)$ cells, which it may do, since S_1 is fully constructible. Then M_2 simulates M_1 on x, accepting if and only if M_1 accepts without using more than $S_1(|x| + i)$ cells. Clearly M_2 is $S_1(n)$ space bounded.

What we have done is to take a set L_1 in NSPACE($S_1(f(n))$) and pad the strings with $\$$'s so that the padded version L_2 is in NSPACE($S_1(n)$). Now by the hypothesis that NSPACE($S_1(n)$) $\subseteq$ NSPACE($S_2(n)$), there is a nondeterministic $S_2(n)$ space-bounded TM M_3 accepting L_2.

Finally we construct M_4 accepting the original set L_1 within space $S_2(f(n))$. M_4 marks off $f(n)$ cells and then $S_2(f(n))$ cells, which it may do since f and S_2 are fully constructible. As $S_2(n) \geq n, f(n) \leq S_2(f(n))$, so M_4 has not used more than $S_2(f(n))$ cells.

Next M_4 on input x simulates M_3 on $x\$^i$ for $i = 0, 1, 2, \ldots$ To do this, M must keep track of the head location of M_3 on $x\$^i$. If the head of M_3 is within x, M_4's head is at the corresponding point on its input. Whenever the head of M_3 moves into the $\$$'s, M_4 records the location in a counter. The length of the counter is at most $\log i$.

If during the simulation, M_3 accepts, then M_4 accepts. If M_3 does not accept, then M_4 increases i until the counter no longer fits on $S_2(f(|x|))$ tape cells. Then M_4 halts. Now, if x is in L_1, then $x\$^i$ is in L_2 for i satisfying $S_1(|x| + i) = S_1(f(|x|))$. Since $f(n) \geq n$, this equality is satisfied by $i = f(|x|) - |x|$. Thus the counter requires $\log(f(|x|) - |x|)$ space. Since $S_2(f(|x|)) \geq f(|x|)$, it follows that the counter will fit. Thus x is in $L(M_4)$ if and only if $x\$^i$ is in $L(M_3)$ for some i. Therefore $L(M_4) = L_1$, and L_1 is in NSPACE($S_2(f(n))$). □

Note that we can relax the condition that $S_2(n) \geq n$, requiring only that $S_2(n) \geq \log_2 n$, provided that $S_2(f(n))$ is fully space constructible. Then M_4 can lay off $S_2(f(n))$ cells without having to lay off $f(n)$ cells. As $S_2(f(n)) \geq \log f(n)$, there is still room for M_4's counter.

Essentially the same argument as in Lemma 12.2 shows the analogous results for DSPACE, DTIME, and NTIME.

Example 12.5 Using the analogous translation result for deterministic time we can prove that DTIME(2^n) $\subsetneq$ DTIME($n2^n$). Note that this result does not follow from Theorem 12.9, as

$$\inf_{n \to \infty} \frac{2^n \log 2^n}{n2^n} = 1.$$

Suppose that

$$\text{DTIME}(n2^n) \subseteq \text{DTIME}(2^n).$$

Then letting $S_1(n) = n2^n$, $S_2(n) = 2^n$, and $f(n) = 2^n$, we get

$$\text{DTIME}(2^n 2^{2^n}) \subseteq \text{DTIME}(2^{2^n}). \tag{12.6}$$

Similarly by letting $f(n) = n + 2^n$ we get

$$\text{DTIME}((n + 2^n)2^n 2^{2^n}) \subseteq \text{DTIME}(2^n 2^{2^n}). \tag{12.7}$$

Combining (12.6) with (12.7), we obtain

$$\text{DTIME}((n + 2^n)2^n 2^{2^n}) \subseteq \text{DTIME}(2^{2^n}). \tag{12.8}$$

However,

$$\inf_{n \to \infty} \frac{2^{2^n} \log 2^{2^n}}{(n + 2^n)2^n 2^{2^n}} = \inf_{n \to \infty} \frac{1}{n + 2^n} = 0.$$

Thus Theorem 12.9 implies that (12.8) is false, so our supposition that $\text{DTIME}(n2^n) \subseteq \text{DTIME}(2^n)$ must be false. Since $\text{DTIME}(2^n) \subseteq \text{DTIME}(n2^n)$, we conclude that $\text{DTIME}(2^n) \subsetneq \text{DTIME}(n2^n)$.

Example 12.6   The translation lemma can be used to show that $\text{NSPACE}(n^3)$ is properly contained in $\text{NSPACE}(n^4)$. Suppose to the contrary that $\text{NSPACE}(n^4) \subseteq \text{NSPACE}(n^3)$. Then letting $f(n) = n^3$, we get $\text{NSPACE}(n^{12}) \subseteq \text{NSPACE}(n^9)$. Similarly letting $f(n) = n^4$, we get $\text{NSPACE}(n^{16}) \subseteq \text{NSPACE}(n^{12})$, and $f(n) = n^5$ gives $\text{NSPACE}(n^{20}) \subseteq \text{NSPACE}(n^{15})$. Putting these together yields $\text{NSPACE}(n^{20}) \subseteq \text{NSPACE}(n^9)$. However, we know by Theorem 12.11 that $\text{NSPACE}(n^9) \subseteq \text{DSPACE}(n^{18})$, and by Theorem 12.8, $\text{DSPACE}(n^{18}) \subsetneq \text{DSPACE}(n^{20})$. Thus combining these results, we get

$$\text{NSPACE}(n^{20}) \subseteq \text{NSPACE}(n^9) \subseteq \text{DSPACE}(n^{18})$$

$$\subsetneq \text{DSPACE}(n^{20}) \subseteq \text{NSPACE}(n^{20}),$$

a contradiction. Therefore our assumption $\text{NSPACE}(n^4) \subseteq \text{NSPACE}(n^3)$ is wrong, and we conclude $\text{NSPACE}(n^3) \subsetneq \text{NSPACE}(n^4)$.

A nondeterministic space hierarchy

Example 12.6 can be generalized to show a dense hierarchy for nondeterministic space in the polynomial range.

Theorem 12.12   If $\epsilon > 0$ and $r \geq 0$, then

$$\text{NSPACE}(n^r) \subsetneq \text{NSPACE}(n^{r+\epsilon}).$$

Proof If r is any nonnegative real number, we can find positive integers s and t such that $r \leq s/t$ and $r + \epsilon \geq (s + 1)/t$. Therefore it suffices to prove for all positive integers s and t, that

$$\text{NSPACE}(n^{s/t}) \subsetneq \text{NSPACE}(n^{(s+1)/t}).$$

Suppose to the contrary that

$$\text{NSPACE}(n^{(s+1)/t}) \subseteq \text{NSPACE}(n^{s/t}).$$

Then by Lemma 12.2 with $f(n) = n^{(s+i)t}$, we have

$$\text{NSPACE}(n^{(s+1)(s+i)}) \subseteq \text{NSPACE}(n^{s(s+i)}) \tag{12.9}$$

for $i = 0, 1, \ldots, s$. As $s(s + i) \leq (s + 1)(s + i - 1)$ for $i \geq 1$, we know that

$$\text{NSPACE}(n^{s(s+i)}) \subseteq \text{NSPACE}(n^{(s+1)(s+i-1)}). \tag{12.10}$$

Using (12.9) and (12.10) alternately, we have

$$\text{NSPACE}(n^{(s+1)(2s)}) \subseteq \text{NSPACE}(n^{s(2s)})$$

$$\subseteq \text{NSPACE}(n^{(s+1)(2s-1)}) \subseteq \text{NSPACE}(n^{s(2s-1)})$$

$$\subseteq \cdots \subseteq \text{NSPACE}(n^{(s+1)s}) \subseteq \text{NSPACE}(n^{s^2}).$$

That is,

$$\text{NSPACE}(n^{2s^2+2s}) \subseteq \text{NSPACE}(n^{s^2}).$$

However, by Savitch's theorem,

$$\text{NSPACE}(n^{s^2}) \subseteq \text{DSPACE}(n^{2s^2}),$$

and by Theorem 12.8,

$$\text{DSPACE}(n^{2s^2}) \subsetneq \text{DSPACE}(n^{2s^2+2s}).$$

Clearly,

$$\text{DSPACE}(n^{2s^2+2s}) \subseteq \text{NSPACE}(n^{2s^2+2s}).$$

Combining these results, we get

$$\text{NSPACE}(n^{2s^2+2s}) \subsetneq \text{NSPACE}(n^{2s^2+2s}),$$

a contradiction. We conclude that our assumption

$$\text{NSPACE}(n^{(s+1)/t}) \subseteq \text{NSPACE}(n^{s/t})$$

was wrong. Since containment in the opposite direction is obvious, we conclude

$$\text{NSPACE}(n^{s/t}) \subsetneq \text{NSPACE}(n^{(s+1)/t})$$

for any positive integers s and t. $\qquad\qquad\qquad\qquad\qquad\qquad\qquad\square$

Similar dense hierarchies for nondeterministic space can be proved for ranges higher than the polynomials, and we leave some of these results as exercises. Theorem 12.12 does not immediately generalize to nondeterministic time, because of the key role of Savitch's theorem, for which no time analog is known. However, a time analog of Theorem 12.12 has been established by Cook [1973a].

12.6 PROPERTIES OF GENERAL COMPLEXITY MEASURES: THE GAP, SPEEDUP, AND UNION THEOREMS

In this section we discuss some unintuitive properties of complexity measures. While we prove them only for deterministic space complexity, they will be seen in the next section to apply to all measures of complexity.

Theorems 12.8 and 12.9 indicate that the space and time hierarchies are very dense. However, in both theorems the functions are required to be constructible. Can this condition be discarded? The answer is no: the deterministic space and time hierarchies have arbitrarily large gaps in them.

We say that a statement with parameter n is true *almost everywhere* (a.e.) if it is true for all but a finite number of values of n. We say a statement is true *infinitely often* (i.o.) if it is true for an infinite number of n's. Note that both a statement and its negation may be true i.o.

Lemma 12.3   If L is accepted by a TM M that is $S(n)$ space bounded a.e., then L is accepted by an $S(n)$ space-bounded TM.

Proof   Use the finite control to accept or reject strings of length n for the finite number of n where M is not $S(n)$ bounded. Note that the construction is not effective, since in the absence of a time bound we cannot tell which of these words M accepts.   □

Lemma 12.4   There is an algorithm to determine, given TM M, input length n, and integer m, whether m is the maximum number of tape cells used by M on some input of length n.

Proof   For each m and n there is a limit t on the number of moves M may make on input of length n without using more than m cells of any storage tape or repeating an ID. Simulate all sequences of up to t moves, beginning with each input of length n.   □

Theorem 12.13 (*Borodin's Gap Theorem*)   Given any total recursive function $g(n) \geq n$, there exists a total recursive function $S(n)$ such that $\text{DSPACE}(S(n)) = \text{DSPACE}(g(S(n)))$. In other words, there is a "gap" between space bounds $S(n)$ and $g(S(n))$ within which the minimal space complexity of no language lies.

Proof   Let M_1, M_2, ... be an enumeration of TM's. Let $S_i(n)$ be the maximum number of tape cells used by M_i on any input of length n. If M_i always halts, then $S_i(n)$ is a total function and is the space complexity of M_i, but if M_i does not halt on some input of length n, then $S_i(n)$ is undefined.† We construct $S(n)$ so that for each k either

1) $S_k(n) \leq S(n)$ a.e., or

2) $S_k(n) \geq g(S(n))$ i.o.

That is, no $S_k(n)$ lies between $S(n)$ and $g(S(n))$ for almost all n.

In constructing $S(n)$ for a given value of n, we restrict our attention to the finite set of TM's $M_1, M_2, \ldots, M_n$. The value for $S(n)$ is selected so that for no i between 1 and n does $S_i(n)$ lie between $S(n)$ and $g(S(n))$. If we could compute the largest finite value of $S_i(n)$ for $1 \leq i \leq n$, then we could set $S(n)$ equal to that value. However, since some $S_i(n)$ are undefined, we cannot compute the largest value. Instead, we initially set $j = 1$ and see if there is some M_i in our finite set for which $S_i(n)$ is between $j + 1$ and $g(j)$. If there is some such $S_i(n)$, then set j to $S_i(n)$ and repeat the process. If not, set $S(n)$ to j and we are done. As there is but a finite number of TM's under consideration, and by Lemma 12.4 we can tell whether $S_i(n) = m$ for any fixed m, the process will eventually compute a value for j such that for $1 \leq i \leq n$ either $S_i(n) \leq j$ or $S_i(n) > g(j)$. Assign $S(n)$ this value of j.

Suppose there were some language L in DSPACE$(g(S(n))$ but not in DSPACE$(S(n))$. Then $L = L(M_k)$ for some k where $S_k(n) \leq g(S(n))$ for all n. By the construction of $S(n)$, for all $n \geq k$, $S_k(n) \leq S(n)$. That is, $S_k(n) \leq S(n)$ a.e., and hence by Lemma 12.3, L is in DSPACE$(S(n))$, a contradiction. We conclude that DSPACE$(S(n))$ = DSPACE$(g(S(n)))$. $\qquad\square$

Theorem 12.13 and its analogs for the other three complexity measures have a number of highly unintuitive consequences, such as the following.

Example 12.7   There is a total recursive function $f(n)$ such that

$$\text{DTIME}(f(n)) = \text{NTIME}(f(n)) = \text{DSPACE}(f(n)) = \text{NSPACE}(f(n)).$$

Clearly DTIME$(f(n))$ is contained within NTIME$(f(n))$ and DSPACE$(f(n))$. Similarly, both NTIME$(f(n))$ and DSPACE$(f(n))$ are contained within NSPACE$(f(n))$. By Theorem 12.10, for all $f(n) \geq \log_2 n$, if L is in NSPACE$(f(n))$, then there is a constant c, depending only on L such that L is in DTIME$(c^{f(n)})$. Therefore, $L = L(M)$ for some TM M whose time complexity is bounded above by $f(n)^{f(n)}$ a.e. By the DTIME analog of Lemma 12.3, L is in DTIME$(f(n)^{f(n)})$. Finally, the DTIME analog of Theorem 12.13 with $g(x) = x^x$ establishes the existence of $f(n)$ for which DTIME$(f(n))$ = DTIME$(f(n)^{f(n)})$, proving the result.

Similarly, if one has two universal models of computation, but one is very simple and slow, say a Turing machine that makes one move per century, and the other is very fast, say a random-access machine with powerful built-in instructions for multiplication, exponentiation, and so on, that performs a million operations

---

† We identify an undefined value with infinity, so an undefined value is larger than any defined value.

per second, it is easily shown that there exists a total recursive $T(n)$ such that any function computable in time $T(n)$ on one model is computable in time $T(n)$ on the other.

The speed-up theorem

Another curious phenomenon regarding complexity measures is that there are functions with no best programs (Turing machines). We have already seen that every TM allows a linear speed up in time and compression in space. We now show that there are languages with no "best" program. That is, recognizers for these languages can be sped up indefinitely. We shall work only with space and show that there is a language L such that for any Turing machine accepting L, there always exists another Turing machine that accepts L and uses, for example, only the square root of the space used by the former. This new recognizer can of course be replaced by an even faster recognizer and so on, *ad infinitum*.

The basic idea of the proof is quite simple. By diagonalization we construct L so that L cannot be recognized quickly by any "small" machine, that is, a machine with a small integer index encoding it. As machine indices increase, the diagonalization process allows faster and faster machines recognizing L. Given any machine recognizing L, it has some fixed index and thus can recognize L only so fast. However, machines with larger indices can recognize L arbitrarily more quickly.

Theorem 12.14 (*Blum's Speed-up Theorem*)   Let $r(n)$ be any total recursive function. There exists a recursive language L such that for any Turing machine M_i accepting L, there exists a Turing machine M_j accepting L such that $r(S_j(n)) \leq S_i(n)$, for almost all n.

Proof   Without loss of generality assume that $r(n)$ is a monotonically nondecreasing fully space-constructible function with $r(n) \geq n^2$ (see Exercise 12.9). Define $h(n)$ by

$$h(1) = 2, \qquad h(n) = r(h(n-1)).$$

Then $h(n)$ is a fully space-constructible function, as the reader may easily show.

Let $M_1, M_2, \ldots$ be an enumeration of all off-line TM's analogous to that of Section 8.3 for single-tape TM's. In particular, we assume that the code for M_i has length $\log_2 i$. We construct L so that

1) if $L(M_i) = L$, then $S_i(n) \geq h(n-i)$ a.e.;
2) for each k, there exists a Turing machine M_j such that $L(M_j) = L$ and $S_j(n) \leq h(n-k)$.

The above conditions on L assure that for each M_i accepting L there exists an M_j accepting L with

$$S_i(n) \geq r(S_j(n)) \qquad \text{a.e.}$$

To see this, select M_j so that $S_j(n) \le h(n - i - 1)$. By (2), M_j exists. Then by (1),

$$S_i(n) \ge h(n - i) = r(h(n - i - 1)) \ge r(S_j(n)) \qquad \text{a.e.}$$

Now let us construct $L \subseteq \mathbf{0}^*$ to satisfy (1) and (2). For $n = 0, 1, 2, \ldots$ in turn, we specify whether 0^n is in L. In the process, certain M_i are designated as "canceled." A canceled TM surely does not accept L. Let $\sigma(n)$ be the least integer $j \le n$ such that $S_j(n) < h(n - j)$, and M_j is not canceled by $i = 0, 1, \ldots, n - 1$. When we consider n, if $\sigma(n)$ exists, $M_{\sigma(n)}$ is designated as canceled. Then 0^n is placed in L if and only if $\sigma(n)$ exists and 0^n is not accepted by $M_{\sigma(n)}$.

Next we prove that L satisfies condition (1), namely: if $L(M_i) = L$, then $S_i(n) \ge h(n - i)$ a.e. Let $L(M_i) = L$. In constructing L, all TM's M_j, for $j < i$, that are ever canceled are canceled after considering some finite number of n's, say up to n_0. Note that n_0 cannot be effectively computed, but nevertheless exists. Suppose $S_i(n) < h(n - i)$ for some $n > \max(n_0, i)$. When we consider n, no M_j, $j < i$, is canceled. Thus $\sigma(n) = i$, and M_i would be canceled had it not been previously canceled. But a TM that is canceled will surely not accept L. Thus $S_i(n) \ge h(n - i)$ for $n > \max(n_0, i)$, that is, $S_i(n) \ge h(n - i)$ a.e.

To prove condition (2) we show that there exists, for given k, a TM $M = M_j$ such that $L(M) = L$, and $S_j(n) \le h(n - k)$ for all n. To determine whether 0^n is in L, M must simulate $M_{\sigma(n)}$ on 0^n. To know what $\sigma(n)$ is, M must determine which M_i's have already been canceled by 0^ℓ for $\ell < n$. However, constructing the list of canceled TM's directly requires seeing if M_i uses more than $h(\ell - i)$ space for $0 \le \ell \le n$ and $1 \le i \le n$. For $i < k + \ell - n$, this requires more than $h(n - k)$ space.

The solution is to observe that any TM M_i, $i \le k$, that is ever canceled, is canceled when we consider some ℓ less than a particular n_1. For each $\ell \le n_1$, incorporate into the finite control of M whether 0^ℓ is in L, and also incorporate a list of all TM's M_i canceled by any $\ell \le n_1$. Thus no space at all is needed by M if $n \le n_1$. If $n > n_1$, to compute $\sigma(n)$ and simulate $M_{\sigma(n)}$ on 0^n, it will only be necessary to simulate TM's M_i on input 0^ℓ, where $n_1 < \ell \le n$ and $k < i \le n$, to see whether M_i is canceled by ℓ.

To test whether M_i is canceled by ℓ, we need only simulate M_i using $h(\ell - i)$ of M_i's cells, which is less than $h(n - k)$, as $\ell \le n$ and $i > k$. As $n > n_1$, it must be that $\sigma(n)$, if it exists, is greater than k. Thus simulating $M_{\sigma(n)}$ on input 0^n takes $h(n - \sigma(n))$ of $M_{\sigma(n)}$'s cells, which is less than $h(n - k)$ cells.

Lastly, we must show that M can be made to operate within space $h(n - k)$. We need only simulate TM's M_i for $k < i \le n$ on inputs 0^ℓ, $n_1 \le \ell \le n$, to see whether they get canceled, so we need represent no more than $h(n - k - 1)$ cells of M_i's tape for any simulation. Since $i \le n$, the integer code for M_i has length no more than $\log_2 n$. Thus any tape symbol of M_i can be coded using $\log_2 n$ of M's cells. As $r(x) \ge x^2$, we know $h(x) \ge 2^{2^x}$. Also, by the definition of h, $h(n - k) \ge [h(n - k - 1)]^2 \ge 2^{2^{n-k-1}} h(n - k - 1)$. As $2^{2^{n-k-1}} \ge \log_2 n$ a.e., $h(n - k)$ space is sufficient for the simulation for almost all n.

In addition to the space required for simulating the TM's, space is needed to maintain the list of canceled TM's. This list consists of at most n TM's, each with a code of length at most $\log_2 n$. The $n \log n$ space needed to maintain the list of canceled TM's is also less than $h(n - k)$ a.e. By Lemma 12.3, M can be modified to recognize words 0^n, where $n \log_2 n < h(n - k)$ or $2^{2^{n-k-1}} < \log_2 n$ in its finite control. The resulting TM is of space complexity $h(n - k)$ for all n, and is the desired M.   □

The union theorem

The last theorem in this section, called the *union theorem*, has to do with the naming of complexity classes. By way of introduction, we know that each polynomial such as n^2 or n^3 defines a space complexity class (as well as complexity classes of the other three types). However, does polynomial space form a complexity class? That is, does there exist an $S(n)$ such that $\mathrm{DSPACE}(S(n))$ contains all sets recognizable in a polynomial space bound and no other sets? Clearly, $S(n)$ must be almost everywhere greater than any polynomial, but it also must be small enough so that one cannot fit another function that is the space used by some TM between it and the polynomials, where "fit" must be taken as a technical term whose meaning is defined precisely in the next theorem.

Theorem 12.15   Let $\{f_i(n) \mid i = 1, 2, \ldots\}$ be a recursively enumerable collection of recursive functions. That is, there is a TM that enumerates a list of TM's, the first computing f_1, the second computing f_2, and so on. Also assume that for each i and n, $f_i(n) < f_{i+1}(n)$. Then there exists a recursive $S(n)$ such that

$$\mathrm{DSPACE}(S(n)) = \bigcup_{i \geq 1} \mathrm{DSPACE}(f_i(n)).$$

Proof   We construct a function $S(n)$ satisfying the following two conditions:

1) For each i, $S(n) \geq f_i(n)$ a.e.
2) If $S_j(n)$ is the exact space complexity of some TM M_j and for each i, $S_j(n) > f_i(n)$ i.o., then $S_j(n) > S(n)$ for some n (and in fact, for infinitely many n's).

The first condition assures that

$$\bigcup_i \mathrm{DSPACE}(f_i(n)) \subseteq \mathrm{DSPACE}(S(n)).$$

The second condition assures that $\mathrm{DSPACE}(S(n))$ contains only those sets that are in $\mathrm{DSPACE}(f_i(n))$ for some i. Together the conditions imply that

$$\mathrm{DSPACE}(S(n)) = \bigcup_i \mathrm{DSPACE}(f_i(n)).$$

Setting $S(n) = f_n(n)$ would assure condition (1). However, it may not satisfy condition (2). There may be a TM M_j whose space complexity $S_j(n)$ is greater than each $f_i(n)$ i.o. but less than $f_n(n)$ for all n. Thus there may be sets in $\mathrm{DSPACE}(f_n(n))$

not in $\bigcup_i$ DSPACE($f_i(n)$). To overcome this problem we construct $S(n)$ so that it dips below each $S_j(n)$ that is i.o. greater than each $f_i(n)$, and in fact, $S(n)$ will dip below $S_j(n)$ for an infinity of n's. This is done by guessing for each TM M_j an i_j such that $f_{i_j}(n) \geq S_j(n)$ a.e. The "guess" is not nondeterministic; rather it is subject to deterministic revision as follows. If at some point we discover that the guess is not correct, we guess a larger value for i_j and for some particular n define $S(n)$ to be less than $S_j(n)$. If it happens that S_j grows faster than any f_i, S will infinitely often be less than S_j. On the other hand, if some f_i is almost everywhere greater than S_j, eventually we shall guess one such f_i and stop assigning values of S less than S_j.

In Fig. 12.6 we give an algorithm that generates $S(n)$. A list called LIST of "guesses" of the form "$i_j = k$" for various integers j and k is maintained. For each j, there will be at most one guess k on LIST at any time. As in the previous theorem, $M_1, M_2, \ldots$ is an enumeration of all off-line TM's, and $S_j(n)$ is the maximum amount of space used by M_j on any input of length n. Recall that $S_j(n)$ may be undefined (infinite) for some values of n.

```
        begin
1)          LIST := empty  list
2)          for n = 1, 2, 3, ... do
3)              if for all "i_j = k" on LIST, f_k(n) ≥ S_j(n) then
4)                  add "i_n = n" to LIST and define S(n) = f_n(n)
                else
                    begin
5)                      Among all guesses on LIST such that f_k(n) < S_j(n), let "i_j = k" be the
                        guess with the smallest k, and given that k, the smallest j;
6)                      define S(n) = f_k(n);
7)                      replace "i_j = k" by "i_j = n" on LIST;
8)                      add "i_n = n" to LIST
                    end
        end
```

Fig. 12.6   Definition of $S(n)$.

To prove that

$$\text{DSPACE}(S(n)) = \bigcup_i \text{DSPACE}(f_i(n))$$

we first show that $S(n)$ satisfies conditions (1) and (2). Consider condition (1). To see that for each m, $S(n) \geq f_m(n)$ a.e. observe that $S(n)$ is assigned a value only at lines (4) and (6) of Fig. 12.6. Whenever $S(n)$ is defined at line (4) for $n \geq m$, the value of $S(n)$ is at least $f_m(n)$. Thus for the values of $S(n)$ defined at line (4), $S(n) \geq f_m(n)$ except for the finite set of n less than m. Now consider the values of $S(n)$ defined at line (6). When n reaches m, LIST will have some finite number of guesses. Each of these guesses may subsequently cause one value of $S(n)$, for some $n > m$, to be less than $f_m(n)$. However, when that happens, line (7) causes that guess to be replaced by a guess "$i_j = p$" for some $p \geq m$, and this guess, if selected at line (5), does not cause $S(n)$ to be made less than $f_m(n)$, since $f_p(n) \geq f_m(n)$ whenever $p \geq m$. Thus from line (6) there are only finitely many n greater than m (at most the length of LIST when $n = m$) for which $S(n) < f_m(n)$. Since there are only a finite number of n's less than m, $S(n) \geq f_m(n)$ a.e.

Next we must show condition (2), that if there exists TM M_j such that for each i, $S_j(n) > f_i(n)$ i.o., then $S_j(n') > S(n')$ for infinitely many n'. At all times after $n = j$, LIST will have a guess for i_j, and LIST is always finite. For $n = j$ we place "$i_j = j$" on LIST. As $S_j(n) > f_j(n)$ i.o., there will be arbitrarily many subsequent values of n for which the condition of step (3) does not hold. At each of these times, either our "$i_j = j$" is selected at line (5), or some other one of the finite number of guesses on LIST when $n = j$ is selected. In the latter case, that guess is replaced by a guess "$i_p = q$" with $q > j$. All guesses added to LIST are also of the form "$i_p = q$" for $q > j$, so eventually our "$i_j = j$" is selected at step (5), and for this value of n, we have $S_j(n) > f_j(n) = S(n)$. Thus condition (2) is true.

Lastly we must show that conditions (1) and (2) imply

$$\text{DSPACE}(S(n)) = \bigcup_i \text{DSPACE}(f_i(n)).$$

Suppose L is in $\bigcup_i \text{DSPACE}(f_i(n))$. Then L is in $\text{DSPACE}(f_m(n))$ for some particular m. By condition (1), $S(n) \geq f_m(n)$ a.e. Thus by Lemma 12.3, L is in $\text{DSPACE}(S(n))$. Now suppose that L is in $\text{DSPACE}(S(n))$. Let $L = L(M_j)$, where $S_j(n) \leq S(n)$ for all n. If for no i, L is in $\text{DSPACE}(f_i(n))$, then by Lemma 12.3, for every i, each TM M_k accepting L has $S_k(n) > f_i(n)$ i.o. Thus by condition (2) there is some n for which $S_k(n) > S(n)$. Letting $k = j$ produces a contradiction.

$\square$

Example 12.8   Let $f_i(n) = n^i$. Then we may surely enumerate a sequence of TM's $M_1, M_2, \ldots$ such that M_i, presented with input 0^n, writes 0^{n^i} on its tape and halts. Thus Theorem 12.15 says that there is some $S(n)$ such that

$$\text{DSPACE}(S(n)) = \bigcup_i \text{DSPACE}(n^i).$$

As any polynomial $p(n)$ is equal to or less than some n^i a.e., $\text{DSPACE}(S(n))$ is the union over all polynomials $p(n)$, of $\text{DSPACE}(p(n))$. This union, which in the next chapter we shall call PSPACE, and which plays a key role in the theory of intractable problems, is thus seen to be a deterministic space complexity class.

12.7   AXIOMATIC COMPLEXITY THEORY

The reader may have observed that many theorems in this chapter are not dependent on the fact that we are measuring the amount of time or space used, but only that we are measuring some resource that is being consumed as the computation proceeds. In fact one could postulate axioms governing resources and give a completely axiomatic development of complexity theory. In this section we briefly sketch this approach.

The Blum axioms

Let M_1, M_2, ... be an enumeration of Turing machines defining among them every partial recursive function. For technical reasons we consider the M_i's as computing partial recursive functions ϕ_i rather than as recognizing sets. The reason is that it is notationally simpler to measure complexity as a function of the input rather than of the length of the input. Let $\phi_i(n)$ be the function of one variable computed by M_i, and let $\Phi_1(n)$, $\Phi_2(n)$, ... be a set of partial recursive functions satisfying the following two axioms (*Blum's axioms*).

Axiom 1 $\Phi_i(n)$ is defined if and only if $\phi_i(n)$ is defined.

Axiom 2   The function $R(i, n, m)$ defined to be 1 if $\Phi_i(n) = m$ and 0 otherwise, is a total recursive function.

The function $\Phi_i(n)$ gives the complexity of the computation of the ith Turing machine on input n. Axiom 1 requires that $\Phi_i(n)$ is defined if and only if the ith Turing machine halts on input n. Thus one possible Φ_i would be the number of steps of the ith Turing machine. The amount of space used is another alternative, provided we define the space used to be infinite if the TM enters a loop.

Axiom 2 requires that we can determine whether the complexity of the ith Turing machine on input n is m. For example, if our complexity measure is the number of steps in the computation, then given i, n, and m, we can simulate M_i on 0^n for m steps and see if it halts. Lemma 12.4 and its analogs are claims that Axiom 2 holds for the four measures with which we have been concerned.

Example 12.9   Deterministic space complexity satisfies Blum's axioms, provided we say $\Phi_i(n)$ is undefined if M_i does not halt on input 0^n, even though the amount of space used by M_i on 0^n may be limited. Deterministic time complexity likewise satisfies the axioms if we say $\Phi_i(n)$ is undefined whenever M_i runs forever or halts without any 0^j on its tape. To compute $R(i, n, m)$, simply simulate M_i for m steps on input 0^n.

We may establish that nondeterministic time and space satisfy the axioms if we make an intelligent definition of what it means for an NTM to compute a function. For example, we might say that $\phi_i(n) = j$ if and only if there is some sequence of choices by M_i with input 0^n that halts with 0^j on the tape, and no sequence of choices that leads to halting with some 0^k, $k \neq j$, on the tape.

If we define $\Phi_i(n) = \phi_i(n)$, we do not satisfy Axiom 2. Suppose $R(i, n, m)$ were recursive. Then there is an algorithm to tell if M_i with input 0^n halts with 0^m on its tape. Given any TM M, we may construct $\hat{M}$ to simulate M. If M halts with any tape, $\hat{M}$ erases its own tape. If i is an index for $\hat{M}$, then $R(i, n, 0)$ is true if and only if M halts on input 0^n. Thus if $R(i, n, m)$ were recursive, we could tell if a given TM M halts on a given input, which is undecidable (see Exercise 8.3).

Recursive relationships among complexity measures

Many of the theorems on complexity can be proved solely from the two axioms. In particular, the fact that there are arbitrarily complex functions, the speed-up theorem, the gap theorem, and the union theorem can be so proved. We prove only one theorem here to illustrate the techniques. The theorem we select is that all measures are recursively related. That is, given any two complexity measures Φ and $\hat{\Phi}$, there is a total recursive function r such that the complexity of the TM M_i in one measure, $\hat{\Phi}_i(n)$, is at most $r(n, \Phi_i(n))$. For example, Theorems 12.10 and 12.11 showed that for the four measures of complexity with which we have been dealing, at most an exponential function related any pair of these complexity measures. In a sense, functions that are easy in one measure are "easy" in any other measure, although the term "easy" must be taken lightly, as r could be a very rapidly growing function, such as Ackermann's function.

Theorem 12.16   Let Φ and $\hat{\Phi}$ be two complexity measures. Then there exists a recursive function r such that for all i,

$$r(n, \Phi_i(n)) \geq \hat{\Phi}_i(n) \quad \text{a.e.}$$

Proof   Let

$$r(n, m) = \max_i \{\hat{\Phi}_i(n) \,|\, i \leq n \quad \text{and} \quad \Phi_i(n) = m\}.$$

The function r is recursive, since $\Phi_i(n) = m$ may be tested by Axiom 2. Should it be equal to m, then $\phi_i(n)$ and $\hat{\Phi}_i(n)$ must be defined, by Axiom 1, and hence the maximum can be computed. Clearly $r(n, \Phi_i(n)) \geq \hat{\Phi}_i(n)$ for all $n \geq i$, since for $n \geq i$, $r(n, \Phi_i(n))$ is at least $\hat{\Phi}_i(n)$.   □

Although the axiomatic approach is elegant and allows us to prove results in a more general framework, it fails to capture at least one important aspect of our intuitive notion of complexity. If we construct a Turing machine M_k that first executes M_i on n and then executes M_j on the result, we would expect the complexity of M_k on n to be at least as great as M_i on n. However, there are complexity measures such that this is not the case. In other words, by doing additional computation we can reduce the complexity of what we have already done. We leave the construction of such a complexity measure as an exercise.

EXERCISES

12.1   The notion of a crossing sequence—the sequence of states in which the boundary between two cells is crossed—was defined in Section 2.6 in connection with two-way finite automata. However, the notion applies equally well to single-tape TM's. Prove the following basic properties of crossing sequences.

a) The time taken by single-tape TM M on input w is the sum of the lengths of the crossing sequences between each two cells of M's tape.

b) Suppose M is a single tape TM that, if it accepts its input, does so to the right of the cells on which its input was originally written. Show that if M accepts input $w_1 w_2$, and the crossing sequence between w_1 and w_2 is the same as that between x_1 and x_2 when M is given input $x_1 x_2$, then M accepts $x_1 w_2$.

*12.2   Use Exercise 12.1 to show that the languages

S a) $\{wcw^R \mid w \text{ is in } (\mathbf{a} + \mathbf{b})^*\}$ b) $\{wcw \mid w \text{ is in } (\mathbf{a} + \mathbf{b})^*\}$

each require kn^2 steps on some input of sufficiently large odd length n, for some constant $k > 0$. Thus the bound of Theorem 12.5 is in a sense the best possible.

*12.3   The notion of crossing sequences can be adapted to off-line TM's if we replace the notion of "state" by the state, contents of storage tapes, and positions of the storage tape heads. Theorem 12.8, the space hierarchy, applied only to space complexities of log n or above. Prove that the same holds for fully space-constructible $S_2(n)$ below log n. [*Hint:* Using a generalized crossing sequence argument, show that $\{wc^iw \mid w \text{ is in } (\mathbf{a} + \mathbf{b})^* \text{ and } |w| = 2^{S_2(i + 2|w|)}\}$ is in DSPACE$(S_2(n))$ but not in DSPACE$(S_1(n))$.]

*12.4   Show, using generalized crossing sequence arguments, that if L is not a regular set and L is in DSPACE$(S(n))$, then $S(n) \geq \log \log n$ i.o. Show the same result for nondeterministic space. Thus for deterministic and nondeterministic space there is a "gap" between 1 and $\log \log n$.

12.5   Show that Lemma 12.2, the "translation lemma," applies to

a) deterministic space
b) deterministic time, and
c) nondeterministic time.

12.6   Show that DTIME$(2^{2^n + n})$ properly includes DTIME(2^{2^n}).

12.7   Show that NSPACE$((c + \epsilon)^n)$ properly includes NSPACE(c^n) for any $c > 1$ and $\epsilon > 0$.

12.8   What, if any, is the relationship between each of the following pairs of complexity classes?

a) DSPACE(n^2) and DSPACE$(f(n))$, where $f(n) = n$ for odd n and n^3 for even n.
b) DTIME(2^n) and DTIME(3^n)
c) NSPACE(2^n) and DSPACE(5^n)
d) DSPACE(n) and DTIME$(\lceil \log_2 n \rceil^n)$

12.9   Show that if r is any total recursive function, then there is a fully space-constructible monotonically nondecreasing r' such that $r'(n) \geq r(n)$, and $r'(x) \geq x^2$ for all integers x. [*Hint:* Consider the space complexity of any TM computing r.]

12.10   Show that there is a total recursive function $S(n)$ such that L is in DSPACE$(S(n))$ if and only if L is accepted by some c^n space-bounded TM, for $c > 1$.

12.11   Suppose we used axioms for computational complexity theory as it pertains to languages rather than functions. That is, let M_1, M_2, ... be an enumeration of Turing machines and L_i the language accepted by M_i. Replace Axiom 1 by:

Axiom 1': $\Phi_i(n)$ is defined if and only if M_i halts on all inputs of length n.

Reprove Theorem 12.16 for Axioms 1' and 2.

12.12 Show that the speed-up and gap theorem hold for NSPACE, DTIME and NTIME. [*Hint:* Use Theorem 12.16 and the speed-up and gap theorems for DSPACE.]

12.13 Show that the following are fully time and space constructible:

a) n^2 b) 2^n c) $n!$

12.14 Show that the following are fully space constructible:

a) $\sqrt{n}$ b) $\log_2 n$

**Sc) Some function that is bounded above by $\log_2 \log_2 n$ and that is bounded below by $c \log_2 \log_2 n$, for some $c > 0$, infinitely often.

12.15 Show that if $T_2(n)$ is time constructible, and

$$\inf_{n \to \infty} \frac{T_1(n) \log T_1(n)}{T_2(n)} = 0,$$

then there is a language accepted by a $T_2(n)$ time-bounded one-tape TM, but by no $T_1(n)$ time-bounded one-tape machine. [*Hint:* To simulate a one-tape TM M_i by a one-tape machine, move the description of M_i so that it is always near the tape head. Similarly, carry along a "counter" to tell when M_i has exceeded its time limit.]

**12.16 Show that if $T_2(n)$ is time constructible and

$$\inf_{n \to \infty} \frac{T_1(n) \log^* T_1(n)}{T_2(n)} = 0,$$

then for all k, there is a language accepted by a k-tape T_2 time-bounded TM but by no k-tape $T_1(n)$ time-bounded TM, where $\log^*(m)$ is the number of times we must take logarithms base 2 of m to get to 1 or below. For example, $\log^*(3) = 2$ and $\log^*(2^{65536}) = 5$. Note that this exercise implies Exercise 12.15.

*12.17 Show that for any complexity measure Φ satisfying the Blum axioms there can be no total recursive function f such that $\Phi_i(n) \leq f(n, \phi_i(n))$. That is, one cannot bound the complexity of a function in terms of its value.

**12.18 The speed-up theorem implies that for arbitrarily large recursive functions r we can find a language L for which there exists a sequence of TM's $M_1, M_2, \ldots$, each accepting L, such that the space used by M_i is at least r applied to the space used by M_{i+1}. However, we did not give an algorithm for finding such a sequence; we merely proved that it must exist. Prove that speed up is not effective, in that if for every TM accepting L, there is an M_i on the list using less space, then the list of TM's is not recursively enumerable.

*12.19 Which of the following are complexity measures?

a) $\Phi_i(n) =$ the number of state changes made by M_i on input n.

b) $\Phi_i(n) =$ the maximum number of moves made by M_i without a state change on input n.

c) $\Phi_i(n) = 0$ for all i and n.

d) $\Phi_i(n) = \begin{cases} 0 & \text{if } \phi_i(n) \text{ is defined,} \\ \text{undefined} & \text{otherwise.} \end{cases}$

**12.20 (*Honesty theorem for space*). Show that there is a total recursive function r such that for every space complexity class $\mathscr{C}$, there is a function $S(n)$ such that DSPACE$(S(n)) = \mathscr{C}$ and $S(n)$ is computable in $r(S(n))$ space.

*12.21 Theorem 12.7 shows that given $S(n)$, there is a set L such that any TM recognizing

L uses more than $S(n)$ space i.o. Strengthen this result to show there is a set L' such that any TM recognizing L' uses more than $S(n)$ space a.e.

12.22   Let Φ be a complexity measure and let $c(i, j)$ be any recursive function such that when $\phi_i(n)$ and $\phi_j(n)$ are defined then so is $\phi_{c(i,j)}(n)$. Prove there exists a recursive function h such that
$$\Phi_{c(i,j)}(n) \leq h(n, \Phi_i(n), \Phi_j(n)) \quad \text{a.e.}$$

12.23   Show that if $f(n)$ is fully space constructible then $\text{DTIME}(f(n) \log f(n)) \subseteq \text{DSPACE}(f(n))$.

12.24   Exhibit a TM that accepts an infinite set containing no infinite regular subset.

*12.25**   Consider one-tape TM's that use a constant one unit of ink each time they change a symbol on the tape.

   a) Prove a linear "speed-up" theorem for ink.
   b) Give an appropriate definition of a "fully ink-constructible" function.
   c) How much of an increase in the amount of ink is necessary to obtain a new complexity class?

12.26   A Turing machine is said to be *oblivious* if the head position at each time unit depends only on the length of the input and not on the actual input. Prove that if L is accepted by a k-tape $T(n)$ time-bounded TM, then L is accepted by a 2-tape $T(n) \log T(n)$ oblivious TM.

*12.27**   Let $L \subseteq (0 + 1)^*$ be the set accepted by some $T(n)$ time-bounded TM. Prove that for each n there exists a Boolean circuit, with inputs $x_1, \ldots, x_n$, having at most $T(n) \log T(n)$ two-input gates and producing output 1 if and only if the values of $x_1, \ldots, x_n$ correspond to a string in L. The values of $x_1, \ldots, x_n$ *correspond* to the string x if x_i has value true whenever the ith symbol of x is 1 and x_i has value false whenever the ith symbol of x is 0. [*Hint:* Simulate an oblivious TM.]

12.28   *Loop programs* consist of variables that take on integer values and statements. A *statement* is of one of the forms below.

   1) $\langle \text{variable} \rangle := \langle \text{variable} \rangle$
   2) $\langle \text{variable} \rangle := \langle \text{variable} \rangle + 1$
   3) **for** $i := 1$ **to** $\langle \text{variable} \rangle$ **do** statement;
   4) **begin** $\langle \text{statement} \rangle$; $\langle \text{statement} \rangle$; $\ldots$ $\langle \text{statement} \rangle$ **end**;

In (3) the value of the variable is bound before the loop, as in PL/I.
   a) Prove that loop programs always terminate.
   b) Prove that every loop program computes a primitive recursive function.
   c) Prove that every primitive recursive function is computed by some loop program.
   d) Prove that a TM with a primitive recursive running time can compute only a primitive recursive function.

*12.29**   Let F be a formal proof system in which we can prove theorems about one-tape TM's. Define a complexity class
$$C_{T(n)} = \{L(M_i) \,|\, \text{there exists a proof in } F \text{ that } T_i(n) \leq T(n) \text{ for all } n\}.$$

Can the time hierarchy of Exercise 12.16 be strengthened for provable complexity? [*Hint:* Replace the clock by a proof that $T_i(n) \leq T(n)$.]

Solutions to Selected Exercises

12.2(a)   Consider any string wcw^R of length n and let $\ell_{w,i}$ be the length of the crossing sequence between positions i and $i + 1$, for $1 \le i < n/2$, made by some one-tape TM M with s states. Suppose the average of $\ell_{w,i}$ over all words w of length $(n - 1)/2$ is $p(i)$. Then for at least half of all w's, $\ell_{w,i} \le 2p(i)$. The number of w's is $2^{(n-1)/2}$, so there are at least $2^{(n-3)/2}$ w's for which $\ell_{w,i} \le 2p(i)$. As the number of crossing sequences of length $2p(i)$ or less is

$$\sum_{j=0}^{2p(i)} s^j \le s^{2p(i)+1},$$

there must be at least $2^{(n-3)/2}/s^{2p(i)+1}$ w's with the same crossing sequence between positions i and $i + 1$. There are $2^{(n-1)/2-i}$ sequences of a's and b's that may appear in positions $i + 1$ through $(n - 1)/2$ in these words, so if

$$\frac{2^{(n-3)/2}}{s^{2p(i)+1}} > 2^{(n-1)/2-i} \tag{12.11}$$

Then two words with the same crossing sequence differ somewhere among the first i positions. Then by Exercise 12.1(b), M accepts a word it should not accept.

Thus (12.11) is false, and $s^{2p(i)+1} \ge 2^{i-1}$. Therefore,

$$p(i) \ge \frac{i - 1}{2 \log_2 s} - \frac{1}{2}$$

Surely there is some word w such that when presented with wcw^R, M takes at least average time. By Exercise 12.1(a), this average is at least

$$\sum_{i=1}^{(n-1)/2} p(i) \ge \sum_{i=1}^{(n-1)/2} \frac{i - 1}{2 \log_2 s} - \frac{n-1}{4} \ge \frac{1}{4 \log_2 s}\left(\frac{n-3}{2}\right)\left(\frac{n-1}{2}\right) - \frac{n-1}{4}$$

12.14(c)   We may design an off-line TM M of space complexity $S(n)$ to test for $i = 2, 3, \ldots$ whether its input length n is divisible by each i, stopping as soon as we encounter a value of i that does not divide n. As the test whether i divides n needs only $\log_2 i$ storage cells, $S(n)$ is the logarithm of the largest i such that $2, 3, \ldots, i$ all divide n. If we let $n = k!$, we know that $S(n) \ge \log_2 k$. As $k! \le k^k$, we know that

$$\log_2 n \le k \log_2 k$$

and

$$\log_2 \log_2 n \le \log_2 k + \log_2 \log_2 k \le 2 \log_2 k.$$

Thus for those values of n that are $k!$ for some k, it follows that

$$S(n) \ge \tfrac{1}{2} \log_2 \log_2 n.$$

We must show that for all n, $S(n) \le 1 + \log_2 \log_2 n$. It suffices to show that the smallest n for which $S(n) \ge k$, which is the least common multiple (LCM) of $2, 3, \ldots, 2^{k-1} + 1$, is at least $2^{2^{k-1}}$. That is, we need the fact that $\text{LCM}(2, 3, \ldots, i) \ge 2^{i-1}$. A proof requires results in the theory of numbers that we are not prepared to derive, in particular that the probability that integer i is a prime is asymptotically $1/\ln i$, where $\ln$ is the natural logarithm (see Hardy and Wright [1938]). Since $\text{LCM}(2, 3, \ldots, i)$ is at least the product of the primes between 2 and i, a lower bound on the order of e^i for $\text{LCM}(2, 3, \ldots, i)$ for large i is easy to show.

BIBLIOGRAPHIC NOTES

The study of time complexity can be said to begin with Hartmanis and Stearns [1965], where Theorems 12.3, 12.4, 12.5, and 12.9 are found. The serious study of space complexity begins with Hartmanis, Lewis, and Stearns [1965], and Lewis, Stearns, and Hartmanis [1965]; Theorems 12.1, 12.2, and 12.8 are from the former. Seiferas [1977a,b] presents some of the most recent results on complexity hierarchies. A number of earlier papers studied similar aspects of computation. In Grzegorczyk [1953], Axt [1959], and Ritchie [1963] we find hierarchies of recursive functions. Yamada [1962] studies the class of real-time computable functions $[T(n) = n]$. Rabin [1963] showed that two tapes can do more than one in real time, a result that has since been generalized by Aanderaa [1974] to k versus $k - 1$ tapes.

Theorem 12.6, showing that logarithmic slowdown suffices when one goes from many tapes to two is from Hennie and Stearns [1966]. Theorem 12.11, the quadratic relationship between deterministic and nondeterministic time, appears in Savitch [1970]. Translational lemmas were pioneered by Ruby and Fischer [1965], while Theorem 12.12, the nondeterministic space hierarchy, is by Ibarra [1972]. The nondeterministic time hierarchy alluded to in the text is from Cook [1973a]. The best nondeterministic hierarchies known are found in Sieferas, Fischer, and Meyer [1973]. Book and Greibach [1970] characterize the languages in $\bigcup_{c>0}$ NTIME(cn).

The study of abstract complexity measures originates with Blum [1967]. Theorem 12.13, the gap theorem, is from Borodin [1972] and (in essence) Trakhtenbrot [1964]; a stronger version is due to Constable [1972]. (Note that these and all the papers mentioned in this paragraph deal with Blum complexity measures, not solely with space, as we have done.) Theorem 12.14, the speed-up theorem, is from Blum [1967], and the union theorem is from McCreight and Meyer [1969]. Theorem 12.16, on recursive relationships among complexity measures, is from Blum [1967]. The honesty theorem mentioned in Exercse 12.20 is from McCreight and Meyer [1969]. The simplified approach to abstract complexity used in this book is based on the ideas of Hartmanis and Hopcroft [1971].

Crossing sequences, discussed in Exercises 12.1 and 12.2, are from Hennie [1965]. The generalization of crossing sequences used in Exercises 12.3 and 12.4 is developed in Hopcroft and Ullman [1969a], although Exercise 12.4 in the deterministic case is from Hartmanis, Lewis, and Stearns [1965]. Exercise 12.14(c) is from Freedman and Ladner [1975]. Exercise 12.16, a denser time hierarchy when TM's are restricted to have exactly k tapes, is from Paul [1977]. Exercise 12.18, showing that speed up cannot be made effective, is from Blum [1971]. Exercise 12.22 is from Hartmanis and Hopcroft [1971]. Exercise 12.23 is from Hopcroft, Paul, and Valiant [1975]. See also Paul, Tarjan, and Celoni [1976] for a proof that the method of Hopcroft *et al.* cannot be extended. Oblivious Turing machines and Exercises 2.26 and 2.27 are due to M. Fischer and N. Pippenger. Loop programs and Exercise 2.28 are from Ritchie [1963] and Meyer and Ritchie [1967].

INTRACTABLE
PROBLEMS

In Chapter 8 we discovered that one can pose problems that are not solvable on a computer. In this chapter we see that among the decidable problems, there are some so difficult that for all practical purposes, they cannot be solved in their full generality on a computer. Some of these problems, although decidable, have been proved to require exponential time for their solution. For others the implication is very strong that exponential time is required to solve them; if there were a faster way of solving them than the exponential one, then a great number of important problems in mathematics, computer science, and other fields—problems for which good solutions have been sought in vain over a period of many years—could be solved by substantially better means than are now known.

13.1 POLYNOMIAL TIME AND SPACE

The languages recognizable in deterministic polynomial time form a natural and important class, the class $\bigcup_{i \geq 1} \text{DTIME}(n^i)$, which we denote by $\mathcal{P}$. It is an intuitively appealing notion that $\mathcal{P}$ is the class of problems that can be solved efficiently. Although one might quibble that an n^{57} step algorithm is not very efficient, in practice we find that problems in $\mathcal{P}$ usually have low-degree polynomial time solutions.

There are a number of important problems that do not appear to be in $\mathcal{P}$ but have efficient nondeterministic algorithms. These problems fall into the class $\bigcup_{i \geq 1} \text{NTIME}(n^i)$, which we denote by $\mathcal{NP}$. An example is the Hamilton circuit problem: Does a graph have a cycle in which each vertex of the graph appears exactly once? There does not appear to be a deterministic polynomial time algorithm to recognize those graphs with Hamilton circuits. However, there is a simple nondeterministic algorithm; guess the edges in the cycle and verify that they do indeed form a Hamilton circuit.

The difference between $\mathscr{P}$ and $\mathscr{NP}$ is analagous to the difference between efficiently finding a proof of a statement (such as "this graph has a Hamilton circuit") and efficiently verifying a proof (i.e., checking that a particular circuit is Hamilton). We intuitively feel that checking a given proof is easier than finding one, but we don't know this for a fact.

Two other natural classes are

$$\text{PSPACE} = \bigcup_{i \geq 1} \text{DSPACE}(n^i)$$

and

$$\text{NSPACE} = \bigcup_{i \geq 1} \text{NSPACE}(n^i).$$

Note that by Savitch's theorem (Theorem 12.11) PSPACE = NSPACE, since $\text{NSPACE}(n^i) \subseteq \text{DSPACE}(n^{2i})$. Obviously, $\mathscr{P} \subseteq \mathscr{NP} \subseteq \text{PSPACE}$, yet it is not known if any of these containments are proper. Moreover, as we shall see, it is unlikely that the mathematical tools needed to resolve the questions one way or the other have been developed.

Within PSPACE we have two hierarchies of complexity classes:

$$\text{DSPACE}(\log n) \subsetneqq \text{DSPACE}(\log^2 n) \subsetneqq \text{DSPACE}(\log^3 n) \subsetneqq \cdots$$

and

$$\text{NSPACE}(\log n) \subsetneqq \text{NSPACE}(\log^2 n) \subsetneqq \text{NSPACE}(\log^3 n) \subsetneqq \cdots.$$

Clearly $\text{DSPACE}(\log^k n) \subseteq \text{NSPACE}(\log^k n)$ and thus by Savitch's theorem

$$\bigcup_{k \geq 1} \text{NSPACE}(\log^k n) = \bigcup_{k \geq 1} \text{DSPACE}(\log^k n).$$

Although one can show that

$$\mathscr{P} \neq \bigcup_{k \geq 1} \text{DSPACE}(\log^k n),$$

containment of either class in the other is unknown. Nevertheless

$$\text{DSPACE}(\log n) \subseteq \mathscr{P} \subseteq \mathscr{NP} \subseteq \text{PSPACE},$$

and at least one of the containments is proper, since $\text{DSPACE}(\log n) \subsetneqq \text{PSPACE}$ by the space hierarchy theorem.

Bounded reducibilities

Recall that in Chapter 8 we showed a language L to be undecidable by taking a known undecidable language L' and *reducing* it to L. That is, we exhibited a mapping g computed by a TM that always halts, such that for all strings x, x is in

L' if and only if $g(x)$ is in L. Then if L were recursive, L' could be recognized by computing $g(x)$ and deciding whether $g(x)$ is in L.

By restricting g to be an easily computable function, we can establish that L' is or is not in some class such as $\mathscr{P}$, $\mathscr{NP}$, or PSPACE. We shall be interested particularly in two types of reducibility: polynomial time reducibility and log-space reducibility. We say that L' is *polynomial-time reducible* to L if there is a polynomial-time bounded TM that for each input x produces an output y that is in L if and only if x is in L'.

Lemma 13.1 Let L' be polynomial-time reducible to L. Then

a) L' is in $\mathscr{NP}$ if L is in $\mathscr{NP}$,

b) L' is in $\mathscr{P}$ if L is in $\mathscr{P}$.

Proof The proofs of (a) and (b) are similar. We prove only (b). Assume that the reduction is $p_1(n)$ time bounded and that L is recognizable in time $p_2(n)$, where p_1 and p_2 are polynomials. Then L' can be recognized in polynomial time as follows. Given input x of length n, produce y using the polynomial-time reduction. As the reduction is $p_1(n)$ time bounded, and at most one symbol can be printed per move, it follows that $|y| \le p_1(n)$. Then, we can test if y is in L in time $p_2(p_1(n))$. Thus the total time to tell whether x is in L' is $p_1(n) + p_2(p_1(n))$, which is polynomial in n. Therefore, L' is in P. □

A *log-space transducer* is an off-line TM that always halts, having log n scratch storage and a write-only output tape on which the head never moves left. We say that L' is *log-space reducible* to L if there is a log-space transducer that given input x, produces an output string y that is in L if and only if x is in L'.

Lemma 13.2 If L' is log-space reducible to L, then

a) L' is in $\mathscr{P}$ if L is in $\mathscr{P}$,

b) L' is in NSPACE($\log^k n$) if L is in NSPACE($\log^k n$),

c) L' is in DSPACE($\log^k n$) if L is in DSPACE($\log^k n$).

Proof

a) It suffices to show that a log-space reduction cannot take more than polynomial time, so the result follows from Lemma 13.1(b). In proof, note that the output tape contents cannot influence the computation, so the product of the number of states, storage tape contents, and positions of the input and storage tape heads is an upper bound on the number of moves that can be made before the log-space transducer must enter a loop, which would contradict the assumption that it always halts. If the storage tape has length log n, the bound is easily seen to be polynomial in n.

There is a subtlety involved in the proofs of (b) and (c). We prove only (c), the proof of (b) being essentially the same as for (c).

c) Let M_1 be the log-space transducer that reduces L' to L, and let M_2 be a $\log^k n$ space bounded TM accepting L. On input x of length n, M_1 produces an output of length bounded by n^c for some constant c. Since the output cannot be written in $\log^k n$ space, M_1 and M_2 cannot be simulated by storing the output of M_1 on a tape. Instead the output of M_1 can be fed directly to M_2, a symbol at a time. This works as long as M_2 moves right on its input. Should M_2 move left, M_1 must be restarted to determine the input symbol for M_2, since the output of M_1 is not saved.

We construct M_3 to accept L' as follows. One storage tape of M_3 holds the input position of M_2 in base 2^c. Since the input position cannot exceed n^c, this number can be stored in $\log n$ space. The other storage tapes of M_3 simulate the storage tapes of M_1 and M_2. Suppose at some time M_2's input head is at position i, and M_2 makes a move left or right. M_3 adjusts the state and storage tapes of M_2 accordingly. Then M_3 restarts the simulation of M_1 from the beginning, and waits until M_1 has produced $i - 1$ or $i + 1$ output symbols if M_2's input head moved left or right, respectively. The last output symbol produced is the new symbol scanned by M_2's head, so M_3 is ready to simulate the next move of M_2. As special cases, if $i = 1$ and M_2 moves left, we assume that M_2 next scans the left endmarker, and if M_1 halts before producing $i + 1$ output symbols (when M_2 moves right), we assume that M_2 next scans the right endmarker. M_3 accepts its own input whenever M_2 accepts its simulated input. Thus M_3 is a $\log^k n$ space bounded TM accepting L'. $\qquad\square$

Lemma 13.3 The composition of two log-space (resp. polynomial-time) reductions is a log-space (resp. polynomial-time) reduction.

Proof An easy generalization of the constructions in Lemmas 13.1 and 13.2.

$\qquad\square$

Complete problems

As we have mentioned, no one knows whether $\mathcal{NP}$ includes languages not in $\mathcal{P}$, so the issue of proper containment is open. One way to find a language in $\mathcal{NP} - \mathcal{P}$ is to look for a "hardest" problem in $\mathcal{NP}$. Intuitively, a language L_0 is a hardest problem if every language in $\mathcal{NP}$ is reducible to L_0 by an easily computable reduction. Depending on the exact kind of reducibility, we can conclude certain things about L_0. For example, if all of $\mathcal{NP}$ is log-space reducible to L_0, we can conclude that if L_0 were in $\mathcal{P}$, then $\mathcal{P}$ would equal $\mathcal{NP}$. Similarly, if L_0 were in DSPACE($\log n$), then $\mathcal{NP} = $ DSPACE($\log n$). If all of $\mathcal{NP}$ were polynomial-time reducible to L_0, then we could still conclude that if L_0 were in $\mathcal{P}$, then $\mathcal{P}$ would equal $\mathcal{NP}$, but we could not conclude from the statement L_0 is in DSPACE($\log n$) that $\mathcal{NP} = $ DSPACE($\log n$).

We see from the above examples that the notion of "hardest" may depend on the kind of reducibility involved. That is, there may be languages L_0 such that all languages in $\mathcal{NP}$ have polynomial-time reductions to L_0, but not all have log-space reductions to L_0. Moreover, log-space and polynomial-time reductions do not exhaust the kinds of reductions we might consider. With this in mind, we define the notion of hardest (*complete*) problems for a general class of languages with respect to a particular kind of reduction. Clearly the following generalizes to an arbitrary type of reduction.

Let $\mathcal{C}$ be a class of languages. We say language L is *complete for $\mathcal{C}$ with respect to polynomial-time* (resp. *log-space*) *reductions* if L is in $\mathcal{C}$, and every language in $\mathcal{C}$ is polynomial-time (resp. log-space) reducible to L. We say L is *hard for $\mathcal{C}$ with respect to polynomial-time* (resp. *log-space*) *reductions* if every language in $\mathcal{C}$ is polynomial-time (resp. log-space) reducible to L, but L is not necessarily in $\mathcal{C}$. Two special cases are of primary importance, and we introduce shorthands for them. L is *NP-complete* (*NP-hard*) if L is complete (hard) for $\mathcal{NP}$ with respect to log-space reductions.† L is *PSPACE-complete* (*PSPACE-hard*) if L is complete (hard) for PSPACE with respect to polynomial time reductions.

In order to show a first language L_0 to be *NP*-complete, we must give a log-space reduction of each language in $\mathcal{NP}$ to L_0. Once we have an *NP*-complete problem L_0, we may prove another language L_1 in $\mathcal{NP}$ to be *NP*-complete by exhibiting a log-space reduction of L_0 to L_1, since the composition of two log-space reductions is a log-space reduction by Lemma 13.3. This same technique will be used for establishing complete problems for other classes as well.

13.2 SOME *NP*-COMPLETE PROBLEMS

The significance of the class of *NP*-complete problems is that it includes many problems that are natural and have been examined seriously for efficient solutions. None of these problems is known to have a polynomial-time solution. The fact that if any one of these problems were in $\mathcal{P}$ all would be, reinforces the notion that they are unlikely to have polynomial-time solutions. Moreover, if a new problem is proved *NP*-complete, then we have the same degree of confidence that the new problem is hard that we have for the classical problems.

The first problem we show to be *NP*-complete, which happens to be historically the first such problem, is satisfiability for Boolean expressions. We begin by defining the problem precisely.

The satisfiability problem

A *Boolean expression* is an expression composed of variables, parentheses, and the operators $\wedge$ (logical AND), $\vee$ (logical OR) and $\neg$ (negation). The precedence of these operators is $\neg$ highest, then $\wedge$, then $\vee$. Variables take on values 0 (false) and 1 (true); so do expressions. If E_1 and E_2 are Boolean expressions, then the

---

† Many authors use the term "*NP*-complete" to mean "complete for $\mathcal{NP}$ with respect to polynomial time reductions," or in some cases, "with respect to polynomial time Turing reductions."

value of $E_1 \wedge E_2$ is 1 if both E_1 and E_2 have value 1, and 0 otherwise. The value of $E_1 \vee E_2$ is 1 if either E_1 or E_2 has value 1, and 0 otherwise. The value of $\neg E_1$ is 1 if E_1 is 0 and 0 if E_1 is 1. An expression is *satisfiable* if there is some assignment of 0's and 1's to the variables that gives the expression the value 1. The *satisfiability problem* is to determine, given a Boolean expression, whether it is satisfiable.

We may represent the satisfiability problem as a language L_{sat} as follows. Let the variables of some expression be $x_1, x_2, \ldots, x_m$ for some m. Code x_i as the symbol x followed by i written in binary. The alphabet of L_{sat} is thus

$$\{\wedge, \vee, \neg, (,), x, 0, 1\}.$$

The length of the coded version of an expression of n symbols is easily seen to be no more than $\lceil n \log_2 n \rceil$, since each symbol other than a variable is coded by one symbol, there are no more than $\lceil n/2 \rceil$ different variables in an expression of length n, and the code for a variable requires no more than $1 + \lceil \log_2 n \rceil$ symbols. We shall henceforth treat the word in L_{sat} representing an expression of length n as if the word itself were of length n. Our results will not depend on whether we use n or $n \log n$ for the length of the word, since $\log(n \log n) \leq 2 \log n$, and we shall deal with log-space reductions.

A Boolean expression is said to be in *conjunctive*† *normal form* (*CNF*) if it is of the form $E_1 \wedge E_2 \wedge \cdots \wedge E_k$, and each E_i, called a *clause* (or *conjunct*), is of the form $\alpha_{i1} \vee \alpha_{i2} \vee \cdots \vee \alpha_{ir_i}$, where each α_{ij} is a *literal*, that is, either x or $\neg x$, for some variable x. We usually write $\bar{x}$ instead of $\neg x$. For example, $(x_1 \vee x_2) \wedge (\bar{x}_1 \vee x_3 \vee \bar{x}_4) \wedge \bar{x}_3$ is in CNF. The expression is said to be in *3-CNF* if each clause has exactly three distinct literals. The above example is not in 3-CNF because the first and third clauses have fewer than three literals.

Satisfiability is *NP*-complete

We begin by giving a log-space reduction of each language in $\mathcal{NP}$ to L_{sat}.

Theorem 13.1 The satisfiability problem is *NP*-complete.

Proof The easy part of the proof is that L_{sat} is in $\mathcal{NP}$. To determine if an expression of length n is satisfiable, nondeterministically guess values for all the variables and then evaluate the expression. Thus L_{sat} is in $\mathcal{NP}$.

To show that every language in $\mathcal{NP}$ is reducible to L_{sat}, for each NTM M that is time bounded by a polynomial $p(n)$, we give a log-space algorithm that takes as input a string x and produces a Boolean formula E_x that is satisfiable if and only if M accepts x. We now describe E_x.

Let $\#\beta_0 \# \beta_1 \# \cdots \# \beta_{p(n)}$ be a computation of M, where each β_i is an ID consisting of exactly $p(n)$ symbols. If acceptance occurs before the $p(n)$th move, we allow the accepting ID to repeat, so each computation has exactly $p(n) + 1$ ID's.

---

† "Conjunctive" is an adjective referring to the logical AND operator (*conjunction*). The term *disjunctive* is similarly applied to logical OR.

In each ID we group the state with the symbol scanned to form a single composite symbol. In addition, the composite symbol in the ith ID contains an integer m indicating the move by which the $(i + 1)$st ID follows from the ith. Numbers are assigned to moves by arbitrarily ordering the finite set of choices that M may make given a state and tape symbol.

For each symbol that can appear in a computation and for each i, $0 \le i < (p(n) + 1)^2$, we create a Boolean variable c_{iX} to indicate whether the ith symbol in the computation is X. (The 0th symbol in the computation is the initial #.) The expression E_x that we shall construct will be true for a given assignment to the c_{iX}'s if and only if the c_{iX}'s that are true correspond to a valid computation. The expression E_x states the following:

1) The C_{iX}'s that are true correspond to a string of symbols, in that exactly one C_{iX} is true for each i.

2) The ID β_0 is an initial ID of M with input x.

3) The last ID contains a final state.

4) Each ID follows from the previous one by the move of M that is indicated.

The formula E_x is the logical AND of four formulas, each enforcing one of the above conditions. The first formula, stating that for each i between 0 and $(p(n) + 1)^2 - 1$, exactly one C_{iX} is true is

$$\bigwedge_i \left[\bigvee_X C_{iX} \wedge \neg \left(\bigvee_{X \ne Y} (C_{iX} \wedge C_{iY}) \right) \right].$$

For a given value of i the term $\bigvee_X C_{iX}$ forces at least one C_{iX} to be true and $\neg \bigvee_{X \ne Y} (C_{iX} \wedge C_{iY})$ forces at most one to be true.

Let $x = a_1 a_2 \cdots a_n$. The second formula expressing the fact that β_0 is an initial ID is in turn the AND of the following terms.

i) $c_{0\#} \wedge c_{p(n)+1,\#}$. The symbols in positions 0 and $p(n) + 1$ are #.

ii) $c_{1Y_1} \vee c_{1Y_2} \vee \cdots \vee c_{1Y_k}$, where $Y_1, Y_2, \ldots, Y_k$ are all the composite symbols that represent tape symbol a_1, the start state q_0, and the number of a legal move of M in state q_0 reading symbol a_1. This clause states that the first symbol of β_0 is correct.

iii) $\bigwedge_{2 \le i \le n} c_{ia_i}$. The 2nd through nth symbols of β_0 are correct.

iv) $\bigwedge_{n < i \le p(n)} c_{iB}$. The remaining symbols of β_0 are blank.

The third formula says that the last ID has an accepting state. It can be written

$$\bigvee_{p(n)(p(n)+1) < i < (p(n)+1)^2} \left(\bigvee_{X \text{ in } F} c_{iX} \right),$$

where F is the set of composite symbols that include a final state.

To see how to write the fourth formula stating that each ID β_i, $i \geq 1$, follows from β_{i-1} by the move appearing in the composite symbol of β_{i-1}, observe that we can essentially deduce each symbol of β_i from the corresponding symbol of β_{i-1} and the symbols on either side (one of which may be #). That is, the symbol in β_i is the same as the corresponding symbol in β_{i-1} unless that symbol had the state and move, or one of the adjacent symbols had the state and move, and the move caused the head position to shift to where the symbol of β_i in question was. Note that should this symbol of β_i be the one representing the state, it also represents an arbitrary legal move of M, so there may be more than one legal symbol. Also note that if the previous ID has an accepting state, the current and previous ID's are equal.

We can therefore easily specify a predicate $f(W, X, Y, Z)$ that is true if and only if symbol Z could appear in position j of some ID given that W, X, and Y are the symbols in positions $j - 1$, j, and $j + 1$ of the previous ID [W is # if $j = 1$ and Y is # if $j = p(n)$]. It is convenient also to declare $f(W, \#, X, \#)$ to be true, so we can treat the markers between ID's as we treat the symbols within ID's. We can now express the fourth formula as

$$\bigwedge_{p(n) < j < (p(n)+1)^2} \left(\bigvee_{\substack{W,X,Y,Z \text{ such} \\ \text{that } f(W,X,Y,Z)}} \left(c_{j-p(n)-2,W} \wedge c_{j-p(n)-1,X} \wedge c_{j-p(n),Y} \wedge c_{jZ} \right) \right).$$

It is easy, given an accepting computation of M on x to find truth values for the c_{iX}'s that make E_x true. Just make c_{iX} true if and only if the ith symbol of the computation is X. Conversely, given an assignment of truth values making E_x true, the four formulas above guarantee that there is an accepting computation of M on x. Note that even though M is nondeterministic, the fact that a move choice is incorporated into each ID guarantees that the next state, symbol printed, and direction of head motion going from one ID to the next will all be consistent with some one choice of M.

Furthermore, the formulas composing E_x are of length $O(p^2(n))$ and are sufficiently simple that a log-space TM can generate them given x on its input. The TM only needs sufficient storage to count up to $(p(n) + 1)^2$. Since the logarithm of a polynomial in n is some constant times log n, this can be done with $O(\log n)$ storage. We have thus shown that every language in *NP* is log-space reducible to L_{sat}, proving that L_{sat} is *NP*-complete. □

We have just shown that satisfiability for Boolean expressions is *NP*-complete. This means that a polynomial-time algorithm for accepting L_{sat} could be used to accept any language in $\mathcal{NP}$. Let L be the language accepted by some $p(n)$ time-bounded nondeterministic Turing machine M, and let A be the log-space (hence polynomial-time) transducer that converts x to E_x, where E_x is satisfiable if and only if M accepts x. Then A combined with the algorithm for L_{sat}

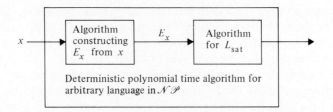

Fig. 13.1   Algorithm for arbitrary set L in $\mathcal{NP}$ given algorithm for L_{sat}.

as shown in Fig. 13.1 is a deterministic polynomial-time algorithm accepting L. Thus the existence of a polynomial-time algorithm for just this one problem, the satisfiability of Boolean expressions, would imply $\mathcal{P} = \mathcal{NP}$.

Restricted satisfiability problems that are *NP*-complete

Recall that a Boolean formula is in conjunctive normal form (CNF) if it is the logical AND of clauses, which are the logical OR of literals. We say the formula is in *k-CNF* if each clause has exactly k literals. For example, $(x \vee y) \wedge (\bar{x} \vee z) \wedge (y \vee \bar{z})$ is in 2-CNF.

We shall now consider two languages, L_{csat}, the set of satisfiable Boolean formulas in CNF, and $L_{3\text{sat}}$, the set of satisfiable Boolean formulas in 3-CNF. We give log-space reductions of L_{sat} to L_{csat} and L_{csat} to $L_{3\text{sat}}$, showing the latter two problems *NP*-complete by Lemma 13.3. In each case we map an expression to another expression that may not be equivalent, but is satisfiable if and only if the original expression is satisfiable.

Theorem 13.2 L_{csat}, the satisfiability problem for CNF expressions, is *NP*-complete.

Proof   Clearly L_{csat} is in $\mathcal{NP}$, since L_{sat} is. We reduce L_{sat} to L_{csat} as follows. Let E be an arbitrary Boolean expression of length n.† Certainly, the number of variable occurrences in E does not exceed n, nor does the number of $\wedge$ and $\vee$ operators. Using the identities

$$\neg(E_1 \wedge E_2) = \neg(E_1) \vee \neg(E_2),$$
$$\neg(E_1 \vee E_2) = \neg(E_1) \wedge \neg(E_2), \tag{13.1}$$
$$\neg\neg E_1 = E_1,$$

we can transform E to an equivalent expression E', in which the $\neg$ operators are applied only to variables, never to more complex expressions. The validity of Eqs. (13.1) may be checked by considering the four assignments of values 0 and 1 to E_1

---

† Recall that the length of a Boolean expression is the number of characters, not the length of its code, and recall that this difference is of no account where log-space reduction is concerned.

and E_2. Incidentally, the first two of these equations are known as *DeMorgan's laws*.

The transformation can be viewed as the composition of two log-space transformations. As a result of the first transformation, each negation symbol that immediately precedes a variable is replaced by a bar over the variable, and each closing parenthesis whose matching opening parenthesis is immediately preceded by a negation sign is replaced by $)\vdash$. The symbol $\vdash$ indicates the end of the scope of a negation. This first transformation is easily accomplished in log-space using a counter to locate the matching parentheses.

The second transformation is accomplished by a finite automaton that scans the input from left to right, keeping track of the parity (modulo 2 sum) of the *active* negations, those whose immediately following opening parenthesis but not closing parenthesis has been seen. When the parity of negations is odd, x is replaced by $\bar{x}$, $\bar{x}$ by x, $\vee$ by $\wedge$, and $\wedge$ by $\vee$. The symbols $\neg$ and $\vdash$ are deleted. That this transformation is correct may be proved using (13.1) by an easy induction on the length of an expression. We now have an expression E' in which all negations are applied directly to variables.

Next we create E'', an expression in CNF that is satisfiable if and only if E' is satisfiable. Let V_1 and V_2 be sets of variables, with $V_1 \subseteq V_2$. We say an assignment of values to V_2 is an *extension* of an assignment of values to V_1 if the assignments agree on the variables of V_1. We shall prove by induction on r, the number of $\wedge$'s and $\vee$'s in an expression E', all of whose negations are applied to variables, that if $|E'| = n$, then there is a list of at most n clauses, $F_1, F_2, ..., F_k$, over a set of variables that includes the variables of E' and at most n other variables, such that E' is given value 1 by an assignment to its variables if and only if there is an extension of that assignment that satisfies $F_1 \wedge F_2 \wedge \cdots \wedge F_k$.

Basis $r = 0$. Then E' is a literal, and we may take that literal in a clause by itself to satisfy the conditions.

Induction   If $E' = E_1 \wedge E_2$, let $F_1, F_2, ..., F_k$ and $G_1, G_2, ..., G_l$ be the clauses for E_1 and E_2 that exist by the inductive hypothesis. Assume without loss of generality that no variable that is not present in E' appears both among the F's and among the G's. Then $F_1, F_2, ..., F_k, G_1, G_2, ..., G_l$ satisfies the conditions for E'.

If $E' = E_1 \vee E_2$, let the F's and G's be as above, and let y be a new variable. Then $y \vee F_1, y \vee F_2, ..., y \vee F_k, \bar{y} \vee G_1, \bar{y} \vee G_2, ..., \bar{y} \vee G_l$ satisfies the conditions. In proof, suppose an assignment of values satisfies E'. Then it must satisfy E_1 or E_2. If the assignment satisfies E_1, then some extension of the assignment satisfies $F_1, F_2, ..., F_k$. Any further extension of this assignment that assigns $y = 0$ will satisfy all the clauses for E'. If the assignment satisfies E_2, a similar argument suffices. Conversely, suppose all the clauses for E' are satisfied by some assignment. If that assignment sets $y = 1$, then all of $G_1, G_2, ..., G_l$ must be satisfied, so E_2 is satisfied. A similar argument applies if $y = 0$. The desired expression E'' is all the clauses for E' connected by $\wedge$'s.

To see that the above transformation can be accomplished in log-space, consider the parse tree for E. Let y_i be the variable introduced by the ith $\vee$. The final expression is the logical AND of clauses, where each clause contains a literal of the original expression. In addition, if the literal is in the left subtree of the ith $\vee$, then the clause also contains y_i. If the literal is in the right subtree of the ith $\vee$, then the clause contains $\bar{y}_i$. The input is scanned from left to right. Each time a literal is encountered, a clause is emitted. To determine which y_i's and $\bar{y}_i$'s to include in the clause, we use a counter of length $\log n$ to remember our place on the input. We then scan the entire input, and for each $\vee$ symbol, say the ith from the left, we determine its left and right operands, using another counter of length $\log n$ to count parentheses. If the current literal is in the left operand, generate y_i; if it is in the right operand, generate $\bar{y}_i$, and if in neither operand, generate neither y_i nor $\bar{y}_i$.

We have thus reduced each Boolean expression E to a CNF expression E'' that is in L_{csat} if and only if E is in L_{sat}. Since the reduction is accomplished in log-space, the NP-completeness of L_{sat} implies the NP-completeness of L_{csat}. $\square$

Example 13.1   Let

$$E = \neg(\neg(x_1 \vee x_2) \wedge (\neg x_1 \vee x_2)).$$

Applying DeMorgan's laws yields

$$E' = (x_1 \vee x_2) \vee (x_1 \wedge \bar{x}_3).$$

The transformation to CNF introduces variables y_1 and y_2 to give

$$E'' = (x_1 \vee y_1 \vee y_2) \wedge (x_2 \vee \bar{y}_1 \vee y_2) \wedge (x_1 \vee \bar{y}_2) \wedge (\bar{x}_3 \vee \bar{y}_2)$$

Theorem 13.3 $L_{3\text{sat}}$, the satisfiability problem for 3-CNF expressions, is NP-complete.

Proof   Clearly, $L_{3\text{sat}}$ is in $\mathcal{NP}$, since L_{sat} is. Let $E = F_1 \wedge F_2 \wedge \cdots \wedge F_k$ be a CNF expression. Suppose some clause F_i has more than three literals, say

$$F_i = \alpha_1 \vee \alpha_2 \vee \cdots \vee \alpha_\ell, \qquad \ell > 3.$$

Introduce new variables $y_1, y_2, \ldots, y_{\ell-3}$, and replace F_i by

$$(\alpha_1 \vee \alpha_2 \vee y_1) \wedge (\alpha_3 \vee \bar{y}_1 \vee y_2) \wedge (\alpha_4 \vee \bar{y}_2 \vee y_3) \wedge \cdots$$
$$\wedge (\alpha_{\ell-2} \vee \bar{y}_{\ell-4} \vee y_{\ell-3}) \wedge (\alpha_{\ell-1} \vee \alpha_\ell \vee \bar{y}_{\ell-3}). \quad (13.2)$$

Then F_i is satisfied by an assignment if and only if an extension of that assignment satisfies (13.2). An assignment satisfying F_i must have $\alpha_j = 1$ for some j. Thus assume that the assignment gives literals $\alpha_1, \alpha_2, \ldots, \alpha_{j-1}$ the value 0 and α_j the value 1. Then $y_m = 1$ for $m \leq j - 2$ and $y_m = 0$ for $m \geq j - 1$ is an extension of the assignment satisfying (13.2).

Conversely, we must show that any assignment satisfying (13.2) must have $\alpha_j = 1$ for some j and thus satisfies F_i. Assume to the contrary that the assignment gives all the α_m's the value 0. Then since the first clause has value 1, it follows that $y_1 = 1$. Since the second clause has value 1, y_2 must be 1, and by induction, $y_m = 1$ for all m. But then the last clause would have the value 0, contradicting the assumption that (13.2) is satisfied. Thus any assignment that satisfies (13.2) also satisfies F_i.

The only other alterations necessary are when F_i consists of one or two literals. In the latter case replace $\alpha_1 \vee \alpha_2$ by $(\alpha_1 \vee \alpha_2 \vee y) \wedge (\alpha_1 \vee \alpha_2 \vee \bar{y})$, where y is a new variable, and in the former case an introduction of two new variables suffices. Thus E can be converted to a 3-CNF expression that is satisfiable if and only if E is satisfiable. The transformation is easily accomplished in log-space. We have thus a log-space reduction of L_{csat} to L_{3sat} and conclude that L_{3sat} is *NP*-complete. □

The vertex cover problem

It turns out that 3-CNF satisfiability is a convenient problem to reduce to other problems in order to show them *NP*-complete, just as Post's correspondence problem is useful for showing other problems undecidable. Another *NP*-complete problem that is often easy to reduce to other problems is the vertex cover problem. Let $G = (V, E)$ be an (undirected) graph with set of vertices V and edges E. A subset $A \subseteq V$ is said to be a *vertex cover* of G if for every edge (v, w) in E, at least one of v or w is in A. The *vertex cover problem* is: Given a graph G and integer k, does G have a vertex cover of size k or less?

We may represent this problem as a language L_{vc}, consisting of strings of the form: k in binary, followed by a marker, followed by the list of vertices, where v_i is represented by v followed by i in binary, and a list of edges, where (v_i, v_j) is represented by the codes for v_i and v_j surrounded by parentheses. L_{vc} consists of all such strings representing k and G, such that G has a vertex cover of size k or less.

Theorem 13.4 L_{vc}, the vertex cover problem, is *NP*-complete.

Proof To show L_{vc} in $\mathcal{NP}$, guess a subset of k vertices and check that it covers all edges. This may be done in time proportional to the square of the length of the problem representation. L_{vc} is shown to be *NP*-complete by reducing 3-CNF satisfiability to L_{vc}.

Let $F = F_1 \wedge F_2 \wedge \cdots \wedge F_q$ be an expression in 3-CNF, where each F_i is a clause of the form $(\alpha_{i1} \vee \alpha_{i2} \vee \alpha_{i3})$, each α_{ij} being a literal. We construct an undirected graph $G = (V, E)$ whose vertices are pairs of integers (i, j), $1 \leq i \leq q$, $1 \leq j \leq 3$. The vertex (i, j) represents the jth literal of the ith clause. The edges of the graph are

1) $[(i, j), (i, k)]$ provided $j \neq k$, and
2) $[(i, j), (k, \ell)]$ if $\alpha_{ij} = \neg \alpha_{k\ell}$.

Each pair of vertices corresponding to the same clause are connected by an edge in (1). Each pair of vertices corresponding to a literal and its complement are connected by an edge in (2).

G has been constructed so that it has a vertex cover of size $2q$ if and only if F is satisfiable. To see this, assume F is satisfiable and fix an assignment satisfying F. Each clause must have a literal whose value is 1. Select one such literal for each clause. Delete the q vertices corresponding to these literals from V. The remaining vertices form a vertex cover of size $2q$. Clearly for each i, only one vertex of the form (i, j) is missing from the cover, and hence each edge in (1) is incident upon† at least one vertex in the cover. Since edges in (2) are incident upon two vertices corresponding to some literal and its complement, and since we could not have deleted both a literal and its complement, one or the other of these vertices is in the cover. Thus we indeed have a cover of size $2q$.

Conversely, assume we have a vertex cover of size $2q$. For each i the cover must contain all but one vertex of the form (i, j), for if two such vertices were missing, an edge $[(i, j), (i, k)]$ would not be incident upon any vertex in the cover. For each i assign value 1 to the literal α_{ij} corresponding to the vertex (i, j) not in the cover. There can be no conflict, because two vertices not in the cover cannot correspond to a literal and its complement, else there would be an edge in group (2) not incident upon any vertex of the cover. For this assignment F has value 1. Thus F is satisfiable. The reduction is easily accomplished in log-space. We can essentially use the variable names in the formula F as the vertices of G, appending two bits for the j-component in vertex (i, j). Edges of type (1) are generated directly from the clauses, while those of type (2) require two counters to consider all pairs of literals. Thus we conclude that L_{vc} is NP-complete.   □

Example 13.2   Consider the expression

$$F = (x_1 \vee x_2 \vee x_3) \wedge (\bar{x}_1 \vee x_2 \vee x_4) \wedge (\bar{x}_2 \vee x_3 \vee x_5) \wedge (\bar{x}_3 \vee \bar{x}_4 \vee \bar{x}_5).$$

The construction of Theorem 13.4 yields the graph of Fig. 13.2. $x_1 = 1$, $x_2 = 1$, $x_3 = 1$, $x_4 = 0$ satisfies F and corresponds to the vertex cover $[1, 2]$, $[1, 3]$, $[2, 1]$, $[2, 3]$, $[3, 1]$, $[3, 3]$, $[4, 1]$, and $[4, 3]$.

The Hamilton circuit problem

The *Hamilton circuit problem* is: Given a graph G, does G have a path that visits each vertex exactly once and returns to its starting point? The *directed Hamilton circuit problem* is the analogous problem for directed graphs. We represent these problems as languages L_h and L_{dh} by encoding graphs as in the vertex cover problem.

---

† An edge (v, w) is *incident upon* v and w and no other vertices.

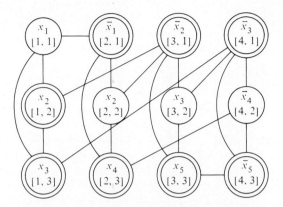

Fig. 13.2 Graph constructed by Theorem 13.4.
Double circles indicate vertices in set cover.

Theorem 13.5 L_{dh}, the directed Hamilton circuit problem, is *NP*-complete.

Proof To show L_{dh} in $\mathcal{NP}$, guess a list of arcs and verify that the arcs form a simple cycle† through all the vertices. To show L_{dh} is *NP*-complete, we reduce 3-CNF satisfiability to L_{dh}.

Let $F = F_1 \wedge F_2 \wedge \cdots \wedge F_q$ be an expression in 3-CNF, where each F_i is a clause of the form $(\alpha_{i1} \vee \alpha_{i2} \vee \alpha_{i3})$, each α_{ij} being a literal. Let $x_1, \ldots, x_n$ be the variables of F. We construct a directed graph G that is composed of two types of subgraphs. For each variable x_i there is a subgraph H_i of the form shown in Fig. 13.3(a), where m_i is the larger of the number of occurrences of x_i and $\bar{x}_i$ in F. The H_i's are connected in a cycle, as shown in Fig. 13.3(b). That is, there are arcs from d_i to a_{i+1}, for $1 \le i < n$ and an arc from d_n to a_1.

Suppose we had a Hamilton circuit for the graph of Fig. 13.3(b). We may as well suppose it starts at a_1. If it goes next to b_{10}, we claim it must then go to c_{10}, else c_{10} could never appear on the cycle. In proof, note that both predecessors of c_{10} are already on the cycle, and for the cycle to later reach c_{10} it would have to repeat a vertex. (This argument about Hamilton circuits occurs frequently in the proof. We shall simply say that a vertex like c_{10} "would become inaccessible.") Similarly, we may argue that a Hamilton circuit that begins a_1, b_{10} must continue $c_{10}, b_{11}, c_{11}, b_{12}, c_{12}, \ldots$ If the circuit begins a_1, c_{10}, then it descends the ladder of Fig. 13.3(a) in the opposite way, continuing $b_{10}, c_{11}, b_{11}, c_{12}, \ldots$ Likewise we may argue that when the circuit enters each H_i in turn it may go from a_i to either b_{i0} or c_{i0}, but then its path through H_i is fixed; in the former case it descends by the arcs $c_{ij} \rightarrow b_{i,j+1}$, and in the latter case by the arcs $b_{ij} \rightarrow c_{i,j+1}$. In what follows, it helps to think of the choice to go from a_i to b_{i0} as making x_i true, while the opposite choice makes x_i false. With this in mind, observe that the graph of Fig. 13.3(b) has

---

† A *simple* cycle has no repeated vertex.

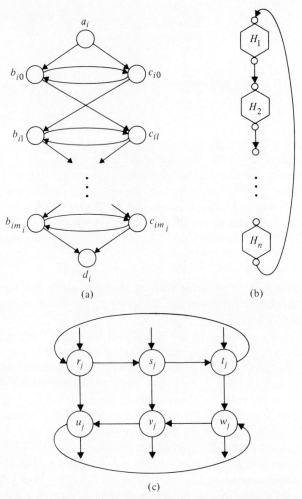

Fig. 13.3 Graphs concerned with directed Hamilton circuits.

exactly 2^n Hamilton circuits that correspond in a natural way to the 2^n assignments to the variables of F.

For each clause F_j we introduce a subgraph I_j, shown in Fig. 13.3(c). I_j has the properties that if a Hamilton circuit enters it at r_j, it must leave at u_j; if it enters at s_j, it must leave at v_j; and if it enters at t_j, it must leave at w_j. In proof, suppose by symmetry that the circuit enters I_j at r_j.

CASE 1   The next two vertices on the circuit are s_j and t_j. Then the circuit must continue with w_j, and if it leaves at w_j or v_j, u_j is inaccessible. Thus in this case it leaves at u_j.

CASE 2   The next two vertices on the circuit are s_j and v_j. If the circuit does not next go to u_j, then u_j will be inaccessible. If after u_j it goes to w_j, vertex t_j cannot appear on the circuit because its successors are already on the circuit. Thus in this case the circuit also leaves by u_j.

CASE 3   The circuit goes directly to u_j. If it next goes to w_j, the circuit cannot include t_j, because its successors are already used. So again it must leave by u_j.

Observe that the above argument holds even though the circuit may enter I_j more than once. Finally, the graph I_j has the additional property that entering I_j at r_j, s_j, or t_j, it can traverse all six vertices before exiting.

To complete the construction of the graph, connect the I_j's to the H_i's as follows. Suppose the first term in F_j is x_i. Then pick some c_{ip} that has not yet been connected to any I_k and introduce an arc from c_{ip} to r_j and from u_j to $b_{i,p+1}$. If the first term is $\bar{x}_i$, pick an unused b_{ip} and introduce arcs $b_{ip} \to r_j$ and $u_j \to c_{i,p+1}$. Make analogous connections with s_j and v_j for the second term of F_j, and analogous connections with t_j and w_j for the third term. Each H_i was chosen sufficiently long that enough pairs of b_{ij}'s and c_{ij}'s are available to make all the connections.

If the expression F is satisfiable, we can find a Hamilton circuit for the graph as follows. Let the circuit go from a_i to b_{i0} if x_i is true in the satisfying assignment, and from a_i to c_{i0} otherwise. Then, ignoring the I_j's, we have a unique Hamilton circuit for the subgraph of Fig. 13.3(b). Now, whenever the constructed circuit uses an arc $b_{ik} \to c_{i,k+1}$ or $c_{ik} \to b_{i,k+1}$, and b_{ik} or c_{ik}, respectively, has an arc to an I_j subgraph that has not yet been visited, visit all six vertices of I_j, emerging at $c_{i,k+1}$ or $b_{i,k+1}$, respectively. The fact that F is satisfiable implies that we can traverse I_j for all j.

Conversely, we must show that the existence of a Hamilton circuit implies F is satisfiable. Recall that in any Hamilton circuit an I_j entered at r_j, s_j, or t_j must be left at u_j, v_j, or w_j, respectively. Thus as far as paths through the H_i's are concerned, connections to an I_j look like arcs in parallel with an arc $b_{ik} \to c_{i,k+1}$ or $c_{ik} \to b_{i,k+1}$. If excursions to the I_j's are ignored, it follows that the circuit must traverse the H_i's in one of the 2^n ways which are possible without the I_j's; that is, it may follow the arc $a_i \to b_{i0}$ or $a_i \to c_{i0}$ for $1 \le i \le n$. Each set of choices determines a truth assignment for the x_i's. If one set of choices yields a Hamilton circuit, including the I_j's, then the assignment must satisfy all the clauses. For example, if we reach I_j from b_{ik} in the circuit, then $\bar{x}_i$ is a term in F_j, and it must be that the circuit goes from a_i to c_{i0}, which corresponds to the choice $x_i = 0$. Note that if the circuit goes from a_i to b_{i0}, then it must traverse $b_{i,k+1}$ before $c_{i,k+1}$ and we could not traverse I_j between b_{ik} and $c_{i,k+1}$, as $b_{i,k+1}$ could never be included in the circuit.

As a last remark, we must prove we have a log-space reduction. Given F, we can list the vertices and arcs of H_i simply by counting occurrences of x_i and $\bar{x}_i$. We can list the connections between the H_i's and I_j's easily as well. Given a term like x_i in F_j, we can find a free pair of vertices in H_i to connect to I_j by counting occurrences of x_i in F_1, F_2, ..., F_{j-1}. As no count gets above the number of variables or clauses, $\log n$ space is sufficient, where n is the length of F. $\qquad\Box$

Example 13.3 Let F be

$$(x_1 \vee x_2 \vee x_3) \wedge (\bar{x}_1 \vee \bar{x}_2 \vee x_3).$$

The graph constructed from F by Theorem 13.5 is shown in Fig. 13.4. A Hamilton circuit corresponding to the assignment $x_1 = 1$, $x_2 = 0$, $x_3 = 0$ is drawn in heavy lines.

Finally we show that the Hamilton circuit problem is NP-complete by reducing the directed Hamilton circuit problem to it.

Theorem 13.6 L_h, the Hamilton circuit problem for undirected graphs, is NP-complete.

Proof To show that L_h, is in $\mathcal{NP}$, guess a list of the edges and verify that they form a Hamilton circuit. To show L_h NP-complete we reduce L_{dh} to it. Let $G = (V, E)$ be a directed graph. Construct an undirected graph G' with vertices v_0, v_1, and v_2 for each v in V, and edges

1) (v_0, v_1) for each v in V,
2) (v_1, v_2) for each v in V,
3) (v_2, w_0) if and only if $v \to w$ is an arc in E.

Each vertex in V has been expanded into three vertices. Vertices with subscript 1 have only two edges, and since a Hamilton circuit must visit all vertices, the subscript of the vertices in any Hamilton circuit of G' must be in the order 0, 1, 2, 0, 1, ... or its reverse. Assume the order is 0, 1, 2, ... Then the edges whose subscript goes from 2 to 0 correspond to a Hamilton circuit in G. Conversely, a Hamilton circuit in G may be converted to a Hamilton circuit in G' by replacing an arc $v \to w$ by the path from v_0 to v_1 to v_2 to w_0. Thus G' has a Hamilton circuit if and only if G has a Hamilton circuit. The reduction of G to G' is easily accomplished in log-space. Thus we conclude that L_h is NP-complete. $\qquad\Box$

Integer linear programming

Most known NP-complete problems are easily shown to be in $\mathcal{NP}$, and only the reduction from a known NP-complete problem is difficult. We shall now give an example of a problem where the opposite is the case. It is easy to prove that integer linear programming is NP-hard but difficult to show it is in $\mathcal{NP}$. The *integer linear programming problem* is: Given an $m \times n$ matrix of integers A and a column vector **b** of n integers, does there exist a column vector of integers **x** such

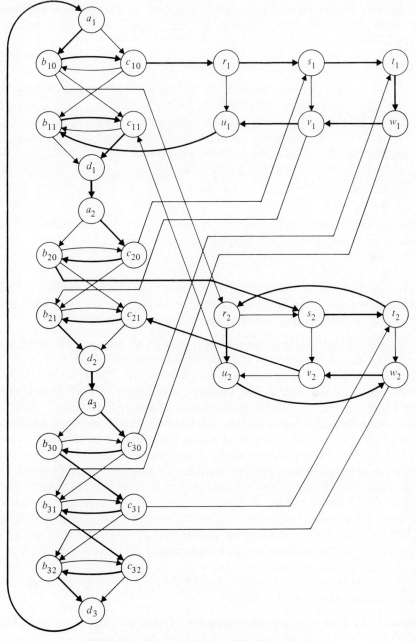

Fig. 13.4 Graph constructed for Example 13.3.

that $A\mathbf{x} \geq \mathbf{b}$? The reader may formalize this problem as a language in an obvious way, where the words of the language are the elements of A and $\mathbf{b}$ written in binary.

Lemma 13.4   Integer linear programming is NP-hard.

Proof   We reduce 3-CNF satisfiability to integer linear programming. Let $E = F_1 \wedge F_2 \wedge \cdots \wedge F_q$ be an expression in 3-CNF, and let $x_1, x_2, \ldots, x_n$ be the variables of E. The matrix A will have a column for each literal x_i or $\bar{x}_i$, $1 \leq i \leq n$. We may thus view the inequality $A\mathbf{x} \geq \mathbf{b}$ as a set of linear inequalities among the literals. For each i, $1 \leq i \leq n$, we have the inequalities

$$x_i + \bar{x}_i \geq 1, \qquad x_i \geq 0,$$
$$-x_i - \bar{x}_i \geq -1, \qquad \bar{x}_i \geq 0,$$

which has the effect of saying that one of x_i and $\bar{x}_i$ is 0, the other is 1. For each clause $\alpha_1 \vee \alpha_2 \vee \alpha_3$, we have the inequality

$$\alpha_1 + \alpha_2 + \alpha_3 \geq 1,$$

which says that at least one literal in each clause has value 1. It is obvious that A and $\mathbf{b}$ can be constructed in log-space and the inequalities are all satisfied if and only if E is satisfiable. Thus linear integer programming is NP-hard. $\square$

To show integer linear programming is in $\mathcal{NP}$, we may guess a vector $\mathbf{x}$ and check that $A\mathbf{x} \geq \mathbf{b}$. However, if the smallest solution has elements that are too large, we may not be able to write $\mathbf{x}$ in polynomial time. The difficulty is to show that the elements of $\mathbf{x}$ need not be too large, and for this we need some concepts from linear algebra, specifically determinants of square matrices, the rank of a matrix, linear independence of vectors, and Cramer's rule for solving simultaneous linear equations, with all of which we expect the reader to be familiar.

In what follows, we assume matrix A and vector $\mathbf{b}$ form an instance of the integer linear programming problem and that A has m rows and n columns. Let α be the magnitude of the largest element of A or $\mathbf{b}$. Note that the number of bits needed to write out A and $\mathbf{b}$ is at least $mn + \log_2 \alpha$, and we shall use this quantity as a lower bound on the input size; our nondeterministic solution finder will work in $\text{NTIME}(p(mn + \log_2 \alpha))$ for some polynomial p. Further, we define $\mathbf{a}_i$, for $1 \leq i \leq m$, to be the vector of length n consisting of the ith row of A. We let b_i be the ith element of $\mathbf{b}$ and we let $\mathbf{x} = (x_1, x_2, \ldots, x_n)$ be a vector of unknowns. We use $|i|$ for the magnitude of integer i and $\det B$ for the determinant of matrix B. A series of technical lemmas is needed.

Lemma 13.5   If B is a square submatrix of A, then $|\det B| \leq (\alpha q)^q$, where $q = \max(m, n)$.

Proof   Recall that the determinant of a $k \times k$ matrix is the sum or difference of $k!$ terms, each of which is the product of k elements. Therefore, if B is a $k \times k$

submatrix, $k! \alpha^k$ is an upper bound on $|\det B|$. As $k! \leq k^k$ and $k \leq q$, we have our lemma. ☐

Lemma 13.6 Let A have rank r.† If $r < n$, then there is an integer vector $\mathbf{z} = (z_1, z_2, \ldots, z_n)$, $\mathbf{z}$ not identically zero, such that $A\mathbf{z} = \mathbf{0}$ ($\mathbf{0}$ is a vector of all 0's) and no z_j exceeds $(\alpha q)^{2q}$ in magnitude, where $q = \max\ (m, n)$.

Proof Assume without loss of generality that B, the $r \times r$ submatrix of A in the upper left corner, has a nonzero determinant. Let C be the first r rows of A and let D be the last $m - r$ rows of A. As any $r + 1$ rows of A are linearly dependent, and the rows of C are linearly independent (because B has a nonzero determinant), each row of D can be expressed as a linear combination of rows of C. That is, $D = EC$ for some $(m - r) \times r$ matrix E. Then $A\mathbf{z} = \mathbf{0}$ if and only if $C\mathbf{z} = \mathbf{0}$ and $EC\mathbf{z} = \mathbf{0}$. It suffices, therefore, to show that we can make $C\mathbf{z} = \mathbf{0}$. If we choose $z_n = -1$, and $z_{r+1} = z_{r+2} = \cdots = z_{n-1} = 0$, then $C\mathbf{z} = \mathbf{0}$ if and only if $B\mathbf{y} = \mathbf{w}$, where $\mathbf{y}$ is the vector $(z_1, z_2, \ldots, z_r)$ and $\mathbf{w}$ is the nth column of C. By Cramer's rule, $B\mathbf{y} = \mathbf{w}$ is satisfied if we take $z_i = \det B_i/\det B$, where B_i is B with the ith column replaced by $\mathbf{w}$. By Lemma 13.5, these determinants do not exceed $(\alpha q)^q$ in magnitude. The resulting $\mathbf{z}$ may not have integer components, but if we multiply all components by $\det B$, they will be integers, and will still satisfy $A\mathbf{z} = \mathbf{0}$. When we do so, $z_n = -\det B$; the magnitudes of the first r components of $\mathbf{z}$ do not exceed $((\alpha q)^q)^2 = (\alpha q)^{2q}$, and components $r + 1$ through $n - 1$ are 0. ☐

It follows that the solution $\mathbf{z}$ can be written with a number of bits that is at most the second power of $mn + \log_2 \alpha$, the size of the problem statement.

Lemma 13.7 Let A be a matrix with at least one nonzero element. If there is a solution to $A\mathbf{x} \geq \mathbf{b}$, $\mathbf{x} \geq \mathbf{0}$, then there is a solution in which for some i, $b_i \leq \mathbf{a}_i\mathbf{x} < b_i + \alpha$, where α is the magnitude of the largest element of A.

Proof Let $\mathbf{x}_0$ be a solution to $A\mathbf{x} \geq \mathbf{b}$. Suppose $\mathbf{a}_i\mathbf{x}_0 \geq b_i + \alpha$ for all i. Adding or subtracting 1 from some component of $\mathbf{x}_0$ must reduce some product $\mathbf{a}_i\mathbf{x}_0$. Furthermore, no product can decrease by more than α. Thus the new $\mathbf{x}$ is also a solution. The process cannot be repeated indefinitely without obtaining a solution $\mathbf{x}$ for which there is an i such that $b_i \leq \mathbf{a}_i\mathbf{x} < b_i + \alpha$. ☐

Theorem 13.7 Integer linear programming is *NP*-complete.

Proof By Lemma 13.4 we have to show only that the problem is in $\mathcal{NP}$. We begin by guessing the signs of the x_i's in some hypothetical solution and adding n constraints $x_i \leq (\geq)0$ depending on the sign guessed. Then guess a row i and a constant c_i in the range $b_i \leq c_i < b_i + \alpha$ such that in some solution $\mathbf{x}_0$, we have $\mathbf{a}_i\mathbf{x}_0 = c_i$. Now suppose that after reordering rows if necessary, we have correctly

---

† Recall that the *rank* of r is equivalently defined as the maximum number of linearly independent rows, the maximum number of linearly independent columns, or the size of the largest square submatrix with a nonzero determinant.

guessed $c_1, c_2, \ldots, c_k$ such that

1) $b_i \leq c_i < b_i + (\alpha q)^{2q+1}$, and
2) $Ax \geq \mathbf{b}$ has a nonnegative integer solution if and only if

$$\mathbf{a}_i \mathbf{x} = c_i, \qquad 1 \leq i \leq k,$$

$$\mathbf{a}_i \mathbf{x} \geq b_i, \qquad k < i \leq m,$$

has such a solution.

Let A_k be the first k rows of A, and let $\mathbf{c}$ be the vector $(c_1, c_2, \ldots, c_k)$.

CASE 1   The rank of A_k is less than n. By Lemma 13.6 there is an integer vector $\mathbf{z}$, $\mathbf{z} \neq \mathbf{0}$, none of whose components has a magnitude greater than $(\alpha q)^{2q}$, such that $A_k \mathbf{z} = 0$. Therefore, if $A_k \mathbf{x}_0 = \mathbf{c}$, it follows that $A_k(\mathbf{x}_0 + d\mathbf{z}) = \mathbf{c}$ for any integer d. If it is also true that $\mathbf{a}_i \mathbf{x}_0 \geq b_i + (\alpha q)^{2q+1}$ for all $i > k$, then we may repeatedly add or subtract 1 from d until for some $j \geq k$, $\mathbf{a}_j(\mathbf{x}_0 + d\mathbf{z})$ drops below $b_j + (\alpha q)^{2q+1}$. Since $\mathbf{z}$ has some nonzero component, the row $\mathbf{a}_\ell$ [corresponding to a constraint $x_i \leq (\geq)0$] that is all zero except for a one in that component, must have $\ell \geq k$. Thus some $\mathbf{a}_j(\mathbf{x}_0 + d\mathbf{z})$ for $j \geq k$ must eventually drop below $b_j + (\alpha q)^{2q+1}$. Since each component of $\mathbf{z}$ is bounded in magnitude by $(\alpha q)^{2q}$, changing d by 1 cannot change any $\mathbf{a}_j(\mathbf{x}_0 + d\mathbf{z})$ by more than $\alpha n(\alpha q)^{2q}$, which is no more than $(\alpha q)^{2q+1}$. Therefore $\mathbf{a}_j(\mathbf{x}_0 + d\mathbf{z}) \geq b_j$. By reordering rows, we may assume $j = k + 1$ and repeat the above process for $k + 1$ in place of k.

CASE 2   The rank of A_k is n. In this case, there is a unique $\mathbf{x}$ satisfying $A_k \mathbf{x} = \mathbf{c}$. By Cramer's rule, the components of $\mathbf{x}$ are ratios of two determinants whose magnitudes do not exceed $q^q(\alpha + (\alpha q)^{2q+1})\alpha^{q-1}$, which is less than $(2\alpha q)^{3q+1}$. We may check whether this $\mathbf{x}$ consists only of integers and satisfies $\mathbf{a}_j \mathbf{x} \geq b_j$ for $j > k$.

The nondeterministic process of guessing c_i's repeats at most n times, and for any sequence of choices requires a number of arithmetic steps that is polynomial in q [since Cramer's rule can be applied in $0(r^4)$ arithmetic steps to $r \times r$ matrices] applied to integers whose length in binary is polynomial in αq. The arithmetic steps that are multiplication or division of integers can be performed in time proportional to the square of the length of the integers in binary† and addition and subtraction can be performed in linear time. Thus the entire process takes time that is polynomial in the input length, since that length is at least $mn + \log_2 \alpha$.   □

Other NP-complete problems

There is a wide variety of other known NP-complete problems. We shall list some of them here.

---

† Actually in considerably less time (see Aho, Hopcroft, and Ullman [1974]), although this is of no importance here.

1) *The Chromatic Number Problem.* Given a graph G and an integer k, can G be colored with k colors so that no two adjacent vertices are the same color?

2) *The Traveling Salesman Problem.* Given a complete graph with weights on the edges, what is the Hamilton circuit of minimum weight? To express this problem as a language, we require the weights to be integers and ask whether there is a Hamilton circuit of weight k or less. This problem is NP-complete even if we restrict the weights to 0 and 1, when it becomes exactly the Hamilton circuit problem.

3) *The Exact Cover Problem.* Given a collection of sets $S_1, S_2, \ldots, S_k$, all being subsets of some set U, is there a subcollection whose union is U such that each pair of sets in the subcollection is disjoint?

4) *The Partition Problem.* Given a list of integers $i_1, i_2, \ldots, i_k$, does there exist a subset whose sum is exactly $\frac{1}{2}(i_1 + i_2 + \cdots + i_k)$. Note that this problem appears to be in $\mathcal{P}$ until we remember that the length of an instance is not $i_1 + i_2 + \cdots + i_k$, but the sum of the lengths of the i_j's written in binary or some other fixed base.

Among the NP-complete problems are many, including the ones mentioned in this section, for which serious effort has been expended on finding polynomial-time algorithms. Since either all or none of the NP-complete problems are in $\mathcal{P}$, and so far none have been found to be in $\mathcal{P}$, it is natural to conjecture that none are in $\mathcal{P}$. More importantly, if one is faced with an NP-complete problem to solve, it is questionable whether one should even bother to look for a polynomial-time algorithm. We believe one is much better off looking for heuristics that work well on the particular kinds of instances that one is likely to encounter.

Extended significance of NP-completeness

We have inadvertently implied that the only issue regarding NP-complete problems was whether they required polynomial or exponential time. In fact, the true answer could be between these extremes; for example, they could require $n^{\log n}$ time. If all languages in $\mathcal{NP}$ are log-space or even polynomial-time reducible to L, and L is in, say DTIME($n^{\log n}$), then every language in $\mathcal{NP}$ is in DTIME($n^{c \log n}$) for some constant c. In general, if L were log-space or polynomial-time complete for $\mathcal{NP}$, and L were in DTIME($T(n)$), then

$$\mathcal{NP} \subseteq \bigcup_{c > 0} \text{DTIME}(T(n^c)).$$

13.3 THE CLASS CO-$\mathcal{NP}$

It is unknown whether the class $\mathcal{NP}$ is closed under complementation. Should it turn out that $\mathcal{NP}$ is not closed under complementation, then clearly $\mathcal{P} \neq \mathcal{NP}$, since $\mathcal{P}$ is closed under complementation. There is no NP-complete problem whose complement is known to be in $\mathcal{NP}$. For example, to determine non-satisfiability for a Boolean formula with n variables, it appears necessary to test every one of the 2^n possible assignments, even if the algorithm is nondeterministic. In fact if any NP-complete problem is discovered to have its complement in $\mathcal{NP}$, then $\mathcal{NP}$ would be closed under complementation, as we show in the next theorem.

Theorem 13.8 $\mathcal{NP}$ is closed under complementation if and only if the complement of some NP-complete problem is in $\mathcal{NP}$.

Proof   The "only if" part is obvious. For the "if" part let S be an NP-complete problem, and suppose $\bar{S}$ were in $\mathcal{NP}$. Since each L in $\mathcal{NP}$ is log-space reducible to S, each $\bar{L}$ is log-space reducible to $\bar{S}$. Thus $\bar{L}$ is in $\mathcal{NP}$.   □

We shall define the class co-$\mathcal{NP}$ to be the set of complements of the languages in $\mathcal{NP}$. The relationship between $\mathcal{P}$, $\mathcal{NP}$, co-$\mathcal{NP}$ and PSPACE is shown in Fig. 13.5, although it is not known for certain that any of the regions except the one labeled $\mathcal{P}$ are nonempty.

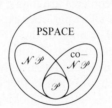

Fig. 13.5   Relations among some language classes.

The problem of primality

It is interesting to consider a problem in $\mathcal{NP}$ such as "nonprimeness" for which there is no known polynomial time algorithm† and furthermore which is not known to be NP-complete.‡ To test an integer to see if it is not a prime, one simply guesses a divisor and checks. The interesting observation is that the complementary problem is in $\mathcal{NP}$, which suggests that there may be sets in the intersection of $\mathcal{NP}$ and co-$\mathcal{NP}$ that are not in $\mathcal{P}$.

We now consider a nondeterministic polynomial-time algorithm for testing whether an integer is prime.

Lemma 13.8   Let x and y be integers, with $0 \le x, y < p$. Then

1) $x + y \pmod{p}$ can be computed in time $0(\log p)$;

---

† Although Miller [1976] presents strong evidence that one exists.

‡ This is another problem that appears to be in $\mathcal{P}$ until one remembers that the size of input p is $\log_2 p$, not p itself.

2) $xy \pmod p$ can be computed in time $O(\log^2 p)$;

3) $x^y \pmod p$ can be computed in time $O(\log^3 p)$.

Proof (1) and (2) are obvious since an integer mod p requires only log p bits. For (3) compute x^y by repeated squaring to get x^2, x^4, x^8, ..., x^{2^i} mod p, where $i = \lfloor \log_2 y \rfloor$, then multiply the appropriate powers of x to get x^y. $\qquad\square$

We shall, in what follows, make use of Fermat's theorem: $p > 2$ is a prime if and only if there exists an x of order $p - 1$, that is, for some x, $1 < x < p$,

1) $x^{p-1} \equiv 1 \bmod p$, and

2) $x^i \not\equiv 1 \bmod p$, for $1 \le i < p - 1$.

Theorem 13.9 The set of primes is in $\mathcal{NP}$.

Proof If $x = 2$, then x is prime. If $x = 1$ or x is an even integer greater than 2, then x is not prime. To determine if p is prime for odd p greater than 2, guess an x, $0 < x < p$, and verify that

1) $x^{p-1} \equiv 1 \bmod p$, and

2) $x^i \not\equiv 1 \bmod p$ for all i, $1 \le i < p - 1$.

Condition (1) is easily checked in $O(\log^3 p)$ steps. We cannot check condition (2) for each i directly since there are too many i's. Instead, guess the prime factorization of $p - 1$. Let the factorization be $p - 1 = p_1 p_2 \cdots p_k$. Recursively verify that each p_j is a prime. Verify that $p - 1$ is the product of the p_j's. Finally verify $x^{(p-1)/p_j} \not\equiv 1 \bmod p$. Observe that if $x^{p-1} \equiv 1 \bmod p$, then the least i satisfying $x^i \equiv 1 \bmod p$ must divide $p - 1$. Furthermore, any multiple of this i, say ai, must also satisfy $x^{ai} \equiv 1 \bmod p$. Thus, if there is an i such that $x^i \equiv 1 \bmod p$, then for some p_j, $x^{(p-1)/p_j} \equiv 1 \bmod p$.

Assume that the nondeterministic time to recognize that p is prime is bounded by $c \log^4 p$. Then we need only observe that

$$\sum_{j=1}^{k} c \log^4 p_j + \sum_{i=1}^{k} c_1 \log^3 p_i + c_1 \log^3 p \le c \log^4 p$$

for some sufficiently large constant c. $\qquad\square$

13.4 PSPACE-COMPLETE PROBLEMS

We now show several problems to be complete for PSPACE with respect to polynomial time.

Quantified Boolean formulas

Quantified Boolean formulas (QBF) are built from variables, the operators $\wedge$, $\vee$, and $\neg$, parentheses, and the quantifiers $\exists$ ("there exists") and $\forall$ ("for all"). When defining the QBF's recursively, we find it useful simultaneously to define *free* occurrences of variables (occurrences to which no quantifier applies), *bound* occurrences of variables (occurrences to which a quantifier applies), and the scope of a quantifier (those occurrences to which the quantifier applies).

1) If x is a variable, then it is a QBF. The occurrence of x is free.

2) If E_1 and E_2 are QBF's, so are $\neg(E_1)$, $(E_1) \wedge (E_2)$, and $(E_1) \vee (E_2)$. An occurrence of x is free or bound, depending on whether the occurrence is free or bound in E_1 or E_2. Redundant parentheses can be omitted.

3) If E is a QBF, then $\exists x(E)$ and $\forall x(E)$ are QBF's. The scopes of $\exists x$ and $\forall x$ are all free occurrences of x in E. (Note that there may also be bound occurrences of x in E; these are not part of the scope.) Free occurrences of x in E are bound in $\exists x(E)$ and $\forall x(E)$. All other occurrences of variables in E are free or bound, depending on whether they are free or bound in E.

A QBF with no free variable has a value of either **true** or **false**, which we denote by the Boolean constants 1 and 0. The value of such a QBF is determined by replacing each subexpression of the form $\exists x(E)$ by $E_0 \vee E_1$ and each subexpression of the form $\forall x(E)$ by $E_0 \wedge E_1$, where E_0 and E_1 are E with all occurrences of x in the scope of the quantifier replaced by 0 and 1, respectively. The *QBF problem* is to determine whether a QBF with no free variables has value **true**.

Example 13.4 $\forall x\, [\forall x[\exists y(x \vee y)] \wedge \neg x]$ is a QBF. The scope of the inner $\forall x$ is the first occurrence of x; the scope of the outer $\forall x$ is the second occurrence. To test the truth of the above formula, we must check that $\forall x[\exists y(x \vee y)] \wedge \neg x$ is true when free occurrences of x (that is, the second occurrence only) are set to 0 and also when set to 1. The first clause $\forall x(\exists y(x \vee y))$ is seen to be true, as when this x is 0 or 1 we may choose $y = 1$ to make $x \vee y$ true. However, $\neg x$ is not made true when $x = 1$, so the entire expression is false.

Note a Boolean expression E with variables $x_1, x_2, \ldots, x_k$ is satisfiable if and only if the QBF $\exists x_1 \exists x_2 \cdots \exists x_k(E_k)$ is true. Thus the satisfiability problem is a special case of the problem of whether a QBF is true, which immediately tells us that the QBF problem is *NP*-hard. It does not appear that QBF is in $\mathcal{NP}$ however.

PSPACE-completeness of the QBF problem

Lemma 13.9 QBF is in PSPACE.

Proof A simple recursive procedure EVAL can be used to compute the value of a QBF with no free variables. In fact, EVAL will handle a slightly more general problem, where the Boolean constants 0 and 1 have been substituted for some variables. If the QBF consists of a Boolean constant, EVAL returns that constant.

If the QBF consists of a Boolean operator applied to subformula(s), then EVAL evaluates the subformulas recursively and then applies the operator to the result(s). If the QBF is of the form $\exists x(E)$ or $\forall x(E)$, then EVAL replaces all occurrences of x in E that are in the scope of the quantifier by 0 to obtain E_0 and then evaluates E_0 recursively. Next EVAL replaces the occurrences of x by 1 to obtain E_1, and evaluates E_1 recursively. In the case of $\exists x(E)$, EVAL returns the OR of the two results. In the case of $\forall x(E)$, EVAL returns the AND.

Since the number of operators plus quantifiers is at most n for a QBF of length n, the depth of recursion is at most n. Using a Turing tape for the stack of activation records (as in Theorem 12.11), we see that the tape need never grow longer than the square of the length of the original QBF. Thus the QBF problem is in PSPACE. $\qquad \square$

Theorem 13.10 The problem of deciding whether a QBF is true is PSPACE complete.

Proof By Lemma 13.9, we need show only that the language L_{qbf} of coded true QBF's is PSPACE-hard. That is, we must show that every language in PSPACE is polynomial-time reducible to L_{qbf}.

Let M be a one-tape polynomial space-bounded DTM accepting a language L. Then for some constant c and polynomial p, M makes no more than $c^{p(n)}$ moves on inputs of length n. We can code ID's of M as in Theorem 13.1, using the Boolean variables c_{iX}, $1 \leq i \leq p(n)$, and X a tape symbol or a composite symbol representing a symbol and the state of M. Since M is deterministic, there is no need to code a choice of moves in the composite symbol. Our goal is to construct for each j, $0 \leq j \leq p(n)\log c$, a QBF $F_j(I_1, I_2)$, where

1) I_1 and I_2 are each distinct sets of variables, one for each i, $1 \leq i \leq p(n)$, and each tape symbol or composite symbol X, analogous to the c_{iX}'s of Theorem 13.1. Say

$$I_1 = \{c_{iX} \mid 1 \leq i \leq p(n) \quad \text{and } X \text{ is such a symbol}\},$$

and

$$I_2 = \{d_{iY} \mid 1 \leq i \leq p(n) \quad \text{and } Y \text{ is such a symbol}\}.$$

2) $F_j(I_1, I_2)$ is true if and only if I_1 and I_2 represent ID's β_1 and β_2 of M, that is, for each i, exactly one c_{iX} and d_{iX} is true, and $\beta_1 \overset{*}{\vdash} \beta_2$ by a sequence of at most 2^j moves, where $\beta_1 = X_1 X_2 \cdots X_{p(n)}$, $\beta_2 = Y_1 Y_2 \cdots Y_{p(n)}$, and X_i and Y_i are the symbols such that c_{iX_i} and d_{iY_i} are true.

Then given x of length n we may write a QBF

$$Q_x = \exists I_0 \, \exists I_f [F_{p(n)\log c}(I_0, I_f) \wedge \text{INITIAL}(I_0) \wedge \text{FINAL}(I_f)],$$

where $\exists I_0$ and $\exists I_f$ stand for a collection of existentially quantified variables, one for each symbol X and integer i, $1 \leq i \leq p(n)$, as above. $\text{INITIAL}(I_0)$ is a propositional formula that says the variables in the set I_0 represent the initial ID of M

with input x, and $FINAL(I_f)$ expresses the fact that I_f represents an accepting ID of M. Then Q_x is true if and only if x is in $L(M)$. INITIAL and FINAL can be written in time that is polynomial in n using the techniques of Theorem 13.1.

We now show how to construct, for each j, the formula $F_j(I_1, I_2)$. The basis, $j = 0$, is easy. Using the technique of Theorem 13.1, we have only to express as a Boolean formula the facts that

1) I_1 and I_2 represent ID's, say β_1 and β_2; that is, exactly one variable for each position in β_1 and β_2 is true.
2) Either $\beta_1 = \beta_2$ or $\beta_1 \vdash \beta_2$.

For the induction step, we are tempted to write

$$F_j(I_1, I_2) = (\exists I)[F_{j-1}(I_1, I) \wedge F_{j-1}(I, I_2)].$$

However, if we do so, F_j has roughly double the length of F_{j-1}, and the length of $F_{p(n)\log_2 c}$ will be at least $c^{p(n)}$, and therefore cannot be written in polynomial time.

Instead we use a trick that enables us to make two uses of an expression like F_{j-1} in only a small amount (polynomial in n) more space than is required for one use. The trick is to express that there exist J and K such that if $J = I_1$ and $K = I$ or $J = I$ and $K = I_2$, then $F_{j-1}(J, K)$ must be true. The QBF for this is

$$F_j(I_1, I_2) = \exists I[\exists J[\exists K[(\neg(J = I_1 \wedge K = I)$$
$$\wedge \neg (J = I \wedge K = I_2)) \vee F_{j-1}(J, K)]]]. \tag{13.3}$$

We use expressions like $J = I_1$ to mean that for each pair of corresponding variables in the sets J and I_1 (those representing the same position and symbol), both are true or both are false. Equation (13.3) states that whenever the pair (J, K) is either (I_1, I) or (I_1, I_2), then $F_{j-1}(J, K)$ must be true. This allows us to assert that both $F_{j-1}(I_1, I)$ and $F_{j-1}(I, I_2)$ are true using only one copy of F_{j-1}. Intuitively, F_{j-1} is used as a "subroutine" that is "called" twice.

The number of symbols in F_j, counting any variable as one, is $O(p(n))$ plus the number of symbols in F_{j-1}. Since (13.3) introduces $O(p(n))$ variables (in the sets I, J, and K), the number of variables in F_j is $O(jp(n))$. Thus we can code a variable with $O(\log j + \log p(n))$ bits. It follows by induction on j that F_j can be written in time $O(jp(n)(\log j + \log p(n)))$. If we let $j = p(n) \log c$ and observe that for any polynomial $p(n)$, $\log p(n) = O(\log n)$, we see that Q_x can be written in $O(p^2(n) \log n)$ time. Thus there is a polynomial time reduction of $L(M)$ to L_{qbf}. Since M is an arbitrary polynomial space-bounded TM, we have shown that L_{qbf} is PSPACE-complete. □

Context-sensitive recognition

Another PSPACE-complete problem worth noting is: Given a CSG G and a string w, is w in $L(G)$? This result is surprising, since the CSL's occupy the "bottom" of PSPACE, being exactly $NSPACE(n)$ and contained in $DSPACE(n^2)$.

However, the "padding" technique used in the translation lemma (Lemma 12.2) makes a proof possible.

To begin, pick a straightforward binary code for grammars as we have done for Turing machines. Let L_{cs} be the language consisting of all strings $x\#w$, where x is the code for a CSG G_x and w is a coded string from the input alphabet of G_x. Assume that for a given grammar, all grammar symbols are coded by strings of the same length. It is easy to design an LBA that, given input $x\#w$, guesses a derivation in G_x such that no sentential form exceeds the length of the string coded by w. The coded sentential form can be stored on a second track under the cells holding w. Moves are determined by consulting the x portion of the input (to see how this may be done it helps to assume the existence of a second tape). We see that L_{cs} is in NSPACE(n) and thus in PSPACE.

Theorem 13.11 L_{cs}, the CSL recognition problem, is PSPACE-complete.

Proof   We already know L_{cs} to be in PSPACE. Let L be an arbitrary member of PSPACE; say L is accepted by M, a DTM of space complexity $p(n)$. Define L' to be $\{y\$^{p(|y|)} \mid y$ is in $L\}$, where $\$$ is a new symbol. It is easy to check that L' is in DSPACE(n) and therefore is a CSL. Let G be a CSG for L', and let x be the binary encoding of G. Then the polynomial-time mapping that takes y to $x\#w$, where w is the encoding of $y\$^{p(|y|)}$, is a reduction of L to L_{cs}, showing L_{cs} is PSPACE-complete.   □

13.5   COMPLETE PROBLEMS FOR $\mathscr{P}$ AND NSPACE(LOG n)

It is obvious that DSPACE(log n) $\subseteq \mathscr{P}$ by Theorem 12.10. Could it be that $\mathscr{P} = $ DSPACE(log n), or perhaps $\mathscr{P} \subseteq$ DSPACE(log$^k n$) for some k? Similarly, it is obvious that DSPACE(log n) $\subseteq$ NSPACE(log n). Could these two classes be equal? If so, then by a translation analogous to Lemma 12.2, it follows that NSPACE(n) $\subseteq$ DSPACE(n), that is, deterministic and nondeterministic CSL's are the same.

We shall exhibit a language L_1 in $\mathscr{P}$ such that every language in $\mathscr{P}$ is log-space reducible to L_1. Should this language be in DSPACE(log$^k n$) for some k, then $\mathscr{P}$ is contained in DSPACE(log$^k n$). Similarly we exhibit an L_2 in NSPACE(log n) such that every language in NSPACE(log n) is log-space reducible to L_2. Should L_2 be in DSPACE(log n), then DSPACE(log n) would equal NSPACE(log n). There is, of course, no known way to recognize L_1 in log$^k n$ space and no known way to recognize L_2 deterministically in log n space.

Languages complete for NSPACE(log n) or for $\mathscr{P}$ are not necessarily hard to recognize, and in fact, the languages L_1 and L_2 are relatively easy. The results of this section serve merely to reinforce the idea that many complexity classes have complete problems. They do not suggest intractability the way NP-completeness or PSPACE-completeness results do.

Context-free emptiness

Define L_{cfe} to be the language of coded CFG's whose languages are empty. L_{cfe} is the language L_1 alluded to above. We shall show that $\mathscr{P}$ is log-space reducible to L_{cfe}.

Theorem 13.12 L_{cfe}, the emptiness problem for CFG's, is complete for $\mathscr{P}$ with respect to log-space reductions.

Proof We shall reduce an arbitrary language L in $\mathscr{P}$ to L_{cfe} using only log n space. Specifically we shall design a log-space transducer M_1. Given input x of length n, M_1 writes a grammar G_x such that $L(G_x) = \varnothing$ if and only if x is in L. Let $\bar{M}$ be a $p(n)$ time-bounded TM accepting the complement of L. Since $\mathscr{P}$ is effectively closed under complementation, we can find $\bar{M}$. Intuitively, a derivation of G_x corresponds to a valid computation of $\bar{M}$ on x. The nonterminals of G_x are all symbols of the form A_{Xit}, where

1) X is a tape symbol of $\bar{M}$, a pair $[qY]$, where q is a state and Y a tape symbol, or the marker symbol # used to denote the ends of ID's;
2) $0 \le i \le p(n) + 1$;
3) $0 \le t \le p(n)$.

The intention is that $A_{Xit} \overset{*}{\Rightarrow} w$ for some string w if and only if X is the ith symbol of the ID of $\bar{M}$ at time t. The symbol S is also a nonterminal of G_x; it is the start symbol.

The productions of G_x are:

1) $S \to A_{[q_f Y]it}$ for all i, t, and Y, where q_f is a final state.
2) Let $f(X, Y, Z)$ be the symbol in position i of the tth ID whenever XYZ occupies positions $i - 1$, i, and $i + 1$ of the $(t - 1)$th ID. Since $\bar{M}$ is deterministic, $f(X, Y, Z)$ is a unique symbol and is independent of i and t. Thus for each i and t, $1 \le i, t \le p(n)$, and for each triple X, Y, Z with $W = f(X, Y, Z)$, we have the production

$$A_{Wit} \to A_{X,i-1,t-1} A_{Y,i,t-1} A_{Z,i+1,t-1}.$$

3) $A_{\#0t} \to \epsilon$ and $A_{\#,p(n)+1,t} \to \epsilon$ for all t.
4) $A_{Xi0} \to \epsilon$ for $1 \le i \le p(n)$ if and only if the ith symbol of the initial ID with input x is X.

Any easy induction on t shows that for $1 \le i \le p(n)$, $A_{Wit} \overset{*}{\Rightarrow} \epsilon$ if and only if W is the ith symbol of the ID at time t. Of course, no terminal string but ϵ is ever derived from any nonterminal.

Basis The basis, $t = 0$, is immediate from rule (4).

Induction If $A_{Wit} \overset{*}{\Rightarrow} \epsilon$, then by rule (2) it must be that for some $X, Y,$ and Z, W is $f(X, Y, Z)$ and each of $A_{X,i-1,t-1}$, $A_{Y,i,t-1}$, and $A_{Z,i+1,t-1}$ derive ϵ. By the inductive hypothesis the symbols in the ID at time $t - 1$ in positions $i - 1, i$, and $i + 1$ are X, Y, and Z, so W is the symbol at position i and time t by the definition of f.

Conversely, if W is the symbol at position i and time $t \geq 1$, then $W = f(X, Y, Z)$, where X, Y, and Z are the symbols at time $t - 1$ in positions $i - 1, i$, and $i + 1$. By the inductive hypothesis, or by rule (3) if $i = 0$ or $i = p(n) + 1$,

$$A_{X,i-1,t-1} \, A_{Y,i,t-1} \, A_{Z,i+1,t-1} \overset{*}{\Rightarrow} \epsilon.$$

Thus by rule (2), $A_{W_{it}} \overset{*}{\Rightarrow} \epsilon$.

Then by rule (1), $S \overset{*}{\Rightarrow} \epsilon$ if and only if $\bar{M}$ accepts x.

Finally we need show that the productions of G_x can be produced by M_1 with input x of length n. First of all, recall that $\log_2 p(n) \leq c \log_2 n$ for some constant c, since $p(n)$ is a polynomial. Therefore M_1 can count from $i = 0$ to $p(n)$ in $\log n$ scratch storage. Similarly M_1 can count from $t = 0$ to $p(n)$ in $\log n$ space. The productions of G_x are easily generated by a double loop on i and t.

Now G_x is in L_{cfe} if and only if $\bar{M}$ does not accept x and hence if and only if x is in L. Thus L_{cfe} is complete for $\mathscr{P}$ with respect to log-space reductions. ☐

The reachability problem

Now we shall give a problem that is complete for NSPACE($\log n$) with respect to log-space reductions. The *graph reachability problem* is, given a directed graph with vertices $\{1, 2, \ldots, n\}$ determine if there is a path from 1 to n.

Theorem 13.13 The graph reachability problem is log-space complete for NSPACE($\log n$) with respect to log-space reductions.

Proof The formalization of this problem as a language is left to the reader. First we show that the graph reachability problem is in NSPACE($\log n$). A nondeterministic TM M can guess the path vertex by vertex. M does not store the path, but instead verifies the path, storing only the vertex currently reached.

Now, given a language L in NSPACE($\log n$) we reduce it in $\log n$ space deterministically to the language of encoded digraphs for which a path from the first vertex to the last exists. Let M be a $\log n$ space-bounded nondeterministic offline TM accepting L. An ID of M can be represented by the storage tape contents, which takes $\log n$ space to represent, the storage tape head position and state, which may be coded with the storage contents via a composite symbol $[qX]$, and the input head position, which requires $\log n$ bits.

We construct a log-space transducer M_1 that takes input x and produces a digraph G_x with a path from the first to the last vertex if and only if M accepts x. The vertices of G_x are the ID's of M with input x (but with the input head position, rather than with x itself) plus a special vertex, the last one, which represents acceptance. The first vertex is the initial ID with input x. M_1 uses its $\log n$ storage to cycle through all the ID's of M. For each ID I, M_1 positions its input head at the correct input position, so it can see the input symbol scanned by M. M_1 then generates arcs $I \to J$ for all the finite number of J's such that I can become J by one move of M. Since M_1 has I available on its storage tape, and J can be easily constructed from I, this generation requires no more than log n space. If I is an accepting ID, M_1 generates the arc $I \to v$, where v is the special vertex.

It is straightforward to check that there is a path in G_x from the initial ID to v if and only if M accepts x. Thus each language in NSPACE(log n) is log-space reducible to the reachability problem. We conclude that the reachability problem is complete for NSPACE(log n) with respect to log-space reductions.   □

13.6 SOME PROVABLY INTRACTABLE PROBLEMS

Up to now we have strongly implied that certain problems require exponential time by proving them NP-complete or PSPACE-complete. We shall now prove that two problems actually require exponential time. In one case, we reduce to our problem a language which, by the space hierarchy theorem, is known to require exponential space and hence exponential time. In the second case, we show how to reduce to our problem all languages in nondeterministic exponential time and then argue by a nondeterministic time hierarchy theorem [Cook 1973a] that among them there must be one that really requires, say, 2^n space.

We shall now consider a problem about regular expressions that is somewhat contrived so that (a) at least $2^{cn/\log n}$ space is required to solve it and (b) this requirement can be readily proved. After that, we consider a problem in logic that is not contrived in that it had been considered long before its complexity was analyzed, and where proof of exponentiality is far from straightforward.

Regular expressions with exponentiation

Let us consider regular expressions over an alphabet assumed for convenience not to contain the symbols $\uparrow$, 0, or 1. Let $r \uparrow i$ stand for the regular expression $rr \cdots r$ (i times), where i is written in binary. The expression r may include the $\uparrow$ (exponentiation) operator. For example, $(\mathbf{a} \uparrow 11 + \mathbf{b} \uparrow 11) \uparrow 10$ stands for

$$\{aaaaaa, aaabbb, bbbaaa, bbbbbb\}.$$

We assume $\uparrow$ has higher precedence than the other operators. The problem we shall show requiring essentially *exponential space*, that is, $2^{p(n)}$ space for some polynomial $p(n)$, is whether a regular expression with exponentiation denotes all strings over its alphabet (remember $\uparrow$, 0, and 1 are used as operators and are not part of the alphabet). First we give an exponential-space algorithm for the problem.

Theorem 13.14 The problem whether a regular expression with exponentiation denotes all strings over its alphabet can be solved in exponential space.

Proof Given a regular expression of length n, we shall expand the $\uparrow$'s to obtain an ordinary regular expression and show that it has length at most $n2^n$. Then we shall convert this expression to an NFA of at most $n2^{n+2}$ states and test whether that NFA accepts Σ^*. (Note that this latter step must be done without conversion to a DFA, since the DFA might have $2^{n2^{n+2}}$ states). To eliminate the $\uparrow$'s we work from inside out. We prove by induction on j that an expression with $\uparrow$'s, having length m, with j 0's and 1's, has an equivalent ordinary regular expression of length at most $m2^j$.

Basis $j = 0$. The result is immediate.

Induction Scan the expression r of length m from the left until the first $\uparrow$ is encountered. Then scan back until the left argument r_1 of that $\uparrow$ is found. We assume $\uparrow$ has highest precedence, so its argument must be a single symbol or be surrounded by parentheses; hence this extraction is easy. Let the expression be $r = r_2 r_1 \uparrow i r_3$. Replace r by $r' = r_2 r_1 r_1 \cdots r_1 r_3$, where r_1 is written i times. By the inductive hypothesis, r' has an equivalent ordinary regular expression of length at most $(m + (i - 1)|r_1|)2^{j - \log_2 i}$ symbols. Since $2^{j - \log_2 i} = 2^j/i$, and since $|r_1| \leq m$, we see that

$$(m + (i - 1)|r_1|)2^{j - \log_2 i} = \frac{m + (i - 1)|r_1|}{i} \times 2^j \leq m2^j.$$

If r is of length n, then surely $m = n$ and $j \leq n$, so the equivalent ordinary regular expression has length at most $n2^n$.

Now, using the algorithm of Theorem 2.3, we can produce an equivalent NFA of at most $4n2^n = n2^{n+2}$ states. Nondeterministically guess symbol by symbol an input $a_1 a_2 \cdots$ that the NFA does not accept. Using $n2^{n+2}$ cells we can, after each guess, compute the set of states entered after the NFA reads the sequence of symbols guessed so far. The input need not be written down, since we can compute the set of states entered from this set on any input symbol. If we ever guess an input sequence on which no accepting state of the NFA is entered, we accept; the original expression does not denote Σ^*. By Savitch's theorem we may perform this process deterministically using space $n^2 4^n$. It is easy to devise an encoding of the NFA that can be stored in $O(n^3 2^n)$ cells, since about n bits suffice to code a state, and the input alphabet is no larger than n. As $n^2 4^n > n^3 2^n$, it follows that $n^2 4^n$ is an upper bound on the required space. $\square$

We shall now provide a lower bound of $2^{cn/\log n}$ for some constant c on the space required for the above problem. Observe that proving a certain amount of space is required also proves that the same amount of time is required (although the opposite is not true).

Theorem 13.15 There is a constant $c > 0$ such that every TM accepting the language L_{rex} of regular expressions with exponentiation that denote Σ^* takes more than $2^{cn/\log n}$ space (and therefore $2^{cn/\log n}$ time) infinitely often.

Proof Consider an arbitrary 2^n space bounded single-tape deterministic TM M. For each input x of length n, we construct a regular expression with exponentiation E_x that denotes Σ^*, where Σ is the alphabet of E_x, if and only if M does not accept x. We do so by making E_x denote all invalid computations of M on x. Let Σ consist of all tape symbols of M, the composite symbols $[qX]$, where q is a state and X a tape symbol, and the marker symbol #. Assume that $\uparrow$, 0, and 1 are none of these symbols.

A string y in Σ^* is not an accepting computation of M on x if and only if one or more of the following are true.

1) The initial ID is wrong.
2) There is no accepting state.
3) One ID does not follow from the previous by a move of M.

In what follows, we use sets of symbols to represent the regular expression that is the sum of those symbols. Thus, if $\Sigma = \{a_1, a_2, \dots, a_n\}$, then we use Σ as a shorthand for the regular expression $a_1 + a_2 + \cdots + a_n$. Similarly we also use $\Sigma - a$ to stand for the regular expression that is the sum of all the symbols in Σ except a.

A regular expression denoting all strings that do not begin with the initial ID is given by

$$\text{START} = \epsilon + (\Sigma - \#)\Sigma^* + A_1 + A_2 + \cdots + A_n$$
$$+ \Sigma \uparrow (n+1)(\Sigma + \epsilon) \uparrow (2^n - n - 1)(\Sigma - B)\Sigma^*$$
$$+ \Sigma \uparrow (2^n + 1)(\Sigma - \#)\Sigma^*,$$

where

$$A_1 = \Sigma \uparrow 1(\Sigma - [q_0 a_1])\Sigma^*,$$

and for $2 \le i \le n$,

$$A_i = \Sigma \uparrow i(\Sigma - a_i)\Sigma^*.$$

The next-to-last term denotes Σ^{n+1} followed by up to $2^n - n - 1$ symbols followed by anything but a blank, and denotes strings such that some position between $n + 1$ and 2^n of the first ID does not contain a blank. Since n and $2^n - n - 1$ are written in binary, the length of this term is proportional to n. The last term denotes strings in which the $(2^n + 1)$th symbol is not #. It is also of length proportional to n. The remaining terms are proportional to $\log n$ in length, and there are $n + 3$ such terms. Thus the length of the expression is proportional to $n \log n$. Curiously, the length of the expression denoting false initial ID's dominates the length of the other terms in E_x.

A regular expression enforcing the condition that there is no accepting state is given by

$$\text{FINISH} = (\Sigma - \{[qX] \mid q \text{ is a final state}\})^*.$$

This expression is of constant length depending only on M.

Finally, let $f(X, Y, Z)$ denote the symbol Z such that if W, X, and Y are at positions $i - 1$, i, and $i + 1$ of one ID, then Z will be at position i of the next ID. Then let

$$\text{MOVE} = \underset{(W,X,Y)}{+} \ \Sigma^* W X Y \Sigma \uparrow (2^n - 1)(\Sigma - f(W, X, Y)\Sigma^*.$$

That is, MOVE is the sum, over the finite number of triples (W, X, Y) of symbols in Σ, of those strings with W, X, and Y occupying consecutive positions in an ID that has a wrong next symbol 2^n positions to the right. As the length of each term is linear in n, the length of MOVE is linear in n.

The desired expression is $E_x = \text{START} + \text{FINISH} + \text{MOVE}$. If M accepts x, then the accepting computation is not in E_x. If some string y is not in E_x, then it must begin $\#[q_0 a_1]a_2 \cdots a_n B^{2^n - n}\#$, each ID must follow the previous by one move of M, and acceptance must occur somewhere along the way. Thus M accepts x. Therefore $E_x = \Sigma^*$ if and only if M does not accept x.

Now, let M be a Turing machine accepting language L that can be accepted in 2^n space but not in $2^n/n$ space. The hierarchy theorem for space assures us that such an M exists. Suppose there were an $S(n)$ space-bounded TM accepting the set L_{rex} of regular expressions with exponentiation denoting Σ^*, suitably coded so L_{rex} has a finite alphabet. Then we could recognize L as follows.

1) From x of length n, construct E_x, whose length is proportional to $n \log n$. We can construct E_x in space proportional to $n \log n$ in an obvious way.

2) Code E_x into the alphabet of L_{rex}. As M has a finite number of symbols, the length of the coded E_x is $cn \log n$ for some constant c.

3) In $S(cn \log n)$ space, determine whether E_x is in L_{rex}. If so, reject x; if not, accept x.

The total amount of space is the maximum of $n \log n$ and $S(cn \log n)$. As no TM using less than $2^n/n$ space and accepting L exists, it must be that

$$n \log n + S(cn \log n) > 2^n/n \quad \text{i.o.,} \tag{13.4}$$

else L could be accepted in $2^n/n$ space by Lemma 12.3. There exists a constant $d > 0$ such that if $S(m)$ were less than $2^{dm/\log m}$ for all but a finite set of m, then (13.4) would be false. It follows that $S(m) \geq 2^{dm/\log m}$ for some constant d and an infinite number of m's. □

Corollary L_{rex} is complete for exponential space with respect to polynomial-time reduction.

Proof In Theorem 13.15, we gave a polynomial time reduction to L_{rex} that works for every language L in $\text{DSPACE}(2^n)$. We could easily have generalized it to reduce any language in $\text{DSPACE}(2^{p(n)})$, for polynomial p, to L_{rex}. □

We should observe that the $n \log n$ bound on the length of E_x is critical for Theorem 13.15, although for its corollary we could have allowed the length to be any polynomial in $|x|$. If, for example, we could only prove that $|E_x| \leq |x|^2$, then our lower bound on the space required by L_{rex} would have been $2^{d\sqrt{n}}$ instead.

Complexity of first-order theories

Now we shall consider a problem that requires at least 2^{cn} time, nondeterministically, and is known to be solvable in exponential space and doubly exponential time. As the problem can also be shown nondeterministic exponential time-hard with respect to polynomial time reductions, proving a better lower bound regarding the amount of nondeterministic time would improve on Theorem 12.10, which is most unlikely.

A *first-order language* consists of a *domain* (for example, the nonnegative integers), a set of *operations* (for example, $+$, $*$) a set of *predicates* (for example, $=$, $<$), a set of *constants* chosen from the domain, and a set of *axioms* defining the meaning of the operators and predicates. For each theory we can define the language of true expressions over the constants, operators, predicates, variables, the logical connectives, $\wedge$, $\vee$, and $\neg$, and the quantifiers $\exists$ and $\forall$.

Example 13.5 $(\mathbf{N}, +, *, =, <, 0, 1)$, where $\mathbf{N}$ stands for the nonnegative integers, is known as number theory. Godel's famous incompleteness theorem states that the language of true statements in number theory is undecidable. While Godel's result predated Turing machines, it is not hard to show his result. If a TM M accepts when started on blank tape, it does so by a computation in which no ID is longer than some constant m. We may treat an integer i, in binary, as a computation of M with ID's of length m.

The statement that M accepts ϵ, which is known to be undecidable, can be expressed as $\exists i \exists m(E_m(i))$, where E_m is a predicate that is true if and only if i is the binary encoding of a computation leading to acceptance of ϵ with no ID longer than m. (Some of the details are provided in Exercise 13.37.) Thus, number theory is an undecidable theory.

There are a number of decidable theories known. For example, $(\mathbf{R}, +, =, <, 0, 1)$, the *theory of reals with addition*, is decidable, and we shall show that it inherently requires nondeterministic exponential time. If the reals are replaced by the rationals, we get the same true statements, since without multiplication, it is impossible to find a statement like $\exists x(x * x = 2)$ that is true for the reals but not the rationals. The theory of integers with addition $(\mathbf{Z}, +, =, <, 0, 1)$, called *Presburger arithmetic*, is decidable, and is known to require doubly exponential nondeterministic time. That is, $2^{2^{cn}}$ is a lower bound on the nondeterministic time complexity of Presburger arithmetic.

Example 13.6 Before proceeding, let us consider a number of examples in the theory of reals with addition. $\forall x \exists y(y = x + 1)$ is true: it says that $x + 1$ is a real whenever x is.

$$\forall x \forall y [x = y \vee \exists z(x < z \wedge z < y) \vee \exists z(y < z \wedge z < x)]$$

is also true: it states that between two different reals we can find a third real; that is, the reals are *dense*. The statement

$$\exists y \forall x (x < y \vee x = y)$$

is false, since for every real number y there is a greater real. Note that we have not told how to decide whether a statement is true; the decision depends on knowing the properties of real numbers, with which we assume the reader is familiar.

A decision procedure for the reals with addition

We shall begin our study of the reals with addition by giving a decision procedure that requires exponential space and doubly exponential time. To begin, let us put our given statement in prenex normal form, where all quantifiers apply to the whole expression. It is easy to obtain an expression in this form if we first rename quantified variables so they are unique, and then apply the identities

$$\neg(\forall x(E)) = \exists x(\neg E) \qquad \forall x(E_1) \vee E_2 = \forall x(E_1 \vee E_2)$$

and four similar rules obtained from these by interchanging $\forall$ and $\exists$ and/or replacing $\vee$ by $\wedge$. This process does not more than double the length of the expression; the only symbols that might be added to the expression are a pair of parentheses per quantifier.† Now we have a formula

$$Q_1 x_1 Q_2 x_2 \cdots Q_m x_m F(x_1, x_2, \ldots, x_m), \tag{13.5}$$

where the Q_i's are quantifiers, and the formula F has no quantifiers. F is therefore a Boolean expression whose operands are atoms, an *atom* being a Boolean constant or an expression of the form E_1 **op** E_2, where **op** is $=$ or $<$ and E_1 and E_2 are sums of variables and the constants 0 and 1. We know F is of this form because no other combination of operators make sense. That is, $+$ can be applied only to variables and constants, $<$ and $=$ relate only arithmetic expressions, and the Boolean operators can be applied sensibly only to expressions that have true/false as possible values.

To determine the truth or falsehood of (13.5) we repeatedly substitute for the innermost quantifier a bounded quantification, which is the logical "or" (in place of $\exists$) or "and" (for $\forall$) of a large but finite number of terms. Suppose in (13.5) we fix the values of $x_1, x_2, \ldots, x_{m-1}$. Every atom involving x_m can be put in the form

---

† Technically the renaming of variables may increase the length of the formula by a log n factor when we encode in a fixed alphabet. However, the complexity depends on the original number of symbols and not the length of the encoded string.

x_m **op** t, where **op** is $<$, $=$, or $>$ and t is of the form

$$c_0 + \sum_{i=1}^{m-1} c_i x_i,$$

where the c_i's are rationals. Suppose all these atoms are x_m **op** t_i, $1 \le i \le k$, where $t_1 \le t_2 \le \cdots \le t_k$ for the given values of $x_1, \ldots, x_{m-1}$. For any value of x_m in the range $t_i < x_m < t_{i+1}$, each atom has the same truth value. Thus the truth of (13.5) is independent of the actual value of x_m in this range. This leads us to the observation that the t_i's partition the real line into a finite number of segments, and the truth of (13.5) depends only on the segment in which x_m lies, and not on the actual value of x_m. Thus we can test (13.5) by trying one value of x_m from each of a finite number of regions as suggested in Fig. 13.6.

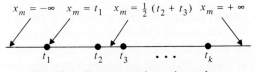

Fig. 13.6   Representative values of x_m.

As the values of $x_1, \ldots, x_{m-1}$ will vary, we do not really know the order of the t_i's. However, trying $x_m = t_i$ for each i, $x_m = \frac{1}{2}(t_i + t_j)$ for each $i \ne j$, and $x_m = \pm\infty$,† we know that no matter what the order of the t_i's, we are sure to have a representative x_m in each interval of Fig. 13.6 and also at the t_i's themselves, where atoms with the $=$ operator may become true.

It follows that if $Q_m = \exists$, then $\exists x_m F(x_1, \ldots, x_m)$ may be replaced by

$$F'(x_1, \ldots, x_{m-1}) = \bigvee_{\substack{x_m = t_i \text{ or} \\ x_m = (1/2)(t_i + t_j) \\ \text{or } x_m = \pm\infty}} F(x_1, \ldots, x_m), \tag{13.6}$$

that is, by the logical "or" of $k(k+1)/2 + 2$ terms, each of which is F with a substitution for x_m. If $Q_m = \forall$, a similar replacement, with $\wedge$ substituting for $\vee$, may be made.

If F has k atoms, F' has $k[k(k+1)/2 + 2]$ atoms, which is at most k^3 atoms for $k \ge 3$. Also, if the coefficients in the atoms of F are each the ratio of integers of at most r bits each, then after grouping terms, solving for x_m, and computing the average of two t_i's, we find that the coefficients in the atoms of F' will be ratios of integers with no more than $4r + 1$ bits. This follows since if a, b, c, and d are r-bit integers,

$$\frac{a}{b} \frac{c}{d} = \frac{ac}{bd}$$

---

† If $x_m = +\infty$, then $x_m = t$ and $x_m < t$ are false, and $x_m > t$ is true independently of t. If $x_m = -\infty$ analogous simplifications occur.

is the ratio of integers with at most $2r$ bits, and

$$\frac{a}{b} \pm \frac{c}{d} = \frac{ad \pm bc}{bd}$$

is the ratio of a $(2r + 1)$-bit integer and a $2r$-bit integer. For $r \geq 1$, then, the coefficients in F' are no more than five times the length of the coefficients in F.

If we repeat the above process to eliminate all the quantifiers and variables, we eventually produce a formula with only logical operators, $=$, $<$, and constants. The constants are ratios of integers with at most $5^m r$ bits. The number of atoms is at most

$$\underbrace{(\dots ((k^3)^3) \dots)^3}_{m \text{ times}} = k^{3^m}.$$

As each atom is a relation between constants of $5^m r$ bits, and k, m, and r are less than n, the length of the expression is at most $2^{2^{cn}}$ for some constant c (note that $n^{3^n} \leq 2^{2^{2n}}$). We may evaluate an atom of the form $a/b < c/d$ by computing $ad - bc$ and comparing it with 0. Thus the entire final expression may be evaluated in the square of its length. Hence our decision procedure takes $2^{2^{dn}}$ time for some constant d.

The procedure as we have given it also takes doubly exponential space. However, we can reduce the space to a single exponential by evaluating F recursively. We have already seen that we need consider only a finite set of values for each x_i. The values for x_i are given by a formula of the form $a_0 + \sum_{j=1}^{i-1} a_j x_j$, where the a_j's are rationals that are ratios of 5^{m-j+1} r-bit integers, where r is the number of bits in the largest constant of the original formula, F; note $r \leq \log n$. Thus values for x_1 are rationals that are at most ratios of $5^m r$-bit integers, the values for x_2 are ratios of at most $5^{m+1} r$-bit integers, etc. Thus we need only cycle through values for each x_i that are at most $5^{2m} r$ bits. We use a recursive procedure EVAL(G) that determines whether G is true when the variables take on the values $\pm \infty$ and any ratio of $5^{2m} r$-bit integers.

If G has no quantifiers, then it consists only of arithmetic and logical relations among rationals, so its truth can be determined directly. If $G = \forall x(G')$, EVAL(G) calls EVAL(G'') for all G'' formed from G' by replacing x by $\pm \infty$ or a ratio of $5^{2m} r$-bit integers. EVAL(G) is true if EVAL(G'') returns **true** for all these expressions G''. If $G = \exists x(G')$, we do the same, but EVAL(G) returns **true** whenever some EVAL(G'') is true.

It is easy to check that no more than m copies of EVAL are active simultaneously. The arguments for the active calls to EVAL can be put on a stack, and this stack takes $0(m5^{2m} r)$ space. Thus, if F is an expression of length n, we may evaluate F in space 2^{cn} and time $2^{2^{dn}}$ for some constants c and d.

A lower bound

We now show that the theory of reals with addition requires essentially non-deterministic exponential time. A series of lemmas are needed showing that multiplication and exponentiation by limited size integers can be expressed by short formulas.

Lemma 13.10 There exists $c > 0$ such that for each n there is a formula $M_n(x, y, z)$ that is true if and only if x is a nonnegative integer strictly less than 2^{2^n}, and $xy = z$. Furthermore, $|M_n(x, y, z)| < c(n + 1)$, and $M_n(x, y, z)$ can be constructed from n in time polynomial in n.

Proof For $n = 0$, $2^{2^0} = 2$. Thus $M_0(x, y, z)$ can be expressed as $(x = 0 \land z = 0) \lor (x = 1 \land z = y)$.

Inductive step: (Construction of M_{k+1} from M_k). Let x be an integer less than $2^{2^{k+1}}$. There exist integers $x_1, x_2, x_3, x_4 < 2^{2^k}$ such that $x = x_1 x_2 + x_3 + x_4$. In proof, let $x_1 = x_2 = \lfloor \sqrt{x} \rfloor$. Now $z = xy$ can be expressed by $z = x_1(x_2 y) + x_3 y + x_4 y$. Thus

$$M_{k+1}(x, y, z) = \exists u_1 \cdots \exists u_5 \exists x_1 \cdots \exists x_4 [M_k(x_1, x_2, u_1)$$
$$\land x = u_1 + x_3 + x_4 \land M_k(x_2, y, u_2) \land M_k(x_1, u_2, u_3) \land M_k(x_3, y, u_4)$$
$$\land M_k(x_4, y, u_5) \land z = u_3 + u_4 + u_5] \tag{13.7}$$

That is,
$$u_1 = x_1 x_2, \qquad x = x_1 x_2 + x_3 + x_4,$$
$$u_2 = x_2 y, \qquad u_3 = x_1 x_2 y, \qquad u_4 = x_3 y, \qquad u_5 = x_4 y,$$
and
$$z = x_1 x_2 y + x_3 y + x_4 y.$$

The condition that each x_i is an integer less than 2^{2^k} is enforced by each x_i being the first argument of some M_k.

Formula (13.7) has five copies of M_k, so it appears that M_{k+1} must be at least five times as long as M_k. This would make the length of M_n exponential in n, not linear as we asserted. However, we can use the "trick" of Theorem 13.10 to replace several copies of one predicate by a single copy. That is, we may write

$$M_{k+1}(x, y, z) = \exists_1 \cdots \exists u_5 \exists x_1 \cdots \exists x_4$$
$$[x = u_1 + x_3 + x_4 \land z = u_3 + u_4 + u_5$$
$$\land \forall r \, \forall s \, \forall t [\neg r = x_1 \land s = x_2 \land t = u_1)$$
$$\land \neg (r = x_2 \land s = y \land t = u_2)$$
$$\land \neg (r = x_1 \land s = u_2 \land t = u_3)$$
$$\land \neg (r = x_3 \land s = y \land t = u_4)$$
$$\land \neg (r = x_4 \land s = y \land t = u_5)$$
$$\lor M_k(r, s, t)]],$$

which has a constant number of symbols more than M_k does.

One minor point is that if we introduce new variable names for each M_k, we shall eventually introduce a log n factor into the length of M_n, since variable names must be coded in a fixed alphabet in the language of true formulas. However, the scope rules for quantified formulas allow us to reuse variables subject to the restriction that the twelve new variables introduced in M_k don't conflict with the free variables x, y, and z. Thus M_n requires only 15 different variables, and its coded length is proportional to the number of symbols. □

Observe that $M_n(x, 0, 0)$ states that x is an integer less than 2^{2^n}. Thus we can make statements about small integers in the theory of reals with addition by using very short formulas.

Lemma 13.11 There exists a constant $c > 0$ such that for every n there is a formula $P_n(x, y, z)$ that is true if and only if x and z are integers in the range $0 \le x$, $z < 2^{2^n}$ and $y^x = z$. Furthermore $|P_n| \le c(n + 1)$ and P_n can be constructed from n in time polynomial in n.

Proof We construct by induction on k a sequence of formulas $E_k(x, y, z, u, v, w)$ such that E_k has both exponentiation and multiplication built into it. The reason for doing this is that we wish to express E_k in terms of several copies of E_{k-1} and then use universal quantification to express E_k in terms of one copy of E_{k-1}. We could not do this with P_k, since a formula for P_k involves both P_{k-1} and M_{k-1}.

The formula $E_k(x, y, z, u, v, w)$ will be true if and only if x, z, and u are integers, $0 \le x$, $z < 2^{2^k}$, $z = y^x$, $0 \le u < 2^{2^n}$, and $uv = w$.

Basis For $k = 0$,

$$E_0 = (x = 0 \wedge z = 1) \vee (x = 1 \wedge y = 0 \wedge z = 0)$$
$$\vee (x = 1 \wedge y = 1 \wedge z = 1) \wedge M_0(u, v, w).$$

Induction To construct $E_{k+1}(x, y, z, u, v, w)$ we can use the fact that

$$E_k(0, 0, 0, u, v, w) = M_n(u, v, w)$$

to express the conditions on u, v, and w as in Lemma 13.10. Using several copies of E_k, we may assert that there exist integers x_1, x_2, x_3, x_4 in the range $0 \le x_i < 2^{2^k}$ such that

$$x = x_1 x_2 + x_3 + x_4 \qquad \text{and} \qquad y^x = (y^{x_1})^{x_2} y^{x_3} y^{x_4}.$$

Finally, we use the "trick" of Theorem 13.10 to express E_{k+1} in terms of one copy of E_k and a constant number of additional symbols. Last, we may write

$$P_n(x, y, z) = E_n(x, y, z, 0, 0, 0).$$

This asserts that $z = y^x$, and x and z are integers in the range $0 \le x$, $z < 2^{2^n}$.

□

To improve readability of what follows, we use the abbreviations 2 for $1 + 1$, $2x$ for $x + x$, $x \le y$ for $x < y \vee x = y$, and $x \le y < z$ for $(x = y \vee x < y) \wedge y < z$.

Expanding an abbreviated formula results in at most multiplying the length by a constant factor. In addition to the above abbreviations, we shall use constants like 2^n and multiplications like ab in formulas. Technically these must be replaced by introducing an existentially quantified variable, say x, and asserting $x = 2^n$ or $x = ab$ by $P_n(n, 2, x)$ or $M_n(a, b, x)$. This can also increase the length of the formula by a constant factor.

We intend to encode Turing machine computations as integers. Let M be a 2^n time-bounded NTM. If the total number of tape symbols, composite symbols, and the marker $\#$ is b, then a computation of M is an integer x in the range $0 \le x < b^{(2^{n+1})^2 + 1}$. Asserting that an integer is a computation is facilitated by a predicate that interrogates the ith digit in the b-ary representation of x.

Lemma 13.12   For each n and b there exists a constant c, depending only on b, such that there is a formula $D_{n,b}(x, i, j)$ that is true if and only if x and i are integers, $0 \le x < b^{(2^{n+1})^2 + 1}$, $0 \le i < 2^n$, and x_i, the $(i + 1)$th digit of x counting from the low-order end of the b-ary representation of x, is j. Furthermore $|D_{n,b}| \le c(n + 1)$, and $D_{n,b}$ can be constructed from n and b in time polynomial in n and b.

Proof   For each b there exists a constant s such that $b^{(2^{n+1})^2 + 1} \le 2^{2^{sn}}$ for all n. Thus that x is an integer in the correct range can be expressed by $\exists m[P_{sn}((2^n + 1)^2, b, m) \wedge 0 \le x < m]$. (Recall our previous remarks concerning constants like 2^n and their expansions.) That i is an integer in the range $0 \le i < 2^n$ can be expressed by $M_n(i, 0, 0) \wedge (0 \le i < 2^n)$. Now x in base b has zeros in positions $1, 2, \ldots, i + 1$ if and only if it is divisible by b^{i+1}. Thus $x_i = j$ if and only if there exist integers q and r such that $x = qb^{i+1} + r$ and $jb^i \le r < (j + 1)b^i$. This fact is easily expressed using P_{sn} and M_{sn}.   □

Theorem 13.16   Any nondeterministic algorithm to decide whether a formula in the first-order theory of reals with addition is true must, for some constant $c > 0$, take 2^{cn} steps for an infinite number of n's.

Proof   The proof is quite similar in spirit to that of Theorem 13.1. Let M be an arbitrary 2^n-time bounded NTM. Here ID's in a computation of M consist of 2^n symbols rather than $p(n)$ as in Theorem 13.1. Let the total number of tape symbols, composite symbols, and $\#$'s be b. Then a computation of M on input of length n consists of $[(2^n + 1)^2 + 1]$ b-ary digits. We may consider this computation to be an integer i in the range $0 \le i < 2^{2^{sn}}$ for some constant s. For convenience, we take the low-order digits of i to be at the left end of the computation.

Let x be an input of length n to M. We construct a formula F_x that is true if and only if M accepts x. F_x is of the form $\exists i(\ldots)$, where the formula within the parentheses asserts i is an accepting computation of x. This formula is analogous to that in Theorem 13.1. The first $n + 1$ symbols of the computation are

$$\#[q_0, a_1, m]a_2 \cdots a_n,$$

assuming that $x = a_1 a_2 \cdots a_n$, q_0 is the initial state, and m is any choice of first move. To say that the first $n + 1$ symbols of the computation are correct, we say that there exist u and j such that the value of u represents $\#[q_0, a_1, m]a_2 \cdots a_n$ for some m, and $i = b^{n+1}j + u$ for some integer j.

We must write this formula in $0(n)$-space in time that is polynomial in n. By induction on $k = 2, 3, \ldots, n + 1$ we can write a formula $C_k(v)$ with free variable v, which asserts that the value of v is the numerical value of the first k symbols of the computation. For the basis, $k = 2$, we simply write a formula

$$C_2(v) = (v = p_1 \vee v = p_2 \vee \cdots \vee v = p_n),$$

where the p_j's are the integers represented by $\#[q_0, a_1, m]$ for the finite set of values of m. For the induction,

$$C_k(v) = \exists w (C_{k-1}(w) \wedge v = bw + a_{k-1}),$$

where a_{k-1} is taken to be the numerical value of tape symbol a_{k-1}. To avoid using n variables to express C_{n+1}, which would make its length $0(n \log n)$, we alternate between two variables, such as v and w, as we construct $C_2, C_3, \ldots, C_{n+1}$.

The desired formula asserts $C_{n+1}(u)$ and $i = b^{n+1}j + u$ for integer j. The latter assertion is similar to what was done in Lemma 13.12, and the technique will not be repeated here.

To express that the initial ID was correct in Theorem 13.1 required asserting that "approximately" $p(n)$ cells contained the blank symbol. This was accomplished by the logical $\vee$ of $p(n)$ items. We must now assert that about 2^n cells contain the blank symbol, and thus we cannot use a logical $\vee$ of 2^n formulas; this would be too long a formula. Instead we use the quantifier $\forall j$ and assert that either j is not an integer in the range $n + 2 < j \leq 2^n + 1$ or the jth symbol is the blank, which we denote by 0. Thus we write

$$\forall j [\neg M_{sn}(j, 0, 0) \vee \neg(n + 2 \leq j \leq 2^n + 1) \vee D_{n,b}(i, j, 0)].$$

The formulas that force the last ID to contain a final state and force each ID to follow from the previous ID because of the choice of move embedded in the previous ID are similarly translated from the techniques of Theorem 13.1. Having done this, we have a formula E_x, whose length is proportional to n, that is true if and only if M accepts x.

Suppose M accepts a language L in time 2^n not accepted by any $2^{n/2}$ time-bounded NTM. (The existence of such a language follows from the NTIME hierarchy of Cook [1973a], which we have not proved.) We can recognize L as follows. Given x of length n, produce the formula E_x that is true if and only if x is in L. Now, if $T(n)$ nondeterministic time suffices to accept the set of true formulas in the first-order theory of reals with addition, we may determine whether x is in L in time $p(n) + T(cn)$. Then $p(n) + T(cn) > 2^{n/2}$ for an infinity of n's, else by Lemma 12.3 we could recognize L in time at most $2^{n/2}$, for all n. It follows that $T(n) \geq 2^{dn}$ i.o. for some $d > 0$. □

Corollary   The theory of reals with addition is nondeterministic exponential time-hard with respect to polynomial time reductions.

Proof   The proof is an easy generalization of the foregoing reduction of a 2^n nondeterministic time TM.   □

13.7   THE $\mathscr{P} = \mathscr{N}\mathscr{P}$ QUESTION FOR TURING MACHINES WITH ORACLES: LIMITS ON OUR ABILITY TO TELL WHETHER $\mathscr{P} = \mathscr{N}\mathscr{P}$

The reader should recall from Section 8.9 our discussion of Turing machines with oracles. These TM's had associated languages, called oracles, and had special states in which the membership of the string written to the left of their head could be tested in one step for membership in the oracle. Any oracle TM can have any oracle "plugged in," although its behavior will naturally vary depending on the oracle chosen. If A is an oracle, we use M^A for M with oracle A. The time taken by an oracle TM is one step for each query to the oracle and one step for each ordinary move of the TM.

We define $\mathscr{P}^A$ to be the set of languages accepted in polynomial time by DTM's with oracle A. Also define $\mathscr{N}\mathscr{P}^A$ to be the set of languages accepted by NTM's with oracle A in polynomial time. We shall prove that there are oracles A and B for which $\mathscr{P}^A = \mathscr{N}\mathscr{P}^A$ and $\mathscr{P}^B \neq \mathscr{N}\mathscr{P}^B$. This result has implications regarding our ability to solve the $\mathscr{P} = \mathscr{N}\mathscr{P}$ question for TM's without oracles. Intuitively all known methods to resolve the question one way or the other will work when arbitrary oracles are attached. But the existence of A and B tells us that no such method can work for arbitrary oracles. Thus existing methods are probably insufficient to settle whether $\mathscr{P} = \mathscr{N}\mathscr{P}$. We shall provide details along these lines after we see the constructions of A and B.

An oracle for which $\mathscr{P} = \mathscr{N}\mathscr{P}$

Theorem 13.17 $\mathscr{P}^A = \mathscr{N}\mathscr{P}^A$, where $A = L_{qbf}$, the set of all true quantified Boolean formulas (or any other PSPACE-complete problem).

Proof   Let M^A be nondeterministic polynomial time bounded, and let $L = L(M^A)$. Then M^A queries its oracle a polynomial number of times on strings whose lengths are bounded by a polynomial of the length of the input to M^A. Thus we may simulate the oracle computation in polynomial space. It follows that $\mathscr{N}\mathscr{P}^A \subseteq \text{PSPACE}$. However, any language L in PSPACE is accepted by some DTM M^A that reduces L to A in polynomial time and then queries its oracle. Thus $\text{PSPACE} \subseteq \mathscr{P}^A$. But clearly $\mathscr{P}^A \subseteq \mathscr{N}\mathscr{P}^A$, so $\mathscr{P}^A = \mathscr{N}\mathscr{P}^A$.   □

An oracle for which $\mathscr{P} \neq \mathscr{N}\mathscr{P}$

We now show how to construct an oracle $B \subseteq (0 + 1)^*$ for which $\mathscr{P}^B \neq \mathscr{N}\mathscr{P}^B$. B will have at most one word of any length; exactly which words will be discussed later. We shall be interested in the language

$$L = \{0^i \,|\, B \text{ has a word of length } i\}.$$

We may easily construct an NTM with oracle B that, given input 0^i, guesses a string of length i in $(0 + 1)^*$ and queries its oracle about the guessed string, accepting if the oracle says "yes." Thus L is in $\mathscr{N}\mathscr{P}^B$. However, we can construct B so that the string of each length, if any, is so cleverly hidden that a DTM with oracle B cannot find it in polynomial time.

Theorem 13.18   There is an oracle B for which $\mathscr{P}^B \neq \mathscr{N}\mathscr{P}^B$.

Proof   We shall give a procedure to enumerate the set B. Set B will have at most one word of any length. As we generate B, we keep a list of forbidden words; these words are ruled out of consideration for possible membership in B. Assume an enumeration of DTM's with oracle and input alphabet $\{0, 1\}$, in which each TM appears infinitely often. We consider each M_i, $i = 1, 2, \ldots$, in turn. When M_i is considered we shall have generated some forbidden words and a set B_i of words so far in B. There will be at most one word in B_i of length $0, 1, \ldots, i - 1$, and no longer words. Furthermore, no other words of length less than i will subsequently be put in B. We simulate $M_i^{B_i}$ on input 0^i. If M_i queries a word of length less than i, we consult B_i, which is all words in B so far, to see if the oracle responds "yes" or "no." If M_i queries a word y of length i or more, we assume that y is not in B (i.e., answer "no") and to make sure y is not later placed in B, add y to the list of forbidden words.

The simulation of $M_i^{B_i}$ on 0^i continues for $i^{\log i}$ steps. Afterwards, whether or not M_i has halted, we make a decision about a word to put in B. If within $i^{\log i}$ steps, $M_i^{B_i}$ halts and rejects 0^i, then we put a word of length i that is not on the forbidden list in B, provided there is such a word. The word may be picked arbitrarily, say the lexicographically first word that is not forbidden. If $M_i^{B_i}$ does not reject 0^i within $i^{\log i}$ steps, then no word of length i is placed in B.

There is also no word of length i in B if all words of length i are forbidden by the time we finish simulating $M_i^{B_i}$. However, the number of steps simulated for $M_j^{B_j}$ is $j^{\log j}$, so the total number of words of all lengths forbidden by $M_1, M_2, \ldots, M_i$ is at most

$$\sum_{j=1}^{i} j^{\log j} \leq i(i^{\log i}) \leq i^{1 + \log i}.$$

As there are 2^i words of length i, we know that not all words of length i are forbidden if $2^i > i^{1 + \log i}$, that is, if $i > (1 + \log i)\log i$. But the latter relation holds for $i \geq 32$, so it is only for a finite number of small i's that all words of length i could be forbidden.

Having finished the simulation of $M_i^{B_i}$ on 0^i for $i^{\log i}$ steps, we generate the selected word, if there is one, obtaining us a new set B_{i+1} of generated words. We are now ready to repeat the process for $M_{i+1}^{B_{i+1}}$ on 0^{i+1}.

Next we define a language L that is in $\mathcal{N}\mathcal{P}^B - \mathcal{P}^B$. Let

$$L = \{0^i \mid B \text{ has a word of length } i\}.$$

We may easily construct a linear time NTM with oracle B that, given input 0^i, nondeterministically guesses string w of length i in $(0 + 1)^*$ and queries its oracle about w, accepting if the oracle says "yes." Thus L is in $\mathcal{N}\mathcal{P}^B$.

Suppose L is in $\mathcal{P}^B$. Let M_k^B accept L, where M_k^B is a deterministic polynomial $p(n)$ time-bounded TM with oracle B. As each TM has arbitrarily long codes, we may pick k such that $k \geq 32$ and $k^{\log k} \geq p(k)$. If M_k^B accepts 0^k, then 0^k is in L, so B has a word of length k. That means $M_k^{B_k}$ rejects 0^k. But M_k^B and $M_k^{B_k}$ must behave identically on input 0^k, since B and B_k agree on words shorter than k, and B has no word of length k or more that is queried by $M_k^{B_k}$ on 0^k. Thus M_k^B rejects 0^k, a contradiction.

If M_k^B rejects 0^k, so 0^k is not in L, then $M_k^{B_k}$ cannot reject 0^k within $k^{\log k}$ steps. This follows since $k \geq 32$, and had $M_k^{B_k}$ rejected 0^k within $k^{\log k}$ steps, there would still be a word of length k not on the forbidden list, and that word would be in B. Thus 0^k would be in L. Hence M_k^B does not reject 0^k within $k^{\log k}$ steps. But as $k^{\log k} \geq p(k)$, M_k^B does not reject 0^k at all, another contradiction. We conclude that L is in $\mathcal{N}\mathcal{P}^B - \mathcal{P}^B$. $\qquad\qquad\square$

Significance of oracle results

Let us consider the ways used in this book to show two language classes to be the same or different, and see why Theorems 13.17 and 13.18 suggest that these methods will fail to resolve the $\mathcal{P} = \mathcal{N}\mathcal{P}$ question. We showed certain classes to be the same by simulation. For example, Chapter 7 contains many simulations of one type of TM by another. Chapter 5 contained simulations of PDA's by CFG's and conversely.

Suppose we could simulate arbitrary polynomial time-bounded NTM's by polynomial time-bounded DTM's. (Note that giving a polynomial-time algorithm for any one NP-complete problem is in effect a polynomial-time simulation of all NTM's.) It is likely that the simulation would still be valid if we attached the same oracle to each TM. For example, all the simulations of Chapter 7 are still valid if we use oracle TM's. But then we would have $\mathcal{P}^B = \mathcal{N}\mathcal{P}^B$, which was just shown to be false.

Other classes of languages were shown unequal by diagonalization. The hierarchy theorems, Theorems 12.8 and 12.9, and the proof that L_u is an r.e. set but not a recursive set are prime examples. Diagonalizations also tend to work when oracles are attached, at least in the three examples cited above. If we could diagonalize over $\mathcal{P}$ to show a language to be in $\mathcal{N}\mathcal{P} - \mathcal{P}$, then the same proof might well work to show $\mathcal{N}\mathcal{P}^A - \mathcal{P}^A \neq \varnothing$. This would violate Theorem 13.17.

We also used translation lemmas to refine time and space hierarchies in Chapter 12. Could these help show $\mathcal{P} \neq \mathcal{N}\mathcal{P}$? Probably not, because the translation lemmas also hold when oracles are attached.

Lastly, we can use closure properties to show a difference between two languages. For example, the DCFL's are contained in the CFL's, but the DCFL's are closed under complementation and the CFL's are not. This proves that there is a CFL that is not a DCFL. Could we find a closure property of $\mathscr{P}$ that is not shared by $\mathscr{N P}$? This at first appears the most promising approach. While proofs that $\mathscr{P}$ is closed under an operation are likely to show also that $\mathscr{P}^A$ is closed under that operation, a nonclosure result for $\mathscr{N P}$ might not carry over to $\mathscr{N P}^A$. On the other hand, showing $\mathscr{N P}$ not closed under an operation involves showing a particular language not to be in $\mathscr{N P}$. This proof might be accomplished by diagonalization, but then it would likely carry over to $\mathscr{N P}^A$. It might be done by developing a pumping lemma for $\mathscr{N P}$, but this seems well beyond present capability. Finally, we might develop some *ad hoc* argument, but again, no such arguments have been found, and they appear very difficult.

EXERCISES

13.1   Suppose there is a 2^n time-bounded reduction of L_1 to L_2, and L_2 is in DTIME(2^n). What can we conclude about L_1?

13.2   Which of the following Boolean formulas are satisfiable.

a) $\bar{x}_1 \wedge x_3 \wedge (\bar{x}_2 \vee \bar{x}_3)$

*b) $\bigwedge_{i_1, i_2, i_3} (x_{i_1} \vee x_{i_2} \vee x_{i_3}) \wedge \bigwedge_{i_1, i_2, i_3} (\bar{x}_{i_1} \vee \bar{x}_{i_2} \vee \bar{x}_{i_3})$

where (i_1, i_2, i_3) ranges over all triples of three distinct integers between 1 and 5.

13.3   A *clique* in a graph G is a subgraph of G that is complete; i.e., each pair of vertices is connected by an edge. The clique problem is to determine if a given graph G contains a clique of given size k.

a) Formulate the clique problem as a language recognition problem.
b) Prove that the clique problem is NP-complete by reducing the vertex cover problem to the clique problem.

[*Hint*: Consider a graph G and its complement graph $\bar{G}$, where $\bar{G}$ has an edge if and only if G does not have that edge.]

13.4   Given a graph G and integer k, the *clique cover problem* is to determine if there exist k cliques in G such that each vertex of G is in at least one of the k cliques. Prove that the clique cover problem is NP-complete by reducing the vertex cover problem to the vertex cover problem for graphs without triangles, thence to the clique cover problem. [*Hint*: Consider graphs $G = (V, E)$ and

$$G' = (E, \{(e_1, e_2) | e_1, e_2 \text{ are incident upon the same vertex in } G\})].$$

13.5   Does the graph of Fig. 13.7

a) have a Hamilton circuit?
b) a vertex cover of size 10?
c) a vertex coloring with 2 colors such that no two adjacent vertices are the same color?

13.6   Prove that the chromatic number problem is NP-complete by reducing the 3-CNF satisfiability problem to the chromatic number problem. [*Hint*: The graph in Fig. 13.8 can

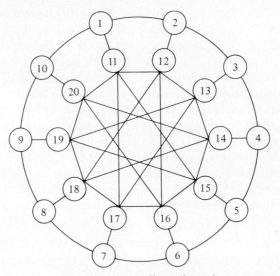

Fig. 13.7 An undirected graph.

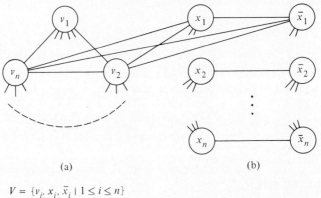

$V = \{v_i, x_i, \bar{x}_i \mid 1 \leq i \leq n\}$

$E = \{(v_i, v_j) \mid i \neq j\} \cup \{(x_i, \bar{x}_i) \mid 1 \leq i \leq n\} \cup \{v_i, x_j), (v_i, \bar{x}_j) \mid i \neq j\}$

Fig. 13.8 Graph used to show chromatic number problem *NP*-complete. (a) Complete graph on n vertices; (b) x_i and $\bar{x}_i$ are connected to all v_j for which $i \neq j$.

be used as a subgraph in your construction. Note that each v_i must be colored with a distinct color, say color i. The entire graph can be colored with $n + 1$ colors if and only if for each i, $1 \leq i \leq n$, one of x_i and $\bar{x}_i$ is colored with color i and the other is colored with color $n + 1$.]

13.7 Show that the following problems are *NP*-complete.

a) Given a graph G, with integer distances on the edges, and two integers f and d, is there a way to select f vertices of G on which to locate "firehouses," so that no vertex is at distance more than d from a firehouse?

**b) *The one-register code generation problem.* Suppose we have a computer with one register and instructions

    LOAD m bring the value in memory location m to the register

    STORE m store the value of the register in memory location m

    OP m apply OP, which may be any binary operator, with the register as left argument and location m as right argument; leave the result in the register.

Given an arithmetic expression, each of whose operands denotes a memory location and given a constant k, is there a program that evaluates the expression in k or fewer instructions?

**c) *The unit execution time scheduling problem.* Given a set of *tasks* $T_1, \ldots, T_k$, a number of *processors* p, a *time limit* t, and a set of *constraints* of the form $T_i < T_j$, meaning that task T_i must be processed before T_j, does there exist a *schedule*, that is, an assignment of at most one task to any processor at any time unit, so that if $T_i < T_j$ is a constraint, then T_i is assigned an earlier time unit than T_j, and within t time units each task has been assigned a processor for one time unit?

**d) *The exact cover problem.* Given a set S and a set of subsets $S_1, S_2, \ldots, S_k$ of S, is there a subset $T \subseteq \{S_1, S_2, \ldots, S_k\}$ so that each x in S is in exactly one S_i in T?

13.8   *The spanning tree problem.* Determine whether a tree T is isomorphic to some spanning tree of G.

a) Give a log-space reduction of the Hamilton circuit problem to the spanning tree problem.

*b) Give a direct log-space reduction of 3-CNF satisfiability to the spanning tree problem.

13.9

a) An *n-dimensional grid* is a graph $G = (V, E)$ where

$$V = \{(i_1, i_2, \ldots, i_n) \mid 1 \le i_j \le m_j, \ 1 \le j \le n\}$$

and $E = \{(v_1, v_2) \mid v_1$ and v_2 differ in only one coordinate, and the difference in v_1 and v_2 in that coordinate is one$\}$. For what values of m_j and n does G have a Hamilton circuit?

*b) Let G be a graph whose vertices are the squares of an 8×8 chess board and whose edges are the legal moves of the knight. Find a Hamilton circuit in G.

13.10   Prove that the Hamilton circuit problem is *NP*-complete even when restricted to planar graphs. [*Hint:* First show that the Hamilton circuit problem is *NP*-complete for planar graphs with "constraints," by reducing $L_{3\mathrm{sat}}$ to it. In particular, consider the class of planar graphs with constraint arrows connecting certain pairs of edges. Constraint arrows are allowed to cross each other but cannot cross edges of the graph. Show that the existence of Hamilton circuits that use exactly one edge from each pair of constrained edges is *NP*-complete. Then replace the constraint arrows one by one by graph edges by the substitution of Fig. 13.9(a). In the process, a constraint arrow may cross a graph edge but only if the graph edge must be present in any Hamilton circuit. These crossings can be removed by the substitution of Fig. 13.9(b). The graph of Fig. 13.10 may be helpful in the first step of the hint to represent a clause $x + y + z$.]

13.11   A graph is *4-connected* if removal of any three vertices and the incident edges leaves the graph connected. Prove that the Hamilton circuit problem is *NP*-complete even for 4-connected graphs. [*Hint:* Construct a subgraph with four distinguished vertices that can replace a vertex in an arbitrary graph G so that even if additional edges are added from the

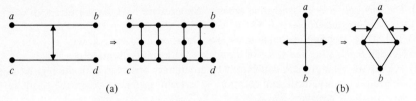

Fig. 13.9   Transformations for Exercise 13.10.

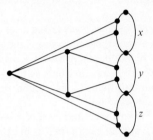

Fig. 13.10   Graph used in the construction of Exercise 13.10.

four distinguished vertices to other vertices of G, the resulting graph will have a Hamilton circuit if and only if G did.]

*13.12   Prove that the problem of determining whether a set of linear equations $A\mathbf{x} = \mathbf{b}$ has a solution with k components of $\mathbf{x}$ equal to zero is NP-complete. [*Hint:* If the x_i are constrained to 0 or 1, then an inequality of the form $x_1 + x_2 + x_3 \geq 1$ can be replaced by an equation of the form $y + x_1 + x_2 + x_3 = 4$, provided y is constrained to be 1, 2, or 3. The system of equations $y + z_1 + z_2 = 3$, $y = z_3 + z_4$, and $z_i + \bar{z}_i = 1$, $1 \leq i \leq 4$, has no solution with more than four variables zero and has a solution with exactly four variables zero if and only if $y = 1, 2,$ or 3.]

*13.13   A *kernel* of a directed graph is a set of vertices such that

1) there is no arc from a vertex in the kernel to another vertex in the kernel, and
2) every vertex is either in the kernel or has an arc into it from the kernel.

Prove that determining whether a directed graph has a kernel is NP-complete. [*Hint:* Observe that a cycle of length two or three may have only one vertex in a kernel.]

13.14   Prove that the traveling salesman problem is NP-complete.

**13.15   Consider approximations to the traveling salesman problem. Show that the existence of a polynomial-time algorithm that produces a tour within twice the cost of the optimal tour would imply $\mathcal{P} = \mathcal{NP}$.

*S13.16   Consider the traveling salesman problem where the distances satisfy the triangle inequality, that is

$$d(v_1, v_3) \leq d(v_1, v_2) + d(v_2, v_3).$$

Give a polynomial-time algorithm to find a tour that is within twice the cost of the optimal tour.

*13.17 Suppose there exists a polynomial-time algorithm for finding a clique in a graph that is of size at least one-half the size of the maximal clique.

a) Prove that there would exist a polynomial-time algorithm for finding a clique which is of size at least $1/\sqrt{2}$ times the size of the maximal clique. [*Hint:* Consider replacing each vertex of a graph by a copy of the graph.]

b) Prove that for any $k < 1$ there would exist a polynomial-time algorithm for finding a clique which is of size at least k times the size of the maximal clique.

*13.18 Prove that it is *NP*-complete to determine whether the chromatic number of a graph is less than or equal to 3. [*Hint:* The graph of Fig. 13.11 can be used as a weak form of an OR gate when only three colors are available, in the sense that the output can be colored "true" if and only if at least one input is colored "true."]

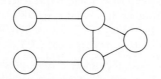

Fig. 13.11 Graph used in Exercise 13.18.

**13.19 For $n \geq 6$, let $G_n = (V_n, E_n)$ be the graph where

$$V_n = \{(i, j, k) \mid i, j, k \text{ are distinct elements of } \{1, 2, \ldots, n\}\},$$

$$E_n = \{(u, v) \mid u \text{ and } v \text{ are disjoint triples}\}.$$

a) Let $X_m(G)$ be the minimum number of colors needed to assign m distinct colors to each vertex of G so that no two adjacent vertices have a color in common. Prove for $n \geq 6$ that $X_3(G_n) = n$ and $X_4(G_n) = 2n - 4$.

b) Suppose there were a polynomial-time algorithm to color a graph G with at most twice the minimum number of colors needed. Then prove that $\mathscr{P} = \mathscr{NP}$. [*Hint:* Combine part (a) with Exercise 13.18.]

**13.20 Construct an algorithm for finding a Hamilton circuit in a graph that under the assumption that $\mathscr{P} = \mathscr{NP}$, will find a Hamilton circuit in polynomial time whenever such a circuit exists. If no Hamilton circuit exists, the algorithm need not run in polynomial time. Note it is not sufficient to design a nondeterministic algorithm and then use the hypothesis $\mathscr{P} = \mathscr{NP}$ to claim that there is a deterministic polynomial-time algorithm. You must actually exhibit the potentially deterministic polynomial-time algorithm.

**13.21 If $\mathscr{P} \neq \mathscr{NP}$ prove it is undecidable for L in $\mathscr{NP}$ whether L is in $\mathscr{P}$.

**13.22 Prove that the existence of an *NP*-complete subset of 0^* implies $\mathscr{P} = \mathscr{NP}$.

*13.23 An integer n is composite if and only if there exists an $a, 1 < a < n$, such that either

1) $a^{n-1} \neq 1 \bmod n$, or
2) there exist integers b and i where $n - 1 = 2^i b$ and a^b and n have a common divisor.

If n is composite, at least one-half of the integers between 1 and n satisfy (1) or (2). Give a randomized algorithm that with high probability will determine whether a number is prime in polynomial time.

*13.24 Suppose there exists a function f mapping integers of length k onto integers of length k such that

1) f is computable in polynomial time;
2) f^{-1} is not computable in polynomial time.

Prove that this would imply

$$A = \{\langle x, y \rangle \mid f^{-1}(x) < y\} \text{ is in } (\mathcal{NP} \cap \text{Co-}\mathcal{NP}) - \mathcal{P}$$

13.25 Show that the following problems are PSPACE-complete.

a) Does a given regular expression (with only the usual operators $\cdot$, $+$, and $*$) define all strings over its alphabet? [*Hint:* The proof parallels Theorem 13.14.]

**Sb) *The Shannon switching game.* Given a graph G with two distinguished vertices s and t, suppose there are two players SHORT and CUT. Alternately, with SHORT first, the players select vertices of G other than s and t. SHORT wins by selecting vertices that, with s and t, form a path from s to t. CUT wins if SHORT cannot make such a path. Can SHORT force a win on G no matter what CUT does?

**13.26 Show that if PSPACE $\neq \mathcal{P}$, then there exists a proof by diagonalization. That is, there is an enumeration $L_1, L_2, \ldots$ of $\mathcal{P}$, and a computable function f from integers to strings and a set L in PSPACE such that for each i, $f(i)$ is in L if and only if $f(i)$ is not in L_i.

13.27 Give a polynomial-time algorithm for converting a quantified Boolean formula to prenex normal form $Q_1 X_1 Q_2 X_2 \cdots Q_k X_k(E)$, where E is a Boolean expression in 3-CNF.

*13.28 Can any QBF be converted in polynomial time to an equivalent formula with at most ten distinct variables?

13.29 Show that the following problems are complete for $\mathcal{P}$ with respect to log-space reductions.

a) Is x in $L(G)$ for string x and CFG G?

**b) The *circuit value problem.* Encode a circuit as a sequence $C_1, C_2, \ldots, C_n$, where each C_i is a variable $x_1, x_2, \ldots$ or $\wedge(j, k)$ or $\neg(j)$ with j and k less than i. Given an encoding of a circuit and an assignment of true and false to the variables, is the output of the circuit true?

**13.30 Show that the following problems are complete for NSPACE($\log n$) with respect to log-space reductions.

a) Is a Boolean expression in 2-CNF not satisfiable?

b) Is a directed graph strongly connected?

c) Is $L(G)$ infinite for CFG G without ϵ-productions or useless nonterminals?

*13.31 Given CFG's G_1 and G_2 and integer k, show that the problem of determining whether there are words w_1 in $L(G_1)$ and w_2 in $L(G_2)$ that agree on the first k symbols, is complete for nondeterministic exponential time with respect to polynomial-time reductions.

**13.32 Show that the problem of determining whether a regular expression with the intersection operator permitted denotes all strings in its alphabet requires time $2^{c\sqrt{n}}$ i.o., for some $c > 0$ and can be solved in time 2^{dn}.

13.33

a) Write a formula in the theory of integers under addition expressing that every integer greater than 5 is the sum of three distinct positive integers.

b) Write a formula in number theory expressing that d is the greatest common divisor of a and b.

**c) Write a formula in number theory expressing that $z = x^y$.

13.34 Apply the decision procedure of Section 13.6 for the theory of reals to decide whether the formula

$$\exists y \ \exists x[(x + y = 14) \land (3x + y = 5)] \text{ is true.}$$

13.35

a) Show that the theory of Presburger arithmetic (the integers with $+$, $=$, and $<$) requires nondeterministic time $2^{2^{cn}}$ i.o., for some $c > 0$. [*Hint:* Develop the following formulas of size proportional to n:
   1) $R_n(x, y, z)$: $0 \leq y < 2^{2^n}$, and z is the residue of x mod y.
   2) $P_n(x)$: $0 \leq x < 2^{2^n}$, and x is a prime.
   3) $G_n(x)$: x is the smallest integer divisible by all primes less than 2^{2^n}.
   4) $M_n(x, y, z)$: x, y, and z are integers in the range 0 to $2^{2^{2^n}} - 1$, and $xy = z$.]

b) Show that Presburger arithmetic can be decided in $2^{2^{cn}}$ space and $2^{2^{2^{dn}}}$ time.

c) Use the algorithm of part (b) to decide

$$\exists y \ \exists x[(x + y = 14) \land (3x + y = 5)].$$

13.36 Extend Presburger arithmetic to allow quantification over arrays of integers. Thus we could write formulas such as

$$\forall A \ \forall n \ \exists B \ \forall i[\neg(1 \leq i \leq n) \lor [\exists j(1 \leq j \leq n) \land A(i) = B(j)]].$$

Prove that the theory of Presburger arithmetic with arrays is undecidable.

13.37 To show that number theory is undecidable, it is convenient to encode a sequence of length $n + 1$, $x_0, x_1, \ldots, x_n$, into an integer x such that each x_i can be obtained from x by a formula.

a) Let $m = \max\{n, x_0, x_1, \ldots, x_n\}$. Prove that the set of $u_i = 1 + (i + 1)m!$, $0 \leq i \leq n$, are pairwise relatively prime and that $u_i > x_i$. This implies that there exists an integer $b < u_0 u_1 \cdots u_n$ such that $b = x_i$ mod u_i, $0 \leq i \leq n$.

b) Express Gödel's β function

$$\beta(b, c, i) = b \bmod [1 + (i + 1)c]$$

as a predicate.

c) Prove that number theory is undecidable.

13.38 Show that there are oracles C, D, and E, for which

a) $\mathcal{P}^C$, $\mathcal{NP}^C$, and co-$\mathcal{NP}^C$ are all different.

b) $\mathcal{P}^D \neq \mathcal{NP}^D$ but $\mathcal{NP}^D = \text{Co-}\mathcal{NP}^D$.

c) $\mathcal{P}^E = \mathcal{NP}^E$ is independent of the axioms of number theory.

*13.39** Show that $\mathcal{P} = \mathcal{NP}$ if and only if $\mathcal{P}$ is an AFL.

Solutions to Selected Exercises

13.16 Construct a minimum cost spanning tree by sorting the edges by increasing cost, selecting edges starting with the lowest cost edge, and discarding any edge that forms a cycle. Let T_{opt} be the minimum cost of a Hamilton circuit and let T_s be the cost of the minimum cost spanning tree. Clearly $T_s \leq T_{\text{opt}}$, since a spanning tree can be obtained from a Hamilton circuit by deleting an edge. Construct a path through all vertices of the graph by traversing the spanning tree. The path is not a Hamilton circuit, since each edge of the spanning tree is traversed twice. The cost of this path is at most $2T_s \leq 2T_{\text{opt}}$. Traverse the path until encountering some edge e_1 leading to a vertex for the second time. Let e_2 be the edge immediately following e_1 on the path. Replace the portion of the path consisting of e_1 and e_2 by a single direct edge. By the triangle inequality this cannot increase the cost. Repeat the process of replacing pairs of edges by a single edge until a Hamilton circuit is obtained.

13.25b   First we show that the Shannon switching game is in PSPACE. Consider a game tree. The root indicates the initial game position. Assume SHORT moves first. The sons of the root correspond to each possible game position after a move of SHORT. In general, a vertex in the tree corresponds to the moves so far (which determine a game position) and the sons of the vertex correspond to the board position after each possible additional move.

A position is a winning position if SHORT has a forced win from the position. Thus a leaf is a winning position only if SHORT has a path from s to t. We can recursively define winning positions as follows. If vertex v is not a leaf and corresponds to a position in which it is SHORT's move, then v is a winning position if there exists a son that is a winning position. If it is CUT's move, then v is a winning position only if every son is a winning position. Since the tree has depth at most n, the number of vertices of G, a recursive algorithm to determine if the root is a winning position requires space at most n. Thus the problem is in PSPACE.

To show that the Shannon switching game is PSPACE-complete, we reduce the quantified Boolean formula problem to it. Consider a quantified Boolean formula and without loss of generality assume that the quantifiers alternate (otherwise add dummy quantifiers and variables)

$$\exists x_1 \, \forall x_2 \, \exists x_3 \, \cdots \, \forall x_{n-1} \, \exists x_n F(x_1 \cdots x_n).$$

Consider the graph, called a ladder, shown in Fig. 13.12, where $n = 3$. There will be additional edges (see dashed lines) but they are unimportant for the first observation. SHORT plays first. He must at some time select either $x_1(1)$ or $\bar{x}_1(1)$. This corresponds to SHORT selecting a value for the existentially quantified variable x_1. The next four moves are forced, ending up with SHORT having selected $x_1(1)$, $x_1(2)$, and $\exists x_1$ and CUT having selected $\bar{x}_1(1)$ and $\bar{x}_2(2)$, or SHORT having selected $\bar{x}_1(1)$, $\bar{x}_1(2)$, and $\exists x_1$ and CUT having selected $x_1(1)$ and $x_2(2)$. If SHORT does not select one of $x_1(1)$, $\bar{x}_1(1)$, $x_1(2)$, $\bar{x}_1(2)$, or $\exists x_1$, then CUT wins. If SHORT selects $\exists x_1$, then CUT is given the advantage in selecting $x_1(1)$ or $\bar{x}_1(1)$. The purpose of the vertex $\exists x_1$ is to consume an additional move of SHORT, thereby allowing CUT the first selection from the set $\{x_2(1), \bar{x}_2(1), x_2(2), \bar{x}_2(2)\}$. This means that CUT selects the value for the universally quantified variable x_2, and so on.

Once the values for $x_1, x_2, \ldots, x_n$ have been selected, the dashed portion of the graph, which corresponds to the quantifier-free portion of the formulas, comes into play. Without loss of generality we can assume that $F(x_1, \ldots, x_n)$ is in conjunctive normal form. Let $F = F_1 \wedge F_2 \wedge \cdots \wedge F_n$, where each F_i is a clause. Construct the tree of Fig. 13.13. Identify the root 1 with vertex $\exists x_n$ in Fig. 13.12. From vertex F_i add an edge to vertex $x_j(1)$ or $\bar{x}_j(1)$ if x_j or $\bar{x}_j$, respectively, appears in F_i. Now observe that SHORT selects vertex 1. CUT can select either F_1 or 2, and SHORT selects the other. Clearly SHORT can build a path to at

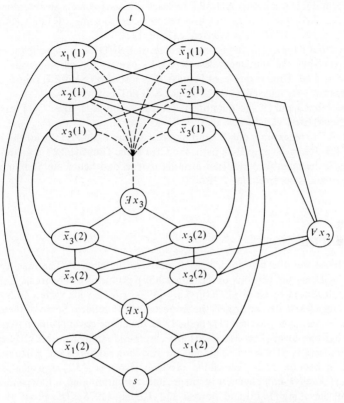

Fig. 13.12 A ladder for the Shannon switching game.

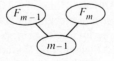
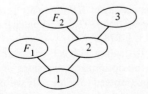

Fig. 13.13 The tree for formula $F = F_1 F_2 \cdots F_m$.

least one F_i, and CUT can force SHORT to reach only one F_i and can determine which F_i. Now SHORT has a path from s to t if F_i is connected to some $x_j(1)$ or $\bar{x}_j(1)$ which "has value one"; that is, SHORT has selected $x_j(1)$ or $\bar{x}_j(1)$.

Observe that if the quantified formula is true, then SHORT can specify the existentially quantified variables, so that regardless of CUT's choices for the universally quantified variables, F is true. Thus regardless of which F_i is forced on SHORT, that F_i is true and hence connected to a selected x_j or $\bar{x}_j$. Hence SHORT can win.

On the other hand, if the quantified Boolean formula is false, CUT can select the universally quantified variables so that for the assignment to the x's, F is false. Then CUT forces SHORT to reach only one F_i, and in particular an F_i that is false for the assignment. Thus SHORT does not complete a path, and CUT wins. Thus SHORT is guaranteed a win if and only if the quantified Boolean formula is true, and hence the Shannon switching game on vertices is complete for PSPACE.

BIBLIOGRAPHIC NOTES

Cobham [1964] was the first to devote attention to the class $\mathscr{P}$. The first NP-complete problems, including the versions of the satisfiability problems in Theorems 13.1, 13.2, and 13.3, were introduced by Cook [1971b]. Karp [1972] gave a wide variety of NP-complete problems, and clearly demonstrated the importance of the idea. Some of these problems include the vertex cover problem (Theorem 13.4), the clique cover problem (Exercise 13.4), the exact cover problem (Exercise 13.7d), the chromatic number problem (Exercise 13.6), the Hamilton circuit (Theorem 13.6), and the traveling salesman and partition problems mentioned in Section 13.2. The clique problem (Exercise 13.3) is from Cook [1971]. Theorem 13.7, the NP-completeness of integer linear programming, is independently due to Gathen and Sieveking [1976] and Borosh and Treybig [1976]. The proof given is from Kannan and Monma [1978].

An enormous number of problems have since been shown NP-complete, and those problems come from a wide variety of areas. Garey and Johnson [1978] attempt to catalog such problems, and we shall here mention only a sample of the work that has been done and the areas that have been covered. Sethi [1975], and Bruno and Sethi [1976] cover code generation problems (Exercise 13.7b appears in the latter). Scheduling problems are considered in Coffman [1976] and Ullman [1975]; the solution to Exercise 13.7(c) can be found in both. Garey, Johnson, and Stockmeyer [1976], and Garey, Graham, and Johnson [1976] provide a variety of powerful results, principally for graph problems. Papadimitriou [1976] and Papadimitriou and Steiglitz [1977] study path problems in graphs. Exercise 13.18 is taken from Stockmeyer [1973], Exercise 13.10 from Garey, Johnson, and Tarjan [1976], and Exercise 13.12 is by J. E. Hopcroft.

A number of results showing large classes of NP-complete problems appear in Hunt and Szymanski [1976], Hunt and Rosenkrantz [1977], Kirkpatrick and Hell [1978], Lewis [1978], Schaefer [1978], and Yannakakis [1978].

Among the promising approaches to dealing with NP-complete problems is the idea of considering *approximate algorithms* to the optimization versions of problems. These algorithms run in polynomial time but are guaranteed to come only within some specified range of the optimum. Johnson [1974] considered approximation algorithms for some of the

NP-complete problems appearing in Karp [1972]. Sahni and Gonzalez [1976] were the first to prove the approximation to an NP-complete problem to be NP-complete itself (Exercise 13.15), while Garey and Johnson [1976] showed that coming within less than a factor of two of the chromatic number of a graph (number of "colors" needed to ensure that each vertex be colored differently from adjacent vertices) is NP-complete (Exercise 13.19). Exercise 13.17 on improving an approximation to a maximal clique is also from Garey and Johnson [1976]. Rosenkrantz, Stearns, and Lewis [1977] studied approximations to the traveling salesman problem (Exercise 13.16). Christofides [1976] has improved on their results.

A number of papers have attempted to explore the structure of $\mathcal{NP}$ on the hypothesis that $\mathcal{P} \neq \mathcal{NP}$. Ladner [1975a] shows, for example, that if $\mathcal{P} \neq \mathcal{NP}$, then there are problems that are neither in $\mathcal{P}$ nor NP-complete. Adleman and Manders [1977] show that certain problems have the property that they are in $\mathcal{P}$ if and only if $\mathcal{NP} = \mathrm{co}\text{-}\mathcal{NP}$. Book [1974, 1976] shows inequality among certain complexity classes, such as $\mathrm{DTIME}(n^k)$ or $\mathrm{DSPACE}(\log^k n)$. Exercise 13.39, relating $\mathcal{P} = \mathcal{NP}$ to AFL theory, is from Book [1970]. Berman and Hartmanis [1977] look at density-preserving reductions of one problem to another. Exercise 13.22 is from Berman [1978], and Exercise 13.20 is from Levin [1973].

Particular attention has been given to the complexity of recognizing primes. It is easy to show that the nonprimes (written in binary) are in $\mathcal{NP}$, but it was not known that the primes are in $\mathcal{NP}$ until Pratt [1975]. Thus, if the recognition of primes is NP-complete, then by Theorem 13.8, $\mathrm{co}\text{-}\mathcal{NP} = \mathcal{NP}$. Miller [1976] gives strong evidence that the recognition of primes written in binary is in $\mathcal{P}$. Exercise 13.23, which shows an efficient test determining primality with high probability, is from Rabin [1977]. A similar result is found in Solovay and Strassen [1977]. Exercise 13.24 is from Brassard, Fortune, and Hopcroft [1978].

The first PSPACE-complete problems were introduced by Karp [1972], including CSL recognition (Theorem 13.11) and "$= \Sigma^*$" for regular expressions (Exercise 13.25a). PSPACE-completeness of quantified Boolean formulas was shown by Stockmeyer [1974]. Exercise 13.25(b), PSPACE completeness of the Shannon switching game, is by Even and Tarjan [1976]. Stockmeyer [1978] gives a hierarchy of problems between $\mathcal{NP}$ and PSPACE, on the assumption that $\mathcal{NP} \neq$ PSPACE.

Problems complete for $\mathcal{P}$ with respect to logarithmic space reductions have been considered by Cook [1973b], Cook and Sethi [1976], Jones [1975], Jones and Laaser [1976] (including Theorem 13.12) and Ladner [1975b] (Exercise 13.29b). Problems complete for NSPACE($\log n$) with respect to log space reductions are considered in Savitch [1970], including Theorem 13.13 (on reachability), Sudborough [1975a,b], Springsteel [1976], and Jones, Lien, and Laaser [1976]. Exercise 13.30 is from Jones, Lien, and Laaser [1976].

The first problem proved to require exponential time (in fact, exponential space) was presented by Meyer and Stockmeyer [1973]. The problem is similar in spirit to that of Theorem 13.15. The lower bounds on the complexity of the theory of reals with addition (Theorem 13.16) and of Presburger arithmetic (Exercise 13.35) are from Fischer and Rabin [1974]. The upper bounds for these problems are from Cooper [1972], Ferrante, and Rackoff [1975], and Oppen [1973]. Berman [1977]; and Bruss and Meyer [1978] put what are, in a sense, more precise bounds (outside the usual time-space hierarchies) on these problems. The undecidability of Presburger arithmetic with arrays is from Suzuki and Jefferson [1977].

The literature contains a number of papers that deal with the complexity of a variety of problems and their special cases, dividing problems into groups, principally: polynomial,

NP-complete, PSPACE-complete, and provably exponential. A sample of the areas covered include Diophantine equations in Adleman and Manders [1976], asynchronous computation in Cardoza, Lipton, and Meyer [1976], problems about regular expressions in Hunt [1975] (including Exercise 13.32), Hunt, Rosenkrantz, and Szymanski [1976], and Stockmeyer and Meyer [1973], problems about context-free grammars in Hunt and Rosenkrantz [1974, 1977], Hunt and Szymanski [1975, 1976], and Hunt, Szymanski, and Ullman [1975] (including Exercise 13.31), and game theory in Schaefer [1976].

The results of Section 13.7 and Exercise 13.38, on the $\mathcal{P} = \mathcal{NP}$ question in the presence of oracles, are from Baker, Gill, and Solovay [1975]. However, Kozen [1978] presents another viewpoint on the issue. Exercise 13.26 is from there. Ladner, Lynch, and Selman [1974] studied the different kinds of bounded reducibility, such as many-one, Turing, and truth tables. Another attack on the $\mathcal{P} = \mathcal{NP}$ question has been the development of models whose deterministic and nondeterministic time-bounded versions are equivalent. The vector machines (Pratt and Stockmeyer [1976]) are the first, and other models have been proposed by Chandra and Stockmeyer [1976] and Kozen [1976]. The reader should also note the equivalence for space-bounded versions of the "auxiliary PDA's" discussed in Section 14.1.

14

HIGHLIGHTS OF OTHER IMPORTANT LANGUAGE CLASSES

Numerous models and classes of languages have been introduced in the literature. This chapter presents a few of those that appear to be of greatest interest.

Section 14.1 discusses auxiliary pushdown automata, which are PDA's with two-way input and additional general purpose storage in the form of a space-bounded Turing tape. The interesting property of auxiliary PDA's is that for a fixed amount of extra storage, the deterministic and nondeterministic versions are equivalent in language-recognizing power, and the class of languages accepted by auxiliary PDA's with a given space bound is equivalent to the class of languages accepted by Turing machines of time complexity exponential in that space bound.

Section 14.2 is concerned with stack automata, which are PDA's with the privilege of scanning the stack below the top symbol, but only in a read-only mode. Languages accepted by variants of the two-way stack automaton turn out to be time- or space-complexity classes.

Section 14.3 is devoted to indexed languages, since they arise in a number of contexts and appear to be a natural generalization of the CFL's. Finally, Section 14.4 introduces developmental systems, which attempt to model certain biological patterns of growth.

14.1 AUXILIARY PUSHDOWN AUTOMATA

An $S(n)$ *auxiliary pushdown automaton* (*APDA*) is pictured in Fig. 14.1. It consists of

1) a read-only input tape, surrounded by the endmarkers, ¢ and $,

2) a finite state control,

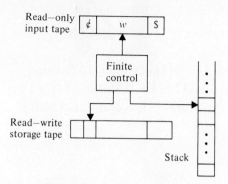

Fig. 14.1 Auxiliary PDA.

3) a read-write storage tape of length $S(n)$, where n is the length of the input string w, and

4) a stack.

A move of the APDA is determined by the state of the finite control, along with the symbols scanned by the input, storage, and stack heads. In one move, the APDA may do any or all of the following:

1) change state,

2) move its input head one position left or right, but not off the input,

3) print a symbol on the cell scanned by the storage head and move that head one position left or right,

4) push a symbol onto the stack or pop the top symbol off the stack.

If the device is nondeterministic, it has a finite number of choices of the above type. Initially the tape heads are at the left end of the input and storage tapes, with the finite control in a designated initial state and the stack consisting of a designated start symbol. Acceptance is by empty stack.

Equivalence of deterministic and nondeterministic APDA's

The interest in APDA's originates from the discovery that deterministic and nondeterministic APDA's with the same space bound are equivalent, and that $S(n)$ space on an APDA is equivalent to $c^{S(n)}$ time on a Turing machine. That is, the following three statements are equivalent.

1) L is accepted by a deterministic $S(n)$-APDA.

2) L is accepted by a nondeterministic $S(n)$-APDA.

3) L is in $\mathrm{DTIME}(c^{S(n)})$ for some constant c.

These facts are established in the following series of lemmas.

Lemma 14.1 If L is accepted by a nondeterministic $S(n)$-APDA A with $S(n) \geq \log n$, then L is in $\text{DTIME}(c^{S(n)})$ for some constant c.

Proof Let A have s states, t storage symbols, and p stack symbols. Given an input of length n, there are $n + 2$ possible input head positions, s possible states, $S(n)$ possible storage head positions, and $t^{S(n)}$ possible storage tape contents, for a total of

$$\hat{s}(n) = (n + 2)sS(n)t^{S(n)}$$

possible configurations.† As $S(n) \geq \log n$, there is a constant d such that $\hat{s}(n) \leq d^{S(n)}$ for all $n \geq 1$.

Construct a TM M that performs the following operations on input w of length n.

1) M constructs a PDA P_w that on ϵ-input simulates all moves of A on input w.

2) M converts P_w to a CFG G_w by the algorithm of Theorem 5.4.

For fixed A, P_w is a different PDA for each w, with the state and contents of input and storage tapes of A encoded in the state of P_w. $N(P_w)$ is $\{\epsilon\}$ or ϕ depending on whether or not A accepts w.

P_w has at most $\hat{s}(n) \leq d^{S(n)}$ states and p stack symbols. Therefore G_w has at most $pd^{2S(n)} + 1$ variables. As A can push only one symbol, no right side of a production of G_w has more than two variables, so there are at most $rd^{S(n)}$ productions for any nonterminal of G_w, where r is the maximum number of choices that A has in any situation. Thus the test of Theorem 6.6, to tell whether $L(G_w)$ is empty, takes time proportional to $rp^2 d^{5S(n)}$, at most. Since r, p, and d are constants, there is a constant c such that M can determine in time at most $c^{S(n)}$ whether $L(G_w)$ is nonempty, i.e., whether w is accepted by A. □

Lemma 14.2 If L is in $\text{DTIME}(T(n))$, then L is accepted in time $T^4(n)$ by a one-tape TM M that traverses its tape, making a complete scan in one direction, reaching the first cell it has never before scanned, reversing direction and repeating the process, as shown in Fig. 14.2.

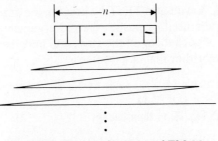

Fig. 14.2 Traversal pattern of TM M.

---

† Note that a "configuration" in the sense used here does not include the stack contents.

Proof By Theorems 12.3 and 12.5, L is accepted by a $\frac{1}{2}T^2(n)$ time-bounded one-tape TM M_1. M simulates M_1, marking on a second track M_1's head position and the cells which M_1 has already scanned. As long as the head of M_1 travels in the same direction as M's head, M can simulate a move of M_1 with each of its own moves. When M_1 moves in the opposite direction, M leaves the head marker, completes its scan and simulates that move on the return pass. Thus M simulates at least one move of M_1 per pass, taking at most $\sum_{i=0}^{(1/2)T^2(n)} n + i \leq T^4(n)$ moves to complete the simulation of M_1.   □

Lemma 14.3 If L is in DTIME($c^{S(n)}$) for any constant c, then L is accepted by a deterministic $S(n)$-APDA.

Proof By Lemma 14.2, L is accepted by a $c^{4S(n)}$ time-bounded one-tape TM M with the traversal pattern of Fig. 14.2. Define $d = c^4$ so that M is $d^{S(n)}$ time bounded. Let the triple (q, Z, t) stand for the statement that at time t,† M is in state q scanning symbol Z, where $t \leq d^{S(n)}$. Note that since the head motion of M is independent of the data, the cell scanned at time t is easily calculated from t.

The heart of the construction of a deterministic $S(n)$-APDA A that accepts L is the recursive procedure TEST of Fig. 14.3, which assigns value true to the triple (q, Z, t) if and only if

1) $t = 0$, q is the start state, and Z is the symbol in the first tape cell of M, or

2) M scans some cell for the first time at time t, Z is the original symbol in that tape cell, and there is a triple $(p, X, t - 1)$ that is true and implies that M enters state q after one move, or

3) M previously scanned the cell visited at time t and there are true triples $(p_1, X_1, t - 1)$ and (p_2, X_2, t') such that the first triple implies that state q is entered after one move, and the second implies that Z was left on the tape cell the last time the tape cell was scanned. Recall that the head motion of M is uniform, and thus the time t' at which the cell was last visited is easily calculated from t.

As TEST only calls itself with smaller third arguments, it eventually terminates. The $S(n)$-APDA A evaluates TEST by keeping the arguments on the storage tape. When TEST calls itself, A pushes the old arguments onto the stack, and when TEST returns, A pops them off the stack and puts them on the storage tape.

The complete algorithm that A executes is

> **for** each triple (q, Z, t) such that q is an accepting state
> and $0 \leq t \leq d^{S(n)}$ **do**
> **if** TEST(q, Z, t) **then** accept   □

Theorem 14.1 The following are equivalent for $s(n) \geq \log n$.

1) L is accepted by a deterministic $S(n)$-APDA.

---

† "At time t" means "after t moves have elapsed," so initially, $t = 0$.

---

procedure TEST(q, Z, t);
begin
    if $t = 0$, q is the initial state of M and Z is the first input symbol **then return true**;
    if $1 \leq t < n$ and Z is the tth input symbol, or $t = in + i(i - 1)/2$ for some integer $i \geq 1$
    and $Z = B$ **then**
        for each state p and symbol X **do**
            if M enters state q when scanning X in state p, and TEST$(p, X, t - 1)$ **then return**
            true;
    /* the times $in + i(i - 1)/2$ are exactly the times when M scans a new cell */
    if $t \geq n$ and $t \neq in + i(i - 1)/2$ for any integer $i \geq 1$ **then**
        begin
            let t' be the previous time M scanned the same cell as at time t;
            for all states p_1 and p_2 and symbols X_1 and X_2 **do**
                if M enters state q when scanning X_1 in state p_1 and M writes Z when scanning
                    X_2 in state p_2 and TEST$(p_1, X_1, t - 1)$ and TEST(p_2, X_2, t') **then return true**
        end;
    return false
end

Fig. 14.3 The procedure TEST.

2) L is accepted by a nondeterministic $S(n)$-APDA.

3) L is in DTIME$(c^{S(n)})$ for some constant c.

Proof That (1) implies (2) is obvious. Lemma 14.1 established that (2) implies (3) and Lemma 14.3 established that (3) implies (1). $\square$

Corollary L is in $\mathscr{P}$ if and only if L is accepted by a log n-APDA.

14.2 STACK AUTOMATA

The *stack automaton* (SA) is a PDA with the following two additional features.

1) The input is two-way, read-only with endmarkers.

2) The stack head, in addition to push and pop moves at the top of the stack can enter the stack in read-only mode, traveling up and down the stack without rewriting any symbol.

A stack automaton is shown in Fig. 14.4, in read-only mode.

    A move of an SA is determined by the state, the input, and stack symbols scanned, and whether or not the top of the stack is being scanned by the stack head. In either case, in one move the state may change and the input head may move one position left or right. If the stack head is not at the top of the stack, a move may also include a stack head motion, one position up or down the stack. If the stack head is at the top, the permissible stack actions are:

1) push a symbol onto the stack,

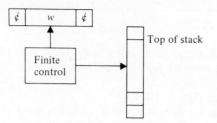

Fig. 14.4   A stack automaton.

2) pop the top symbol off the stack, or

3) move one position down the stack without pushing or popping.

In actions (1) and (2) the stack head stays at the top; in action (3) it leaves the top of stack and enters the read-only mode, which it may leave only by returning to the top of the stack.

Initially, the input head is at the left end, the finite control is in a designated initial state, and the stack consists of a single designated start symbol. Acceptance is by final state.

If there is never more than one move in any situation, the device is deterministic (a DSA); if there is a finite number of choices of moves in any situation, the automaton is nondeterministic (an NSA). If the device never pops a symbol it is *nonerasing* (an NEDSA or NENSA). If the input head never moves left, the stack automaton is *one-way* (a 1DSA, 1NENSA, and so on). In the absence of any statement to the contrary, we shall assume an SA is two-way, deterministic, and permits erasing.

Example 14.1   Let $L = \{0^n 1^n 2^n \mid n \geq 1\}$. We design an SA to accept L as follows. The input head moves right at each move. While 0's are encountered, they are pushed onto the stack above the bottom marker (start symbol) Z_0. The stack head remains at the top of stack in read-write mode. Fig. 14.5(a) shows the situation after reading 0's. On seeing the first 1, the stack head moves down, entering the read-only mode. As successive 1's are read, the stack head moves one position down for each 1 (but if the first 2 is not seen at the same time the stack head reaches the bottom marker, there is no next move, and the SA does not accept). The situation in which the SA then finds itself is shown in Fig. 14.5(b). As 2's are scanned on the input, the stack head moves up one position for each 2. A move to an accepting state is permissible only when the stack head is at the top and $ is scanned on the input, as in Fig. 14.5(c). Of course, the state from which this move can be made is only entered after we have seen 2's, so we cannot accept inputs like ¢$ or ¢00$.

Note that the SA we have described is one-way, deterministic, and nonerasing.

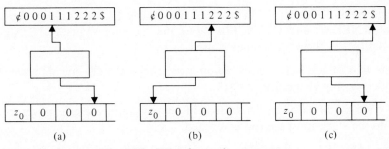

Fig. 14.5 ID's of a stack automaton.

Transition tables

In the remainder of the section we give proof sketches for a number of the fundamental results characterizing the languages accepted by the varieties of SA. One of the central ideas is the simulation of stack automata by other devices by means of a *transition table*, which is a succinct representation of a stack (actually the stack except for the top symbol). Suppose a deterministic stack automaton is in state q with the input head at position i and the stack head at the next-to-top symbol. Then the SA is in read-only mode and the stack cannot change until the stack head reaches the top. For a particular sequence of stack symbols, the stack head may never reach the top, or it will first reach there in some state p with input head in position j. For each q and i the transition table tells whether the stack head ever moves to the top and if so gives the state p and input head position j when the top is reached. Thus the transition table completely characterizes the effect of the sequence of stack symbols below the top, provided acceptance does not occur when the stack head is inside the stack.

The number of distinct transition tables for an SA with input of length n (excluding endmarkers) and with s states is thus $[s(n + 2) + 1]^{s(n+2)}$. With input positions encoded in binary, a transition table requires only $cn \log n$ bits for some constant c that depends on the number of states of the given SA.

If the SA is nondeterministic, then for each q and i, the transition table must give the set of (p, j) pairs such that started in state q, with input position i, and the stack head at the next-to-top stack symbol, the top of stack can be reached in state p and input position j. The number of possible transition tables for an s state NSA with input of length n is $[2^{s(n+2)+1}]^{s(n+2)} \leq 2^{cn^2}$, so such a transition table can be encoded in cn^2 bits, where c depends only on the number of states of the NSA.

Characterization of stack languages by time and space complexity classes

We shall show that a deterministic SA can be simulated by an $n \log n$-APDA and conversely that an $n \log n$-APDA can be simulated by a DSA establishing the equivalence of DSA and $n \log n$-APDA. In a similar manner we establish the equivalence of NSA and n^2-APDA. For nonerasing SA we establish the equivalence of NEDSA and DSPACE(n log n) and the equivalence of NENSA and NSPACE(n^2). A series of lemmas is used.

Lemma 14.4 Each type of stack automaton is equivalent to one of the same type that accepts only at the top of stack.

Proof We modify a given SA so that in any accepting state it moves its stack head up the stack until the top is reached. □

Lemma 14.5 If L is accepted by an NEDSA, then L is in DSPACE(n log n).

Proof Given an NEDSA A that accepts only at the top of the stack, we construct a Turing machine M that simulates A by keeping track of A's state, input head position, top stack symbol, and the transition table for the portion of the stack below the top symbol. The initial transition table is the table associated with the empty string ("undefined" for all q and i). We need only explain how to construct the transition table T' associated with the stack string $X_1 X_2 \cdots X_m$ given the table T for $X_1 X_2 \cdots X_{m-1}$.

For each state q and input position i, execute the algorithm of Fig. 14.6. The algorithm keeps track of the sequence of state-input-position pairs (p, j) in which X_m is scanned. Each time the stack head moves to X_{m-1}, T is consulted to determine the next state-position pair in which X_m will be scanned if any. The variable COUNT checks that the length of the sequence of (p, j)'s does not exceed the product of s, the number of states, and $n + 2$, the number of input positions. If so, A is surely in a loop, so that value of $T'(q, i)$ is "undefined."

```
begin
    COUNT := 0;
    (p, j) := (q, i);
    while COUNT < s(n + 2) do
        begin
            COUNT := COUNT + 1
            suppose A in state p, scanning stack symbol Xₘ, at input position j enters
                state r, moves the input head to position k and the stack head in direc-
                tion D;
            if D = "up" then return (r, k);
            if D = "stationary" then (p, j) := (r, k);
            if D = "down" then
                if T(r, k) = "undefined" then return "undefined"
                    else (p, j) := T(r, k)
        end
    return "undefined"
end
```

Fig. 14.6 Algorithm to compute transition table for NEDSA.

Note that for given (q, i) the algorithm of Fig. 14.6 requires only $0(\log n)$ space to hold the value of COUNT. Thus T' can be computed from T and X_m in the space it takes to store T and T', which is $n \log n$. The TM M has only to simulate A directly when the stack head is at the top of the stack, consult the current transition table when the stack head leaves the top, and compute a new transition table (throwing away the old) when a stack symbol is pushed. As stack symbols are never erased, we need not preserve the stack. ☐

Lemma 14.6 If L is accepted by a NENSA, then L is in NSPACE(n^2).

Proof The proof is similar to that of the previous lemma, save that n^2 space is needed to store the transition matrix, and the simulation must be nondeterministic. ☐

Lemma 14.7 If L is accepted by DSA, then L is accepted by a $n \log n$-APDA.

Proof The proof is again similar to that of Lemma 14.5. The APDA uses its stack (which it may not enter in read-only mode, of course) to hold the stack of the DSA. Between each DSA stack symbol the APDA stores a transition table. The transition table above a particular stack symbol corresponds to the entire stack, up to and including that symbol. The topmost stack symbol and the table for the stack below it are placed on the storage tape. When the DSA pushes a symbol, the APDA pushes the table that is on its storage tape along with the old top stack symbol onto its own stack, and computes the new table as in Lemma 14.5. When the DSA pops a symbol, the APDA discards the top stack symbol and then moves the top table to its storage tape. ☐

Lemma 14.8 If L is accepted by an NSA, then L is accepted by an n^2-APDA.

Proof The proof is a combination of the ideas introduced in Lemmas 14.6 and 14.7. Note that by Theorem 14.1 the APDA may be made deterministic. ☐

We now turn to the simulation of space-bounded devices by stack automata. The key idea here is that the SA can use its input of length n to count n symbols or "blocks" of symbols down its stack. A sequence of ID's representing a computation of a space-bounded device is constructed on the stack by successively copying the top ID onto the stack, making changes represented by one move of the space-bounded device. The ability to count down n symbols or "blocks" of symbols allows the SA to copy the current ID onto the top, symbol by symbol.

As a simple introduction consider the simulation of a deterministic linear bounded automaton M by an NEDSA A. Given input $w = a_1 \cdots a_n$, A pushes $[q_0 a_1]a_2 \cdots a_n\#$ onto its stack, where q_0 is the start state and $\#$ is a special symbol separating ID's. The state is combined with the symbol scanned, so an ID is always exactly n symbols long. Suppose A has constructed a stack that is a sequence of ID's, including the first i symbols of the next ID:

$$\cdots \#X_1 X_2 \cdots X_n\#X_1 X_2 \cdots X_i.$$

(Actually one or two of the X's in the ID being constructed may differ from the corresponding symbols in the ID below, due to the move made by M). Starting at the left end of the input, A repeatedly moves one position right on the input and one position down the stack, until the right endmarker is reached on the input. At this point A's stack head will be $n + 1$ symbols from the top of the stack, scanning X_{i+1} of the last complete ID. A looks one symbol above and below X_{i+1} to see if X_{i+1} changes in the next ID because of the move made by M. A then moves to the top of the stack and pushes either X_{i+1} or the symbol replacing X_{i+1} in the next ID due to the move of M. A accepts if and only if M enters an accepting state.

Actually a stack automaton can simulate devices with ID's of length greater than n by more clever use of the input. In particular, a DSA can manipulate ID's of length $n \log n$, and an NSA can manipulate ID's of length n^2. The nondeterministic case is easier, so we present it first.

Lemma 14.9   If L is in NSPACE(n^2), then L is accepted by a NENSA.

Proof Since n^2 is greater than n we may assume L is accepted by a one-tape TM rather than an off-line TM. An ID of length n^2 is represented by listing the tape symbols, combining the state with the symbol scanned by the tape head. A marker $*$ is inserted after every n symbols. The n symbols between $*$'s make up a *block*. Successive ID's are placed on the stack as in the description of the LBA above. Suppose j blocks and i symbols of the $(j + 1)n$th block have been copied. The input tape is used to measure n $*$'s down the stack to the $(j + 1)n$th block of the previous ID. A position k, $1 \leq k \leq n$, in the $(j + 1)n$th block is guessed. Checking one symbol above and below determines if the symbol is affected by a move of the TM. If so, a move is guessed, provided a move for this ID has not been guessed previously; otherwise the symbol is recorded in the state of the SA. The input tape is then used to record k by alternately moving the input head one symbol left (starting at the right end) and the stack head one symbol down until a $*$ is encountered. Next the stack head moves to the top of the stack and compares k with i, the number of symbols of the jth block already copied. If $k \neq i + 1$, this sequence of choices "dies." If $k = i + 1$, then the next symbol of the new ID is placed on top of the stack. The input is then used to determine if $i + 1 = n$. If so a $*$ is printed, and then it is checked whether $j + 1 = n$. In the case $j + 1 = n$, a # is placed on the stack marking the end of an ID. Acceptance occurs if the symbol copied includes a final state. Otherwise the next symbol is copied.

A small but important point is that once a move is guessed in copying an ID, the guess cannot be changed on copying a subsequent symbol in that ID. Otherwise an invalid successor ID may be constructed.   □

Theorem 14.2   The family of languages accepted by nondeterministic, nonerasing stack automata is exactly NSPACE(n^2).

Proof Immediate from Lemmas 14.6 and 14.9.   □

Theorem 14.3 The family of languages accepted by nondeterministic stack automata is exactly $\bigcup_{c>0}$ DTIME(c^{n^2}).

Proof By Theorem 14.1, L is in $\bigcup_{c>0}$ DTIME(c^{n^2}) if and only if L is accepted by an n^2-APDA. By Lemma 14.8, if L is accepted by an NSA then L is accepted by a deterministic n^2-APDA. Thus it suffices to show that a deterministic n^2-APDA A can be simulated by an NSA S.

We assume that the input of A is kept on the storage tape of A rather than on a read-only input, since n^2 exceeds n. The stack of S will hold the stack of A as well as a sequence of ID's representing the storage tape of A. Suppose S has the current contents of A's storage tape on top of its stack, and A pushes a symbol. S guesses the tape contents of A when that symbol is popped and places its guess on top of the stack. Then S pushes the symbol pushed by A and creates the new current tape contents of A from the old, as in Lemma 14.9. The guessed ID intervening is ignored while running up and down the stack; its symbols can be chosen from a separate alphabet, so S can skip over it.

If A pops a symbol, S checks that the guessed ID below that symbol is correct; that is, the guessed ID is the storage tape of A after the pop move. The current ID of A held on top of S's stack is popped one symbol at a time, and each symbol popped is compared with the corresponding symbol of the guessed ID by a method similar to that of Lemma 14.9. If the guess is correct, the guessed ID becomes the current storage tape content of A, and the simulation of A proceeds; if not, this sequence of choices by S "dies." S accepts if and only if A empties its stack. $\square$

Corollary L is accepted by an NSA if and only if L is accepted by an n^2-APDA.

Proof The "only if" portion was established in Lemma 14.8. The "if" follows immediately from Theorems 14.1 and 14.3. $\square$

In the deterministic case the function n^2 is replaced by $n \log n$ in the analogs of Theorems 14.2 and 14.3. The reason for this is that in the construction of Lemma 14.9 the NSA made an essential use of its nondeterminism in copying ID's of length n^2. A DSA is able only to copy ID's of length $n \log n$.

Lemma 14.10 If L is in DSPACE$(n \log n)$, then L is accepted by an NEDSA.

Proof Let L be accepted by some one-tape TM M that uses exactly $n \log n$ cells. Let t be the number of symbols of the form X or $[qX]$, where X is a tape symbol and q a state. These symbols are identified with the digits $1, 2, \ldots, t$ in base $t + 1$. Strings of $\lfloor \log_{t+1}(n) \rfloor$ such symbols of M are encoded as blocks of between 0 and $(n-1)$ 0's. There is an integer c, depending only on M, such that an ID of M may be represented by cn blocks of 0's, each block coding $\lfloor \log_{t+1}(n) \rfloor$ symbols, provided $n > t$.

Design a stack automaton S to construct a sequence of ID's of M, each ID being a sequence of cn blocks of between 0 and $(n - 1)$ 0's separated by markers, $*$. Blocks are copied to the top of the stack by using the input to count cn $*$'s down the stack, measuring the length of the block to be copied on the input, moving to the top of stack and pushing an equal number of 0's onto the stack.

Before a new block is placed on the stack, it is necessary to determine which, if any, symbols change. To do so, decode 0^k by repeatedly dividing by $t + 1$, the successive remainders being the successive symbols of the ID. The division is accomplished by measuring k on the input and then moving the input back to the endmarker, placing an X on the stack for every $t + 1$ positions the input head moves. The X's are not part of an ID. The finite control computes k mod $(t + 1)$, and the resulting digit is placed above the X's. The block of X's is then measured on the input and the process repeated until the block of X's has length zero. The digits written on the stack between blocks of X's are the desired block of the ID.

S checks whether the head is scanning a symbol in the block and also notes if the head moves into an adjacent block. The blocks are re-encoded into strings of 0 to $(n - 1)$ 0's, making the necessary changes to reflect the move of M. The process of re-encoding is the reverse of that just described. Note that since S is nonerasing, it never gets rid of the X's or digits on its stack; they are simply ignored in subsequent computation. Also, before copying a block, S must decode the block above, to see whether the head of M moves left into the present block.

S initializes its stack by coding its own input as an ID of M. The details of this process are omitted. S accepts if it discovers that M enters an accepting state.

$\square$

Theorem 14.4 L is accepted by a deterministic nonerasing stack automaton if and only if L is in $\mathrm{DSPACE}(n \log n)$.

Proof   From Lemmas 14.5 and 14.10. $\square$

Theorem 14.5 L is accepted by a deterministic stack automaton if and only if L is in $\bigcup_{c>0} \mathrm{DTIME}(n^{cn})$.

Proof   Note that $n^{cn} = 2^{cn \log n}$. By Theorem 14.1, L is in $\bigcup_{c>0} \mathrm{DTIME}(n^{cn})$ if and only if L is accepted by an $n \log n$-APDA. By Lemma 14.7, if L is accepted by a DSA, then L is accepted by a deterministic $n \log n$-APDA. Thus it suffices to show that if L is accepted by a deterministic $n \log n$-APDA A, then L is accepted by a DSA S. Again we assume that A's input tape is combined with its storage tape. The proof parallels Theorem 14.3, using the techniques of Lemma 14.10 to represent storage tapes of A and simulate moves of A. However, when A pushes a symbol X onto its stack, S, being deterministic, cannot guess the storage tape contents of A when A eventually pops that X. Instead S cycles through all possible ID's systematically. If it has made the wrong choice, it generates the next possible ID and restarts the simulation of A from the time X was pushed by A. The fact that A empties its stack to accept assures that if A accepts, S will eventually get a chance to generate the correct choice. $\square$

Corollary L is accepted by a DSA if and only if L is accepted by an $n \log n$-APDA.

Proof The "only if" portion was established in Lemma 14.7. The "if" follows immediately from Theorems 14.1 and 14.5. □

One-way stack automata are not powerful enough to simulate tape-bounded devices. However, there is one important containment relation, which we state without proof.

Theorem 14.6 If L is accepted by a 1NSA, then L is in DSPACE(n).

14.3 INDEXED LANGUAGES

Of the many generalizations of context-free grammars that have been proposed, a class called "indexed" appears the most natural, in that it arises in a wide variety of contexts. We give a grammar definition here. Other definitions of the indexed languages are cited in the bibliographic notes.

An indexed grammar is a 5-tuple (V, T, I, P, S), where V is the set of variables, T the set of terminals, I the set of *indices*, S in V is the start symbol, and P is a finite set of productions of the forms

1) $A \to \alpha$,   2) $A \to Bf$,   or   3) $Af \to \alpha$,

where A and B are in V, f is in I, and α is in $(V \cup T)^*$.

Derivations in an indexed grammar are similar to those in a CFG except that variables may be followed by strings of indices. (Terminals may not be followed by indices.) When a production such as $A \to BC$ is applied, the string of indices for A is attached to both B and C. This feature enables many parts of a sentential form to be related to each other by sharing a common index string.

Formally, we define the relation $\Rightarrow$ on *sentential forms*, which are strings in $(VI^* \cup T)^*$, as follows. Let β and γ be in $(VI^* \cup T)^*$, δ be in I^*, and X_i in $V \cup T$.

1) If $A \to X_1 X_2 \cdots X_k$ is a production of type (1) then

$$\beta A \delta \gamma \Rightarrow \beta X_1 \delta_1 X_2 \delta_2 \cdots X_k \delta_k \gamma,$$

where $\delta_i = \delta$ if X_i is in V and $\delta_i = \epsilon$ if X_i is in T. When a production of type (1) is applied, the string of indices δ distributes over all the variables on the right side.

2) If $A \to Bf$ is a production of type (2), then $\beta A \delta \gamma \Rightarrow \beta B f \delta \gamma$. Here f becomes the first index on the string following variable B, which replaces A.

3) If $Af \to X_1 X_2 \cdots X_k$ is a production of type (3), then

$$\beta A f \delta \gamma \Rightarrow \beta X_1 \delta_1 X_2 \delta_2 \cdots X_k \delta_k \gamma,$$

where $\delta_i = \delta$ if X_i is in V and $\delta_i = \epsilon$ if X_i is in T. The first index on the list for A is consumed, and the remaining indices distribute over variables as in (1).

We let $\overset{*}{\Rightarrow}$ be the reflexive and transitive closure of $\Rightarrow$ as usual, and define $L(G)$ to be $\{w \mid S \overset{*}{\Rightarrow} w$ and w is in $T^*\}$.

Example 14.2   Let $G = (\{S, T, A, B, C\}, \{a, b, c\}, \{f, g\}, P, S)$, where P consists of

$$S \to Tg, \qquad Af \to aA, \qquad Ag \to a,$$
$$T \to Tf, \qquad Bf \to bB, \qquad Bg \to b,$$
$$T \to ABC, \qquad Cf \to cC, \qquad Cg \to c.$$

An example derivation in this indexed grammar is

$$S \Rightarrow Tg \Rightarrow Tfg \Rightarrow AfgBfgCfg$$
$$\Rightarrow aAgBfgCfg \Rightarrow aaBfgCfg \Rightarrow aabBgCfg$$
$$\Rightarrow aabbCfg \Rightarrow aabbcCg \Rightarrow aabbcc.$$

In general,

$$S \overset{*}{\Rightarrow} Tf^i g \Rightarrow Af^i g Bf^i g Cf^i g \overset{*}{\Rightarrow} a^{i+1} b^{i+1} c^{i+1}.$$

As the only freedom in derivations of G consists of trivial variations in order of replacement and the choice of how many times to apply $T \to Tf$, it should be clear that

$$L(G) = \{a^n b^n c^n \mid n \ge 1\}.$$

This language is not context free, of course.

We state without proof two major results about indexed languages.

Theorem 14.7   (a) If L is accepted by a one-way nondeterministic stack automaton, then L is an indexed language. (b) If L is an indexed language, then L is a context-sensitive language.

In fact, (a) can be strengthened by defining a generalization of an SA, called a "nested stack automaton," whose one-way nondeterministic variety exactly characterizes the indexed languages. The nested SA has the capability, when the stack head is inside its stack in read-only mode, to create a new stack. However, this stack must be destroyed before the stack head can move up in the original stack. The process of creating new stacks is recursive and allows the creation of new stacks to an arbitrary depth.

14.4   DEVELOPMENTAL SYSTEMS

The application of grammars to the study of growth in cellular organisms introduced new grammar families called *L*-systems. These grammar families differ from the Chomsky grammars in that

1) no distinction between terminals and nonterminals is made, and

2) at each step in a derivation, a production is applied to each symbol of a sentential form, rather than to just one symbol or a short substring.

The modeling of organisms by L-systems allows the testing of hypotheses concerning the mechanisms behind certain observable biological phenomena. Here we content ourselves with defining only the most basic family of these grammars, called 0L-systems. (The 0 stands for zero symbols of context; the L acknowledges Arvid Lindenmeyer, who first used these grammars to study growth in organisms.)

A 0L-grammar is a triple $G = (\Sigma, P, \alpha)$, where Σ is a finite alphabet called the *vocabulary*, α is a string in Σ^+ called the *start string*, and P is a set of productions of the form $a \to \beta$, where a is in Σ and β is in Σ^*. The relation $\Rightarrow$ is defined by

$$a_1 a_2 \cdots a_n \Rightarrow \alpha_1 \alpha_2 \cdots \alpha_n$$

if $a_i \to \alpha_i$ is in P for $1 \le i \le n$. Note that $a_i \to a_i$ might be a production, permitting us to avoid substituting for a_i. Otherwise, a substitution must be made for each symbol. The substitution for different occurrences of the same symbol need not be the same. The relation $\overset{*}{\Rightarrow}$ is the reflexive, transitive closure of $\Rightarrow$, and $L(G)$ is defined to be $\{\beta \mid \alpha \overset{*}{\Rightarrow} \beta\}$.

Example 14.3 Let $G = (\{a, b\}, P, a)$, where P consists of $a \to b$ and $b \to ab$. In this case, there is only one production for each symbol, so there is really only one (infinite length) derivation, and every word in the language appears in that derivation. The derivation is

$$a \Rightarrow b \Rightarrow ab \Rightarrow bab \Rightarrow abbab \Rightarrow bababbab \Rightarrow \cdots.$$

Note that the length of words in $L(G)$ are exactly the Fibonacci numbers defined by $f_1 = f_2 = 1$ and $f_i = f_{i-1} + f_{i-2}$ for $i \ge 3$. One can prove by induction on $i \ge 3$ that the ith word in the derivation has f_{i-1} b's and f_{i-2} a's, a total of f_i symbols.

Example 14.4 The language $\{a, aa\}$ is not a 0L-language. Suppose $L(G) = \{a, aa\}$, where $G = (\{a\}, P, \alpha)$. Then α must be a or aa. Now all productions are of the form $a \to a^i$ for some $i \ge 0$. Suppose $\alpha = a$. Surely there cannot be a production $a \to a^i$, for $i \ge 3$. Then there must be a production $a \to aa$, else aa could never be generated. But then $a \Rightarrow aa \Rightarrow aaaa$, a contradiction. Suppose next that $\alpha = aa$. There must be a production $a \to \epsilon$, else all strings in $L(G)$ are of length two or more. But then $aa \Rightarrow \epsilon$, so $L(G) \ne \{a, aa\}$ again.

A basic result about 0L-languages is the following.

Theorem 14.8 If L is a 0L-language, then L is an indexed language.

Proof Let $G_1 = (\Sigma, P_1, \alpha)$ be a 0L-grammar. Define indexed grammar $G_2 = (V, \Sigma, \{f, g\}, P_2, S)$, where

$$V = \{S, T\} \cup \{A_a \mid a \text{ is in } \Sigma\},$$

and P_2 contains

$$S \rightarrow Tg,$$

$$T \rightarrow Tf,$$

$$T \rightarrow A_{a_1} A_{a_2} \cdots A_{a_k} \quad \text{if} \quad \alpha = a_1 a_2 \cdots a_k,$$

$$A_a f \rightarrow A_{b_1} A_{b_2} \cdots A_{b_j} \quad \text{for each production } a \rightarrow b_1 b_2 \cdots b_j \text{ in } P_1,$$

$$A_a g \rightarrow a \quad \text{for each } a \text{ in } \Sigma.$$

Informally the string of f's counts the number of steps in a derivation of G_1, and index g marks the end of an index string, allowing a variable to be replaced by the terminal it represents. An easy induction on the length of a derivation shows that

$$S \overset{*}{\Rightarrow} Tf^i g \overset{*}{\Rightarrow} A_{b_1} f^{i-j} g A_{b_2} f^{i-j} g \cdots A_{b_k} f^{i-j} g$$

in G_2 if and only if $\alpha \overset{*}{\Rightarrow} b_1 b_2 \cdots b_k$ by a derivation of j steps in G_1. Thus

$$S \overset{*}{\Rightarrow} A_{b_1} g A_{b_2} g \cdots A_{b_k} g \overset{*}{\Rightarrow} b_1 b_2 \cdots b_k$$

if and only if $\alpha \overset{*}{\Rightarrow} b_1 b_2 \cdots b_k$.   □

14.5 SUMMARY

Figure 14.7 shows the various equivalences and containments proved or stated in this chapter, plus some others that are immediate from definitions. Containments are indicated by upward edges.

EXERCISES

14.1

a) Design a one-way DSA to recognize the language $\{0^n 1^{n^2} \mid n \geq 1\}$.

b) Design a one-way NSA to recognize the language $\{ww \mid w \text{ is in } (0 + 1)^*\}$.

*14.2   Design a two-way DSA to accept the set of binary strings whose value, treated as an integer, is a power of 3.

**14.3   Since every CFL can be recognized in polynomial time by the CYK algorithm, the corollary to Theorem 14.1 implies that every CFL is recognized by some deterministic log n-APDA. Give a direct construction of such an APDA from a CFG.

14.4   Show that the family of 1NSA languages and the family of 1NENSA languages form full AFL's.

14.5   Show that the families of 1DSA languages and 1NEDSA languages are closed under:

a) intersection with a regular set,   b) inverse GSM mappings,

c) complementation,   ****d) quotient with a regular set.

14.6   Give indexed grammars generating the following languages.

Sa) $\{0^n \mid n \text{ is a perfect square}\}$ b) $\{0^n \mid n \text{ is a power of 2}\}$

c) $\{0^n \mid n \text{ is not a prime}\}$ d) $\{ww \mid w \text{ is in } (0 + 1)^*\}$

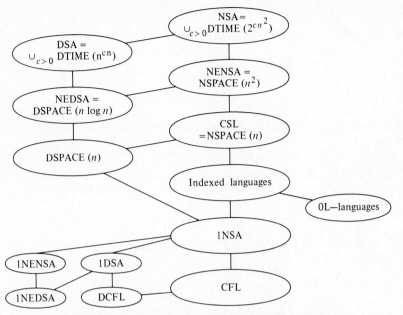

Fig. 14.7 Containments among classes of languages.

14.7 Give 0L-grammars generating the following languages.

a) $\{a^n \mid n \text{ is a power of 2}\}$ b) $\{wcw^R \mid w \text{ is in } (0 + 1)^*\}$

*S14.8 Give a 0L-grammar with the property that every string generated is of length a perfect square and furthermore for every perfect square there is at least one string of that length generated.

*14.9 Of the eight subsets of $\{\epsilon, a, aa\}$, how many are 0L-languages?

**14.10 Show that the family of 0L-languages is not closed under any of the AFL operations.

**14.11 Show that it is decidable whether the language generated by an indexed grammar is empty.

*14.12 Show that Greibach's theorem (Theorem 8.14) applies to the 1NEDSA languages, and that "$= \Sigma^*$" is undecidable for this class.

**14.13 Show that it is undecidable whether two 0L-languages are equivalent.

Solutions to Selected Exercises

14.6 a) We make use of the fact that the nth perfect square is the sum of the first n odd integers. The indexed grammar with productions

$$S \rightarrow Ag$$

$$A \rightarrow Af$$

$$A \rightarrow B$$

$$B \to CD$$

$$Df \to B$$

$$Dg \to \epsilon$$

$$Cf \to 00C$$

$$Cg \to 0$$

generates $\{0^n \mid n$ is a perfect square$\}$. The derivations are trivial variations of the following derivation.

$$S \Rightarrow Ag \overset{*}{\Rightarrow} Af^{n-1}g \Rightarrow Bf^{n-1}g$$

$$\Rightarrow Cf^{n-1}gDf^{n-1}g \Rightarrow Cf^{n-1}gBf^{n-2}g$$

$$\Rightarrow Cf^{n-1}gCf^{n-2}gDf^{n-2}g$$

$$\Rightarrow Cf^{n-1}gCf^{n-2}gBf^{n-3}g \Rightarrow \cdots$$

$$\Rightarrow Cf^{n-1}gCf^{n-2}g \cdots CfgCgDg$$

$$\Rightarrow Cf^{n-1}gCf^{n-1}g \cdots CfgCg$$

$$\overset{*}{\Rightarrow} 0^{2n-1}Cf^{n-1}g \cdots Cf_g C_g \overset{*}{\Rightarrow} \cdots$$

$$\overset{*}{\Rightarrow} 0^{2n-1}0^{2n-3} \cdots 0^3 0^1 = 0^{n^2}$$

14.8   We again make use of the fact that the nth perfect square is the sum of the first n odd integers. Consider the $0L$-grammar $(\{a, b, c\}, \{a \to abbc, b \to bc, c \to c\}, a)$. A simple induction shows that the nth string generated has one a, $2(n-1)$ b's, and $(n-1)^2$ c's. Thus the length of the nth string is $1 + 2(n-1) + (n-1)^2$ or n^2.

BIBLIOGRAPHIC NOTES

The auxiliary pushdown automaton and Theorem 14.1 are from Cook [1971a]. Earlier, Mager [1969] had considered "writing pushdown acceptors," which are n-APDA's. Stack automata were first considered by Ginsburg, Greibach, and Harrison [1967a, b]. Theorems 14.2 and 14.4, relating nonerasing stack automata to space complexity classes, are from Hopcroft and Ullman [1967a], although the fact that the CSL's are contained in the NEDSA languages was known from Ginsburg, Greibach, and Harrison [1967a]. Theorems 14.3 and 14.5, relating stack languages to APDA's and time complexity classes, are by Cook [1971a].

The basic closure and decision properties of one-way stack languages were treated in Ginsburg, Greibach, and Harrison [1967b]. Exercise 14.5(d), the closure of 1DSA languages under quotient with a regular set, is by Hopcroft and Ullman [1968b]. Theorem 14.6, containment of the 1NSA languages in DSPACE(n) is by Hopcroft and Ullman [1968c]. Ogden [1969] gives a "pumping lemma" for one-way stack languages. Beeri [1975] shows that two-way SA's are equivalent to two-way nested stack automata.

Indexed grammars were first studied by Aho [1968]. Theorem 14.7(b), the containment within the CSL's, is from there, as in Exercise 14.11, decidability of emptiness. A variety of other characterizations of the indexed languages are known. Aho [1969] discusses one-way nested stack automata, an automaton characterization. Fischer [1968] discusses macro grammars, Greibach [1970] provides another automaton characterization—a device with a stack of stacks, and Maibaum [1974] presents an algebraic characterization. These alternative formulations lend credence to the idea that the indexed languages are a "natural" class. Hayashi [1975] gives a "pumping lemma" for indexed languages.

L-systems originated with Lindenmayer [1968], and the $0L$-systems, on which we have concentrated, were considered by Lindenmayer [1971]. Exercise 14.10, on nonclosure properties of these languages, is from Herman [1974]. Exercise 14.13, the undecidability of equivalence of $0L$-languages, is implied by a stronger result of Blattner [1973], that it is undecidable whether the sets of sentential forms generated by two CFG's are the same. Much has been written on the subject, and the interested reader is referred to Salomaa [1973] and Herman and Rozenberg [1975].

We have but touched on some of the multitude of species of automata and grammars that have been studied. Rosenkrantz [1969] is representative of another early step in this direction, and Salomaa [1973] covers a variety of classes not touched upon here.

BIBLIOGRAPHY

Aanderaa, S. O. [1974]. "On k-tape versus $(k - 1)$-tape real time computation," *Complexity of Computation* (R. M. Karp, ed.). Proceedings of SIAM-AMS Symposium in Applied Mathematics.

Adleman, L., and K. Manders [1976]. "Diophantine complexity," *Proc. Seventeenth Annual IEEE Symposium on Foundations of Computer Science*, pp. 81–88.

Adleman, L., and K. Manders [1977]. "Reducibility, randomness and intractability," *Proc. Ninth Annual ACM Symposium on the Theory of Computing*, pp. 151–163.

Aho, A. V. [1968]. "Indexed grammars—an extension of context-free grammars," *J. ACM* **15**: 4, 647–671.

Aho, A. V. [1969]. "Nested stack automata," *J. ACM* **16**: 3, 383–406.

Aho, A. V., and M. J. Corasick [1975]. "Efficient string matching: an aid to bibliographic search," *Comm. ACM* **18**: 6, 333–340.

Aho, A. V., J. E. Hopcroft, and J. D. Ullman [1968]. "Time and tape complexity of pushdown automaton languages," *Information and Control* **13**: 3, 186–206.

Aho, A. V., J. E. Hopcroft, and J. D. Ullman [1974]. *The Design and Analysis of Computer Algorithms*, Addison-Wesley, Reading, Mass.

Aho, A. V., and S. C. Johnson [1974]. "LR parsing," *Computing Surveys*, **6**: 2, 99–124.

Aho, A. V., and J. D. Ullman [1970]. "A characterization of two-way deterministic classes of languages," *J. Computer and Systems Sciences* **4**: 6, 523–538.

Aho, A. V., and J. D. Ullman [1972]. *The Theory of Parsing, Translation and Compiling*, Vol. I: *Parsing*, Prentice Hall, Englewood Cliffs, N.J.

Aho, A. V., and J. D. Ullman [1973]. *The Theory of Parsing, Translation and Compiling*, Vol. II: *Compiling*, Prentice Hall, Englewood Cliffs, N.J.

Aho, A. V., and J. D. Ullman [1977]. *Principles of Compiler Design*, Addison-Wesley, Reading, Mass.

Arbib, M. A. [1970]. *Theories of Abstract Automata*, Prentice Hall, Englewood Cliffs, N.J.

Arden, D. N. [1960]. "Delayed logic and finite state machines," *Theory of Computing Machine Design*, pp. 1–35, Univ. of Michigan Press, Ann Arbor, Mich.

Axt, P. [1959]. "On a subrecursive hierarchy and primitive recursive degrees," *Trans. AMS* **92**, 85–105.

Backus, J. W. [1959]. "The syntax and semantics of the proposed international algebraic language of the Zürich ACM-GAMM conference," *Proc. Intl. Conf. on Information Processing*, pp. 125–132, UNESCO.

Baker, B. S., and R. V. Book [1974]. "Reversal bounded multipushdown machines," *J. Computer and Systems Sciences* **8**: 3, 315–332.

Baker, T., J. Gill, and R. Solovay [1975]. "Relativizations of the $P = ?NP$ question," *SIAM J. Computing* **4**: 4, 431–442.

Bar-Hillel, Y., M. Perles, and E. Shamir [1961]. "On formal properties of simple phrase structure grammars," *Z. Phonetik. Sprachwiss. Kommunikationsforsch.* **14**, 143–172.

Bauer, M., D. Brand, M. J. Fischer, A. R. Meyer, and M. S. Paterson [1973]. "A note on disjunctive form tautologies," *SIGACT News* **5**: 2, 17–20.

Beeri, C. [1975]. "Two-way nested stack automata are equivalent to two-way stack automata," *J. Computer and Systems Sciences* **10**: 3, 317–339.

Beeri, C. [1976]. "An improvement on Valiant's decision procedure for equivalence of deterministic finite-turn pushdown automata," *Theoretical Computer Science* **3**: 3, 305–320.

Berman, L. [1977]. "Precise bounds for Presburger arithmetic and the reals with addition," *Proc. Eighteenth Annual IEEE Symposium on Foundations of Computer Science*, pp. 95–99.

Berman, L., and J. Hartmanis [1977]. "On isomorphisms and density of NP and other complete sets," *SIAM J. Computing* **6**: 2, 305–322.

Berman, P. [1978]. "Relationship between density and deterministic complexity of NP-complete languages," *Fifth International Symposium on Automata, Languages, and Programming*, Udine, Italy.

Bird, M. [1973]. "The equivalence problem for deterministic two-tape automata," *J. Computer and Systems Sciences* **7**: 2, 218–236.

Blattner, M. [1973]. "The unsolvability of the equality problem for sentential forms of context-free grammars," *J. Computer and Systems Sciences* **7**: 5, 463–468.

Blum, M. [1967]. "A machine-independent theory of the complexity of recursive functions," *J. ACM* **14**: 2, 322–336.

Blum, M. [1971]. "On effective procedures for speeding up algorithms," *J. ACM* **18**: 2, 290–305.

Boasson, L. [1973]. "Two iteration theorems for some families of languages," *J. Computer and Systems Sciences* **7**: 6, 583–596.

Book, R. V. [1972]. "On languages accepted in polynomial time," *SIAM J. Computing* **1**: 4, 281–287.

Book, R. V. [1974]. "Comparing complexity classes," *J. Computer and Systems Sciences* **9**: 2, 213–229.

Book, R. V. [1976]. "Translational lemmas, polynomial time, and $(\log n)^j$ space," *Theoretical Computer Science* **1**: 3, 215–226.

Book, R. V., and S. A. Greibach [1970]. "Quasi-realtime languages," *Math. Systems Theory* **4**: 2, 97–111.

Book, R. V., S. A. Greibach, and B. Wegbreit [1970]. "Time- and tape-bounded Turing acceptors and AFL's," *J. Computer and Systems Sciences* **4**: 6, 606–621.

Borodin, A. [1972]. "Computational complexity and the existence of complexity gaps," *J. ACM* **19**: 1, 158–174.

Borosh, I., and L. B. Treybig [1976]. "Bounds on positive integral solutions of linear Diophantine equations," *Proc. AMS* **55**, 299–304.

Brainerd, W. S., and L. H. Landweber [1974]. *Theory of Computation*, John Wiley and Sons, New York.

Bruno, J. L., and R. Sethi [1976]. "Code generation for a one-register machine," *J. ACM* **23**: 3, 502–510.

Bruss, A. R., and A. R. Meyer [1978]. "On time-space classes and their relation to the theory of real addition," *Proc. Tenth Annual ACM Symposium on the Theory of Computing*, pp. 233–239.

Brzozowski, J. A. [1962]. "A survey of regular expressions and their applications," *IEEE Trans. on Electronic Computers* **11**: 3, 324–335.

Brzozowski, J. A. [1964]. "Derivatives of regular expressions," *J. ACM* **11**: 4, 481–494.

Bullen, R. H., Jr., and J. K. Millen [1972]. "Microtext—the design of a microprogrammed finite-state search machine for full text retrieval," *Proc. 1972 Fall Joint Computer Conference*, pp. 479–488, AFIPS Press, Montvale, N.J.

Cantor, D. C. [1962]. "On the ambiguity problem of Backus systems," *J. ACM* **9**: 4, 477–479.

Cardoza, E., R. J. Lipton, and A. R. Meyer [1976]. "Exponential space complete problems for Petri nets and commutative semi-groups: preliminary report," *Proc. Eighth Annual ACM Symposium on the Theory of Computing*, pp. 50–54.

Chandler, W. J. [1969]. "Abstract families of deterministic languages," *Proc. First Annual ACM Symposium on the Theory of Computing*, pp. 21–30.

Chandra, A. K., and L. J. Stockmeyer [1976]. "Alternation," *Proc. Seventeenth Annual IEEE Symposium on Foundations of Computer Science*, pp. 98–108.

Chomsky, N. [1956]. "Three models for the description of language," *IRE Trans. on Information Theory* **2**: 3, 113–124.

Chomsky, N. [1959]. "On certain formal properties of grammars," *Information and Control* **2**: 2, 137–167.

Chomsky, N. [1962]. "Context-free grammars and pushdown storage," *Quarterly Prog. Rept. No. 65*, pp. 187–194, MIT Res. Lab. Elect., Cambridge, Mass.

Chomsky, N. [1963]. "Formal properties of grammars," *Handbook of Math. Psych.*, Vol. 2, pp. 323–418, John Wiley and Sons, New York.

Chomsky, N., and G. A. Miller [1958]. "Finite state languages," *Information and Control* **1**: 2, 91–112.

Chomsky, N., and M. P. Schutzenberger [1963]. "The algebraic theory of context free languages," *Computer Programming and Formal Systems*, pp. 118–161, North Holland, Amsterdam.

Christofides, N. [1976]. "Worst case analysis of a new heuristic for the traveling salesman problem," *Algorithms and Complexity: New Directions and Recent Results* (J. Traub, ed.), p. 441, Academic Press, New York.

Church, A. [1936]. "An unsolvable problem of elementary number theory," *Amer. J. Math.* **58**, 345–363.

Church, A. [1941]. "The Calculi of Lambda-Conversion," *Annals of Mathematics Studies* **6**, Princeton Univ. Press, Princeton, N.J.

Cobham, A. [1964]. "The intrinsic computational difficulty of functions," *Proc. 1964 Congress for Logic, Mathematics, and Philosophy of Science,* pp. 24–30, North Holland, Amsterdam.

Coffman, E. G., Jr. (ed.) [1976]. *Computer and Job Shop Scheduling Theory,* John Wiley and Sons, New York.

Cole, S. N. [1969]. "Pushdown store machines and real-time computation," *Proc. First Annual ACM Symposium on the Theory of Computing,* pp. 233–246.

Constable, R. L. [1972]. "The operator gap," *J. ACM* **19**: 1, 175–183.

Conway, J. H. [1971]. *Regular Algebra and Finite Machines,* Chapman and Hall, London.

Cook, S. A. [1971a]. "Characterizations of pushdown machines in terms of time-bounded computers," *J. ACM* **18**: 1, 4–18.

Cook, S. A. [1971b]. "The complexity of theorem proving procedures," *Proc. Third Annual ACM Symposium on the Theory of Computing,* pp. 151–158.

Cook, S. A. [1971c]. "Linear time simulation of deterministic two-way pushdown automata," *Proc. 1971 IFIP Congress,* pp. 75–80, North Holland, Amsterdam.

Cook, S. A. [1973a]. "A hierarchy for nondeterministic time complexity," *J. Computer and Systems Sciences* **7**: 4, 343–353.

Cook, S. A. [1973b]. "An observation on time-storage trade off," *Proc. Fifth Annual ACM Symposium on the Theory of Computing,* pp. 29–33.

Cook, S. A., and R. A. Reckhow [1973]. "Time bounded random access machines," *J. Computer and Systems Sciences* **7**: 4, 354–375.

Cook, S. A., and R. Sethi [1976]. "Storage requirements for deterministic polynomial time recognizable languages," *J. Computer and Systems Sciences* **13**: 1, 25–37.

Cooper, C. D. [1972]. "Theorem proving in arithmetic without multiplication," *Machine Intelligence 7* (Melzer and Mitchie, eds.), pp. 91–99, John Wiley and Sons, New York.

Cremers, A., and S. Ginsburg [1975]. "Context-free grammar forms," *J. Computer and Systems Sciences* **11**: 1, 86–117.

Cudia, D. F. [1970]. "General problems of formal grammars," *J. ACM* **17**: 1, 31–43.

Cudia, D. F., and W. E. Singletary [1968]. "Degrees of unsolvability in formal grammars," *J. ACM* **15**: 4, 680–692.

Davis, M. [1958]. *Computability and Unsolvability,* McGraw-Hill, New York.

Davis, M. (ed.) [1965]. *The Undecidable,* Raven Press, New York.

De Remer, F. L. [1969]. "Generating parsers for BNF grammars," *Proc. 1969 Spring Joint Computer Conference,* pp. 793–799, AFIPS Press, Montvale, N.J.

De Remer, F. L. [1971]. "Simple LR(k) grammars," *Comm. ACM* **14**: 7, 453–460.

Earley, J. [1970]. "An efficient context-free parsing algorithm," *Comm. ACM* **13**: 2, 94–102.

Eilenberg, S., and C. C. Elgot [1970]. *Recursiveness,* Academic Press, New York.

Even, S., and R. E. Tarjan [1976]. "A combinatorial problem which is complete in polynomial space," *J. ACM* **23**: 4, 710–719.

Evey, J. [1963]. "Application of pushdown store machines," *Proc. 1963 Fall Joint Computer Conference,* pp. 215–227, AFIPS Press, Montvale, N.J.

Ferrante, J., and C. Rackoff [1975]. "A decision procedure for the first order theory of real addition with order," *SIAM J. Computing* **4**: 1, 69–76.

Fischer, M. J. [1968]. "Grammars with macro-like productions," *Proc. Ninth Annual IEEE Symposium on Switching and Automata Theory,* pp. 131–142.

Fischer, M. J. [1969]. "Two characterizations of the context-sensitive languages," *Proc. Tenth Annual IEEE Symposium on Switching and Automata Theory*, pp. 157–165.

Fischer, M. J., and M. O. Rabin [1974]. "Super-exponential complexity of Presburger arithmetic," *Complexity of Computation* (R. M. Karp, ed.). Proceedings of SIAM-AMS Symposium in Applied Mathematics.

Fischer, P. C. [1963]. "On computability by certain classes of restricted Turing machines," *Proc. Fourth Annual IEEE Symp. on Switching Circuit Theory and Logical Design*, pp. 23–32.

Fischer, P. C. [1965]. "On formalisms for Turing machines," *J. ACM* **12**: 4, 570–588.

Fischer, P. C. [1966]. "Turing machines with restricted memory access," *Information and Control* **9**: 4, 364–379.

Fischer, P. C., A. R. Meyer, and A. L. Rosenberg [1968]. "Counter machines and counter languages," *Math. Systems Theory* **2**: 3, 265–283.

Fischer, P. C., A. R. Meyer, and A. L. Rosenberg [1972]. "Real-time simulation of multihead tape units," *J. ACM* **19**: 4, 590–607.

Floyd, R. W. [1962a]. "On ambiguity in phrase structure languages," *Comm. ACM* **5**: 10, 526–534.

Floyd, R. W. [1962b]. "On the nonexistence of a phrase structure grammar for ALGOL 60," *Comm. ACM* **5**: 9, 483–484.

Floyd, R. W. [1964]. "New proofs and old theorems in logic and formal linguistics," Computer Associates Inc., Wakefield, Mass.

Floyd, R. W. [1967]. "Nondeterministic algorithms," *J. ACM* **14**: 4, 636–644.

Freedman, A. R., and R. E. Ladner [1975]. "Space bounds for processing contentless inputs," *J. Computer and Systems Sciences* **11**: 1, 118–128.

Friedman, A. [1975]. *Logical Design of Digital Systems*, Computer Science Press, Potomac, Md.

Friedman, E. P. [1976]. "The inclusion problem for simple languages," *Theoretical Computer Science* **1**: 4, 297–316.

Friedman, E. P. [1977]. "The equivalence problem for deterministic context-free languages and monadic recursion schemes," *J. Computer and Systems Sciences* **14**: 3, 344–359.

Gabriellian, A., and S. Ginsburg [1974]. "Grammar schemata," *J. ACM* **21**: 2, 312–226.

Garey, M. R., R. L. Graham, and D. S. Johnson [1976]. "Some *NP*-complete geometric problems," *Proc. Eighth Annual ACM Symposium on the Theory of Computing*, pp. 10–22.

Garey, M. R., and D. S. Johnson [1976]. "The complexity of near-optimal graph coloring," *J. ACM* **23**: 1, 43–49.

Garey, M. R., and D. S. Johnson [1978]. *Computers and Intractability: A Guide to the Theory of NP-Completeness*, H. Freeman, San Francisco.

Garey, M. R., D. S. Johnson, and L. J. Stockmeyer [1976]. "Some simplified NP-complete problems," *Theoretical Computer Science* **1**: 3, 237–267.

Garey, M. R., D. S. Johnson, and R. E. Tarjan [1976]. "The planar Hamilton circuit problem is *NP*-complete," *SIAM J. Computing* **5**: 4, 704–714.

Gathen, J., and M. Sieveking [1976]. "A bound on the solutions of linear integer programs," Unpublished notes.

Ginsburg, S. [1962]. "Examples of abstract machines," *IEEE Trans. on Electronic Computers* **11**: 2, 132–135.

Ginsburg, S. [1966]. *The Mathematical Theory of Context-Free Languages*, McGraw Hill, New York.

Ginsburg, S. [1975]. *Algebraic and Automata-Theoretic Properties of Formal Languages*, North Holland, Amsterdam.

Ginsburg, S., and S. A. Greibach [1966a]. "Deterministic context-free languages," *Information and Control* **9**: 6, 563–582.

Ginsburg, S., and S. A. Greibach [1966b]. "Mappings which preserve context-sensitive languages," *Information and Control* **9**: 6, 563–582.

Ginsburg, S., and S. A. Greibach [1969]. "Abstract families of languages," *Studies in Abstract Families of Languages*, pp. 1–32, Memoir No. 87, American Mathematical Society, Providence, R.I.

Ginsburg, S., and S. A. Greibach [1970]. "Principal AFL," *J. Computer and Systems Sciences* **4**: 3, 308–338.

Ginsburg, S., S. A. Greibach, and M. A. Harrison [1967a]. "Stack automata and compiling," *J. ACM* **14**: 1, 172–201.

Ginsburg, S., S. A. Greibach, and M. A. Harrison [1967b]. "One-way stack automata," *J. ACM* **14**: 2, 389–418.

Ginsburg, S., and J. E. Hopcroft [1970]. "Two-way balloon automata and AFL," *J. ACM* **17**: 1, 3–13.

Ginsburg, S., and H. G. Rice [1962]. "Two families of languages related to ALGOL," *J. ACM* **9**: 3, 350–371.

Ginsburg, S., and G. F. Rose [1963a]. "Some recursively unsolvable problems in ALGOL-like languages," *J. ACM* **10**: 1, 29–47.

Ginsburg, S., and G. F. Rose [1963b]. "Operations which preserve definability in languages," *J. ACM* **10**: 2, 175–195.

Ginsburg, S., and G. F. Rose [1966]. "Preservation of languages by transducers," *Information and Control* **9**: 2, 153–176.

Ginsburg, S., and E. H. Spanier [1963]. "Quotients of context free languages," *J. ACM* **10**: 4, 487–492.

Ginsburg, S., and E. H. Spanier [1966]. "Finite turn pushdown automata," *SIAM J. Control*, **4**: 3, 429–453.

Ginsburg, S., and J. S. Ullian [1966a]. "Ambiguity in context-free languages," *J. ACM* **13**: 1, 62–88.

Ginsburg, S., and J. S. Ullian [1966b]. "Preservation of unambiguity and inherent ambiguity in context free languages," *J. ACM* **13**: 3, 364–368.

Graham, S. L. [1970]. "Extended precedence languages, bounded right context languages and deterministic languages," *Proc. Eleventh Annual IEEE Symposium on Switching and Automata Theory*, pp. 175–180.

Graham, S. L., M. A. Harrison, and W. L. Ruzzo [1976]. "On-line context-free language recognition in less than cubic time," *Proc. Eighth Annual ACM Symposium on the Theory of Computing*, pp. 112–120.

Gray, J. N., M. A. Harrison, and O. Ibarra [1967]. "Two-way pushdown automata," *Information and Control* **11**: 1–2, 30–70.

Greibach, S. A. [1963]. "The undecidability of the ambiguity problem for minimal linear grammars," *Information and Control* **6**: 2, 117–125.

Greibach, S. A. [1965]. "A new normal form theorem for context-free phrase structure grammars," *J. ACM* **12**: 1, 42–52.

Greibach, S. A. [1966]. "The unsolvability of the recognition of linear context-free languages," *J. ACM* **13**: 4, 582–587.

Greibach, S. A. [1968]. "A note on undecidable properties of formal languages," *Math Systems Theory* **2**: 1, 1–6.

Greibach, S. A. [1970]. "Full AFL's and nested iterated substitution," *Information and Control* **16**: 1, 7–35.

Greibach, S. A. [1973]. "The hardest context-free language," *SIAM J. Computing* **2**: 4, 304–310.

Greibach, S. A., and J. E. Hopcroft [1969]. "Independence of AFL operations," *Studies in Abstract Families of Languages*, pp. 33–40, Memoir No. 87, American Mathematical Society, Providence, R.I.

Greibach, S. A., and J. E. Hopcroft [1969]. "Scattered context grammars," *J. Computer and Systems Sciences* **3**: 3, 233–247.

Griffiths, T. V. [1968]. "The unsolvability of the equivalence problem for Λ-free nondeterministic generalized machines," *J. ACM* **15**: 3, 409–413.

Gross, M. [1964]. "Inherent ambiguity of minimal linear grammars," *Information and Control* **7**: 3, 366–368.

Grzegorczyk, A. [1953]. "Some classes of recursive functions," *Rosprawy Matematyczne* **4**, Instytut Matematyczne Polskiej Akademie Nauk, Warsaw, Poland.

Haines, L. [1965]. "Generation and recognition or formal languages," Ph.D. thesis, MIT, Cambridge, Mass.

Hardy, G. H., and E. M. Wright [1938]. *An Introduction to the Theory of Numbers*, Oxford Univ. Press, London.

Hartmanis, J. [1967]. "Context-free languages and Turing machine computations," *Proc. Symposia in Applied Math.* **19**, American Mathematical Society, Providence, R.I.

Hartmanis, J. [1968]. "Computational complexity of one-tape Turing machine computations," *J. ACM* **15**: 2, 325–339.

Hartmanis, J. [1969]. "On the complexity of undecidable problems in automata theory," *J. ACM* **16**: 1, 160–167.

Hartmanis, J., and J. E. Hopcroft [1968]. "Structure of undecidable problems in automata theory," *Proc. Ninth Annual IEEE Symposium on Switching and Automata Theory*, pp. 327–333.

Hartmanis, J., and J. E. Hopcroft [1971]. "An overview of the theory of computational complexity," *J. ACM* **18**: 3, 444–475.

Hartmanis, J., and Hopcroft, J. E. [1976]. "Independence results in computer science," *SIGACT News* **8**: 4, 13–23.

Hartmanis, J., P. M. Lewis II, and R. E. Stearns [1965]. "Hierarchies of memory limited computations," *Proc. Sixth Annual IEEE Symp. on Switching Circuit Theory and Logical Design*, pp. 179–190.

Hartmanis, J., and H. Shank [1968]. "On the recognition of primes by automata," *J. ACM* **15**: 3, 382–389.

Hartmanis, J., and R. E. Stearns [1965]. "On the computational complexity of algorithms," *Trans. AMS* **117**, 285–306.

Hayashi, T. [1973]. "On derivation trees of indexed grammars—an extension of the *uvwxy* theorem," *Publications of the Research Institute for Mathematical Sciences* **9**: 1, pp. 61–92.

Hennie, F. C. [1964]. "Fault detecting experiments for sequential circuits," *Proc. Fourth Annual IEEE Symp. on Switching Circuit Theory and Logical Design*, pp. 95–110.

Hennie, F. C. [1965]. "One-tape off-line Turing machine computations," *Information and Control* **8**: 6, 553–578.

Hennie, F. C. [1977]. *Introduction to Computability*, Addison-Wesley, Reading, Mass.

Hennie, F. C., and R. E. Stearns [1966]. "Two-tape simulation of multitape Turing machines," *J. ACM* **13**: 4, 533–546.

Herman, G. T. [1974]. "Closure properties of some families of languages associated with biological systems," *Information and Control* **24**: 2, 101–121.

Herman, G. T., and G. Rozenberg [1975]. *Developmental Systems and Languages*, North Holland, Amsterdam.

Hibbard, T. N. [1974]. "Context-limited grammars," *J. ACM* **21**: 3, 446–453.

Hogben, L. [1955]. *The Wonderful World of Mathematics*, Garden City Books, Garden City, N.Y.

Hopcroft, J. E. [1971]. "An *n* log *n* algorithm for minimizing the states in a finite automaton," *The Theory of Machines and Computations* (Z. Kohavi, ed.), pp. 189–196, Academic Press, New York.

Hopcroft, J. E., W. J. Paul, and L. G. Valiant [1975]. "On time versus space and related problems," *Proc. Sixteenth Annual IEEE Symposium on Foundations of Computer Science*, pp. 57–64.

Hopcroft, J. E., and J. D. Ullman [1967a]. "Nonerasing stack automata," *J. Computer and Systems Sciences* **1**: 2, 166–186.

Hopcroft, J. E., and J. D. Ullman [1967b]. "An approach to a unified theory of automata," *Bell System Technical J.* **46**: 8, 1763–1829.

Hopcroft, J. E., and J. D. Ullman [1968a]. "Decidable and undecidable questions about automata," *J. ACM* **15**: 2, 317–324.

Hopcroft, J. E., and J. D. Ullman [1968b]. "Deterministic stack automata and the quotient operator," *J. Computer and Systems Sciences* **2**: 1, 1–12.

Hopcroft, J. E., and J. D. Ullman [1968c]. "Sets accepted by one-way stack automata are context sensitive," *Information and Control* **13**: 2, 114–133.

Hopcroft, J. E., and J. D. Ullman [1969a]. "Some results on tape-bounded Turing machines," *J. ACM* **16**: 1, 168–177.

Hopcroft, J. E., and J. D. Ullman [1969b]. *Formal Languages and Their Relation to Automata*, Addison-Wesley, Reading, Mass.

Huffman, D. A. [1954]. "The synthesis of sequential switching circuits," *J. Franklin Institute* **257**: 3–4, 161–190, 275–303.

Hunt, H. B., III [1973]. "On the time and tape complexity of languages," *Proc. Fifth Annual ACM Symposium on the Theory of Computing*, pp. 10–19.

Hunt, H. B., III, and D. J. Rosenkrantz [1974]. "Computational parallels between the regular and context-free languages," *Proc. Sixth Annual ACM Symposium on the Theory of Computing*, pp. 64–74.

Hunt, H. B., III, and D. J. Rosenkrantz [1977]. "On equivalence and containment problems for formal languages," *J. ACM* **24**: 3, 387–396.

Hunt, H. B., III, D. J. Rosenkrantz, and T. G. Szymanski [1976]. "On the equivalence, containment and covering problems for regular expressions," *J. Computer and Systems Sciences* **12**: 2, 222–268.

Hunt, H. B., III, and T. G. Szymanski [1975]. "On the complexity of grammar and related problems," *Proc. Seventh Annual ACM Symposium on the Theory of Computing*, pp. 54–65.

Hunt, H. B., III, and T. G. Szymanski [1976]. "Complexity metatheorems for context-free grammar problems," *J. Computer and Systems Sciences* **13**: 3, 318–334.

Hunt, H. B., III, T. G. Szymanski, and J. D. Ullman [1975]. "On the complexity of LR(k) testing," *Comm. ACM* **18**: 12, 707–715.

Ibarra, O. H. [1972]. "A note concerning nondeterministic tape complexities," *J. ACM* **19**: 4, 608–612.

Ibarra, O. H. [1977]. "The unsolvability of the equivalence problem for free GSM's with unary input (output) alphabet," *Proc. Eighteenth Annual IEEE Symposium on Foundations of Computer Science*, pp. 74–81.

Johnson, D. S. [1974]. "Approximation algorithms for combinatorial problems," *J. Computer and Systems Sciences* **9**: 3, 256–278.

Johnson, S. C. [1974]. "YACC—yet another compiler compiler," CSTR 32, Bell Laboratories, Murray Hill, N.J.

Johnson, W. L., J. H. Porter, S. I. Ackley, and D. T. Ross [1968]. "Automatic generation of efficient lexical analyzers using finite state techniques," *Comm. ACM* **11**: 12, 805–813.

Jones, N. D. [1975]. "Space-bounded reducibility among combinatorial problems," *J. Computer and Systems Sciences* **11**: 1, 68–85.

Jones, N. D. [1973]. *Computability Theory: an Introduction*, Academic Press, New York.

Jones, N. D., and W. T. Laaser [1976]. "Complete problems for deterministic polynomial time," *Theoretical Computer Science* **3**: 1, 105–118.

Jones, N. D., E. Lien, and W. T. Lasser [1976]. "New problems complete for nondeterministic log space," *Math. Systems Theory* **10**: 1, 1–17.

Jones, N. D., and S. S. Muchnick [1977]. "Even simple programs are hard to analyze," *J. ACM* **24**: 2, 338–350.

Kannan, R., and C. L. Monma [1977]. "On the computational complexity of integer programming problems," Report 7780-0R, Inst. fur Operations Research, Univ. Bonn, Bonn, West Germany.

Karp, R. M. [1972]. "Reducibility among combinatorial problems," *Complexity of Computer Computations*, pp. 85–104, Plenum Press, N.Y.

Karp, R. M. [1977]. "The probabilistic analysis of some combinatorial search algorithms," *Algorithms and Complexity: New Directions and Recent Results* (J. Traub, ed.), pp. 1–20, Academic Press, New York.

Kasami, T. [1965]. "An efficient recognition and syntax algorithm for context-free languages," *Scientific Report AFCRL-65-758*, Air Force Cambridge Research Lab., Bedford, Mass.

Kasami, T., and K. Torii [1969]. "A syntax analysis procedure for unambiguous context-free grammars," *J. ACM* **16**: 3, 423–431.

Kirkpatrick, D. G., and P. Hell [1978]. "On the completeness of a generalized matching problem," *Proc. Tenth Annual ACM Symposium on the Theory of Computing*, pp. 240–245.

Kleene, S. C. [1936]. "General recursive functions of natural numbers," *Mathematische Annalen* **112**, 727–742.

Kleene, S. C. [1952]. *Introduction to Metamathematics*, D. Van Nostrand, Princeton, N.J.

Kleene, S. C. [1956]. "Representation of events in nerve nets and finite automata," *Automata Studies*, pp. 3–42, Princeton Univ. Press, Princeton, N.J.

Knuth, D. E. [1965]. "On the translation of languages from left to right," *Information and Control* **8**: 6, 607–639.

Knuth, D. E., J. H. Morris, Jr., and V. R. Pratt [1977]. "Fast pattern matching in strings," *SIAM J. Computing* **6**: 2, 323–350.

Kohavi, Z. [1970]. *Switching and Finite Automata Theory*, McGraw-Hill, New York.

Korenjak, A. J. [1969]. "A practical method for constructing LR(*k*) processors," *Comm. ACM* **12**: 11, 613–623.

Korenjak, A. J., and J. E. Hopcroft [1966]. "Simple deterministic languages," *Proc. Seventh Annual IEEE Symposium on Switching and Automata Theory*, pp. 36–46.

Kosaraju, S. R. [1974]. "Regularity preserving functions," *SIGACT News* **6**: 2, 16–17.

Kosaraju, S. R. [1975]. "Context free preserving functions," *Math. Systems Theory* **9**: 3, 193–197.

Kozen, D. [1976]. "On parallelism in Turing machines," *Proc. Seventeenth Annual IEEE Symposium on Foundations of Computer Science*, pp. 89–97.

Kozen, D. [1978]. "Indexing of subrecursive classes," *Proc. Tenth Annual ACM Symposium on the Theory of Computing*, pp. 287–295.

Kuroda, S. Y. [1964]. "Classes of languages and linear bounded automata," *Information and Control* **7**: 2, 207–223.

Ladner, R. E. [1975a]. "On the structure of polynomial time reducibility," *J. ACM* **22**: 1, 155–171.

Ladner, R. E. [1975b]. "The circuit value problem is log-space complete for *P*," *SIGACT News* **7**: 1, 18–20.

Ladner, R. E., N. Lynch, and A. Selman [1974]. "Comparison of polynomial time reducibilities," *Proc. Sixth Annual ACM Symposium on the Theory of Computing*, pp. 110–121.

Landweber, P. S. [1963]. "Three theorems on phrase structure grammars of type 1," *Information and Control* **6**: 2, 131–136.

Landweber, P. S. [1964]. "Decision problems of phrase structure grammars," *IEEE Trans. on Electronic Computers* **13**, 354–362.

Leong, B., and J. Seiferas [1977]. "New real-time simulations of multihead tape units," *Proc. Ninth Annual ACM Symposium on the Theory of Computing*, pp. 239–240.

Lesk, M. E. [1975]. "LEX—a lexical analyzer generator," CSTR 39, Bell Laboratories, Murray Hill, N.J.

Levin, L. A. [1973]. "Universal sorting problems," *Problemi Peredachi Informatsii* **9**: 3, 265–266.

Lewis, J. M. [1978]. "On the complexity of the maximum subgraph problem," *Proc. Tenth Annual ACM Symposium on the Theory of Computing*, pp. 265–274.

Lewis, P. M., II, D. J. Rosenkrantz, and R. E. Stearns [1976]. *Compiler Design Theory*, Addison-Wesley, Reading, Mass.

Lewis, P. M., II, and R. E. Stearns [1968]. "Syntax directed transduction," *J. ACM* **15**: 3, 465–488.

Lewis, P. M., II, R. E. Stearns, and J. Hartmanis [1965]. "Memory bounds for recognition of context-free and context-sensitive languages," *Proc. Sixth Annual IEEE Symp. on Switching Circuit Theory and Logical Design*, pp. 191–202.

Lindenmayer, A. [1968]. "Mathematical models for cellular interactions in development, parts I and II," *J. Theor. Biol.* **18**, 280–315.

Lindenmayer, A. [1971]. "Developmental systems without cellular interaction, their languages and grammars," *J. Theor. Biol.* **30**, 455–484.

Machtey, M., and P. R. Young [1978]. *An Introduction to the General Theory of Algorithms*, North Holland, New York.

Mager, G. [1969]. "Writing pushdown acceptors," *J. Computer and Systems Sciences* **3**: 3, 276–319.

Maibaum, T. S. E. [1974]. "A generalized approach to formal languages," *J. Computer and Systems Sciences* **8**: 3, 409–439.

McCreight, E. M., and A. R. Meyer [1969]. "Classes of computable functions defined by bounds on computation," *Proc. First Annual ACM Symposium on the Theory of Computing*, pp. 79–88.

McCulloch, W. S., and W. Pitts [1943]. "A logical calculus of the ideas immanent in nervous activity," *Bull. Math. Biophysics* **5**, 115–133.

McNaughton, R., and H. Yamada [1960]. "Regular expressions and state graphs for automata," *IEEE Trans. on Electronic Computers* **9**: 1, 39–47.

Mealy, G. H. [1955]. "A method for synthesizing sequential circuits," *Bell System Technical J.* **34**: 5, 1045–1079.

Meyer, A. R., and R. Ritchie [1967]. "The complexity of loop programs," *Proc. ACM Natl. Conf.*, pp. 465–469.

Meyer, A. R., and L. J. Stockmeyer [1973]. "The equivalence problem for regular expressions with squaring requires exponential space," *Proc. Thirteenth Annual IEEE Symposium on Switching and Automata Theory*, pp. 125–129.

Miller, G. L. [1976]. "Riemann's hypothesis and tests for primality," *J. Computer and Systems Sciences* **13**: 3, 300–317.

Minsky, M. L. [1961]. "Recursive unsolvability of Post's problem of 'tag' and other topics in the theory of Turing machines," *Annals of Math.*, **74**: 3, 437–455.

Minsky, M. L. [1967]. *Computation: Finite and Infinite Machines*, Prentice Hall, Englewood Cliffs, N.J.

Minsky, M. L., and S. Papert [1966]. "Unrecognizable sets of numbers," *J. ACM* **13**: 2, 281–286.

Moore, E. F. [1956]. "Gedanken experiments on sequential machines," *Automata Studies*, pp. 129–153, Princeton Univ. Press, Princeton, N.J.

Moore, E. F. (ed.) [1964]. *Sequential Machines: Selected Papers*, Addison-Wesley, Reading, Mass.

Myhill, J. [1957]. "Finite automata and the representation of events," WADD TR-57-624, pp. 112–137, Wright Patterson AFB, Ohio.

Myhill, J. [1960]. "Linear bounded automata," WADD TR-60-165, pp. 60–165, Wright Patterson AFB, Ohio.

Naur, P. *et al.* [1960]. "Report on the algorithmic language ALGOL 60," *Comm. ACM* **3**: 5, 299–314, revised in *Comm. ACM* **6**: 1, 1–17.

Nerode, A. [1958]. "Linear automaton transformations," *Proc. AMS*, **9**, pp. 541–544.

Oettinger, A. G. [1961]. "Automatic syntactic analysis and the pushdown store," *Proc. Symposia in Applied Math.* **12**, American Mathematical Society, Providence, R.I.

Ogden, W. [1968]. "A helpful result for proving inherent ambiguity," *Math. Systems Theory* **2**: 3, 191–194.

Ogden, W. [1969]. "Intercalation theorems for stack languages," *Proc. First Annual ACM Symposium on the Theory of Computing*, pp. 31–42.

Oppen, D. C. [1973]. "Elementary bounds for Presburger arithmetic," *Proc. Fifth Annual ACM Symposium on the Theory of Computing*, pp. 34–37.

Papadimitriou, C. H. [1976]. "On the complexity of edge traversing," *J. ACM* **23**: 3, 544–554.

Papadimitriou, C. H., and K. Steiglitz [1977]. "On the complexity of local search for the traveling salesman problem," *SIAM J. Computing* **6**: 1, 76–83.

Parikh, R. J. [1966]. "On context-free languages," *J. ACM* **13**: 4, 570–581.

Paull, M. C., and S. H. Unger [1968]. "Structural equivalence of context-free grammars," *J. Computer and Systems Sciences* **2**: 4, 427–468.

Paul, W. J. [1977]. "On time hierarchies," *Proc. Ninth Annual ACM Symposium on the Theory of Computing*, pp. 218–222.

Paul, W. J., R. E. Tarjan, and J. R. Celoni [1976]. "Space bounds for a game on graphs," *Proc. Eighth Annual ACM Symposium on the Theory of Computing*, pp. 149–160.

Plaisted, D. A. [1977]. "Sparse complex polynomials and polynomial reducibility," *J. Computer and Systems Sciences* **14**: 2, 210–221.

Post, E. [1936]. "Finite combinatory processes-formulation, I," *J. Symbolic Logic*, **1**, 103–105.

Post, E. [1943]. "Formal reductions of the general combinatorial decision problem," *Amer. J. Math.* **65**, 197–215.

Post, E. [1946]. "A variant of a recursively unsolvable problem," *Bull. AMS*, **52**, 264–268.

Pratt, V. R. [1975]. "Every prime has a succinct certificate," *SIAM J. Computing* **4**: 3, 214–220.

Pratt, V. R., and L. J. Stockmeyer [1976]. "A characterization of the power of vector machines," *J. Computer and Systems Sciences* **12**: 2, 198–221.

Rabin, M. O. [1963]. "Real-time computation," *Israel J. Math.* **1**: 4, 203–211.

Rabin, M. O. [1976]. "Probabilistic algorithms," *Algorithms and Complexity: New Directions and Recent Results* (J. Traub, ed.), pp. 21–40, Academic Press, New York.

Rabin, M. O., and D. Scott [1959]. "Finite automata and their decision problems," *IBM J. Res.* **3**: 2, 115–125.

Rackoff, C. [1978]. "Relativized questions involving probabilistic algorithms," *Proc. Tenth Annual ACM Symposium on the Theory of Computing*, pp. 338–342.

Reedy, A., and W. J. Savitch [1975]. "The Turing degree of the inherent ambiguity problem for context-free languages," *Theoretical Computer Science* **1**: 1, 77–91.

Rice, H. G. [1953]. "Classes of recursively enumerable sets and their decision problems," *Trans. AMS* **89**, 25–59.

Rice, H. G. [1956]. "On completely recursively enumerable classes and their key arrays," *J. Symbolic Logic* **21**, 304–341.

Ritchie, R. W. [1963]. "Classes of predictably computable functions," *Trans. AMS* **106**, 139–173.

Rogers, H., Jr. [1967]. *The Theory of Recursive Functions and Effective Computability*, McGraw-Hill, New York.

Rosenkrantz, D. J. [1967]. "Matrix equations and normal forms for context-free grammars," *J. ACM* **14**: 3, 501–507.

Rosenkrantz, D. J. [1969]. "Programmed grammars and classes of formal languages," *J. ACM* **16**: 1, 107–131.

Rosenkrantz, D. J., and R. E. Stearns [1970]. "Properties of deterministic top-down grammars," *Information and Control* **17**: 3, 226–256.

Rosenkrantz, D. J., R. E. Stearns, and P. M. Lewis, II [1977]. "An analysis of several heuristics for the traveling salesman problem," *SIAM J. Computing* **6**: 3, 563–581.

Rounds, W. C. [1970]. "Mappings and grammars on trees," *Math. Systems Theory* **4**: 3, 257–287.

Ruby, S., and P. C. Fischer [1965]. "Translational methods and computational complexity," *Proc. Sixth Annual IEEE Symp. on Switching Circuit Theory and Logical Design*, pp. 173–178.

Sahni, S. [1974]. "Computationally related problems," *SIAM J. Computing* **3**: 4, 262–279.

Sahni, S., and T. Gonzalez [1976]. "P-complete approximation problems," *J. ACM* **23**: 3, 555–565.

Sakoda, W. J., and Sipser, M. [1978]. "Nondeterminism and the size of two-way finite automata," *Proc. Tenth Annual ACM Symposium on the Theory of Computing*, pp. 275–286.

Salomaa, A. [1966]. "Two complete axiom systems for the algebra of regular events," *J. ACM* **13**: 1, 158–169.

Salomaa, A. [1973]. *Formal Languages*, Academic Press, N.Y.

Savitch, W. J. [1970]. "Relationships between nondeterministic and deterministic tape complexities," *J. Computer and Systems Sciences* **4**: 2, 177–192.

Savitch, W. J. [1972]. "Maze recognizing automata," *Proc. Fourth Annual ACM Symposium on the Theory of Computing*, pp. 151–156.

Schaefer, T. J. [1976]. "Complexity of decision problems based on finite two-person perfect information games," *Proc. Eighth Annual ACM Symposium on the Theory of Computing*, pp. 41–49.

Schaefer, T. J. [1978]. "The complexity of satisfiability problems," *Proc. Tenth Annual ACM Symposium on the Theory of Computing*, pp. 216–226.

Scheinberg, S. [1960]. "Note on the Boolean properties of context-free languages," *Information and Control* **3**: 4, 372–375.

Schutzenberger, M. P. [1963]. "On context-free languages and pushdown automata," *Information and Control* **6**: 3, 246–264.

Seiferas, J. I. [1974]. "A note on prefixes of regular languages," *SIGACT News* **6**: 1, 25–29.

Seiferas, J. I. [1977a]. "Techniques for separating space complexity classes," *J. Computer and Systems Sciences* **14**: 1, 73–99.

Seiferas, J. I. [1977b]. "Relating refined complexity classes," *J. Computer and Systems Sciences* **14**: 1, 100–129.

Seiferas, J. I., M. J. Fischer, and A. R. Meyer [1973]. "Refinements of nondeterministic time and space hierarchies," *Proc. Fourteenth Annual IEEE Symposium on Switching and Automata Theory*, pp. 130–137.

Seiferas, J. I., and R. McNaughton [1976]. "Regularity preserving relations," *Theoretical Computer Science* **2**: 2, 147–154.

Sethi, R. [1975]. "Complete register allocation problems," *SIAM J. Computing* **4**: 3, 226–248.

Shannon, C. E. [1956]. "A universal Turing machine with two internal states," *Automata Studies*, pp. 129–153, Princeton Univ. Press, Princeton, N.J.

Shannon, C. E., and J. McCarthy (eds.) [1956]. *Automata Studies*, Princeton Univ. Press, Princeton, N.J.

Sheperdson, J. C. [1959]. "The reduction of two-way automata to one-way automata," *IBM J. Res.* **3**: 2, 198–200.

Solovay, R., and V. Strassen [1977]. "A fast Monte Carlo test for primality," *SIAM J. Computing* **6**: 1, 84–85. A correction *ibid.* **7**: 1, p. 118.

Springsteel, F. N. [1976]. "On the pre-AFL of [log n] space and related families of languages," *Theoretical Computer Science* **2**: 3, 295–304.

Stanley, R. J. [1965]. "Finite state representations of context-free languages," *Quarterly Prog. Rept. No. 76*, 276–279, MIT Res. Lab. Elect., Cambridge, Mass.

Stearns, R. E. [1967]. "A regularity test for pushdown machines," *Information and Control* **11**: 3, 323–340.

Stearns, R. E., and J. Hartmanis [1963]. "Regularity preserving modifications of regular expressions," *Information and Control* **6**: 1, 55–69.

Stockmeyer, L. J. [1973]. "Planar 3-colorability is polynomial complete," *SIGACT News* **5**: 3, 19–25.

Stockmeyer, L. J. [1974]. "The complexity of decision problems in automata theory and logic," MAC TR-133, Project MAC, MIT, Cambridge, Mass.

Stockmeyer, L. J. [1976]. "The polynomial time hierarchy," *Theoretical Computer Science* **3**: 1, 1–22.

Stockmeyer, L. J., and A. R. Meyer [1973]. "Word problems requiring exponential space," *Proc. Fifth Annual ACM Symposium on the Theory of Computing*, pp. 1–9.

Sudborough, I. H. [1975a]. "A note on tape-bounded complexity classes and linear context-free languages," *J. ACM* **22**: 4, 499–500.

Sudborough, I. H. [1975b]. "On tape-bounded complexity classes and multihead finite automata," *J. Computer and Systems Sciences* **10**: 1, 62–76.

Suzuki, N., and D. Jefferson [1977]. "Verification decidability of Presburger array programs," *A Conference on Theoretical Computer Science*, pp. 202–212, Univ. of Waterloo, Waterloo, Ont., Canada.

Taniguchi, K., and T. Kasami [1976]. "A result on the equivalence problem for deterministic pushdown automata," *J. Computer and Systems Sciences* **13**: 1, 38–50.

Thompson, K. [1968]. "Regular expression search algorithm," *Comm. ACM* **11**: 6, 419–422.

Trakhtenbrot, B. A. [1964]. "Turing computations with logarithmic delay," *Algebra i Logika*, **3**: 4, 33–48.

Turing, A. M. [1936]. "On computable numbers with an application to the Entscheidungsproblem," *Proc. London Math. Soc.*, **2**: 42, 230–265. A correction, *ibid.*, **43**, pp. 544–546.

Ullman, J. D. [1975]. "*NP*-complete scheduling problems," *J. Computer and Systems Sciences* **10**: 3, 384–393.

Valiant, L. G. [1973]. "Decision procedures for families of deterministic pushdown automata," Theory of computation—Report No. 1, Univ. of Warwick, Coventry, Great Britain.

Valiant, L. G. [1974]. "The equivalence problem for deterministic finite-turn pushdown automata," *Information and Control* **25**: 2, 123–133.

Valiant, L. G. [1975a]. "General context-free recognition in less than cubic time," *J. Computer and Systems Sciences* **10**: 2, 308–315.

Valiant, L. G. [1975b]. "Regularity and related problems for deterministic pushdown automata," *J. ACM* **22**: 1, 1–10.

Valiant, L. G., and M. S. Paterson [1975]. "Deterministic one-counter automata," *J. Computer and Systems Sciences* **10**: 3, 340–350.

Wang, H. [1957]. "A variant to Turing's theory of computing machines," *J. ACM* **4**: 1, 63–92.

Wegbreit, B. [1969]. "A generator of context-sensitive languages," *J. Computer and Systems Sciences* **3**: 3, 456–461.

Wise, D. S. [1976]. "A strong pumping lemma for context-free languages," *Theoretical Computer Science* **3**: 3, 359–370.

Yamada, H. [1962]. "Real-time computation and recursive functions not real-time computable," *IEEE Trans. on Electronic Computers* **11**: 6, 753–760.

Yannakakis, M. [1978]. "Node and edge deletion *NP*-complete problems," *Proc. Tenth Annual ACM Symposium on the Theory of Computing*, pp. 253–264.

Yasuhara, A. [1971]. *Recursive Function Theory and Logic*, Academic Press, New York.

Younger, D. H. [1967]. "Recognition and parsing of context-free languages in time n^3," *Information and Control* **10**: 2, 189–208.

INDEX